# Origins *of* Judaism

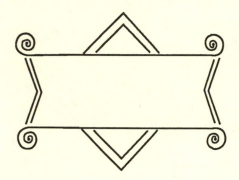

## Religion, History, and Literature in Late Antiquity A Twenty-Volume Collection of Essays and Articles

*Edited by*
Jacob Neusner
*University of South Florida*
*with*
William Scott Green
*University of Rochester*

## A Garland Series

# Origins *of* Judaism

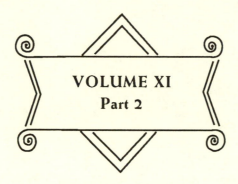

## VOLUME XI
### Part 2

## The Literature of Formative Judaism:
## The Midrash-Compilations

*Edited with a Preface by*
Jacob Neusner

— Garland Publishing, Inc. • New York & London —
1990

The volumes in this series are printed on acid-free, 250-year-life paper.
Printed in the United States.

Library of Congress Cataloging-in-Publication Data

The Literature of formative Judaism. The Midrash-compilations /
edited by Jacob Neusner with William Scott Green.
p. cm. — (Origins of Judaism : vol. 11)
ISBN 0-8240-8182-X (alk. paper)
1. Midrash—History and criticism. 2. Aggada—History and
criticism. I. Neusner, Jacob. II. Green, William scott. III. Series.
Bm177.075 vol. 11
[BM514]
296'.09'015 s—dc20
[296.1'406]                                          90-13899

A complete list of articles in this series, indexed by volume and by
author, may be found at the end of this volume.

# PREFACE

In these volumes we turn to the canon, or holy literature, of Judaism. That literature covers what is called "the Oral Torah." To understand the concept of the Oral Torah, we have to return to the generative myth of the Judaism that has predominated. For that Judaism appeals to a theory of revelation in two media of formulation and transmission, written and oral, in books and in memory. The written Torah is the Pentateuch and encompasses the whole of the Hebrew Scriptures of ancient Israel (the "Old Testament"). The Oral Torah is ultimately contained in and written down as the Mishnah, expanded and amplified by Tosefta, and the two Talmuds, on the one side, and the Midrash-compilations that serve to explain the written Torah, on the other.

Let us then review the myth of the dual Torah and its literary expression. The Judaism that has predominated from ancient times to the present day finds its definitive statement in the myth that, when Moses received the Torah, revelation, from God at Mount Sinai, God gave the Torah through two media, writing and memory. In these volumes we address the canon, or holy books, of that Judaism. The important side is here. The written Torah of this Judaism of the dual Torah is represented by Scripture or the Old Testament. The other Torah, formulated orally and transmitted only in memory, was handed on for many generations, from Moses down to the great sages of the early centuries of the Common Era when it finally reached writing in documents produced by sages, who bore the honorific title, "rabbi," "my lord."

Judaism may best be traced through the unfolding of its writings, because it was in writing, in study in academies, through the teaching of holy men (in contemporary times, women as well) qualified for saintliness by learning—specifically mastery of the Torah through discipleship— that that Judaism took shape. Just as one may write the history of Roman Catholic Christianity by tracing the story of the papacy, though that history would not be complete, and the history of Protestant Christianity through telling the story of the Bible in the world since the Reformation, so the history of the Judaism of the dual Torah takes shape in the tale of its holy books.

A review of the written evidence for the Judaism of the dual Torah makes the leap from the Pentateuch, ca. 450 B.C., to the end of the second century, for the first of these groups of writings begins with the Mishnah, a philosophical law book brought to closure at ca. A.D. 200, later called the first statement of the oral Torah. In its wake, the Mishnah drew tractate Abot, ca. A.D 250, a statement concluded a generation after the Mishnah on the standing of the authorities of the Mishnah; Tosefta, ca. A.D. 300, a compilation of supplements of various kinds to the statements in the Mishnah; and three systematic exegeses of books of Scripture or the written Torah, Sifra to Leviticus, Sifré to Numbers, and another Sifré, to Deuteronomy, of indeterminate date but possibly concluded by A.D. 300. These books overall form one stage in the unfolding of the Judaism of the dual Torah, in which emphasis is on issues of sanctification of the life of Israel, the people, in the aftermath of the destruction of the Temple of Jerusalem in A.D. 70, in which, it was commonly held, Israel's sanctification came to full realization in the rites of sacrifice to God on high.

The second set of the same writings begins with the Talmud of the Land of Israel, or Yerushalmi, generally supposed to have come to a conclusion at ca. A.D. 400, Genesis Rabbah, assigned to about the next half century, Leviticus Rabbah, ca. A.D. 450, Pesiqta deRab Kahana, ca. A.D. 450–500, and, finally, the Talmud of Babylonia or Bavli, assigned to the late sixth or early seventh century, ca. A.D. 600. The two Talmuds systematically interpret passages of the Mishnah, and the other documents, as is clear, do the same for books of the written Torah. The interpretation of Scripture in the Judaism of the dual Torah is collected in documents that bear the title of Midrash (pl.: Midrashim) meaning "exegesis." The single striking trait of Midrash as produced by the Judaism of the dual Torah is the persistent appeal, in interpreting a verse or a theme of Scripture, to some other set of values or considerations than those contained within the verse or topic at hand. On that account rabbinic Midrash compares something to something else, as does a parable, or it explains something in terms of something else, as does allegory. Rabbinic Midrash reads Scripture within the principle that things never are what they seem. In late antiquity rabbinic Midrash-compilation mainly attended to the pentateuchal books, Genesis, Exodus, Leviticus, Numbers, and Deuteronomy. Some other treatments of biblical books important in synagogue liturgy, particularly the Five Scrolls, e.g., Lamentations Rabbati, Esther Rabbah, and the like, are supposed also to have reached closure at this time. This second set of writings introduces, alongside the paramount issue of Israel's sanctification, the matter of Israel's salvation, with doctrines of history, on the one side, and the Messiah, on the other, given prominence in the larger systemic statement.

Let me briefly expand upon this skeletal account of the documents that define the problem solved by the documentary method of the study of Judaism. Between ca. 200, when autonomous government was well established again, and ca. 600, the continuous and ongoing movement of sages, holding positions of authority in the Jewish governments recognized by Rome and Iran, as political leaders of the Jewish communities of the Land of Israel (to just after 400 C.E.) and Babylonia (to about 500 C.E.), respectively, wrote two types of books. One sort extended, amplified, systematized, and harmonized components of the legal system laid forth in the Mishnah. The work of Mishnah-exegesis produced four principal documents as well as an apologia for the Mishnah. This last—the rationale or apologia—came first in time, about a generation or so after the publication of the Mishnah itself. It was tractate Abot ( ca. 250 C.E.), a collection of sayings attributed both to authorities whose names also occur in the Mishnah as well as to some sages who flourished after the conclusion of the Mishnah. These later figures, who make no appearance in that document, stand at the end of the compilation. The other three continuations of the Mishnah were the Tosefta, the Talmud of the Land of Israel (the Yerushalmi), and the Bavli. The Tosefta, containing a small portion of materials contemporaneous with those presently in the Mishnah and a very sizable portion secondary to, and dependent on the Mishnah, reached conclusion some time after ca. 300 and before ca. 400. The Yerushalmi closed at ca. 400. The Bavli, as we said, was completed by ca. 600. All these dates, of course, are rough guesses, but the sequence in which the documents made their appearance is not. The Tosefta addresses the Mishnah; its name means "supplement," and its function was to supplement the rules of the original documents. The Yerushalmi mediates between the Tosefta and the Mishnah, commonly citing a paragraph of the Tosefta in juxtaposition with a paragraph of the Mishnah and commenting on both, or so arranging matters that the paragraph of the Tosefta serves, just as it should, to complement a paragraph of the Mishnah. The Bavli, following the Yerushalmi by about two centuries, pursues its own program, which, as we said, was to link the two Torahs and restate them as one.

The stream of exegesis of the Mishnah and exploration of its themes of law and philosophy flowed side by side with a second. This other river coursed up out of the deep wells of the written Scripture. But it surfaced long after the work of Mishnah-exegesis was well underway and followed the course of that exegesis, now extended to Scripture. The exegesis of the Hebrew Scriptures, a convention of all systems of Judaism from before the conclusion of Scripture itself, obviously occupied sages from the very origins of their group. No one began anywhere but in the encounter with the Written Torah. But the writing down of exegeses of Scripture in a systematic way, signifying also the formulation of a program and a plan for the utilization of the Written Torah in the unfolding literature of the Judaism taking shape in the centuries at hand, developed in a distinct circumstance.

Specifically, one fundamental aspect of the work of Mishnah-exegesis began with one ineluctable question: How does a rule of the Mishnah relate to, or rest upon, a rule of Scripture? That question demanded an answer, so that the status of the Mishnah's rules, and of the

Mishnah itself, could find a clear definition. Standing by itself, the Mishnah bore no explanation of why Israel should obey its rules and accept its vision. Brought into relationship to Scriptures, in mythic language, viewed as part of the Torah, the Mishnah gained access to the source of authority operative in Israel—the Jewish people. Accordingly, the work of relating the Mishnah's rules to those of Scripture got under way alongside the formation of the Mishnah's rules themselves. Collecting and arranging exegeses of Scripture as these related to passages of the Mishnah first reached literary form in the Sifra to Leviticus, and in two books, both called Sifré, one to Numbers, the other to Deuteronomy. All three compositions accomplished much else. For, even at that early stage, exegeses of passages of Scripture in their own context, not just for the sake of Mishnah-exegesis, attracted attention. But a principal motif in all three books concerned the issue of Mishnah-Scripture relationships.

A second, still more fruitful path also emerged from the labor of Mishnah-exegesis. As the work of Mishnah-exegesis got under way, in the third century, exegetes of the Mishnah and others undertook a parallel labor. It was to work through verses of Scripture in exactly the same way—word for word, phrase for phrase, line for line—in which, to begin with, the exegetes of the Mishnah pursued the interpretation and explanation of the Mishnah. To state matters simply, precisely the types of exegesis that dictated the way in which sages read the Mishnah now guided their reading of Scripture as well. And, as people began to collect and organize comments in accord with the order of sentences and paragraphs of the Mishnah, they found the stimulation to collect and organize comments on clauses and verses of Scripture. This kind of work got under way in the Sifra and the two Sifrés. It reached massive and magnificent fulfillment in Genesis Rabbah, which, as its name tells us, presents a line-for-line reading of the book of Genesis.

Beyond these two modes of exegesis and the organization of exegeses in books—first on the Mishnah then on Scripture—lies yet a third. To understand it, we once more turn back to the Mishnah's great exegetes, represented to begin with in the Yerushalmi. While the original exegesis of the Mishnah in the Tosefta addressed the document through a line by line commentary, responding only in discrete and self-contained units of discourse, authors gathered for the Yerushalmi developed another mode of discourse entirely. They treated not phrases or sentences but principles and large-scale conceptual problems. They dealt not alone with a given topic, a subject and its rule, but with an encompassing problem, a principle and its implications for a number of topics and rules. This far more discursive and philosophical mode of thought produced for Mishnah-exegesis, in somewhat smaller volume but in much richer contents, sustained essays on principles cutting across specific rules. And for Scripture the method of sustained and broad-ranging discourse resulted in a second type of exegetical work, beyond that focused on words, phrases, and sentences.

Discursive exegesis is represented, to begin with, in Leviticus Rabbah, a document that reached closure, people generally suppose, sometime after Genesis Rabbah, thus between 400 and 500, one might guess. Leviticus Rabbah presents not phrase-by-phrase systematic exegeses of verses in the book of Leviticus, but a set of thirty-seven topical essays. These essays, syllogistic in purpose, take the form of citations and comments on verses of Scripture to be sure. But the compositions range widely over the far reaches of the Hebrew Scriptures while focusing narrowly upon a given theme. Moreover, they make quite distinctive points about that theme. Their essays constitute compositions, not merely composites. Whether devoted to God's favor to the poor and humble or to the dangers of drunkenness, the essays, exegetical in form, discursive in character, correspond to the equivalent legal essays, amply represented in the Yerushalmi.

Thus in this other mode of Scripture-interpretation, too, the framers of the exegeses accomplished what the Yerushalmi's exegetes of the Mishnah were doing in the same way at the same time. We move rapidly past yet a third mode of Scriptural exegesis, one in which the order of Scripture's verses is left far behind, and in which topics, not passages of Scripture, take over as the mode of organizing thought. Represented by Pesiqta de Rab Kahana, Lamentations Rabbati, and some other collections conventionally assigned to the sixth and seventh centuries, these entirely discursive compositions move out in their own direction, only marginally relating in mode of discourse to any counterparts in the Yerushalmi (or in the Bavli).

At the end of the extraordinary creative age of Judaism, the authors of units of discourse collected in the Bavli drew together the two, up-to-then distinct, modes of organizing thought, either around the Mishnah or around Scripture. They treated both Torahs, oral and written, as equally available in the work of organizing large-scale exercises of sustained inquiry. So we find in the Bavli a systematic treatment of some tractates of the Mishnah. And within the same aggregates of discourse, we also find (in somewhat smaller proportion to be sure, roughly 60% to roughly 40% in a sample made of three tractates) a second principle of organizing and redaction. That principle dictates that ideas be laid out in line with verses of Scripture, themselves dealt with in sequence, one by one, just as the Mishnah's sentences and paragraphs come under analysis, in cogent order and one by one. So much for the written evidence that forms the arena of inquiry.

There are three distinct modes of organizing sustained discourse in the canon of the Judaism of the dual Torah. These statements are, respectively, those built around the exegesis of the oral Torah, the Mishnah (hence the Tosefta and two Talmuds), second, those that serve to amplify the written Torah, the Midrash-compilations, and, finally, those that find cogency in the life and teaching of a given sage or group of sages. No collections of stories and sayings about sages emerged in the formative age, as counterparts to the Gospels, for example. There were three modes of organizing large-scale discourse in the Judaism of the dual Torah. One was to make use of books or verses or themes of Scripture. A second was to follow the order of the Mishnah and compose a systematic commentary and amplification of that document. This was the way, for example, of those who created the Talmud of the Land of Israel a century or so before. A third was to organize stories about and sayings of sages. These were framed around twin biographical principles, either as strings of stories about great sages of the past or as collections of sayings and comments drawn together solely because the same name stands behind them.

Ths Midrash-compilations performed a distinctive task in the formation of the Judaism of the dual Torah. The Midrash produced by the Judaism of the dual Torah from the fourth century onward, in particular Genesis Rabbah and Leviticus Rabbah, took as its set of urgent questions the issue defined by Christianity as it assumed control of the Roman empire; it provided as self-evident valid answers a system, that derived its power from the Torah, was read by sages, embodied by sages, exemplified by sages, and served as the reply. In this enormous intellectual enterprise we confront the counterpart to the evangelists' rereading of Scripture so as to answer the urgent question facing first century Christians: who it is that people say I am? In both cases an extraordinary experience—the one in the encounter with a man beyond time, the other in the meeting of an age beyond all expectation—required the rereading of Scripture in the light of what, in each circumstance, people grasped as the ultimate issue of eternity.

The verses that are quoted in rabbinic Midrash ordinarily shift from the meanings they convey to the implications they contain, thus speaking about something, anything, other than what they seem to be saying. The as-if frame of mind brought to Scripture renews Scripture, with the sage seeing everything with fresh eyes. The result of the new vision was a re-imagining of the social world depicted by the document at hand, the everyday world of Israel in that difficult time. For what the sages now proposed was a reconstruction of existence along the lines of the ancient design of Scripture as they read it. What this meant was that, from a sequence of singular, and linear events, everything that happened was turned into a repetition of known and already experienced paradigms—hence, once more, a mythic being. The source and core of the myth, of course, derive from Scripture—Scripture reread, renewed, reconstructed along with the society that revered it.

Reading one thing in terms of something else, the builders of the document systematically adopted for themselves the reality of the Scripture, its history, and doctrines. They transformed that history from a sequence of one-time events. No longer was there one Moses, one David, one set of happenings of a distinctive and never- to-be-repeated character. Now whatever these thinkers propose to take into account must enter into that established and ubiquitous pattern and structure founded in Scripture. It is not that biblical history repeats itself. Rather, biblical history no longer constitutes history as a story of things that happened once, long ago, and pointed toward some one moment in the future. Rather it becomes an account of things that happen every day—hence, an ever-present mythic world. That is why, in Midrash in the Judaism of the dual Torah, Scripture as a whole does not dictate the order of discourse, let alone its character. In this document they chose a verse here, a phrase there. In the more mature Midrash-compilations, such as Leviticus Rabbah and Pesiqta deRab Kahana, these presented the pretext for propositional discourse quite out of phase with the cited passage.

Since biblical events exemplify recurrent happenings, sin and redemption, forgiveness and atonement, they lose their one-time character. At the same time and in the same way, current events find a place within the ancient, but eternally present, paradigmatic scheme. So no new historical events, other than exemplary episodes in lives of heroes, demand narration because, through what is said about the past, what was happening in the times of the framers of Midrash in the Judaism of the dual Torah would also come under consideration. This mode of dealing with biblical history and contemporary events produces two reciprocal effects. The first is the mythicization of biblical stories, their removal from the framework of ongoing, unique patterns of history and sequences of events and their transformation into accounts of things that happen all the time. The second is that contemporary events too lose all of their specificity and enter the paradigmatic framework of established mythic existence. Thus the Scripture's myth happens every day, and every day produces reenactment of the Scripture's myth.

This brings us to the final and authoritative statement of the Judaism of the dual Torah, the Talmud of Babylonia or Bavli. A tripartite corpus of inherited materials awaiting composition in a cogent composite document found its way into the Bavli. Prior to that time, the framers of documents had tended to resort to a single principle of organization, whether scriptural, mishnaic, or biographical. The authors of the Bavli took up materials, in various states and stages of completion, pertinent to the Mishnah or to the principles of laws that the Mishnah had originally brought to articulation. Second, they had received materials, again in various conditions, pertinent to the Scripture, both as the Scripture related to the Mishnah and as the Scripture laid forth its own narratives. Finally, they collected and arranged sayings of and stories about sages. But this third principle of organizing discourse took a position subordinated to the other two. The framers of the Bavli organized it around the Mishnah. But they adapted and included vast tracts of antecedent materials organized as scriptural commentary. These they inserted whole and complete, not at all in response to the Mishnah's program. And, finally, while making provision for compositions built upon biographical principles, preserving strings of sayings from a given master (and often a given tradent of a given master) as well as tales about authorities of the preceding half millennium, they did nothing new. That is to say, the ultimate authors of the canonical documents never created redactional compositions, of a sizable order, that focused upon given authorities, even though sufficient materials lay at hand to allow doing so. God's will reached Israel through Scripture, Mishnah, sage—that is, by the evidence and testimony of each of these three media equally. That is the premise of the Judaism of the entire rabbinic canon, of each of the stories that appeal to a verse of Scripture, a phrase or sentence of the Mishnah, or a teaching or action of a sage. Recognizing the three components of the single canon, the written Torah, the oral Torah, and the sage as the living Torah, leads us to the articles collected in the volumes on the literature of Judaism in late antiquity. We address the Mishnah and Tosefta, the two Talmuds, the Midrash-compilations, the translations of Scripture into Aramaic called "Targumim," and the translation into Greek called "the Septuagint." In all of these ways the canonical heritage of the Judaism that was forming at this time came into being.

# CONTENTS

❦ ❧

## VOLUME 11 (PART 1)

## VOLUME 11 (PART 2)

# Contents

# ACKNOWLEDGMENTS

Goldin, Judah, "Reflections on Translation and Midrash," *Proceedings of American Academy for Jewish Research*, 1975, 41–42:87–104. Reprinted with the permission of the American Academy for Jewish Research. Courtesy of the American Academy for Jewish Research.

Goldin, Judah, "The Two Versions of *Abot de Rabbi Nathan*," *Hebrew Union College Annual*, 1946, 19:97–120. Reprinted with the permission of the Hebrew Union College-Jewish Institute of Religion. Courtesy of Yale University.

Heinemann, Joseph, "Profile of a Midrash; the Art of Composition in Leviticus Rabba," *Journal of the American Academy of Religion*, 1922, 39:141–50. Courtesy of New York Public Library.

Kadushin, Max, "Aspects of the Rabbinic Concept of Israel: A Study in the Mekilta," *Hebrew Union College Annual*, 1946, 19:57–96. Reprinted with the permission of the Hebrew Union College-Jewish Institute of Religion. Courtesy of Yale University.

Kagan, Zipporah, "Divergent Tendencies and Their Literary Moulding in the Aggadah," *Scripta Hierosolymitana*, 1971, 22:151–70. Reprinted with the permission of *Scripta Hierosolymitana*. Courtesy of Yale University.

Kohler, K., "Abba, Father: Title of Spiritual Leader and Saint," *Jewish Quarterly Review—Old Series*, 1901, 13:567–80. Courtesy of Yale University.

Kohler, K., "The Pre-Talmudic Haggada, Part I," *Jewish Quarterly Review—Old Series*, 1893, 5:399–419. Courtesy of Yale University.

Kohler, K., "The Pre-Talmudic Haggada, Part II," *Jewish Quarterly Review—Old Series*, 1895, 7:581–606. Courtesy of Yale University.

Kohut, A., "Zeus in Mishnah, Talmud, and Midrash," *Jewish Quarterly Review—Old Series*, 1891, 3:552–54. Courtesy of Yale University.

Lauterbach, Jacob Z., "The Two Mekiltas," *Proceedings of American Academy for Jewish Research*, 1933, 4:113–29. Courtesy of Yale University.

Loewe, Raphael, "The 'Plain' Meaning of Scripture in Early Jewish Exegesis," *Annual of the Institute of Jewish Studies*, London (London, 1964), I:140–85. Courtesy of Yale University.

Mandelbaum, Bernard, "Prolegomenon to the Pesikta," *Proceedings of American Academy for Jewish Research*, 1954, 23:41–58. Reprinted with the permission of the American Academy for Jewish Research. Courtesy of the American Academy for Jewish Research.

Mihaly, Eugene, "A Rabbinic Defense of the Election of Israel. An Analysis of Sifre Deuteronomy, 32:9, Pisqa 312," *Hebrew Union College Annual*, 1964, 35:103–43. Reprinted with the permission of the Hebrew Union College-Jewish Institute of Religion. Courtesy of Yale University.

Neusner, Jacob, "History and Midrash," *Judaism*, 1960, 9(1):47–54. Reprinted with the permission of *Judaism*. Courtesy of Yale University.

Neusner, Jacob, "The Development of the *Merkavah* Tradition," *Journal for the Study of Judaism*, 1971, 2(2) 149–60. Courtesy of Yale University.

Slonimsky, Henry, "The Philosophy Implicit in the Midrash," *Hebrew Union College Annual*, 1956, 27:235–90. Reprinted with the permission of the Hebrew Union College-Jewish Institute of Religion. Courtesy of Yale University.

Towner, W. Sibley, "Hermeneutical Systems of Hillel and the Tannaim: A Fresh Look," *Hebrew Union College Annual*, 1983, 53:101–35. Reprinted with the permission of the Hebrew Union College-Jewish Institute of Religion. Courtesy of Yale University.

Wacholder, Ben Zion, "The Date of the Mekilta de-Rabbi Ishmael," *Hebrew Union College Annual*, 1969, 39:117–44. Reprinted with the permission of the Hebrew Union College-Jewish Institute of Religion. Courtesy of Yale University.

Wright, Addison G., "The Literary Genre Midrash," *Catholic Biblical Quarterly*, 1966, 28(2):105–38; 1966, 28(4):417–457. Reprinted with the permission of the *Catholic Biblical Quarterly*. Courtesy of Yale University.

# REFLECTIONS ON TRANSLATION AND MIDRASH

by Judah Goldin

*For Morton Smith on his birthday
because he prefers the originals*

Although the verb *targem* occurs only once in Scripture, and in a rather late book at that, the word is apparently no parvenu in Semitic, as the lexicons and my smart friends instruct me. The Akkadian *targumanu* was an interpreter, and that is what the translator has always been. As Professor S. Lieberman underscored for a later period, "... the first rudiment of the interpretation of a text is the ἑρμηνεία, the literal and exact equivalent of the Hebrew תרגום, which means both translation and interpretation." And the OED informs me that once upon a time the very English word "interpret" was used also for "to translate." When we ask, What is the oldest Midrash that has been preserved, the scholars answer, The Septuagint.

No less than the word, the activity of translation is hardly a newcomer on the cultural scene. From the middle of the second millenium B.C. there have come down fragments of an Akkadian recension of the Gilgamesh epic current in the Hittite Empire, and, continues Speiser, "the same Boğazköy archives have yielded also important fragments of a Hittite translation, as well as a fragment of a Hurrian rendering of the epic." Tablet XII of that epic is, according to the experts, "a literal translation from the Sumerian." None of this should be surprising. The first translation in history probably occurred when the first reader began his first rereading of the first author's composition, and he, the reader, wanted to make sure that he understood what the text said. When Jacob said גלעד he was already behaving like many before him. And maybe in the mind of the author of the Genesis story, על כן קרא שמו גלעד reflects what happens repeatedly in cultural history, to wit, once a translation is proposed it tends to be adopted and is

1

treated as though it alone were the correct interpretation. "When the book of Jonah was read in a Christian church in Africa from Jerome's new Latin version, there was an uproar, because the miraculous plant (4.6), which in the older translation was based upon the Greek had been rendered 'gourd,' was now identified with the 'ivy.'" When several years ago a "mist" ceased to rise from the earth, in the second Creation story, this omission caused a tumult for months on end.

If the Mishnah goes to the trouble to declare that when one translates ומזרעך לא תתן להעביר למלך ומזרעך לא תתן לאעברא as באָרמיותא, he is not only to be silenced but rebuked (משתקין אותו בנזיפה), it is wittingly or unwittingly admitting that a translation and interpretation the Sages resent, are popular in certain quarters: the translation and interpretation have taken hold (of some Karaites two centuries later), are passing for the real thing, and pretty soon every one may begin to think that this is how the original reads.

Translation — because it really equals translation plus interpretation — is in truth effective. Because that is so, a kind of literary hybris tends to develop, and it may be demanded that the translation be treated no less solemnly than the original. When the Greek translation of the Pentateuch had been executed and read to τὸ πλῆθος τῶν Ἰουδαίων εἰς τὸν τόπον, there was a great ovation (a μεγάλη ἀποδχή), and then the priests, the elders of the translators, some of the corporate body and the leaders of the people rose and said, "'Inasmuch as the translation has been well and piously made and is in every respect accurate (καὶ κατὰ πᾶν ἠκριβωμένως), it is right that it should remain in its present form and that no revision of any sort take place.' When all had assented to what had been said, they bade that an imprecation be pronounced, according to their custom, upon any who should revise the text by adding or transposing anything whatever in what had been written down, or by making any excision; and in this they did well, so that the work might be preserved imperishable and unchanged always."

It may be that on hearing these words the author of Deuteronomy would be taken aback, as perhaps also the Vizier Ptah-Hotep (though some have questioned the current rendition) and still another bureaucrat who spoke of how to deliver a message. It doesn't matter. Nor does it matter whether Aristeas is writing fiction or history. What does matter is the expression of an attitude, Don't underestimate translation.

Nor, to take one further step, do the talmudic Sages disagree with that view. I shall try to spend a little time with their views shortly. And we have already seen, they actively tried to silence a translator whose translation they disliked — evidently a sign of their not underestimating the damage a poor translation (from their point of view) can do. But it would be very far from the truth to present the talmudic Sages as unqualified opponents of translation. Again the Mishnah. It is describing the procedure of blessings and curses at Gerizim and Ebal; afterwards an altar to be built, and שנאמר וכתבו עליו את כל דברי התורה בשבעים לשון, באר היטב. Targum Jonathan and Targum Yerushalmi and Neofiti are prepared to endorse this. Whether there should have been a holiday or fast day when the Torah was translated into Greek, for the author of the Mishnah statement, it was certainly desirable to have the contents of the Torah translated and broadcast to the nations of the world in all the languages. What is באר היטב? To write out all the words of the Torah בשבעים לשון. When you want to make your work known, you translate (= translate and interpret) it into as many languages as you can. Even for domestic consumption you invent the role of the dragoman. Of course, you also lay down rules as to how he is to act his part: may he or may he not resort to a script, when may he speak up and when shut up? But apparently you need him and you use him.

Before proceeding with our principal discussion and examination of the attitudes of the talmudic Sages in some detail, there are three problems related to our subject which I am deliberately excluding because in my opinion they don't belong here.

First, the permissibility or prohibition of using a translation in public service. What must be recited in the original and what need not? Or what may or may not be the practice in the synagogues

3

of לעוזות? And so forth. These reveal of course the presence of the possibilities of translation, but they are halakic-institutional problems. When you have a community, and especially an extensively spread-out community, how much liberty in the use of languages can you afford to permit, or accept *faute de mieux*? The Roman Church is rediscovering today how complicated and dissolving this can be. I must say, I admire the Sages for liberating important expressions from their original cultic framework, I also admire them for their courage to allow the recitation of the Shema, the Tefillah, and the Grace after meals in any language. One of these days they'll visit Caesarea, and maybe then they will appreciate how sweet and risky are the uses of diversity. But that's their problem, not ours. It, therefore, is out of bounds for our reflections.

Another problem to be excluded is the relation of oral targums to written targums, or the apparent displeasure of any particular leading or run-of-the-mill sage with any particular targum text on the Temple-mount or anywhere else. Again, this may be partly halakic — what status should such written documents enjoy when there is a likely transgression of a biblical injunction — and partly an individual's taste for a specific style. Anyway, that's out, as is a third and inherently interesting problem; but it requires brief digression.

Most of the time when our sources speak of translation they have the Scriptures in mind. Not always, witness the grandson of Sirach who in the second century B.C. translated a book, his grandfather's, not yet or ever to be part of the canon — did he hope to create the feeling that possibly the book ought to be included, and therefore a Greek translation would suggest that like the canonical works, his grandfather's maxims also deserved publication and in more than the original version?

Or another example. A very good case has been made for the possibility that a little more than a century before Sirach's grandson produced his work, a Jew who admired an Aramaic work undertook to translate it into Hebrew, with what results, Professor H. L. Ginsberg has already demonstrated. It is not impossible that

the translator too thought that Solomon was the author of that
cheerful treatise. No matter. While he was at work on his translation, it was still not part of the canon, though if it were already
being attributed to Solomon, it would enjoy esteem in some
circles. But it was then not yet catalogued in the library of כתבי הקדש.
That is all I care to underline, my point being that the fingerprints
of translation can be detected even on literary works that are not
in the category of the sacred. Probably I'm belaboring the obvious.
Be this as it may: It is understandable that translation of *sacred*
scriptures might be undertaken, even though their custodians
might be less than jubilant at the prospect of having to publicize,
superficially at least, the esoteric messages in these writings:
because if you want to circulate your truth among your neighbors
and their neighbors, and among your own kindred whom you're
determined to indoctrinate, how can you do it without translation
and interpretation? But it is certainly interesting to recall that
translation goes on even when writings are not sacred. And the
problem which I wish to exclude from consideration is this, the
relation of translation of the sacred to translation of the profane.

Hence we may revert to our principal discussion, which is,
translation-as-such, the activity of translating and interpreting;
and it's not with the ancients only that I'm concerned, although I
shall refer to them and help myself to examples from some of
their texts: my concern is with the activity itself.

And the first thing to be said about it is that (except in one
respect) it is a thoroughly frustrating and unrewarding occupation:
I recommend it to anyone eager to develop an inferiority complex.
Here is Sirach's grandson apologizing, entreating his readers "to
be indulgent, if in any part of what we have labored to interpret
we may seem to fail in some of the phrases." That's the Greek
for הנני העני ממעש. He is obviously frightened that the savants in
Alexandria will publish reviews in which they will point out that
you cannot transfer the Hebrew to the Greek idiom. Hopeless,
hopeless, for the simple fact is, the job can't be done: what's
Greek is Greek and what's Hebrew is Hebrew, and if you try to say
in one what is said in the other, you're misleading.

And the translators of the King James Version have this to say: "It hath pleased God in his Divine Providence, here and there to scatter words and sentences of that difficulty and doubtfulness ... that fearfulness would better beseem us than confidence..."

And here is A.J. Arberry:"... the rhetoric and rhythm of the Arabic of the Koran are so characteristic, so powerful, so highly emotive, that any version whatsoever is bound in the nature of things to be but a poor copy of the glittering splendour of the original. Never was it more true than in this instance that *traduttore traditore*."

שבכל דור ודור עומדים עלינו. It's the same with every measure and every period of time. "All translations are reputed females, delivered at second hand," writes John Florio in his Dedicatory Epistle of his translation of Montaigne; and in his preface to the "courteous reader" he proceeds to list one apology and excuse after another: "Shall I apologize translation? Why but some holde (as for their free-hold) that such conversion is the subversion of Universities." So he tries to explain that the citadels of learning will not come down if works in one language are made accessible in another. After a number of other possible protests, he comes to this one: "Why but who ever did well in it?" He takes care of that and still other criticisms. He confesses ("and let confession make halfe amends") that every language has its own "Genius and inseparable forme." He fears that he has made "of good French no good English." And of course he prays and entreats "you for your owne sake to correct as you reade; to amend as you list." In short, he knows he's in for it. You'll never get the footnote aficionados to approve because indeed they don't need the translation and they would rather not be annoyed by the static of a bad translation.

But this is not all. Even more resentful of the translation is none other than the author. He simply cannot be pleased, though he would like to be. He is both grateful and heartbroken, for he cannot help noting that his precious nuances have vanished alas.

In the introduction to his wonderful translation of Cervantes' *Don Quixote*, Samuel Putnam quotes Cervantes on *his* attitude toward translation: "But for all that, it appears to me that translating from one language into another, unless it be from one of those two queenly tongues, Greek and Latin, is like gazing at a Flemish tapestry with the wrong side out: even though the figures are visible, they are full of threads that obscure the view and are not bright and smooth as when seen from the other side." You'll never get the author happy (about the concrete translation, that is) because, naturally, he knows all the words he rejected before he decided on just that one, and the translator can't take his eyes off it.

And if you think you'll fare any better with the public, you're living, beg pardon, in a fool's paradise. Nobody with any intelligence, particularly one who is engaged in translation, would deny that you can't go on interminably with the antiquated. The translator above all is no pillar of obscurity or devout unintelligibility, even if he happens to have a taste for that which has aged. The fact remains that the public, like the scholar and author, is unfriendly to translation. What it wants is jazz and prose that puts no strain on the mind: pop digest: which have their place in society, but these are not translation. "You look terrific!" is not a translation of "Shall I compare thee to a summer's day? /Thou art more lovely and more temperate." From the way a man translates you can tell whether he loves his source or his public. Ignore the exact meaning of words, start resorting to paraphrase, and you still can transmit more or less accurately the substance of the source: but you're not translating. You're after *tachlis*, quick returns, but not exegesis or science or art. כי זה. והחסידות האמתי הנרצה והנחמד רחוק מציור שכלנו. דבר פשוט, מילתא דלא רמיא עליה דאינש לאו אדעתיה. The following translation is not misleading: "We find it difficult properly to conceive true saintliness, since we cannot grasp that to which we give no thought." For all their bad grammar, I miss that הנרצה והנחמד. I miss כי זה דבר פשוט. And to me that translation says, Come on now, let's get this over with! "We find it difficult properly to conceive" is Report of the Dean's Committee; רחוק מציור שכלנו is style. I shall not quote Franz Rosenzweig — why, I don't know; or maybe I do. But I will quote from W. H. Auden, though you may think his problem is not ours. He writes (I'm not quoting in full):

"I don't know if it is any better with the Anglican Church in England, but the Episcopalian Church in America seems to have gone stark raving mad." He then gives several examples of a proposed reformed Holy Communion service, and the fourth is: "Worst of all, the Epistle and Gospel are read in some appalling 'modern' translation. In one such, the Greek word which St. Paul uses in Romans VIII and which the Authorized Version translates as *flesh* turns into *our lower nature*, a concept which is not Christian, but Manichean." Then Auden concludes: "And why? The poor Roman Catholics have had to start from scratch, and, as any of them with a feeling for language will admit, they have made a cacophonous horror of the Mass. We had the extraordinary good fortune in that our Book of Common Prayer was composed at exactly the right historical moment. The English language had already become more or less what it is today, so that the Prayer Book is no more difficult to follow than Shakespeare, but the ecclesiastics of the sixteenth century still possessed a feeling for the ritual and ceremonious which today we have almost entirely lost. Why should we spit on our luck?"

Nowhere is translation welcomed with open arms, and among the Jews (by whom I mean from hereon out the midrashic-talmudic rabbis and others), among the Jews it is no different. The attitude seems to be, With one hand keep at a distance and pull towards you with the other. To say that the Jews are afraid of it, is true; why shouldn't they be? How well they knew what havoc a translation can work! God be with you if you introduce a *parthenos* where it isn't too safe even for an *almah*. Centuries of polemics and worse-than-polemics may follow. Translation is certainly hazardous; but then what isn't? To say, or even to imply, however, that the Sages rejected translation is unwarranted when it isn't worse than that. Of Hillel's eighty disciples — thirty of whom could have done with the sun what Joshua did! — of these disciples, who was the greatest? Jonathan ben Uzziel! Wouldn't you know. And to recall what this signifies, all that is necessary to remember is that the least of that fellowship was Rabban Yohanan ben Zakkai. Hyperbole, obviously, and a lot more than translation is behind and all over that statement. But if translator had meant traducer, גדול שבהם or גדול שבכולם could never have been Jonathan ben Uzziel; or better put it the other way around, had translator-interpreter meant traducer, Pseudo-Jonathan could never have acquired so fancy a name and reputation. The way some people avoid translation, you'd think birds were flying overhead.

But what of R. Judah's (or, R. Eliezer's) statement that המתרגם פסוק כצורתו (or, בצורתו), הרי זה בדי, והמוסיף הרי זה מגדף (or, מחרף ומגדף)? To begin with, the statement in the talmudic context is clearly being invoked for a halakic purpose, and that is not our problem, as we decided earlier. Second, the Sage is speaking of translation of sacred scriptures and that too, as we have detected, may bring on institutional shingles. However, we need not hesitate to consider the remark against the widest possible background. For what R. Judah or R. Eliezer is saying is absolutely true, and there isn't a translator in the business who would contradict him. At least the first half of that statement is verbatim what Walter Benjamin once said: "A translation that strove to be exactly similar to its original would not be a true translation." For this indeed is *the* fundamental challenge and frustration and hoped-for triumph beckoning the translator: When do you translate with strict literalness and when dare you not do so? When do you shrink or stretch the original and when dare you not do so? If I may use Onkelos as an example, in the same chapter, and in all reverence if you please: When do I content myself with three words exactly as in the original and say, לפורקנך סברית ה', and when do I seemingly go on and on, for example, "Israel shall go round his city, the people shall build his temple, the righteous ones shall surround him and study (or, carry out) the Torah in instruction with him, precious purple shall his garment be and his clothing wool, crimson-colored wool, yea, clothing splendid with color?" In the interior of that chapter the first, not the second, is astonishing.

Any way you translate you're sunk, whether you translate literally or expansively. But that's the assignment, to get it done properly (to the best of your ability); you're between the monster of lying and that female of blasphemy: go, navigate.

9

For there is no formula you can formulate in advance, except of course the resolution, I may never be dishonest — let's be perfectly clear about that. And even that supposedly noble end, literal translation, that is, reproduce faithfully what the original wishes to say, how fugitive it is! ימצאהו בארץ מדבר, ובתהו ילל ישמן and so on, says the verse in Deuteronomy. One interpretation has it, ד״א ימצאהו בארץ מדבר, הכול מצוי ומסופק להם במדבר, באר עולה להם. In להם, מן יורד להם, שליו מצוי להם, ענני כבוד מקיפות עליהם וכו׳ וכו׳. other words, ימצאהו is being interpreted as though it read ימציאהו. Homiletical exaggeration? I don't suppose that with some people the testimony of Onkelos, סופיק צורכייהון, will count for much; but here is the Septuagint translating αὐτάρκησεν αὐτόν. Somebody, evidently, thinks this is *peshat*.

Times change, styles of translation change, and this is as it should be if the voice of the classic is to be heard in our land. Changes there may be and will be; yet I believe three things are constant in all translations:

(1) The way translation begins. It is a purely personal, unsocial, private act. Of course it can take on public and institutional interests, and there may even be at the outset a commission from a monarch or a society or publisher to undertake the job. But that is not the beginning of translation. Translation begins the moment I discover that I'm not sure I understand the text I'm reading; the moment I begin to suspect that all I'm getting out of my reading or study is general impressions, a kind of smog of comprehension. Nothing is precise, everything is only vaguely familiar, darkly intelligible, or mechanically hand-me-down. But if I ask myself, Just what exactly is the text saying, and why is it saying it this way and not another, and cannot answer the question cleanly — no self-bluff or deception — then I know I have no alternative. I must clear the atmosphere. I must begin to translate. That will speedily disclose to me what I know and what I don't know: for what I *thought* I knew equals what I don't know. If the words *gemilut* — or even by chance *gemilot* — *ḥasadim* always meant acts of lovingkindness, who in his right mind would

ask, How could they be practised in Babylon where animal sacrifices were forbidden; or who would say in illustration of them that Daniel prayed three times a day? אין עזי אלא תוקפי, the Midrash enlightens me. Fine. What do I know now I did not know before? If again and again and again the reading crops up הוי שקוד ללמוד מה שתשיב לאפיקורוס, what does that mean, precisely?

Translation is for oneself, entirely, for me to gain correct understanding. That is all, and let no one tell you otherwise: especially that it is for the benefit of the world. A time may well come when the translator wishes to pass on his translation to the public. But that's no more than a biological reflex he shares with all who fill their bellies with learning or poetry or scientific theories or gossip: they can't keep it to themselves. The fear of one's own ignorance is the beginning of translation.

Shortly before the second World War there lived in London a gentleman (שמריה מנשה הכהן אדלר) who seems to have been a *lamdan*. That he knew a respectable amount of Talmud and rabbinics is clear, but it is also clear that he was a formidable *nudnik*. Had his mouth been just a little cleaner, he might have deserved A + for his attacks on the Establishment, the chief rabbinate and boards of beth-din and so on. What a delight it is to see the way he writes out טשיף ראביי in Hebrew characters! Or to keep coming upon one of his favorite expressions, מסוה דקדושה מזוייפת. Bravo. Now, when the Soncino translation of the Talmud began to appear, this valiant gent came out with an attack על גודל הפירצה כזו (הזו?) דבאמת פעולה כזו היא יסוד ושורש גדול לחורבן קיום האומה אחכ״י and the ב״ד דפה לונדון who are גמורה נינהו בגדר ע״ז באמת.. כפי המוסכם בתורה שבע״פ ובכל הפוסקים בלי שום חולק. Into the battle he even dragged the Gaon of Dvinsk and of course the opinions of still other *geonim addirim shalita*, all to the single effect that it is absolutely forbidden to translate תורה שבעל פה into a foreign language. Would indeed that even the written Torah had remained only in the original: ומי יתן והיתה תורה אתנו בני ישראל אמון מוצנע כאשר מלפנים אפילו אחאב לא רצה לתתה למלך ארם, כי כל הצרות נמשכו אחר זה. He can't forgive rabbis and reverends who study foreign languages. In Jephthah's generation how impatient he would have been for Samuel's coming!

There are, needless to say, many fine points to establish — for example, whom are you translating for, us or them: what's the translation for; will you use a Hebrew alphabet or another; and other subjects too come in by association, like who is qualified to be a *dayyan*, or why Resh Lakish seems to have changed his mind regarding supporting or not supporting דייני בור, or whether he ever was a brigand, and so forth. I am not the person to discuss the halakic finesse or applicability of our friend's view, and I know that I am unable to read his hysterical prose and insults without wanting to laugh. That's my prejudice. But one complaint of his is surely justified. He reports — and I find no reason to disbelieve him, though in the heat of righteousness he may be exaggerating — that from the speeches at the gala celebration מפורש עיקר כוונתם דעי״ז יתקרבו ויתדבקו בקשר של קיימא חיבה וריעות ישראל לב״נ ובזה ישראל נושע תשועת עולמים, אוי לאזנים שככה שומעות. I agree fully. The motive for genuine translation is not to prove to the next person how pretty my text is: though that may come later. As we saw, the impulse if anything comes from an almost completely opposite direction.

(2) The basic unit of translation. What is it? It cannot be the single word. That seldom has a life of its own. A word I can look up, but I cannot translate it. That's why interlinears are trots but not translations. I don't doubt that Aquila pleased several important scholars; maybe subconsciously they hoped that after one hour with such Greek, a man would cry out, Give me Hebrew or give me death; or maybe those were still the early days of computer translation. With a single word, it's a little like what the Midrash says, ועדין הדבר תלי בדלא תלי ואין אנו יודעים. A word acquires its specific gravity from the context it's in.

What then? Shall I take the sentence as a whole? That is generally too long. It may give me the overall sense, but it tends to devaluate the individuality of many terms it contains. Consider this:

וּכְנֵטֶף בַּיָּם כֵּן נֹאבֵדָה

עֲרִירִים בֵּין אַלְפֵי רְבָבָה —

מָה רַב, הוֹי, מָה רַב הַשִּׁמָּמוֹן

בָּאָרֶץ הָרֵיקָה, הָרְחָבָה

Now an English version:

> And like a drop of water in the sea
>
> We'll sink, and none will reckoning demand.
>
> Can loneliness more utter be
>
> Than in this wide, this empty land?"

I get the idea, but I don't get the poem: instead of sipping, the translator gulps.

What then is the proper unit? Sometimes it is the phrase but most often and likely the clause. Here I see the word in its relation to its immediate neighbors and the unit is not too big for my embrace.

נשמת כל חי תברך את שמך, ה׳ אלהינו, ורוח כל בשר תפאר ותרומם זכרך מלכנו תמיד. מן העולם ועד העולם אתה אל, ומבלעדיך אין לנו מלך גואל ומושיע, פודה מציל ומפרנס ומרחם בכל עת צרה וצוקה.

> The breath of all that lives shall bless Thy Name,
>
> O Lord our God; the spirit of all flesh
>
> Shall sing remembrance unto Thee, our King.
>
> From everlasting unto everlasting
>
> Thou wert and art the Lord; and but for Thee
>
> We have no King, and no deliverer,
>
> No savior, no redeemer, no provider,
>
> No fount of mercy in an evil day.

This translator is reading בכונה.


(3) The right *English* word and syntax. It is alas overlooked again and again by well-meaning people that the test of translation is met or missed — despite learning and despite virtue — in the choice of the right word, the exact word, and the proper arrangements of the language one translates *into*, not the language one translates *from*. And beware of prepositions! They're merciless. Verbal equivalence by itself is not the way. A gift of flesh and blood

13

comes from a butcher shop. I cannot for the life of me believe that
Joshua ben Perahya ever said, "And when thou judgest any man
incline the balance in his favor," though he might have said, "tip
the scale in his favor." "Incline the balance in his favor," forsooth.
It's like the famous sermon once delivered (I'm told) in the Seminary synagogue on the text, "Israel is a nut." Or like that master-
piece-rendering of שנים מי יודע, which ran, "Who knows the meaning
of number two?" Unfortunately, I do. The language translated
*into* is the test we must pass. And it is only a slight exaggeration
(if that!) to say that a knowledge of that is more important than a
knowledge of the original. For this is the question the translator
must ask of himself every syllable along the way: If Akiba or Yohanan ben Zakkai or Joshua ben Levi or whoever had spoken
American English the way (let us say) E.B. White or Auden writes
it, how would he have said what he wanted to say? Like a translation out of Jastrow? Like the trilingual posters in Meah Shearim
admonishing women how to dress? Because he knows the English
language superbly, though he does not know Swedish, Auden
could translate Dag Hammarskjöld's *Markings* with the help
of a Swede, Leif Sjöberg. The postscript to his Foreword is a
lesson to us all.

These are the three constants, and with industry they are attainable, it seems to me, by any student who loves his text. But
there is one element which is not to be had by industry alone.
That is why it cannot be a constant. It comes from an eardrum
מן השמים: if one is lucky to be born with it, how fortunate for him;
if one is not lucky, he may still be a competent journeyman — but
don't expect miracles.

I would like to illustrate what I mean by a negative example, so
to speak. In his delightful volume, *In Praise of Yiddish*, Mr.
Maurice Samuel tries to explain why it is impossible to translate
into English the monologues of Sholom Aleichem's Tevye. "To
clarify the nature of Tevye's gnomic mutilations," he writes, "we
must imagine an American college graduate addressing an audience
of his intellectual peers. We must further imagine that all of them
once took a course in Latin, and have preserved in their memories

the familiar tags with which 'cultivated' essays were peppered a
century or two ago. The speaker throws them in from time to
time accompanying them with English paraphrases and explications
which are sometimes utterly nonsensical, sometimes ingeniously
tangential, sometimes both, and always with a vague suggestion of
authenticity and relevance." Then come, what Samuel calls, some
"imperfect examples":

> *Sic transit gloria mundi*, Here today and gone tomorrow.
> *Reductio ad absurdum*, A fool and his money are soon parted....
> *De mortuis nisi nil bonum*, Once you're dead it's for good.
> *Ars longa vita brevis*, That's the long and the short of it. ...
> *Delenda est Cartago*, Neither a borrower nor a lender be.
> *Carpe diem*, Shoot the works.
> *Non compos mentis*, Look who's talking. ...

And so on. Sweat and possibly tears too lie behind this, but they
did not create it.

Now, that midrashic texts should prove attractive, even irresis-
tible, to translators is no surprise. There is, after all, a natural
affinity between translation which is interpretation (as we saw
from the outset) and Midrash which is commentary. Please allow
me to italicize something immediately, lest we be swept away by
some gothic nonsense, sentimental or pietistic. Regardless of what
the case may have been in antiquity, for the modern student
translation and the received interpretations of the Midrashim will
coincide only to their mutual annihilation, except on rare, and
possibly accidental, occasions: despite rightly-to-be-treasured
felicities like אין פסיחה אלא חייס. There is a profound distinction
between modern translation and the ancient Midrash, and to
ignore it is to vulgarize or neo-hasidize our thinking and speech.
What is it, therefore, that modern translation and the inherited
Midrash share? The ambition to recapture the reverberations of
the original. אם הוא בן גרים לא יאמר לו, זכור מעשה אבותיך, שנאמר,
וגר לא תונה ולא תלחצנו. If a translation of Exodus 22:20 does not
capture something of the moral tremor, it's diminished the charity
of that verse. Beautiful as it is, I cannot be persuaded that Abba
Saul's interpretation of ואנוהו is what Moses and the children of

Israel had in mind at the Reed Sea. Contemporary fashion seems once again to prefer the suggestion of Yose son of the Damascene. In either event, both men are responding to the same wonder: What in the world are that peculiar verb and suffix doing here? Something of that wonder should survive. It may not distort, make either more or less of the original; but it must be within reach of the original. ויאידך? If genuinely imaginative, the result is a sermon (no mean literary accomplishment!); otherwise, humbug.

But now our concern is not with midrashic interpretation of Scripture; it is with translating the Midrash, and that deserves, and requires, the same thoughtfulness as we bring to a biblical verse.

For the longest time I thought that the reason translators were drawn to Midrash — by which I mean specifically haggadic midrash — was because it was easier than halakah. Tackle a halakic subject, *sugya*, and you know at once that it demands your whole tensed intellect: try as a refresher the *sugya* of יי׳ נסך ‎. There is a hardness to this material that is of an altogether different order from even a difficult midrashic passage. In the latter it may be a term we do not understand, or the connection of the prooftext with the statement or comment proposed; or the comment seems plain silly at first; or the mangled state of the text drives you to despair. Halakic material, on the other hand, may be inherently so complex, so involved and casuistical, it's uphill work even when every term is intelligible and the text impeccable.

Only an idiot would deny this. Yet I dare to propose that as regards translation, it is often easier to translate a straight halakic discussion of the Talmud than many, many Midrashim. I'm not saying this to be provocative. I actually made the experiment once: curious to see the outcome. What you need to do is saturate yourself for about three months (if you can stand it) with Bacon's *Essays* till some of his lapidary constructions affect your own speech, and then let yourself go. (Please excuse me for the mixed metaphor which may be present here.) Be sure to paragraph as you would if you were reproducing dialogue in English composition. Punctuate as though your life depended on it: commas, periods, question marks, quotation marks. Don't be frightened that in the end the discussion is still unintelligible. Remember, so is the original. Were it not for Rashi, who would know where the Tanna *is* standing, what this is all about. In other words, halakic discussion or text is far from being untranslatable. It's unreadable, not incomprehensible. What it requires is the very thing the original too cannot do without: a running commentary: and nothing less than that. In this field much not only remains to be done, much can be done.

Perhaps the following is as close to the truth as I can get: If translation and Midrash find that there is a real kinship between them, it is no more than what was always true, that they were both engaged in interpretation. But there may be one aspect of Midrash that especially attracts the modern translator, and that is: Haggadic Midrash is the one branch of talmudic literature which *approaches* the character of belles-lettres. Midrash is not belles-lettres: it does not care to reflect on the beautiful for its own sake; it does not tell its stories for the sake and delight of the story itself (this may be an exaggeration); its poetry is not for the pleasure to be had from the poem itself. But in the reflections and parables and homilies of the Midrash, in the very daring to fly far beyond the literal as it creates hortatory exegesis, in the initiative it takes to explain the biblical past with the help of the present — beloved are anachronisms! — and the present as a prolongation of the biblical past, in the determination to prove appealing to scholar and non-scholar alike (though there were occasions when the Sage directed his remarks specifically to a non-scholarly audience), in the way it enjoys quoting biblical verses, one after the next and the next — thus stirring in the mind sounds and memories that would otherwise vanish, the surrealistic way it catches sight of signs of the future in biblical figures of speech: in all these ways it leads the modern man toward the discourse which has come to mean so much to him, the discourse of the humane and beautiful, the discourse that tries to satisfy a desperate *human* need: the need for flight from surrounding ugliness, the need to escape from the crushing commonplace. Who can resist, אם עשית רצונו כרצונך, לא עשית רצונו כרצונו. ואם עשית רצונו שלא כרצונך, עשית רצונו כרצונו.

17

רצונך שלא תמות, מות עד שלא חמות. רצונך שתחיה, אל תחיה, עד שתחיה.
מוטב לך למות מיתה בעולם הזה, שעל כרחך אתה מת, מלמות מיתה לעתיד
כי אתה עשית Or this, as commentary on לבא, שאם תרצה אי אתה מת?
of Lamentations 1:21? משל למלך שנשא למטרונה; אמר לה, אל תשיחי
עם חברותיך ואל תשאלי מהן ואל תשאילי להן. לימים כעס עליה המלך
וטרדה חוץ לפלטין, וחזרה על כל שכנותיה ולא קבלו אותה; וחזרה לפלטין.
אמר לה המלך, אקשית אפיך? אמרה המטרונה למלך, אדני, אלולי הייתי
משאילה להן ושואלת מהן... לא הוון מקבלין לי? So Israel says to God,
First you order me ולא תתחתן בם, בתך לא תתן לבנו ובתו לא תקח
לבנך. You cut me off from the whole world fraternity, and now
you decide to get rid of me? There is even a dear halakic irony
embedded in this!

There are numerous, numerous other examples (as who should
know better than an audience of the Academy?), some so incisive
in honesty and unostentatiousness of diction, so graceful in their
movements away, away from the strictly literal, and in total yet
dignified submission to what God may decree, only the eloquence
of prayer can equal it.

מי כמכה באלים ה׳

מי כמכה באילמים ה׳

מי כמוך

רואה בעלבון בניך ושותק

To respond to it is to want to understand as completely as possible:
word for word and then the whole of it as a unity. Here translation
begins, and lingers.

# THE TWO VERSIONS OF *ABOT DE RABBI NATHAN**

By JUDAH GOLDIN, Duke University, Durham, N. C.

## To Professor Louis Ginzberg

EVER since Solomon Schechter published his edition of *Abot de Rabbi Nathan* (1887), it has been customary to refer to the two forms of this midrash on *Abot* as two versions of one treatise.[1] The idiom, in fact, was employed by Schechter and he has been followed by all subsequent students. This is not to say that differences between the versions were overlooked. Schechter himself called attention to variants, despite his conclusion that basically "both are one book (not like the *Tanna d'be Eliahu Rabbah* and *Zuta* or *Derek Erez Rabbah* and *Zuta*)."[2] And although after repeated study that conclusion has been modified by some scholars[3] the view still is current that substantially both versions — regardless of the fact that each contains material which does not occur in the other; that even when both express the same general thought, hardly if ever do the readings strictly coincide — present the same ideological commentary on *Abot*. The relationship between the two versions is reduced in effect to this: sometimes the one, sometimes the other retains the better reading; sometimes one supplements the other; sometimes one preserves a more original order.

The fact is, however, that a careful examination of the two versions of *Abot de Rabbi Nathan* reveals a relationship of more than "textual" nature. There is nothing wrong in regarding these treatises as versions, so long as we are not led to overlook

---

* I wish to express my thanks to Professors Louis Ginzberg and Alexander Marx, who were kind enough to read this paper and make several suggestions. Responsibility for the views here expressed, however, rests with me.

[1] It should be recalled that as early as 1872 Solomon Taussig published a substantial portion of the second version in נוה שלום.

[2] *Abbot de Rabbi Nathan*, ed. Schechter, Vienna 1887, Introduction, p. XX.

[3] Cf. Kaufmann in *M.G.W.J.*, Vol. 36, 1887, p. 382–83; Finkelstein, *J.B.L.*, Vol. LVII, Part I, pp. 39 ff.

a very interesting *thematic* difference between them. Indeed, had Schechter recognized the theme of his texts, he would have been spared a number of difficulties with several passages.

Now, "theme" may possibly strike many as a strange word where a text like *Abot de Rabbi Nathan* is concerned. Is it a story, or an essay, or a logical treatise of any sort? Does not *Abot de Rabbi Nathan*, like *Abot*, contain material on a multitude of subjects? Does it not read like a collection of various epigrams with commentary thereon, rather than like a dissertation on some one specific proposition? All this is true. Nevertheless, a recurring note in the treatises as they read today is hardly accidental, and the feeling is inescapable that *Abot de Rabbi Nathan* has more than various reflections on numerous subjects; it is more than a catalogue of maxims with illustrations.

It is almost tempting to suggest that in the difference of theme may lie an explanation for the existence of two separate versions of one treatise. Louis Finkelstein is essentially correct, I feel, when he says that "the two versions of ARN are independent from one another."[4] The question is, Why should two versions have developed from one tradition? Did the respective compilers perhaps wish to deduce different emphases or make prominent different concepts? Be that as it may — since it is very difficult to discover just how collections of oral traditions were undertaken — the treatises today do present a significant divergence in thought.

One word more, before stating this theme, and presenting the evidence. By the word "theme" I mean in effect something like "emphasis," or perhaps what Max Kadushin would call "point of reference."[5] The theme, in other words, is that idea which is repeatedly emphasized, and/or that idea in relation to which other ideas are studied. When an idea becomes so central in treatment, it is entitled to be a "theme."

The theme or emphasis of version I of *Abot de Rabbi Nathan* is the study of Torah. Again and again throughout the text our version goes out of its way to underscore the importance of Torah

[4] Finkelstein, *op. cit.*
[5] Cf. his *Theology of Seder Eliahu,* p. 33–34, and "Organic Thinking," passim.

study. And this emphasis is so strong as to leave the impression that version I is primarily concerned with the study of Torah, while version II would underline "good works" or "good deeds." In any event, this strong insistence upon Torah study is characteristic of version I only.

To the evidence we shall turn in a moment; and naturally the only evidence that may be introduced is evidence derived from passages which occur in *both* versions. Unless a paragraph or a maxim is presented in both versions, there is little opportunity for comparison. Here, however, something must be said lest the hypothesis is misunderstood.

It would be preposterous to say that version I only is interested in the study of Torah. Was not the editor or were not the editors of version II anxious for תלמוד תורה? Could a Jew, with any sensitivity toward his tradition, be indifferent to that "crown" which above all others raised his people from commonness? Or, on the other hand, was there ever a devoted Jew who regarded מעשים טובים as inconsequentials? Was the editor, or were the editors, of version I contemptuous of practical virtues? Patently, no! And if this categorical reply needs proof, both versions of *Abot de Rabbi Nathan* stand ready to demonstrate that the study of Torah *and* good works must be part of every Jew's equipment. Nevertheless, even in unanimity there are differences of inflection. Version I and version II would agree on what makes the perfect Jew. But version I presents an emphasis which is lacking in II. Version I, with a certain emphasis in mind, is always — or almost always — referring whatever it discusses to this central idea. And this central idea, as I have said, is the study of Torah.[6]

a) Perhaps the most striking passage — indeed, it was the first to catch my attention — in all the evidence is the comment of version I on Rabbi Jose's saying, "Let all thy deeds be for the sake of Heaven."[7] This is the comment:[8] "And let all thy deeds be for the sake of Heaven: for the sake of Torah; as it is said, 'In

---

[6] Professor Ginzberg notes, "דרכן של‎ = II ;‏דרכן של תלמידי חכמים‎ = I כל בני אדם‎!"

[7] I, 17, p. 65; II, 30, p. 65. Cf. *Abot* 2.12.

[8] I, 17, p. 66.

all thy ways acknowledge Him (רעהו) and He will direct thy paths' (Prov. 3.6).'' ''For the sake of Torah'' is certainly not ''for the sake of Heaven'' unless one's regard for Torah is extraordinary. Indeed, if we look to the parallel passage in version II we meet no such extravagant interpretation. ''And let all thy deeds be for the sake of Heaven,'' reads version II,[9] ''like Hillel. When Hillel used to go forth to [some] place, [people] would say to him, 'Whither art thou going?' [He would reply,] 'I go to perform a commandment.' 'Which commandment, Hillel?' [they would ask.] [He would reply,] 'I am going to the privy.' 'Is this, then, a commandment?' He would say to them, 'Indeed! so that the body do not deteriorate.'

''[Moreover, men would say to Hillel,] 'Where art thou going, Hillel?' [He would reply,] 'I go to perform a commandment.' 'Which commandment, Hillel?' 'I am going to the bath house.' 'Is this, then, a commandment?' He would say to them, 'Indeed! To clean the body. Know thou that it is so: if he, that is appointed to polish and clean the statues which stand in the palaces of kings, receives a stipend each and every year; moreover, he is magnified together with the magnates of the kingdom — how much more so we that have been created in the image and likeness [of God]; as it is said, 'For in the image of God made He man' (Gen. 9.6).' ''

The comment of version II is not only a lesson on the proximity of cleanliness to godliness, but certainly less forced than the one offered by our version. Only on the basis of the assumption that version I is emphasizing the study of Torah, can we understand what has happened.[10]

[9] II, 30, p. 66.

[10] Schechter was apparently bewildered by this passage; cf. his note 19, p. 66.

A note is perhaps in place at this point. Some may feel that the text is very likely corrupt. לשם שמים, it may be said, is definitely not לשם תורה, and the reading is, to say the least, suspicious.

Now, Dr. Schechter in his note (19) observes that the Oxford ms. reads וכל מעשיך יהיו לשם תורה. Furthermore, Editio Princeps (so too the Zolkiev edition) of *Abot de Rabbi Nathan* has לשם שמים שנא' בכל דרכיך דעהו והוא יישר אורחותיך. Is this not further evidence that our text does not read properly?

Before explaining why I consider the text correct, I think it profitable to point out that even if the reading had been otherwise, the theory offered

b) On the statement of Nittai the Arbelite,[11] "Consort not with the wicked,"[12] version I gives us two interpretations.[13] The

here serves to explain how such a "corruption" could occur. If scholars recognized that version I of *Abot de Rabbi Nathan* was stressing Torah study, a late editor would without embarrassment interpret לשם שמים as לשם תורה.

However, I do not believe that our text ever read otherwise. In the first place, the Oxford ms. is obviously wrong since we have no statement from R. Jose וכל מעשיך יהיו לשם תורה. True, the phrase וכל מעשיך יהיו לשם שמים, at the beginning of the chapter, has been added to our edition by Schechter, on the basis of the Mishnah reading. Nevertheless, where is there a statement by R. Jose which reads like the epigram recorded in the Oxford ms.? Version II can at least serve us as an aid in establishing the general maxim! Version II reads clearly וכל מעשיך יהיו לשם שמים.

The form in Editio Princeps is absolutely unwarranted. It may be urged that the verse from Proverbs proves that not Torah study is involved. I am not sure about that. Perhaps the emphasis is on דעהו — *know* Him! It is worth noticing, for example, that version II (*ibid.*) gives the same verse at the end of the next paragraph, which reads: "Rabbi Eleazar (not Eliezer) says, Be diligent in the study of Torah, and know how to reply to an unbeliever (אפיקורס) in words of Torah, so that they be not destroyed (reading יסתרו — cf. Bacher, *Agada der Tannaiten*, I, p. 72, n. 5; see also Felix Perles in *Jewish Studies in Memory of Israel Abrahams*, p. 382). And know before whom thou toilest and who is author of the covenant with thee; as it is said, 'In all thy ways acknowledge Him (דעהו)' (Prov. 3.6)."

My reluctance to yield on this point — though the hypothesis is in no way weakened, as I observed — is due to the fact that the term לשם שמים *is* used in association with an activity centering around the study of Torah. For thus we read (I, 40, p. 129; cf. *Abot* 5.17; see also II, 46, p. 128): כל מחלוקת שהיא לשם שמים סופה להתקיים ... אי זו מחלוקת שהיא לשם שמים, זו מחלוקת הלל ושמאי. If the controversies of Hillel and Shammai might be described — as they unquestionably deserve to be — as controversies לשם שמים, it is not, I feel, impossible to associate deeds לשם שמים with the concept לשם תורה.

Professor Ginzberg adds the following note: "As to the interchange between שמים and תורה, comp. the use of רחמנא, 'the All Merciful,' one of the names of God in Palestinian sources, while in Babli it stands — hundreds of times! — for אוריתא, Torah. A very intersting discussion on the identity of שם שמים=שם תורה is found in נפש החיים, chap. iv by R. Hayyim Volozhin, the famous pupil of the Gaon. There are many places in Rabb. Literature where תורה and הקב'ה are used interchangeably; the idea is that the will of God is expressed in the Torah. It is quite possible that לשם תורה was used for לשם שמים for another reason, to avoid the two almost identical syllables שָם and שָם."

[11] II, 16, p. 35 attributes it to Rabbi (!) Joshua ben Perahiah.
[12] I, 9, p. 38; cf. *Abot* 1.7.    [13] I, 9, p. 42.

first is an exhortation, with illustrations from biblical history, not to associate with evil or wicked persons. The second reads tersely as follows: "Another interpretation: Consort not with the wicked, even for Torah!"[14] A glance at the comments — and there are several — of version II on אל תתחבר_לרשע reveals some interesting thoughts, but nothing even remotely resembling our treatise at this point.[15] Version I, indeed, I feel, has a significant variant from the statement in the *Mekilta*[16] and *Yalkut*,[17] which resembles ours. These latter read אפילו. לקרבו לתורה, which conceivably might mean: "Consort not with the wicked, even to bring him close to those things for which Torah stands, those lessons which Torah teaches."[18] That לקרבו לתורה does not necessarily refer to Torah study is evident from the comment on ומקרבן לתורה of Hillel's saying.[19] The reading, however, of version I indicates that again and again Torah study is the author's point of reference. The full meaning of the passage seems to be, Although Torah is so very, very important, none the less consorting with the wicked is hazardous — certain men cannot be taught Torah.[20]

c) A very subtle distinction between the readings of our two versions in one of the early chapters throws into sharp focus the motives of the different editors. Like God, like Adam, like Torah and others, we are told, the Sages too made a hedge about their words. Now, asks version I,[21] "What is the hedge which the Sages made about their words? For the Sages say, The recitation of the evening *shema* [may take place] until midnight. Rabban Gamaliel says, Until the cock crows. How is that?[22] When a man returns

[14] In a translation which is to appear shortly I have rendered the phrase, "even for [the study of] Torah."

[15] Cf. II, 16, p. 36.

[16] Mekilta, מסכתא דעמלק, 3, ed. Lauterbach, II, p. 166.

[17] Yalkut Joshua, 1, ¶ 3.

[18] On the other hand, the reading in Aknin's ספר מוסר, ed. Bacher, Berlin, 1910, p. 14, is ואפילו לקרבו לתורה. Is this perhaps a case of אשנרא דלישנא?

[19] Cf. I, 12, p. 53. But see II, 26, p. 53. This passage is to be discussed below in the appendix.

[20] Cf., on the other hand, the attitude of the school of Hillel, I, 3, p. 14–15, and II, 4, *ibid*.

[21] I, 2, p. 14.

[22] That is, What is the hedge which the Sages made?

from his work, let him not say, I will eat a bit, and drink a bit, and nap a while, and afterwards I shall recite the *shema* — for thus he will sleep through the night and not recite the *shema*. Rather, when a man returns from his work in the evening, let him go to the synagogue or to the house of study. If he is accustomed to study Scripture, let him study Scripture; and if he is accustomed to study Mishnah, let him study Mishnah; and if not, let him recite the *shema* and pray."

And now let us look at version II.[23] "Whence do we learn that the Sages made a hedge about their words? For the Sages said that the [evening] *shema* may be recited until midnight. Rabban Gamliel says, Until the cock crows. [And why do the Sages say, Until midnight?] For a man should not say, Since I am permitted to recite the [evening] *shema* all night, I shall go to sleep; whenever I please, I will recite the *shema*: [because] sleep will overtake him, and he will not have recited it. Lo, such a one is guilty against his own soul! Hence the Sages said, When a man mounts his couch let him recite [the *shema*]; if he is a scholar, let him first recite the *shema*, and then if he wishes to study, let him study."

Version II certainly makes more sense than does our version. The hedge, let us remember, is a hedge connected with the reading of the *shema*. The first thing, therefore, one should do in the evening is recite the *shema*. What is the meaning, then, of If he is accustomed to study, let him study; "and if not, let him recite the *shema* and pray?" Is study perhaps more important than prayer? Is prayer only for those who cannot study?[24]

Moreover, what fears pursue version II, that it should declare pointedly — after stating what all men must do — "if he is a scholar, let him first recite the *shema*, and *then* if he wishes to study, let him study?" Is this version afraid lest scholarship reduce prayer to secondary significance? The variant reading in Doctor Schechter's note[25] makes all the more emphatic the duty to recite the *shema* first: a scholar must first recite the *shema* and *afterwards* (ואח״כ) if he wished to study he might do so.

---

[23] II, 3, p. 14.

[24] Notice how the commentators have called attention to the fact that the parallel reading of this passage (Berakot 4b) does not record ואם לאו.

[25] II, 3, p. 14, n. 24.

Can this variant between the two versions be described as a mere accident?[26]

d) Many are the sayings attributed by *Abot de Rabbi Nathan* to Hillel. The form of one of these will be of immediate interest. In Babylonian he said, according to version I,[27] "And he that does not attend the Sages is worthy of death." In order to amplify this brief remark, our text, shortly thereafter, tells a story of a priest whose efforts at piety were of no avail, since he had neglected to attend the Sages, that is, to study under them.[28] Version II,[29] on the other hand, adds one further saying to Hillel's credit: "And he that does not attend the Sages is worthy of death; and he that attends the sages but does not practice (ולא מקיים) is worthy of the death of deaths." Like the previous version, version II tells the story of the priest who did not attend the Sages.[30] The story, in other words, is the same in both instances; but the final moral deduced differs in each version. Our version is anxious to demonstrate that he that fails to study with the Sages is mortally guilty, while version II leaves the whole subject with the words, "he that attends [the Sages] but does not practice is worthy of the death of deaths!" Do not the two versions appear to be underscoring different themes?

e) Not very far from Hillel's maxim, in our version, is recorded a saying of Shammai.[31] "Make thy [study of] Torah,"

---

[26] Moreover, I feel that Aknin (*op. cit.*, p. 3) sensed the difficulty created by the reading of version I: although he quotes *Abot de Rabbi Nathan* to illustrate the various hedges, for the hedge of the Sages he gives the reading from *Berakot* 1.1! Did Aknin too recognize that the reading of version I did not quite apply to the saying of the Men of the Great Assembly? One could of course say that Aknin preferred to refer to the Mishnah directly; but that would be forced. If he is quoting A. R. N. throughout and substantially the same illustration in this instance too occurs in A. R. N., why suddenly express a preference for the Mishnah reading?

[27] I, 12, p. 55.

[28] Cf. I, 12, p. 56.

[29] Cf. II, 27, p. 56.

[30] Cf. II, 27, p. 56–57. Incidentally, the very conclusion of the chapter, [סכאן] אמרו חכמים (!), needs examination.

[31] I, 13, p. 56; cf. *Abot* 1.15. On the significance of the order in versions I and II in which Hillel and Shammai are quoted, see Schechter's introduction to his edition, p. XX–XXI.

Shammai used to say, "a fixed habit." And this is the comment: "Make thy [study of] Torah a fixed habit: how is that? This teaches us that if a man has heard something from a sage in the house of study, let him not treat it casually (אל יעשה אותו עראי),[32] but let him treat it attentively (קבע); and what a man learns let him practice himself, and then teach others that they may practice it; as it is said, 'That ye may learn them and observe to do them.' (Deut. 5.1). And so too in Ezra it says, 'For he had set his heart to seek the law of the Lord, and to do it.' And afterwards, 'And to teach in Israel statutes and ordinances' (Ezra 7.10).[33]

Now, version II,[34] on the same phrase, has this to say: "Make thy [study of] Torah a fixed habit: Be thou not lenient with thyself and severe with others, or lenient with others and severe with thyself. Instead, even as thou art lenient with thyself, so shalt thou be lenient with others; and even as thou art severe with thyself, so shalt thou be severe with others. As it is said, 'For Ezra had set his heart to seek the law of the Lord and to do it.' And afterwards, 'And to teach in Israel statutes and ordinances' (Ezra 7.10)"

In the first place, it is interesting to notice that the verse from Ezra applies more smoothly to version I than it does to version II — although, even in the latter instance, the Ezra passage is not altogether irrelevant. Secondly, however, version II has but one understanding of Shammai's teaching. Version II sees in Shammai's words an exhortation to consistent practice only. Version I would have no quarrel with such an attitude; but it relates Shammai's counsel to study as well as to practice. First our version, at Shammai's suggestion, recommends what a man is to do when he hears something from a sage in a school; then, it prescribes what he is to do if he hopes to teach others.

f) Another slight yet significant variant in the light of the present hypothesis, is reflected in the statement of Rabbi Ishmael. According to version I[35] Rabbi Ishmael said, "He that

---

[32] That this is the proper meaning is, I feel, clearly brought out by the continuation of the paragraph. In the latter half, practice is spoken of.

[33] I shall have additional comments on this passage in the forthcoming translation, *ad loc.*

[34] II, 23, p. 47.     [35] I, 27, p. 84; cf. *Abot* 4.5.

studies in order to teach, it is granted him to study and teach; and he that studies in order to practice, it is granted him to study and to teach and to practice." Version II,[36] on the other hand, quotes Rabbi Ishmael to this effect: "He that studies in order to teach, it is not granted him to study and to teach. But he that studies in order to practice, it is granted him to study and to teach, to observe and to practice." Again it is clear that both versions I and II agree that practice is the culmination of study. But version I insists that study for the purpose of teaching will bear fruit; to this version II objects.

g) After all these examples — and before proceeding with others — one may introduce as evidence a passage which has all the earmarks of later interpolation. The point is, of course, that we now have an explanation for such an interpolation. Only he who recognized the emphasis of version I would have felt no compunctions in inserting such a thought.

Early in our text,[37] where Moses' independent decisions are described, and they are said to have had God's unqualified approval, we read as follows: "He broke the tables [of the Commandments]. How is that? It was said, When Moses went up to heaven to receive the tables [of the Commandments], which had been inscribed and put away since the six days of Creation — as it is said, 'And the tables were the work of God, and the writing was the writing of God, graven upon the tables' (Ex. 32.15): read not *harut* (graven), but *herut* (freedom), for whosoever studies Torah is a free man — at that time, the ministering angels conspired against Moses," and so forth.

None of this interpolation אל תקרי הרות אלא חירות שכל מי שעוסק בתורה הרי הוא בן חורין לעצמו is in the parallel passage of the second version[38] — and as a result, indeed, it reads more fluently. Merely to dismiss the passage as a later addition to our text is to overlook, I feel, the theme which the later editor detected in the treatise. With such a theme easily recognizable to him, why should he have felt any scruples in adding more material? This

[36] II, 32, p. 68.
[37] I, 2, p. 10.
[38] II, 2, p. 10-11.

was very likely his sentiment; and even when we recognize his intrusion, we ought to understand his motives.

h) One interpolation leads to another; and so it may not be unprofitable to compare the account in the two versions of Ben Zoma's saying. "Who is wise," we read in version I:[39] "He that learns from all men; as it is said, 'From all my teachers have I got understanding.'[40] (Ps. 119.99). Who is most humble? He that is as humble as Moses our master; as it is said, 'Now the man Moses was very meek' (Num. 12.3). Who is most rich? He that rejoices in his portion; as it is said, 'When thou eatest the labour of thy hands, happy shalt thou be, and it shall be well with thee.' (Ps. 128.2). Who is most mighty? He that subdues his evil *yezer*; as it is said, 'He that is slow to anger is better than the mighty; and he that ruleth his spirit than he that taketh a city' (Prov. 16.32). And whoever subdues his evil *yezer* is accounted as though he had subdued a city full of mighty men; as it is said, 'A wise man scaleth the city of the mighty, and bringeth down the stronghold wherein it trusteth' (Prov. 21.22). And the mighty are none but the mighty of Torah; as it is said, 'Ye mighty in strength that fulfill His word, hearkening unto the voice of His word' (Ps. 103.20)."

The passage gives two other possible interpretations of נבורים but these need not concern us especially at this point. What is immediately interesting is the expansion of the term "mighty." The mighty, in short, are not only those who subdue their passions, but the "Torah-braves." An examination of version II is now appropriate. Here[41] we read: "Ben Zoma says, Who is wise? He that learns from all men; as it is said, 'From all my teachers have I got understanding' (Ps. 119.99). Who is honored? He that honors mankind; as it is said, 'For them that honor Me I will honor and they that despise Me shall be lightly esteemed' (I Sam. 2.30).[42] Who is mighty? He that subdues his evil *yezer*; as it is

---

[39] I, 23, p. 75; cf. *Abot* 4.1.

[40] See, on the other hand, the regular translation in the J. P. S. Bible.

[41] II, 33, p. 72.

[42] On the proof offered by this verse, cf. the commentary of R. Obadiah of Bertinoro to *Abot* 4.1. See also the commentary *ad loc.* in Mahzor Vitry, Rabbenu Jonah, ps. Rashi, etc.

said, 'He that is slow to anger is better than the mighty' (Prov.
16.32). Who is rich? He that rejoices in his portion; as it is said,
'When thou eatest the labour of thy hands, happy shalt thou be,
and it shall be well with thee' (Ps. 128.2): happy shalt thou be in
this world, and it shall be well with thee in the world to come.''

Not only does version II read more like *Abot*, but it reads
better than does our version. What happened to version I can
be explained, I believe, by the hypothesis which each of these
examples is intended to substantiate.

i) Very instructive, I feel, will be an analysis of what the two
versions of *Abot de Rabbi Nathan* do with a saying by Elisha ben
Abuyah. This time we quote first from version II. It reads:[43]
"Elisha ben Abuyah says, He that studies Torah in his youth, to
what may he be likened? To lime which is spread on stones: even
if all the rains come down, they do not injure it. But he that
studies Torah in his old age, to what may he be likened? To lime
which is spread over bricks: as soon as one drop of water falls on
it, it disintegrates and is washed away (והולך לו — literally,
'disappears').

"A parable is told: to what may this be likened? To a king
who said to his servant, 'Protect [this] bird for my son.' The king
said to his servant, 'If thou dost protect the bird, thou dost protect thine own life; but if thou dost destroy the bird, thou dost
destroy thine own life.' [The servant] protected the bird. . . Thus
says the Holy One blessed be He to Israel: 'My children, if you
keep[44] the Torah, you keep your own lives; but if you destroy the
Torah, you destroy your own lives.' So too, whoever keeps one
word of the Torah, keeps his own life; but whoever destroys one
word of the Torah, destroys his own life; as it is said, 'Only take
heed to thyself, and keep thy soul diligently, [lest thou forget the
things which thine eyes saw].' (Deut. 4.9)."

Does this parable have anything to do with Elisha's statement? The editor, in fact, seems to have had a very strange
conception of analogies.[45] Both the tale and the conclusion em-

---

[43] II, 35, p. 77.

[44] The word is משמר — the same as the word translated "protect."

[45] Schechter (II, 35, p. 77–78, note 2) also observed the difficulty. Taking
a hint from the Gaon, he suggests that possibly the parable illustrates the

phasize "observance" of Torah — in other words, the practical implication of Torah — while the statement of Elisha had as its theme study. Is the same, perhaps, true of version I? Let us see.

Version I has no single passage which runs completely parallel to the Elisha passage of II. For example, the metaphor of lime on stones, our version employs in the description of men with Torah and with or without good deeds.[46] The parable of the king with the bird, our version attaches to a statement concerning those who stimulate others to good works. This is, however, what version I does have on the subject of studying in youth and in old age:[47] "He that studies Torah as a child, the words of Torah are absorbed in his blood[48] and they come forth from his mouth distinctly. But he that studies Torah in his old age, the words of Torah are not absorbed in his blood and do not come forth from his mouth distinctly. And thus the maxim goes (אומר — literally, 'says'): If in thy youth thou didst not desire them, how shalt thou acquire them in thine old age?"

The reading of our text is obviously better, more logical. And I believe that once more we have an instance of version I clinging to its point of reference, study; version II, on the other hand, takes the theme of study and turns it into a sermon on the importance of observing Torah.

Here we have an opportunity to repeat the caution recommended at the very outset of this paper. There is a danger that in focussing evidence on a theory, the picture as a whole may be blurred. To say that version I of *Abot de Rabbi Nathan* is emphasizing Torah study is not to imply that this treatise prescribes a neglect of practice. The chapter in which Elisha's views are recorded is an excellent case in point. Most of the paragraphs in it emphasize the incompleteness of study alone. The man without

saying of Rabbi Dostai (*Abot* 3.8) which should come into our text. I do not agree at all. Notice, incidentally, the difficulty with this parable in I, 24, p. 78, and there too no word is heard of R. Dostai. For a more detailed discussion see note 51, below.

[46] Cf. I, 24, p. 77.

[47] I, 24, p. 77-78.

[48] Bacher, *op. cit.*, I, p. 432, n. 5, alludes to the Roman proverb, "in succum et sanguinem." As for the maxim, see Ecclus. 25.3.

מעשים טובים, Elisha tells us again and again — and who knew it better than he — is like a stone structure atop brick foundations, or like lime poured on bricks, or like a cup without a flat base, or like the rider of an unbridled horse. None of these would one choose to be. The point is, that our version, while admitting all this, seeks to underline the concept of study of Torah; as a result it stresses that theme, or relates other ideas to it, or refrains from turning it into other directions.

The thesis is here restated because version I affords us the occasion in this instance to examine how it applies the parable which II had attached to a statement on study. In our version too,[49] truth be told, the parable is not without its problems.[50] Nevertheless, here the parable is said to illustrate, not "study," but the statement, "Whoever makes his fellow perform some commandment, the verse accounts it to him as though he has performed it himself."[51]

j) After having observed the two versions in their treatment of Elisha's statement, it is interesting to notice the variants in their description of them that frequent the house of study. "There are four types," we read in our version,[52] "among them that frequent the house of study: [there is one] that draws near

[49] I, 24, p. 78.

[50] See *ibid.*, Schechter's note 24; see also my note in the forthcoming translation *ad loc.*

[51] Is not the following a possible explanation of what happened in version II? The statement of Elisha unquestionably discussed "study." The editor of version II, however, being principally concerned with good works, determined to read his theme into the words of Elisha. Consequently he attached the parable and the concluding sentences to Elisha's dictum. For there was a particularly good reason to do so in this case! The author of the saying was none other than *Aher*. Was he not a splendid example of those who do not "keep the Torah?" Moreover, Elisha's own career seemed to belie his words: הלמד תורה בנערותו למה הוא דומה, לסיד שהוא טוח על גבי אבנים, אפילו כל הגשמים יורדין אין מזיקין אותו. But Elisha had studied in his youth! Not study at too late a date was the stumbling block of this man; probably he failed to supplement his many studies with good deeds. That was the cause for his failure.

In the light of this, perhaps we can understand too why version II quotes so little from Elisha, while version I gives a goodly number of his statements.

[52] I, 40, p. 126.

[the sage] and sits down, [and] has a portion [of reward]; [there is one] that draws near and sits down, [and] has no portion [of reward]; [there is one] that keeps at a distance and sits down, [and] has a portion [of reward]; [there is one] that keeps at a distance and sits down, [and] has no portion [of reward]. [There is one] that asks and replies, [and] has a portion [of reward]; [there is one] that asks and replies, [and] has no portion [of reward]; [there is one] that sits and keeps quiet, [and] has a portion [of reward]; [there is one] that sits and keeps quiet, [and] has no portion [of reward]."

The text then proceeds to explain what distinguishes one man from the next. The individuals to be rewarded are those who approach the sage in order the better to hear his lesson, or keep at a distance out of sincere humility, or ask questions the better to understand, or do not interrupt the lecture with questions the better to hear. Those who go without reward are the ones who come up front out of arrogance, or keep at a distance out of false modesty, or ask questions to leave the impression that they are wise, or keep quiet to indicate their independence of the sage.

The "catalogue" and description, in brief, are devoted to an analysis of various types of behavior at study. Some students belong to one category, some to another, but the categories are descriptive of conduct at study.

The "four types among them that frequent the house of study" presented by version II,[53] are entirely different. They are, significantly enough, as follows: "He that goes[54] and practices, is a saintly man. He that neither goes nor practices, is a wicked man. He that goes but does not practice, has the reward for going. He that practices and does not go, has the reward for practice." The word עשה has changed the complexion of the passage. We are dealing with something else entirely; we are dealing with a different perspective. The הולכי בית המדרש are examined for different qualities by the two versions.[55]

---

[53] II, 45, p. 126.
[54] I. e., to school.
[55] See, incidentally, II, 46, p. 129, where different types of "frequenters" are described.

k) The theme of version I of *Abot de Rabbi Nathan* will perhaps serve us in understanding a passage in the text which has
baffled many scholars. We read toward the end of the treatise:[56]
"The sword comes upon the world because of the delaying of
justice and the perverting of justice; and because of them המורין
בתורה שלא כהלכה." Before translating this last clause, as it is
understood by version I, it is necessary to examine the story
which follows our sentence. We are told that when Rabbi Simeon
ben Gamaliel and Rabbi Ishmael[57] were being led to their execution, Rabbi Simeon wept. He could not understand why it was
destined for him to be treated like a criminal. Yet God could not
be unjust! Therefore Rabbi Ishmael advised him to think of certain sins in his lifetime which conceivably warranted the present
punishment. The conversation deserves more than a paraphrase.

> " 'Perhaps,' " said Rabbi Ishmael to him, " 'when thou
> didst settle down to dinner, poor men came and stood at
> thy door, and thou didst not permit them to enter and eat?'
> [Rabbi Simeon] said to him, 'By Heaven, I did not do thus!
> Rather, I had guards sitting at the door. When the poor
> would come, they would be brought in to me, and they
> would eat and drink with me and recite a blessing in the name
> of Heaven.'[58] [Rabbi Ishmael] said to him, 'Perhaps when
> thou didst sit expounding on the Temple Mount, and all
> the hosts of Israel sat before thee, thou didst grow
> proud?' He said to him, 'Ishmael, my brother, Man is
> destined to receive the punishment [he deserves].' "[59]

The narrative then goes on with the execution proper; finally it
brings the verses from Zechariah (3.17) and from Exodus (22.33)
which speak of slaughter by the sword.

The question is, What is this story intended to illustrate?
Its connection with the introductory statement of the paragraph
is far from clear. The commentators have gone to no end of

---

[56] I, 38, p. 114; cf. *Abot* 5.8.

[57] Cf. Finkelstein, *The Ten Martyrs*, in *Essays and Studies in Memory of Linda R. Miller*, New York, 1938, pp. 29–55.

[58] I. e., recite the Grace.

[59] The text reads מוכן אדם ייקבל את פגעו. The phrase is not without its difficulties. Nonetheless, it does not affect what is here involved. There will be a note in the translation *ad loc.*

trouble to relate the statement about the sword and the story to
each other.[60] Their suggestions, though fine, fail to explain what
has happened to our text.

As usual, when the text gives one trouble, he turns to the
parallel passage of the second version. The reading here[61] is of
great assistance.

"The sword comes upon the world because of the perversion
of justice and the delaying of justice."[62] Immediately thereafter
comes the story of the execution of Rabbi Simeon ben Gamaliel
and Rabbi Ishmael, with the details of which we are already
familiar. Nevertheless, it will be instructive to eavesdrop on
their conversation.

> " 'Shall I not weep,' " said Rabbi Simeon, " 'when I am
> being led forth to be killed like them that worship idols,
> and like them that commit incest, and like them that shed
> [innocent] blood, and like them that profane the Sabbath?'
> Rabbi Ishmael said to him, 'Is it, [then,] for naught? Did
> never a woman come to ask thee concerning her menstrua-
> tion, or a man concerning his vow, and thou wast asleep,
> or at dinner, or perhaps thy time was not free, or perhaps
> the servant did not permit him to enter?'[63] [Rabbi Simeon]
> said to him, 'Whether I was asleep or at dinner, the servant
> was commanded that no man be prevented from entering.
> Yet,[64] it is not for naught! Once, as I was sitting down, men
> stood before me[65] and my heart swelled within me.' Rabbi
> Ishmael said to him, 'We deserve to be led forth to be
> killed.' "

From version II, in other words, we learn that the story of the
execution of the two sages is an illustration of the consequences
of עִנּוּי הַדִּין — particularly is this clear from the reading in the
*Menorat Hamaor*. Is it not significant that the second version,

---

[60] See Schechter's note 7, *ibid*. See also what the Gaon recommends.

[61] II, 41, p. 114.

[62] See also II, 41, p. 116.

[63] See the reading at this point in Al-Nakawa, *Menorat Ha-Maor*, ed.
Enelow, IV, p. 189–90, which makes the connection to the introductory statement sufficiently obvious.

[64] I am following the reading of *Menorat Ha-Maor, ibid.*, which omits אִ״ל
here and the very next one. My feeling is that Rabbi Simeon is saying all this.

[65] At this point *Menorat Ha-Maor, ibid.*, adds pointedly לָדִין.

substantially, does so read, while version I reads כשהיית יושב
ודורש בהר הבית? Moreover, the form in version I is all the more
impressive when we inspect other sources in which the story
occurs. Most of them[66] say nothing of "expounding on the Temple
Mount." Only one manuscript[67] resembles the idiom in our
treatise: שמא כשהיית דורש ברבים היה לבך שמח והנאה (לכך) [לבך] אמ'
[ניחמתני] לו (ניוומתי). Another source[68] has this interesting expression: שמא כשהיית יושב בדין ודורש וכל אכלוסי ישראל יושבין לפניך שמא זהת
דעתך עליך. Apparently there were two forms in which the conversation between Rabbi Simeon and Rabbi Ishmael was handed
down, and our last source represents an effort to combine them
both.[69]

In any event — and particularly if the last assumption is true
— the story in version I reflects the emphasis which it is constantly making. Either the phrase was deliberately changed to
כשהיית יושב ודורש בהר הבית or that form was selected by version
I because Torah study — and hence an activity, "expounding,"
related to it — was its point of reference.[70]

If the interpretation offered thus far is plausible, we may
return to the clause המורין בתורה שלא כהלכה. The words, in this
instance, are extremely difficult, particularly since I believe
that the story about the execution of the sages (in version I) is

[66] Cf. Mekilta, *Mishpatim*, מסכתא דנזיקין, 18, III, p. 142; *Semahot*, ed.
Higger, Ch. 8, p. 153; *Tanna d'be Eliahu*, ed. Friedmann, Ch. 30, p. 153; Yalkut
Exodus, 349 (these references are given by Schechter, I, 38, p. 115, n. 7).
For other references see Higger, *op. cit.*, p. 36–38.

[67] סדר חיבור ברכות, p. 266 — quoted by Higger, *op. cit.*, p. 38.

[68] *Exempla of the Rabbis*, ed. M. Gaster, Passage 76, p. 51. See incidentally,
Büchler, *Studies in Sin and Atonement*, p. 199, n. 1.

[69] I must confess that this is indeed my feeling about the passage in the
*Exempla*. There seems to have been one tradition which regarded the tragic
end of R. Simeon as a punishment not for עוני הדין, but as a punishment for
lack of humility. Witness the account in סדר חיבור ברכות (I quote in full so that
the context be clear): כשיצאו רשב'ג ור' ישמעאל כהן גדול ליהרג אמ' לו רשב'ג לר' ישמעאל,
אחי אוי לי שאיני יודע למה אני יוצא ליהרג, אמ' לו שמא כשהיית דורש ברבים היה לבך
שמח והנאה (לכך) [לבך] אמ' לו (ניוומתי) [ניחמתני]. על כן כשעושה אדם מעשים טובים יעשם
בצניעות, ואל יהנה בפני העולם שנוטל שכרו בזה העולם.

[70] The difficulty felt by Schechter (note 7, p. 114–15) thus becomes clear,
and his suggested reading is altogether unnecessary.

meant as an illustration not of עני הדין but of 'המורין בתורה וכו.
Although Professor Ginzberg informs me that in rabbinic litera-
ture מורין is always "decide" — not merely "teach" — perhaps,
*Abot de Rabbi Nathan*, for purposes of *derush*,[71] amplifies the
meaning of the word in this connection to instruction in general.
Moreover, שלא כהלכה here means "improperly" and has nothing
to do with the *halakah* as such.[72] The clause would then mean,
The sword comes upon the world because of them that teach
Torah with improper conduct. The teacher who is proud is not
behaving well, for humility must characterize him at all times.

I am thoroughly aware of the serious objections to such an
interpretation.[73] Nevertheless, the crux of the evidence resides
not in the validity of my understanding of 'המורין בתורה וכו, nor
in the hypothesis that the story illustrates that principle; the
important factor is the variant between the readings in version I
and version II of the cause of Rabbi Simeon's punishment.

1) Every example introduced thus far has been taken from
such passages as both versions of *Abot de Rabbi Nathan* discuss.
This was deliberately done, for, as was early observed, some
comparative standard is necessary. The next, and last illustration, however, represents material in two separate paragraphs
which occur in version I only. Nevertheless, more than passing
significance, I believe, is theirs.

At the very beginning of version I,[74] immediately after the
controversy between Rabbi Jose the Galilean and Rabbi Akiba,
Rabbi Nathan — allegedly the author-editor of this treatise[75] —
is quoted. Rabbi Nathan offers a reason why Moses was detained
six days before the word of God came to him. With that view,
apparently, Rabbi Mattiah ben Heresh cannot agree; conse-

---

[71] See, for example, what the text does to Jose ben Johanan's statement
in I, 7, p. 34 and II, 14, p. 33.

[72] See, for example, II, 40, p. 111 and also p. 112 where the phrase (in
describing the clod) ושואל שלא כראוי ומשיב שלא כענין occurs as a contrast to שואל
כענין ומשיב כהלכה.

[73] Incidentally, neither is the passage in II, 41, p. 116 בעון בטול תורה ועוות
הדין חרב בא לעולם וכו' of much assistance. For, is pride an instance of בטול תורה?

[74] I, 1, p. 1.

[75] See my note in the translation, *ad loc.*

quently, he explains otherwise what happened with Moses. This done, the paragraph concludes as follows: "It once happened that Rabbi Josiah and Rabbi Mattiah ben Heresh sat together engaged in the study of Torah. Rabbi Josiah withdrew to attend to his occupation. Said Rabbi Mattiah to him, 'Master, why dost thou leave the words of the living God to pursue an occupation? Now, although thou art my master and I am thy pupil, [I declare] it is not good to leave the words of the living God and pursue an occupation.' It was said [of them], So long as they sat studying Torah, they acted as though they were jealous of each other: but when they departed, they were like friends from childhood on."

On this note the first paragraph in our treatise ends. The theme calls attention to itself quite adequately, and needs no amplification on my part. The connection, likewise, of this brief story with the preceding material is not far fetched.

Nothing like this story is to be found at the beginning of version II.[76]

And now we turn to the very last paragraph of our work.[77] "Rabbi Hannaniah ben Akashya said, It pleased the Holy One blessed be He to grant merit to Israel; therefore, He gave them Torah and commandments in abundance; as it is said, 'The Lord was pleased for his[78] righteousness' sake, to make Torah great and glorious.' (Is. 42.21)." Certainly the theme here is clear enough, and the verse from Isaiah is as felicitous for our hypothesis as it is for a peroration of the volume.

The sentiment expressed at the conclusion of version II[79] is unquestionably noble; moreover it is a tribute to scholars, those "philosophers-kings" of Israel. But an emphasis on Torah it is not.

Now, Doctor Schechter[80] is very likely correct in assuming that the saying of Rabbi Hananiah ben Akashya is a late conclusion attached to our treatise. Nevertheless, "And there is no doubt that these words were added here either by the copyists

[76] Cf. II, 1, p. 1.
[77] I, 41, p. 134.
[78] I. e,. Israel's. Cf. translation *ad loc.*
[79] Cf. II, 48, p. 134.
[80] I, 41, p. 134, n. 27.

or by the printers in order to conclude on a happy note" is not enough of an answer. There are many "happy endings" in the literature of Israel. The conclusion of version II, for example, leaves nothing to be desired. The question is, Why was this particular passage with this particular theme employed?[81] The question is not petulant; for my feeling is that both the opening and closing paragraphs of a treatise are often strategic. There the author or compiler can make a deeper impression than almost anywhere else in his work. The fact that version I strikes the note of Torah both at its start and its finish indicates (when all the other facts are added to this one) that at one time students recognized what this text was emphasizing throughout: in other words, the closing paragraph of the book became the closing paragraph of the book because its appropriateness was evident to the later editors. And when Torah is the keynote, the beginning and the end are becoming unto the treatise (to use the idiom of the prayer) even as it is becoming unto them.[82]

[81] It is of course with this passage, as is well known, that each chapter of *Abot* is concluded in the synagogue service. But the centrality of Torah to *Abot* has likewise been observed. See especially Herford, *Pirke Aboth*, New York, 1925, p. 15-16 and Mordecai M. Kaplan in *Jewish Education*, Vol. 14, No. 2, p. 72-73.

[82] The passages discussed in this section do not exhaust all the evidence. Of course, I have selected the most impressive (or what I thought to be the most impressive) examples, so that the hypothesis be most clearly presented. Nevertheless, it is not unprofitable to examine every passage in the text very carefully. Some "minor" variants between the readings of the two versions are, I feel, extremely illuminating. To give just one more example: I. 26, p.82 reads ולא עם הארץ חסיד, while II, 33, p. 72 reads אין עם הארץ חסיד [פירוש] (פירוש) [פרוש] Why this qualification in version II? Why is version II almost all alone amongst sources (cf. Mekilta de R. Simeon, p. 169; the reading in Mekilta de R. Ishmael בסכתא דעסלק, I, II, p. 139-140, is very interesting!) to read נ' חזרו לסקומן, ישראל והתורה(!) וכו' (II, 47, p. 130; cf. I, 41, p. 133)? These and other passages might be analysed, but the point is well enough taken. Again I must state that in both I and II there are certain passages on Torah which cannot serve our immediate purpose since these occur in only one of the treatises. I have not referred to any of these (except for the last example in the body of the paper). I has many which II does not have; II, on the other hand, has many which I does not have. Only comments which occur on passages common to both texts can help us at this stage. And in addition to all the examples in the paper, and the two hinted at earlier in this note, one would do well to inspect

## APPENDIX

The discussion of any hypothesis is never complete unless all available evidence, favorable and unfavorable, has been examined. Perhaps where there is no contradictory material, a hypothesis is almost superfluous. In any event, there are two passages in version II which must be referred to at this point, because they raise embarrassing questions. Unlike many other passages which occur in this version only, there is no material in version I to cancel them out of existence.

The first of these passages occurs in the commentary of version II upon a saying of Hillel. Hillel had said, "Be of the disciples of Aaron, loving peace and pursuing peace, loving mankind and bringing them nigh to Torah."[83] Each of the versions records this beautiful epigram and each comments on its separate clauses.

the following: II, 3, p. 12 (though scholars are talked of, prayer is emphasized); I, 3, p. 14 f. and II, 4, p. 14; I, 4, p. 18 and II, 5, p. 18 (see also II, 8, p. 22); II, 12, p. 28 and I, 6, p. 27; II, 13, p. 30 and I, 16, p. 64; II, 15, p. 34 f. (but see Schechter's note); I, 10, p. 43; I, 11, p. 47 and II, 22, p. 47 (see also I, 11, p. 48 — מים הרעים כמשמעו — and Schechter's note); I, 12, p. 55; I, 12, p. 56 and II, 27, p. 56; I, 14, p. 58 and II, 29, p. 58 and II, 31, p. 56; I, 16, p. 62 (ד'א עין הרע); I, 16, p. 64 (but see II, 13, p. 30); I, 17, p. 65 (notice the difficulty in the passage ד'א יהי ממון; incidentally, the Zolkiev edition gives this as the only (!) interpretation of R. Jose's saying); I, 17, p. 66 and II, 30, p. 66; II, 31, p. 67 and I, 22, p. 74 f. (notice here the emphasis on מעשים in II); II, 31, p. 68 and I, 28, p. 85; II, 31, p. 68 and I, 24, p. 78; II, 32, p. 68 and I, 20, p. 70 f (see too I, 29, p. 87, ד'ח על השוקד כל); II, 32, p. 68 and I, 27, p. 83; II, 32, p. 69 and I, 22, p. 74 (notice the length to which II goes to emphasize מעשים טובים); II, 32, p. 70 and I, 22, p. 75; II, 32, p. 70 and I, 22, p. 75 (שמעון בנו); II, 33, p. 71 and I, 26, p. 82; II, 33, p. 73 (see I, 29, p. 87; notice, incidentally, how II adds to *Abot* 4.10); I, 21, p. 73 f and II, 34, p. 73 (II simply gives R. Dosa's statement); I, 22, p. 75 and II, 34, p. 75; II, 34, p. 75 (R. Hananiah) and I, 29, p. 87 (see also II, 35, p. 79); II, 34, p. 76 and I, 24, p. 77; II, 35, p. 81 and I, 26, p. 82 and I, 29, p. 88; II, 35, p. 82 and I, 30, p. 89; II, 35, p. 82 f (see I, 24, p. 78); I, 26, p. 82 and II, 35, p. 87; I, 27, p. 84 and II, 35, p. 84 (see too I, 27, p. 84); I, 28, p. 85 and II, 48, p. 132; I, 28, p. 86 and II, 35, p. 87 (the statements are not really parallel, yet they are interesting; above all see Schechter's note 22, p. 86), One of the things always to keep in mind is: Is it Torah study which is emphasized, or the efficacy of Torah? For an excellent analysis of these terms see Kadushin's *Organic Thinking*, pp. 68–79. (Even in this list I have often omitted. passages which occur in only one version.)

[83] II. 24. p. 48; cf. I, 12, p. 48 and *Abot* 1.12.

However, version II, in its comment on the last clause,[84] reads as follows: "And bringing them nigh to the study (!) of Torah."

This is certainly strange, particularly in the second version. Moreover, a glance at the reading of the comments on the same thought in version I,[85] reveals that it — the version which is so preoccupied with Torah study, according to the theory — has simply, "And bringing them nigh to Torah." What follows resembles essentially the ideas expressed in version II.[86] What shall we say, therefore?

My feeling is that the text of version II is corrupt. This is usually the easiest and most unoriginal way out of a difficulty; but there are indices in the treatise to make what I say plausible.

In the first place, nowhere do we find attributed to Hillel the phrase ומקרבן לתלמוד תורה. The reading in Tosefta *Horayot*[87] to which Schechter refers[88] contains the idea expressed in our passage, but no mention is made of Hillel. Thus the Tosefta: מנין שכל המשנה לחבירו מעלין עליו כאילו יצרו וריקמו והביאו לעולם שנ' אם תוציא יקר מזולל כפי תהיה באותו הפרק שזרק בו נשמה באדם, כך כל המכניס בירי"א אחת תחת כנפי השמים מעלין עליו כאילו יצרו וריקמו והביאו לעולם, יקר זו תורה שנ' יקרה היא מפנינים וכל חפצים לא ישוו בה וא' יש זהב ורב פנינים וכלי יקר שפתי דע'.

In the second place, at the beginning of chapter 24, where the complete saying of Hillel is first quoted by our version, the reading is explicitly ומקרבן לתורה — not ומקרבן לתלמוד תורה.

In the third place, the text in version II already reveals some tampering with. As we have it, the phrase goes ומקרב לתלמוד תורה. Schechter is quite right when he corrects ומקרב to ומקרבן — the word may easily have been an abbreviation of ומקרבן. Nevertheless, since on other accounts the reading is suspect, the additional problem must be reckoned with.

How, however, did the expression enter the text?[89] This question cannot be answered with certainty. Perhaps originally the reading was ומקרבן לתורה כל המכניס בריה וכו'. A later scholar,

[84] II, 26, p. 53.     [85] I, 12, p. 53.
[86] Cf. II, 26, p. 53 and II, 26, p. 54 (the last paragraph of the chapter).
[87] II:7.     [88] II, 26, p. 53, n. 12.
[89] I. e., if it is not a mere slip of the pen, since Talmud Torah is so common a combination.

reading this passage, suddenly remembered the Tosefta idiom
כל המשנה לחבירו. In order to make the phrase of Hillel all the more
clear, he inserted the word תלמוד.[90] Nevertheless, the wording at
the beginning of the chapter, where Hillel is quoted directly,
he did not touch.

Regardless of how convincing this explanation is, the fact
that the text should read ומקרבן לתורה is, I feel, indubitable.

The second of the difficult passages is likewise connected
with Hillel. We read in version II:[91] "He (i. e. Hillel[92]) used to
say, The more wives, the more witchcraft; the more bondswomen,
the more lewdness; the more bondsmen, the more theft; the more
witchcraft, the more evils; the more possessions, the more toil;[93]
the more flesh, the more worms; the more Torah, the more life;
he that acquires a good name, has acquired it for himself, he that
acquires the words of Torah for himself, has acquired for himself
the life of the world to come."

After such a passage, the reading in version I is a disappointment. Here[94] we have, "He used to say, The more one eats, the
more one eliminates; and the more flesh, the more worms and
maggots; and the more one performs good works, the more he
brings peace upon himself."[95] Is there no word about Torah?

It is significant that the reading of the Rome manuscript[96]
is as follows: הוא היה אומר כל המרבה מעשים טובים משים שלום בנופו
וכל המרבה תורה מרבה חכמה.
I do not know how to explain what has happened.

Despite the difficulties created by these two passages, my
feeling still is that the hypothesis presented in the body of this
paper is correct: namely, that the theme of version I of *Abot de
Rabbi Nathan* as it reads today is the study of Torah, while the
theme of version II is "piety" and good works.

---

[90] He may also have inserted, therefore, the story which follows: II, 26, p. 54.

[91] II, 31, p. 67; cf. *Abot* 2.7.

[92] Notice, incidentally, that he is here called Rabbi(!) Hillel.

[93] Our text reads יניעה. I wonder whether the reading might not have been
originally דאנה.

[94] I, 28, p. 86.

[95] The last phrase is משים שלום בנופו. The phrase is peculiar; see my note
in the translation *ad loc.*

[96] See Appendix II in Schechter's edition of *Abot de Rabbi Nathan*, p. 157.

# Profile of a Midrash

## The Art of Composition in Leviticus Rabba

### Joseph Heinemann

THE unknown, fifth-century author of Leviticus Rabba[1] has produced a highly individual piece of work, original in conception and executed skillfully and imaginatively. Even though he was but a compiler of traditional material, which he collected and arranged, and although he did not, presumably, create any *aggadot* of his own—in this respect he was not different from the authors of the other old *midrashim*—he undoubtedly succeeded in leaving the imprint of his personality on his work.

For one thing, consider the choice of the biblical book to which he devoted his compilation. There can hardly be a less promising field for aggadic treatment than Leviticus, most of which is devoted to details of sacrificial ritual, laws of impurity, lists of forbidden and permitted fowl, and the like. The first part of the book, comprising more than half, would appear extremely barren ground for developing themes concerning faith or creeds, moral behavior or piety, or the suffering of Israel and its hope of redemption. There seems to be little opportunity here to present sermons of more general significance, which would be likely to appeal to a wide circle of readers, who expect not intricate and involved details of *halakhah*—most of it no longer even applicable in practice after the destruction of the Temple!—but edification, religious insights, and words of hope and encouragement relevant to their own situation of increasing despondency and despair under Roman-Christian rule, which became more and more oppressive as time went on. Surely it is no mean feat to provide all that and more in homilies based on texts dealing with the details of meal-offerings and sin-offerings, with cloven-footed beasts that are chewing the cud, or with

[1] Cf. M. Margulies, *Midrash Wayyikra Rabba* V (Introduction), 1960, p. XXXI f.; Ch. Albeck, "Midrash Wayyikra Rabba," *Louis Ginzberg Jubilee Volume* (Hebrew Part), New York: The American Academy for Jewish Research 1946, p. 42.

JOSEPH HEINEMANN (M.A., University of Manchester, England; Ph.D., Hebrew University, Jerusalem) is Senior Lecturer for Talmudic and Midrashic Literature at the Hebrew University. During the first semester of 1970/1 he was Visiting Professor for Judaica at the Department of Religious Studies, Brown University. His *Prayer in the Period of the Tanna'im and the Amora'im* (Hebrew) was published in 1964 by the Magnes Press, The Hebrew University. He has published articles on Liturgy, Midrash, and Talmudic Literature in *Tarbiz*, *JJS*, *JSS*, and elsewhere. A comprehensive study of *Leviticus Rabba* is due to appear in *Ha-Sifrut* (University of Tel Aviv).

141

uncleanness due to childbirth or leprosy. Not only did our author succeed in evolving from such texts sermons on Moses and his prophecy, God's love for the poor and their sacrifices, drunkenness and its dangers and Israel's superiority over the Gentiles, but also in relating these subjects to the specific problems and situation of his time. This he did mostly by suggestion and by implications, based on the arrangement of the material and emerging from between the lines. All this is presented in a lively, popular manner; parables and entertaining folk-tales abound, and the work as a whole is eminently readable.

Nor was the choice of Leviticus for the text of the work inevitable. As far as we know, only one of the major, "classical" aggadic *midrashim* preceded *Leviticus Rabba*, viz., *Genesis Rabba*, which was compiled probably some two or three generations earlier.[2] Hence our author could have chosen books such as Exodus or Deuteronomy, which would have provided far more fertile ground for the type of work he had in mind; or he could have presented a collection of homilies for festivals and special Sabbaths, as did the author of *Pesiqta de Rav Kahana*—who appears to have been his younger contemporary[3]—which would have given him far more scope to create a *midrash* dealing with subjects of wide, popular appeal. His choice of Leviticus must have been deliberate, the acceptance of a challenge, out of the conviction that no part of the Torah is devoid of meaning and all of it capable of providing inspiration and guidance. "Some sections of the Torah, though they appear too repulsive and ugly for reciting in public, such as the laws relating to issues, leprosy and childbirth, 'are nevertheless', says the Holy One, 'pleasing to Me'" (*Lev. Rabba* XIX.3); if so, it must be possible to compose homilies on such subjects which will be attractive, interesting, and inspiring—as those found in *Leviticus Rabba* indeed are.

.His original approach is evident also in the arrangement of his material and the structure of the chapters of his *midrash*. As has been stated, the only aggadic *midrash* which is older than *Leviticus Rabba*, and which our author may have known, is *Genesis Rabba*, apart from the tannaitic *midrashim*, which contain mainly halakhic material (as, e.g., the *Sifra* to Leviticus, in which, in striking contrast to *Leviticus Rabba*, aggadic themes are hardly touched upon at all). All these, however, belong to the category which is known as expositional *midrashim*, whereas our author appears to have compiled the first homiletical *midrash*[4] and thus invented a new literary genre. The difference, in brief, is that the former collect expositions, interpretations and comments—as many as they can find—on each biblical verse or even on each word or phrase and ar-range them consecutively according to the order of the biblical text, the result

    [2] Margulies, *ibid.*, p. XIII, XXXII; Ch. Albeck, *Bereschit Rabba* III (Introduction), 1931, p. 96.
    [3] Margulies, *ibid.*, Albeck, *Ginzberg Jubilee Volume*, p. 36 f., p. 42; cf. also my article "Chapters of Doubtful Authenticity in Leviticus Rabba" (Hébrew), *Tarbiz* XXXVII (1968), p. 343 f.
    [4] *Cf.* H. Strack, *Introduction to the Talmud and Midrash*, Philadelphia: The Jewish Publication Society, 1945, p. 204 f.

being that more often than not there is no connection at all between the individual items that follow one another, because each of them refers to a different verse or phrase. But in *Leviticus Rabba* (and in other, later, homiletical *midrashim*, such as *Tanḥuma or Pesiqta*) no attempt is made to provide a running commentary on the whole of the biblical text; instead, each chapter or homily is devoted to one pericope and deals almost exclusively with its first verse or verses. Since each chapter limits itself to one brief passage, it can be devoted to one clearly defined, specific subject, aspects of which are developed throughout the entire sermon. The pericopes are based on the lectionary which was in vogue in Palestine at the time, where the reading of the entire Pentateuch on Sabbaths was completed during a period of over three years.[5] The 37 chapters of *Leviticus Rabba* (a few of which may not be part of the original work) thus correspond to the beginnings of the weekly readings from Leviticus (though the Midrash reflects a division of pericopes somewhat different from the "triennial cycle" as known to us from other sources).[6]

Although an expositional *midrash* neither possesses nor requires any specific structure other than a rough-and-ready division of the material into chapters, in this new type of *midrash* it was both possible and imperative to arrange each homily according to a definite pattern, to give it order and coherence, and to strive towards the integration of the many dozens of individual comments, stories, and expositions of which it is made up into a larger entity. Even though in *Genesis Rabba*—but not in the tannaitic *midrashim*—an attempt is made to mark the beginning of most chapters by one or more short proems, the bulk of the material following them is just a hodgepodge of disjointed *aggadot*, devoid of any shape or form. In striking contrast, the homilies of *Leviticus Rabba*, are not only, on the whole, homogeneous as far as their contents are concerned, they also possess a clear, formal structure: Each of them opens with a number of proems—mostly of considerable length and intricate pattern—followed by the "body of the sermon," which enlarges upon the themes touched on in the former, concluding with a brief peroration, devoted mostly to the messianic hope. Although it seems certain that these various component parts are not original creations of the author but rather parts of sermons actually delivered in the Synagogue, which came down to him through oral tradition, undoubtedly the welding-together of these separate and often heterogeneous parts into one organic entity must be ascribed to him.[7] In fact, we may look upon him as the creator of a new form, which was adopted subsequently by authors of other homiletical *midrashim*, which might be called the "literary homily."

[5] *Cf.* my articles "The Triennial Cycle and the Calendar" (Hebrew), *Tarbiz* XXXIII (1964), p. 362 f.; "On the Triennial Lectionary Cycle", *JJS* XIX (1968), p. 41 f.

[6] *Cf.* Albeck, *Ginzberg Jubilee Volume*, p. 27 and my article in Tarbiz XXXVII, p. 340 f.

[7] J. Mann, in *The Bible as read and preached in the Old Synagogue*, Cincinnati: Hebrew Union College, 1940, *passim*, fails to distinguish clearly between live sermons actually preached in the Synagogue and literary compilations; this is but one of the many weaknesses of his hypothesis. Cf. my article in *JJS*, as above, p. 46 f.

This is evident especially in his use of the proem. A proem is a rhetorical form which opens with a verse from Scripture—mostly from Psalms or the "Wisdom-books"—not obviously connected with the subject-matter of the homily, viz., the beginning of the pericope.[8] The preacher's task is gradually to establish a link with the latter through a series of interpretations, stories, and so on and to finish by quoting the first (or second) verse of the pericope (wholly or in part). It stands to reason that in an actual, live sermon, delivered to an audience, the preacher would use no more than one such proem. What purpose would be served by opening a sermon with a series of introductions, each complete in itself and unconnected with the others and each leading, again and again, up to the same point which had already been reached with the first one? It is precisely because of its striking rhetorical qualities, which make it certain that the proem originated in the live sermon, that we cannot accept the idea that any preacher would use more than one proem in his sermon; otherwise he would entirely destroy its carefully planned rhetorical effect of building up interest by proceeding step by step from the opening verse, chosen apparently at random, to the beginning of the pericope.[9] Hence the very fact that in our Midrash almost invariably a number of proems are collected at the beginning of each homily proves conclusively that the author drew his material from a variety of sermons known to him; he was aiming, so it seems, at presenting homilies of more ambitious dimensions than those actually delivered in the Synagogue. Obviously, the reader of a written work can absorb more complex and extensive homilies than the audience of a sermon given orally; for the former can always return to the book and re-read what he failed to comprehend the first time.

It may have been this new form—a composite of material drawn from different sermons knit together into a new literary entity—that enabled the author to shape his *midrash* as he did, to arrange the traditional material to suit his own purposes, and to deal with subjects suitable for a wider circle of readers. By focusing the entire homily on the first verse or verses of the pericope, or even only on some words or phrases of it, he freed himself from the bondage to the subject of the lection itself. While the first chapter of Leviticus deals with details of burnt-offerings, its first verse reads, "And the Lord called unto Moses and spoke unto him out of the tent of meeting, saying" and thus provides an opening for a discourse on Moses and his prophecy. Chapter 16 deals with the sacrificial cult on the Day of Atonement but opens with the words "After the death of the two sons of Aaron"; hence, a homily may be constructed dealing with this subject only. Even a single phrase from the first verse may be isolated, e.g., "Drink no wine nor strong drink" and made the occasion for a sermon on drunkenness, completely disregarding the fact that this prohibition is addressed to Aaron and his sons and applies during the performance of the sacrificial

---

[8] I do not accept Mann's thesis regarding the hidden link between the *haftarah* and the proem-verse; cf. my articles in *JJS, ibid.*, and in *Tarbiz* XXXVII, p. 354.

[9] *Cf.* my article "The *petihtot* in aggadic *midrashim*, their origin and function", (Hebrew), *Fourth World Congress of Jewish Studies—Papers*, II (1968), 43 f.

service only. Still more clearly is the freedom of the author in his choice of subject demonstrated, when in his homily on Lev. 14:1-2 he concentrates exclusively on the one word *mezora'*, but interprets it not as leper, but as *mozi ra'*, i.e., one who utters evil reports, and devotes the entire discourse to denouncing slander and the "evil tongue." In his homily on Lev. 2, dealing with the meal-offering he assumes—rightly—that the inexpensive meal-offering is for all practical purposes the sacrifice of the poor; hence, instead of dealing with ritual details, he devotes his sermon to the special love God has for the poor and their prayers.

However, the art and skill of the author of the *midrash* emerge fully only when we consider the arrangement of material in, and the inner structure of, each homily. In the one mentioned last—chapter III of *Leviticus Rabba*—the first proem elucidates Eccl. 4:6 in a variety of ways, interpreting it in its concluding (and relevant) section: "'Better is a handful of quietness', that is a handful of flour of the meal-offering of a poor man, 'than two handfuls of labour and striving after wind', that is the incense of spices of the congregation . . ." (on the basis of two plays on words: *nahat* and *minhah*, *ruah* and *reah*, i.e., "a sweet savour"). The second proem opens with Ps. 22:24 f. and concludes: "For he hath not despised nor abhorred the affliction (*'enuth* is understood, apparently, in the sense of utterance) of the lowly'; even as he despises not his prayer, he despises not his offering." The third proem emphasizes that God "pardons abundantly" (Isa. 55:7), hence, he provided us with an additional—inexpensive—means of obtaining forgiveness, namely the tenth of an ephah of flour making up the meal-offering. The body of the sermon begins here—by no means the patterns of all homilies—with the question, "What is written prior to this matter?" and refers to the end of chap. 1, dealing with the burnt-offering of a fowl, which, being comparatively cheap, may also be considered a poor man's sacrifice. This serves as a connecting link for introducing the charming folktale of King Agrippas who, on a certain day, had commanded the High Priest: "Let no man other than myself offer sacrifices today." Nevertheless, the priest accepted two turtle-doves from a poor man, who told him: "I catch four doves every day, two I offer up, and with the other two I sustain myself. If you do not accept them, you cut off my means of livelihood." This is followed by two more stories about poor people and their sacrifices, the last one about a woman who brought a handful of fine flour, and the priest insulted her by saying, "What is there in this to eat? What is there in this to offer up?" This leads us back to the actual subject of the homily, viz., the meal-offering. This tale of the real grievance of a poor woman against the haughty priests has its counterpart in one about a man who brought his meal-offering from a far-away country: "When he saw that the priest took off a handful and ate the rest, he said 'Woe unto me! All this trouble I have gone to was for the benefit of this man!'"—an unjustified complaint, for the Torah states explicitly, "He shall take thereout his handful of the fine flour to offer up," and not "all the fine flour." And, indeed, those present pacified the aggrieved pilgrim: If the priest has the right to enjoy the meal-offering in return for the little trouble he has taken in offering up some of it, how much more so will you, who have come such a long way, receive great reward for your trouble? Here we come to a turning-point in the homily: The tales which illustrate the contempt felt by the aristocracy and especially by the priests for the meager sacrifices offered by the poor are counterbalanced by a hymn of praise for the ideal priest: The priests who are without a share in the land and take their portion from the hand of God Himself are truly themselves the poorest of the poor and yet devote themselves whole-heartedly to the service of God; hence, they are worthy of the praise bestowed upon them by the prophet Malachi: "For the priest's lip should keep knowledge, and they should seek the law at his mouth; for he is the messenger (or: angel!) of the Lord of Hosts."

This last section of the homily relates to verse 3 of the pericope: "And that which is left of the meal-offering shall be Aaron's and his sons'." But the author would not have introduced this material just because it is connected with another verse of the same chapter, had he not been able to integrate it into the structure of the homily and, indeed, use it for creating its climax. Similarly, the section dealing with a burnt-offering of a fowl following upon the proems, is introduced by the technical device of referring back to the preceding pericope; but again it turns out that the material is pertinent to the subject of the sermon and provides the necessary transition to the series of tales about poor men's sacrifices, which vividly present its central thesis.

Just as in this case different parts of one and the same homily express, through their juxtaposition, contrasting and even contradictory aspects of the theme, so also different homilies are at times linked together dialectically to complement each other. Thus the picture drawn here of the ideal priest is again qualified in chapter 5 (relating to 4:13, the passage dealing with the sin-offering of the congregation),[10] where the merits of the plain people and their true leaders—the sages—are extolled (§7-8), as opposed to the shortcomings of the priests, who frequently failed in their high office and, at times, even led the people astray (§5-6). It is not to them that the people must look for atonement, but instead they can rely on their own good deeds—especially their generosity in providing funds for scholars (§4)—and their prayers, "for Israel know how to placate their Creator" (§9); thus atonement is assured to them in their own right (even now, when sacrifices of atonement can no longer be offered).

Even though all homilies have a certain formal pattern in common, as described before, the author does not by any means mechanically construct all his sermons exactly along the same lines. The organization of the material is not contrived by technical devices only, but, as we have seen, it is dictated by the inner logic of the theme and the need to attain coherence and integration. Let us illustrate this by outlining the structure of one more homily. The whole

---

[10] In the printed editions, including the one of Marqulies, p. 97, this chapter is identified, erroneously, as a homily on Lev. 4:1; cf. my article in *Tarbiz* XXXVII, p. 349 f.

of chapter XIII, relating to Lev. 11:1f., dealing with beasts clean and unclean, i.e., fit or unfit for eating, is undoubtedly an organic unity (except for the first proem, which relates to verse 1 and does not appear to link up with what follows). The second proem opens with "He rose and measured the earth, and He released nations" (Hab. 3:6), which is taken to mean that the heathen were released from obligations such as the dietary laws because they were unable to endure even the seven Noahide precepts given to them. Moreover, a parable is told of a physician who had two patients, one who would live and one who would certainly die; to the one who would live he said: "This you may eat, that you may not eat," but regarding the one about to die he said: "Give him whatever he asks!" Thus the dietary restrictions were given only to the people of Israel, who are destined for the life of the World-to-Come. Furthermore, these (and all other) precepts were given for the purpose of purifying them. From here we pass to detailed descriptions of the marvels of the Time-to-Come: Behemoth and Leviathan will engage in a wild-beast contest for the entertainment of those who have not been spectators at the wild-beast contests of the heathen nations of this world; they will eventually slaughter each other to provide a banquet for the righteous, who refrained from eating ritually forbidden meat in this world. When God said: "These are the living things which you may eat," he implied, "if you will prove yourselves worthy, you will eat, but if not, you will be eaten (consumed) by the heathen empires." All the prophets foresaw the empires engaged in their activities; a point demonstrated by a series of proof-texts, concluding with "Moses foresaw the empires engaged in their activities," for which a daring allegorical interpretation of our chapter, dealing with the unclean animals, is offered as proof: The camel alludes to Babylon, . . . the rockbadger alludes to Media, . . . the hare alludes to Greece, . . . the swine alludes to Edom (i.e., Rome). . . . Why is Edom compared to a swine? To tell you that just as the swine, when reclining, puts forward its cloven hooves, as if to say "See that I am clean," so, too, does the empire of Edom boast, as it commits violence and robbery, that it is but executing justice. It is not content with not exalting the righteous, it also slays them. But while each preceding empire brought in its train another one, no other empire will follow Rome; hence, it is called *ḥazir*, because it will restore (*haḥazir*) the crown to its rightful owner, as it is written, "And saviours shall come on Mount Zion to judge the mount of Esau; and the kingdom shall be the Lord's" (Obad. 21).

All sections of this homily refer, in one way or another, to animals and the eating of their meat; yet, instead of dealing with details of the precepts, they put the entire chapter into an utterly new perspective. Far from being a burden, the dietary laws are a token of distinction for Israel, a means by which they are set apart from other nations and will, eventually, inherit life in the World-to-Come. If they refrain from participating in the wild-beast contests and from eating forbidden meat in this world, incomparably greater pleasures are in store for them in the future. And this very chapter, apparently but enumerating the list of forbidden animals, is in truth foretelling the messianic redemption. In this as in other homilies the author deals by implication with acute problems of his time. Not only does he hold up the hope of redemption and demonstrate that Israel's subjugation to Roman rule is but temporary, he also summarily rejects the idea that the commandments are but a yoke and a burden—as was claimed by Christianity in its polemics against Judaism.[11] Elsewhere (I.1) he extolls those who observe the commandments loyally, e.g., the precepts of the Sabbatical year, in spite of economic hardships, and calls them "You mighty in strength, that fulfill His word." Other chapters he devotes to demonstrating that only seemingly is any sacrifice involved in observing the commandments for "'Who has given Me anything beforehand, and I shall repay him'. . . . Who set apart pe'ah (the corner of the field) for My sake before I gave him a field? Who set aside an offering for Me before I gave him cattle?" (XXVII.2). Another question, arising again and again, is the great suffering of Israel in the past and in the present; here, too, a number of answers are suggested in different homilies. Other sermons (e.g., chapter V, dealt with above) pose the problem of atonement after the destruction of the Temple and the suspension of the sacrificial cult; again different answers are given in various parts of the midrash, as e.g., in ch. 7, relating to the passage about the burnt-offering (6:1f.), but developing themes such as "The sacrifices of God are a broken spirit" and "Love covers all transgressions".

Perhaps no less striking is the attitude taken by the author of the midrash towards any attempt to bring about Israel's liberation from the Roman yoke by means of armed rebellion. Not only does he carefully refrain from mentioning any military action when describing the coming of the future redemption, he also disregards, minimizes, and plays down deeds of military prowess and heroism in the past. Thus, all that is told of Saul is his tragic death; how "he was afraid" and asked Samuel, whom the witch had conjured up, "But if I flee, shall I be saved?" His death was due but to his own grievous sins, and the only thing that our midrash has to say in his favor is this: "This man goes out to battle and, though he knows that he will be killed . . . he faces cheerfully the just punishment which is overtaking him" (XXVI.7). Again, in ch. XXVIII.4, all the great victories of the past, including those of Moses, Joshua, and Deborah, are reviewed, but each one is summed up with the same refrain: "Neither with weapon nor with shield (was the victory achieved) but with prayer and supplication." There is a clear message in these and similar passages, which, far from glorifying military action, discourage and even discredit it. Still more remarkable is the silence of our author on one aspect of the eschatalogical theme, on which he elaborates on so many occasions: When will Redemption come and how can it be speeded up? While he describes the joys and splendors of the messianic days in glowing colors and does not tire of repeating to his readers that Israel's future salvation is certain to come, he never refers to the question of time: Is there or is there not a predestined time for Redemption? Can it be

[11] Cf., inter alia, A. J. Heshel, Theology of Ancient Judaism II, (Hebrew), London and New York: The Soncino Press, 1965, p. 189-190.

known beforehand? Can it be brought about earlier? By what means? He does point out, time and again, that the observance of certain commandments will cause the Messiah to come. But in each of those many passages a different commandment is named; hence, no specific action having the power to bring redemption nearer is suggested.[12] And this in spite of the wealth of statements, undoubtedly known to the author of *Leviticus Rabba*, by the Sages of the second, third, and fourth centuries, in which all these questions are hotly debated: By what signs can we tell the generation in which the Son of David will come? Does redemption depend on Israel's repentance? Will salvation come "in its own time" or can it be speeded up? Can "the end" be calculated?[13] Although opportunities abound in our *midrash* to bring up these matters, the author keeps utter silence—undoubtedly because after the bitter defeats of the past and the tragic disappointments which had been caused, time and again, by "calculating the end," he prefers to avoid this entire discussion and not to encourage, even indirectly, further illusions and vain hopes.

The most outstanding feature in the composition of this *midrash* is the tendency of the author to present his themes in all their complexity and with all their manifold implications. He does not see any virtue in simplification, still less in over-simplification; he looks upon his subjects not just from one angle, but from all possible angles; he likes to bring out contrasts and to emphasize opposites. What we might term his "dialectical approach" is manifest throughout the work in a variety of ways. For one thing when he is obliged to use heterogeneous material for building up one of his homilies, he often achieves integration by stressing the contrast between different interpretations and thus creates a relationship between them of thesis and antithesis. In ch. 25 the verse "And when you shall come into the land and shall plant all manner of trees . . ." (Lev. 19:23) is taken first allegorically: the Torah is called a tree, as it is written "She is a tree of life to them that lay hold upon her" (Prov. 3:18), and the importance of the study of the Torah is elaborated; then there is an abrupt transition, and we are told that the people of Israel are commanded to engage in the planting of trees just as God himself planted trees (in the Garden of Eden) at the time of creation. The two interpretations of the "tree," offered side by side, are not only different but also, in a sense, contradictory; one implies that the supreme duty of Israel is the study of Torah, while the second exhorts them to engage *derekh erez* (the way of the land). But "if a man will plough at the time of ploughing, and sow at the time of sowing . . .

---

[12] *E.g.*, kindling the eternal lamp (XXXI.11); the taking of the *lulav, ethrog*, etc. on Sukkot (XXX.16); *cf.* also XXIII.13, etc. The commandment of the "sheaf of the first-fruits" is cited as having brought about Israel's salvation in many instances in the past (XXVIII.6); hence, by analogy, it should be expected to do so also in the future. Note that some of the examples concern commandments connected with the Temple, which can no longer be observed. The reference to them as a means of bringing about Messianic redemption is, therefore, of no practical value.

[13] *E.g.*, *Mishnah Sotah*, end; b. *Sanhedrin* 97 a-b; *j Ta'an.* I, 63 d. It is noteworthy that the *Pesiqta de Rav Kahana*, in contrast to *Lev. Rabba*, quotes some of these statements at length; *cf.* Buber's edition, p. 51 a-b.

and reap at the time of reaping . . . what shall become of the (study of the) Torah?" (b. *Berakhot* 35.b). The bold juxtaposition of the two opposing concepts suggests its own solution: In spite of the apparent contradiction between the two demands, they are not essentially incompatible, but "An excellent thing is the study of the Torah combined with *derekh erez*. . . ." (*Avot* II.2).

Often the emphasis on contrasts and opposites is first and foremost a stylistic device for knitting together more closely the different *aggadot* making up the constituent parts of the homily. Towards the beginning of chap. 9, elaborating mainly on the theme of peace, the story is told of R. Yannai who had invited a man to his house, believing him to be scholar, and then, on discovering him to be an ignoramus, insulted him: "A dog has eaten of Yannai's food!"; but at the end of the same homily we have another tale, of R. Meir, who, to the consternation of his disciples, allowed himself to be insulted in order "to make peace between a man and his wife." Surely these two anecdotes were interwoven into the same chapter because there is between them a relationship both of analogy and of contrast and because each of them gains in depth by being viewed against its counterpart. Elsewhere the author of the *midrash* presents one and the same subject from a variety of points of view, even though they conflict with one another. In chap. 10:3, Aaron is cleared of all guilt in making a golden calf and immediately afterwards we are told that for this very reason the death of his sons was decreed. But in chap. 27 the sin of the golden calf is ascribed to the mixed multitude; Israel had no part in it—Aaron still less. Chap. 23 sings a hymn of praise for the people of Israel in Egypt, who were worthy of redemption because they were not contaminated by the immorality prevailing there, even though "both these and those were uncircumcised . . . these wore garments made of a mixture of wool and linen and those wore garments made of a mixture of wool and linen"; and the same motif recurs again in chap. 32:5. "Israel were redeemed from Egypt . . . because none of them was found to be immoral." But in chap. 21:4 the "princes of the nations" accuse Israel of being no different from the gentiles: "These are idol-worshipers and those are idol-worshippers; these commit sexual immorality and those commit sexual immorality; these are shedders of blood and those are shedders of blood"— in exactly the same style used in chap. 23 to proclaim Israel's superiority over heathen nations!

There are many more passages where we find this tendency of emphasizing contrasts and opposites, of presenting contradictory or conflicting viewpoints. Some of these may, of course, have been inherent in the traditional material of which the author of *Leviticus Rabba* made use. But even so, had he wished to do so, he could easily have avoided a good many of the "contradictions" contained in his work, harmonized opposing ideas or omitted them. Far from doing so, he appears to delight in demonstrating to his readers the complexity of the Torah, which may be expounded "by adducing forty-nine reasons for declaring a thing unclean and forty-nine for declaring it clean" (XXVI.2), and in making manifest the many facets of the one divine truth. For, in spite of all seeming contradictions, "Both these and those are the words of the living God" (b. Eruvin 13b).

# ASPECTS OF THE RABBINIC CONCEPT OF ISRAEL[1]
## A STUDY IN THE MEKILTA[2]

By MAX KADUSHIN, New York City

## I.

### THE CONCEPT OF ISRAEL[3]

ISRAEL designates in rabbinic literature, and to us, a specific people, the Jews. It is the concept which expressed and evoked throughout all the stages of this people's history its sense of nationhood. "Scripture," say the Rabbis, "designates them as a nation, as it says 'And who is like Thy people Israel, a nation one in the earth' (I Chron. 17.21),"[4] the Rabbis thus adducing sound Scriptural warrant for their own national self-consciousness. In whatever respects the rabbinic concept of Israel may differ from its biblical antecedent, the core of the concept, the awareness of nationhood, remains the same. Without the concept of Israel, or some other equivalent, there would have been no Jewish people, no Bible, no rabbinic literature. It is an excellent example of the way in which an organic concept interprets, organizes and oft-times creates the facts of experience.

The rabbinic concept of Israel, however, has an individuality of its own, certain qualities which distinguish it from its biblical antecedent.[5] The Rabbis' high regard for the dignity of Israel,

---

[1] I wish to thank Professor Louis Ginzberg for his annotations to these pages; like his annotations to my books *The Theology of Seder Eliahu* and *Organic Thinking*, they are marked here with his initials. *The Theology of Seder Eliahu* is referred to hereafter as TE and *Organic Thinking* as OT.

[2] References by volume and page are to *Mekilta de Rabbi Ishmael*, ed. Jacob Z. Lauterbach (Philadelphia, 1933–1935, 3 vols.). I have also utilized the translation in this edition, though occasionally departing from it.

[3] ישראל is the term used throughout in the *Mekilta*; כנסת ישראל occurs once — II, 29.

[4] II, 206.

[5] See OT, Chap. IV, section V.

57

for instance, results in a kind of equalitarianism that practically nullifies the biblical institution of the Hebrew slave. Menial personal services by the Hebrew slave, such as washing the feet of the master, or helping the latter with his shoes, or carrying him in a litter, are forbidden, though the master's son or pupil, significantly enough, are permitted to do these things.[6] The master may not even change the trade of the Hebrew slave, let alone force him to engage in any sort of "humiliating" work.[7] The Rabbis interpret "Because he (the slave) fareth well with thee" (Deut. 15.16) to mean that he must fare *equally* as well as the master, and this interpretation is then applied to the matters of food and drink and bed.[8] Indeed, the question is raised whether he should be called "slave" at all, since it is a term of opprobrium.[9] Again, to the Rabbis, love for one another is implicit in the very term "Israel" itself. "Thine enemy" (Ex. 23.4), they say therefore, cannot really apply to an Israelite at all, and if it does the enmity is such as between a father and son who have quarreled, fleeting and temporary.[10] Let us present but one more indication that the rabbinic concept differs, in certain respects, from the biblical concept of Israel. The tremendous importance of Israel, in the eyes of the Rabbis, renders significant every detail of its history, and so the Rabbis endeavor to make definite and specific what may be indefinite and blurred

[6] III, 5–6.

[7] III, 6. The passage also discusses other conditions of labor for the Hebrew slave.

[8] III, 14. The master must also provide food for the Hebrew slave's wife and children — III, 9–10.

[9] III, 4. In these statements concerning the Hebrew slave, we have an illustration of the manner in which rabbinic theology is imbedded in the Halakah.

"On the Hebrew slave see my lectures on קדושין where I show that the tannaitic tradition had no longer any 'facts' about the institution of Hebrew slavery. The tannaitic statements about the עבד עברי prove nothing but that later generations tried to explain from their point of view conditions of the past" — L. G. We have been endeavoring to present "the point of view" of the "later generations" — the rabbinic — and to indicate that that point of view *differed* from the one which governed and made possible "the conditions of the past," namely, the biblical institution of the Hebrew slave.

[10] III, 163–4.

in the biblical account. The year in which Israel went out of Egypt did not have to be intercalated;[11] they went out in the day-time;[12] they went out armed;[13] and, the biblical "six hundred thousand. . . beside children" (Ex. 12.37) means, according to one authority, exclusive of women, children and infants whilst another takes it to be exclusive of women, children and old men.[14]

The rabbinic concept of Israel has a distinct individuality of its own, then, differs from the biblical concept, despite the unbroken continuity of national self-consciousness. In the preceding paragraph, we did no more than to suggest this difference, only touching on a few of the distinctive qualities of the rabbinic concept. The national self-consciousness of Israel in the rabbinic period is, however, like a texture woven of many strands, each with its own rich color yet blending harmoniously with all the rest. In other words, Israel is an organic concept. Its significance is manifold, for it takes on meanings, shadings, connotations, from the other concepts interwoven with it in the rabbinic complex of thought. More, Israel is a fundamental organic concept. It possesses, therefore, a number of aspects varied and definite enough in their own right to be crystallized into terms, which we characterize as sub-concepts.[15] Only by tracing the pattern made by the interrelation of Israel and its sub-concepts with all the other concepts can we begin to grasp the meaning of the concept; but that alone is not sufficient. We must also study the leit-motifs running through the complex as a whole and which affect Israel as they do all the other concepts. These leit-motifs, or emphatic trends as we have called them elsewhere, account, among other things, for such differences between the biblical and the rabbinic concepts of Israel as we have noticed above. In sum, there can be no succinct definition of the concept of Israel. We can merely indicate its relationships and depict its qualities, and by doing this shed light on the manner of its effectiveness.

11 I, 141.     12 I, 74.
13 I, 174.     14 I, 109.
15 On the relation of the fundamental concept to its sub-concepts, see OT, pp. 181–4.

Nationality went hand-in-hand with universality in rabbinic thought, as the modern authorities have noticed.[16] What made this "two-fold character" of rabbinic thought possible was not only the universal quality of certain rabbinic concepts but the fact that *all* the rabbinic concepts, including the concept of Israel, were organically interrelated. Rabbinic thought is a unitary complex. If, therefore, we recognize certain concepts such as God's love, His justice, Man, *Derek Erez*, to be patently universal in scope we may be sure that this universal quality is not confined to these concepts alone but affects the other concepts as well. We shall learn that Israel, the very concept expressive of nationality, is strongly affected by the quality of universality. The latter frequently acts as a check upon the former. The organic complex of rabbinic thought is extremely flexible, allowing now one concept to be stressed, now another, particularly in the case of the fundamental concepts. Thus, there are occasions when Torah, or God's love, or God's justice are stressed rather than Israel. A concept may then be so heavily accented, so distinctly individualized, that it is entirely dissociated, for the time being, from Israel. Sometimes Israel is even subordinated to another fundamental concept, or vice versa. But universality does more than act as a check upon nationality in rabbinic thought. It combines with nationality in the concept of *Gerim*, Proselytes, which is a sub-concept of Israel. Rabbinic thought, hence, owes its "two-fold character" to the organic coherence of the concepts as well as to the specific qualities exhibited by the individual concepts. The national self-consciousness, expressed through the concept of Israel, itself had the two-fold character of nationality and universality. Broad enough to take universal humanity into its orbit, it also possessed the inestimable advantages of being focussed in the common life and daily experience of a living people, the advantages, in other words, of an organic concept.

Israel is one of the four fundamental concepts of rabbinic thought, the others being Torah, God's loving-kindness and

---

[16] See G. F. Moore, *Judaism*, Vol. I, pp. 219 ff. Cf. the references cited *ibid.*, p. 219, note 1.

God's justice. They are not fundamental in the sense of being more essential to the rabbinic outlook than the other rabbinic concepts. In an organic complex of thought, all the concepts are equally essential, for the pattern would not be the same were a single concept missing. We have called them fundamental, however, because by tracing the relationships or connections of these four concepts with each other and with the rest of the rabbinic concepts, we can demonstrate the organic interconnectedness of all the concepts in the complex. The four fundamental concepts are constitutive of each other and of all the remaining concepts as well. Since all the concepts are thus interrelated by reason of their common constitutive elements, any concept can combine with any other concept. This interrelation of concepts makes a full analysis of our topic a very long and arduous task. The interweaving of the concept of Israel with the universal concept of God's love, for example, draws into the pattern the concepts of *Shekinah*, the righteous, the Nations of the World, God's justice — in fact all the concepts of the complex. In this essay, however, we are not offering a full treatment of the topic. We wish merely to suggest the manner in which the concept of Israel, apart from any of its sub-concepts, is affected by the quality of universality in rabbinic thought. For that purpose it is enough to demonstrate the interweaving of Israel only with the other three fundamental concepts.

## II. Torah and Israel

The Torah was given to Israel. All the other matters involving Torah and Israel flow from this essential relationship. This relationship looms large enough, indeed, to be included on its own accord in another rabbinic concept — the concept of מתן תורה, the giving of Torah.

The entire Torah, except for certain specific commandments first given to Adam and "the sons of Noah,"[17] was given to Israel.

---

[17] II, 211. For the six commandments given Adam and the seven given Noah see Genesis R. 16.6 (ed. Theodor, p. 149) and *ibid.*, 26.5 (ed. Theodor, p. 244). Cf. also the references cited by Theodor. Cf. also II, 235. "The מצות 'ז

It was not given them at one time. Besides the revelation at Sinai, there were other occasions, both before and after Sinai, when Israel received definite laws and even religious lore. The revelation at Sinai occurred on the sixth day of the third month. The Rabbis declare, however, that "And he took the book of the covenant and read in the hearing of the people" (Ex. 24.7) refers to the fifth day, that is, to the day before the revelation.[18] There was, then a "book of the covenant" before the Ten Commandments were promulgated; and in the different opinions of what this book contained, all brought forward in the same passage, we have both a summary of what the Rabbis regarded as earlier revelations and a good illustration of the non-dogmatic character of rabbinic thought. According to one authority, Moses read to Israel "from the beginning of Genesis up to here," whilst another, R. Ishmael, proves from Lev. 26.46 that the book from which Moses read contained the laws concerning "the sabbatical years and the jubilees" as well as "the blessings and the comminations."[19] The third opinion, second in order in the passage, is that of Rabbi Judah, the Prince, who says, "He read to them the *mizwot* (commandments) commanded to Adam and the *mizwot* commanded to the sons of Noah, and the *mizwot* given Israel in Egypt and at Marah, and (all the rest of the *mizwot?*)."[20] As

---

בני נח is an old tradition and a very important one while that concerning the commandments given to Adam is a later Haggadah (not known to the authorities of the Mishnah) of very little consequence"— L. G.

[18] II, 210–11.

[19] *Ibid.*, 211.

[20] *Ibid.* This opinion is rightly placed second in the passage because it represents a midway position. Like the first in following the textual order of the Bible, it is nevertheless like that of R. Ishmael in its selection of the laws and exclusion, apparently, of the lore.

"The text has ושאר כל המצות כלן, which cannot mean the *mizwot* which 'had already been given' (as rendered by Lauterbach). Comp. Horovitz (*Mechilta d'Rabbi Ismael*, ed. Horovitz-Rabin, Frankfurt-am-Main, 1928–31, p. 211) who calls attention to Midrash Tannaim where the reading is מבראשית עד לעיני כל ישראל. Hoffman's emendation is not acceptable since chap. 24 of Exodus narrates that that took place after the revelation on Sinai (v. 18) and there can be no doubt that according to רבי the Torah was completely known to the Patriarchs and Moses before it was revealed — but it was *not given* up to a later day"— L. G. But see Horovitz-Rabin, *ibid.*, note 13.

to the nature of the *mizwot* given in Egypt[21] and at Marah,[22] —
at Marah "He made for them a statute and an ordinance" (Ex.
15.25)—, there was again no consensus. But besides the laws
given before the revelation at Sinai, there were also laws given
in "the tent of meeting," after Sinai, and these are also characterized as *diberot*, the very term used to designate the Ten
Commandments.[23] Similarly, "the giving of Torah," an expression
usually reserved for the Sinaitic revelation, is also employed to
describe the imposition of the Sabbath before that revelation.[24]
The occasions, both before and after Sinai, when Israel received
Torah were thus, in rabbinic thought, of the same nature as the
revelation at Sinai — were, indeed, regarded as so many revelations. That these revelations could be subject to widely differing opinions is of no little significance. It emphasizes that we
have to do here not with religious dogmas but with a pattern
of religious thought which encouraged differences of opinion.

How did the Rabbis regard the revelation at Sinai? We have
just learned that it was by no means regarded as the only revelation of Torah to Israel. This conclusion is confirmed by a closer
examination of the term, "the giving of Torah." True, this term
(with the necessary grammatical variations) ordinarily refers to
the Sinaitic revelation. Jethro heard of "the giving of Torah"
and thereupon came to Israel in the Wilderness;[25] the earth
trembled, and the kings of the Nations of the World were greatly
frightened until Balaam assured them God was bringing upon
the world neither a flood of water nor a flood of fire but was
simply "giving Torah to His people Israel";[26] it was on the sixth

---

[21] I, 33–4 and 36–8.

[22] II, 94. According to R. Joshua, the Sabbath was among the commandments imposed upon Israel at Marah (cf. also II, 121). An anonymous opinion
has it, however, that it was first imposed on the twenty-second day of Iyyar
and after Marah though before the revelation at Sinai.

[23] II, 215.

[24] *Ibid.*, 99 — שנתנה להם תורה לישראל. "Reading very doubtful and Lauterbach had no right to put it into the text." — L. G.

[25] II, 162 — מתן תורה; *ibid.*, 174 — שנתן תורה לעמו ישראל. See Zebaḥim
116a for the opinions as to whether Jethro came before or after the revelation
at Sinai. Cf. also Ibn Ezra and Naḥmanides on Ex. 18.1.

[26] II, 233–34 — נותן תורה לעמו ישראל; *ibid.*, 162–3 — הורה נותן לעמו; cf. also
*ibid.*, 198.

day of the third month, *Siwan*, which fell on a Friday, that "Torah was given to Israel."[27] In these and in other passages[28] the term refers to the revelation on Sinai; indeed, in the passages concerning Jethro the term actually stands for, without any additional hint, that revelation. We must not fail to notice, however, that our term does not read "the giving of the Torah" but just "the giving of Torah," that the word "Torah" is *not* preceded by the definite article.[29] It is a general term, not the designation of a single, particular event. Even when standing for the Sinaitic revelation, the term implies, then, that this revelation is only one of a number of revelations of Torah to Israel.[30]

There was a distinction, nevertheless, between the revelation at Sinai and all the other revelations. At Sinai, according to both the Bible and rabbinic theology, Torah was not only revealed to Israel but in the presence of Israel; the revelation was thus experienced by the entire people. The Rabbis, as usual, enlarge upon the biblical narrative. The earth shook, and all the Nations of the World were frightened.[31] The people of Israel, too, stand-

[27] *Ibid.*, 99 — ניתנה תורה לישראל. "The day of the giving of Torah" — יום מתן תורה — *ibid.*, 202.

[28] II, 198, 236.

[29] See the term as given in the preceding references. Lauterbach, reflecting the common conception, always translates the term as "the giving of the Torah."

The Rabbis use the definite article התורה (the Torah), only when they wish to convey the idea of the Torah as a whole. Examples: "They will neglect the Torah" (בטלים מן התורה) — I, 171; "they will absorb the Torah" (והתורה נבללת בגופן) — *ibid.*; R. Simon ben Yoḥai's statement — *ibid.*; "will you accept the Torah" (מקבלים אתם את התורה) — II, 234 (*bis*). I do not think that there is any violation of the rule in the phrase "for the purpose of giving them the Torah" (כדי ליתן להם את התורה) — I, 174. This phrase does not have reference to the Sinaitic revelation only but to all the other revelations in the Wilderness, as well. R. Joshua, its author, insists that the commandments to observe the Sabbath and to honor one's parents were given at Marah, a revelation that preceded the one on Sinai — II, 94.

[30] "Comp. however: אמרה ת ו ר ה — without the definite article though it means Scripture. This shows that תורה is sometimes treated as personified, and hence no article is added." — L. G. But is it found here as a personification? Is it active in any way? When the Rabbis wish to convey the idea of the Torah as a whole, they do employ the article, as demonstrated in the previous note.

[31] See above.

ing huddled together, were terrified by the earthquakes, thunder and lightning.[32] The thunder and lightning were not of the ordinary kind but were heard by each Israelite according to his own powers.[33] The people stood literally "below the mount" (Ex. 19. 17), for "the mount was pulled up from its place and the people came near and stood under it."[34] Again, "stood afar off" (Ex. 20. 18) is to be taken literally, for they moved backward twelve miles and then forward again twelve miles as each Commandment was pronounced.[35] So overpowering was the whole experience that more than the Ten Commandments — given in ten sounds "mouth to mouth"[36]— the people simply had not the strength to receive.[37] Conceived as the great spiritual experience in which the *entire* people shared and hence depicted in the most vivid and dramatic imagery, the revelation at Sinai was the most memorable of all the revelations. In contrast to all other revelations, says Ginzberg, it was a *direct* revelation.[38] All this implies, obviously, that the Sinaitic revelation possessed, for the Rabbis, a significance greater than that of the other revelations of Torah;[39] and that would account for the fact that when the term "the giving of Torah" is used it ordinarily refers to the Sinaitic revelation. The term is essentially, however, of a general character, inclusive of all the occasions when, according to the Rabbis, there were revelations of Torah to Israel.[40]

[32] II, 219.
[33] *Ibid.*, 266–67.
[34] *Ibid.*, 219.
[35] *Ibid.*, 269; cf. also *ibid.*, 202.
[36] *Ibid.*, 95.
[37] *Ibid.*, 269–70.
[38] "The revelation on Sinai was, in contrast to all other revelations, a *direct* one. The Rabbis insisted that this revelation was *not* through an angel; comp. my remarks in *Eine unbekannte jüdische Sekte* (New York, 1922), p. 246 f." — L. G.
[39] This bears out the analysis of the relation of significance to the emphatic trends in OT pp. 246–7. Here there is a combination of emphatic trends.
[40] אלה המצות (ולקוטא, הקצ'ו) in his ר' צבי ה' חיות, Chap. 11, seeks to demonstrate the thesis that all the *miẓwot* previously revealed were again confirmed on Sinai. Even according to Chajes' reasoning, however, the revelation at Marah apparently possessed a character similar to that of the revelation on

Israel accepted the commandments of God, again not at one time but on the various occasions when these were revealed. They accepted the Sabbath when it was given them sometime before the revelation at Sinai.[41] When Moses finished reading the book of the covenant to them, on the day before the revelation on Sinai, the people declared, "We accept upon ourselves." Thereupon, Moses sprinkled on the people from the blood of the sacrifice and uttered the formula, "Now you are bound, held and tied," and told them to come on the morrow and receive "all the *mizwot*."[42] The people accepted the Ten Commandments by responding to each one as it was given.[43] The whole-hearted acceptance of Torah by Israel is contrasted with rejections just as positive by the Nations of the World, none of them being willing to obey any of the Ten Commandments that forbade their ordinary mode of living.[44] Logically, of course, the acceptance of God's decrees or commandments presupposes the awareness or acceptance of God's sovereignty, and this logical procedure is, in fact, attributed by the Rabbis to Israel.[45] Obviously, having accepted the Torah, Israel was henceforth committed to the practice of it. "The words of Torah are obligatory upon you."[46]

The revelations of Torah but gave Israel the possibility, afforded the people the opportunity, to acquire Torah. Actual acquisition of Torah was achieved only through the process of laborious and painstaking study. Moses was told by God that

Sinai, for, as Chajes points out, the Rabbis say that at Marah certain *mizwot* previously given were confirmed again.

Chajes' approach to the entire question is decidedly rationalistic. The corner-stone of his argument is the view of Maimonides, and he utilizes again and again the latter's statement that the Patriarchs and the others vouchsafed divine commandments prior to the revelation on Sinai, attempted to impart these *mizwot* to mankind, not on the basis that they were divine commands, but by means of argumentation, teaching, reason.

[41] II, 122–3; cf. II, 119.

[42] II, 210–11. "נעשה ונשמע" (Ex. 24.7) means according to the Rabbis: We shall do what we shall hear" — L. G.

[43] II, 229. " 'Let me hear thy voice' (Song of Songs 2.14), that is, (when responding to) the Ten Commandments" — II, 219.

[44] II, 234–5.

[45] II, 237–8.

[46] III, 179.

it was not sufficient simply to present the Torah with its ordinances to Israel but that, instead, he must teach it to them a second, a third, and a fourth time until they learned it. Nor was this sufficient: they must not only learn the Torah but must be able to repeat it. Nor was even this sufficient: they must be taught until everything is clear to them, orderly, "like a set table."[47] It was that Israel might absorb the Torah that God had them take a circuitous route in the Wilderness. "God said: If I bring Israel into the Land now, every man will immediately take hold of his field or his vineyard and neglect the Torah. But I will make them go round about in the Wilderness forty years so that, having the manna to eat and the water of the well to drink, they will absorb the Torah."[48] In the Wilderness, the study of Torah by Israel followed, apparently, each revelation. At Elim (Ex. 15.27), before reaching Sinai, they were occupied, according to R. Eleazar, with the words of the Torah which had been given them at Marah.[49]

Only by the study and practice of the Torah can Israel remain a spiritual people. The Torah is the covenant between God and Israel, annulled when all the commandments are broken or idolatry practiced.[50] To be God's people means to be altogether absorbed with the Torah. "Then ye shall be Mine" (Ex. 19.5) means according to the Rabbis, "you shall be turned to Me and be occupied with the words of the Torah and not be occupied with other matters."[51] Israel's acceptance of the Torah is, therefore, linked with their love of God "with all their heart and with

[47] III, 1.

[48] I, 171. See Lauterbach, note #4, ibid.

[49] II, 98.

[50] I, 36–38. Several individual commandments and practices are also described by the term "covenant": "The covenant of the Sabbath," "The covenant of circumcision" and the injunction against idolatry — II, 204. The Sabbath is, of course, also "a sign" between God and Israel (Ex. 30.13), and the Rabbis add the comment, "But not between Me and the Nations of the World" — III, 199 and 204.

According to R. Ishmael, God made three covenants with Israel: one at Horeb (Sinai), one in the plains of Moab and one on Mt. Gerizim and Mt. Ebal — III, 187.

[51] II, 204.

all their soul,"[52] for it is the concrete evidence of that love. Israel is God's people only if they are holy. "If you are holy then you are Mine." But what confers holiness upon Israel? "With every new *miẓwah* which God issues to Israel He adds holiness to them."[53] This involves, of course, the practice of these commandments. The observance of the Sabbath, for example, "adds holiness to Israel."[54] On the other hand, when Israel cease to engage in Torah, they tend to lose their spiritual character. They became rebellious soon after they left Egypt, "because they had been without words of Torah for three days."[55] In fact, unless they occupy themselves with the words of the Torah, Israel cannot exist as a people at all.[56]

When the Rabbis extol Israel they frequently do so in terms of Israel's relation to Torah. Thus, the generation that went out of Egypt loved the Torah and the *miẓwot*, according to the Rabbis. Upon leaving Egypt, the people took the unleavened dough, "their kneading-troughs being bound up in their clothes upon their shoulders" (Ex. 12.34) despite their having with them many beasts of burden. This indicates, says R. Nathan, that "Israel cherished the *miẓwot*."[57] Although elsewhere the people journeyed with dissension and encamped with dissension, this was not true when they encamped before Mt. Sinai. Here, as inferred from the word *vayyiḥan*, a singular form, all the people were united, of one accord concerning the acceptance of Torah.[58] Before the giving of the Ten Commandments, "all the people answered together and said, 'All that the Lord hath spoken we will do' (Ex. 19.8)." The Rabbis add: "They did not give this answer with hypocrisy, nor did they get it one from the other, but all of them made up their minds alike."[59] God, Himself, ex-

[52] II, 53. The term for God here is השם.
[53] III, 157.
[54] III, 200.
[55] II, 90. This is the reason given here for the institution of reading from the Torah in the synagogue on the Sabbath and on Mondays and Thursdays.
[56] II, 135.
[57] I, 104.
[58] II, 200.
[59] II, 207; cf. also *ibid.*, 230, where such unanimity is spoken of as an "excellence" of Israel.

pressly approves Israel's response on similar occasions — when they declare "all that the Lord hath spoken we will do and obey" (Ex. 24.7)[60] and when they say, "If we hear the voice of the Lord our God any more, then we shall die" (Deut. 5.22). "Happy the people whose words God has approved!"[61] We have already seen how the Rabbis depict Israel as accepting the laws on every occasion these have been revealed and how they contrast Israel's acceptance with the Nations' rejection of the Torah. The people or generation that received the Torah were not an ordinary people, in the Rabbis' view. Standing before Mt. Sinai, Israel possessed marked "excellence": They interpreted the divine word as soon as they heard it, and there were neither blind nor dumb nor deaf nor lame nor fools among them.[62] At that time, honoring the Torah, Israel was "the most beautiful among the nations."[63]

There can be wide differences of opinion in rabbinic thought, due largely to the different emphasis on one or another of the organic concepts. The following statements, when placed side by side, contradict each other no doubt, but the "contradiction" is merely an instance of the flexibility of organic thinking. Is there a necessary, exclusive, inherent relationship between Torah and Israel? The Rabbis express the idea that there is an inherent relationship between four things, among them Torah and Israel, by observing that Scripture designates each of them by the same term, the common term being "possession" according to one passage[64] and "inheritance" according to a kindred passage.[65] Again, in contradistinction, say the Rabbis, to the things given Israel conditionally — such as the Temple, for example, which was later destroyed — the Torah was one of the things given unconditionally.[66] This statement, too, can only mean that a necessary, inherent bond unites Torah and Israel, and that even

---

[60] II, 229.

[61] II, 270–1. The same biblical verse (Deut. 5.17) is used as warrant in both midrashim.

[62] II, 267.

[63] II, 270. "Sweet is thy voice and thy countenance is comely" (Song of Songs 2.14), refers to Israel when engaged in Torah — II, 219 and I, 211.

[64] II, 75–6.     [65] *Ibid.*; 77–8.     [66] II, 188–9.

a temporary rupture between them, comparable to the temporary loss of the Temple,[67] is impossible. The opposite view, however, is implied by other passages. "When I gave it (i. e., the Torah) from the very start, I gave it not in the place of a land of darkness, not in a secret place, not in an obscure place. 'I said not: It is unto the seed of Jacob' (Isa. 45.19)— that is, to these *only* will I give it."[68] "To three things is the Torah likened: To the desert, to fire and to water. This is to tell you that just as these three things are free to all who come into the world, so also are the words of the Torah free to all who come into the world."[69] Do such statements imply that Torah and Israel are inherently related? We have before us, manifestly, two opinions, each the antithesis of the other, and the organic complex is flexible enough to leave room for both. The opinion affirming that there is an inherent bond between Israel and Torah emphasizes the concept of Israel, whilst in the contrary opinion the concept of Torah is accented in such a way as to be dissociated from Israel.[70] In the former, the element of nationality comes to the fore; in the latter, the element of universality. The "contradiction" presented by these two opinions goes back, very likely, to differences in temperament between two individuals, or perhaps even to the differences in mood of a single individual.

Either Israel or Torah may be emphasized also in such manner as to render one subordinate to the other. When Amalek came to attack Israel, says R. Joshua, Moses' plea to God was that if Israel is destroyed, "who then will read that Book of the Torah which Thou hast given them?"[71] In this plea Torah is definitely emphasized, Israel's very existence being justified on the ground of its service in behalf of Torah. The same is obviously

[67] The Rabbis believed that the Temple would be ultimately restored.

[68] II, 199. For םינפ, see Ginzberg, *Legends of the Jews*, VI (Philadelphia, 1928), p. 32, note 185.

[69] II, 237. See, *ibid.*, Lauterbach's note #12.

[70] Commenting on Ex. 12.26, the Rabbis say "Evil tidings were announced to Israel at that time, namely, that the Torah would ultimately be forgotten" — I, 94. Here the meaning is that knowledge of the Torah would be rare among Israel, but not that it would disappear for then there would be nobody even to tell of the law. "Comp. Shabbat 138b." — L. G.

[71] II, 158.

true of the following midrash: " 'Thou hast guided them in Thy strength' (Ex. 15.13) — for the sake of (i. e., because of) the Torah which they were later to accept."[72] On the other hand, Israel is emphasized, and a primary law of the Torah made altogether subordinate to Israel, in the famous midrash, "The Sabbath is given to you but you are not surrendered to the Sabbath."[73] The organic complex allows emphasis now on this and now on that concept of the complex.

In this section we have demonstrated how the concepts of Israel and Torah interweave in rabbinic thought. The Rabbis tell of a number of revelations of Torah to Israel, though the one at Sinai possessed for them the greatest significance. The Rabbis say further that Israel accepted the various commandments on these occasions and that the actual acquisition of Torah was achieved only by painstaking study. Through study and practice of Torah, they declare, does Israel remain a spiritual, holy people; and, when they wish to extol Israel, do so in terms of Israel's relation to Torah. We also found that Torah and Israel can each be accented over the other at different times, thus allowing, on occasion, the element of universality to come to the fore.

## III. God's Loving-kindness[74] and Israel

God loves Israel. He is their "Father who is in heaven,"[75] and they are "His children"[76] or "His sons."[77] Parental love is but one form, however, taken by God's all-embracing love for Israel,

---

[72] II, 70.

[73] III, 199 and 198. "The contrast is not between the Sabbath and Israel but between the commandment and the instrument (man!) to fulfill it."—L.G. The statement on p. 198 occurs in conjunction with the discussion that demonstrates that the duty of saving life supersedes the Sabbath laws.

[74] The חסד of God — II, 69. מדת רחמים — II, 28. For the terms מידה של חסד and מידה של רחמים see TE, p. 108 and p. 114.

[75] II, 93, 158 (twice), 290 — אביהם שבשמים.

[76] I, 57, 216, 222, 243, II, 21 (twice), 42, 45, 158, 223, 274 — all in the forms of either בני or בניך or בניו.

[77] I, 219 — "sons" because of the parable introducing the idea refers to a "son."

though the form most often apprehended by the Rabbis. God is also Israel's Brother[78] and Israel God's loving friends.[79] Once, when speaking to Moses, according to the Midrash, God fondly designates Israel as the "congregation of holy men."[80] This designation is reflective of Israel's religious status and function; of like character are the references to Israel as God's "servants"[81] and "ministers."[82] For most of these terms there is good biblical warrant; and the following list occurring as a single block is unequivocally biblical: "Thy people, Thy herd, Thy flock, the flock of Thy pasture, the seed of Abraham Thy friend, the children of Isaac Thine only one, the congregation of Jacob, Thy first-born son, the vine which Thou didst pluck up out of Egypt and the stock which Thy right hand hath planted."[83] When the Rabbis depict God's love for Israel by means of such terms of endearment they have, therefore, sound biblical authority, although a certain tender, personal quality is rather more pronounced in the rabbinic terms. We must keep in mind, however, that in the rabbinic view God's love is not limited to Israel. It extends to all men: "Thy right hand is stretched forth to all those who come into the world."[84]

Israel is precious to God, even as a treasure is precious to a man.[85] Not only is the people as a whole dear to God but every individual in Israel. When Israel stood before Mt. Sinai, God told Moses to warn the people "lest they break through. . . and many of them perish" (Ex. 19.21). The Rabbis interpret the word *rab* in that verse to mean that "every one of them that might be taken away is of as great account to Me as the whole

---

[78] I, 221 — אח.

[79] III, 139 — אוהבים.

[80] I, 216 — עדת קדושים.

[81] III, 138 — עבדים; *ibid.*, 23 — עבדיי הם מכל מקום.

[82] III, 139.

[83] II, 80. The passage as given both here and in Horovitz-Rabin, *op. cit.*, p. 150, is textually corrupt, but Horovitz-Rabin calls attention to the parallel in the *Mechilta de R. Simon* the text of which is certainly more reasonable. The terms of endearment, however, remain the same.

[84] II, 39.

[85] II, 204.

work of creation."[86] God's profound love, tender and personal, as felt by the Rabbis, is here portrayed in the strongest manner possible.

Israel is God's especially beloved people. God is "The Lord, the God of all flesh" (Jer. 32.27), the Rabbis point out, but add with emphasis that "He associated His name particularly with Israel."[87] "I am God for all those who come into the world, nevertheless I have associated My name particularly with My people Israel."[88] "The whole world is Thine, and yet Thou hast no other people than Israel," say the Rabbis, offering sound proof from the Bible.[89] Israel is designated as God's "possession" and as God's "inheritance," sharing that distinction only with the Land of Israel, the Temple and the Torah, things which are themselves bound up with Israel.[90] Of special significance is the word "nevertheless" (אף על פי כן) which occurs in one of the passages just quoted. It indicates that, although the Rabbis recognized the anomaly of the God of the universe making one particular people for His own, this anomaly was to them only astounding evidence of God's love for Israel. The exalted place of Israel was both deserved and established in the very nature of the universe. It was deserved: "He has proclaimed me of special distinction and I (Israel) have proclaimed Him of special distinction."[91] And it has been ordained from the beginning: "Have they not already from the time of the six days of creation been designated to be before Me? For it says, 'If these ordinances depart from before Me, saith the Lord, then the seed of Israel

[86] II, 225. The biblical proof-text is "For the Lord's is the eye of man and all the tribes of Israel" (Zech. 9.1), "the eye of man" apparently being taken to mean the world in general which man sees.

[87] III, 184 — ייחד שמו ביותר.

[88] Ibid., 185.

[89] II, 69, 75. The proof-texts are: "The people that Thou hast redeemed" (Ex. 15.13), "The people that Thou hast gotten" (Ex. 15.16), "The people which I formed for Myself" (Isa. 43.21).

"But were they not God's people?"— II, 4; the proof-text here is: "Yet they are Thy people and Thine inheritance" (Deut. 9.29).

[90] II, 75-6, 77-8.

[91] II, 23.

also shall cease from being a nation before Me forever' (Jer. 31. 35)."[92]

God identifies Himself with Israel, in a sense. Israel's troubles, are as it were, His troubles and their joys His joys.[93] So strongly did the Rabbis feel God's close sympathy with Israel that, on the basis of it, they not only reinterpret but actually reconstruct a biblical text. R. Judah declares, though with circumspection, that Zech. 2.12 originally read: "Surely he that toucheth you toucheth the apple of Mine eye."[94] Israel's enemies are thus God's enemies. "And who are they that rose up against Thee? They that rose up against Thy children."[95] And the midrash goes on to say that as to him who helps Israel it is as though "he helps Him who spake and the world came to be."[96] In these midrashim the Rabbis ascribe to God attitudes which they also ascribe to *Shekinah*. The same is true of many of the deeds in behalf of Israel depicted in the following paragraphs.

God, in His loving-kindness, protects and helps Israel. To portray this phase of God's love, the Rabbis tell a parable of a man who was walking in the way with his son in front of him. Let robbers, who seek to capture the lad, attack in front, the father acts as shield by placing the son behind him; let a wolf attack from behind, the father again acts as shield by placing the lad once more before him; let robbers attack in front and wolves behind, the father takes the son up in his arms.[97] Repeated in another section, this parable is introduced there with the following poignant image: " 'And how I bore you on eagles' wings' (Ex. 19.4) — How is the eagle distinguished from all other birds? The rest of the birds carry their young between their feet, being

[92] I, 222; compare also the statement of R. Simon the son of Yoḥai, *ibid.*, 217–18.

[93] II, 160.

[94] II, 43. See Lauterbach, *ibid.*, note #1. R. Judah employs circumlocution so as not to make the actual change in text. The change from the original reading would be out of regard for the majesty of God, not because of fear of anthropomorphism.

"I have no doubt that עיני was the original reading."— L. G.

[95] II, 42, 45.

[96] II, 45.

[97] I, 224–5.

afraid of other birds flying higher above them. The eagle, however, is afraid only of men who might shoot at him. His intention,
therefore, is to let (the arrow) lodge in him rather than in his
children."[98] God indeed protects Israel and always fights for
them against their enemies.[99] Israel's troubles are manifold and
"later troubles cause the former ones to be forgotten," but God
delivers them from all evil.[100] He caused the sea to be divided
before them, declaring on that occasion, "I am a Brother to
Israel when they are in trouble."[101] Not only did He cause them
to pass over the sea but in the same way over the Jordan and
also, apparently, over the rivers of Arnon.[102] He led them un-
harmed through such places as the Wilderness of Kub, a long and
dreadful territory, full of serpents and scorpions.[103] "You call
in secret and I answer you in the open and cause the whole
world to be shaken on your account."[104]

The Bible speaks of "the pillar of cloud by day and the pillar
of fire by night" (Ex. 13.22), by means of which God led Israel
in the Wilderness. The pillar of fire began to gleam, say the Rabbis, while the pillar of cloud was still there.[105] More frequently
the Rabbis refer to the biblical "pillar of cloud" by their term
"clouds of glory." Thus the idea of *Sukkot*, which may be taken
to mean "canopies," suggests to R. Akiba "the clouds of glory."[106]
The "clouds of glory" literally enveloped and protected Israel:
There were four on the four sides of them, one above and one
beneath them, "and one that advanced before them, raising the

---

[98] II, 202–3. The repeated parable is given with slight textual variations.
[99] I, 215.
[100] I, 133.
[101] I, 221.
[102] II, 75; cf. I, 182.
[103] II, 87–89. This wilderness contained one kind of viper, people say,
which had but to look at (or cross) the shadow of a bird flying overhead for
that bird to fall down in pieces. Lauterbach reads מכרכר, but Horovitz-Rabin,
p. 154, reads ומתהבר אל צלו, reserving a still better reading — מיד הוא מתחבל —
for the notes there.
[104] II, 196 — ומרעים עליך את כל העולם.
[105] I, 187.
[106] I, 108, 182. "The underlying idea of R. Akiba is connected with the
ככות of water referred to in Ps. 18.12." — L. G.

depressions and lowering the elevations; . . . it also killed the
snakes and the scorpions, and swept and sprinkled the road before them." According to this statement, there were seven "clouds
of glory;" another opinion sets them at thirteen, still another
at four and still another at two.[107] God's protection of Israel in
this wise presents to the Rabbis an anomaly similar to the one
we noticed above, and once more because of their recognition
of the universality of God. " 'And the Lord went before them
by day' etc. (Ex. 13.21) — Is it possible to say so? Has it not
already been said, 'Do I not fill heaven and earth? saith the Lord'
(Jer. 23.24)?" The answer here, too, is that this anomaly is but
astounding evidence of God's love for Israel, an answer illustrated by the parable of Antoninus himself lighting the way for
his sons although the courtiers, the great men of the Empire,
expressed their eagerness to do so.[108]

God is the Redeemer of Israel. He redeemed them from the
bondage of Egypt. "Through the strength (of God) did Israel
go out of Egypt."[109] The Exodus could not have taken place save
for direct divine intervention; never had a slave, it was said,
been able to run away from Egypt, yet on this occasion God
brought out six hundred thousand people.[110] The final redemption
of Israel "from the hand of Egypt" resembled the escape of a
bird from out of a man's hand when only a slight pressure could
have choked the bird, and the drawing out of a new-born calf
from a cow's womb.[111] Indeed the deliverance from Egypt "is
equal to all the miracles and mighty deeds which God has done
for Israel."[112]

God's love for Israel was also manifest in the details and
circumstances of the redemption. As soon as the designated "end"
came — designated on that fifteenth of *Nisan* at night when
God "did speak with Abraham our father at the covenant be-

---

[107] I, 183. To fight Amalek, Joshua had to get out from under the protection of the cloud — II, 141.
[108] I, 185–6.
[109] I, 141.
[110] II, 176.
[111] I, 249.
[112] II, 105.

tween the parts"— He did not delay them an instant: the people of Israel went out of Egypt also at night on the fifteenth of *Nisan*.[113] The month of *Nisan* itself, "the month of *Abib*," was chosen by God because it was the season most convenient for Israel, for then the sun is mild and there are no rains.[114] Even before the Exodus was God's kindness to Israel manifest. While Israel was in Egypt, a woman would give birth to six children at one delivery,[115] no doubt to offset the cruel decimation of Israel by the Egyptians. And God encouraged the people at the brink of the redemption by announcing the good tidings that "they were destined to see children and children's children."[116] According to one authority, "God skipped over the houses of his children in Egypt" (when the last plague was visited upon Egypt), and this action was a further manifestation of His love — "Hark! my Beloved! behold, He cometh leaping upon the mountains . . . behold, He standeth behind our wall," etc. (Song of Songs 2.8–9).[117] God is the salvation of Israel. "Thou art the salvation of all who come into the world but of me (Israel) especially,"[118] say the Rabbis, again linking the universality of God's love with His especial concern for Israel. God was and will be the salvation of Israel.[119]

[113] I, 112–13, 116. God's covenant with Abraham "between the parts"— Gen. chap. 15.

[114] I, 139–140.

[115] I, 95, 175.

[116] I, 94.

[117] I, 57 — אל תקרי ופסחתי אלא ופסעתי. This implies of course, that the ח and ע were interchangeable in their pronunciation. Naḥmanides uses this example among a number of others to prove this very point; and he insists that it is true not only of rabbinic but also of biblical times for, although all of his examples are rabbinic, he brings them as proof that the עוים (Deut. 2.23) were the חוים. See the comments on Deut. 2.10 and 2.23 in his Commentary to the Pentateuch. "Naḥmanides showed fine philological sense. We know now that the Assyrian transliterated the Hebrew ע by ח"— L. G.

Incidentally, most of the Rabbis declare the blood on the lintel was on the inside not the outside of the house, and all agree that it was not meant as a sign for God — I, 56, 84.

[118] II, 24.

[119] *Ibid.*

The universality of God's love and His especial concern with Israel are once more linked by the Rabbis when depicting God's providence. "Thou art Helper and Supporter of all who come into the world but of me (Israel) especially."[120] In that parable referred to above wherein the father protects his son with his own body, the father also attends to each of the lad's needs. When the lad begins to suffer from the sun, his father spreads his cloak over him; when the lad is hungry, he feeds him, thirsty, he gives him to drink. "So, (too), did the Holy One blessed be He do (to Israel):" "He spread a cloud for a screen" (Ps. 105.39); He fed them bread (Ex. 16.4); He gave them water to drink (Ps. 78.16).[121] After the many years of servitude, the Israelites did not leave Egypt empty-handed, but "the Lord gave the people favour in the sight of the Egyptians" (Ex. 12.36). The Rabbis offer various comments on this verse, all of them illustrating the willingness of the Egyptians to part with their gold and silver and raiment; in fact, according to one comment, the Egyptians let them have things for which they did not even ask.[122] "There was not a single Israelite," says another authority, "who did not bring up with him (from Egypt) ninety asses laden with gold and silver."[123] The "plunder" at the Red Sea was, however, even greater than that taken out of Egypt.[124] After leaving Egypt, God provided Israel with food and drink during their long sojourn in the Wilderness. "On the day the Holy One blessed be He created His world He created there (at Elim) twelve springs, corresponding to the twelve tribes of Israel, and seventy palm-trees, corresponding to the seventy elders."[125] He gave them the manna because of His love, not because it was due them.[126] He brought Israel not by the straight road in order that the Canaa-

[120] II, 23.

[121] I, 225.

[122] I, 105–6. "With great substance" (Gen. 15.4) — God's promise to Abraham — is interpreted to mean "I will fill them with silver and gold" (I, 109).

[123] II, 139.

[124] I, 106.

[125] II, 98.

[126] II, 102.

nites might arise and repair all the damage they had done to the seeds, trees, buildings and wells upon hearing that Israel was about to enter the land; and thus Israel came not "to a desolate land but to a land full of all good things."[127] And when He brought them to the Land, He gave each tribe its proper place and portion so that Israel was "like a vineyard that is planted in rows."[128]

God's love for Israel is also manifested in the moral sphere. "Thou hast shown us loving-kindness (חסד) for we possessed no (meritorious) deeds ... And the world from its very beginning was created only by loving-kindness."[129] Here, it is worth noticing, though God's universal love and Israel are again linked, there is no greater emphasis on Israel than on "the world" in general. God's mercy alone enabled Israel to leave Egypt, not their own virtue. "They were rebellious but He dealt with them charitably."[130] He exercised His mercy and forgave them when they repented after having angered Him — this both at Rephidim and in the Wilderness of Sinai.[131] God's love is enduring and compassionate, and needs must be in the face of human frailty and weakness. It was revealed before Him that they would deal falsely with Him in the future; "yet He helped them — was their Saviour — not as people who would in the future provoke Him but as people who would never prove faithless to Him."[132]

In this section, we have described, to some degree, how the concept of God's loving-kindness intertwines with the concept of Israel. God loves Israel, and Israel is precious to Him. Israel is God's especially beloved people and He identifies Himself, in a sense, with that people. He protects and helps Israel and is the Redeemer of Israel. His providence sustains them. His mercy and forgiveness never fail them. These aspects of God's love for

[127] I, 171–2.
[128] II, 77.
The ark was a means of blessing, of invoking God's providence, the Rabbis emphasize, not as the people were wont to say, after the incidents of Uzzah and the men of Beth-Shemesh, a means of punishment — II, 132.
[129] II, 69.
[130] I, 141.
[131] II, 195–6.
[132] II, 197.

Israel have, however, not been given here in all their fulness, for we have confined our description to the manner in which only two concepts combine. When we shall take up combinations of three or more concepts, there will emerge a somewhat fuller description of these as well as of other aspects of God's love for Israel.

We have, hence, thus far not told the complete story. It is important to bear this in mind when evaluating the effect upon the national consciousness of linking the universality of God with His special relation to the people of Israel. The people felt that Israel alone, in a largely pagan world, were the bearers of the Word of God; God's special relation to Israel was therefore vindicated both by the Bible and by their own experience. This view, moreover, gave them stregnth to withstand the buffeting and persecution which was so often their lot. Nevertheless, had this view not been checked, continuously, by other elements in the organic complex, it would doubtless have led to arrant chauvinism. One of these checks was the concept of God's justice. Its interplay with the concept of Israel is the theme of the following section.

## IV. God's Justice[133] and Israel

The justice of God, like His loving-kindness, is universal in scope.[134] It is manifested toward Israel, as toward all nations and individuals, both in reward and in punishment. Thus, if the people of Israel act according to the will of God, they are rewarded; if not, they are punished. When they do God's will, "they make His left hand to be like a right hand" (a symbol for strength and protection), but when they do not, "they make His right hand to be like a left" (a symbol for withdrawal of protection); when they do God's will, "there is no sleep before Him, as it says 'Behold, He that keepeth Israel doth neither slumber nor sleep' (Ps. 121.4)," but when they do not, "there is, as it were, sleep before Him, as it says 'Then the Lord awaked

---

[133] מדת הדין — II, 28. For this term, cf. TE, pp. 163-6.
[134] See TE, Chap. VI, for an analysis of the concepts of God's justice.

as one asleep' (Ps. 78.65);" when they do God's will, "there is no anger before Him," but when they do not, "there is, as it were, anger before Him;" and when they do God's will, "He fights for them," but when they do not, "He fights against them, — and not that alone but they even make the Merciful One cruel."[135] Here God's protection of Israel is associated with His justice, whereas in the preceding section we saw that it was integrated with God's love. We can begin to perceive, therefore, how the organic quality of rabbinic thought acts as a check upon any development of complacent nationalism. For in this midrash the national welfare is made dependent upon Israel's acting according to the will of God, and on that alone.

God's justice decides Israel's economic welfare; national prosperity depends upon Israel's "doing God's will." When Israel do God's will, says R. Ishmael, they have to observe only the Sabbatical year required by the law (Ex. 23.10–11 and Lev. 25. 2–4), but when they do not, adverse conditions force upon them four such "Sabbatical" years in a septennate.[136] Another midrash has it that ease, or freedom from work, apparently regarded a symbol of national prosperity, is Israel's reward for doing God's will, and exploitation by others Israel's punishment for not doing it. "When Israel do God's will . . . their work is done for them by others . . . but when Israel do not God's will . . . they themselves must do their own work, and not only that but even the work of others is done by them, as it is said, 'Thou shalt serve thine enemy' (Deut. 28.48)."[137] Now above we saw that national prosperity — food, shelter, riches — was a gift of God's love, a manifestation of His providence. Here we find it to be contingent upon Israel's deeds and a manifestation of God's justice. We thus have

---

[135] II, 41–2. The terms לפניו, "before Him," and כביכול, "as it were," mitigate the anthropomorphisms. But we ought to notice that the anthropomorphism of right and left hand is not so mitigated, and that כביכול is employed here to soften only the anthropomorphisms expressing punishment. See the remarks on the use of these precautionary terms in OT, p. 217. These terms, as we have pointed out there, do not imply a philosophic approach to God.

[136] III, 173.

[137] III, 202 and 206–7. There is a slight difference between the two versions.

another example of that "inconsistency"— more properly, that flexibility — to which attention was called in the preceding paragraph. Matters interpreted by means of the concept of God's love could be — and also were — interpreted by means of the concept of God's justice. This check upon the development of a complacent nationalism is, therefore, not sporadic but inherent in the organic nature of rabbinic thought.

Reward is promised Israel for moral sensitiveness and punishment for the lack of it. " 'And Moses came and told the people all the words of the Lord, and all the ordinances' (Ex. 24.3) — he told them: If you will accept with joy the stipulated penalties, you will obtain reward; but if not, you receive punishment. And they accepted with joy the stipulated penalties."[138] This passage does have for its subject moral sensitiveness, despite the threat involved. Joy cannot be coerced.

The term employed in the midrash above for reward is *sakar* and for punishment *puranut*.[139] More often these sub-concepts are referred to as *midat ha-tovah* and *midat ha-puranut*.[140]

God rewards Israel as a people, and the tribes individually, for doing His will or for exhibiting zeal. Regarding Ex. 15.1 — "The horse and his rider hath he thrown into the sea"— the Rabbis ask, "But was there only one horse and one rider?" And they answer, "When Israel do the will of God, their enemies are before them as but one horse and one rider."[141] On that same memorable occasion at the Red sea, but before the waters were divided, the tribes wrangled with one another in their zeal to be the first to enter the sea, each one saying, "I will go down into the sea first." The tribe of Benjamin did not wait for a decision, however, but jumped into the sea first, whereupon the princes of Judah, in sore disappointment, began hurling stones at them. Since it was nought but zeal for God that caused this

---

[138] II, 208–9.

[139] II, 209 — שכר and פורענות.

[140] Cf., e. g., I, 55, 103 — מדת הטובה and מדת הפורענות. "פורענות is a neutral term: the payment one receives for his deeds — reward for the good and punishment for the evil."— L. G. Nevertheless, in all the instances to be found in this text, *puranut* carries with it always the connotation of punishment.

[141] II, 19.

quarrel, both tribes were rewarded: The *Shekinah* (referring here to the Divine Presence in the Temple in Jerusalem) rested in the portion of the tribe of Benjamin, and royalty (referring to David and his dynasty) was given the tribe of Judah for its merit.[142]

God's justice is visited upon Israel not only in reward but also, and apparently more frequently, in punishment. And the Rabbis discern the manifestation of God's punitive justice in the times close to them and in the events of their own day no less than in the distant past of Israel, as we shall soon learn. Being a commentary on a portion of the Book of Exodus, our Midrash depicts God's punishment of Israel whilst they were in Egypt and in the Wilderness. Even according to a conservative opinion, only one out of five Israelites went out of Egypt, the rest being slain by God during the Three Days of Darkness.[143] Because "the sons of Ephraim" took matters in their own hand and went forth out of Egypt without waiting for "the end"— that is, the time set by God — the Philistines were enabled to slay them all, two hundred thousand strong.[144] Before the Red Sea was divided, Israel were placed in judgment as to whether or no they should be destroyed together with the Egyptians.[145] There is certainly a suggestion here that Israel were not without guilt, perhaps only less so than the Egyptians. Israel and the Egyptians are not on totally different planes. Indeed, one of the punishments meted out to the Egyptians was later to be visited on Israel as well. Referring to the last plague, the Midrash says, " 'When I smite the land of Egypt' (Ex. 12.15) — then there will be no plague (upon you) but there will be at a future time."[146]

---

[142] I, 232–3.

[143] I, 95, 175. Other views set the number as one out of fifty and one out of five hundred, and R. Nehorai declares that not even one out of five hundred went out.

[144] I, 172–3; II, 71–3. The biblical warrant is from I Chron. 7.20–1 and Ps. 78.9. The time set by God was in the covenant with Abraham. (Gen. 15. 13–16).

[145] I, 225–6. *Elohim* occurring in the proof-text. Ex. 14.19, is taken by the Rabbis always to refer to God's justice. See Lauterbach, I, 226, note #5, and also the references in Horovitz-Rabin a. l.

[146] I, 58.

In the Wilderness, too, Israel were punished for wrong-doing. They had asked for bread and it was granted them, since it is not possible for man to live without bread. "But now you turn around," God tells Moses to say to Israel, "and, out of a full stomach, you ask for meat. Behold, I shall give it to you. . . But though I am giving it to you, I shall later punish you. 'And ye shall know that I am the Lord your God' (Ex. 16.12) — I am a judge to exact punishment of you."[147] According to some authorities, Amalek's attack upon Israel was a punishment for the ingratitude of Israel: "Let Amalek the ungrateful come and punish the people who were ungrateful."[148] It would seem, however, that the severest penalty of all was meted out to Israel for the sin of making the golden calf, for the penalty consisted of a permanent change in the status of the mass of the people. Before they made the golden calf, the entire people were designated as 'a holy nation" (Ex. 19.6). This leads the Rabbis to say, "(The whole people of) Israel, before they made the (golden) calf, were eligible to eat of the holy things; but after they made the (golden) calf these were taken from them and given to the priests (exclusively)."[149] There was thus, originally, no distinction between

---

[147] II, 107–8. "Your God" is a form of *Elohim*. See above, note 145. We are thus confirmed in our statement that the passage to which that note refers, I, 225–6, implies guilt on Israel's part.

R. Eleazar of Modi'im interprets the phrase "Come near" (Ex. 16.9) to refer to the incident of the quail and to mean, "Come near, to give account" — II, 106.

[148] II, 137.

[149] II, 205. I had thought to question Lauterbach's interpretation of להיות כיוצאי מצרים לו בנים. "The commentators whom Lauterbach follows are quite correct in interpreting כיוצאי מצרים as referring to the large number and not to their holy character. Not only has Midrash Tehillim XLV, end, explicitly explained כיוצאי מצרים by ששים רבוא (comp. also Tanḥuma, Toledot 9), but the remark in the *Mekilta* יכול דווים וסנופים has no sense if כיוצאי מצרים means holy, as they — holy people — are not 'wretched and afflicted.' It is, however, possible that in the *Mekilta* the meaning is: as many children as were procreated by those who went out of Egypt — and not, as understood by the later Midrashim, as many (600,000) as those who left Egypt.

"By the way, the passage יכול. כהגים בטלנים means: I might think כהגים has in this passage the meaning of בטלנים, i. e., people who enjoy life without need to work."— L. G.

priests and people; all were eligible to eat of "the holy things," and hence all were priests. The demarcation between priests and people, with the reduction in status for the mass which this entailed, came only as penalty for the sin of making the golden calf.[150]

But God's punitive justice is manifest throughout Israel's history, not alone in the remote past. The Rabbis find occasion, even in this commentary on the Book of Exodus, to interpret later events and those of their own day in the light of God's universal justice. Three things — the Land of Israel, the Temple, and the kingship of the House of David — were given conditionally, they assert, and were taken away when the conditions, consisting of loyalty to God and His commandments, were not fulfilled.[151] All the disasters that came upon Israel were justified, according to the Rabbis, were, in fact, punishments inflicted by God. He punished the tribes of Judah and Benjamin, they say, apparently referring to the First Exile, and he also punished the Ten Tribes, scattering them abroad.[152] Israel's wickedness brought about the destruction of the Temple, so that they were obliged to count from its destruction instead of from its construction; it likewise brought about foreign domination, so that they were obliged to count according to the era of others instead of their own.[153] Interpretations in like vein gave significance to the tragic circumstances of the Rabbis' own times. In a passage following immediately upon the one last cited, we are told of how R. Joḥanan ben Zakkai once justified Israel's dire poverty and their degrading servitude to Rome and to other, inferior, nations.

[150] "The rabbinic concept of Israel widens the biblical ideal of Israel as a priest-people until the demarcation between the priest-class and the rest of Israel is all but eliminated"— OT, p. 222. See *ibid.* for other examples. The rabbinic concepts, as that section demonstrates, are much wider in application than their biblical antecedents.

[151] II, 188. The conditions were, respectively, those given in Deut. 11.16 f., I Ki. 6.12 and 9.8, and Ps. 132.12 together with *ibid.*, 89.33.

[152] I, 230. The juxtaposition of the tribes of Judah and Benjamin with the scattering of the Ten Tribes leaves no doubt that the punishment of the former was the First Exile. The scattering of the Ten Tribes is adduced from the proof-text (Jer. 18.17).

[153] II, 193.

He was going up to Emmaus in Judea when he saw a Jewish girl picking barley-corn out of the excrements of a horse that, he was told, belonged to an Arab. The scene was symbolic to him of the state of all Israel, and he declared, "You are unwilling to be subject to Heaven (God), behold now you are subjected to the most inferior of the nations, the Arabs; you were unwilling to pay the head-tax of Heaven, 'a beka a head' (Ex. 38.26), behold now you are paying a head-tax of fifteen shekels under a government of your enemies; you were unwilling to repair the roads and streets leading up to the Temple, behold now you have to keep in repair the posts and stations on the roads to the royal cities." God's stern justice is further emphasized by the close of the passage in a lesson drawn from Deut. 28.47–48: " 'Because thou dist not serve the Lord thy God' with love, 'therefore shalt thou serve thine enemy' with hatred; 'because thou didst not serve the Lord thy God' when thou hadst plenty, 'therefore shalt thou serve thine enemy' 'in hunger and in thirst'; 'because thou didst not serve the Lord thy God' when thou wast well-clothed, 'therefore shalt thou serve thine enemy' 'in nakedness'; 'because thou didst not serve the Lord thy God' by reason of the abundance of all things: 'therefore shalt thou serve thine enemy' 'in want of all things.' "[154] The Rabbis thus attribute the general state of Israel to God's punitive justice. Nor do they refrain from interpreting by means of the same concept specific national catastrophes of their own day, such as the disastrous revolt under Trajan.[155]

God punishes Israel for the sins committed by the nation as a whole. The concept of God's justice also includes, however, the aspect of corporate justice whereby the whole group is held accountable, and therefore punished, for the sins of the individual.[156] This aspect of God's justice, the Rabbis feel, is applied in all its rigorousness especially to the people of Israel: " 'A nation one

[154] II, 193–5.

[155] I, 213–14. Other things mentioned here are trafficking with Egypt during the period of Sennacherib and in the days of Joḥanan the son of Kareah. For the revolt under Trajan, see the references given by Horovitz-Rabin, p. 95.

[156] For corporate justice, see OT, pp. 10–11, and TE, pp. 179–184. The group, conversely, is also rewarded for the good deeds performed by the individual.

in the earth' (I Chron. 17.21) — One of them commits a sin and all of them are punished."[157]

The concept of God's justice interweaves with the concept of Israel. The people of Israel are rewarded or punished, according as they do God's will. Moral sensitiveness and zeal are rewarded. But the history of Israel, as the Rabbis view it, is replete with instances of God's punitive justice. Moreover, the Rabbis interpret numerous events and circumstances of their own day as so many punishments for wrong-doing on the part of Israel. Indeed, the more rigorous application of God's punitive justice is particularly the burden of Israel. Thus interwoven with the concept of God's justice, the concept of Israel could not have made, with any degree of consistency, for a complacent nationalism. This interplay of concepts demonstrates, in other words, how the element of universality acts as a check upon the element of nationality whilst both are given simultaneous expression.

## V. Integration of the Fundamental Concepts

The fundamental concepts interweave with one another, as has been demonstrated in the sections above. But this integration is even more thorough-going than we have as yet had the opportunity to perceive. We have noticed, thus far, how any one fundamental concept can combine with any other, the fundamental concepts in any combination being only two. Frequently, however, three fundamental concepts are interlaced with each other in a single passage, and sometimes even all four.

God's love, His justice, and Israel are the fundamental concepts woven together in each of the midrashim now to be considered. The Rabbis interpret the words "My God (Eli) ... my father's God" (Ex. 15.2) to mean that Israel declared, "With me He dealt according to the rule (or quality) of mercy, while with my fathers He dealt according to the rule (or quality) of

---

[157] II, 205–6. The text here is obviously corrupt, although the sentence אחד מהן חוטא וכולן נענשין is clear enough. Lauterbach is forced into an ambiguous translation by the rest of the text as given here. I have taken the passage as it occurs in *Mechilta de Rabbi Simon*, ed. Hoffman, p. 95, which offers no difficulty.

justice."[158] In this interpretation of a verse from the song at the
Red Sea, the people of Israel give thanks to God and contrast
God's mercy toward themselves, undeserved and thus simply a
manifestation of His loving-kindness, with God's strict justice
toward their ancestors.[159] God, out of His love, provided Israel
with manna during the period of the Wilderness; but, though
He also gave them the meat for which they asked, that request
was uncalled for and brought punishment. "The manna was given
Israel with 'a bright countenance': the quail, because they asked
for it out of a full stomach, was given them with 'a frowning
countenance.' "[160] The same agency employed by God on one
occasion as the instrument of His punitive justice is also employed by Him on another occasion in the manifestation of His
love. For, unlike man, "the Holy One Blessed be He. . . heals
with the very same thing with which He smites." When he exiled
Israel, He exiled them by means of clouds (Lam. 2.1), and when
He assembles them again, He will assemble them by means of
clouds (Isa. 60.8); when He scattered them, He scattered them
like doves (Ezek. 7.16), and when He brings them back, He will
bring them back like doves (Isa. 60.8).[161] In each of these midrashim, the fundamental concepts of God's love, His justice, and
Israel are in combination. We must also mark, however, that
although they combine, the individual concepts here stand out
rather boldly, quite clear and distinct: God manifested His mercy
toward Israel at the Red Sea whereas He acted toward their
ancestors with punitive justice; God provided Israel with manna,
a manifestation of His love, and He punished them for asking
for the quail, a manifestation of His justice; God exiled Israel
by means of clouds and scattered them like doves, manifestations

[158] II, 28. The word *El*, as this midrash goes on to explain, always refers
to God's mercy. Contrasted with *El* in the proof-text, according to the rabbinic interpretation, is *Elohim*, or rather its genitive, which, as we have
noticed above, note 145, stands for God's justice.

[159] "This refers to the suffering of the Patriarchs because of 'slight' sins
they had committed."— L. G.

[160] II, 105 (twice); cf. *ibid.*, 108. The midrash also says that Israel was
justified in asking for the manna.

[161] I, 239–40.

of His justice, and He will assemble them by means of clouds and bring them back like doves, future manifestations of His love.

But the individuality of each of the fundamental concepts is not always so definite and clear-cut when the concepts are in combination. Sometimes concepts blend into one another, so thorough-going is their integration. This is true of God's love and His justice in the following midrashim, each of which again presents the fundamental concepts of God's love, His justice, and Israel in combination. " 'Ye are standing this day all of you ... your little ones' etc. (Deut. 29.9–10) — Now what do the little ones know about distinguishing between 'good' and 'evil' (Deut. 30.15)? It was but to give the parents reward for bringing their children, thus increasing the reward of those who do His will."[162] The people of Israel are to be given additional reward for bringing their children to the assemblage, but it was God's love that made for the inclusion of the children in the assemblage at all. Two fundamental concepts are thus mingled: God's love here makes for the occasion of the exercise of His rewarding justice. The homily concludes with ·a statement, immediately following on the section already quoted, that practically says this in so many words. "This confirms what has been said: 'the Lord was pleased for His love's sake' etc. (Isa. 42.21)."[163] When God issues decrees concerning Israel, says another midrash, the execution is reported back to Him if it be for good and is not reported back to Him if it be for evil.[164] This distinction obviously proceeds out of God's love; again the two concepts are mingled. The promised redemption of Israel is to come at the end of four hundred years, according to one verse (Gen. 15.13), and according to another (*ibid.*, 15.16) "in the fourth generation." "How

---

[162] I, 132. Lauterbach does not in his translation hold to the text he gives — ליתן שכר בנים לאבות — which is the reading of the MSS, but offers the sense rather of the reading in the printed editions, לסביאיהם. Horovitz-Rabin prefers the latter.

[163] *Ibid.* We translate צדקו as "His love." The whole context is additional proof that the larger meaning of צדקה in rabbinic literature is love; cf. OT, pp. 132–3 and 303, notes 193 and 194.

[164] *Ibid.*, 11–13. Proof is given from Ezek. 9.2–7 and 11.

can both these passages be maintained?" asks Rabbi Judah the
Prince. And he answers, "The Holy One blessed be He said: If
they repent I will redeem them after the number of generations,
and if not, I will redeem them after the number of years."[165]
Israel's redemption, whenever it comes, is a manifestation of
God's love, as we saw above, but the redemption will nevertheless be hastened in reward for repentance. Thus once more the
concepts of God's love and His justice are mingled.

Another combination of fundamental concepts consists of
God's love, Torah, and Israel. At Sinai, when the Ten Commandments were given, "God came forth to receive Israel as a bridegroom comes forth to meet the bride."[166] God spoke to Israel
at that time, according to the Rabbis, in the tender phrases of
the Song of Songs: "Let me hear thy voice" (Song of Songs 2.14)
that is, when responding to the Ten Commandments; "for sweet
is thy voice" (ibid.) — after having received the Ten Commandments; "and thy countenance is comely" (ibid.) — when "all
the congregation drew near and stood before the Lord" (Lev.
9.5).[167] There was a purpose to the revelation which again indicates God's love for Israel — "God has come in order to make
you (Israel) great among the Nations."[168]

This combination of God's love, Torah, and Israel does not
always make for interpretations which glorify Israel. When Israel
stood at Sinai, they sought to deceive God by saying "All that
the Lord hath spoken we will do and obey" (Ex. 24.7), and God
was silent and forgave them. " 'They beguiled Him. . . for their
heart was not steadfast with Him' (Ps. 78.36–7) and yet 'He,
being full of compassion, forgiveth iniquity' etc. (ibid., 78.38)."[169]
Here God's love is stressed as it manifests itself in forgiveness
of Israel's iniquity. Another midrash contrasts God's love for
Israel, expressed in various ways, with Israel's utter ingratitude,
demonstrated in their refusal to obey the laws. "I have brought

[165] Ibid., III.
[166] II, 218–19.
[167] II, 219–20. See Horovitz-Rabin, p. 215, note #1.
[168] II, 272. On the use of נסות, comp. ibid., 94, ושם נסהו.
[169] III, 105–6. "God was silent" we deduce from ננב ומחריש. Notice that
Horovitz-Rabin, p. 295, does not read לקבל את התורה.

you out of Egypt, I have divided the sea for you, I have sent
down the manna for you, I have caused the well to come up for
you, I have driven up the quail for you, I have fought the battle
of Amalek for you — how long will you refuse to observe My commandments and My laws (ותורותי)? Perhaps you will say that I
have imposed upon you many commandments. I have imposed
upon you the observance of this (commandment of the) Sabbath
since Marah, and you have not kept it."[170]

The combination of God's justice, Torah, and Israel occurs
frequently, God's justice having the aspects of reward and punishment, and Torah the aspect of *mizwot*, or conduct, and study.
The great deeds done in Israel's behalf by God were deserved,
and were rewards for the observance of definite *mizwot*. When
the first-born of Egypt were slain, the people of Israel were spared.
R. Ishmael declares that they were spared "in reward for the
*mizwah*" performed when they struck the lintel and the two side-
posts with the blood, as they had been commanded to do.[171] Until
the last Israelite had finished his paschal sacrifice, R. Jose the
Galilean says, the whole people were in danger of being destroyed
in Egypt;[172] the observance of this commandment, then, saved
Israel. For adhering to the rite of circumcision, according to one
opinion, God brought Israel out of Egypt;[173] according to another,
that adherence earned for them the division of the Red Sea.[174]
Various other reasons, however, are also assigned for the division of the Red Sea, among them Israel's observance of the *mezuzah* and of the *tefillin*.[175] And Israel received not only physical
but spiritual rewards, as well, for observing *mizwot*. Moses told
Israel, says R. Joshua, that if they would succeed in keeping the

[170] II, 121.

[171] I, 56, 87. On p. 56, מצוה, the singular is used, referring to this particular
מצוה; on p. 87, the plural is used.

[172] I, 94. See Lauterbach, *ibid.*, note #2. Implied in this midrash is, of
course, the idea of corporate justice.

[173] I, 140–1.

[174] I, 218.

[175] I, 237, 247, 248 (R. Akiba's opinion). On p. 247, another reason given
is Israel's future acceptance of the Torah and Israel's prayer.

"The assumption is that Israel observed the commandments before they
were revealed on Sinai"— L. G.

Sabbath, God would give them the festivals of Pesaḥ, Shabuot
and Sukkot, whilst according to R. Eleazar of Modi'im, the reward will consist of six good portions — the Land of Israel, the
World to Come, the "New World," the kingdom of the House
of David, the priesthood, and the Levites' offices.[176] Anything
for which Israel laid down their lives — for example, the Sabbath,
circumcision, the study of Torah and the ritual of immersion —
was preserved among them; but anything for which they did
not lay down their lives — for example, the Temple, civil courts,
the Sabbatical and jubilee years — was not preserved among
them.[177] In this paragraph, we have seen that the Rabbis interpreted the events in Egypt and on the Red Sea by means of the
concepts of God's justice, Torah, and Israel whereas previously
we noticed that they interpreted the same events by means of
the concepts of God's love and Israel.

God rewards Israel when they study Torah. "The words of
the Torah which I have given you are life unto you. . . they are
health unto you."[178] The prophet Jeremiah conveyed to his generation a similar idea by using as a reminder the jar of manna,
kept since the days of the Wilderness. Jeremiah had rebuked
Israel for not occupying themselves with Torah, and the people
had replied, "If we occupy ourselves with the words of the Torah,
how will we get our sustenance?" Jeremiah thereupon brought
forth the jar of manna, saying, "See with what your forefathers,
who occupied themselves with the words of the Torah, were provided! You, too, if you will occupy yourselves with the words
of the Torah — God will provide you, too, with sustenance of
this sort."[179]

---

[176] II, 119–20, 122. As to the term the "New World": "Comp. Isa. 66.22
הארץ החדשה, and hence עולם חדש."— L. G.
[177] III, 204–5. See Lauterbach, ibid., note #8. In view of the heroic defense of the Temple, it is curious that this institution was looked upon by the
Rabbis as one for which Israel did not lay down their lives. "The reference
is to Israel's sacrifices at the time of עזר — comp. Shabbat 130a: בשעת גזירת
המלכות; and after the destruction of the Temple only one serious attempt was
made to reëstablish the Temple."— L. G.
[178] II, 96.
[179] II, 125–6.

God also punishes Israel for not studying Torah or for not observing *mizwot*. "Is it possible for the rush to grow without mire and without water? . . . So also is it impossible for Israel to exist unless they occupy themselves with words of Torah. And because they separated themselves from words of Torah, the enemy came upon them, for the enemy comes only because of sin and transgression; therefore it says, 'Then came Amalek,' (Ex. 17.8)."[180] The attack by Amalek is but one instance of the general rule that "the enemy comes (upon Israel) only because of (their) relinquishing their hold on the Torah."[181] Another instance given is the attack by Shishak, king of Egypt (I Ki. 14. 25–26), for at that time Rehoboam "forsook the law of the Lord and Israel with him" (II Chron. 12.1).[182] Some authorities, holding that "And he feared not God" (Deut. 25.18) refers not to Amalek but to Israel, interpret that verse to mean that Amalek's attack was a punishment for Israel's lack of *mizwot*.[183] The general idea that the enemy comes upon Israel because of Israel's deficiency in Torah is here made more specific by the depiction of Israel as lacking in *mizwot*, as deficient in conduct. The same general idea is also made more specific by describing the deficiency in Torah as deficiency in study. " 'Therefore shalt thou serve thine enemy . . . in want of all things' (Deut. 28.48) — 'in want of all things': They were deficient in the study of Torah."[184]

God's justice in its aspect of corporate justice combines with the concepts of Torah and Israel. We learned above that this

---

[180] II, 135. Similarly, *ibid.*, 139, 129. See the following note.

[181] II, 139. The general rule is drawn from the word רפידים, the name of the place where Amalek attacked Israel. The Rabbis interpret the word רפידים to be רפיון ידים, which Lauterbach wrongly translates as "feebleness of hands." This rabbinic interpretation is implied on II, 135, though it is not given there. The full *derashah* can be seen from the parallel on II, 129, where the verse is given, "And . . . Israel journeyed from the Wilderness of Sin . . . and encamped in Rephidim" (Ex. 17.9). The Rabbis take "Sin" to be Sinai, thus Torah, and the verse is given the meaning that they left the Torah, and this meaning is corroborated, according to them, by the phrase "encamped at Rephidim," which is taken to be רפיון ידים.

[182] II, 139.

[183] II, 136.

[184] II, 195.

aspect of God's justice, the Rabbis felt, is applied in all its rigorousness especially to the people of Israel. When the people stood
before Mt. Sinai to receive the Ten Commandments, had one
person defied the warning not to "break through unto the Lord"
(Ex. 19.21) he would have brought disaster upon all. "This teaches
that even one individual can impair the whole group."[185] Corporate justice, however, is not necessarily punitive in its character for it also underlies concepts of corporate reward.

The two aspects of God's justice — reward and punishment
— are occasionally found both together in combination with the
concepts of Torah and Israel. "Israel stood up before Mt. Sinai,"
says R. Jose, "on condition that the Angel of Death should have
no power over them — 'I said: Ye are godlike beings,' etc. (Ps.
82.6). (But) you corrupted your conduct — 'Surely ye shall die
like men' (ibid., 82.7)."[186] As reward for accepting the Torah, this
midrash states, Israel was to be granted eternal life, but their
conduct later was so corrupt that it brought upon them the punishment of death. Similarly, the observance of the mizwah of the
mezuzah should have prevented "the destroyer" (i. e., death)
from entering their homes; "but what caused it to be otherwise?
Our sins."[187] The reward for the observance of this mizwah was
to have been eternal life; the punishment meted out instead, in
view of the actual sins committed, was death. Early death is
the punishment with which the husbands and fathers in Israel
are threatened when they violate justice, and longevity is to be
their reward when they execute it. "If for merely refraining from
violating justice your reward will be that your wives will not
become widows and your children will not be fatherless, how
much more so when you actually execute justice. . . your days
will be lengthened in this world and you will live to see children
and grandchildren and you will merit the life of the World to
Come."[188]

[185] II, 225. The text offers difficulties. See Horovitz-Rabin, p. 217.
[186] II, 272. "Ye are godlike beings" means that like the angels Israel would
have been immortal.
[187] I, 88–9.
[188] III, 144–6.

All four fundamental concepts are sometimes combined, inex-
tricably interwoven in a single midrash. When this occurs, the
concepts of God's love and His justice usually flow into each
other, blend, as in the following instances. Why did Scripture
require that Israel purchase the paschal lamb four days prior
to its slaughtering? Because, says one authority, the time had
arrived, in accordance with God's oath to Abraham, for Israel's
redemption, yet they were without *miẓwot* by virtue of which
they might be redeemed from Egypt. "The Holy One blessed
be He therefore gave them two *miẓwot* — the *miẓwah* of the
paschal sacrifice and the *miẓwah* of circumcision — which they
should perform that they might be redeemed. . . For one cannot
obtain reward except for the deed."[189] The granting of the *miẓwot*
(Torah) necessary for Israel's redemption was a manifestation
of God's love toward Israel, for the redemption itself could only
be in reward for the performance of *miẓwot*, a manifestation of
God's justice. All the four fundamental concepts are present here
but there is a blending of the concepts of God's love and His
justice. Again, because of God's love, reward for *miẓwot*, which
is a manifestation of His justice, at times precedes actual performance by Israel of these *miẓwot*. "Even before I (God) gave
them the *miẓwot* I advanced them the rewards for them (i. e., for
the *miẓwot*)." Thus, before Israel observed the Sabbath, they
received a double portion of manna on the day preceding; and
before the Sabbatical year, the sixth year was blessed; and " 'He
gave them the lands of the nations' (Ps. 105.44) — what for?
'That they might keep His statutes and observe His laws' (*ibid.*,
105.45)."[190] In this midrash, God's love and His justice blend
once more, whilst the other two fundamental concepts also figure.
A third instance involves the aspect, or sub-concept, of corporate
justice. According to an anonymous opinion, Israel would have

[189] I, 33–4. The verse from which the interpretation is drawn is Ezek. 16.8.
[190] II, 199. The emphatic note in this passage is God's loving-kindness to
Israel, all the instances cited demonstrating how God advanced His reward
for the *miẓwot* before Israel performed them. Now this passage is introduced
by the biblical verse אני ד' דובר צדק וכו' (Isa. 45.19). We have here, therefore,
another proof that *ẓedaḳah* has the connotation of love in rabbinic theology.
See above note 163, and the reference there.

been unworthy of receiving (the Torah) at Sinai had a single person been missing, whereas according to R. Jose, it would have
been sufficient had only twenty-two thousand been present.[191]
R. Jose's statement follows immediately upon the anonymous
opinion, and contains a mitigation of the latter's extreme application of corporate justice. The concepts involved in R. Jose's
statement, then, are Torah, Israel, and God's justice as it is
mitigated by God's love.

The concept of Israel is thoroughly integrated with all of the
other fundamental concepts. It combines with all of the other
fundamental concepts, be the combination that of two, or three,
or even of all four fundamental concepts. Such intertwining can
only mean that the fundamental concepts act almost as a unit;
indeed, two concepts, God's love and His justice, sometimes
actually blend into one another. The fundamental concepts have,
therefore, the tendency to act as checks upon each other, a tendency which allows no one concept, Israel included, to be permanently stressed. Israel may thus be stressed on occasion within
any given combination of concepts, such as God's love, Torah
and Israel; properly so, too, since it is one of the fundamental
concepts. By the same token, however, it may, on other occasions,
be subordinated, and this within the very same combination of
concepts. The national self-consciousness acted in concert with
factors, just as powerful, that were broad and universal.

[191] II, 212–13. See Lauterbach, *ibid.*, note #5

# DIVERGENT TENDENCIES AND THEIR LITERARY MOULDING IN THE AGGADAH

## ZIPPORAH KAGAN

Aggadah is literature and should be treated as such. Its significance lies in the meaning which it bestows upon the human situation contained in it; in the answer it gives to the problems it raises. All this is given within a literary framework, hence the necessity to examine both the conceptual and the artistic aspects of the Aggadah. Conceptual differences create artistic differences according to the maxim: "The contents represent the question, the form its answer"[1]. Consequently two formulations of the same Aggadah constitute two creations different in their contents as well as in their form. The appearance of variants in the Aggadah[2] derives from man's inherent need to give different expression to different view-points. Every variant expresses its own view of life — the outcome of a period, a society or a creative personality. Every variant of an Aggadah is an independent literary creation in is own right. Its significance is revaled in all aspects of the literary creation: in the characters, plot, structure and idea. The variants of the story about the early life of Rabbi Eliezer ben Hyrcanus to be analysed in this article will serve as an example. We also hope to establish the chronology of these variants by textual and literary analysis. The criterion of the time when the various Midrashim where edited is not sufficient for our present purpose, both, because the inclusion of a certain Aggadah in an early Midrash and of its variant in a late Midrash is not enough in itself for establishing the respective times of composition, and because, as happens to be the case in our example, two variants belonging to different periods may appear in the very same Midrash. Let us therefore examine the literary aspects of the Aggadah: the fashioning of its characters, the development of the plot and the structure of the Aggadah, as regards its adherence to the historical truth on the one hand, and to the conceptual tendency on the other — all

---

[1] According to the formulation of S. Ẓemaḥ, *Sheti Wa-'erev*, (Tel Aviv 1959), p. 7.

[2] I am distinguishing between a *version* meaning the same story with slight unessential changes; while a *variant* is also the same story but with essential changes — a result of a different view of life. The *variant* differs in essence, ideology and artistic character, which is clearly visible in the plot, the character and in the idea.

this in the light of the assumption that a different formulation expresses different orientation manifested both in contents and form.

We shall discuss five Aggadot[3] about the beginnings of Rabbi Eliezer ben Hyrcanus (R.E.) according to the following sources:

1. *Avot de Rabbi Nathan* (ARN)[4] ed. Schechter, I, Ch. 6.
2. *Avot de Rabbi Nathan* (ARN), ed. Schechter, II, Ch. 13.
3. *Genesis Rabba* (Gen. R.), xlii.
4. *Tanḥuma Buber*, (Tan. B.), (lekh-lekha, 10).
5. *Pirqey de Rabbi Eliezer* (PRE)[5], Chs. 1 and 2.

### ARN I, CHAPTER 6

What were the beginnings of Rabbi Eliezer ben Hyrcanus? He was twenty two years old and had not yet studied Torah. One day he said: 'I will go and study Torah with Rabban Yoḥanan ben Zakkai'. Said his father Hyrcanus to him: 'You shall not get a taste of food before you have ploughed the entire furrow'. He rose early in the morning and ploughed the entire furrow. They said, it was the eve of the Sabbath, he went and ate at his father-in-law's. And others say, he tasted nothing from six hours on the eve of the Sabbath until six hours after the end of the Sabbath. As he was walking along he saw a stone, lifted it up and put it in his mouth; and some say that it was cattle dung. He went and spent the night at his inn. Then he

---

[3] Horowitz, in *Bet 'Eqed Aggadot* (Frankfurt a/M 1881), gives seven versions and variants of our Aggadah.

[4] Schechter, who discovered and published ARN II from manuscripts in the libraries of Rome and Parma — isolated fragments of it, Ms. Munich, were published before in *Newe Shalom* — was of the opinion that versions I and II on the whole constitute only one version and that the differences between them are the work of the traditionists who handed the work down from generation to generation. We do not possess the original version. In his view, ARN II is close to the original since the changes and additions there are fewer in comparison with the changes in I which is quite corrupt. Since then additional manuscripts of ARN I have been discovered, as well as many additional passages from I and II, both in Genizah fragments and in the works of early scholars, and we can no longer accept Schechter's generalization that ARN II is invariably closer to the original. A. L. Finkelstein, *Introduction to the Tractates of Aboth and Aboth de Rabbi Nathan*, (New York 1951) writes that one cannot employ one single yard-stick, but that each passage must be treated separately since in certain passages I and in others II is closer to the original. For that reason Finkelstein divided ARN into five parts (according to the tractate Avot) and dealt with each part separately. This is not the place to discuss his method about which there are different opinions. His conclusion that occasionally I is the earlier, and not always II, is important to us since we also intend to prove the antiquity of the variant in ARN I as against II, though in an entirely different way.

[5] I do not give the text as it appears in PRE, but only the Aggadah in ARN II. Cf. note 11.

went and sat before Rabban Yoḥanan ben Zakkai in Jerusalem, until a bad smell came from his mouth. Said R. Yoḥanan ben Zakkai to him: 'Eliezer, my son, have you eaten nothing today?' He was silent. He told him once more, and he was silent. He sent to his inn and said: 'Didn't Eliezer eat with you at all'? They said: 'We thought he was probably eating with my Master'. He answered them: 'Thus I also thought that he was probably eating with you; between me and between you, we nearly destroyed Rabbi Eliezer'. He said to Him: 'Just as bad breath went forth from your mouth, so shall a good name go forth for you in the Torah'.

Hyrcanus, his father, heard about him that he was studying Torah with R. Yoḥanan ben Zakkai, he said: 'I shall disinherit my son Eliezer'. They said that on that day R. Yoḥanan ben Zakkai sat and expounded in Jerusalem and all the great of Israel sat before him. When he heard that he was coming, he set up guards and told them: 'If he comes, do not permit him to sit down'. He came to sit down, and they did not let him. He pushed and went up until he came to Ben Ẓiẓit Ha-keset, to Nakdimon ben Gorion and Ben Kalba Savu'a. He sat down among them and trembled.

They said, on that day R. Yoḥanan ben Zakkai directed his eyes towards R. Eliezer and told him: 'Give an exposition'. He answered: 'I cannot begin'. He pressed him and the disciples pressed him, so he stood up and began an exposition the like of which ears had never heard. With every word that came forth from his mouth R. Yoḥanan ben Zakkai stood upon his feet and kissed him on his head and said to him: 'R. Eliezer, my master, you have tought me a truth'. Before the time had come to go out, Hyrcanus, his father, got up on his feet and said: 'My masters, I only came to disinherit my son Eliezer, now all my possessions are to be given to my son Eliezer and all his brothers are dismissed (disinherited) and they have nothing of them'.

And why was he called Ẓiẓit Ha-keset? Because he used to recline on a a bed of silver at the head of all the great men of Israel.

ARN II, CHAPTER 13

"And he drinks their words thirstily" — it is said concerning R. Eliezer ben Hyrcanus that at the time when he wanted to study Torah, his father had many plowmen, and he was at the time ploughing on stony ground, and he sat down and cried. His father said to him: "My son, why do you cry? Are you perhaps aggrieved that you are ploughing on stony ground? Come tomorrow and you shall plough on ground already furrowed". He sat down on the furrowed ground and cried. Said his father to him: "Why do you cry?". He said: "Because I want to study Torah". Said his father: "[But you are twenty-eight years old, and yet you are desirous of studying Torah?]

go and take yourself a wife and beget sons from her and send them to school". Eliezer grieved for three weeks, until Elijah appeared to him, and told him: "Go up to Jerusalem to Ben Zakkai." [He went up] and he sat down and cried. R. Yoḥanan ben Zakkai said to him: "Whose son are you?" Eliezer refused to tell him. "Why do you cry? What is your wish?". Said he: "To study Torah". Ben Zakkai asked: "Have you never been to school? Have you never learnt to read the *Shema'*, or the Eighteen Benedictions, or the Grace after a meal?" He replied: "No". So he forthwith tought him all three. Then he asked: "What is your wish, to study the Bible or to study the Oral Law?" He replied: "To study the Oral Law". So he taught him two Halakhot each week-day, and on Sabbath he would go over them once more and link them together.

He spent thus eight days, but had nothing to eat, until a bad breath rose from his mouth, and Ben Zakkai sent him away. Again he sat down and cried. Ben Zakkai asked him: "Why do you cry?" He replied: "Because you made me appear like one plagued with boils". Asked he: "Whose son are you?" He replied: "I am the son of Hyrcanus". Ben Zakkai said: "Truly, you are a son of one of the great of this world, and you did not tell me? Today you shall dine at my house". Said he: "I have already dined at my hosts". R. Yoḥanan sent to the people of his inn and asked: "Has Eliezer eaten with you today?" They replied: "No, and it is now eight days that he has not eaten anything". Then R. Joshua ben Hananiah, R. Yose Ha-Kohen, and R. Simeon ben Netanel went and told R. Yoḥanan ben Zakkai that he had not eaten anything for eight days.

When R. Yoḥanan ben Zakkai heard this, he went and rent his garments and said to him: "Woe upon you, R. Eliezer, that you were cast out from our midst!" (But I say to you) just as the bad breath from your mouth rose in my presence, so the teaching of your mouth shall go forth from one end of the world to the other. [With reference to you I recite the verse] 'And the name of the One was Eliezer'."

The sons of Hyrcanus said to their father: "Go and disinherit Eliezer from your possessions". So he went up to Jerusalem in order to disinherit him from his prossessions, and there found it was a day of celebration in honour of R. Yoḥanan ben Zakkai, and all the great of the city were sitting at table with him. And they were: Ben Zizit Ha-keset, Nakdimon ben Gorion and Ben Kalba Savu'a. R. Joshua and R. Simeon went and told R. Yoḥanan ben Zakkai that R. Eliezer's father had arrived. He said to them: "Prepare a place for him". They prepared a place for him, and made him sit down between them next to him. Then R. Yoḥanan ben Zakkai said: "Eliezer, tell us one thing of the Torah". He replied: "I shall tell to you a parable: What do I resemble? A cistern, which cannot produce more water than has been put in it". "Let me then propound a parable to you", said R. Yoḥanan, "what is the proper comparison? A well that makes water gush forth by its own power — thus you are able to say more words of the Torah than have ever been told to Moses on Mt. Sinai". [He asked him two and even three times, but R. Eliezer would not respond. Thereupon R. Yoḥanan ben Zakkai went out and left, and now R. Eliezer sat town and expounded more matters that had ever been told to Moses on Mt. Sinai.] His face was shining like the sun, and rays of light were coming forth from it like those that shone on Moses' face, and people did not know whether it was day or night. R. Joshua and R. Simeon ben Netanel went and told R. Yoḥanan ben Zakkai: "Come and look how R. Eliezer is sitting and expounding more matters than have ever been told to Moses on Mt. Sinai, and how his face is shining like the sun, and rays of light come forth from it like those that shone on the face Moses, and people do not know whether it is day or night". So R. Yoḥanan ben Zakkai came up to him from behind, and kissed him upon his head, and said: "Joy unto you, [Abraham], Isaac, and Jacob, that this man has come forth from your loins". R. Eliezer's father asked them: "About whom are you saying that?" They replied: "About your son, Eliezer". Said he: "Is that what you should say: 'Joy to you, Abraham, Isaac and Jacob, that this man has come forth from your loins' — you should have wished me joy that he has come forth from my loins!" R. Eliezer went on sitting there and expounding the Law, while his father was standing up, and he said to him: "Father, I cannot sit and expound and say words of the Torah, while you are on your feet standing." Forthwith he made him sit down at his side.

Said the father: "My son, I did not come for all this glory. What I came for, was to ban you from my possessions. Now that I have come and seen you and rejoiced in your teaching, your brothers are banned from my possessions, and I give them to you as a gift". Said he: "I am protected (?), so that I have an equal share with all of them". Then he went on: "If I had asked God to grant me silver and gold, He would have been able to grant me my wish, for it is said 'Mine is the silver, and Mine the gold, saith the Lord of Hosts' (Haggai ii:8). Had I asked Him to grant me landed property, He would have given it to me, as it is said: 'The earth is the Lord's and the fulness thereof'. I, however, only asked Him that I may be granted the Torah, as it is said, 'Therefore I esteem all Thy precepts concerning all things to be right, every false way I hate'."

## GENESIS RABBA, xlii

The story is told about R. Eliezer ben Hyrcanus whose brothers were ploughing in the plain, while he ploughed on the mountain, when his cow fell and was injured. He said: 'It is for my good that my cow was injured'. He fled and went to Rabban Yoḥanan ben Zakkai, where he ate clods of earth until his mouth produced a bad smell. They went and told Rabban Yoḥanan ben Zakkai: 'The smell of R. Eliezer's mouth is hard (to bear)'. He told him: 'Just as the smell from your mouth has become malodorous over the Torah, so the odour of your learning will travel from one end of the world to the other'. Some time later his father came up to disinherit him from his possessions, and found him sitting and expounding, with the great of the land sitting before him: Ben Ẓiẓit Ha-keset, Nakdimon ben Gorion and Ben Kalba Savu'a. He found him sitting and expounding the following verse: 'The wicked have drawn out their sword, and have bent their bow' (Ps. xxxvii. 14) — this refers to Amraphel and his companions — 'To cast down the poor and the needy' (ib.) — this is Lot — 'To slay such as are upright in the way' (ib.) — this is Abraham — 'Their sword shall enter into their own heart' (ib.) — 'And he divided himself against them by night, he and his servants, and smote them. etc.' (Gen. xiv:15). Said his father to him: 'I only came up here to disinherit you, now all my possessions are given to you for a gift'. He replied: 'Let them be a ban upon me, I shall only share them equally with my brothers'.

### TANHUMA (ED. BUBER)
### (Lekh Lekha, par. 10, vol. I, pp. 67–69)

The story of Rabbi Eliezer ben Hyrcanus, who was a son of the 'Pilot' and his father was close to the government and to affairs of high army officers. Once upon a time R. Eliezer's father went to another place, and as soon as it was noticed that they were coming, he said to his sons: 'Let us rise and flee from them', and forthwith he called to his slaves and attendants to bring the cattle and the camels and to load his chattels upon the camels. Hyrcanus and his sons fled, but R. Eliezer did not go with his father, but fled to Jerusalem, without carrying with him as much as one *Kikkar* or one *Maneh,* but arrived in Jerusalem like a beggar. He saw R.Yoḥanan ben Zakkai sitting and teaching Torah, while the pupils were sitting before him during the discourse. When he had finished the chapter, he taught them Aggadah, and then he taught Mishnah. Eliezer went in and sat down before R. Yoḥanan ben Zakkai, and spent two or three weeks thus sitting before him, and started to speak up in discussion with the other pupils. They could smell the bad breath from his mouth, but they kept silent and said nothing, and yet again he would speak and they kept silent and said nothing. R. Yoḥanan ben Zakkai realized that the odour of his mouth did not come from anything bad that was in his mouth, but from hunger, as he had not eaten anything. R. Yoḥanan ben Zakkai said to the pupils: "Upon your life, investigate the matter and find out what is the matter with this pupil, whether he is starving, and what he is eating". They went all over Jerusalem, and asked each innkeeper whether he had a scholar among his lodgers, but they replied in the negative. Then they came to a certain woman, and asked her: "Is there a scholar here as lodger", and she replied, "Yes". They asked her: "Has he got anything here?", and she answered: "He has one bag". They said: "Let us see it", and she forthwith brought it to them. They opened it, but found in it sand; he used to put his head inside and suck it like a skin full of wine. So they went back to R. Yoḥanan ben Zakkai and told him, and he was astounded, and appreciated the righteousness of R. Eliezer, that he had not demanded of anyone to give him anything. Immediately he alloted to him a large sum, so that he should eat good food, as he used to do in his father's house. He ate and drank well, until his bad breath was cured.

R. Eliezer spent a year or two before R. Yoḥanan ben Zakkai until his father returned to his old home. When the father had returned, and been there for a month or two, and his son R. Eliezer did not come, he was loth to say to himself that he had abandoned him and let him go to Jerusalem, [and the brothers of R. Eliezer kept saying to their father: "Just look at your son Eliezer, what he has done; he has abandoned you and gone off to Jerusalem, where he eats fattened calves, while you had to leave your house and go abroad. If anything untoward were to happen, would he not jump to take his inheritance? Look at the difference between us and your son. We endangered our lives for you and did not abandon you, but he did not even come to witness the distress. Now, as soon as he hears that anything has happened to you, he will come to us to share with us." Straightaway he said to them: "Whatever happened, he will not inherit anything from me". Said they: "How will you keep him away once you are dead?" He said: "Call a notary", but they replied: "Nothing will help; there is a Patriarch in Jerusalem, called R. Yoḥanan ben Zakkai, [and he helps him], and as soon as you are dead, he will come without fail, and he will say, 'who says that his father dishinherited him'? and we produce the document, and he will say, 'It is forged, and you yourselves have fabricated it, and I do not recognize it as valid, unless we bring the matter to court'." Said the father: "Since you say thus before me, that R. Yoḥanan ben Zakkai is so proud of him, I am certainly going to disinherit him". Immediately his sons put him upon a carriage (?), and he arrived in Jerusalem on the eve of the Sabbath. He said: "I shall disinherit him [on the Sabbath] in the House of Learning, when all the congregation is assembled". He entered and sat down in the House of Learning, and all Israel came in to study, in order to hear the lecture which R. Eliezer used to deliver in public, sitting on a *cathedra*, with the Ḥazzan standing before him. His father saw him wrapped in his *Tallit* (and the phylacteries upon his head), he realized that he had been thinking all along that his son had fallen into bad ways. Now that he saw him sitting upon the *cathedra* and expounding, Hyrcanus stood on a bench and proclaimed before the inhabitants of Jerusalem: "I came to Jerusalem to ban you, my son Eliezer, even to disinherit you, but now herewith I give you two shares, more than any of your brothers".

A comparison of the five Aggadot shows that we have here four variants, the last one — PRE — being merely a version of ARN II. The relationship between the last two is that of versions, i.e. narrative and ideological identity (see note 2), while the relationship between the other Aggadot is that of variants, four different manifestations of one story, of one set of circumstances. The variants can therefore be set out as in the tables following on pp. 160–162.

The comparative table shows us that the five Aggadot (four variants) are divided into two groups.[6] Group A includes ARN I and Gen. R., Group B — ARN II (and PRE), with the unique variant in Tan. B.[7] revealing a close affinity to Group A and a lesser one to Group B (cf. below).

### THE CHARACTERS

*The figure of the father — Hyrcanus*

Hyrcanus' figure is differently treated in the two groups. In the first group — ARN I and Gen. R. — we have a tough, patriarchal figure, a landed farmer whose greatest concern in life is for the family property. This accounts for his violent objection to the aspiration of his son Eliezer to go and study the Torah. The father's opposition in these sources is fundamental, admits of no compromise and is accompanied by suitable sanctions: "You shall not get a taste of food before you have ploughed the entire furrow" (ARN I), while in the second group — ARN II and PRE — we are introduced to a tolerant father who understands his son's wish and whose objection to the study of the Torah is more "technical" and reasonable: "He said to him: 'Are you not twenty-eight years old and you wish to learn Torah? Instead,

---

[6] A similar examination which I made of the variants of the Aggadah concerning "The beginnings of Rabbi Akiba" led to an identical conclusion; there too, various tendencies were at work which were responsible for the different moulding of the characters and the course taken by the plot. The reason for this is the attitude to the part his wife played in the career of this illustrious Tanna, which in some sources (ARN I, T. B. Ket. 66 and the second part in T. B. Ned. 50) is positive and enthusiastic, while in the rest of the sources (ARN II, Ned. 50, Part I) it is cool and reserved. This difference also pervades the late sources: *Gaster, Ḥibbur Yafeh Me-Ha-Yeshu'a* and *'Oseh Fele*.

[7] Only the first part of the story in Tan. B. is different from the other variants of our Aggadah, while the continuation is the same.

go, take yourself a wife, beget sons and you shall take them to school"
(PRE).

Hyrcanus' later reaction and conduct agree with the above starting-
point. According to the first group Hyrcanus goes to Jerusalem to disinherit
his son Eliezer on his own initiative:

> Hyrcanus, his father, heard about him that he was studying Torah with
> Rabban Yoḥanan ben Zakkai, he said: 'I shall disinherit my son Eliezer'
> (ARN I).

> After some time his father came up to disinherit him (Gen. R.).

It is the father who is responsible for the decision and its execution. That is
how an authoritative father reacts to a slighting of his authority and disregard
for the preservation of the family's property. Hyrcanus' reaction can be
understood in the light of his longstanding opposition to his son's ambition
to study Torah. The situation differs in Group B. Here one might well
ask: if the father's resistance was, in fact, not on a matter of principle, but
"technical" — the advanced age at which R.E. was moved to go and
study — what, then, was it which made the father react in so violent and
revengeful a manner? The authors of the Aggadah were aware of this weak
point and realized that a softening of the father's image necessitated a
softening of his reaction and that is why they shifted the centre of gravity
from the father to the sons. According to ARN II and PRE it is not Hyrcanus
who wishes to disinherit R.E., but his sons who goad him on to go to
Jerusalem and give legal force to the act of depriving him of his share of the
family's property.

> The sons of Hyrcanus said to their father: 'Go disinherit Eliezer from your
> possessions' (ARN II).

> The sons of Hyrcanus said to their father: 'Go up to Jerusalem and disin-
> herit Eliezer from your possessions'. So he went to Jerusalem to disinherit
> him (PRE).

On this point the variant in Tan. B. is close to Group B. According to
Tan. B., not only did the sons make the suggestion, but they went so far as to
prove its justice to their father:

> Just look at your son Eliezer, what he has done; he has abandoned you and
> gone off to Jerusalem, where he eats fattened calves... if anything untoward
> were to happen, would he not jump to take his inheritance? (Tan. B.).

They prevailed upon him to go up to Jerusalem to the law-court in order to
give legal authority to his will so that after his death R. Yoḥanan ben
Zakkai, R. Eliezer's patron, would not come and claim that the will is a
forgery. In Tan. B. the interference of the sons is not merely an incidental

*A Comparison between the Five Aggadot about Eliezer ben Hyrcanus*

| Subject | ARN I | Gen. R. | Tan. B. | ARN II (PRE) |
|---|---|---|---|---|
| R. Eliezer's family | Agricultural background alluded to in one sentence. | Agricultural family. Several sons, R. Eliezer is discriminated against in the ploughing by his brothers. | Different background. Roman rule. Refugees flee from Roman oppression. | Farming family. Several sons. R. E. discriminated against by his brothers in the ploughing. |
| Conversation between R. Eliezer & his father | Briefly | Missing | Missing | Repeated several times and accompanied by R. E.'s weeping. |
| Revelation of the Prophet Elijah | Missing | Missing | Missing | Elijah appears before R. E. (here too he weeps) & advises him to go to R. Y. b. Z.'s Bet Midrash in Jerusalem. |
| R. Eliezer & R. Yoḥanan ben Zakkai | This central subject appears in all the sources with many differences (cf. below) | | | |
| Difficulties in studying | Missing | Missing | Missing | Difficulties in study (taught two Halakhot) accompanied by R. E.'s weeping. |

| | | | | |
|---|---|---|---|---|
| R.Y. b. Z.'s reaction to R.E.'s bad breath | Shows anxiety. Sends to inn whether R.E. has eaten. | Missing | Shows anxiety. Sends to inn whether R.E. has eaten. | Sends him away. "You made me appear like one affected with boils", (spoken by R.E.). Shows anxiety & sends to inn whether he has eaten, only after he knows whose son he is. |
| Promise of future reward | "Just as bad breath" etc. | "Just as the smell of your mouth became unpleasant for the sake of the Torah, so will the odour of your learning go from one end of the world to the other." | Immediate reward of much money so he could eat well. | "Just as the breath… so the teaching of your mouth shall go forth from one end of the world to the other." |
| Good family of Hyrcanus | Not mentioned at all. | Not mentioned at all. | Not mentioned at all. | Stressed. After R.Y. b.Z. knows whose son R.E. is, "A son of one of the great of this world", he changes his attitude, invites him for a meal & is anxious on his account. |
| Hyrcanus' trip to Jerusalem | Goes to Jerusalem on his own initiative. | Goes to Jerusalem on his own initiative. | Goes at the wish of his sons who *insist* that he disinherit R.E. at a law-court. | Goes at his sons' advice, that he disinherit R.E. |

*A Comparison between the Five Aggadot about Eliezer ben Hyrcanus*

| Subject | ARN I | Gen. R. | Tan. B. | ARN II (PRE) |
|---|---|---|---|---|
| Hyrcanus' reception in the House of Study | R.Y.b.Z. orders the guards not to let him sit down. Hyrcanus pushes ahead, sits down and trembles. | Missing | Missing | Hyrcanus sits among Jerusalem's great men. |
| R.E. in his greatness. | At length | Briefly | Briefly | At great length. |
| Comparison to Moses | Missing | Missing | Missing | Mentioned with great emphasis. |
| Hyrcanus' announcement | Came to disinherit him. Now *all his property* is to go to R.E. and nothing to his brothers. | Came to disinherit him. Now *all his property* is to go to R.E. as a gift. | Came to disinherit him. Now he is to get *two parts*, more than his brothers. | Came to disinherit him. Now his brothers are disinherited and *all his property* is to go to R.E. as a gift. |
| R.E.'s reaction | No reaction (No refusal) | Let them be a ban upon me, I shall only share them equally with my brothers. | No reaction (No refusal) | *Explicitly rejects the inheritance.* "Had I asked Him to grant me landed property, He would have given it, ... if silver and gold... *I, however, only asked Him that I may be granted the Torah.*" |

addition, but constitutes the central subject of the Aggadah which deals with the problem of inheritance — the will.[8]

A further difference of the father's image in the two groups is brought about by the social position of his family and his relationship to the scholarly world of his time. Group A (and Tan. B) makes no mention of any closeness between him and the Torah and its teachers, on the contrary, one notices antagonism between the two sides:

> When he R.Y.b.Z. heard that he was coming, he set up guards and told them: 'If he comes, do not permit him to sit down'. He came to sit down, and they did not let him. He pushed and went up until he came to Ben-Zizit Ha-Keset, to Nakdimon ben Gorion and Ben Kalba Savu'a. He sat down among them and trembled (ARN I).

In Tan. B. the father and his sons have some harsh things to say against R. Yoḥanan ben Zakkai who assisted the son when he had deserted his father and his family at a time of distress:

> 'As soon as you are dead, he will come without fail, and he will say: Who says that his father disinherited him? And we produce the document, and he will say: It is forged, and you yourselves have fabricated it, and I do not recognize it as valid, unless we bring the matter to court'. Said the father: 'Since you say thus before me, that R. Yoḥanan ben Zakkai is so proud of him, I am certainly going to disinherit him' (Tan.B.).

In Group B this tension has disappeared. Here Hyrcanus enjoys an important social status and Eliezer is no unknown young man, but "a son of one of the great". Hyrcanus is known to the scholars and close to them:

> Asked he: 'Whose son are you'? He replied: 'I am the son of Hyrcanus'. He told him: 'Truly you are a son of one of the great of this world, and you did not tell me' (ARN II).

And with a slight change of the wording also in PRE:

> 'And you did not tell me. Upon your life, today you dine with me'.

In Group A (ARN I), at R.Yoḥanan's command, Hyrcanus is not to sit among Jerusalem's great men and scholars, and though the aggressive Hyrcanus refuses to obey this order, impudently forces his way and sits amongst them, still: "He sat down among them and trembled" — that is how the Aggadists imagined the feelings of a man who sat himself down in

---

[8] In this connection the variant in Tan. B. is discussed by E.E. Urbach, "Inheritance Laws and After-life" *The Fourth World Congress of Jewish Studies-Papers*, Vol. I (Jerusalem 1967), pp. 263 f. (Hebrew).

the wrong place. However, in Group B the attitude towards him is radically different. Thus R. Yoḥanan ben Zakkai to his pupils:

'Prepare a place for him', and they prepared a place for him and made him to sit down next to him (PRE).

... and made him sit down next to him between them (ARN II).

Further on in the Aggadah Hyrcanus sits among the scholars and Jerusalem's great men, in his rightful place, without any trembling, and his intervention in the discussion amazes neither the listeners present nor the latterday readers. He is considered a great man amongst the great and a man of ¡mportance among the important — a man in his place.

### THE HERO OF THE AGGADAH — R. ELIEZER BEN HYRCANUS

From the different evaluation of the father's personality follows the different treatment of the son's image in the two groups, which demonstrates the literary understanding of the various authors and editors in preserving the intrinsic relationship of the various components of the Aggadah.

Vis-à-vis the aggressive character of the father in Group A there is the stubborn and forceful character of the son. R. Eliezer obeys his father only until he has reached adulthood, given here as a certain age (twenty-two or twenty-eight years). As he got older, he rebelled against his father's authority to force on him a way of life which was opposed to his wishes, and of his own accord he left his father's house and went up to Jerusalem in order to realize his ambition and learn Torah in the Bet Midrash of R. Yoḥanan ben Zakkai. His strong personality is also brought out by his conduct during his period of learning when he bears hunger and poverty in silence, does not tell a soul, nor seeks any help. In the two variants in Group A — ARN I and Gen. R. — the father and son are placed opposite each other, two strong personalities whose similar character serve a different *Weltanschauung*. This increases the visible and the concealed narrative tension. In Group A the conflict is sharp and elemental and takes place in several spheres at the same time: in the family sphere (father vis-à-vis son, brothers vis-à-vis brother); in the social sphere (farmers vis-à-vis scholars), and in the conceptual sphere (a materialistic and realistic outlook on life vis-à-vis an idealistic and spiritual outlook).

In Group B — ARN II and PRE — R. Eliezer's image is altogether different. He is portrayed as being passive and hesitant, needing to be encouraged and urged on. He lacks independent power of decision at crucial moments; at the encounters with his father, the Prophet Elijah and R. Yoḥanan ben Zakkai — fateful encounters — R. Eliezer just sits and weeps. Even his going to Jerusalem, to the Bet Midrash of R.Y.b.Z. is not a result of his own decision. This step in his life he takes on the decisive advice of a higher power, that of Elijah the Prophet who appears to him and plainly tells him:

'If you wish to learn Torah, go up to Jerusalem to R. Yoḥanan ben Zakkai' (PRE).

'Go up to Jerusalem to Ben Zakkai' (ARN II).

R. E. was in need of spiritual help also during his years of study in Jerusalem. Apart from his poverty at this time (according to both groups), he was assailed — according to Group B only — by psychological problems of acquiring knowledge. In ARN II and in PRE much is made of his being an unlettered ignoramus who had never learnt to recite the *Shema'* or Grace after Meals and who was a complete *'Am Ha'arez'*[9]. There are allusions that as a result he found it difficult to study in the beginning and therefore

... he sat down and cried. He asked him: 'Why do you cry?' He replied: 'Because I wish to learn Torah'. So he taught him two Halakhot every day of the week and he repeated them and assimilated them.[10]

### THE PLOT

The plot is the outward embodiment of the spiritual processes of the *dramatis personae* and is determined by their character and their consciousness. These two aspects, the figures and the plot, express, each one in its own way, the idea of the composition. In the plot the author expresses his view of the development of the events and their inner consistency.

A few examples of differences in the plot between the Aggadot in Group A and in Group B will serve as an illustration.

A first difference — Hyrcanus' good family, which is emphasized in Group B and is missing in Group A, influences the attitude of R.Y.b.Z. towards R. Eliezer. When R.Y.b.Z. realizes that R. Eliezer is the "son of one of the great men", the son of Hyrcanus, he immediately invites him to dine with him. This expansion of the plot in Group B is certainly significant for it expresses a *Weltanschauung* which appreciates good family connections and a social position.

---

[9] "Our Rabbis tought: Who is an *'Am ha-arez'*? Anyone who does not recite the *Shema'* morning and evening — arcording to the words of R. Eliezer" (Ber. 47).

[10] The commentators found it difficult to consider this a lack of quick understanding, and already R. David Luria in his commentary on PRE states: "It does not seem that R. Eliezer who was a 'plastered cistern which loses not a drop, etc.' needed to repeat two halakhot every day of the week... a more likely explanation is that on every day of the week he taught him two new halakhot since it was his way to teach his pupils two halakhot every day, as it is said in *Lev. Rabba*, xix: 'I study two halakhot today, two halakhot tomorrow...'

A second difference — Hyrcanus' conduct at the end follows naturally from his behaviour at the beginning. In Group A we understand his violent reaction — the decision to disinherit R. Eliezer — as resulting from his basic objection from the beginning. In Group B, however, there is no room for a furious and vengeful reaction since his objection to the study of the Torah had been softened to quite a degree. The editors of the Aggadah understood this and introduced changes into the plot, such as shifting the centre of gravity from the father to the sons. It was not the father who instigated the disherison, but his sons, Eliezer's brothers.

A third difference — the softening of the father's image in Group B, led to a softening of the father and son conflict in the entire Aggadah and hence to many changes in the plot. First of all, R. Eliezer does not rebel against his father's authority and does not disobey him even though his father's command opposes his aspirations. His opposition does not express itself in deeds, but merely in heartache. "He sits and weeps." Only when the Prophet Elijah appears before him and advises him what to do he dares to go off. The plot in this group stresses the positive aspect of his action, namely, obeying the representative of God, the instruction from on High which has the force of a decree. Here, the confrontation is not between the will of the father and the will of the son, but between the forces of this world and the above. In this manner the conflict was removed from the family sphere and transferred to a higher one, to that of Divine Providence which directs man's movements.

The difference in the plot expresses a different view of the world. The variants in Group A place man in their centre, in the centre of the plot. His self-knowledge reveals his destiny to him, which he fulfils on the strength of his decision and by his own force. While Group B has a higher power at the centre of its plot which directs the step of man by means of its messenger — the Prophet Elijah.

A fourth difference — the extension of the plot in Group B, is brought about by means of agreement with R. Eliezer's views which were well known to the Aggadists. This shows us how the late Aggadists worked. For example: R. Eliezer's refusal to sit down and give his exposition so long as his father stood up:

> 'Father, I cannot sit and expound and say words of the Torah while you are standing on your feet'. He stood up and made him sit down at his side (ARN II & PRE)

fits in with R. Eliezer's extreme view of honouring one's father. He praised a Gentile for honouring his father (Qidd. 31a), even though in general he is known for his harsh attitude to foreigners. We also know his ruling (*ibid.*):

If my father says, Give me water to drink, and my mother says: Give me water to drink, which one comes first? He said to him: Forgo honouring your mother and observe the honour of your father, since both you and your mother are obliged to honour your father.

Of a similar nature is his refusal to begin his discourse until R. Yoḥanan ben Zakkai had gone out:

He (R.Y.b.Z.) said to him: 'Lest you feel ashamed because of me, I shall get up and go away from you'. Rabbi Yoḥanan got up and went outside (PRE).

We are reminded of R. Eliezer's saying:

Any pupil who teaches Halakhah in the presence of his teacher deserves death (P.T. Gitt. V 2).

Almost certainly, the comparison with Moses, only given in Group B, is connected, even if only by association, with the following Aggadah:

Said R. Aḥa tn the name of R. Ḥanina: When Moses went up to the high heavens he heard the voice of the Holy One blessed be He, sitting and discussing the red heifer, quoting Halakhah in the name of its originator: 'R. Eliezer says...'. Said Moses to the Holy One blessed be He: 'Master of the Universe...Would that he should come forth from my loins'. He said to him: 'Upon your life, he will come forth from your loins'. This is what is written: "And the name of the other was Eliezer" (Exod. xviii:4) that same, particular Eliezer (*Pesiqta de R. Kahana*, Parah, ed. Buber, 40a).

## THE SIGNIFICANCE OF THE STRUCTURE OF THE AGGADAH

The structural aspect, too, in its own way, has its contribution to make to the significance of the Aggadah. Our Aggadah consists of three different parts which are distinguished from one another by the ideological concepts embodied in them.

| | Group A | Group B |
|---|---|---|
| Part I | Rabbi E. in his father's house. | R.E. in his father's house |
| | | R.E. and the Prophet Elijah. |
| Part II | R.E. in the Bet Midrash of R. Yoḥanan ben Zakkai. The agony of hunger. | R.E. in the Bet Midrash of R. Yoḥanan ben Zakkai. The agony of hunger. The agony of learning. Good family connections. |
| Part III | The exposition. | The exposition. Comparison to Moses. |
| | The proposal. | The proposal. Rejection. |

109

Part I — The family circle is dominated by materialistic and economic considerations and is characterized by rigid relationships, hard physical labour and the dissatisfaction of R.E. with his way of life.

Part II — The spiritual circle is characterized by economic hardship which the hero accepts readily.

Part III — The meeting of the two circles ends in the victory of the Torah over physical labour, of the spirit over material matters, of R. Eliezer over his father and his brothers.

In group A the Aggadah is shorter and more concise; it describes the events realistically, while the emphasis is on earthly motifs and people.

In Group B the Aggadah was expanded and took in supernatural motifs which were intended to enhance the hero and raise the struggle to the highest degree, with forces from above taking part in it: The Prophet Elijah actively and Moses merely in an associative capacity. Here the conflict is between the heavenly realm and that of this world, hence, the different end: The absolute rejection of all material possessions.

## THE CHRONOLOGICAL SEQUENCE IN THE AGGADAH

We thus have two groups. The first one — ARN I and Gen. R. — is earlier and more authentic. The Aggadah in Group A was told close to the time when the events took place and for that reason it preserved a more realistic view of the figures, the plot and numerous details. The Aggadah in Group B, on the other hand, — ARN II and PRE — was composed at a later time than the historical event.[11] The later editors who wished to enhance the hero and clothe him in shining armour (legend), were free to introduce changes and additions in the light of this tendency without being tied to the factual and historical yardstick or any need to consider it.

The tendency of Group B is to glorify the image of R. Eliezer as well as his origin. The result is a softening of the father's character.[12] At a time close to the actual events it was obviously impossible to alter his rigid

---

[11] The chronological criterion — the time when the Midrashim were edited — can help us a little, but not decisively. ARN and Gen. R. were finally edited still in the fifth century; PRE in the eighth (or ninth) century. According to our conclusions, the Aggadah in ARN I is early, while that in ARN II is late and many changes were made in it, compared with the original. The Aggadah in PRE is merely a version of ARN II.

[12] A similar attempt was made in the sources with R. Akiba's father-in-law Kalba Savu'a. It does not require much imagination, nor knowledge, to see that originally this is a nickname — and not a complimentary one at that. The explanation of the Aggadists "Ben Kalba Savu'a, because whoever entered his house as hungry as a dog left it satisfied (Save'a)" (Gitt. 56, ARN I, Ch. 6), is extremely tenuous, and in contrast we might do well to quote the note of Schechter to ARN I, Ch. 6 which he found in Ms. Epstein: "That whoever entered his house, left it satisfied like a dog". The description in the

personality and to blur his hostile attitude to the study of the Torah and to its teachers. Many generations later it was possible to represent him as a great man.

The variant in Tan. B. is unique as we have shown above. The principal changes took place as the result of adjusting the historical background to the period in which it was composed: In place of the agricultural background we have a political one with its lack of security and fugitives fleeing from fear of the Roman rule. The matter of property and transfer of possessions was very serious at this time, which accounts for its position in the centre of the Aggadah. The expansion of the Aggadah here is realistic at the beginning and homiletical at the end.

Thus the different representation of the figures, plot and structure are the result of different tendencies, a process which intensifies as time goes on and expresses itself in all aspects of the composition. The main difference in the orientation is in the contents and form. The Aggadot in Group A are more reliable and their contents more realistic, also their outlook is feasible to quite an extent: The hero attains both the Torah and riches. The Aggadot in Group B, on the other hand, emphasize the study of the Torah as the supreme and exclusive value in the life of the holy man. All the elements which make up the composition were worked over for this purpose, the characters, plot, sturcture and literary genre.

The Aggadah in Group A embodies elements of a *Sage*, while that in Group B bears a clearly legendary character. A legend aims at enhancing its heroes and for that reason tends to interweave miraculous motifs which are meant to demonstrate through the agency of its holy heroes on this earth connections between this world and the world above. The appearance of Elijah, and R.E. being compared to Moses:

> R. Eliezer sat down and expounded, and his face shone like the light of the sun and the rays shone like the rays of Moses so that no man knew whether it was day or night (PRE)

also bestow a noble and exalted sanctity upon the hero and not merely Torah and wisdom as in Group A.

In both groups the end constitutes a resounding victory for the Torah and its teachers. But while in Group A R. Eliezer does not reject the worldly possessions which Hyrcanus leaves him as his inheritance, his absolute rejection of them is stressed in Group B.

Aggadah — the people are dying of hunger and the granaries of Kalba Savu'a are full of all the best; and not until they came to burn all did he suggest distributing it — also gives an idea which is the literal meaning and which the homiletical interpretation.

In Group A — ARN I, Gen. R. and in Tan. B. — there is no rejection, and in my view this is the authentic and factual reaction. Here there is material reward side by side with spiritual reward, while in Group B, in the legend, R. Eliezer rejects the entire inheritance with an expression of scorn for the possessions of this world. Here, the idealistic conception which does not come to any terms with reality celebrates its victory:

> He said to him: 'Indeed, I am not equal to one of them. If I had requested land from the Holy One blessed be He, He would have been able to give it to me, as it is said: "The earth is the Lord's, and the Fulness thereof"; and if I had requested silver and gold he would have given it to me, as it is said: "Mine is the silver, and Mine the gold, saith the Lord of Hosts". I, however, only asked for the Torah from the Holy One blessed be He (PRE)

The end fits the tendencies. In Group A the moral lesson is realistic: He who forgoes riches and choses the Torah, in the end attains both crowns, while in Group B the moral is idealistic. They share the same central ideology, namely, a demonstration that Torah learning is the supreme value in human life. But in Group B this is exclusive and uncompromising: He who chooses the realm of the spirit turns his back on the material world, and so does a great man like R. Eliezer ben Hyrcanus.

# ABBA, FATHER.

## TITLE OF SPIRITUAL LEADER AND SAINT.

In his well-known rebuke of Pharisean ostentatiousness and love of public recognition (Matt. xxiii. 1–10) Jesus says to his disciples: "They love to be called of men Rabbi. But be ye not called Rabbi; for one is your teacher, and all ye are brethren. And call no man your father on the earth; for one is your father, which is in heaven. Neither be ye called masters, for one is your master, even the Christ." Lightfoot already observed that reference is here made to the three titles by which the leaders of the school were addressed in Talmudical times: Rabbi, Abba, and Moreh (see *Maccoth*, 24 a). Still, a careful glance at the New Testament passage reveals the fact that the text has been tampered with, since Jesus cannot well have spoken of himself in this manner.

Let us then consider the three titles and the judgment passed on them: (1) the title most in use certainly was *Rabbi*, my master, or master, and gradually this became a standing title for every recognized teacher. The title *Rab*, master, which in its fuller form *Ribbon*, Great Master, was often applied to God in prayer, implies submission and awe. "Let fear of thy master be like the fear of God (heaven)" is the rule of the early fathers (*Pirke Aboth*, IV, 7), and *Shimmush hakamim*, "servile attendance of the wise," is one of the conditions of acquiring knowledge of the Torah. If the disciple, therefore, happen to be at the side of the teacher when he goes to the bath-house, he is bound to carry his clothes for him. Against such claims of superiority Jesus remonstrated, laying down the

113

principle of perfect equality. Instead of bidding his
disciples to wash his feet before reclining at the supper
table, as he might have done, he humbly washed the feet
of each of them, as the Gospel of John relates. Accordingly he did not claim the rank of master for himself.
He wanted, on the contrary, to reserve the name of *Rab*,
master, for him who is the Master of the world, *Ribbono
shel Olam*, and therefore they were to drop the name of
Rabbi altogether: "One is your Master, and that is God."
The Greek word *Didascalos*, teacher, is incorrect. Likewise is the sentence, "And all ye are brethren," misplaced;
it belongs to the following verse which refers to *Abba*.

(2) The second title in use was *Abba*, "father." With
reference to this Jesus says: "Call none of you on earth
*Abba*, father, for one is your Father, he who is in heaven,
and all ye are brethren." Who it was that the people
addressed by this name, we shall see immediately. Let us
first dispose of the third title.

(3) Next to Rabbi we find the title of *Moreh* (Aram.
*Malfono*), teacher or guide, for which the Greek equivalent
*Katechetes* was quite common in the philosophical schools.
Of it Jesus says: "Neither let yourselves be addressed as
teachers (or guides), for there is but one Guide, and that
is . . . . . ." Obviously the name of Christ has been substituted here by the compilers for another word, and that
is, in all probability, *the Holy Spirit* (compare Isa. xxx. 20,
where the word *Moreh* is twice translated in the Targum
by *Shekhina*). "God through his interpreter, the Holy
Spirit, is your only Guide."

Coming now to our main object, the explanation of the
title *Abba*, we can dismiss all that has been thus far
written on the subject as decidedly unsatisfactory. Frankel's
note to Abba Saul in his *Hodegetica in Mishnam*, p. 176,
which says: "It is a title of honour, but less than rabbi,"
referring to Rashi, *Br'achoth*, 16 b, has been repeated by
Jastrow and others without further inquiry. The head
slave was called *Abba*, also, but that has no bearing upon

our question. Dr. Buechler, in *Die Priester und der Cultus*, pp. 31–33, referring to a number of passages containing traditions concerning the temple and its mode of worship preserved by Tannaites bearing the title of *Abba*, comes to the conclusion that the title originated in priestly circles who had their chief seat—presumably after the destruction of the temple—in the South. But this does not explain the origin in the least.

Beginning with the Bible, we find the title of *Ab*, father, given not only to the originator, as in Gen. iv. 20, 21 (where the Targum translates *rab*), but also to an adviser (Gen. xlv. 8; Judges xvii. 10, where Targum has also *Ab*). Thus do also the young prophets call their master *Ab*, father (1 Sam. x. 12; 2 Kings ii. 12; vi. 21). In like manner are Hillel and Shammai called the "fathers of the world" (*Eduyoth*, I, 4), and also their schools (*Yerush. Haggiga*, II, p. 77 d); also R. Jishmael and R. Akiba (*Yerush. Shkalim*, III, 47 b); and, like Moses, R. Tarfon is called "father of entire Israel" (*Yer. Yoma*, I, 38 d).

"The fathers" became, therefore, the standing name for the ancient masters of the law, as is not only shown by the name of the treatise *Pirke Aboth*, "The Sayings of the Fathers," but the very word for tradition preserved both in the Talmud and by Josephus (*Ant.*, XIII, 10, 6) is Masoreth *Aboth*, Tradition of the Fathers (see Hoffmann, *Die erste Mishnah*, p. 6; 267).

There is little doubt that the Church, in according to their heads the name of *fathers*, simply followed in the footsteps of the Synagogue[1].

But the question is, whether particular individual teachers of the Law received the title of *Abba*, "father," and who?

Let us then take up the list of the men called *Abba* in the Talmudical literature, one after the other, and inquire into their peculiar merit.

[1] The *Falashas* also call their leaders *Abba*, and they represent a branch of the Hasideans of the old school.

Before doing so, however, we must take notice of one spoken of as "father of the Jews" in the second book of the Maccabees (xiv. 37–46). The passage has not received the attention it deserves, because the name of the saint whose tragic end is there related, *Razis*, is, owing to the hand of a copyist, no longer to be recognized. Only Frankel, in his *Monatschrift*, 1852, p. 106, has noted the identification. He is described as one of the elders of Jerusalem, a lover of his fellow citizens, and a man of very great renown, and on account of his extreme piety called "a father of the Jews." He "encouraged the separation of Judaism from the Gentiles, and imperilled body and soul by his steadfastness to Judaism." In other words, then, he was the actual leader of the Hasideans, and, while he escaped when the other sixty were slain by Bacchides and Alkimos (1 Macc. vii. 16), he was now made the object of an especial attack by Nicanor, the friend of Alkimos, who sent five hundred men to capture him. He, however, preferred a cruel death by his own hands. Whatever legend may have added to the facts, there can be little doubt that the personality of the martyr is historical, and, if so, it can be no other than Jose ben *Joezer* of Sereda, the uncle of Alkimos, whose martyrdom is related in *Bereshith Rabba*, § 65. He was the spiritual head of the Pharisees, and remained their highest authority (see *Sota*, 47 a). The people called him by the endearing name of "father." But we may go a step further. According to the Rabbinical tradition he and Jose ben Johanan were the chiefs of the Sanhedrin. This tradition, however, which speaks of two Pharisean chiefs, does not stand the test of historical scrutiny, as was shown by Kuenen and others. The real chief, or *Nasi*, was the high priest, the head of the nation, while, on the other hand, it seems quite natural that the Pharisean, or Hasidean party, furnished the highest court of justice with a spiritual head, one distinguished (Mufla) by learning and saintliness. He, by his authority, was to decide the difficult cases in place of the high priest, since the oracle of the *Urim we-Tumim* had ceased to voice the will of God. He had the rank and title of *Ab Beth Din*, "father of the court of Justice," and Josephus, whose remark on this point has been strangely overlooked by the historians, speaks of him as "the prophet" alongside of the high priest (*Ant.*, IV, 8, 4). We find the title "father" and "prophet," for the head of religious bodies, frequently on inscriptions of the time (see Schuerer, *Gesch. d. jüdischen Volkes*, III, 3, 50). It is quite likely that a combination of the two powers represented by the high priest and the leader of the Hasideans was brought about in this form of a double régime (זוג Zeugos) under Judas Maccabee. Cp. Rappoport, *Erck Millin*, and Loewy, *Talmudisches Lexicon*, s. v. Ab Beth Din.

(2) The first man of distinction known to us as Abba is *Abba Hilkia*, the grandson of Onias the Saint, the story of whose martyrdom Josephus relates, while the memory of his miraculous power of intercession for rain in a time of great dearth is preserved alike by Josephus and the Mishna (see *Ant.*, XIV, 31, and *Taanith*, 19 a). Like Onias, who, according to Midrash Tanhuma (*Vaera*, ed. Buber, II, 37), traced his pedigree back to Moses, Hilkia also succeeded in bringing down rain in a time of drought by the prayer he and his pious wife offered, but he humbly refused to acknowledge that it was due to his merit that the rain came (see *Taanith*, 23 a, b). Singularly enough, it escaped the notice of the historians that this Abba Hilkia is none other than "Helkias the Great," of whom Josephus tells that he and Aristobulus, the brother of King Agrippa, went at the head of a deputation of Jews to Petronius, the Governor of Syria, to ask him to interfere in favour of the people with the Emperor Caligula that he should withdraw his edict concerning the erection of his statue in the temple, and when he showed his kind disposition to them, a miracle happened which greatly impressed the governor. It had not rained for a whole year, and in the midst of the great drought, behold, there

P p 2

came out of a clear sky great showers of rain, which
convinced the heathen governor of God's special favour
and providential care for his people (*Ant.*, XVIII, 8, 4–6).
Evidently the Talmudical legend and Josephus point to
the same fact and to the same personality.

(3) There is a similar story related in the Talmud of
another grandson of Onias, which throws light on the title
of Abba: There was another great drought in the land,
and the rabbis sent the little children to Hanan the
Hidden One, to ask him to pray for rain, as he would not
leave his hiding-place and join them. And when these
little ones came to him, and said: "Abba, Abba, Father!
Father! give us rain!" the saint knelt down in prayer,
and cried: "O Master of the world! For the sake of these
innocent ones, who know not how to discriminate between
the Father who giveth rain and the father who cannot
give, but only ask for rain, hear our prayer!" and, behold,
rain came.

Concerning the name "the Hidden One," it should be
observed that of his grandfather Onias, too, Josephus tells
us that he kept himself hidden, and the reason given there
(*Ant.*, XIV, 21) is a political one. It is much more likely,
however, that it was the common practice of these Essene
saints to keep themselves concealed and excluded from
the world, exactly as John the Baptist did long before
his life was imperilled. Elsewhere (Tosefta, *Rosh Hashana*,
IV, 11) our Hanan is mentioned as Honi (Onias) the Little,
or younger one. Our story, however, shows that the
people called him Abba, father, in view of his saintly life.

(4) Another Abba who lived before the destruction of
the temple exhibits traits which stamp him as Ḥasid,
or Essene, viz. *Abba Saul, the son of Bathnith.* He was
extremely scrupulous, giving full measure to such as
bought the wine he produced, and when he died, he held
his right hand up, saying, "See whether this hand was
not clean and righteous!" He denounced in the following
scathing terms the corruption and greed of the ruling

houses of the priesthood of his time: "Woe cometh unto me from the house of Boethus; woe from their club! Woe cometh unto me from the house of Kantharos; woe from their pen! Woe cometh unto me from the house of Ishmael ben Phabi; woe from their fist (grasp), for they fill the offices of high priests, and their sons are treasurers, their sons-in-law inspectors, while their servants go about beating us with their rods" (see Tosefta, *Menahot*, XIII, 21; *Babli Pesachim*, 57 a; and the remarks of Bacher, *Agada der Tannaiten*, I, 50, 377, note).

Two other *Abbas* are mentioned there also in that connexion.

(5) *Abba ben Hanin*, who either joined Abba Saul of Bathnith in denouncing the priesthood in the above words, or spoke in his name. He has preserved traditions concerning the temple (*Middoth*, II, 6; *Derech Eretz Zutta*, IX; *Sifra*, 9 a).

(6) *Abba Saul* also denounced the ruling priesthood as "the men of violence who appropriated other people's property" (Tosefta, *Menahoth eodem*), and his traditions concerning temple and priesthood were regarded as of especial value and weight. His ethical teachings have an Essene character: "As God is merciful, so be thou merciful" (*Sabbath*, 133 b). He also enjoins on the business man scrupulous care in selling goods, lest the buyer be misled (*Baba Metzia*, IV, 12). Regarding also the various trades and their influence on character, Abba Saul expresses an opinion which characterizes him as Essene. See *Jerushalmi Kiddushim*, IV, at the close (where the correct reading of Mishna is preserved). *Abba Gorion* of Sidon says in the name of *Abba Saul*: "A man should not train his son to be a driver of ass or camel, a potter, a barber, or a mariner, a herdsman, or a merchant, because each of these trades easily leads to some sort of dishonesty." It is superfluous to say that this is exactly *Essene* teaching. His warning against the use of the Tetragrammaton (Mishn., *Sanhedrin*, X, 1), and his rigid

view of the Levirate (*Tosefta Yebamoth*, VI, 11), betray also his Essene leanings.

(7) Another *Abba* famous for his *Hasidean* virtue was *Abba Jose ben Kitunta*, "the humble one." Of him they said: "When Abba Jose the Humble One departed, Hasidean virtue departed." (See Tosefta, *Sota*, XV, 5; Bacher, *Agada d. Tanaim*, II, 371).

(8) Of *Abba Hosaya of Tirayah* we are told that, when he died, the people saw his bier carried through the air heavenward, and they said: "No one was beloved by God like him" (Midrash Rabba, *Leviticus Emor*, 30). He was to his age sun and shield (*Kohelet Rabba*, Ve sarah hashemesh). He is also especially lauded for his scrupulous care in dealing with other people's property (Tosefta, *Baba Kama*, XI, 14; *Jerushalmi* B. K. 7 c and *Baba Metziah*, II, 4; Midrash Thillim, XII: he is called "a Hasid").

(9) Another *Abba*, whose name has been greatly disfigured, and undeservedly cast into obscurity, is *Abba Halifa ben Karuyah*. Of him we read that Rabban Gamaliel the Younger went to him, saying: "Pray for me!" whereupon he replied in the words of the Psalmist: "May the Lord give thee according to thy heart!" (Midrash Thillim, Ps. xx). That he must have been known for his piety and saintliness is evidenced by this very fact. In Mass. *Derech Eretz*, I, the same Abba Halifa gives in the name of *Abba Higra* the following *Hasidean* precepts: "Be not rash in making vows, lest thou violate an oath; nor be the guest of an ignorant priest, lest thou eat things holy to God; nor indulge in speaking with woman, lest thou mayest come to lust after her." In Tosefta, *Maaser Sheni*, IV, 5, and *Machshirin*, III, 3, he furnishes Hasidean rules regarding the tithes and Levitical purity. Tosefta, *Baba Kama*, IX, 31, it is Abba Halifa (not Rabbi Hilfai ben Agra, as the copyists have it) of whom the strange utterance is preserved by R. Johanan ben Nuri: "He who tears his hair or his garments, his furniture or other valuables in his anger, is like one who serves an idol, for he

obeys the spirit of evil." See also the dialogue between God and the angels at the destruction of the temple given by R. [Abba] Halifa Midrash Thillim, Ps. cxxxvii (ed. Buber, p. 176, note 33), and *Pesiktha Rabbathi*, 28 (ed. Friedman, 135 b); also Abba Halifa b. Karuyah in *Tos. Maaser Sheni*, IV, 5, *Tos. Makshirin*, III, 3.

(10) *Abba Jose ben Dosai* (often quoted in Tosefta and Midrash as Rabbi Jose ben Dosai of Tzaitor), for both Hagadic and Halachic utterances, had communion with the spirits, and the following story is told of him (*Tanhuma*, and Midrash, *Rabba Kedoshim*, and Midrash Thillim, Ps. xx): A *Hasid*, Abba Jose ben Dosai of Tzaitor, passed a spring, when the spirit of the well came to him, saying: "For many years I have dwelt here without doing harm to any creature, and now another spirit wants to drive me off and inflict harm upon the people. For their sake aid me in killing my opponent." "How can I do so?" asked Abba Jose. "Go thou and tell all thy disciples (townsmen) to come hither with iron spits or hammers and beat upon the surface of the water, crying forth, 'Ours is the victory; Ours is the victory!' and when you notice the following morning at daybreak a drop of blood in the water, be sure that the evil spirit is dead." Abba Jose did as he was told, and they saw the blood in the water. The evil spirit was dead. Here also the title of *Abba* had something to do with the powers attributed to him as saint by the people. Cp. for Halakic utterances by Abba Jose ben Dosai Zuckerman's *Tosefta Index*.

(11) Of *Abba Tahna* (or Tehinna) the Pious (Hasida) the following story is told in Midrash, *Koheleth Rabba*, IX, 7: He came back to town with his heavy bundle upon his shoulder, on a Friday afternoon, shortly before the beginning of the Sabbath, when he met a disease-stricken man unable to move, who asked him to have pity on him and bring him into town where he could be attended to. He pondered for a while whether he could afford to lay down his bundle, containing the provisions for his house-

hold for the Sabbath and attend to the sick man, thereby leaving his people without food, or whether he should provide for his household and leave the unfortunate man in his perilous condition. He decided to aid the sick man, and after he had brought him to a safe place, he went back to get his bundle. Meanwhile it had grown dark. The Sabbath had approached, and people who saw him carrying his bundle on his shoulder, wondered, saying: "Is this father Tahna the pious?" He felt conscience-stricken at having violated the sanctity of the Sabbath, when a miracle happened. The sun came forth shining again, and a voice was heard saying: "Go, eat thy bread in joy, and drink thy wine with gladness of heart, for God has accepted favourably thy work." Here again the title Abba was a tribute given by the people to the saint.

(12) Another popular saint distinguished by his great philanthropy was *Abba Yudan*. R. Eliezer, R. Joshua, and R. Akiba—so we are told in Midrash, *Vayikra Rabba*, 5, and *Yerush. Horioth*, III, 7, p. 48 a—on a tour collecting money for charity, came to the district of Antioch, where Abba Yudan lived. Abba Yudan had then by reverses in business lost wellnigh his whole fortune, and he was much distressed at the thought of his inability to give his full share as usual, but his wife, who was even more generous-hearted than he, advised him to sell the acre of land he still possessed and give half of the proceeds to the great teachers. He did so, and they blessed him, saying: "May God compensate your loss!" After a while they came again on the same errand and inquired after Abba Yudan. The townspeople said: "Abba Yudan, the owner of slaves, of cattle, goats and camels; Abba Yudan, the master of an immense fortune, he is inaccessible to the people!" Yet, no sooner did he learn of their arrival than he went to see them, and said: "My prosperity is all due to your blessing, your prayer was heard"; and he gave them in full measure. To which they answered: "Even when you gave no more than others the last time,

we placed you with your gift at the head of all. Your heart was large when you gave." Here, too, the name "father" was a popular recognition of the man's merit.

(13) *Abba Jose the Builder* (Banai) was famous for his intimacy with the mysteries of Creation—an especial privilege of the Essenes. The following is related of him in *Shmoth Rabba*, 13: Oenomaos of Gadara, the pagan philosopher, asked the rabbis: "How was the earth created at the beginning?" They answered: "None among us is familiar with these things except Abba Jose the Builder. Go and ask him." He went and found him working on the scaffold of a building. He addressed him, saying: "May I ask you a question?" "I am hired for a day's work and cannot leave here," he replied, "but you may ask while I remain up here." The philosopher repeated his question, and received the answer: "God took dust from beneath the throne of his glory and cast it into the primeval waters, and it thickened into earth, and the clods grew into hills and mountains" (according to Job xxxviii. 38).

(14) Another Abba shows his *Essene* views in a different way: *Abba Benjamin*, in a *Baraitha Berakot*, 5 b, gives his opinion concerning the position of the bed and the phylacteries [1] to be suspended over the same, concerning demons and the right time and place for prayer in order to be received favourably.

(15) Of one Abba we have a remarkable utterance of decidedly Essene character. *Abba Hanin*, pupil of R. Eliezer the great Shammaite saint, in whose name he preserved many traditions concerning the temple, says, not without reference to the priests of the last temple period: "Nadab and Abihu, the sons of Aaron, sinned by their false family pride, as no house seemed good enough for them to marry a daughter thereof, and so they remained single" (*Tanhuma Ahare Moth*, ed. Buber, III, 63; cf.

[1] Not prayer. Compare Schechter's *Aboth S. R. Nathan*, 165, and *Berachoth*, 24 a.

*Pesikta R. Cahana*, 172 b, and Midrash Thillim, Ps. lxxviii. 18).

(16) *Abba Jose the Hauranite* (*Tos. Mikvaoth*, III, 14), perhaps identical with R. Jose ha Horem, *Sifra Emor*, III a.

(17) *Abba Jose of Mahoz* (see Tosefta, *Mikvaoth*, III, 14; Mechiltha to Exod. xiv. 15; and Bruell in Frankel's *Monatsschr.*, 375, 1868).

(18) *Abba Elazar* (*Sifra*, II, 2). Cp. Abba Elazar of Bene B'rak, *Shir Nashirim Sutta*, ed. Buber, p. 40.

(19) *Abba Pnemon* (*Jerush. Terumma*, III, p. 42 b) is only mentioned as giving traditions concerning temple practice, and views concerning Moses' great powers, and concerning the evil spirit, &c.

(20) While all these, with the exception of Abba Hoshaya, belong to the age of the Tannaim, we see a new class of Abbas rise in the second century, viz. Meturgemans or preachers who receive the title of Abba, father. R. Juda ha Nasi had a preacher or Meturgeman by the name of *Abba Yudan* (*Bereshith Rabba*, 10), whose name was also contracted into Abdan (*Jerushalmi Berachot*, VII a; *Babli Jebamoth*, 105 b). To this class of preachers entitled " father" belonged, probably in a preceding age,—

(21) *Abba Gorion* the preacher (cp. Abba Yudan of Gorion, *Shir Nashirim Sutta*, ed. Buber, p. 38), and towards the close of the age of the Amoraim,—

(22) Abba Hoshaya, mentioned above (see Zunz, *G.*, V, 2, 185, and also about Abba, preacher, see Zunz, *G.*, V, 2, pp. 333 and 351). Abba Doresh and Abba bar Zutra, referred to by Zunz, do not belong here, as *Abba* is here a proper noun and not a title. So Abba the Barber in *Taanit.* 21 b.

It will be noticed that *Abba* as title was known only in Palestine, where the ancient Hasidean life continued long after the destruction of the temple. In Babylonia the name Abba occurs only as a proper name, not as a title.

Two more Abbas require explanation :—

(23) *Abba Sikra*, "Father (of) the Sicarian" head of

the zealots (*Gittin*, 56 a), identified by Rappoport (Erech, *Millin*, I, p. 257), Midrash, *Echa Rabbati*, ed. Buber, p. 66, n. 254, with Ben Batiah as nephew of Johanan ben Zakkai (Midrash, *Echa*, I, 5), "the Melon-like" man of robust form. Rappoport compares Athronges, the *Ethrog* or citron-like leader of a sedition soon after the death of King Herod (Josephus, *Ant.*, XVII, 107), but goes too far in identifying him with the same.

(24) Of *Abba Colon* we have a strange legend in *Shir Hashirim Rabba*, I, 6, according to which he was the founder of the island on which Rome was built. He brought earth from the river Euphrates and threw it into the Sea, and so the island was formed. He is therefore called the *Father Colonus*, "founder of the Colony." (Compare the story of Rome built on a piece of land formed by the angel Gabriel, *Sabbath*, 56 a, and the remark of Abba Banai on the formation of the earth above.) The name given to the Essenes by Strabo and Josephus is *Ktistes* or *Polistes*, "founders of townships," that is pioneers, Banaim, and this practice of an older generation of Essenes may have given rise to our odd legend.

Let us now see whether we cannot find some reason for the fact that *Abba*, father, was a favourite title among the Essenes or Hasideans.

Dr. Jastrow in his Dictionary, s. v. אבא, explains the expression "father Elijah" in *Sanhedrin*, 113 b, to be meant "sarcastically." But note that R. Jose was in constant communion with Elijah the prophet. He addressed him when he met him: "My master and teacher," *Rabbi u Mori* (*Brachoth*, 3 a). One day he spoke to his disciples of his impetuousness in his treatment of King Ahab, and he said: "Father Elijah was quick tempered." What happened? For three days Elijah did not appear to him. On the fourth day he again appeared to him, and R. Jose did not hesitate to take this very absence as due to the remark he had made and as corroboration of his statement. Thus far the Talmudical narrative. What sarcasm is there in the title Abba, father? "Väterchen Elias" translates Bacher (*Agada d. Tannaim*, II, 163) similarly, also mistaking the meaning of the word. Neither Bacher nor Jastrow noticed that, just because Elijah often appeared to the initiated in the garb of a venerable saint (as, in fact, he is often called in the Talmud, *hahu Saba*, yonder aged; see *Tosafoth Chollin*, 6 a), he is quoted, like any other teacher, as "father Elijah." Thus we read (Mas., *Calla*, III): "Abba Elijah, may he be remembered for good! said, 'The Torah is explained only to him who is not quick tempered.'" Likewise we read in *Tana de be Elijahu Zuta*, XV: "Abba Elijahu, may he be remembered for good and for blessing! said,' &c. Throughout the whole book *Tana de be Eliahu*, we find Elijah introduced like any other teacher, exactly as the prophet Jeremiah appeared to Philo while the latter was in a state of ecstasy, as a living "teacher and hierophant" (Philo, *Mang.*, I, 147).

Throughout the Bible, especially in the Wisdom literature, the instructor is the father, and the disciples, those that sit at the feet of the wise, his children. This fatherly relation of the teacher to his pupils was maintained also in the early days of the Scribes. Upon it rested the Essene mode of life. Both Josephus (*Wars*, II, 8, 2) and Philo ("The Virtuous being also free," XII) tell us that the young were regarded as children, and the pupils looked up to their teachers as to fathers. This patriarchal system was continued in the ecclesiastical and monastic institutions of the Christian community. As these relations, however, changed in the schools, and the head was invested with the dignity of the master, the title *Abba* became a survival of the ancient practice, an occasional token of honour bestowed upon some popular saint or preacher. This was little understood by later generations, and therefore the title was often dropped or replaced by the name "Rabbi."

K. KOHLER.

# THE PRE-TALMUDIC HAGGADA.

## I.

IN the April number of the JEWISH QUARTERLY REVIEW Professor Bacher gives so lucid an explanation of the term *Haggada*, that it can hardly be disputed any longer. What the מדרש is to the מקרא, the הגדה, " the telling," is to the כתיב, " the written word." It is the exemplified " telling," the facts or doctrines suggested or implied by the Scripture. Still Professor Bacher fails to accentuate sufficiently the popular character of the Haggada, in contrast to the exclusively scholastic nature of the Halacha. The latter is the legal statute,[1] based upon traditional lore and practice; whereas the former contains fanciful " tales " of all kinds, often so loosely connected with the Scripture as to allow no longer the assumption of hermeneutical rules and premises. It has become a homily of either an ethical or a poetical character. The Haggadists are often no longer interpreters of the Law, but preachers of a socialistic temper, like the old prophets. (See Derenbourg, *Palestine*, pp. 163-4, 351.) And while the Halachists, ever since the days of Hillel and Shammai—that is, as far back as our records reach—endeavour to base the legal statutes upon, or to derive them from, the Mosaic letter, the Haggadists create new " tales," with which they expand and embellish the Biblical stories, without caring for Scriptural supports. The Haggada is, at the very outset, a *paraphrase* rather than an interpretation. In

---

[1] הלכה is " walk," derived from הדרך ילכו בה, the road being the road of life, or of צדקה, " righteousness." See Josephus, *Antiq.* XIII. x. 5f. ὁδὸς δικαίη, and *Targum* to דרך *passim*. Between דרך, " the main road," and הלכה, " the single walk " lies פרק—פרשת דרכים, " the cross-way," hence *chapter*. Nidda 69ᵇ read הלכה for חכמה, which error was caused by Tossifta Negaim near the close, and not as Bacher thinks.

fact, the farther back we go in the history of Jewish literature, the more exuberant the Haggadic material becomes;
and the lines between the *Biblical* Midrash, as given in the
book of Jonah and in the prophetic stories of the books of
Kings and of Chronicles, where the word מדרש first occurs,
and the *Rabbinical* one can hardly be clearly and sharply
drawn.

The difficulty of the problem to trace the origin of the
Haggada lies in the fact that the actual Haggadic embellishment and enlargement of the Bible is—exactly as the
real Pharisean practice of the religious ritual handed down
as "Halacha from Moses and the prophets"—by centuries
older than our traditional records.

It is the purpose of this article to call the attention of
scholars to a number of Midrashim that date back to the
Maccabean era, and throw new light on the character of
the ancient *Haggada*.

### A.—The Testaments of the Twelve Patriarchs.

Both Bacher and Guedemann are puzzled by the ancient
tradition preserved in B. Sota 7*b*, Jer. Sota I., 16*d*, and
Sifra Numb. v., 19, § 12 (to which compare Makkoth 11*b*,
and Sifra Deut. xxxiii. 6), according to which the high
court of justice addresses the woman suspected of adultery,
reciting to her—דברי הגדה מעשים שאירעו בכתובים הראשונים
כגון מעשה ראובן בבלהה ומעשה יהודה בתמר אשר חכמים
יגידו אלו ראובן ויהודה, "words of the Haggada, historical
facts which occur in the early writings, as the story of
Reuben regarding Bilhah, and of Jehuda regarding Tamar,
as it says in Job xv. 18: 'The wise ones confess, and conceal
it not; these are Reuben and Jehuda.'" Now Guedemann, in
the *Zunz Jubelschrift*, 116, understands the early writings to
refer to Genesis, and finds in the words of the Haggada as
contrasted with the כהב references to some other tale than
the Biblical one. Bacher, on the other hand, explains the
earlier writings to refer to Job on account of the verse
quoted therefrom. The fact is that the parenthetical words

מעשים שאירעו בכתובים הראשו, disclose to us the source whence the דברי הגדה are taken, viz., the confessions made by both Reuben and Judah, which should form a lesson and an example to the woman accused of adultery, in case she is guilty. The early writings are none other than *the Testaments of the Twelve Patriarchs.*

Before examining these, their contents, and their age, let us take the Mishnaic Code, and see what kind of lesson is given to the accused woman. The president of the high court addresses her, saying, " My daughter, wine often brings great trouble. Lascivious jesting often brings great trouble. Youth often brings trouble. Bad company often brings trouble. Do make confession; for the sake of God's great name, that it may not be wiped out, after having been written in holiness." Add to this, then, the Talmudical comment : " These exhortations should be accompanied by examples illustrating the benefit of confession of the sin committed, and by Haggadic readings to the same effect." Are not we here clearly informed of the existence of an Haggadic book containing these lessons ? *The Testaments of the Twelve Patriarchs answer exactly this purpose,* and, only because the existence of the same was no longer known in Talmudical times, some copyists added the ו'=" and " to the word מעשים, and the meaning of the whole tradition became a puzzle to the interpreters.

The Testaments of the Twelve Patriarchs have been, like numerous other Midrashim, as will be shown later on, preserved exclusively by the Church, and in form so thoroughly Christianized that the original Jewish character escaped the notice of scholars until recently, when Fr. Schnapp published his interesting little work : *Die Testamente der zwoelf Patriarchen untersucht,* Halle, 1884. Yet even this able research of Schnapp has as yet failed to receive the attention of Jewish scholars, probably for the reason that his critical examination of the book is only a negative one. He shows that the Christian elements of the book are the work of a rather awkward interpolator

anxious to make the twelve Patriarchs prophesy the coming
of Jesus from the tribes Judah and Levi on the father's
and the mother's side; whereas the main book is the compilation of two or more Jewish writers. What Schnapp
has as yet failed to do, is to bring out in clear outlines the
object and tendency of the book, and to interpret it in the
light of history.

This much is certain that each of the twelve sons of
Jacob is represented as teaching a great life-lesson in his
last will made to his own children before dying, either in
the shape of a virtue strenuously practised through life or
in the shape of repentance and avoidance of a vice indulged
in formerly. While Joseph holds forth the lesson of chastity
and purity amidst all temptations, Judah and Reuben
make such confessions of their sins that the Mishnaic
allusion to wine and to bad company easily finds its support
there. How old the book is, and how well-known at a
certain time it was, can be learned from the circumstance
that it has gone through the hands of so many Jewish and
Christian interpolators, which would scarcely have been
the case, had it been the work of an obscure writer or
class of writers. But internal evidence shows it to have
been written shortly after the Maccabean wars, or, to state
it more explicitly, in the time of John Hyrcanus. For he
is introduced in the Testament of Levi (cap. 8) as "the
one who, like Malkizedek in the time of Abraham, shall
unite the crowns of royalty and of prophecy with that of
the priesthood, and bring many strangers to the law." (Compare Josephus *Jewish Wars* I. iii.) But the entire warfare
of the sons of Jacob with Esau (=Edom) and his allies
as described in the Testament of Judah, and also in the Book
of Jubilees and the Midrash Vayissau (Jellinek *B. Ham.*
III.), is, to the very names of the places of the battle-fields
*identical* with the Maccabean war (1 Macc. v. 13). Geiger
(*Zeitsch.* vii. 122) finds traces of Sadducean law throughout
the book. The same laws are found also in the Book of
Jubilees, which must be placed at about the same time as

the Testaments, at the age of John Hyrcanus. But it is hardly correct to behold in either of these books a work of Sadducean authors. The constant reference to the heavenly tablets of Henoch, and the part taken by angels and spirits in all the earthly transactions forbid this assumption altogether. No. The *beau-ideal* of the writer of the Testaments is Issachar, the simple-hearted husbandman with his contempt for gold and lust, and his maxim: *Love for God and love for one's fellow man;* also Zebulon, the kind-hearted friend of the poor. It is not my purpose to enlarge here on the single facts, hitherto altogether overlooked. Suffice it to say that a careful investigation places the fact beyond any doubt, that the book is the work of the ancient Essenes, the *Chassidim,* "who, having the praise of God in their mouth and the two-edged sword in their hand," shaped the destiny of the Jewish people and moulded the original *Haggada* and *Halacha,* before the schools of Hillel formulated the hermeneutic rules. Owing to false literary axioms by which a work is placed as far down as *external* criteria indicate, the Palestinian Targum has been declared by centuries younger than the Babylonian, called after the fictitious Onkelos (the Greek Aquilas). The very reverse is the actual truth. The Jerusalem Targum has preserved the true type of the old Haggada. It is in fact the treasury of *Essene* tradition. It is to a great extent, as was partly recognised by Rappoport, *anti-Mishnaic,* and this implies a *pre-Mishnaic* origin. About its truly Essene character we hope to enlarge elsewhere.[1]

---

[1] Josephus' fastidious style of presenting the Jewish systems of belief as philosophical schools has had a most harmful effect upon the correct portraiture of the Essenes. Especially did the comparison with the Pythagoreans work immense mischief among Christian writers. The Essenes—'Εσσηνοί—are none else than the צנועים of the Talmud, those that follow the prophetic maxim הצנע לכת עם אלהיך, the modest walkers in the path of purity and holiness, the *virtuosi* or *uppermost* in their striving for sanctity among the פרישיא=חסידים=Pharisees, forming no sect of their own, only representing the highest degree of holiness. Their

C C 2

Yet both the Targum Jerushalmi and the Testaments of the Twelve Patriarchs together with the Book of Jubilees, offer one striking feature in common. On the one hand, the Biblical heroes are represented as warlike and of gigantic strength. They are inventors of certain industries. For instance, Zebulon is " the first who makes a boat to sail on the sea" (Cf. Midrash to Genes. xlix.). So are Abraham and Moses, so are Seth, Henoch and Noah, inventors of trades, arts, and sciences in the old Haggadic works. And on the other hand, these very men are mystics who know how to use hidden powers, the secrets of God's holy name in war and peril. Whatever Midrashim of a late origin narrate in this direction, has been anticipated by the Haggada of the Hellenists, by Pseudo-Hecataeus, by the Sibylline writers, by the Book of Wisdom. Philo, Josephus, and the New Testament writers are already familiar with all the chief figures and features of the Midrashic expansion of Biblical history. The Adam and Henoch, the Noah and Abraham, the Moses and Elijah they speak of, are no longer the plain and simple Bible

---

retired and quiet manners, particularly in their charity, which led to a sort of communism in their קופה and תמחוי (Ps. viii.), gave them also the name of חשאים =ʼEσσáιοι. By their constant exercise of the rites of purity and holiness in their daily life at their meals and for their prayers, they expected to be imbued with the holy spirit in order to come into close communion with God, be enabled to work miracles by using the holy name of God, and particularly to bring the מלכות שמים, " the kingdom of God," the Messianic time, near. One of their chief characteristics was their priestly purity as eaters of every meat in the utmost holiness of the priesthood : אוכלי חולין בטהרת הקדש. Now here is the remarkable translation of the verse Exodus xxii. 30 : ואנשי קדש תהיון לי, in Targum Jerush. : ואנשי קדישין מעמין חולין ברכותא תהון קדמי. In other words, "Be holy Essenes unto me." Again, Levit. xx. 7:— והתקדשתם והייתם קדושים, Targ.: ותהון קדישין בנופיכון; " Exercise holiness on your body;" to which compare the Boraitha Berachoth, 53b : והתקדשתם — אלו מים ראשונים — והייתם קדושים — אלו מים אחרונים — כי קדוש — זה שמן — אני יי' — זה ברכה. Here we have the entire system of Essene life as described by Philo and Josephus after an original Essene guide-book.

characters. They are figures moulded after a different pattern by, and for, a different class of Bible students, nor are they products of a school like Hillel's and Akiba's.

He who created, for instance, the characters of Adam and Noah did not, as Dr. Kohut believes, simply copy the Jama or Djemshid of the Zoroastrians, but he moulded the entire cycle of the Proto-plastes after the general Mazdean conception of the world, from its beginning to its end in the millennium of Soschiosch. It is, therefore, not enough to single out a few Talmudical parallels and compare them with the Parsee original, in the fashion that Professor Graetz, the Breslau Court-historian, feels tempted to call Zoroaster the "*ape of Moses.*" There are far closer relations between the Haggada of the Book of Enoch and the original Apocalyptic Book of Adam and Eve, of which the Book of Jubilees and the first Sibylline Book are the off-shoots on the one hand, and the Mazdean tradition, recorded in the Bundahish, on the other, and the resemblances become so striking as to leave no doubt as to a common (Persian or Babylonian) origin.

With regard to the characters of Henoch and Seth, again, we are led from Persian to Egyptian influences in the moulding of the same. The original inventor of letters, the divine recorder, the erector of engraved pillars, the assistant of the Deity in the judgment of the souls is the Egyptian *Thot,* and there can be no doubt that Henoch was shaped after his pattern.[1] Also his astrological and

---

[1] We need not, however, go as far as Egypt to find the origin of the Henoch figures, for *Nebo,* the prophet and scribe among the gods of Babylonia, occupied the same position as *Thot* in Egypt. Nebo was the recorder of both the destinies and the sins of man upon the heavenly tables (see *Tiele Assyr.,* 533 ; *Delitzsch und Haupt Beitr.* II., '412), and the inventor of sciences. And as columns with mystic lore engraved thereon were ascribed to Seth and to Kainan in connection with the flood (*Joseph. Antiq.* I. ii., 3 ; *Jubilees* viii. 3), so was the Babylonian flood story found on columns (Jeremias, *Izdubar Nimrod,* p. 45). And so were columns containing profound mystic lore for the Babylonians ascribed to Achiachar, the wise "Haikar of Mohammedan folk-lore, the Ahiahar of

his medical or therapeutic art was derived from him. And why should Noah and his favourite son Shem, or why should Abraham, the great Chaldean sage, stand behind the great Persian, Greek, or Egyptian inventors and heroes of the past? What in the age of Euhemeristic syncretism each tribe or school claimed for its own past, the Jewish sage claimed with equal pride for his. All that was necessary was a fine creative imagination, able to invest the Biblical personages with the attributes of other heroes of hoary antiquity. Here, far more than in the scholastic efforts of Scriptural interpretation, lie the sources of the Haggada. Every new stream of culture, every new channel of wisdom disclosed to the Jew, thus becomes a tributary to enlarge the river-bed of the Midrash. Is it not remarkable, indeed, that the very first word of the oldest Midrash—Bereshit Rabba—alludes to the Egyptian name of the mystic deity *Amun*, "the hidden One"? Ever since the time of Alexander the Great, the Essene colonies bordering on Egypt had imported Persian, Greek and Egyptian ideas and words to a large extent into the Rabbinical Haggada, and, let me add, also Halacha.[1] To illustrate this fact by a very striking instance, I will call attention to another seemingly Christian, but, in fact, genuinely Jewish apocalypse.

---

Tobit xiv. 10 " (see Clemens, *Stromata* I., 15). Achichathra or Xisuthros equal to Flidr, and Henoch equal to Idris, then belong to the same group of heroes known as those transferred to the land of the celestials.

[1] The whole vocabulary of the Mishna, with such strange words as וסת = η δος for נשים דרך or אמצע = ἥμισυ for תוך, and similar ones, cannot be explained as a Palestinian dialect, still less as a literary dialect. The Mishnaic system is the code of life of a Chasidim colony, of an assembly of pious observers of the law in its utmost rigidity, who live in constant contact with new-comers, strangers, or proselytes, yet remote from the political turmoil of the State. A few strange *Halachoth* are preserved in their writings, which were afterwards dropped or forgotten : —1. *Consanguineous marriages* are recommended or enjoined as especially good and holy. Throughout the Book of Jubilees and the Book of Adam and Eve the rule is maintained that each pious man should marry the daughter of his brother (or sister). In fact, the Parsee doctrine which

## B. — The Second Baruch or rather the Jeremiah Apocalypse.

This book was first made known in the year 1866, when Dillmann published the Ethiopic version in his Chrestomathy. The Greek, original under the title " Rest of the Words of Baruch," was published in 1889 in Cambridge, by J. Rendel Harris. This book, too, has been appropriated and worked over by the Christian Church, in a manner to hide its Jewish character so successfully, that even the last editor felt inclined to ascribe it to a Jewish-

---

urges kin-marriage as something sacred, pervades the entire patriarchal history. In like manner we find *Judith*, the Essene woman, married to a kinsman of hers (Judith viii. 1*f*) ; and *the most conspicuous lesson of the Book of Tobit is neither the charity work nor the burial of the dead with which the saint occupies himself*, as has been suggested, but the rule : " Marry a woman of the seed of thy fathers. Take not a strange woman that is not of thy father's tribe for a wife, for we are the children of prophets Noah, Abraham, Isaac, and Jacob. Remember, my son, that our fathers from the beginning all married wives of their own kindred, and were blessed in their own children, and their seed shall inherit the land " (Tobit iv. 12). On this idea of kin-marriage the whole story hinges. (Compare i. 9, v. 13, vi. 12, vii. 16, x. 12, xi. 17.) 2. כסוי ערוה, "the commandment to cover the nakedness of the flesh," often mentioned as a precept conditioning prayer in the Talmud, is declared in the Book of Jubilees to be a commandment written in the tablets of heaven for Adam and Noah, and all those that want to observe the path of life (see Jubilees III., 23-27, and VII., 16, where it forms one of the seven, or ten, commandments of the Noahides). This alone ought to be sufficient testimony to the Essene character of the Book of Jubilees. 3. לעולם אל יפתח אדם פיו לשטן, Berachoth, 19*a*=Paul in Ephes. iv. 27: Μηδὲ δίδοτε τόπον τῷ διαβόλῳ ; Clement in *Hom.* XIX. 2: Μὴ δότε πρόφασιν τῷ πονηρῳ, " Allow not the evil one to rush in," or " Open not thy mouth to Satan." This is given as an especial command to Noah : no one should be the bearer of evil tidings. This is illustrated by the wife of Cham, who, seeing the water coming while she was standing by the oven baking bread, cried, " The word of God has become true." Then Noah said, " Then the flood hath come." Whereupon God said, " Kill not the wife of Cham, for from thy mouth hath begun the destruction." See Hippolytus, *Fragments on Genesis*—after a more complete version of the Book of Adam and Eve. These specimens of the old pre-Talmudic Halacha may suffice for the present.

Christian author of the Post-Hadrianic epoch. But the book not only betrays Haggadic knowledge and style throughout, but it is solely dictated by the Messianic hope of the Jews, and, fragmentary as it probably is, it vents its wrath upon the Samaritan race in an unmistakably national Jewish spirit, whereas the hand of the Christian interpolator betrays itself by its clumsiness. So, for instance, when the blessing given to Abedmelech (ch. v., close), " God conduct thee to the rebuilt city of Jerusalem ! " is changed into the wish, entirely inappropriate for a person desirous to live : " The Lord guide thee to the UPPER Jerusalem ! " or when the hope that " Zion shall rejoice at seeing the house of God restored to new life by the same miraculous power which kept the figs fresh during the sixty-six years of Abedmelech's sleep," is transformed into the hope of " resurrection for the soul that has left the house of clay." But the worst havoc was done to the closing, or rather the main, part of the book, in which Jeremiah's vision of the coming of the Messiah, with the earth and the heaven around renewed, has been so mutilated that only Jesus' name stands out intelligible amidst the hopelessly corrupt passage. Still it can easily be shown that the book was a Jewish work. The first chapters, corresponding in part literally with the other Baruch Apocalypse—which, in our opinion, is much younger than ours—relate the entrance of the destroying hosts of Nebuchadnezzar into the holy city, after the angel of God had trod upon the gate to open it for the invader, and the burning of the Temple, after four angels of God had set fire to the same, so that the heathen should not boast of having destroyed God's house. All this is told in almost identical words in the Pesiktha Rabbathi, ch. xxvi. Also that the prophet Jeremiah cast the keys of the Temple up to the sun, saying, " We have been unworthy guardians; keep thou the keys, until God demands them back ! " is related in the Midrash there, only in place of Jeremiah, the high priest is mentioned, and elsewhere (*Jalkut*, Kings, 249)

King Jehojakin. Also the story that Jeremiah hid the sacred vessels of the Temple in some secret place in the ground, after having conjured the earth by God's holy name to open her mouth and take them, has many parallels in Rabbinical literature. (See 2 Maccabees ii. 5; *Shekalim* vii., p. 9*b*; *Joma*, 54; and the Samaritan tradition.)

The most interesting story, however, of the book is the sleep of Abedmelech, the Ethiopian, during sixty-six years, from the destruction of the Temple until the time when Jeremiah—not Zerubbabel and Jozadak, the high priest!—started the return of the exiles. He had rescued Jeremiah from the pit, though himself but a heathen slave of the king, and so Jeremiah asks God to spare him from the awful sight of the destruction and the fate of captivity. (See Jerem. xxxviii.—xxxix.) At the command of the Lord Jeremiah sent him with a basket of figs to the sick living "in the vineyard of Agrippa."

This anachronistic designation of the name gives us the most welcome clue to ascertain the date of the writer, who cannot have lived long after the destruction of the second Temple, when the place still bore the name of the King Agrippa, most probably Agrippa I., whose gorgeous palace and gardens are described by Josephus (*Wars*, V. iv. 4). It seems that in the neighbourhood was the colony of the *Essenes*, as, indeed the western gate, near by Solomon's Pool, was called *the Gate of the Essenes* (see Josephus, *Wars*, V. iv. 42), and the cloister adjoining the Ophel—perhaps the שער טרי of Midoth (see *Aruch* Kohut טרי) spoken of by Josephus—was probably the hall of the Essenes, לשכת החשאים (*Shekalim* V., 6).

On the road there Abedmelech takes shelter under a tree —it is not unlikely that, instead of the tree, the original story had a *cave*, ἄντρον and δενδρον are easily confounded together. The hot midday sun of the month of Ab had caused his exhaustion, and he falls asleep. On his awakening, on the 12th day of Nissan, sixty-six years later, he finds the world around him changed, and in his great

anxiety, he blesses God like a genuine *Chassid*, חייב אדם
לברך על הרעה כשם שהוא מברך על הטובה (*Berachoth*
IX., 5). But the figs in his basket remained still as fresh as
when he had put them there; and when an old man, whom
he asked after Jerusalem and after Jeremiah, told him that
the city had been destroyed long ago, and that Jeremiah
had gone to Babylonia with his brethren to preach consolation to them in the exile, he would not believe it, until
he learned that this was Nissan, when figs are not ripe, as
those before him were.    Baruch, too, Jeremiah's pupil, who
had been all along in the neighbourhood of Hebron (?)
recognizes in the miracle of Abedmelech's sleep and of the
figs the pledge of God's restored favour to Jerusalem, and
sends a letter to Jeremiah announcing the approaching
return.   The letter is sent to the exiled brethren, exactly
as in the other Baruch Apocalypse, by one of the fabulous
eagles of Persia—the Simurg, who serves as messenger and
as a riding-bird to King Solomon in the Midrash, as it does
for the kings of Persian folk-lore; he is gifted with
divine wisdom and speech, and also with the power of immortality, or resurrection.   And no sooner has he reached
the far-off land, where the exiled live under the guidance
of the prophet Jeremiah, than he, in the sight of all, restores
a dead man, at the moment he was to be buried, to new
life.  This is the best proof that Jerusalem will be restored
to its new glory.   But the letter contains a special Divine
command to Jeremiah : when leading the exiled back, he
should test them at the waters of the (Jordan ?) Chaboras, or
Pallacopas, נהר אהוה' (Ezra viii. 31), and separate those that
have the stain of idolatry upon them through marriage with
Babylonian wives; for worshippers of foreign gods are
not to be admitted to the holy city.  How they should be
tested is not said in our mutilated text.  It is possible that
the Christian reviser purposely omitted all this, and put
the river Jordan in place of the Babylonian stream to
suggest the rite of baptism, of which the Editor of this
book, J. R. Harris, is reminded, although the people to be

excluded are quite distinctly singled out as the Samaritans, the half-heathen Jews. To solve the problem, we must look for Rabbinical analogies in the Midrash. Nor is it difficult to discover these. After the worship of the golden calf, Moses, says the Bible (Exodus xxxii. 20), gave the Israelites water mixed with the ashes of the idol to drink, and the Targum Jerushalmi explains it, better than the Talmud (*Joma* lxxxvii.): the water branded the stain of impurity upon their foreheads, and those thus marked were the three thousand killed by the Levites. In the very same manner the Midrash has Gehazi punished with the sign of leprosy upon the forehead, because he made the golden calf for King Jeroboam. And I should not be surprised if another Midrash will yet be discovered which tells us that Micha, the maker of the idol of Dan (Judges xvii. and xviii.), who, according to the Midrash was, by the help of Satanic power, the real maker of the golden calf, had this mark of leprosy on his forehead. For he is identical with the *Samiri*, or Samaritan of the *Koran*, who has for ever to go about crying out, " *Là misàs*," Touch me not ! טמא טמא יקרא. Here now we find the connecting link. The Samaritans were again tested by Jeremiah, and by the sign of leprosy on their foreheads—as we may now surmise — which has been changed by the Christian interpolator into the sign of a seal, although only the disobedient, as we read, were marked, found to be still addicted to idolatry. Our conjecture will be corroborated, if not verified, by the final act of our story. Jeremiah, the book continues, starts from Babylonia at once, that is, on the *twelfth day of Nissan*, when Ezra started, according to the Scriptures. The failure of Zerubbabel's attempt was probably the reason why Jeremiah's name was connected with Ezra's and Nehemiah's return rather than with the former's (see 2 Mac. i.—ii. ; and Sanhedrin xxxviii., where Nehemiah is identified with Zerubbabel !). Ezra arrived in Jerusalem at the beginning of the month of Ab, and after a three days' rest, he held a great festival

of thanksgiving for the Twelve Tribes of Israel, lasting
TWELVE days exactly, as the Pentateuch law prescribes the
dedication festival in  the wilderness to last (see Ezra
vii. 9 ; viii. 15, 35).   The last of these days was the 15*th*
*of Ab*, noted in the ancient tradition of the Mishnah
(*Taanith* IV., close) as the great *Fire Kindling Festival*,
which enjoyed the greatest popularity in Jerusalem,
equalled only by the Day of Atonement; but the Talmudical authorities are at a loss to account for it.   It is
the summer solstice festival, celebrated also by the Syrians,
and continued to remain a festival of joy until the time
of Roman oppression.   Naturally enough the legend about
the sacred fire taken from the well by Nehemiah, where it
had been placed by Jeremiah the prophet, as narrated in
the Second Book of Maccabees, originated there in connection with the Fire Festival (Comp. *Taanith* 30*b*).

Now, our book makes Jeremiah hold a thanksgiving
festival of nine days, and on the tenth—the day of the
anniversary of the Temple's destruction—Jeremiah offers
a prayer full of allusions to fine wood and incense, and
light of the Fire-kindling Feast—but, alas ! it is too
mutilated to yield any coherent thought—and then he asks
for his end.   But when he lies already in the coma of
death, mourned by the people, his soul comes back again
to bring the celestial message of the coming Messiah.   We
shall see later on that shortly before death the soul of the
saint forecasts the future, and all apocalypses are glimpses
of the world beyond, espied by dying prophets.

About the corrupt and defective condition of the apocalyptic part of our book we have spoken already.   We shall
now also see how the story about the death of the prophet
Jeremiah has undergone alterations under the hand of the
Christian reviser.

The legend about Isaiah's being sawn to death by King
Manasseh, is recognised as an ancient Jewish one. (See
*Jebamoth* iv. 96, according to a Megillath Jochasin—
Setharim " Essene Scroll.")   But there is also some re-

miniscence of Jeremiah's death by the people (see *Pesiktha Rabbathi*, ch. xxvi. 38).

There existed a tradition among the martyr-sect of the Essenes, long before the rise of Christianity, perhaps soon after the martyrdom of Jose ben Yoezer (the "Razi" of the corrupt text of 2 Mac. xiv. 37 *seq.*), the "father of the (Judæi or) Chasidim," and that of Onias the Essene, that the martyr-death is the seal of true saintliness—(*Abel* therefore was revered by them as the first saint)—and consequently the prophets of Jerusalem had to die the martyr's death.[1] Accordingly our book relates that Jeremiah was anxious to commit all the secret lore regarding the end of the world to Baruch and Abedmelech, and, seeing the people bent upon stoning him to death, he told his pupils to bring him a stone, which he, by invoking the light of God's glory, made to reflect his own image, so that the stoning of his image could shield his person for awhile against the assault of the mob. Finally, when his instructions were all given, the stony image addressed the people, saying :—" O ye foolish sons of Israel ! You cast stones at me, believing me to be Jeremiah, while he stands there in your midst." Instantly the people ran after the real Jeremiah, and stoned him to death. Then his pupils buried him, and placed that stone upon his tomb, calling it " the Stone of Help of Jeremiah."

Most probably the tomb of Jeremiah was at the time when the book was written—perhaps originally in Egypt, where, according to some, he was stoned—a place of pilgrimage, and therefore rendered the object of reverence and wondrous awe. Our story refers to Jerusalem as the place of his murder. But as reason for his murder the present narrator has the Jews' hatred of the very announcement of the coming Christ—a presentation of facts so utterly absurd that only the anti-Semitic malice of the Rome-courting Church could venture to give it. Nor does the falsifier of the document conceal the fact that he copied

---

[1] *Cf.* Luke xiii. 33 ff. ; Pesiktha Rabb., §§ 30 and 33.

the Christian Isaiah-Apocalypse, which makes Isaiah also the victim of Jewish Christ-hatred manifested seven centuries before Jesus. But he did not succeed in wiping out altogether the traces of his original. The eighth chapter closes with the following verse: "And Jeremiah sent word to them (the Samaritan seceders), saying: Repent, for the angel of justice will come and lead you back to your high place." That this threat implies some divine outburst of wrath on the great day of judgment is evident. The admonition to repent becomes significant only when such a threat is uttered, and we know from the Samaritan book of Joshua that the great "day of wrath" plays an important *rôle* in their world-drama as well as in the Jewish and Christian one. But the τόπος ὑψηλός "high place," leaves us in no doubt as to the whereabouts of this impending day of wrath. It is the Septuagint translation of the name *Morijah*. In other words, the prophet hints at the great punishment coming over all the heathen peoples at the final war around Jerusalem, where they, the half-heathen Jews, will share the fate of all idol-worshippers, unless they repent. Was this not a sufficient provocation of the anger of the Samaritan people? And let us see how the stony image of Jeremiah addresses the murderers: "O ye foolish sons of Israel!" This is exactly the name given to the Samaritans by the Jews in the time when the Testament of the Twelve Patriarchs and the Book of Sirach were written. See *Test. Levi* 7, and Ecclesiasticus l. 26, "city of fools." It is the very same spirit in which the *Book of Jubilees* and the *Targum Jerushalmi* treat the Samaritans in connection with the people of Shechem and their treatment by Simeon and Levi.

We have, then, clear proofs that our Midrash literature is far younger than these relics of an older Haggada and Halacha are, some belonging to the time of John Hyrcanus, when the hostile spirit against the Samaritans reached its pitch.

But we have not yet considered the main and most

interesting story of our book—*the sixty-six years' sleep of Abedmelech,* the Ethiopian eunuch. The Talmudical Midrash makes no mention of it, and this is undoubtedly, in the estimate of our Rabbinical scholars, sufficient cause to ridicule it, and see in it an imitation of a similar Talmudical story. Let us hear it and examine it. In *Taanith Babl.,* 23*a,* we are told : " Onias, the drawer of magic circles,[1] חוני המעגל, the Essene miracle-worker, saw an old man plant a carob-tree, and said to him, ' Do you expect to eat the fruit of this tree ? Mark well ! It will take seventy years to mature.' Whereupon the old man said : ' My fathers have planted such trees for me, so will I plant them for my children.' Onias, then, went and took his meal, and fell asleep, and slept during seventy years, while the very stones around him had in the meantime yielded moss and brushwood to conceal him from the world around. When he awoke, he asked the man whom he saw plucking the fruit, whether he was the one who had planted the tree, and he replied : ' Not I, but my grandfather planted it.' ' Then, I must have slept seventy years,' exclaimed Onias. But the she-ass, too, which he had with him, had in the meantime given birth to two generations of asses. He then went home to see whether his son was alive, and he learned that his son had died, but his grandson was living. And when in the school-house his name was mentioned, it was accompanied with the remark that the world had been far better, but when he told the people

---

[1] The drawing of a magic circle, ascribed also to the prophet Habakkuk, and even to Plato (see *Z. d. M. L. G.,* XXVIII., 49), and to Moses (*Aboth di R. Nathan,* ed. Schechter, p. 156), is part of the mystic practice of the Gnostics (see Dietrich *Abraxas,* 158). About this esoteric love of the Essenes the instructive work of A. Dietrech, *Abraxas,* 1891, gives interesting information. No one who has read this book will be in doubt any longer that the ספרי המירם, condemned as containing obnoxious heresy, are the *writings of Hermes,* in which Jewish pseudography took a prominent part, and not *Homeros,* as Dr. Kohut, nor ἱμερος, as D. Kassel, nor ἡμερήσια, as Graetz proposed to read. They must have had some sacred character, or else the Mishnah's declaration, *Yadaim* at the close : אין מטמאין את ידים would be more than superfluous.

who he was, they at first would not believe him, and then treated him no longer with the wonted respect. He found himself alone, and said, ' Give me either congenial company or death,' and so God granted him the boon of death." In the Jerusalem Talmud Taanith the story is told differently: " Onias, the grandson of the well-known Onias, went, shortly before the destruction of the Temple, up the hill to look after his labourers in the field, when a mighty storm overtook him and he took shelter in a cave near by, and fell asleep, and slept for seventy years. In the meantime the old Temple was destroyed and the new one built in its stead. And when he came out of his cave again, the world was changed. He no longer knew any one, nor did the world know him. They said of him that the radiancy of his countenance brightened up the whole town." In like manner all the saints in paradise have faces shining like sun, moon, and stars.

Now both Talmudical legends repeated in the Midrash *Shocher Ṭob* Psalm cxxvi., are certainly parallels to the story given in our book of Abedmelech, and they have the advantage of referring to men that stood very high in popular esteem, so as to offer welcome subjects for legend, while Abedmelech seems hardly known outside of the Book of Jeremiah. Still there is one feature in the Onias legend that betrays an older date or origin. In the Babylonian version there is no reason at all given for the seventy years' sleep. In the Palestinian version the seventy years' sleep points to the actual restoration of the Temple, which took place after the seventy years of the Babylonian exile, and which was held forth as encouraging hope to the Jews at the war of Bar-Cochba. Onias, the popular hero then, took in the legend the place of *another* mythical sleeper during the Babylonian exile. Have we then no means to verify the identity of the same with the Abedmelech of our story ? We have.

Already the editor, J. Rendel Harris, called attention to

the Koran legend regarding Ezra and his ass, who, during the time of Jerusalem's destruction, slept a hundred years, and on his awakening took the food and drink that had remained fresh. Strange that an ass occurs in the Babylonian version of the Onias legend! But of Ezra's sleep the Rabbinical sources give no trace, nor is there any likelihood that Ezra, whose age was too well known to the Jews, was made the subject of the seventy or hundred years' sleep legend. But the Talmud has preserved a remarkable tradition which has puzzled the most learned copyists and inquirers. It reads as follows:—תשעה נכנסו בחייהם לגן עדן ואלו הן: חנוך בן ירד ואליהו (משיח) ואליעזר עבד אברהם וחירם מלך צור ועבד מלך הכושי ויונדב בן רכב בן בנו של יהודה ויעבץ ודור מלחם העוף וסרח בת אשר וחירם בת פרעה. ויש אומרים בתיה בת פרעה. 'Nine went alive into Paradise: Henoch the son of Yared, Elijah (and the Messiah), Eliezer the servant of Abraham, Hiram the king of Tyre, Abedmelech the Ethiopian, Jonadab the son of Rechab, and Jabez the grandson of Jehuda, the generation of the bird-Murg (Phœnix), and Serach the daughter of Asher." Others add Bithia the daughter of Pharaoh (and Joshua ben Levi). This last paragraph of the first chapter of *Massecheth Derech Eretz*—an old Essene Mishna—is repeated in the collection of quaint sayings attributed to Sirach (see Steinschneider's *Alphabetum Siracidis*, Berlin, 1858, pp. 27-28 *sqq.*). The very fact that *Henoch* is, contrary to the later Rabbinical opinions (see *Bereschith Rabb.*, § 25), extolled as immortal, evidences the antiquity of this tradition. Still more so do the names mentioned after *Elijah*. *Eliezer*, the servant of Abraham, the grandson of Ham, the son of Nimrod, or, according to another legend of the giant Og, was believed by the Essenes to have lived along with Abraham, probably as "the faithful Eckehart," also in Paradise, the Lazarus of the New Testament according to Geiger (*Zeitsch.* VI. 196 *f*). Hiram, the King of Tyre, is known throughout the entire Patristic and Rabbinical literature (see Mover's *Phœniz.* II., 338, note 40,

VOL. V.          D D

the *Syrian Cave of Treasures*, or the Adam book, and Midrash Jalkut to Ezekiel xxviii. 2), as a sort of Phœnician Friedrich Barbarossa, probably after an original Phœnician legend, though derived from the Cherub, or Phœnix legend of the Prophet Ezekiel, while his palace and gardens high above the sea and the land to challenge the Deity, yet finally to seal his doom—given also in the Koran legend of the gardens of Iram after the Midrash, are both old Chaldean and Jewish folklore tales.

Jonadab ben Rechab and Jabez, the grandson of Jehuda (not רבי יהודה הנשיא) (see 1 Chron. ii. 55 and iv. 9, with Targum), are the real heroes of the Essene schools, the founders and continuators of the Nazirite customs from the *earliest ages,* as may be learned from Pliny and Philo. As such they occur in the very oldest Midrash traditions in connection with the tribe of the Kenites of Jethro, etc.[1] (Comp. also Jabez as contemporary of Ezra in the I. *Baruch Apocalypse*, v. 5.)

The Midrash about the proselytism of the daughter of Pharaoh, and about the long life of Serach, the daughter of Asher, who took part in the finding of Joseph's bones, and again in David's time acted as the אשה חכמה, is familiar to all.[2] Far less so is the bird מלחם. But pseudo-Sirach has preserved the tradition which identifies it with the Phœnix, the חול of Job xxix. 18, who is mentioned also in *Bereshith Rabba* 19 as the bird who alone of all animals refused to eat of the forbidden fruit in Paradise (Cf. Jellinek *Beth Hamid.* VI., p. 12). מלחם is the Persian mercha (Si = bird; murg = the great).

Regarding Abedmelech, the Midrash (*Sifre Behaalothcha*, 99) only speaks of his kind deeds, which beautified his face

---

[1] Compare J. N. Weinstein, *Exile* 3; *Gesch. d. Essaer*, pp. 87-89; *Hilgenfeld Ketzern Geschichte*, p. 102, note 113, 136-139; *Zosimus Apocalypse*, quoted by James in the notes to the Apocalypse of St. Peter, p. 69 ; the blessed ones, the descendants of the Rechabites, the parallels to the sons of Moses in the *Targ. Jerush.* and the *Eldad Had-Dani Romance.* Finally, the Nabatheans in Diodorus xix. 94 with Pliny, *Nat. H.* v. 17.

[2] See Grünbaum, *D. M. L. Z.* XXXI., 299-305.

so that they called him the Ethiopian, to ward off the *mal'oglio*. But the same Midrash which insisted that Jonadab's blessing from the lips of Jeremiah secured for him immortality (see Jer. xxxv. 19), certainly had equal ground for assuming Abedmelech's immortality from Jer. xxxix. 17-18. Only a later tradition was anxious to allot this privilege to Baruch rather than to the Ethiopian, and so the two were identified, and in the end the latter altogether forgotten.

At the bottom of these legends lies the Mazdean belief in the fifteen associates of Soschiosch the Redeemer, as the first ones to rise on the resurrection day. Hence the Essene tendency to include converted heathen men and women in their list, and also the Persian bird of immortality. Was he the original riding-bird of Soschiosch, as Mohammed rides into Paradise on his *Borak*, and as Solomon-Djemschid rides on wondrous eagles? At any rate, the ass of Ezra is generously admitted into Paradise by the Mohammedans; and no less so the calf which Abraham had offered to his angelic guests, and which came to life again after the angels had eaten its flesh without breaking the bones. The same story has now been found in the far older Jewish Apocryphon, about which we shall give our opinion in a succeeding article—"The Testament of Abraham."[1]

K. KOHLER.

---

[1] Since the above was written, I had the good fortune of discovering—through a hint thrown out by Barnes in his notes to the Testament of Abraham, p. 155—a genuine *Jewish Midrash on Job* by far anterior to Aboth di R. Nathan and the Midrash from which S. Buber's *Mayan Gannim*, Berlin, 1889, is taken, written in historical form, and in the cosmopolitan spirit of Hellenic Essenism, every feature of which—except the last line of the copyist—is Jewish. On this and other Midrashim entombed in Christian libraries and books I will speak later on.

D D 2

# The Jewish Quarterly Review.

## JULY, 1895.

## THE PRE-TALMUDIC HAGGADA.

### II.

#### C.—The Apocalypse of Abraham and its Kindred.

Mr. Montague Rhodes James has the merit of having
made the theological world for the first time familiar
with the "Testament of Abraham," which he published in
two versions of the Greek original, with a most valuable
critical and literary introduction and notes.[1] But it is quite
surprising that the learned editor scarcely considered the
probability of the Jewish origin and character of the
Apocryphon, which, in spite of the few traces of Christian
hands mentioned on page 50f, naturally suggests itself to
the Jewish reader. The conception is so entirely Jewish,
and so cosmopolitan in form and spirit, that we do not
hesitate to accord this Apocryphon a rank equalling the
Book of Tobit, not to say the Book of Jonah. The fact that
the story is presented as a romance and that its chronology
does not at all tally with the Bible, speaks rather in
favour of high antiquity and against the supposition that
the work is to be attributed to a Christian author of the
second century, to which Mr. James inclines.

---

[1] *Text and Studies, Contributions to Biblical and Patristic Literature,*
ed. by J. Armitage Robinson. Vol. II., No. 2. *The Testament of Abraham,*
by Montague Rhodes James, with Appendix by W. E. Barnes. Cambridge
University Press, 1892.

"Abraham the just, the beloved friend of God, the friend of strangers"—thus the story begins—now reached the full measure of years allotted to him—995 years!—when God sent his archangel, Michael, to him to prepare him for the last journey. And here we are forthwith introduced into the hospitable tent Abraham had pitched under the Oak of Mamre with a view to the four "high roads beneath to welcome the rich and the poor, kings and beggars, kinsmen and strangers as guests." This feature—prominent also in the life of Job as pictured in the "*Testament of Job*," and in the Midrash *Aboth d. R. Nathan*, ed. Schechter 33f—occurs throughout the Midrash and Talmud (*Sota* 10, *B. Metzia* 86b, *B. Bathra* 16, *Targ. Jerush.* Gen. xxi. 33, and *Beresh. Rabba*, § 49 and 54, and in Hieronymus IV., p. 583, quoted by Chastel *Stud. Christl. Barmherzigkeit*, note 44). It was the Jewish (Essene) system of propaganda still practised by the great mystic Ishmael ben Elisha in the time of Hadrian (*Aboth d. R. Nathan*, ed. Schechter, § 38, 114) and later on adopted by the Christian monks. It finds its significant illustration in a tradition preserved by Philo ("Monarchy," i. 7, ed. Mangey, ii. 220). Speaking of *proselytes*—גרים—who "come over" from the *path of darkness* and folly to the path of light and truth— he makes Moses enjoin the people not to let these men who have renounced their country, their kindred and friends, for the sake of joining the true religion, remain destitute altogether of cities, homes, and friendships, but to have *places of refuge* always ready to receive them. Compare with this Philo's Fragments, note to Exod. xxii. 19 (ed. Mangey, ii. 667) and *Targum Jerushalmi* to Deut. xxiii. 16 (and Exodus xl. 6). We arrive here at the very root of proselytism developing from the hospitium offered to the גר —the stranger.

But Abraham—to continue our story—is, like a true Essene, an agriculturist, and Michael, the archangel, finds him in the field superintending the ploughing. Abraham is struck with the sun-like splendour of the warrior in whose

garb the angel appears ; and, like a true nobleman, offers
his guest one of his horses from the stable to ride home
with him.   But the angel persistently refuses, and they
walk together, when suddenly the huge tamarisk-tree with
its three hundred (and thirty-one=שלא) branches whis-
pers to Abraham, as he passes, the secret that—this seems
to be the meaning of the hopelessly corrupt passage—the
" thrice holy God is about to summon him to himself to be
among those that love him " (the just in Paradise ; see
*Sabb.* 88*b.* and *Targum* to Judges v. 31).   Isaac had in the
meantime informed his mother Sarah—who, by a sort of
anachronism, still lives—of the arrival of a guest of super-
human appearance, and now hastens, as usual, to bring water
to his father to wash the feet of the stranger, when the pre-
sentiment that this was to be the last time he would
perform the sacred act, made Abraham cry bitterly, whereupon Isaac also wept.   The archangel, too, shed tears, and
behold, they turned into pearls, which Abraham was quick
to take and hide under his cloak.   At once the guest-
chamber is arranged in a manner to suit the royal visitor,
yet, before they sit down at the sumptuous table, the archangel leaves the room and rises in the twinkling of the eye
up to heaven to join the praises of the ministering
angels assembled before the throne of God at the time of
sunset, and then, prostrating himself before God, says : " I
cannot bring the sad message of death to the righteous
man whose likeness is not found on earth."   But God tells
him to sit down and eat with Abraham, as some spirit
would do the eating for him, and then a dream would come
upon Isaac, which he, the archangel, should interpret for
Abraham, thus to bring him the tidings.   Accordingly, the
angel sits down to eat, and Abraham offers the benediction,
the angel joining.   Isaac's dream during the night disturbs
him so much as to cause him to rouse all from sleep, and
the cry also reaches Sarah in her room.   At once Sarah
recognises the angel as one of the three heavenly visitors
who had announced the birth of Isaac, and on that occasion

Q Q 2

151

had wrought the miracle of having the calf that had been
served as meat come to life again and run back to its
mother to take suck from her.[1]   But Abraham, on hearing
the message of the angel, refuses to follow.   In this perplexity the archangel Michael again goes up to heaven for
advice, and, on returning, tells Abraham in the name of
God that none of the offspring of Adam, neither prophet
nor ruler, ever escaped death.   The reader certainly misses
here an allusion to Enoch, but it appears that he, too, was
believed to have migrated from the earth to the heavenly
paradise, as Abraham was now expected to do while following the archangel.   " The angel of death," says God, " shall
not strike thee with his sword nor with disease, for, when
once the angel of death is given permission to strike, God
himself no longer interferes. (Cf. כיון שנתן רשות למשחית.)
Michael, my captain, is to lead thee hence."   Whereupon
Abraham asks one favour yet of God (*Mechiltha Ba.* 11). He
wishes " to be allowed to see the inhabited world and the
entire heavenly order of things while yet alive, so as to
depart thereafter in peace."   The wish is granted.   " Whatever he tells thee to do, do for him, for he is my friend,"
says God, and at his bidding Michael takes the heavenly
chariot with the fiery Cherubim surrounded by sixty angels,
and rides with Abraham upon a cloud high above the earth,
so that with one single glance he can overlook all the
doings of men.   All the scenes of earthly existence, all
the grief and gladness, all the weal and woe of human life,
Abraham now surveys in one instant with tender sympathy, rejoicing with the one and sorrowing with the other.
But when he sees all the havoc that is done everywhere by

---

[1] This story, known in Mohammedan folklore, was known also in Essene
circles, and is alluded to in the *Zohar*, Chaye Sarah, p. 127*b*, cf. Yalkut
Reubeni Vayera, the calf showing Abraham the road to the cave of
Machpelah, where the patriarchs lead their immortal life.   Compare also
F. Mannhardt, *Germanische Mythen*, p. 57-74.   Liebrecht, *Gervasius*,
p. 47 and 158, the story of *Hatim Tai*, the generous host and his horse, in
Liebrecht's *Dunlop*, p. 519; and also the *unbroken bones of Jesus*, John
xix. 33-36.

murderous swords and slanderous tongues, and how the peace of households and nations is destroyed by acts of violence and crime of all kind, he is seized with wrath. Beholding robbers ready to commit murder, he exclaims: "O Lord, let wild beasts of the forests come and devour these!" And no sooner was the word spoken than the wild beasts came out of the forest and devoured the murderers. On seeing men and women committing adultery, he cried out: "O Lord, let the earth open her mouth and swallow these up!" and behold, the houses tumbled over the violators of the marriage-vow and buried them under their ruins. And again he sees thieves digging holes through storehouses and carrying off the goods, and he prays: "O Lord, let fire fall from heaven and consume these!" and immediately fire falls upon the thieves and consumes them.

But instantly a voice from heaven stopped them in their ride; God says to the archangel: "Turn back lest Abraham by his wrath destroy all my creatures. *For behold, Abraham did not sin, and therefore has no pity on sinners. Yet I, who am the Maker of the world, do not wish to destroy a single creature of mine, but defer the death of the sinner, until he repent and live. Go, therefore, and show unto Abraham the judgments and retributions behind the Eastern gate of heaven, that he may have compassion on the souls of those sinners whom he killed in his wrath.*"

With these words of incomparable beauty and grandeur, the like of which have never been uttered by any prophet or preacher since the days of Ezekiel, and which lie at the root of the tenderest sayings of the silver-tongued teacher of Nazareth, God sends Abraham with the archangel Michael to view Paradise and Hell.

A grand scene now opens before the gaze of the patriarch. *Two roads,* one *wide* and one *narrow,* stretch on either side, ending at two gates correspondingly large and small, and a large procession of souls is led by angels along the former, and a few walk along the other; and before the two gates Adam, a man of wondrous figure, sits on a golden throne, weeping and tearing his hair in distress at the sight of the multitude going through the wide gate, and again smiling and exulting at the sight of the few entering the narrow gate. "For the one leads to destruction, the other to eternal bliss, and against seven thousand that walk on the road of perdition, there is hardly one soul that walks on the path of righteousness without blemish to find salvation."

The writer, probably himself entranced as he opens his vision, continues, as if relating in the name of Abraham : "While I was still speaking, behold, there were two angels of fiery face and fierce looks, who drove before them ten thousand souls through the wide gate to perdition, while a single soul was led by one angel. Following the many through the gate, we beheld a man of marvellous stature and sun-like appearance, resembling a son of God sitting on a throne of crystal, and before him stood a table of crystal inlaid with chrysolith and beryl"—the reading of the corrupt text is conjectural !—" with a scroll of six cubits' length and ten cubits' width, while two angels held paper and ink and pen in their hands; and on the other side sat one angel of light with a pair of scales in his hand, and one angel of fire of relentless mien, holding a vessel with fire to probe the sinners. The man upon the throne judged the souls that approached, and pronounced their fate, the two angels opposite weighing and testing them, and the two other angels recording the verdict, the one the righteous acts and the other the sins." " This, O holy Abraham," says the heavenly captain Michael, " is the judgment and the retribution." The one that pronounces the judgment is the first saintly martyr, Abel, the son of Adam. " *Man shall be judged by man* " (cp. Genesis ix. 6, and *Targ. Jerush.*), saith God ; "therefore the power was given to him until the time when God himself will come and give the final judgment, which is everlasting and unchangeable. For each man having sprung forth from the first created, all are first judged here by his son, and after the second appearance of the great Ruler to"—I adopt here

at once the reading suggested by the context in place of
the Christianised version of the text"—*the twelve tribes of
Israel*, all breath and all creation will be judged by the
great Ruler, the God of all. Then the end hath come, and
awful is the verdict, and no one can undo it." And as to the
archangel who holds the scales of justice, this is *Dokiel* (accurate weigher=דוקיאל), and the one who holds the probing
fire that is *Purael* (the chastiser from πυρ=fire, or=פורעטאל,
from פורען, punishment). Further the vision does not lead.
By the true inspiration of art we are spared the shocking
sight of agony and horror in the torture-chambers of hell,
and likewise the spectacle of revels in paradisaical life which
appeal only to the senses, although we might have expected
some such revelations. We are still in touch with the
lofty, prophetic spirit, if, instead of all that, we are called
to witness the following striking scene: The single soul,
under the guidance of the one angel mentioned before, is
brought before Abel, the great judge, who now says: "Open
for me the scroll here, and give account of the sins of this
soul!" whereupon the angels find the number and weight
of both the sins and the righteous deeds of the soul to be
exactly alike. Forthwith the soul is neither handed over
to chastisement nor to salvation, but put into the middle
state—בינוני, as is the Talmudical term for the one who is
neither צדיק nor רשע. And when inquiring after the
reason, Abraham is told by his heavenly guide: "Because
the judge here can neither condemn her for her sins nor
grant her salvation for her righteous acts, she must remain
here until God, the Judge of all, comes at the end of time
and decides her fate." "What can be done for that poor
soul?" asks Abraham, compassionately. "If she would
but possess a single righteous deed above her sins, she
would enter salvation," replied the archangel. "*Then let us
offer a prayer* on her behalf, and see whether God will hear
us," said Abraham, and fell on his knees, the archangel
joining him; and when they rose from their supplication,
behold, the soul was no longer in the middle state (the

Purgatory). "She has been saved through thy righteous prayer," said the angel to Abraham. A light-encircled angel had brought her into Paradise, whereupon Abraham exclaimed: "I give praise to the name of God the Most High, and to his mercy, to which there is no bound." Compare the Kaddish : יהא שמיה רבא מברך לעלם.

But this very act of kindness and of soul-saving grace brought, with all the keener pangs of remorse, the memory of those souls whom his wrath had killed before, back to his mind, and he invoked God amid tears to forgive him his sins and to restore those persons to life again; and God granted him forgiveness, and restored the dead to life, so that those criminals might meet their due punishment there.

It is time to make mention also of the second version of our text, which is both shorter and more recent. There Enoch, "the writer of righteousness, the teacher of heaven and earth," appears at the side of Abel, the judge, as the one who writes down the verdict, and Cherubim hold the scrolls and unroll them before these judges. Then there is first the soul of a woman introduced who had murdered her own daughter, but declared herself to be guiltless, when the scrolls unfolded showed her to have committed adultery with the husband of her daughter and then to have killed her, and many other crimes she had committed. And as they were read, she cried : " Woe to me! I have forgotten all these sins, but they are not forgotten here," and then she is handed over to the torturing demons. We observe here a progress, to be sure, towards the view of the latter Apocalypses; but we fail to find the least trace of Christian ideas, far less of New Testament influences. On the contrary, the Jewish idea of strict justice pervades, until Abraham, the same who pleaded for the living sinners of Sodom, also feels compassion for that one unredeemed soul, and his prayer rescues her. Christ has no place there, neither as a judge in the nether world, as the first Christians took him to be, nor as an atoning high priest who obtains mercy for the sinner by his vicarious sacrifice. In fact, it is easy to show that the Abraham of our Apocalypse has not a tinge of either Christian or of late Rabbinical colour about him. He represents the *cosmopolitan humanity of the Jews of the Ptolemean period,* just as the Book of Aristeas does, for which, strangely enough, the historiographer Graetz has no place except as a stupid forgery.

But before examining the main tenor and tendency of our Apocalypse, we must follow the patriarch to his blissful end. Abraham's hours are numbered. He manifests the same reluctance to depart this life, as does Moses in the Midrash. He persists in refusing to follow Michael to heaven, and the archangel comes complaining before God, saying : " I dare not touch him, because he is Thy friend, *and there is none like him on earth except Job, the marvellous man.*" This occasional reference to the heathen saint Job is altogether remarkable, as it points to a very old conception *intentionally* refuted in Talmud and Midrash, all of which place Job beneath Abraham (compare the passages referred to above), but maintained with great emphasis in the *Testament of Job,* a work of equal age and equal merit to ours, as will be shown later on, and in the Apocalypse of Paul, the sources of which are decidedly Jewish and pre-Christian. Finally, the angel of death, simply called Θάνατος, is sent to take the soul of Abraham. "Thou whose name is bitterness and ferocity, the brazen-faced, and the evil-eyed—עזזאל and עין רע—cast aside thy terrific aspect and impurity ('stench' of Ahriman in the Avesta), and appear in the garb of an angel of light, exhaling the beauty and perfume of Paradise." Exactly so does Satan appear in the garb of an angel of light to Adam in the Book of Adam, to which Paul refers in 2 Cor. xi. 14. Consequently Abraham goes to meet him and welcome him as guest, taking him to be Michael, the archangel ; and the angel of death approaches him bowing, and says : " Peace upon thee, O righteous soul, friend of the Most High, who received holy angels as guests under his hospitable roof!" (cf.

Epistle to the Hebrews xiii. 2, and similar Midrashic expressions passim). But when the patriarch, full of admiration for his guest, asks after his land and destination, the angel of death says: " I am the bitter cup of death," an allusion to the name of *Samael* סם המות. Abraham first hesitates to believe that one so beautiful could be Death, then bids him leave his house; and, when this is of no avail, resorts, like Moses in the similar Moses Apocalypse, after true Essene fashion, to exorcism. By invoking the name of the deathless God he desires him to disclose to him all the secrets of death. He is told that his own virtue and righteousness became a crown of light upon the head of the angel of death, to make him appear like a divine messenger of peace, while to sinners he appears in utmost terror, bitterness, and unbearable odour of impurity. Abraham, desirous to behold Death in his most terrific sight, then arms himself with the *magic power of the holy name* of God, and tells Death to show himself in all his bitterness and cruelty. With seven fiery heads of dragons, and fourteen different aspects, one more ferocious than the other, Death now unmasks himself before him, so that at his very breath seven thousand children die in the neighbourhood, while Abraham swoons away in a fright. At the prayer of Abraham, in which even the angel of death joined, the children were restored again to life, and Abraham praises God on high.

Finally Abraham yielded, promising to give up his soul to the archangel Michael; but asked first for an explanation of the seven dragon heads, and the fourteen aspects of death, which the angel of death gives, while referring to the different modes of death men undergo. In the meantime exhaustion sets in, and, while clasping the hands of Abraham, the angel of death lures away his soul. And instantly Michael comes down from heaven with a multitude of angels to carry the precious soul upward. His body is put in heaven-spun linen, and anointed with paradisaical incense, and after three days buried *under the tree of Mamre.* The soul, however, is amidst hymns and praises to the thrice holy God, carried up by the angels and placed before the throne of God, where Abraham prostrated himself before his Eternal Father, and God the Father says: "Carry my friend Abraham into Paradise to the dwellings of my righteous ones, the abodes of my holy ones, where there is neither labour, nor mourning, nor grief, but peace, and joy, and life without end."

It is very likely that the original work had here a brief description of the bliss of the Paradise, which is altogether wanting in our Apocalypse. The mention of the bosom of Isaac and Jacob at the entrance of Abraham into Paradise is a blunder too gross for the original author. The entire end of the book, which closes with an exhortation to imitate the hospitality of Abraham and the Christian Doxology, seems to betray a Christian hand. Still the whole Requiem idea with the presentation of the soul to God, and the reception of the same in Paradise, must have emanated from the Jewish *Essenes.* For, according to Mone (*Lat. und Griech. Messen*, p. 23f), the formula remained down to the third century: "In *the bosom of Abraham, Isaac, and Jacob our fathers,*" which goes back to the second pre-Christian century, as is seen from 4 Mac. xiii.; also James, in his notes to our book, p. 129, quotes at least one formula: "In sinibus Abrahæ, Isaac, et Jacob *patriarchorum tuorum,*" which corresponds with אבותינו.

At any rate, the omission of Christ as the lamb, as the first-born son of God, the Word, or as the Judge, excludes a Christian authorship. A still stronger argument against the Christian authorship of our Apocalypse is offered by the manner in which Death is introduced. He is the ancient angel of death as we find him in the Books of Chronicles, with a few Persian and Babylonian traits attached, but this "world - destroyer" is simply a natural power without the malignity of the Ahrimanian Satan, and altogether free from the inherence of sin. He is the personification of physical evil with its fourteen forms of death and seventy-two forms of disease (cp. *Apoc. of Moses*, or *Adam-book*; and the Avestas' 99,999 diseases of Ahriman), but not of moral evil, as in the Gnostic system of Paul and his followers, or predecessors. He is an agent, not a counterpart of God and of the principle of goodness.

Neither does Adam, as portrayed here, make the impression of being in need of a redeeming Christ to rescue him from the curse of the first sin. Abel, his son, too, is but beginning to claim especial reverence for his martyrdom. "The blood of Abel" is not yet rendered an object of sanctification or sacrament, as it became in the Books of Adam and Enoch, and in circles related to early Christianity. Our Apocalypse is from beginning to end *Jewish.* And in all probability the *Moses Apoc.*, the Midrash on Moses' departure (Jellinek, *Beth Ham.*, I. 115-129; cp. *Sifre Bam.*, 136, and *Deb.*, 338 and 354-57), has drawn material from the one now before us. (See also *Mech. Amalek* II.)

In the Moses Apocalypse the prophet is also shown the whole earth, Paradise and Hell, being lifted up by Metatron (*Mithra*), who often takes the places of the ἀρχιστράτηγος, "the captain of the heavenly host," the archangel Michael, who drives Abraham around the world in the cherubim chariot. The same is told of Enoch (*Book of Enoch*, lxx. 2). Dillmann compares it to Elijah's ascent in 2 Kings ii. 12. Still Elijah only rode up to heaven, but did not view Paradise and Hell, as Enoch and Abraham did, to see the first-created ones, the righteous ones of old. We cannot but think here of the sun-chariot of *Mithra*, which played a prominent part in the mystic practices of the Persians, the Mandæans or Gnostics, and Neoplatonists (S. Windischman, *Zoroastr. Stud.*, 309-312; Reville, *Religion of Rome under the Severi*, Germ. Trans., 89, 144, 161, 181; *Philostratus Apollonius*, III. 15; Rhode, *Griech. Roman.* 180*f*). We have here the "mystery of the מעשה מרכבה," "the practical use of the divine chariot," about which the oldest Rabbinical traditions, *Hagiga* 13-14, *Shir Hash. Rabba* ad צואר

בחרוזים, and the *Hekhaloth* in Jellinek's *Beth Hamidrash* II., XVI.*ff.*, p. 64, and the Kabbalists, the יורדי מרכבה, speak so characteristically as of an actual miracle-working power. Cp. טטראמולין the *Midrash* and *Hekhaloth*. Let us not forget that in the Adam Book (*Apoc. of Moses*) God rides in the *cherub-wagon* when appearing to Adam, and all the mystics are actually described as riding through the air on the celestial ὄχημα. So does Alexander the Great when carried by cherub-like eagles, and the earth beneath appears to him like a ball, and the sea like a pot, as he looks down from above (*Jerush. Aboda Zara*, III. 1). And now we learn from the cuneiform documents that this heavenly ride upon the eagle to look down upon earth and heaven from immeasurable heights, and then to reach Hades—in other words, the flight upon the cherub up to heaven and down to hell—goes back to the giant *Etan*, of hoary Babylonian antiquity (see Harper in *Delitzsch and Haupt's Beitr.* II. 2, pp. 391*ff.*). We need not be surprised, then, to find the ride down to Hades by Seth, or Sithil, the son of Adam, in the Mandæan lore. Ancient mythology becomes mysticism to a latter age. This is the key to the מעשה מרכבה, and the Essenes were the keepers of this lore— these נסתרות. Strange that when addressing his disciples on the Mount of Olives, through the opened heavens, invoking the Holy Spirit upon them, Christ also uses the word הנסתרות (this is the *Anetharath*) in the Bartholomean Apocalypse given by Tischendorf, *Apocalyps Apocryph.* p. 25.

The Midrash has not only preserved the memory of Abraham's ride above the vault of heaven (cp. also *Ber. Rabb.* 82: אמר רש[ב][ל](קיש) האבות הן הן המרכבה העלה אורו למעלה מכיפת הרקיע, *Beresch. Rabba*, § 48), but tells us expressly, with especial reference also to Moses *Mechiltha Amalek* 2, and without reference to Moses *Bereschith Rabba* 62, that, in order to have the righteous ones die in peace, God discloses to them previous to their death the secrets of the world to come while they are yet alive. The Midrash continues mentioning Rabbis who saw Paradise and their own reward there before dying (Cf. Midrash *Shocher Tob*, Psalm xi.; at the close the vision of the dying Essene martyr יוסי בן יועזר). No doubt, then, there existed a Midrash פטירת אברהם, and probably also a פטירת יצחק ויעקב as well as a פטירת משה, if not in writing, at least as an oral Haggada (cf. Jellinek, *B. Hammidrash*, V. 50 and VI. xxxviii. And this is our Apocalypse. It is the work of an *Essene.* This is shown by its whole angelology and eschatology. And need we further proof that Abraham was endowed with all the virtues of an *Essene?* In his conversation with the angel of death, we have seen him using the holy name of God as a charm. That he ate his meat in priestly purity like an Essene (*B. Metzia*, 87a) was pointed out by Baer (*Leben Abr.*, p. 208). That he taught his children from Keturah the use of magic art by the names of the angels of evil, מסר להם שם הטומאה (*Sanhedrin*, 91a) is also an Essene trait. And the very fact that the Kabbalistic book ספר יצירה was attributed to Abraham shows that, like Moses, he formed the centre of mystic lore. In fact, Enoch and Abraham are as far back as 140 before the Christian era, praised by Eupolemos as teachers of astrology, who had learned all about the stars from angels, which tradition throws some light upon the age of our Apocalyptic literature (Euseb. *Praep. Evang.*, IX. 17f).

On the other hand we know, from both the New Testament and the Jewish writings (Luke xvi. 13; *Kiddushin* 72b; and 4 Mac. xiii.), that "to sit in the lap of Abraham" means to enjoy the bliss of Paradise. Hence Abraham became a prominent figure there, as soon as Adam, Abel, and Enoch had stepped into the background; that is, when the seal of circumcision had become the pledge of life, and Abraham had to acknowledge the circumcised as his own at the gate (*Beresh. Rabba*, 48; *Shemoth Rabba*, 19; *Erubin*, 19a). For the cosmopolitan view of heaven and hell taken in our Apocalypse was narrowed down to sectarian Judaism in the Talmudical age, which tended, more or less, to belittle the piety of Job and Enoch, and to behold in Adam the progenitor of a sinful race. This latter view, exhibited already in IV. Esra, grew into large proportions in Pauline Christianity, so that the poison of sin זוהמא של נחש (*Jebamoth*, 103*b*), worked, in consequence, less mischief in the Jewish dogma regarding the צדיקי אומות העולם than it did in the Church.

Let us now take a glance at the Paradise and Hell of the Talmudists, and see how they compare with our Apocalypse and with those of Peter and Paul. It is Joshua ben Levi, of the third Christian century, who, like Abraham, held previous to his death a conversation with the angel of death, God having given the angel of death the same instructions he had given the angel Michael regarding Abraham: "Do for him whatever he wishes," and who was privileged, like him, to see both *Paradise and Hell*, a description of which is given in the treatise bearing his name (see Jellinek's *Beth Hammidrash*, II. xviii., and 48-53; cf. I. 147-149). Zunz, it is true, finds this treatise to be of a very recent date (*S. Gottesd. Vortr.*, 179); but R. Joshua ben Levi appears throughout the Talmudical and Midrashic literature as the chief recorder of eschatological lore, as will be seen in the following, and his *Paradise* and *Inferno* have their analogies everywhere in the tradition (see *Midr. Konen*, Jellinek, *Beth Hammidrash*, II. 28-32, in תסכת גן עדן. III. 131-140, 67-76, v. 42-51 and 172*f*, and elsewhere).

At Gehenna's gate Joshua ben Levi saw (ib. I. 148, cf. Exodus Rabba, § 40) persons hung up by their noses, others by their hands some by their tongues, some by their eyelids and feet, women by their breasts. At one place men were devoured by worms that die not: at another, coals of fire burnt up their inner parts. Some ate dust that broke their teeth— they had lived on stolen goods; and others were cast from flames into ice, and back again. Each sin had its own chastising angel, the three deadly sins mentioned being adultery, insulting a fellow-man in public, and abusing the name of God. All the faces were *black*, and in the very midst of their suffering the Jewish sinners would declare God to be a just Judge, and be rescued after twelve months, while the heathen, failing to do so, would have their punishment renewed every six months. From Friday eve to the close of Sabbath, however, the fires of Gehenna are cooled down, and they themselves find a cooling place between two mountains of snow. Gan Eden he describes (II. 92) as a city with two gates of carbuncle, above which sixty myriads of angels, with faces like the firmament, stand with crowns of gold and precious stones, and with myrtle-wreaths in their hands, to welcome each righteous man as he enters, and lead him to his tent, where wine and honey from the world's beginning are spread before him on costly tables. Four rivers—one of wine, one of honey, one of balsam, and one of oil—flow through the city, where is light eternal and the beauty of continual rejuvenation, the soul going ever anew through the three ages of child-hood, manhood, and venerable old age. Trees of all kinds surround the Tree of Life, exhaling wondrous perfume, and *seven* partitions there are for the various classes. About these seven partitions of the city of Paradise we learn (II. 28) that the *first*, made of cedar-wood, harbors the proselytes under the captainship of Obadiah the prophet (probably originally Abedmelech the Ethiopian, *see* JEWISH QUARTERLY, V. 417) ; the *second*, made of silver, contains the *repentant* sinners, under Manasseh's leadership ; the *third*, made of gold, and precious stones, with the Tree of Life in the centre, and the patriarchs, the twelve sons of Jacob, David, and Solomon, and all the rulers of the ages under its shade, Kilab the son of David (cf. *B. Bathra*, 17a; *Derech Eretz Zutta* I.) being the leader, while Moses and Aaron perform the function of teachers, all being seated on golden thrones, there singing the praise of God. The *fourth* department, built of olive-wood, is inhabited by the multitude of those sons of Israel whose lives were made as bitter by oppression as is the olive tree, yet gave forth pure light. The *fifth* department, built of onyx and jasper, was that in which both Messiahs, the son of David and the son of Joseph, dwelt in company with Elijah. About the sixth and seventh the Midrash Conen is silent, most likely because, according to the Persian system there were originally but three, with the fifth (or fourth) as the inmost part, and only the Babylonian or Mandæan system had *seven.* Compare also Wolf, *Muhammedanische Eschatologie,* pp. 167-197.

Gehenna, according to the same tradition (page 30), also has but *three* large gates, under the rule of *Kipud,* of Neged sagiel (?) and of Samael, but *seven* departments, in the lowest of which Elisha ben Abuyah, the Gnostic, אחר, is placed; in the sixth, the idolater Micah; in the fifth, Ahab; in the fourth, Jeroboam; in the third, Korah; in the second, Absalom; for the first the name is omitted, but all except *Acher* are said to be released.

This seems to prove that the Midrash belongs to the age of Gnosticism. It is, therefore, quite possible that the tradition given as Elijah's communication to *R. Simeon ben Jochai* (Cod. III. 67*ff.*) goes back to that great mystic, from whose son Eliezer, Joshua ben Levi probably derived his lore. Among these נסהרות we can at least verify a very important one as Simon ben Jochai's teaching, and trace it far back to pre-Christian Essenism, *Sifre Debarim,* 10*a,* 47 (cf. Midrash *Shocher Tob,* Psalms xii. 6, seven heavens and seven hells). R. Simeon ben Jochai teaches that there are *seven* classes of righteous ones, who will see God's majesty in the world to come: first, ". his loving ones are like the *sun;* the next class like the *moon;* the third like the *firmament;* the fourth like the *stars;* the fifth like the *lightning;* the sixth like the *lilies;* and the seventh like the golden candlestick with the olive-trees about it." Now, it is remarkable that the Biblical expression, ואהביו כצאת השמש (Judges v. 31), is not only in the Talmud constantly—(see *B. Bathra,* 8*b; Joma,* 23*a;* Targ. Jerus., and *Sifre* ibid.)—applied to the foremost in piety; but the

New Testament writers use it as a well-accepted term. See James i. 12: "The Lord has promised [*the crown of life*] to those *who love* him," and 2 Tim. iv. 8: "The Lord, the righteous judge, shall on that day give the crown of righteousness not only unto me, but unto all *who love* his presence" πάσι τοῖς ἠγαπηκόσι τὴν ἐπιφάνειαν αὐτοῦ. Resh—who, by the bye, in his very instructive work on the *Agrapha*, construes an original Hebrew Gospel *upon the false premise* that the apostolic quotations are *Christ's sayings*, while, in fact, they are *pre-Christian*, and *chiefly Essene expressions*, to a large extent *traceable also through Talmudic and Hellenistic Judaism!*—fails to see the Biblical allusion (page 253). Likewise must our New Testament exegetes fail to understand the words of the apostle in 1 Cor. xv. 40*ff*, where Paul, speaking of the σώματα ἐπουράνια, in contrast to the σώματα ἐπίγεια, says, "Different is the δόξα of the *sun* from that of the *moon* and that of the *stars*, for each star differs from the others in δόξα. And so is the resurrection of the dead. The generation of Adam is earthly, that of the Messiah heavenly." The apostle evidently alludes to the different classes of the just in Paradise, ranking in degree and in light by their very *faces*, as mentioned by Simon ben Jochai.

How old and constant this tradition was—and this constancy necessitates a class of mystics reaching up to high antiquity!—may also be learned from the following:—In 1 Cor. ii. 9, Paul quotes as sacred writing (καθὼς γέγραπται), "Eye hath not seen and ear not heard, nor hath it entered the heart of any man what God hath prepared for those who love him." Resh (*Agrapha*, page 154*ff*, cf. 281), shows that the words עין לא ראתה, Isaiah lxiv. 3, and lxv. 17, could not have been meant by the apostle, but that an Elijah Apocalypse existed, containing the quoted verse, which he claims to be based upon a specific Christ-saying, although the same verse occurs in different forms elsewhere. The fact is that the Isaianic verse, עין לא ראתה occurs regularly in the apocalyptic description of the bliss of the righteous in Paradise. (See *Berachoth*, 34*b*, sayings of R. Joshua ben Levi and R. Jochanan—both derived their Eschatology from Simon ben Jochai; and the treatise on Gan Eden in Jellinek's *B. Hammidrash*).

But we are in a position to give some information about the origin of the glories of "sun," "moon," and "stars" belonging to the souls in Paradise. The Persian book, *Ardai Viraf* (ed. and transl. by Haugh and West), the contents of which go back to the time of Plato and Pythagoras, also introduces a righteous man taking a glance at heaven and hell; and there heaven and hell are presented according to the original Aryan division into the *three* grades of good or bad *thoughts, words,* and *actions,* and an uppermost heaven, full of light, for the *good God Ahuramazda* with those souls that are godly, and an undermost and darkest hell for the bad spirit *Ahriman* and his evil associates. The three divisions of heaven bear the characteristic names of stations of the *sun,* of the *moon,* and of the *stars;* and above that of the sun, the highest of these, there is the dwelling-place of Ahuramazda, the seat of the Endless Lights, "the House of Song," mentioned already in the oldest Zoroastrian hymns. There are the same rivers of oil and the wine of the new life (a drink from the stream of forgetfulness, יין המשומר), and the perfume of wondrous power with the miraculous trees and the life-bestowing ox (Bundahish, XIX. 13)=Behemoth, as meat for the righteous, and also the same modes of punishment of the wicked, as described in the Apocalypse of Peter and Paul, and in the Jewish treatises on Gehenna, only far more systematically arranged in the Persian system than in any of these. No one familiar with the Avesta literature, from the reports of Theopompus and Plutarch to the vision of Viraf and all the Pahlavi Texts, as translated by West, can read of the wicked in the Peter Apocalypse, how they are hung up by their tongues, breasts, and heads, etc., without feeling certain that the Persian

R R 2

167

conception (if not the Hindoo (Brahmin) one given in
Book XIV., of the Pre-Buddhistic Epic Mahabharata)
is the original and the Christian is a copy.   But between
these stand the Jewish Essenes.   They certainly wrote
the Sibylline books, and of these the second book, verses
260-270, has an indisputable Jewish character.   They are
the prophetical warning to the idolatrous *heathen*, the
pederasts, adulterers, and *usurers !*   There is the original
"gnashing of the teeth" of those in Gehenna, Sibyll.
Book VIII. 350;  II. 306, "the fire" and "the worms," and
the "wailing" of Matt. xiii. 42 and 50, which expression
goes back to Judith xvi. 17.   Consequently, when a
tradition in the name of R. [Joshua ben] Levi, in
*Shir Hashirim Rabba* to v. 15, and *Vayikra Rabb.* § 25,
says that as those that live in concubinage with their
servants are "hung up by their heads in Gehenna"—
exactly as the adulterers are hung up by their heads
in the Peter Apocalypse—and the Rabbinical saying is
based on Psalm lxviii. 22, while the Midrash and Targ.
Jonath. show the entire Psalm applied to the Two
Roads of Life and Death Eternal, Heaven and Hell!—we
see at once that the Christian Apocalypse offers only
*borrowed* views and traditions.   In fact, we possess a
remarkable vision of an Essene, חסיד, of the time of
Simon ben Shetach, a century before the rise of Christianity,
according to which the departed Essene brother enjoys,
under the shade of the trees of Paradise, the bliss of the
streams of life, while the son of a publican nearly suffers
the agonies of Tantalus, standing in the midst of
water, yet unable to quench his thirst (compare *Visio
Pauli*, by Brandes, page 28, and St. Perpetua VII.) and
a saintly woman, Miriam, the daughter of Eli (the
high priest), is at times hedged in under the reeds
[of the Styx river] or hung up by her breasts, because her
fasts had often the air of hypocrisy (see *Jerush. Hagiga* II. 1).
Compare also the thirteen streams of Balsam which R.
Abbahu saw flowing for him to drink from in Paradise

(*Beresh. Rabb.* § 62), and the burning filth in the mouth of the blasphemers (*Gittin* 57a) with the Apocalyptic pictures. Josephus is undoubtedly right when comparing the Paradise and Hell of the Essenes with the Greek Elysium and Hades (*Jewish Wars*, II. viii. 11). But we must not overlook the fact that Plato himself has his description of the Great Judgment in the Nether-world and the two roads leading to Paradise and Hell, the one to the right consisting of seven grades of light—one brighter than the other with a beautiful meadow in the midst, and the other, to the left, of torture chambers, with a " bellowing" beast in the deep, and the " wailing" of the punished ones filling the dark places, derived from the vision of " Er the Pamphylian, the son of Armenios, whose soul came back from the other world and narrated all these things." And this *Er* is identified by Clemens of Alexandria with *Zoroaster*. Compare Plato's *Republic* X., ch. 13 ff., with Clemens Alexandr. *Strom.* V. 14. He is, if not in name, certainly in the main feature identical with Viraf, the Persian saint. Likewise do the names of the judges in Hades, Rhadamanthus and Minos, point to a pre-Hellenic source, the one being Cretan or Semitic, the other the Egyptian god Ra-d'amenthes, " Sun of the Nether-world "; and while the weighing of the souls on the scales before the judgment-seat, found also in the Avesta, has the air of Egyptian thought, the maidens that assist in the judgment, according to the Platonic portraiture, or those that receive the soul at the gate or bridge in the shape of *Virtue* or *Sin* personified, have the original character of Aryan and Teuton Valkyries, and are still found sculptured on the Lykian monuments at Xanthos as soul-carrying *harpies*. In other words, the question of the origin of these *Orphic* conceptions of Hell and Heaven is far more complicated than our theologians or philologists imagine.[1] Egypt and Persia, India and Babylonia must

[1] Including A. Dieterich, whose classic work, *Nekyia*, Leipzig, 1893, is full of interesting facts, but labours under the mistake that the Orphic mysteries can be explained without a study of Babylonia, India, and Ancient Egypt, in short of Semitic origins.

have had an exchange of views regarding these matters ages before the Greeks made the acquaintance of either. The rôle of Judge of the Nether-world ascribed, then, by our Abraham Apocalypse to Adam's son Abel—corresponding with the Jama (Yima) of the Aryans, or with the son of Kayomarth of the Avesta (compare the *Seth* or Sitil of the Mandæans)—refers us to the age of Ptolemean syncretism, in which the Jews (Essenes) took a conspicuous part. The probability is that *Enoch* as Judge or Recorder of the last day, like Hermes (=Tot), Anubis and Mithra, belongs to a later stage, and the Messiah's officiating as judge at the resurrection like Soschiosch to a still later one.

It would lead too far were we to point out single parallels between the Persian and the Jewish Christian *Inferno* with its Wolf (*Kapod Minochird* 27-50 the same as קפוד, *Beth Hammidrash*, II. 30), its *Lake of Tears* (in *Arda Viraf* and עמק הבכא or Mayan Bochim, *Erubin* 19a; *Beth Hammidrash*, II. 147, I. 132), and its בהמות (cf. *Visio Pauli*, by Brandes, p. 26), the Leviathan and Ur of the Mandæans upon whose horns the earth rests corresponding with "the Tartaruchos" and "Themeluchos" of the Christian Apocalypse and the *Paradise* with its rivers and trees, its crowns of glory, and golden thrones for the just. It is the *Purgatory* or middle state, in which the soul with merits equal to her sins must stay, that our Apocalpyse has derived from the Persian system (see *Sacred Books of the East*, West Pahlavi Texts, I. 294), and we find already the schools of Shammai and Hillel—that is the generation preceding the Christian era —in dispute over these ביגונים (see *Tosifta Sanhedrin*, xiii. 3, *Babli Rosh Hashana*, 16b). The *Shammaites* divide men into *three* classes: the wicked ones, the just and those whose sins and good deeds are even—שקולים—the first being at once sent down to Gehenna, the second at once admitted into life eternal, and the third are *tested by fire*. Here we have the same idea of δοκιμάζειν, which forms so prominent a part in the Epistles of Paul as well as in our Apocalypse,

and is based in our Tosefta on Zachariah xiii. 9, את והבאתי
השלישית באש וצרפתים ובחנתים. Here the proving by fire is
emphasised (cf. *Hagiga* 27a). It is probably not too bold to
discern the identical names of the proving angels mentioned
in our Abraham-Apocalypse in דלקיאל and פרעואל also in
the old *Gan Eden* treatise bearing the name of the old Shammaite mystic, R. Eliezer b. Hyrcanos, *B. Hammid.* v. 42-51,
in which Abraham and Isaac sit as judges at the gate in
place of Adam and Abel in the Abrahamic vision. Against
the Shammaites the *Hillelites* maintain that God will have
compassion on the middle class and turn the *scale* in
favour of mercy. The idea of having the scales of judgment turned toward the side of righteousness in our disposition towards our fellow-man, הוה דן את כל אדם לכף זכות
זכות, which occurs in the saying of Joshua ben Parachia 130
B.C.E., shows how old the conception is. *This is exactly the
view taken in our Apocalypse.* It is the cosmopolitan spirit
of non-Palestinian or Hellenistic Judaism which prevails
in the school of Hillel, and made them declare : טוב לאדם
שנברא—"Man with all his shortcomings is not lost," while
the Shammaites held the opposite view: טוב לאדם שלא נברא
משנברא—"It would be better for man in his sinfulness
had he not been born" (*Erubin* 13b).

The idea of divine mercy is emphasised in our Apocalypse
to such an extent that the Christian Apocalypses of Paul,
John, and Esdra could not well adopt it without dealing a
blow to the intermediating power of Christ. Therefore,
they lay all stress on the justice of suffering, sun, moon, and
stars, earth and sea becoming accusers of man's sinfulness
before the throne of God, while the apostles and saints
appear "more merciful than God the Father of all;
until Christ, we presume, releases the imprisoned ones.
The main power of Abraham, however, is manifested in his
*prayer* for the unfortunate inhabitants of Gehenna. His
intercession for the soul he sees held by the angel in the
Purgatory is a specimen of what he shall do after having
entered Paradise. He will always be the מלאך מליץ. This

is the idea underlying our Apocalypse.    And on it the *Kaddish* or *Mass* for the dead rests.

In all the Infernos of the Jews or Christians the cry is heard: "O God, righteous is thy judgment!" (see *Peter Apocalypse*, p. 10; *Paul Apoc.*, pp. 316-18; *Erubin*, 19a; *Taanith*, 11b; *Sifre Haazinn*, 307, צדוק הדין, cf. *Psalms of Solomon*, ii. 16 and viii. 7; 2 Macc. vii. 38, and xii. 41.) In life, justice—מדה כנגד מדה—is not always executed. All the more must the world to come bring about the relentless avenging of wrong, and an exact system of retribution.    Still, even the gates of hell are not shut against the power of mercy when the divine justice of the punishment is humbly acknowledged by the sufferers themselves.    "When the dwellers of Gehenna chant forth their *Amen* at the time when the holy name of God is praised by the congregation in justification of God's ways, the doors of hell yield, and angels carry them in white robes into Paradise on the last day." This is the teaching of R. Eliezer b. Hyrcanos, the great mystic, the last great authority on Essene lore, in *Eliahu Zutta*, ch. xx., and R. Joshua b. Levi, the pupil's pupil of R. Simon b. Jochai, who was the pupil's pupil of *R. Eliezer* has the following remarkable saying, *Sabbath*, 119b.—כל־ העונה אמן בכל כרחו קורעין לו גזר דינו כל׳·····פותחין לו שערי גן עדן, "Whosoever chants the *Amen* of the *Kaddish* with full force will have his verdict of condemnation repealed and the gates of Paradise opened for him" (cf. *Sanhedrin*, 91b, R. J. b. Levi, כל האומר שירה בעה"ז זוכה ואומרה לעה"ב; cf. also Midrash *Shocher Tob*, Ps. xxxi. 8, and Ps. lxxxiv. 3).    It is undoubtedly due also to the *Sabbath* song of the Essene saints at their sacred banquets that the wicked in hell (see *Pesiktha Rabbathi*, 23) were granted a respite on that day from Friday eve to the close of the Sabbath under songs of Amen and Halleluyah, wherefore *Joshua ben Levi,* in the name of /Bar Kappara, pupil of S. b. J., finds the three Sabbath meals to be a safeguard against Gehenna sufferings (*Sabbath*, 118a).    Of course, the

Christian writer of the *Paul Apocalypse* (see Brandes' *Visio Pauli*) had to claim the same respite for the Christian inhabitants of hell on a Sunday instead, as Grand Rabbin Levy in the *Revue des Etudes Juives* suggested. But did not he, as well as the writers of the Christian *Esdra* and of the *Peter Apocalypse*, betray his dependence on Jewish sources in many other ways?

The Acheron, or Acherusian Lake, mentioned as the great river of Hades in Greek mythology, most probably of Semitic origin, found also in the *Sibyll. B.* I., 302, II., 341, appears in the Syriac version of *Paul Apoc.* as the lake Εὐχαριστεία, a rather awkward metamorphosis. The Hebrew words for the forms of hymns, *Th^e hillatha Tushbechatha w^e Nechmatha*, were manifestly no longer understood by the Christian compiler. See Tischendorf, *Apocr. Apoc.* (p. 56). The punishment for disturbance of the devotion during church service is mentioned alike in the Arabian *Moses Apocalypse* (Jellinek, *Beth Hammidrash* I. XIX.), and in the *Paul Apocalypse*, III., 40, a late interpolation). A difficult passage in the newly-discovered *Peter Apocalypse* seems also to find its explanation by recurrence to a Hebrew original. Speaking of the murderers that fall a prey to the evil reptiles of hell, the *Apocalypse* says: "There were set upon them worms like clouds of darkness," v. 10, ἐπέκειντο δὲ αὐτοῖς σκώληκες ὥσπερ νέφελαι σκότους. Harnack confesses his inability to explain this strange simile. As soon, however, as we think of בן הנפילים, and compare the נפילי התהום, a Leviathan-like monster so huge that God, in order to show him to Moses, must shake the ocean, *Shemoth Rabba*, § 15, we have the matter cleared up. But then even the Petrine Apocalypse must have been copied from a Jewish original. And, in fact, no Christian writer would have inflicted so terrible a punishment upon the worshipper of idols as is that of being roasted and burned up like the idol itself. Both he and the Sibylline poet, II., 260-347—whose reference to the Behemoth and Leviathan, v. 292, whose tortures for the usurers, v. 269, and whose three rivers of Paradise with the emphasis of *equality of all* in the participation of bliss : " no slavery, nor poverty, nor riches, nor tyranny," show him to have been an Essene Jew—had older Jewish descriptions as *models*.[1]

The grand topic of the *Divina Comedia*—to sum up our inquiry—occupied the minds of the Jewish Essenes long before the Church took hold of it. The entire view taken of the relation of Judaism to the Church by Zunz and all his followers is, to my mind, utterly false. Before David, the son of Jesse, was placed by the Pauline Apocalyptic in the centre of Paradise as singer of the Hallelujah Psalms, the Essenes had placed their cup of wine into his hands to sing the praise of God at the great banquet of the just (compare *Pauli Apoc.* iii. 30 with *Pesachim* 119*b*). But the New Year's Day, in its character of annual Day of Divine Judgment, turned the mind of the Jew more and more away from prying into the secrets of the hereafter, leaving the subject to the few mystics who maintained the ancient lore, whereas with the Church the question of salvation and doom grew ever of higher moment.

Far, then, from being, as Zunz believed, borrowed from the Church, the Jewish Kaddish, with all the legends connected with it, forms the echo of the last *Amen* of Essene worship, in which the strains of the Orphic song, the Gathas of the Aryan priest and monk, and the Hallelujahs of the ancient Levite, united in praising the Thrice Holy One who dwells unseen above the Cherubim, yet is sought after by all.

K. KOHLER.

---

[1] I will add here that the name of Atarlimos given in the Arabian Testament of Abraham (p. 138) to Death is אנדרלמלסיא equal to ἀνδρολημψία ; see Jastrow's *Dictionary*, s.v., which, like Death הורגת רעים וטובים, *Vayikra Rabb.* § 23, and the Demon Bedargon in *Eisenmenger*, II. 436, mentioned p. 57, is פודגרא, equal to Podagra.

### III.

#### ZEUS IN MISHNAH, TALMUD AND MIDRASH.

We read in the Mishnah [1] : " The blasphemer is not guilty unless he pronounces the name of God. R. Joshua, son of Korcha, said : ' The whole day (as long as the examination of the witnesses lasts) we deal with the witnesses by using the expression יכה יוסה את יוסה, " Jose smote Jose." When judgment is promulgated, we do not sentence by using a surname, but we dismiss every one (of the audience that they should not hear the blasphemy) and say to the first witness : " Tell exactly what did you hear," and he says it,' &c."

In explaining this Mishnah, the Talmud [2] says : " We have learned in the *Boraitha*, he who did not pronounce God's name is not guilty till he pronounces God's *proper* name. Where is this proved ? Samuel says, " For it is written [3] : ' And the son of the Israelitish woman blasphemed the Name and cursed,' and the verb *nakeb* means to pronounce God's proper name." In accordance with this explanation, no death penalty can be executed upon any blasphemer but in the case of his pronouncing God's proper name, the Tetragrammaton. Now, in order to avoid the useless repetition of the blasphemy during the examination of the witnesses, the tribunal introduced a circumlocution, serving as a substitute for the unutterable Name of God. R. Joshua, son of Korcha, thus transmits the formula of this substitute, being the following words : יכה יוסה את יוסה. The reading יוסה is maintained by some sources [4] while others [5] have יוסי. As to the expression itself, it is a *crux interpretum*. Rashi [6] thinks the word has no meaning and was chosen only on account of its having just four letters, and thus recalling the four letters in God's proper name. There is still another reason, namely, that the value of these four letters יוסי expressed in an equivalent of numbers, amounts to 86, the number equivalent of the word אלהים. The latter reason, however, is of no great import, as the blasphemer was not considered to be guilty until God's proper name (יהוה) was pronounced by him. R. Nathan ben Jechiel differs from Rashi, inasmuch as the former suits his explanation to the reading of either

---

[1] *Synh. Mishnah* V., ch. vii.

[2] *Synh.* 56ᵃ.

[3] Levit. xxiv. 11.

[4] Munich MS., Jerus. Talmud, *Sifra*, ch. xviii. of Emor.

[5] Our editions. R. Nathan has both readings of our *Aruch Completum*, iv. 219, and cf. p. 119.

[6] *S nh.* 56ᵃ.

יוסה or יוסי. In the first case, the four letters remind us of God's proper name, consisting likewise of four letters, three of which (יוה) being common. In the second case, three letters of the word יוסי, viz.: יו amount to the number 26, which is at the same time the numerical value of the Tetragrammaton יהוה.

Now it seems improbable to assume that the Mishnah, in choosing the formula above quoted, did so by counting the value of the letters. Moreover, this play with the so-called Geomatria belongs to a later period of Hagadic exegesis.

Another question is, why should just the verb יכה convey the idea of a blasphemy?

J. Levy[1] offers another explanation. He takes יוסי in the double meaning of a Greek and a Hebrew word. The first he thinks υἱὸς = son, the second is יוסי = יוסף, *i.c.*, Joseph, the father of Jesus, so that "Jose smote Jose" imparts the idea: The son smote the father, implying that the son is mightier than the father.

There have been still other attempts to set aright the difficulties, but with the same unsatisfactory results.[2]

In my opinion יוכה is certainly a foreign god, used as a substitute for the Tetragrammaton. The choice is suggestive, as the four letters recall the mystic number, *four*, of יהוה, three of which being identical, as R. Nathan explains. The choice was furthermore a happy one, as Zeus (יוסה), the chief deity of the Greeks, was well-known all over Asia, and the witnesses, in order not to repeat the blasphemy, could with impunity cast their contempt at him. The verb יכה, conveying the idea of blasphemy, is also appropriate and in accordance with the Biblical expression,[3] "And he smites the earth with the rod of his mouth."

The meaning of "Jose smote Jose"—that is, Zeus smote Zeus—is therefore that he blasphemed the highest deity with[4] the highest deity, whereby the highest Jewish deity being expressed by the highest Greek deity, and יהוה substituted by Jose (Zeus), the blasphemy was made a fitting subject of discussion during the examination of the witnesses. That יוכה is not chosen by a mere chance, but for a substitute of יהוה, is expressly remarked by R. Acha b. Jacob in the Talmud,[5] and that blasphemy was only punishable when יהוה by

---

[1] In *Kobuck's Jeshurun* iv., 4.

[2] See Rahmer's *Literaturblatt*, vol. viii.      [3] Isaiah xl. 4.

[4] The particle את in the sentence, יכה יוסה את יוסה, is therefore to be translated "with." See Gen. xv. 18; Exod. i. 1; Judges i. 16; 2 Kings vi. 16.

[5] *Synh.* 60.

יהוה was blasphemed, or, speaking in our formula, Zeus with Zeus (Jose with Jose), has been already mentioned.

A strong confirmation of the view that יוסה alludes to Zeus we find in another passage of the Talmud.[1] Quoting the expression of the Mishnah,[2] " He who curses with a curse," R. Josef says :—" This means יכה קוסם את קוסו, ' he who blasphemed with an oath his Kos,'[3] where Kos, equal to Zeus, is again substituted for יהוה. Kos comes nearer to the word Zeus, besides being a surname of the same, who was called Ζεῦς Κάσιος, and known by the Romans as Jupiter Casius.[4] This name occurs also in a Nabatean inscription as קצין.[5] The Midrash[6] mentions בתי קוצין, houses devoted to the worship of Zeus Kasios, after whom, or in whose honour, the city En Kos was called En Koz.[7] This deity was worshipped also in Idumea. Josephus[8] writes as follows :—" Costobarus was an Idumean by birth, and one of their principal dignitaries, and one whose ancestors had been priests to the Kose,[9] whom the Idumeans had esteemed as a god."

Benjamin Mussafia[10] goes so far as to maintain that the name of the small coin זוז was called thus for bearing the profile of Zeus, and therefore R. Menachem bar Simai never looked at this coin.[11] Zeus' name being so widely spread, we can easily understand why it served as a typical substitute in the case we have been considering.

A. KOHUT.

---

[1] *Synh.* 81ᵇ, 82ᵇ.      [2] *Synh.* 81ᵇ.

[3] This is the proper reading, to be found also in the Munich MS. ; our editions have wrongly קסמו.

[4] *Plinius* v. 14.      [5] *Zeitschrift der D. M. G.* xix. 639.

[6] *Midr. Samuel*, ch. xiv.

[7] *Jerus. Abod. Zara* iii. 43ᵃ; *Tossephta Ab. Zara*, ch. vii. See, too, *Aruch Compl.*, Article כל עין.

[8] *Antiquities* xv. 7, 9.      [9] Koζί. See, too, *Brüll Jahrbücher* i. 140.

[10] Article זוז. A similar view is held by Mussafia with regard to Pallas. See Art. פלס 2.

[11] *Aboda Zara* 50ᵃ.

---

# THE TWO MEKILTAS

## Jacob Z. Lauterbach

The tannaitic Midrash to Exodus which in amoraic and gaonic times formed a part of the *Sifre* or *Sifre debe Rab*[1] came in later gaonic times to be described as "The Tractates on the Book of Exodus" מכילתא דואלה שמות.[2] It was so described because its characteristic feature is that it consists of "tractates" מסכתות,[3] dealing with groups of laws contained, or events recorded, in the book of Exodus. In the course of time this description of the Midrash became its special designation.[4] This special designation מכילתא was then given also to another tannaitic Midrash to Exodus, in contents similar to the first one, though we cannot

---

[1] Even in later medieval times the Mekilta was regarded by many authorities as part of the Sifre. See Lauterbach, The Name of the Mekilta, in Jewish Quarterly Review n.s. XI (Philadelphia 1920) pp. 179–182. To the authorities, cited there, who refer to our Mekilta under the name of Sifre, are to be added the following: Joseph Kara in his commentary to the Book of Kings, published by S. Eppenstein in Jahrbuch der Jüdisch-Literarischen Gesellschaft, volume XIII (Frankfurt a, M. 1920) p. 27, quotes the passage found in the Mekilta de Rabbi Ishmael, Pisḥa XII [ed. Lauterbach, vol. I (Philadelphia 1933) p. 93] and adds the remark: כך היא שנויה בספרי "Thus it is taught in the Sifre." The Tossafists in their commentary on the Torah, הדר זקנים, (Leghorn 1840) p. 29b, quote the passage which is found in the Mekilta de Rabbi Ishmael, Pisḥa XIII, (Lauterbach, vol. I, p. 99) and introduce it by: אמרו בספרי. "They say in the Sifre."

[2] Halakot Gedolot at the end of הלכות הספר (editio Vienna 1810) p. 106a; סידור פרשיות של יסים טובים published by Ch. M. Horowitz in תורתן של ראשונים (Frankfurt a,M. 1881) p. 43; and R. Judah b. Barsilai in his commentary to the Sefer Jezirah, ed. Halberstam (Berlin 1885) p. 14. Also in a Genizah fragment containing statements of Saadya Gaon, cited by Harkavy in Hakedem I (1907) p. 127. Comp. Lauterbach, The Name of the Mekilta, pp. 173–174.

[3] See Lauterbach op. cit. pp. 192–193.

[4] See ibid. p. 193.

113

ascertain whether it likewise was arranged according to tractates.[5] Possibly a slight misunderstanding, on the part of some
authorities, of the designation מכילתא given to the one Midrash,
brought it about that the same designation was also attached
to the other. The word מכילתא forming the designation given to
the one Midrash actually was a plural form to be read Mekilata,
meaning "the tractates" and referring to the nine tractates of
which the Midrash is composed. Some authorities, however,
mistook the word מכילתא for the singular form Mekilta and
understood it as referring not to the tractates composing the
Midrash but to the Midrash as a whole, designating it as a single
tractate or collection of midrashic comments to Exodus.[6] And
when they found a gaonic statement, speaking of "The Tractates
on the Book of Exodus" מכילאתא דואלה שמות or מכילתא דואלה שמות,
in which the form מכילתא was unmistakably plural, they understood it to refer not to the tractates of the one Midrash but to
the two distinct tannaitic Midrashim on the book of Exodus.
The plural form Mekilata, so they understood, simply meant
the two Mekiltas; the singular form Mekilta designated either
of the two Midrashim. Thus the name Mekilta came to serve
as a designation for each one of the two distinct Midrashim to
Exodus. Rabbinic authorities when citing either one of these
two Midrashim would therefore, in most cases, add to the name
Mekilta, common to both Midrashim, a descriptive word or title
indicating which of the two Mekiltas was meant or referred to.

Of these two tannaitic Midrashim to Exodus, called by the
same name Mekilta, the one, usually designated more specifically
as the "Mekilta de Rabbi Ishmael," has been preserved to us
as a separate and complete work in the form and the arrange-

---

[5] As the other Midrash has not been preserved to us in its entirety, it is
impossible to ascertain according to what plan it was arranged.

[6] See Lauterbach op. cit. p. 194 note 23. Joseph Bonfils in his commentary
on Ibn Esra, צפנת פענח, edited by D. Herzog (Heidelberg; part I, 1911; part II,
1930) also seems to have understood the name מכילתא as a singular form; hence
he translates it by the Hebrew מסכת. In part I. p. 229, referring to a passage
found in the Mekilta, he states that it is found במסכת. See Herzog's note
ibid. l. c. Herzog is not correct when he assumes (ibid. l.c. and in his Introduction p. XXXVI) that Joseph Bonfils did not know the Mekilta.

ment given to it by its final redactor.[7] The other, frequently referred to by medieval authorities as "Another Mekilta" מכילתא אחרת[8] or "The Mekilta de Rabbi Simon b. Joḥai," has not been preserved to us in its entirety. The work, in the form and scope given to it by its redactor, has been lost. Only fragments of it have been preserved in various compendia and in quotations found in works by medieval authors. From these fragments and quotations Dr. David Hoffmann has reconstructed a large part of the work and published it under the title "Mechilta de Rabbi Simon b. Jochai."[9]

The titles "Mekilta de Rabbi Ishmael" and "Mekilta de Rabbi Simon b. Joḥai" do not, however, indicate that the two teachers were the respective authors or originators of the works to which their names were attached, even though some rabbinic authorities may have so understood these descriptive titles. Most likely these additional titles were not intended to point to the respective authors or originators of the two Mekiltas. They merely meant to designate each Mekilta more specifically by mentioning, in each case, along with the term Mekilta the name of the teacher mentioned in its opening sentence.[10]

Neither one of these two Mekiltas to Exodus began with the very beginning of the book of Exodus, i.e., with ואלה שמות[11] (Exodus 1:1). The Mekilta de Rabbi Ishmael began, as in our editions, with Exodus 12:1[12] and the Mekilta de Rabbi Simon b. Joḥai began with the third chapter of Exodus which deals with

[7] See Lauterbach, The Arrangement and the Division of the Mekilta in Hebrew Union College Annual I (1924) p. 434, and Introduction to his Mekilta edition (Philadelphia 1933) pp. XXVIII–XXIX.

[8] See D. Hoffmann, Zur Einleitung in die halachischen Midrashim (Berlin 1887) p. 46 and I. Lewy, Ein Wort über die Mechilta des R. Simon (Breslau 1889) p. 3ff.

[9] Frankfurt a,M. 1905.

[10] See Lauterbach, The Name of the Mekilta p. 195 and Hoffmann, Zur Einleitung in die Mechilta de-Rabbi Simon b. Jochai (Frankfurt a,M. 1906) p. 6.

[11] See Lauterbach, The Arrangement and the Division of the Mekilta p. 434, and comp. I. Lewy op. cit. pp. 14–15.

[12] See Lauterbach ibid. l.c. for reference to medieval authorities who designate Ex. 12.1 as the beginning of the Mekilta de Rabbi Ishmael.

the revelation given to Moses from the thorn-bush. Thus since the two Mekiltas began with two different chapters of the book of Exodus they could be distinguished from one another by their opening chapters. In other words, one could, in each case, add to the term Mekilta an indication of the subject treated in the opening chapter. Indeed, some medieval authorities do so differentiate one Mekilta from the other. They designate the Mekilta de Rabbi Simon b. Johai, which in its opening chapter deals with the revelation from the thorn-bush סנה, Aramaic סניא, "The Mekilta of the Thorn-bush" מכילתא דסניא.[13] Thus R. Salomo ben Ha-Jathom in his commentary on the tractate Moed Katon פירוש מסכת משקין, ed. H. P. Chajes, (Berlin 1909), p. 31 gives the reference for a Mekilta passage which he quotes, and which he found in both Mekiltas, by saying: "As it is found in the Mekilta Desanya and in the Mekilta de Rabbi Ishmael." כדאיתא במכילתא דסניא ובמכילתא דרבי ישמעאל. The passage in question is found in the Mekilta de Rabbi Ishmael (Baḥodesh xi, ed. Friedmann 73a; Lauterbach II, p. 284) and is not found in Hoffmann's edition of the Mekilta de Rabbi Simon b. Johai. But R. Salomo did find it also in the Mekilta de Rabbi Simon b. Johai which he calls Mekilta Desanya. Chajes,[14] who was the first one to recognize the identity of the Mekilta Desanya with the Mekilta de R. Simon b. Johai, correctly points out that the passage in question referred to by R. Salomo is also found in *Midrash Tannaim to Deuteronomy* (ed. Hoffmann, p. 54) and originally had its place in the Mekilta de Rabbi Simon b. Johai, though Hoffmann did not embody it in his edition of the latter work.[15]

R. Hillel b. Eljakim also designates the Mekilta de R. Simon b. Johai as Mekilta Desanya. In his commentary on the Baraita

[13] They could not very well designate the Mekilta de Rabbi Ishmael which begins with החרש הזה לכם (Exod. 12.1) as מכילתא דההחרש, since such a designation would have led to a confusion of the Mekilta with the Pesikta which likewise contains a section beginning with החרש הזה לכם. As it is, the two works, Mekilta and Pesikta, are sometimes mistaken for one another and passages from the Pesikta are cited as coming from the Mekilta. See Appendix, No. 10.

[14] In the Introduction to his edition of R. Solomo's work, p. XXII.

[15] Comp. also J. N. Epstein, סנייא, מכילתא דסניא in Tarbiz III. (Jerusalem 1932) pp. 378–79.

of R. Ishmael (ed. A. Freimann in Livre D'Hommage A La Mémoire Du Dr. Samuel Poznanski (Warsaw 1927) Hebrew part p. 178) he says: וטמאי דתני בסניא והיה לכם למשטרת וגו' ר' עקיבא אומר נאמר כאן שמירה ונאמר להלן שמירה מה שמירה האמורה כאן דהיינו פסח שיהו מבקרין אותו ג' ימים קודם שחיטה אף שמירה האמורה להלן דהיינו בת ג' שנים קודם שחיטה [צ"ל ימים]. This saying, though in a slightly different form and not in the name of R. Akiba, is also found in the Mekilta de Rabbi Ishmael (Pisḥa V ed. Lauterbach (Philadelphia 1933) p. 39 and ed. Friedmann 5b). R. Hillel therefore indicates that he does not refer to the latter but that he quotes from the other Mekilta, the one designated as דסניא. This passage, exactly as quoted by R. Hillel, is found in the Midrash Hagadol to Exodus (ed. Hoffmann p. 95) and no doubt belongs to the Mekilta de Rabbi Simon b. Joḥai, even though it is not found in Hoffmann's edition. Again (ibid. l. c.) R. Hillel says: ואשכחן נמי בנין אב מארבעה כתובים דתנן בסנייא[16] ובריש בבא קמא לא השור כהרי המבעה דמייתי בנין אב מד' אבות נזיקין השור והבור והמבעה וההבער בהצד השוה. This passage is found in the Mekilta de Rabbi Simon b. Joḥai (Hoffmann p. 142). And since part of this saying is also found in the Mekilta de Rabbi Ishmael (Nezikin XIV end) R. Hillel who quotes the fuller statement points out that he refers to the passage as found in the Mekilta designated דסניא and not as it is found in the Mekilta de Rabbi Ishmael.

Another authority who designates the Mekilta de Rabbi Simon b. Joḥai as Mekilta Desanya is the Karaite Judah Hadassi. In his אשכול הכופר (Eupatoria 1836) p. 36a he says: וכן כתיב במכילתא דסיינא [דסניא[17] read] החדש הזה לכם וגו' מלמד הראהו הלבנה באצבעו ואמר לו כזה ראה וקדש לראשי חדשים וזה מעשה המנורה הראה למשה מנורה וכן זאת החיה, וזה לכם הטמא הראה לו חיות ושרצים ודגים. This passage is found in the Midrash Hagadol to Exodus (Hoffmann p. 92), introduced by תני רש"ב"י,[18] and no doubt belongs

---

[16] This is the correct reading. See Epstein op. cit. p. 377, note 3. The reading בסכייא in Freimann's edition is a mistake. A. Schwarz, Die Hermeneutische Induktion (Vienna 1909) p. 38, note 1 quotes: דתני בספרא which is also a mistake. The passage is not found in Sifra and R. Hillel did not quote it from Sifra.

[17] See Chajes op. cit. l.c.

[18] See Chajes op. cit. l.c. note 2. The passage is also found in the Pesikta d. R. Kahana (Buber 54b).

to the Mekilta de Rabbi Simon b. Joḥai, though it is not found in Hoffmann's edition of the latter. Since the passage in a slightly different form is also found in the Mekilta de Rabbi Ishmael (Pisḥa II. ed. Lauterbach p. 16 and Friedmann 2b), Hadassi indicates that he does not refer to the Mekilta de Rabbi Ishmael but to the other Mekilta, designated as דסניא.

A Mekilta Desanya is also mentioned in a book list found in a manuscript in the Library of Leningrad, as reported by A. Harkavy in Rahmer's Literaturblatt VII, (1878) p. 43. The item reads: מכילת דסניא הלכות מכתצרה, and Harkavy translates it: "Ein Halachot enthaltendes Compendium der Mechilta." It is more correct, however, to translate it: "A Mekilta (designated) Desanya, containing Halakot." This, no doubt, refers to the Mekilta de Rabbi Simon b. Joḥai, which, as we have seen, is designated דסניא because its opening chapter deals with the revelation from the thorn-bush סנה Aramaic סניא.

That the Mekilta de Rabbi Simon b. Joḥai actually began with the פרשת הסנה,[19] Exodus 3:1 as in Hoffmann's reconstructed edition is implicitly attested by R. Jacob b. Hananel of Sicily, author of the ילקוט תלמוד תורה in manuscript. R. Jacob of Sicily is one of those authorities who designate both tannaitic Midrashim to Exodus just by the name Mekilta without any additional description. In his Yalkut to Genesis[20] he quotes passages from both Mekiltas giving in each case merely the reference מכילתא without further specifying which of the Mekiltas he refers to. In those cases, however, in which the quotations are from the Mekilta de Rabbi Ishmael the reference מכילתא is followed by the word פרק, written out in full, and an accompanying numeral, indicating in which chapter of the Mekilta[21] the passage cited is found. It is different, however, in those cases in which the quotations are from the Mekilta de Rabbi Simon b. Joḥai. The following three Mekilta quotations in the Yalkut

[19] Comp. also J. Mann, Texts and Studies I. (Cincinnati 1931) p. 646 and note 24 on p. 664.

[20] The Ms. of this part of the Yalkut Talmud Torah is found in the Library of the Jewish Theological Seminary in New York.

[21] He considers the whole Mekilta as one single tractate. See Lauterbach, The Arrangement and the Division of the Mekilta op. cit. p. 456ff.

Talmud Torah to Genesis are from the Mekilta de Rabbi Simon b. Joḥai: In the section לך לך he quotes the following passage: מעולם לא יצא עבד או שפחה ממצרים בן חורין אלא הגר בלבד שנאמר ויצו עליו פרעה אנשים וישלחו אותו and מכילתא פר׳ is given as the reference. This passage is actually found in the very opening paragraph of the Mekilta de Rabbi Simon b. Joḥai (Hoffmann p. 1). The abbreviation פר׳, following the reference מכילתא in the Yalkut Talmud Torah, must therefore stand for פרשה ראשונה or פיסקא ראשונה,[22] thus indicating that the passage cited is in the very first section of the Mekilta from which it is quoted, i. e., the Mekilta de Rabbi Simon b. Joḥai.

To Genesis 49:1 he quotes the following passage: האספו ואגידה לכם מה עשה השליך מקל לפניהם ונעשה נחש ואחז בו ונעשה מקל הוציא ידו לפניהם ונעשית כשלו חזר והכניסה לחיקו ונעשית כבשרו אמר להם יודע אני שמצרים משעבדים אתכם ראו שאם יבא אדם ויטעה אתכם ויאמר לכם הגיע זמן אל תאמינו בו ואם יעשה לפניכם כאותות האלה [האמינו בו] וכשבא משה ועשה לישראל אותן האותות מיד האמינו שנאמר ויעש האותות לעיני העם ויאמן העם. The reference for this passage is given as ילמדנו ומכילתא. The passage is also found in Midrash Hagadol to Exodus (on the verse Exodus 4:30, Hoffmann p. 42) and Hoffmann (ibidem note 5) remarks that he could not find the source of this saying מאמר זה לא מצאתי. But there is no doubt that its source is the Mekilta de Rabbi Simon b. Joḥai which R. Jacob of Sicily calls simply Mekilta. Again to Genesis 50:25 he quotes as follows: והעליתם את עצמותי מזה אתכם אמר להם יוסף קברו אותו בכל מקום שתרצו שכן מקובל אני שאיני [שאין] נכנס במערה ליקבר בה אלא ג׳ אבות פוסק הוא [בין] כי׳[23] אשר כריתי לי אמהות דכתיב וג׳ and מכילתא is given as the reference. This passage is from the Mekilta de Rabbi Simon b. Joḥai. It is quoted by Naḥmanides in his Pentateuch-commentary to Genesis 49:31 and introduced by: וראיתי במכילתא דר׳ שמעון בן יוחאי on the basis of which Hoffmann has embodied it in his edition (p. 39–40). But R. Jacob of Sicily calls this Mekilta simply מכילתא.

---

[22] The Mekilta de Rabbi Simon was divided according to chapters, פרשיות, or sections, פיסקאות; see Hoffmann, p. 137, note 4.

[23] The corrections in brackets are according to the readings given by Ramban.

R. Israel Ibn Al-Nakawa in his *Menorat Ha-Maor*[24] likewise quotes passages from both Mekiltas giving in each case merely the reference מכילתא without further specify ing to which of the two Mekiltas he refers.[25]

So also does R. Moses b. Levi Najara in his commentary on the Pentateuch לקח טוב (Constantinople 1571). He quotes passages from the Mekilta de Rabbi Ishmael introducing them merely by ואמר במכילתא "It says in the Mekilta" and he also quotes passages from the Mekilta de Rabbi Simon b. Joḥai and likewise introduces them merely by ואמר במכילתא "It says in the Mekilta."[26]

Thus we see that many medieval authorities do not distinguish at all between these two tannaitic Midrashim to Exodus but call both of them merely by the name Mekilta without any additional description. We also find that even authorities who in most cases do distinguish between these two Mekiltas by calling the one "Mekilta de Rabbi Ishmael" or merely "Mekilta" and the other "Mekilta de Rabbi Simon b. Joḥai" or "Another Mekilta" are not always consistent in so differentiating them. They occasionally drop these additional descriptions and refer to the Mekilta of Rabbi Simon b. Joḥai also by the name Mekilta alone.[27] Now, since so many medieval authorities in so many instances use the name Mekilta also to designate a Midrash to Exodus other than the one usually called "Mekilta de Rabbi Ishmael," it would seem absurd to look only in the latter work for all quotations for which medieval authorities give "Mekilta" as the source. How can one assume that by "Mekilta" they referred only to the Mekilta de Rabbi Ishmael when, as we have seen, in many instances they used this name to designate another work? We certainly have no right to assume that those authorities who quote passages from a Mekilta which are not

[24] Edited by H. G. Enelow, vols. 1–4, New York, 1929–1932.

[25] For all the Mekilta quotations by Al-Nakawa, see Enelow, volume 4, Index, p. 130 and comp. Appendix, Nos. 7–11.

[26] See לקח טוב section משפטים 25d and 33b.

[27] E.g. Nahmanides in his commentary on the Torah, to Num. 25.29. Comp. I Lewy op. cit. pp. 3–4.

found in our Mekilta de Rabbi Ishmael, had before them the
latter work in larger form or scope.

In the first place it must be remembered that the term מכילתא,
while it came to be used as a special designation for the two
tannaitic Midrashim to Exodus, still retained its original meaning
of tractate or compendium and could therefore denote any
collection of halakic, or even agadic sayings. In fact, it is frequently used interchangeably with מסכת to refer to a tractate of
the Mishnah or Tosefta, the Babylonian or Palestinian Gemara.
Hence when medieval authorities quote a Midrashic passage
and give מכילתא as its source we cannot say definitely that they
had in mind either of the two Midrashim to Exodus, especially
so designated. They may just as well have had reference to
any collection of midrashic sayings which they designate as
מכילתא, in the sense of tractate, or compendium. Thus in cases
where we find two different authorities who quote the same
passage, one giving as its source Mekilta and the other referring
it to another work or to just a Midrash,[28] it is more likely that
the one giving as his reference מכילתא meant by it the same
midrashic work which the other authority gives as the source
for the saying than to assume that there is a real conflict between
the two authorities.

Likewise when we find an author who quotes a midrashic
passage in one of his works and gives as its source מכילתא and in
another work quotes the same passage and gives as its source
another Midrash, it is most likely that in the one work where
he gives מכילתא as the reference for the saying quoted, he uses
the term מכילתא in the sense of tractate to designate the very
Midrash named in the other work.[29]

The same explanation would account for the fact that some
authorities, quoting passages from the Pesikta, give as reference
מכילתא.[30] They merely used the latter term in the sense of
tractate or collection. In this case, however, it may also be
that the authorities confused the two works Mekilta and Pesikta

[28] For illustrations see Appendix, No. 7.
[29] For an illustration see Appendix, No. 1.
[30] Comp. above note 13 and see Appendix, Nos. 3 and 10 for illustrations.

with one another, since each consists of a group of tractates or treatises פיסקאות or מסכתות.

In some instances the reference to the Mekilta may be due to an error on the part of the author who quotes from a secondary source. Some authors frequently quote passages which they read only in the Yalkut, but instead of giving as their reference the Yalkut where alone they saw the passage, they give as reference the source whence Yalkut quotes. In some cases, however, the reference to the source for a saying is missing in the Yalkut. The author who quotes such a saying from the Yalkut and wishing to give the source of the Yalkut finds no reference to that source. He concludes—and in some cases, but not in all, such a conclusion is justified—that the source for this saying or passage is the same as the one given by the Yalkut for the saying immediately preceding. If the latter happens to be from the Mekilta, our author concludes that the passage following it was also quoted by the Yalkut from the Mekilta; he accordingly gives the Mekilta as the reference.[31]

Again in many instances a saying of the Mekilta has its parallel in another Midrash where, however, it is enlarged by some additions or elaborations. An author quoting the saying with these additions—or one of the additional sayings found in the parallel alone—and remembering part of the saying from the Mekilta, quotes the whole of it as coming from the Mekilta.[32]

Thus, in many instances when passages not found in our Mekilta are quoted as coming from a Mekilta it is quite likely that the author giving the reference Mekilta either did not have in mind any of the two Midrashim to Exodus so designated but referred to another midrashic collection which he calls מכילתא, or he quoted second hand and had not actually seen the passage in question in the Mekilta itself.

But even in such cases in which there can be no doubt that the author in giving מכילתא as his reference had in mind a Midrash to Exodus so designated in which he actually saw the passage cited, we would not be justified in assuming that he referred to

[31] See for an illustration Appendix No. 16.
[32] See Appendix, No. 4 for an illustration.

that Mekilta which is usually designated as Mekilta de Rabbi
Ishmael and which has been preserved to us in complete form.
He very likely had in mind the other Mekilta, the one frequently
designated as the Mekilta de Rabbi Simon b. Joḥai of which
only part has been preserved to us and which in the parts lost
to us may well have contained the saying quoted by that
author.[33]

---

[33] Comp. Hoffmann, Zur Einleitung in die halachischen Midrashim p. 47.
Even in such cases where במכילתא דרבי ישמעאל is given as the source for a
quotation, we cannot always be certain that the author, quoting the passage,
had reference to the Mekilta de Rabbi Ishmael. The author may have had
in mind the Mekilta de Rabbi Simon b. Joḥai. But his reference, written
in abbreviation במכילתא דר׳ש was mistaken by a copyist for דר׳ יש and then
understood to stand for דר׳ ישמעאל. In some cases the author may have used
the term מכילתא in the sense of tractate or collection, and when he said במכילתא
דריש he meant, "in a collection or tractate it is interpreted." But the word
דריש "it is interpreted" was taken by some copyist for an abbreviation of
דר׳ ישמעאל.

## APPENDIX

The following is a list of passages quoted by rabbinic authorities as being from a Mekilta but not found in our Mekilta de Rabbi Ishmael. It supplements the list published by M. Friedmann in his edition of the Mekilta (Vienna 1870), הוספה שנייה pp. 119–124. Both these lists, however, do not completely exhaust the number of such alleged Mekiltaquotations. Besides the passages cited in this list I have a list of ten other such Mekilta-quotations which, however, largely because of limited space, I cannot discuss here. And, of course, there may be other such alleged Mekilta-quotations which I have not come across. I limit myself in this list to such Mekiltaquotations as illustrate certain points or prove statements made in this essay. The passages are numbered and arranged in the chronological order of the authorities quoting them. Each passage is followed by a brief discussion as to whether the author, giving מכילתא as the source for his quotation had reference to either one of the two Midrashim to Exodus, known by that name, or merely used the term מכילתא, in the sense of tractate or collection, by which he designated some other midrashic work.

(1) Rashi in his commentary to Malachi, 1, 1 says: מכאן דרשו רז״ל בברייתא דמכילתא שכל הנביאים עמדו בסיני ושם נמסרו להם כל הנבואות וכן ישעיה אמר מעת היותה שם אני וגו'. Rashi himself in his commentary to Isaiah 48, 6 quotes this passage as coming from מדרש אגדה ר' תנחומא. Evidently when in his commentary to Malachi he gives as the source of this saying ברייתא דמכילתא he simply means "A Baraita in a midrashic collection" and refers to the Midrash Agada of R. Tanḥuma which he quotes in his commentary to Isaiah.

(2) R. Joseph Kara in his commentary to Kings, ed. Eppenstein in Jahrbuch der Jüdisch-Literarischen Gesellschaft XIII; (Frankfurt a.M. 1920) p. 47 cites the following midrashic saying: טיפה שיצתה מאותו הצדיק מיכיהו שהיכה חבירו הכה ופצוע כפרה על ישראל and adds to it: כן מפורש במכילתא. This saying is not found in the Mekilta nor in any other Midrash known to me (Comp. Eppenstein's remark ibid. l. c. note 5). Kara evidently

used the term מכילתא to designate some compedium or Midrashic collection and not the Mekilta de R. Ishmael. The latter work Kara considered as part of the Sifre and mentions it by the name Sifre. See above, note 1.

(3) R. Samuel b. Meir רשב'ם, in his commentary on the Torah, ed. D. Rosin (Breslau 1881) p. 88, commenting on Exod. 6, 14, says מפרש במכילתא אילו שלשה שבטים שנינה אותם יעקב בעת צוואתו ייחסם עתה הכתוב להודיע שחשובים הם. This saying is not found in our Mekilta de Rabbi Ishmael. It is found in Midrash Hagadol to Exodus (Hoffmann p. 53) and belongs to the Mekilta de Rabbi Simon b. Joḥai which Rashbam designates just by the name Mekilta. The saying is also found in Pesikta Rabbati (Friedmann 28b). Possibly Rashbam used the term מכילתא in the sense of a midrashic collection and refers by it to the Pesikta Rabbati.

(4) R. Moses b. Nachman רמב'ן in his commentary on the Torah, Exod. 12, 31 says: וכך אמרו במכילתא ויקרא למשה ולאהרן לילה ויאמר קומו צאו אמר לו משה כך נצטוינו ואתם לא תצאו איש מפתח ביתו עד בקר וכי גנבים אנחנו שנצא בלילה לא נצא אלא ביד רמה ביד רמה לעיני כל מצרים. Only part of this saying is found in our Mekilta, Pisḥa XIII (Friedmann 13b; Lauterbach I, p. 100). The whole saying, in content exactly as given by Ramban though in wording and arrangement slightly different, is found in Midrash Thillim to Ps. 113.2 (Buber 235a). Ramban evidently quoted from Midrash Thillim (comp. Yalkut to Exod. paragraph 208 where the saying from Midrash Thillim, שוחר טוב, is quoted in the form cited by Ramban). But remembering part of the saying from the Mekilta, he quotes the whole saying as coming from the Mekilta.

(5) R. Shemtob b. Abraham in his מגדל עז to Yad, הלכות גניבה IX says: לשון מכילתא אזהרה לגונב נפש מנין ר' יאשיה אומר מלא תגנוב ר' יונתן אומר מלא ימכרו ממכרת עבד ולא פליני מר קא חשיב לאו דגניבה ומר קא חשיב לאו דמכירה. In this form this Baraita is not found in our Mekilta. R. Shemtob quotes from Talmud Sanhedrin 86a where this Baraita with the Amoraic comment ולא פליני וגו' is found. R. Shemtob either uses the term מכילתא

in the sense of Baraita (comp. Lauterbach, The Name of the Mekilta, op. cit. p. 186), or he uses it in the sense of מסכתא and refers to the מסכת סנהדרין of the Talmud. It is also possible that since the other Baraita following the amoraic comment ולא פליני . . . לאו דמכירה quoted there in Sanhedrin, is from the Mekilta Baḥodesh VIII (Friedmann 70b; Lauterbach II. p. 260–61) R. Shemtob assumed that the first Baraita likewise was from the Mekilta.

(6) R. Jacob Asheri in his commentary on the Torah Exod. 14.11 (Hannover 1838) p. 35d says: ובמכילתא מפרש שמתחלה צעקו לה' לתת בלב פרעה לשוב מעליהם וכשראו שלא היה חוזר וקרב אליהם אמרו לא נתקבלה תפלתנו ונכנסה בלבם להרהר אחר משה. This passage is not found in our Mekilta. The passage in the Mekilta Beshallaḥ III (Friedmann 28a; Lauterbach p. 209) reads only: מאחר שנתנו שאור בעיסה באו לפני משה. R. Jacob Asheri here actually quotes the interpretation given to this short Mekilta passage by Ramban in his Torah commentary Exod. 14.11 [Comp. also R. Tobia b. Eliezer in his לקח טוב to this verse (Buber p. 86) and the Mekilta commentary זה ינחמנו ad loc.]. And when he says: במכילתא מפרש he really refers to Ramban who so interprets the Mekilta.

(7) In R. Israel Al-Nakawa's מנורת המאור (ed. Enelow) II, p. 189, we read: וגרסינן במכילתא ומי כעטך כישראל גוי אחד בארץ, שלשה מעידין זה את זה, הב"ה, הב"ה וישראל ושבת. הב"ה וישראל מעידין על השבת שהוא יום מנוחה, שנא' ושמרו בני ישראל את השבת לעשות את השבת לדורותם ברית עולם ביני ובין בני ישראל אות היא לעולם כי ששת ימים עשה ה' את השמים ואת הארץ וביום השביעי שבת וינפש. הנה בפסוקים האלה שמו של הב"ה וישראל מעידין שברא הב"ה את השמים ואת הארץ וביום השביעי שבת וינפש. ישראל ושבת בהב"ה שהוא אחד, שנא' ועל הר סיני ירדת ודבר עמהם מן השמים ותתן להם משפטים ישרים ותורות אמת חקים ומצות טובים, וכתיב ואת שבת קדשך הודעת להם ומצות וחוקים ותורה צוית להם ביד משה עבדך. הנה שישראל ושבת מעידין בהב"ה. הב"ה ושבת מעידין בישראל שהם יחידים באומות, שנא' והיה אם שמוע תשמעו בקולי ושמרתם את בריתי והייתם לי סגולה מכל העמים. הנה שהב"ה ושבת מעידין בישראל שהם יחידים באומות. Tossafot Ḥagigah 3b s.v. מי כעטך ישראל and Tur Oraḥ Ḥayyim 292 quote this saying from a Midrash. Comp. also Shibbole Ha-Leket 126 (Buber p. 90). Al-Nakawa here uses the term מכילתא merely to designate a midrashic collection.

(8) Ibid. p. 384 we read: כדגרסינן במכילתא ועניתם את נפשותיכם
בתשעה לחדש, יכול בתשעה, ת"ל בערב, אי בערב יכול משתחשך, ת"ל בתשעה.
הא כיצד, מתחיל ומתענה מבעוד יום, מכאן שמוסיפין מחול על הקדש. ואין לי
אלא בכניסתו, ביציאתו מנין, ת"ל מערב עד ערב. This is found in Sifra
Emor XIV (Weiss 102a).

(9) Ibid. III p. 222: כדגרסינן במכילתא בני אם תקח אמרי ומצותי
תצפון אתך. אמ' הב"ה לישראל על הר סיני, אם זכיתם להצפין ולקבל תורתי
ולעשות אותה אני מציל אתכם משלש פורעניות, ממלחמת גוג ומגוג ומחבלו של
משיח ומדינה של גיהנם. In this form the passage is found in Midrash
Mishle 2.1 (ed. Buber p. 48). A similar saying about the reward
for observing the Sabbath is found in our Mekilta Vayassa
(Friedmann 50b; Lauterbach II, Chapter V and p. 120).

(10) Ibid IV p. 208: וגרסינן במכילתא יתום לא ישפוטו וריב אלמנה
לא יבא אליהם. ר' אלעזר אומר, בראשונה היה אדם מת בירושלים והיו ממנין
אפוטרופוס על היתומים, והיתה אלמנה תובעת כתובתה אצל היתומים, והם
הולכים אצל הדיינין ומוצאין אותם עם האפוטרופוס. וריב אלמנה לא יבא
אליהם. א"ר יוחנן, בראשונה היה אדם עולה לדון בירושלים, והיה הדיין אומ'
לו, בקע לי שני בקעיות של עצים, מלא לי שתי חביות מים, והיו יציאותיו כלים,
והיה יוצא בפחי נפש. והיתה האלמנה פוגעת בו בדרך, ואומרת לו, מה נעשה
בדינך, והוא אומר לה על כל יציאותי לא הועילו לו כלום. והיתה אומרת, ומה אם
זה, שהוא איש, לא הועילו לו כלום, אני, שאני אלמנה, על אחת כמה וכמה.
חוזרת לה. הה"ד וריב אלמנה לא יבא אליהם. This passage is found in
the Pesikta d.R. Kahana (Buber p. 123a). But Al-Nakawa
uses the term מכילתא to designate the Pesikta. In II p. 366
and III p. 76 he also quotes passages from the Pesikta and
introduces them by גרסינן במכילתא. About the last two quotations
comp. Friedmann op. cit. p. 123b.

(11) Ibid. IV p. 337: גרסינן במכילתא מעשה ברוכל אחד שהיה מסבב
בעיירות, והיה מכריז ואומר, מי מבקש סם חיים. שמעה בתו של ר' ינאי, נכנסה
לאביה והגידה לו. אמר לה, לכי קראי לו. כיון שבא, אמ' לו ר' ינאי, איזה
כוס של חיים אתה מוכר. אמ' לו, כוס שאני מוכר אתה מוכרו. אמ' לו, אעפ"כ
הודיעני. אמ', והלא כתי' מי האיש החפץ חיים אוהב ימים לראות טוב, נצור
לשונך מרע ושפתיך מדבר מרמה. This passage is found in Tanḥuma
מצורע 5 (Buber p. 45). Al-Nakawa uses the term מכילתא, in the
sense of a midrashic collection, to designate the Tanḥuma
Midrash.

(12) R. Solomo Alkabez in his מנות הלוי (Lemberg 1913) p. 79
quotes as follows: אמרו במכילתא תני בשם ר' נתן ד' אריות ונ' דובים

193

הכה דוד באותו היום דכתיב נם את הארי ארי הארי ואת הארי דוב הדוב וגם הדוב.
This passage is found in Midrash Shemuel ch. XX (Buber
p. 54). Alkabez uses the term מכילתא, in the sense of a midrashic
collection, to designate the Midrash Shemuel.

(13) In a Manuscript in the British Museum, quoted by
Alexander Marx in J.Q.R. n. s. VII (1916–1917) p. 131, there
is found the following passage: אלה תולדות נח קאל פי אל מכילתא
למה נאמר בנח איש צדיק אלא שהיו אנשי דורו כנשים. I could not locate
this saying in any of the known Midrashim. The author no
doubt uses the term מכילתא, in the sense of a compendium and
midrashic collection. We certainly cannot draw any conclusions
from this quotation as to the question whether there ever was
a Mekilta to Genesis (comp. Enelow op. cit. IV, introduction
p. 24, note 2).

(14) In the commentary on the Torah לקח טוב by R. Moses
b. Levi Najara (Constantinople 1571) p. 36a we read as follows:
ועוד איתא במכילתא למה נעשה מעצי שטים שהתורה נקראת עץ חיים שנאמר עץ
חיים היא וכו' ונתנה בתוכו ולמה צפהו זהב לפי שדברי תורה נחמדים מזהב
ומפז רב. This passage is not found in either of our two Mekiltas.
In Yalkut to Exod. paragraph 368 it is quoted from אלה הדברים
זוטא. Najara no doubt uses the term מכילתא, in the sense of a
collection, to refer either to the Yalkut itself, or to the אלה
הדברים זוטא, quoted by the Yalkut.

(15) Ibid. p. 37a: במכלתא ואתה תצוה למדנו שהצווי מיד בשעת מעשה
ולדורות מנין תלמוד לומר צו את בני ישראל ויקחו אליך שמן זית זך הא למדנו
שהצווי מיד ולדורות מצווי הזה נמצינו לכל הצוואות שבתורה. This passage
is found in Siphre Numbers 1 (Friedmann 1a) and Yalkut
to Exodus 337 quotes it from Sifre. Najara probably quoted
from the Yalkut for which he uses the designation מכילתא, in the
sense of a collection (see preceding number). It is also possible
that he quoted from the Sifre, but having noticed that many
authorities call the Mekilta by the name of Sifre, he believed
the two names to be interchangeable; hence he called the Sifre
by the name Mekilta.

(16) In ראשית חכמה by R. Elijah b. Moses De Vidas שער האהבה
ch. VI (Wilna 1911) p. 150 we read: וכן דרשו גם כן במכילתא על
פסוק וישכם יהושע בבקר מלמד שזריזין מקדימין למצות. This passage is

found in Yalkut to Joshua paragraph 13 on the verse 3.1, without any indication of its source. However, preceding it is quoted a saying from the Mekilta Pisḥa XI (Friedmann 11b; Lauterbach I p. 85–86) and following it there is another saying from the Mekilta Beshallaḥ VI (Friedmann ɔ1b–32a; Lauterbach I p. 237–38). Vïdas quoted from the Yalkut. But finding this saying imbedded between the two passages from the Mekilta he concluded that this saying likewise had its source in the Mekilta and accordingly he gives as its source במכילתא.

# The 'Plain' Meaning of Scripture in Early Jewish Exegesis

*by*

RAPHAEL LOEWE

THE HISTORICAL STUDY of biblical exegesis, both Jewish and Christian, is a field in which generalisation is perilous, and any patterns that the investigator may discern he will, if he is wise, postulate but tentatively. In the first place, at the very least until the age of printing our evidence must be incomplete: scribes were not concerned to multiply copies of such of the works of their contemporaries or immediate predecessors as did not command a popular reception, and at the oral stage of transmission similar considerations render survival even more hazardous. Enough fragmentary commentaries and works rarely or uniquely preserved survive to remind us that many more must be deemed to have disappeared. Secondly, for both the Jewish exegete from post-tannaitic times onwards and for his Christian *confrère* from the Carolingian period, an authoritative tradition of interpretation loaded the scales heavily in favour of conservatism. Reform tends to proclaim itself a mere reversion to the authentic teaching of an earlier and purer form of traditional doctrine; innovation is liable to be dissembled, and the author of it prone to convince himself that there is no intrinsic difference between his own views and those of his predecessors, with the result that he may maintain their terminology whilst unavowedly attaching to it an altered signification. All pointers towards the latter process require fresh scrutiny in the case of each individual commentator, and we shall scarcely be justified in ascribing his exegesis to the effect of *Zeitgeist* — e.g. the impact on the Jewish biblical scholar of Christianity, Karaism, or Arabic philosophy — until we have compared his findings with his own terminological description of them. Some framework is, however, essential, for the plotting of such a study as this, and with the *caveat* just mentioned the conventional periods of Jewish historiography may provide it. On the present occasion our *terminus ad quem* will be the end of the amoraic age.

The problem that is here addressed revolves round the isolation of what, if anything, early Jewish biblical exegesis understood by the 'plain' or 'simple' meaning of the text. Did it constitute, for the early exegete, a positive concept the definition of which he could without difficulty adduce? Or was it rather a mere label, convenient as a description of the alternative to any given 'applied' sense — that is to say, a concept that is essentially negative except insofar as the exegete, himself rejecting an 'applied' sense, would invest any alternative description (which he might insist was 'plain') with just that aspect of the matter which carried, for him, supreme validity? If the latter is the case, exegesis allegedly 'plain' will become, in the very moment that objectivity is explicitly claimed for it, as patient of subjective handling as is 'applied'. The investigation must, of course, take note of the fact that for nearly every Jewish exegete the ultimate meaning of the Bible lies in its impact upon Jewish conduct, as response to a divinely vouchsafed opportunity; so that halakhic considerations will frequently obsess the expository endeavours of the Jewish biblical scholar of antiquity and the middle ages, just as the exegetes of Qumran were obsessed, to an even greater extent, by eschatological ones. [1] We shall have to consider whether such obsession is so intense as effectively to distort the natural meaning of such technical terms as the commentator may employ even in contexts where halakhic implication is remote or altogether absent. Consequently, we shall proceed first by asking what area remains over for the 'plain' meaning of scripture after the scope of the allegorical or other 'applied' sense has been either explicitly defined by the exegete himself, or empirically recovered from analysis of his exegesis. We shall also examine the terminology employed, and the treatment accorded to a few sample texts alternative explanations of which were advanced by pairs of controversialists, and attempt such correlation as seems possible. In this way we shall, it is hoped, avoid exposing ourselves to the danger of superimposing on the source material subjective notions as to the meaning of 'plain' exegesis. In case, however, such superimposition has inadvertently been allowed play at any point in the present study, it may help the reader to discount it if the following definition is adduced. That only is properly to be regarded as plain, straightforward, or simple exegesis which corresponds to the totality of

---

1. For the Dead Sea sect the *pesher*, like its corollary *raz*, was the subject of divine revelation and not attainable by means of ordinary, human, intellectual processes; so that even had their interpretation been straightforward rather than eschatological, the method by which it was achieved would have rendered the description 'plain' exegesis scarcely apposite. See F.F. Bruce, *Biblical Exegesis in the Qumran Texts*[2], 1960, pp. 8, 11, 17f., and C. Roth, *The Subject Matter of Qumran Exegesis, Vetus Testamentum* x, 1, 1960.

the meaning(s) intended by the writer; any further significance(s), however emotionally charged, discovered in his message by readers in the
light of subsequent events, lie beyond the purview of 'plain' exegesis. But
the present writer would, in proffering that definition, emphasise its
irrelevance for the investigation here being prosecuted, in which the
evidence must be allowed to speak for itself.

For our present purpose it is not feasible to treat as evidence the various
early translations of the Bible made by Jews for internal Jewish or for
controversial use. The tendencies of these can, it is true, be established;
but since these responsible for them did not provide them with prefaces,
we cannot properly say whether the translators had convinced themselves
that they were invariably expressing the primary meaning of their original
as closely as they might, or were consciously rendering the words in accordance with that sense which, in their opinion, conveyed the ultimate
value of the text. In the unique instance of the prologue to the Greek
*Ecclesiasticus* by Ben Sira's grandson, the latter's plea for the reader's
indulgence wherever he may seem to fail (ἀδυναμεῖν) in choice of language
in any point regarding the interpretation (i.e. translation, ἑρμηνείαν) into
which great pains have been put, [1a] is followed up by the remark that
things said in Hebrew do not retain their meaning accurately (οὐ γὰρ
ἰσοδοναμεῖ) when translated. It is clear that the grandson did not attempt
a slavish translation; and his grandfather's wisdom being direct rather
than allusive, it is improbable that he was much puzzled by problems of
selecting the primary meaning from a number of possible constructions of
the original text. But even disregarding this, the existence of recensional
problems both Hebrew and Greek makes any attempt to reconstruct the
exegetical canons of the younger Ben Sira unprofitable. [2] As regards the
words of *Neh.* viii:8 (ending *wayyavinu ba-Miqra'*), in which rabbinic
comment [3] was able to discover a reference to various hermeneutic and
exegetical processes, the Greek translator, who had a somewhat different
original before him, restricts himself to a bald rendering of the facts; yet

---

1a. ἐφ' οἷς ἂν δοκῶμεν τῶν κατὰ τὴν ἑρμηνείαν πεφιλοπονημένων τισὶν τῶν
λέξεων ἀδυναμεῖν. Cf. J. H. A. Hart, *Ecclesiasticus in Greek*, 1909, p. 267; W. O. E.
Oesterley and G. H. Box in R. H. Charles, *Apocrypha and Pseudepigrapha*, I,
1913, p. 316.

2. Oesterley, *Ecclesiasticus* (Cambridge Bible Series), 1912, p. xcivf. It may be
noted that the secondary Greek text aims, *inter alia*, at greater clarification of the
original; *ibid.*, p. xcviii. M. Z. Segal, *Sefer Ben Sira Ha-Shalem* (Jerusalem, 1953),
p. ‎א—ב. Cf. *infra*, p. 162 f.

3. Babylonian Talmud *Nedarim* 37b, *Meg.* 3a.

in his choice of the word διέστελλεν (= *defined precisely*) [4] it may be that we have an attempt to saddle some underlying derivative of פרש [5] (corresponding to מפרש in the Massoretic text) with the notion of an officially promulgated interpretation of the *Torah* couched in mandatory terms, the verb διαστέλλειν including also amongst its meanings that of *giving orders*. A somewhat similar rabbinic view regarding the authority of the Targum will be discussed below (p. 182f.). Even if this suggestion is correct, the Greek *Esdras* passage is no more than a straw in the wind, evocative of the *halakhah*-laden atmosphere of the Palestinian schools; we cannot apply such incidental pointers as a measuring-rod to the text as it left the translators' hands.

Although there is no need to suppose that rabbinic hermeneutics have an other than internally Jewish origin, our present search may be better orienteed if we begin by summarising the main lines of the Greek approach to the allegorical handling of Homer. The history of Homeric allegorism, which long antedates biblical allegorism, is instructive as indicating something of the reaction against the allegorical method and the limitations that some of the philosophers came to accept or to insist on regarding its application. This will lead us to Philo and thence back to Jewish Palestine.

Homeric allegorism, [6] which ascends to the 6th century B.C.E., was not

---

4. *2 Esdras* xviii:8 καὶ ἀνέγνωσαν ἐν βιβλίῳ νόμου τοῦ θεοῦ, καὶ ἐδίδαξεν Ἔσδρας καὶ διέστελλεν ἐν ἐπιστήμῃ κυρίου, καὶ συνῆκεν ὁ λαὸς ἐν τῇ ἀναγνώσει. The parallel text (*1 Esdras* ix:49) has, corresponding to מפרש ושום שכל ויבינו במקרא, the words 'ἐμφυσιοῦντες ἅμα τὴν ἀνάγνωσιν. 'ἐμφυσιοῦν (= *inspire, instil into*) occurs in biblical Greek elsewhere at v. 55 only (ὅτι καὶ 'ἐνεφυσιώθησαν ἐν τοῖς ῥήμασιν = *Neh.* viii:13 כי הבינו בדברים). ἐμφυσιοῦν should not be confused with ἐμφυσᾶν = *inflate*, which renders נשב, נפח, פוח (*Sirach* xliii:4) as well as standing apparently for פוק (*Nah.* ii:1) and סדר (*1 Kings* xvii:21, cf. also *John* xx:22). It may be observed that in several of the instances of 'ἐμφυσιοῦν listed in the Greek lexicon (*L.* & *S⁹*), the context implies the inculcation of a notion that has *authoritative* backing; cf. e.g. an inscription from Magnesia on the Maeander, referring to a divinely prognosticated sign, *c.* 200 B.C.E., ενεφυσιωσαν τε κ[αι τοις γινομε]νοις εξ εαυτων τημ βουλησιν του θεου την κατα [τον χρησμον]. This may suggest that *1 Esdras* ix:49, in its inclusion of ἐμφυσιοῦντες, reflects a similar recognition of a reference to hermeneutics to that discovered in the text by the rabbinic references cited in note 3, analogously perhaps to διέστελλεν in *2 Esdras*.

5. not elsewhere = διαστέλλειν, but cf. *Ps.* lxvii:15, *1 Sam.* iii:1.

6. On Greek Allegorism see J. Tate, *Classical Review* 41, 1927, p. 214; also *Classical Quarterly*, 23, 1929, pp. 41, 142f.; 24, 1930, p. 1f.; 28, 1934, pp. 105f., 107f. More briefly in the *Oxford Classical Dictionary*, ed. M. Cary etc., 1949, *s.v. Allegory, Greek.* Cf. I. Heinemann, *Altjüdische Allegoristik*, Breslau, 1936, p. 11f.

(it is now thought) in origin an apologetic device invented to account for morally objectionable passages in the poems. The earliest philosophers were reacting against the works of Homer and Hesiod on which they had been brought up, and as their own speculative thought progressed they assumed that the poets had, like themselves, also been speculative thinkers. In revising and appropriating their mythology they were 'correcting' what they held to be the errors of their presumed predecessors. Apologetic allegorism, which became the stock-in-trade of the grammarians, is a secondary development; much play was made of etymology [6a] as a pointer to the supposedly 'true' meaning, and it became an axiom with the grammarians that since Homer cannot lie, he must be deemed to have composed in such terms as to point unmistakeably to the necessity of allegorical interpretation. Rejected in the 2nd century B.C.E. by the Homeric scholar Aristarchus, this negative allegorism nevertheless survived — doubtless sustained by the continued resort to positive allegorism as an instrument of metaphysical speculation on the part of the Stoics.

Philosophy was, indeed, to retain positive allegorism as a tool right up to Neoplatonism. In asserting that they could find their own theories implicitly conveyed in the text of Homer, the allegorists (in particular the Neoplatonists) oscillated between two incompatible presuppositions, which they sometimes nevertheless combined in defiance of logic. Homer's assumed omniscience, on the one hand, gave rise to what has been termed [pseudo-]historic allegorism, i.e. the notion that Homer had of set purpose encoded a philosophically meaningful communication, the truth of which it is the function of the allegorist to disentangle. The alternative assumption regarded Homer as the object of demoniac possession such as affected oracular priests with frenzy, under the inspiration of which he had uttered sayings originating from God Himself. Such a view leads to so-called intrinsic allegorism: the allegorist discards any pretence that the meaning which he claims to identify as integral and essential to the poem bears any necessary relation to the primary meaning of the words used by the poet himself. [7]

See now also E. E. Hallewy in *Tarbiz* xxxi, 2, 1961, p. 157f., on *Biblical Midrash and Homeric Exegesis* (Hebrew, with English summary).

6a. See most recently U. Treu, *Etymologie und Allegorie bei Klemens von Alexandrien, Studia Patristica iv* (= *Texte u. Untersuchungen* 79), Berlin, 1961, p.191f.

7. Cf. T.B. *Soṭah* 12b. Pharaoh's daughter 'prophesies' unconsciously (מתנבאה שלא מדעתה) (R. Yoḥanan); R. Eleazar compares the frenzied ejaculations of necromancers etc.

It was the wrong-headedness of the latter procedure, from the point of view of the responsible philosopher, that elicited from Plato good-humoured disassociation [8]: any allegorical interpretation being necessarily subjective, it can be no valid substitute for reasoned argument through dialectic. If allegorical meanings are indeed present, they are appropriate matter for the meanly educated and rustic intelligence with its exaggerated respect for the written word, but are at best but 'right opinion', not having been scientifically established. As regards education, any myths embodying a reprobate moral code are unacceptable, since the young will not be able to distinguish any underlying meaning (ὑπόνοια[9]: ἀλληγορία and the verb were first used in this sense by the Stoic Cleanthes, 331–232 B.C.E.) from the narrative (λόγος) and the principle implied therein (τύπος, νόμος, δόξα). Aristotle, as one would expect, passes over allegory in silence; Homer is subject to the same literary criteria and humanistic canons as are the philosophers and tragedians, the function of the poet being like that of any other artist, to represent things either as they are (οἷα ἦν ἢ ἔστιν), or as conventionally conceived (οἷά φασιν καὶ δοκεῖ) or as they ought to be (οἷα εἶναι δεῖ) [10].

The inspirational factor which the Greeks conceived as operating on the poets by means of a divine possession was qualitatively different from the divine origin postulated in Judaism for Torah. Law was not, with some local exceptions, held by Greeks to be of divine origin. If the maintenance of the popular religious worship with which the Homeric myths were bound up is commended by Plato, Aristotle, Stoics and Epicureans for reasons of social cohesiveness, no Greek philosopher felt constrained to trim his speculation so as to suit mythological concepts as if the latter corresponded to revealed and established truth. Yet if allegorism as a philosophic method survived Plato's criticism, it was precisely because those who used it could not wholly suppress, either in themselves or in others, 'the prejudice that the ancient poets were the divinely wise and accomplished teachers of mankind'. [11] It was the Stoics in particular, [11a]

8. *Protagoras* 347e, *Apology* 22c, *Ion* 534a, *Phaedrus* 229e, 245a. See Tate, *Classical Quarterly* 23, 1929, pp. 145f., 154.

9. *Republic* 378d.

10. *Poetics* xxv, 1460b; cf. the disparaging reference (*Metaphysics* 1093a, xiii, 6, 7) to τοῖς ἀρχαίοις Ὁμηρικοῖς.

11. Tate, *Classical Quarterly* 24, 1930, p. 10.

11a. Ursula Treu (see n. 6a) refers to K. Barwick, *Probleme der stoischen Sprachlehre und Rhetorik, Abh. der Sächsischen Akad. der Wissenschaften*, Leipzig, Phil.-hist. Klasse, 49, 3, 1957.

especially Chrysippus (early 3rd century B.C.E.), who made much of it, thereby encouraging its continued use for apologetic purposes by the grammarians. But it should be noted that the Stoics did not all insist on the presence throughout Homer of a philosophically meaningful underlying sense however barren the surface meaning might appear; and Seneca, indeed, was to reject the proposition *ab initio*. [12] Such stretches of 'irrational' material Zeno is said to have followed Antisthenes in labelling δόξα, *opinion, unscientific guesswork*, as opposed to truth (ἀλήθεία). The pejorative nuance injected into the term δόξα by Zeno [13] and the Stoics generally [14] is clear from surviving definitions that emanate from them. For the Stoics δόξα meant essentially *ignorance* and *delusion*, and such myths as were held to symbolise truth were never so termed. Even though many Stoics were less hesitant than might appear from the foregoing with regard to the extent to which matter allegorically significant was to be found scattered over the poems, [15] allegory is far from occupying a dominant position in their intellectual armoury. Stoic preoccupation with allegory is but analogous to the willingness of rabbinic methodology to avail itself of an *'asmakhta*.

Stoicism may properly form our bridge to Philo, inasmuch as Philonic thought may be considered an adaption of Platonism and constant critique of the Stoics. [16] Such parallels as can be pointed out between Philo and the Midrash may imply some familiarity on his part with the content of Palestinian Jewish exegesis, and may even contain some slight evidence for his having been aware of such rabbinic processes of hermeneutics as had been evolved by his time. [17] But it is Greek categories that determine

---

12. *Epist.* xiii, 3, (88), 5.

13. Tate, *Classical Quarterly* 23, 1929, p. 42; 24, 1930, pp. 3, 7, 9, 10; 28, 1934, p. 114. Zeno is credited with the definition δόξαν εἶναι τὴν ἀσθενῆ καὶ ψευδῆ συγκατάθεσιν, Sextus Empiricus *adv. Math.* vii (*adv. Logic.* I), 151; see A. Pearson, *The Fragments of Zeno and Cleanthes,* Cambridge, 1891, p. 68, frag. 15. Cf. Dio Chrysostom, *Orat.* liii, 4, lv, 9.

14. Stobaeus, II *Ethica* 7(6), 11m [= II, 231], ed. A. Meineke (Teubner Series, 1864), ii, p. 64, gives two Stoic definitions of δόξα : τὴν μὲν ἀκαταλήπτῳ συγκατάθεσιν (i.e. assent to the incomprehensible) τὴν δ' ὑπόληψιν ἀσθενῆ (tenuous assumption): Pearson, *loc. cit.*

15. Cf. e.g. Strabo i, 2, 7, c. 18 οὐ πάντα τερατευόμενος ἀλλὰ καὶ πρὸς ἐπιστήμην ἀλληγορῶν.

16. H. A. Wolfson, Philo, 1947, i, p. 329; cf. *de Migratione Abr.* 32, [178–]179, 'Chaldaeans' being a disguise for Stoics.

17. Z. Frankel, *Über den Einfluss der palästinischen Exegese auf die Alexandrinische Hermeneutik,* Leipsig, 1851, p. 191, n. *b*. B. Ritter, *Philo und die Halacha,*

his pattern of thinking even though, unlike Plato or Aristotle, Philo is unable to put out of court a body of literature traditionally regarded as being of divine origin, and, unlike the Stoics, requires more of allegory than to furnish 'asmakhta. The central truths of Torah as revealed to Moses being cardinal, philosophy must where necessary accommodate them; its role as 'handmaid of theology' derives from Philo's allegorisation of the relationship of Hagar to Sarah — a notion adapted by him from the Stoic subordination of encyclical studies, i.e. the liberal arts, to philosophy. [18].

In several places Philo makes his attitude to allegory and literalism clear enough. [19] Quoting *Numbers* xxiii:19 in the form οὐχ ὡς ἄνθρωπος ὁ θεός [20], he rejects the literal meaning entirely where anthropomorphism is at issue, holding the language employed to be a mere concession to duller intellects. [21] The creation narratives are allegorically taken, as also anything that might derogate from the dignity of the inspired words of God. This holds good also regarding what is felt to be reprehensible in the legal portions of the Pentateuch, though Philo does not consider the indispensability here of allegory to be a valid reason for abandoning the institution concerned. His argument deserves a fairly full summary. [22] Some, regarding the laws in their literal sense (τοὺς ῥητοὺς νόμους) as symbols, are over-punctilious (ἄγαν ἠκρίβωσαν) regarding the latter and treat the former with easy-going neglect (ῥαθύμως ὠλιγώρησαν). Such casualness (εὐχερείας) he condemns; both aspects, the unseen (τῶν ἀφανῶν) and what is seen (τῶν φανερῶν) require full and exact investigation. As things are, such people live a life as if oblivious of society, overlooking all that the mass of men regard (τὰ δοκοῦντα τοῖς πολλοῖς) and explore reality in its naked absoluteness. Scripture, however, teaches one not to let go customs fixed by divinely empowered men greater than those of

Leipsig, 1879, p. 16, citing also Frankel, *Vorstudien zu der Septuaginta*, Leipzig, 1841, p. 185f.

18. Wolfson, *op. cit.* i, p. 145f.; *de Congressu* 14, 71–80, cf. 4, 14, 20; *de Posteritate Caini* 38, 130. Aristo of Chios (*c.* 250 B.C.E.) following Aristippus (*c.* 435–356) equates encyclical studies with θεραπαίναι, philosophy with δέσποινα or βασίλισσα : Diogenes Laertius ii, 79–80, Stobaeus, *Florilegium* iii, 109, ed. C. Wachsmuth and O. Hense, 1894, iii, p. 24 (ed. A. Meineke, Teubner Series, 1856, iv, p. 110 (?)).

19. Wolfson, *op. cit.* i, p. 116f.

20. *Quod Deus Immutabilis* 13, 62; *de Somniis* i, 40, 237.

21. ἡ [ὁδὸς] πρὸς τὰς τῶν νωθεστέρων δόξας contrasted to ἡ πρὸς τὸ ἀληθὲς ἀπονεύουσα.

22. *De Migratione Abr.* 16, 89–93. Wolfson, *op. cit.* i, p. 127.

our time (μηδὲν τῶν ἐν τοῖς ἔθεσι λύειν ἃ θεσπέσιοι καὶ μείζους ἄνδρες ἢ καθ᾽ ἡμας ὥρισαν). Even though the Sabbath, the Feast of Tabernacles, and the law of circumcision all have a symbolic meaning, that is no occasion to abandon the various institutions accompanying their observance. Such institutions constitute as it were the body; the letter of the law (τῶν ῥητῶν νόμων) needs attention in order to preserve the spirit, which corresponds to the soul. Observance leads to a clearer appreciation of what the institution symbolises (τοῖς δι᾽ ὑπονοιῶν δηλουμένοις) and also obviates the censure and charges that common folk are likely to bring against so intellectualised an approach.

Philo's appreciation of the vital sociological import of *halakhah* is here made obvious enough, [23] but in view of his attitude as expressed elsewhere we should be wrong to assume that the foregoing argument would assert any dependence of *halakhah* upon the literal sense as its indispensable support. His use of παρεμφαίνειν = *to indicate alongside* — in connection with allegory [24] presupposes the parallel legitimacy of literal and allegorical exegesis, the peaceful coexistence of which he can countenance. Indeed, he seems implictly to warn those not intellectually qualified to refrain from meddling with the technical vocabulary of allegorism, a superficial acquaintance with which might have psychologically and sociologically untoward consequences. [25] But the patronising or mildly pejorative tone in the expressions with which the low-brow is contrasted with the philosopher, whose proper approach to the Bible lies through allegory, is unmistakeable. In spite of Plato's emphasis on the unsuitability of allegory as an educational instrument, [26] Philo seems not

23. See Ritter, *op. cit.* (note 17), pp. 9f., 11, quoting Siegfried, *Philo von Alexandria*, Jena, 1875, p. 145, as against Frankel, *Vorstudien* (see note 17), p. 186 (quoted Ritter, p. 13, n.).

24. E.g. *de Abraham* 36, 200, on the binding of Isaac. The occurrence of παρεμφαίνειν here (and elsewhere, *Quis rerum div. heres* 23, 112, *de somniis* ii, 29, 195, 33, 324) perhaps neutralises the suggestion (Wolfson, *op. cit.* i, p. 122) that in countenancing literalism in the *Quaestiones in Gen.* Philo was motivated apologetically in view of the different type of reader there addressed by him. But as employed by Chrysippus (H. von Arnim, *Stoicorum Veterum Fragmenta*, Leipsig, 1903, ii, pp. 52, 245) παρεμφαίνειν and παρέμφασις (= *signification*) seem not to emphasise the force of the prefixed παρά.

25. This seems to be the import of the passages assembled by Wolfson, *op. cit.* i, p. 115f. The following references may be added: the literal (φανερός) sense is μυθοποιΐα (*Leg. Alleg.* i, 14, 43), gullibility (δυσθεράπευτος εὐήθεια, *de Plant.* 8, 32), facile explanation (πρόχειροι ἀποδόσις, *de confusione lingu.* 5, 14). By contrast, allegory or ὑπόνοια is not for the uninitiate (ἀμύητοι, *de fuga* 32, 179).

26. Cf. *supra*, p. 145, note 9.

to have appreciated that his attitude might constitute a long-term danger to the cohesiveness of the Jewish community of Alexandria which embraced both low-brows and intellectuals. And whereas for Plato the literal sense, whatever its merits or demerits, is indissolubly wedded to its own inherent principle (νόμος, τύπος, δόξα) [27], for Philo νόμος is set apart from τύπος and δόξα by virtue of its being used as a term for divine law as embodied in the Pentateuch — a usage likewise current in Jewish Palestine (נימוס[א]). Thus νόμος, approximating sometimes in Philo's language to *halakhah*, stands aside from the literal sense and its inherent meaning: it is to be ranged as a third category, alongside allegory — independent of it indeed but, in sociological terms, of comparable importance.

An approach to the categories presupposed by rabbinic exegesis has something to gain from a brief glance at the philosophical categories acknowledged by Philo, which led him inexorably towards an allegorical treatment of the Bible. He inherited from the Stoics a tripartite division of philosophy which assigned the lowest place to logic, above which were ranged physics and ethics. [28] The relative importance of the latter two in Stoicism is a matter for dispute: right conduct being for the Stoic the aim of philosophy, ethics may be held to occupy first place. Priority is, however, sometimes accorded to physics, inasmuch as the God of Stoicism is held to be immanent in nature. Philo's God, being conceived in essentially Jewish terms, is not immanent in the world in the sense that Stoicism would have Him to be. Theology is consequently assigned to ethics, which Philo defines so as to include 'the knowledge of the maker of the world,' [29] and this supreme branch of philosophy he identifies with the *Torah* as revealed to Moses, and consequently also with the immanent *Logos*.

The major divisions of philosophical thinking which were, for Stoicism, independent of any mythological source-material had led but incidentally to the serious treatment of Homeric allegorism. For Philo, although he remained conscious of their independent origin, these categories had to become subservient to a revelational source-material the inspired quality of which was not open to question: and as a means of achieving a harmony between the two, biblical allegorism consequently became an indispensable device. The difference as between Philo and the

27. Cf. *supra*, p. 145.
28. Wolfson, *op. cit.* i, p. 146.
29. *de mut. nominum* 10. 76, μεταναστάντος ἀπὸ τῆς περὶ τὸν κόσμον θεωρίας πρὸς τὴν τοῦ πεποιηκότος ἐπιστήμην, ἐξ ἧς εὐσέβειαν... ἐκτήσατο. Cf. note 34, *end*.

Stoics on the one side and the rabbis on the other is that, for the latter, the fundamental categories grew out of reflection upon a non-philosophical source-material, instead of having been first elaborated speculatively and then either imposed on or adapted to traditional belief, lore and custom.

Although rabbinic evidence is predominantly later than Philo, the rabbinic scheme of two fundamental categories, *halakhah* and *'aggada,* is both broad enough and of sufficiently marked dominance to justify us in carrying it back, with some confidence, to Philonic times. Insofar as Stoicism makes logic but a necessary substructure for its other two divisions, in the categories of ethics and physics as rearranged by Philo (see p. 149) one might find an approximate parallel to *halakhah* and *'aggada.* If it must be conceded that rabbinic thought places primary emphasis on the former of these, such preoccupation ought not to be exaggerated out of proportion. In the first place, *'aggada, haggadah,* or at the very least its participial counterpart *maggid,* originally meant as a dialectic term nothing more than *exegesis,* and indeed included halakhic as well as aggadic exegesis. [30] Secondly, the division is not watertight; *halakhah* can colour *'aggada,* [31] and *'aggada* may even affect, or at any rate be adduced as embodying considerations pertinent for *halakhah.* [32] Moreover, there seems no doubt that, for rabbinic Judaism, theology must find expression equally within the categories of *halakhah* [33] and *'aggada.* [34] Philo's theology, on the other hand, although considered

30. See W. Bacher in *Jewish Quarterly Review,* O.S., iv, 1892, pp. 406f., especially p. 418.

31. Eg. Bab. Talmud *Yoma* 28b קיים א״א אפילו עירובי תבשילין, cf. Gen. R. §95, 3 אפילו דיקדוקי תורה (ed. Theodor-Albeck, p. 1190). The inclusion here of the word אפילו is significant as betraying a consciousness of the evolutionary character of the institutional element in *halakhah.*

32. E.g. the justification advanced for the mishnaic ruling (*R.H.* 3, 3) that the *shofar* used on New Year ought to be made from a straight, and not a curved ram's horn, Bab. Talmud *R.H.* 26b סבר בראש השנה כמה דפשיט אינש [ומר [ר״ל ת״ק דעתיה טפי מעלי. Rashi *in loc.* refers to *Lam.* iii:41. Cf. *Tosaphoth.* Regarding the absence of a rigid frontier between *halakhah and 'aggada,* cf. H. Loewe's remarks in *A Rabbinic Anthology,* ed. C. G. Montefiore and H. Loewe, 1938, p. xciv.

33. E.g. Bab. Talmud *Shabbath* 133b (Abba Saul) on *Exod.* xv:2 זה אלי ואנוהו הוי דומה לו מה הוא חנון ורחום אף אתה היה חו״ר.

34. E.g. the well-known *dictum* on *Deut.* xi:22 ולדבקה בו (*Sifre, 'Eqev* 49), רצונך להכיר את מי שאמר והיה העולם למוד הגדה שמתוך כך אתה מכיר את מי שאמר והיה העולם ומדבק בדרכיו. J. Z. Lauterbach in *Jewish Quarterly Review,* N.S. i, 1910, p. 305, note, understood *haggadah* here in its wider sense of biblical exegesis (see *supra* note 30). It is true that the foregoing matter is somewhat similar to that

by him part of ethics, is presented entirely within the framework of allegorism. Institutional Judaism is, indeed, indispensable to him, and the law requires for its fulfilment intention and assent; [35] but the language here is Stoic, and in spite of later rabbinic parallels regarding both intention and joyfulness in fulfilment, [36] it seems improbable that on the strength of them we should attribute to Philo any conception of halakhic institutions that would lift them out of the category of *ḥovah* and invest them with the aurora of *miṣwah*. It is significant that the word εὐλογία and its cognates, the main septuagintal rendering of the Hebrew *berakhah*, does not, in Philonic usage, develop semantically beyond the biblical sense, in step with the post-biblical history of the Hebrew ברך. [37]

Our comparison of the respective categories of the rabbis and of Philo and his hellenistic background may be rounded off by the consideration of whether logic, the humble but essential substructure of the two major Stoic divisions of philosophy, has any counterpart on the Jewish side. Logic is for the Greek the basic tool, inasmuch as his true source-material is the accumulated speculation of his predecessors who had all, at any rate since Aristotle, been using the same tool before him. In Philo's hands it has to yield pride of place to allegorism, since philosophy is being imposed upon a discrete body of material held to be of a revelational quality in equal density throughout: thus deprived of the Stoic escape-mechanism which could at will put out of court as δόξα passages of Homer felt not to be susceptible of philosophically meaningful allegorism (see p. 146), Philo was compelled to make his chief instrument a non-logical one. In Jewish Palestine the situation was almost exactly reversed, the subject matter of speculation being identified, at least at a

already given (note 33) as an example of theology in *halakhah*; but the accompanying adducement of adjectives treated as divine appellatives (with which it is organically a unit) marks the passage out as *'aggada*. Moreover, the saying is attributed in L. Finkelstein's critical text (Breslau, 1935, p. 115) to the דורשי הגדות; Lauterbach, in attributing it to the דורשי רשומות, was following what is now shown to be an inferior reading. The remark is strikingly close to Philo, *de mut. nominum*, quoted in note 29.

35. *De post. Cain* 3, 11 τὰ ἐκ προνοίας ἀμείνω τῶν ἀκουσίων κατορθώματα (= *right actions*); *Quod Deus immutabilis* 22, 100 τοὺς ... ἀσυγκαταθέτῳ (= *unassenting*) γνώμῃ πράττοντας ⟨μὴ⟩ ἐθελουσίως βιαζομένους δε... μὴ κατορθοῦν.

36. E.g. Bab. Talmud *Berakhoth* 31a. Cf. Wolfson, *op. cit.* ii, p. 224.

37. Similarly ἐντολή, the main septuagintal rendering of *miṣwah*, is used by Philo in its biblical sense without any of the overtones acquired by *miṣwah* in rabbinic Hebrew. In *de leg. alleg.* i, 29, 93 ἐντολή is distinguished from πρόσταξις and ἀπαγόρευσις and grouped with παραίνεσις, the description of which is to be regarded as Stoic (see von Arnim, *op. cit.*, note 24, iii, p. 139).

popular level, with the source-material, *viz.* the holy books as composed and transmitted by foregoing generations, *plus* (in the case of the Pharisees and the men of Qumran) an agglutinated corpus of institutional *halakhah* and current opinion *('aggada)*. As sophistication revealed a distinction between this source-material and the ultimate goal of the investigation of it, i.e. law and theology, extraneous devices of speculation might come to be applied, at will, to the traditional material in order to extract from it hitherto unexposed knowledge of God and unsuspected possibilities of legal and ethical development. In the hermeneutic *middoth* as they gradually become formalised we may acknowledge something of a counterpart to logic, and a counterpart that possibly owed something to the impact of some established patterns of Greek argumentation, albeit ones derived, probably, not from the philosophical schools or even the popular echo of the dialectic there current, but rather from the language of the law courts. [38]

Yet these hermeneutic processes themselves, by the marked variation in the extent to which they are allowed scope to operate in the spheres of *halakhah* and *'aggada* respectively, at once throw into focus the difference in mental climate as between Jewish Palestine and the west. Jewry has never attempted to produce a definitive code of the *'aggada*, and the 32 exegetical principles that may be applied to its elaboration as ultimately embodied in the post-Sa'adyanic [38a] *'Baraita'* ascribed to R. Eliezer b. Jose the Galilean in effect allow the resourceful aggadist all the scope that he is likely to want. R. Ishmael's 13 rules for halakhic exegesis at once reveal a completely different atmosphere. Such devices as no. 6, כלל ופרט וכלל אי אתה דן אלא כעין הפרט, and the countercheck that came to be placed on any extravagant use of the *gezerah shawah*, [39] seem quite clearly de-

---

38. On this see D. Daube, *Hebrew Union College Annual*, Cincinnati, xxii, 1949, p. 239f., and *H. Lewald Festschrift*, Basle, 1953, p. 27f., on the possible influence of Alexandrian forensic conventions. Cf. also I. Heinemann, *Altjüdische Allegoristik*, p. 37, and, most recently, I. Baer, *On the Problem of Eschatological Doctrine During the Period of the Second Temple* (in Hebrew), *Zion*, xxiii–iv, 1958/9, p. 141f.

38a. On the date, see M. Zucker in the *Proceedings* of the American Academy for Jewish Research, xxiii, 1954 (Hebrew portion), pp. 9, n. 47a, 12–14. Samuel b. Ḥofni, the last *Gaʾon* of Sura, used Saʿadya as the main source for his set of 49 rules (pp. 16–19). Cf. Zucker's (Hebrew) book on Saʿadya's translation of the Pentateuch (New York, 1959), pp. 237f. In *Ha-Doʾar* (New York) xli, 37 (Sept. 8th, 1961), p. 675, Zucker vindicates his conclusions against criticisms expressed by Mirsky in *Peraqim*, 5720 (1960), pp. 43–9.

39. Bab. Talmud *Niddah* 19b אין אדם גוזר ג״ש מעצמו וכו׳. On this see M. Miel-

signed to rig the scales in favour of conservatism. Indeed, the well-known incident concerning Hillel and the Beney Bethera makes abundantly clear a reluctance to allow halakhic validity to the force of sheer logic operating through recognised hermeneutic principles: rebuttals were discovered for all Hillel's arguments from analogy and *a fortiori*, opposition being at once dropped when he abandoned argument in favour of citing precedent. [40] For the Greek, the function of logic was to point the way through mental speculation to the enrichment of man's spirit. Rabbinic Judaism could tolerate this within the realm of *'aggada* inasmuch as independence of mind was not, as a general rule, felt likely to throw undue strain upon the fabric of the Jewish body politic. But where *halakhah* was at issue, the function of logic is almost exactly the reverse; it becomes the machinery for ensuring that changes in social organisation shall be restricted to the essential minimum, especially at such sensitive points as the specifically religious or cultic dimension, and that they shall not be authorised unless social cohesiveness is adequate to sustain them without danger; with the object of preserving traditional Jewish experience in its widest sense as far as possible intact.

The purpose of the foregoing comparison has been to establish, through contrast, what constituted the fundamental object of the scriptural exegesis of the rabbis. It is premature here to discuss examples of the process in action, inasmuch as our concern on the present occasion is with the self-consciousness of the exegete himself as reflected in the descriptions which he attaches to his own endeavour and findings, and by which he stigmatises those of others which he himself disapproves. In considering the extent to which the resultant technical terms of hermeneutics serve to delimit categories of thought, we need to bear in mind that all such divisions must necessarily be patient of subsumption under the major categories of *halakhah=behaviour* and *'aggada=speculation with edification in view* — categories which, as we have suggested, grew out of preoccupation with the contents of the written *Torah* rather than having been applied to them, ready-made, from without. It is significant that

ziner, *Introduction to the Talmud*[2], 1903, p. 151, § 2. Cf. also S. Rosenblatt, *The Interpretation of the Bible in the Mishnah.* Baltimore, 1935, p. 3f., and Bacher, *Terminologie* I (see note 43), p. 110 on מועט.

40. The most instructive source is in the Palestinian Talmud, *Pesaḥim* 6, 1 33a. The following phrases are the most significant: התחיל דורש להן מהיקש ומקו"ח ומג"ש ... אע"פ שהיה יושב דורש להן כל היום לא קיבלו ממנו עד שאמר להן יבוא עלי כך שמעתי משמעיה ואבטליון ... ומינו אותו נשיא עליהן ..... התחיל מקנטרן .... כיון שקנטרן בדברים נעלמה הלכה ממנו .... א"ל הלכה זו שמעתי ושכחתי אלא הניחו אלא לישראל אם אינן

while these two expressions derive fairly naturally from the biblical usage of הלך and נגד (*hiph'il*) respectively, the technical terminology of exegesis, both halakhic and aggadic, if it seldom or never reflects obviously translated borrowings from non-Jewish systems of argument,[41] consists nevertheless of words found in the Hebrew Bible either rarely or not at all; and even where there is a lexical link with biblical vocabulary, the semantic development is far more advanced and far less smooth than it is in the case of the terms *halakhah* and *'aggada*. Such terms as *ribbuy, gezerah shawah*, and *peraṭ* illustrate this point clearly enough. Of the whole corpus of technical terms there are few only of those which, because of their constant use in argument, have been summarised in the lists of halakhic and aggadic principles of hermeneutics, that can point through their linguistic formulation towards the purpose which the individual exegete was setting himself; broadly speaking, these terms represent not the object, but the mechanics of exegesis. For an understanding of the overall plan we have to look for hints embodied in expressions that would not in themselves be serviceable for application as a rule of thumb. In examining them, we must again be constantly asking ourselves whether they would have any independent validity were the categories of *halakhah* and *'aggada* not always in the background.[42] And of the various words generally assumed to indicate the plain, unvarnished meaning of a text as opposed to any more sophisticated elaboration of it, the most obvious from which to commence our investigation is the term פשט.[43]

נביאים בני נביאים הן . . . . כיון שראה את המעשה נזכר את ההלכה אמר כך שמעתי משמעיה ואבטליון.

41. D. Daube had connected סרס with Greek τομή, but subsequently abandoned this in favour of ἀναστροφή in the sense of *interpretation by rearrangement* — *HUCA* p. 261 and *Lewald Festschrift* p. 28 (see note 38). See also Baer (article cited in n. 38), p. 142, who cites some clear cases of terminology translated from Greek.

42. That the rabbis could occasionally dispense with them seems implicit in the use of היישוב [אינו מן] in the sense of οἰκουμένη, Mishnah *Qidd.* 1, 10, where a formulation involving a Torah category would have been apposite enough.

43. The usage of the term דרש, conventionally regarded as the antonym of פשט, does not call for systematic reexamination here, and reference to W. Bacher's treatment must suffice (*die Älteste Terminologie der jüdischen Schriftauslegung, Tan-maiten*, Leipsig 1889, p. 25 f., *Amoräer*, 1905, p. 41 f. (I. Heinmann's study of the semantics of exegetical terminology in *Leshonenu*, 17, pp. 182–9, was unfortunately not available to me). It may, however, be added that Qumranic occurrences of the root run parallel to both biblical and rabbinic use. The following references may be mentioned: *CDC*, ed. S. Schechter, p. 6, 1. 7, C. Rabin, *The Zadokite Fragments*[2], 1958, p. 23, והמחוקק הוא דורש התורה אשר אמר ישעיהו מוציא כלי למעשיהו; *DSD* p. 8, 1. 13f, ed. A. M. Habermann (*Megilloth Mid-*

The fundamental meaning of פשט in biblical Hebrew is to *strip* [a garment], properly to *flatten* it by so doing. [44] Reduced to this primary meaning, it may be brought together with the other basic notion connected with the root in the cognate languages and in later Hebrew, *viz.* *extend, stretch out.* Indeed, the biblical usage of פשט = *make a raid* [45] is best explained as *stretch out* [*scil. hand*, with hostile intent], since פשט יד has frequent rabbinic attestation, albeit mostly without the implication of hostility. [46] Qumranic usage is closely parallel to the biblical. [47] The *hiph'il* and *'aph'el* forms אושט, הושיט in Hebrew and Syriac, conveying the meaning *extend*, have been plausibly connected with the present root rather than with ישט, which does not occur in *Qal* [48] etc.

The notion *extend, flatten*, when used passively, can obviously develope semantically into such meanings as *flat, straight, simple, uncompounded, innocent, unlearned*, all of which are covered by the Syriac פשיט ; the latter thus renders the Greek ἁπλοῦς and near synonyms (e.g. ἄκακος).The use of the term פשיטתא for the Bible version means, according to Payne Smith, [*editio*] *vulgata, communis, popularis*. It is to be emphasized that in Syriac פשט never means to *explain*: and although this meaning can be attested for the corresponding Arabic بـسـط, [49] the metaphorical element of *extending, expatiating on* the subject matter seems there still to be palpable. The Persian lexicon, however, lists among the meanings of the root to *open a discourse, explain*, no qualification being added. [50] It thus appears that, up to the end of the amoraic period, פשט in the sense of *explain* is virtually a solecism of Hebrew and

ללכת למדבר לפנות שם את דרך הואהא ..... הואה מדרש *bar Yehudah*, 1959, p. 68

התורה [אשר] צוה ביד משה לעשות ככול הנגלה עת בעת וכאשר גלו הנביאים ברוח קודשו.

44. So N. H. Torczyner in E. Ben Yehuda's Hebrew *Thesaurus*, xi, 5268, col. 1, note. The biblical Hebrew lexicons of Brown-Driver-Briggs and Gesenius-Buhl[17] compare Assyrian *pašāṭu = expunge.*

45. *Job* i:17, etc. This explanation is superior to that of *stripping off* [*sc. shelter*], proposed by BDB; cf. C. F. Burney, *Judges*[2], p. 282, note, on ix:33.

46. E.g. Mishnah *Sabbath*, i, 1, Palestinian Talmud *Pe'ah* viii, *end*, 21b. But פשט את הרגל (*Keth.* xiii, 5) apparently means [*contemptuous*] *refusal. Pesiqta Kahana, Zakhor* ed. S. Buber 28b פשט יד בכסא [עמלק].

47. It is used of *stripping* the slain and *deploying* into battle order; *DSW* vii, 2, viii, 6. See Y. Yadin's ed., pp. 133–4.

48. Torczyner, *op. cit.* (see note 44), 5267, col. 2, note 4; for the phonetic development see Gesenius' *Hebrew Grammar*, ed. Kautzsch-Cowley, 1910, § 190; in Syriac it is less infrequent, see Nöldeke, *Syr. Grammar*, § 27.

49. Ibn Manṣur, *Lisān el 'Arab*, 9, 1884, p. 127 *supra*.

50. F. Steingass, *s.v.* J. Richardson's dictionary, Oxford, 1777, does not list this meaning.

**211**

Jewish Aramaic, the usage of which must therefore be scrutinised. [51]

The Jewish use of פשט, פשיטא meaning (identically with Syriac) *flat,
undifferentiated* has in rabbinic Hebrew reacted upon the finite verb in
the Qal, so that the latter can mean to *read once only;* [52] while the passive
participle itself stands as the antonym of words meaning *doubled, bent,
circuitous,* [53] or *firstborn.* [54] סבר פנים יפות, *friendly countenance* is once
paraphrased ופניו פשוטים לו. [55] Opposed to צריכא in the sense of צריך עיון,
*in need of investigation,* פשיטא means *clear, plain;* [56] and it can be used
rhetorically ( = *is it [so] clear?*) to invite the rebuttal of an implied
doubt. [57] Of the verbal usages that go beyond the biblical pattern apart
from the special meaning of *explain* here under discussion, particular attention should be paid to the idiomatic sense of *becoming spread, diffused,
and generally accepted,* to be found in the phrase הואיל ופשט איסורו ברוב
ישראל, 'seeing that its prohibition has become diffused among the majority
of Israel.' [58] Alongside this may be mentioned פשיטא = *small coin,* as
being *current, diffused* (cf. *Gen.* xxiii:16 כסף עובר לסוחר), unless this
idiom derives rather from the notion of *undifferentiated* and hence *common* — to which such mediaeval coinage terms as *albus, blanc, weiss-
pfennig* would perhaps be parallel (cf. also Spanish *peseta*).

In the (post tannaitic) [58a] sense of *teach, explain* פשט is used in the
Qal and Pe'al only; and it is to be noted that where it is so used, nothing
constant can be asserted about either the subject matter or the method in
which it is handled. Indeed, it is sometimes interchanged indiscriminately with דרש. Thus R. Yannai is described as having on one occasion
been sitting expounding at his city gate; in the various parallel accounts

51. See W. Bacher, *Terminologie* (see note 43) i, p. 86, ii, p. 170f.

52. E.g. Mishnah *Sukkah,* iii, 11. Geiger, *Zeitschrift für jüdische Theologie* 1,
1844, p. 244, contests this meaning.

53. *Mekhilta, Beshallaḥ, init.,* ed. I. H. Weiss f. 28b, 1, 5, דרך פשוטה opposed to
דרך המדבר.

54. Bab. Talmud *Bekhoroth* 52b.

55. *'Av. de-R. Nathan,* Text B, §23, *end,* ed. S. Schechter f. 24b.

56. E.g. Palestinian Talmud *Sabbạth,* x, end 12d, מה דצריכא לר׳ ירמיה פשיטא ליצחק
בר אוריין, Bab. Talmud *Megillah* 3b פשיטא לי; in *B.M.* 16a it means *it is clear[ly
the case] that;* *Zebaḥim* 55b = *it is settled.* Similarly as opposed to מספקא, *doubtful, Pes.* 83b, *Yoma* 52b.

57. E.g. *B.B.* 137a (followed up by מהו דתימא).

58. Similarly in *Hor.* 3b the printed edd. add the words עד שתפשוט הוראה בכל
עדת ישראל. Also in the *Nithpa'el, Sanh.* 98b עד שתתפשט המלכות על ישראל.

58a. See Bacher, *Terminologie* (see note 43) i, p. 162, n. 3; *Zeitschrift für die
A-Tliche Wissenschaft* 13, 1893, p. 301.

he is described as יתיב מתני [61] ,יושב ושונה [60] ,יושב ודורש [59] ,יושב ופושט [62].
R. Zadok was declared by R. Yoḥanan b. Zakkai to be capable of deliver-
ing disquisitions (ופשיט) running to 100 lectures (or, less probably, sections) on the strength of a single fig. [63] Since the occasion was the end
of the siege of Jerusalem and R. Zadok's emaciated condition is specifically mentioned, עלוהי is here doubtless to be rendered *on the strength
of*; [64] but even if it be rendered [100 lectures] *concerning* [a single fig],
so extended a course can hardly have been restricted to a single type of
approach. פשט לפלך means to *explain to* someone, and is so used even
reflexively. [65] An instructive example, in which explicit reference to the
person instructed has necessarily to be suppressed, occurs in connection
with R. Simeon b. Gamaliel; R. Nathan and R. Me'ir having prearranged
to humiliate him by asking him to lecture *extempore* on the tractate
עוקצין (concerning which he was not well informed), R. Jacob b. Qorshai
saved him from embarrassment by conning the treatise where Simeon
b. Gamaliel would be bound to overhear him, and thus conveyed (פשט)
[to him] both some of the subject-matter and the hint to look it over. [66]

It may be noted that where פשט is used verbally, often an halakhic
issue is involved; [67] and it is significant that in many cases the explanation

59. *Numbers R.* 18, 22, ed. Wilna f. 77b col. 1.

60. *Gen. R.* 10, 7, ed. Theodor-Albeck p. 81.

61. Textual variant *ibid.*

62. *Lev. R.* 16, 2 as quoted by Theodor, *ibid.* (ed. Wilna has ופשט); cf. *Gen. R.*
17, 3, ed. Theodor-Albeck p. 153 יתבין פשטין.

63. *Lam. R.* on i:5, ed. Wilna 15a דאכיל חד גמזוז ופשיט עלוהי מאה פרקין.

64. As e.g. *Deut.* viii:3. Thus, apparently, the commentary *Mattenoth Kehunnah
in loc.* In the context, R. Yoḥanan b. Zakkai tells Vespasian that had Jerusalem
contained but one other such as R. Zadok, the city would not have fallen to a
besieging army twice the size. This suggests that R. Yoḥanan b. Zakkai had in
mind R. Zadok's scholarship rather than his abstemiousness; and he had, when
invited by Vespasian to nominate someone to be allowed to escape the sack of the
city, selected R. Zadok. This may lend some plausibility to the alternative rendering of ופשיט עלוהי admitted above. But פשט ought, where it is used to express
*explain about, concerning* be followed not by על but by ב (e.g. *Menaḥoth* 26b *infra,
Niddah* 34b; Bacher, *Terminologie, Amoräer* (see note 43), pp. 172–3). Similarly
דרש, Mishnah *Ḥagigah* ii, 1).

65. E.g. Bab. Talmud *Ḥullin* 5b, *infra*, cf. also *Ex. R.* 47, 5 of Moses on Sinai
היה למד תורה ביום ופושט אותה בינו לבין עצמו בלילה. Similarly *Tanḥuma, Yithro* 15.

66. Horayoth 13b פשט גרס ותנא גרס ותנא.

67. E.g. Babylonian Talmud, *Bava Meṣiʿa* 18b, of Rabbah giving an halakhic
ruling. In *Midrash Psalms* to Ps. i, § 17, ed. Buber 8b, Bar Kappara's words מה
שהוא רגיל לפשוט בהן are paraphrased by R. Ḥiyya b. ʾAbba as דמוסיף הלכות.

so introduced bases itself upon tannaitic material. [68] Thus, in regard to
the difficulty of construing the words of *Lev.* xxii:7 ובא השמש, appeal
is made to a *baraita* (פשטו ליה מברייתא). [69] Concerning the question of
the permissibility of interposing a layer of material between the threshing
ox and the corn (*Deut.* xxv:4), a *baraita* is quoted to support a proposed affirmative answer, introduced with פשוט מיהא חדא דתניא. [70] Moreover, פשט is even found in an halakhic context where it must mean to
*deduce*: [71] in an aggadic context it occurs to describe results achieved
through analogy by application of the rule of *gezerah shawah*. [72] Again,
it is used of an answer that resolves doubt. [73] Thus, the elders of Nezonia
are found complaining that R. Ḥisda never gives them a [direct] decision
to their questions; [74] R. Ḥamnuna asks them whether he himself has ever
failed to give them a [direct] decision on any point, [75] and when they
take him up with a query as to whether the castration of a slave counts
as an external mutilation, he cannot answer (לא הוה בידיה).

The evidence here set forth, when taken alongside a substantial number of other instances where פשט is used verbally = *explain*, etc., suggests
that the essential notion conveyed by the root at this semantic stage is
*authority*. That is not to say that its employment is intended in every
case to spotlight the authoritative element in the teaching; but I do not
recall having seen any instance that is incompatible with the suggestion
here made. If this is correct, the meaning is but a natural semantic development of the meaning *extend* — *viz.* the extension of an opinion,
received by a teacher or elaborated by himself, over a wider body which
(by acknowledgement thereof) *broadens* the currency of the authority
of the source whence it emanates. Attention has already been drawn

68. In *Gen. R.* 49, 8 on xviii:23, ed. Theodor, p. 506, ויגש אברהם, R. Eleazar
combines the three explanations of R. Judah, R. Nehemiah, and רבנין respectively,
introducing the combination with the phrase פשט ליה (imperative, see Theodor's
note *in loc.*).

69. *Berakhoth*, 2b. Cf. *Zevaḥim* 96b and Bacher, *loc. cit.* at the end of note 67.

70. *Bava Meṣiʿa*, 90b.

71. *Bava Meṣiʿa* 20b ממונא מר איסורא מר פשיט היכי; it is asserted elsewhere that
this deduction is illicit, the operative words being ילפינן לא (*Berakh.* 19b, *Keth.* 40b,
46b; Bacher, *Terminologie, Amoräer* (see note 43), p. 172.

72. Palestinian Talmud *Sanhedrin* ii, 6, *end*, 20d 1. 18, מיציאה יציאה פשטון (ותצא
in *Gen.* xxx:16 and xxxiv: 1).

73. Bacher, *loc. cit.* gives several examples. Cf. also the contrast (פשיטא) מספקא,
*supra*, p. 156, n. 56.

74. *Qidd.* 25a, לן פשט ולא מילתא מיניה בעינן.

75. *Ibid.* לכו פשיטנא ולא מידי מינאי בעיתו מי.

(p. 156) to the use of the verb to indicate, *expressis verbis,* the *spread* of a juridical ruling. The *Qal* and the *Pe'al* forms had to carry the idiomatic sense of *teach* [*authoritatively*] in addition to the literal meaning *extend, spread,* since the *Pi'el* and *Hiph'il* were already taken up with the meaning *strip, flay.* The same phenomenon may be observed in שנה =*repeat* and *teach* [*authoritatively*]. The authority resides either in the prestige of the teacher himself, or the nature of the source-material (Mishnah, etc.) to which he appeals; and the reflexive use (see p. 157, n.65) will mean to convince oneself of what had previously been regarded as questionable or as as taken on trust, thereby extending *over oneself* the authority of one's source or teacher. [76]

The identification of *authority* as the central notion in this use of the root will explain how it comes about that the noun *peshāṭ*, often modified in inflected forms to פשוט, [76a] is used in talmudic and midrashic sources to describe exegesis that is by no means always literal. [77] The latter is the sense in which (it is generally assumed) later commentators used the word; but to read it anachronistically into the exegesis of their predecessors is but to create confusion, [78] and indeed the assumption that *peshāṭ* always means 'plain' exegesis in later times itself requires re-examination. Before we examine some specimens of talmudic exegesis explicitly labelled as פשט, we may notice in the present connection an obscure use of the word in connection with R. Yoḥanan b. Zakkai, [79] who though imprisoned by Vespasian for three days within sevenfold bars (κιγκλίς, latticed gate), was nevertheless able to announce to his jailers the hour of the day or night. The answer given by the Midrash to the question 'how did he know?' is מפשוטיה. [80] If this does not mean '*from* [*the time-table, rhythm, progress of his constant*] *study*' [81] it is

---

76. Cf. T. B. *Shabb.* 63a discussed below p. 166, n. 123 דליגמר איניש והדר ליסבר.

76a. The attempt of M. Gertner (*Terms of scriptural interpretation: a study in Hebrew semantics, Bulletin of the London School of Oriental and African Studies,* xxv, 1, 1962, p. 20) to distinguish *peshaṭ* from *peshuṭ* is in my view not only unsubstantiated, but indeed untenable in the light of such passages as that quoted *infra,* n. 121.

77. Cf Bacher, *Terminologie* ii (see note 43), p. 173, note, and Torczyner, *loc. cit.* (see note 44) xi, pp. 5265, note, and 5274, col. 2, note 2.

78. Rosenblatt (see note 39) senses this point (p. 2), but nevertheless assumes (p. 5f.) that in the Mishnah פשט may be identified with the simple or literal meaning of the text.

79. *Lam. R.* (on *Lam.* i:5) 1, 31, ed. Wilna 14b, col. 2, 1, 6.

80. מנן הוה ידע ריב"ז מפשוטיה.

81. So the commentary of David Luria *in loc.*

just conceivable that it means '*from his authoritative knowledge* [*sc.* of chronometry]. [82]

It is not possible to equate the designation פשט as in such phrases as פשוטיה דקרייא with any single type of biblical exegesis. [82a] The latter phrase can mean the scriptural *order*, as where the order in which the Mishnah [83] lists the categories of civil cases is correlated in the *Gemara* with the text of *Exod.* xxi:1f., a *Baraita* being cited. Nevertheless, occasion is taken in the context to adduce also the exegesis of R. Yosē b. Ḥalafta to the effect that it is the duty of a judge to take the evidence just as he finds it. [84] Reference to the biblical order, with an implied application of the hermeneutic rule of סמוכין, is perhaps what is meant when R. Yannai declares [85] that with regard to the Psalmist's question *What man is he that desireth life?* he had not known how it was to be explained, or possibly how far its explanation extended in the context, [86] until a street peddler had pointed to the succeeding verse, *Keep thy tongue from evil*, etc. In another passage [87] the phrase פשוטיה דקרייא contrasts the explicit reference of the text of *2 Sam.* vi:1 to 30[,000], with the results achieved through hermeneutic treatment of the context whereby 30 is triplicated.

In general, exegesis introduced by the words פשטיה דקרא במאי כתיב is scarcely less oblique than that which it is intended to replace. For example, *Prov.* xxiii:1–2 deal quite plainly with table *étiquette* to be observed in high society. It was quoted [88] by R. Me'ir as conveying a discouragement from the drinking of wine prepared by Samaritans. We have at any rate

---

82. So the first explanation in the *Mattenoth Kehunnah* (ברוב חכמתו ובבקיאותו בטבעי העתים). It is, however, only right to add that the author, who gives a second explanation similar to that of David Luria, implies thereafter hesitancy about both.

82a. This and the following passages were considered by Abraham Dobsewitich, *Ha-meṣaref* (Odessa, 1870), p. xf., who concludes that for the rabbis *peshaṭ* meant the essential truth behind the allegorical form taken by the language of the text (*i.e. entmythologisierung*).

83. *Sanhedrin* i, 1, see Palestinian Talmud *Sanh.* 18a with the commentary פני משה by Moses Margalith *in loc.*

84. The פני משה interprets R. Yosē's thesis as being founded on the emphasising of the words (*Ex.* xxi:1), and claims that [*sc.* in the view of R. Yosē] this (also) constitutes the פשוטיה דקרייא.

85. *Lev. R.* 16, 2, on *Ps.* xxxiv:13, ed. Wilna 22a col. 2.

86. היכן הוא פשט. Probably read, with Torczyner (see note 44), xi, p. 5266, note, היך נפשוט.

87. Palestinian Talmud *Sanh.* x, 2, 29a l. 36 (R. Berekhiah quoting R. 'Abba b. Kahana).

88. *Ḥullin* 6a.

a connection with food and drink here. But the פשט of the text is there-after alleged, by the formula just quoted, to concern the relationship of teacher (identified with the מושל) and pupil, following a *Baraita* of R. Ḥiyya. Again, *Prov.* xxv:20 is understood, implicitly and quite arbi-trarily, to refer to teaching Torah to one who is incapable of appreciat-ing it. [89] When 'Abbayē asked R. Dimi ופשטיה דקרא במאי כתיב, the answer was merely to make the exegesis explicit. [90] The blessing of the patriarch Judah (*Gen.* xlix:12) is construed by R. Dimi [91] with some elaboration as setting forth the agricultural richness of the Land of Israel. If the latter be equated with Judah, the exegesis is natural enough. In contrast thereto stands a different interpretation, which takes the words as a prayer uttered by Israel asking God to vouchsafe them His smiling Presence. [92] It is not the former, but the latter explanation that is introduced by the phrase פשטיה דקרא במאי כתיב, and it is attributed to (presumably the same) R. Dimi. When the area of the courtyard of the Tabernacle is under discussion, [93] 'Abbayē's explanation of the apparently superfluous word חמשים in the dimensions, although described as פשטיה דקרא, can scarcely be said to be any simpler than that which it is intended to super-cede. On the other hand, the same phrase introduces 'Abbayē's more or less plausible explanation for the explicit and apparently redundant men-tion in the laws of incitement to apostasy [94] of [*thy brother*] *the son of thy mother*; the sons of the same mother but different fathers may be less resistant to each other's incitements to apostasy than would be co-heirs of the same father, naturally jealous of each other's patrimony. 'Abbayē's explanation is at least pertinent to the subject matter, whereas R. Yoḥanan quoting R. Ishmael had found in it a רמז ליחד מן התורה. Again, R. Eleazar explained (פשט) a detail in the prescriptions regarding the animals that were to be assembled in the ark; [95] his exegesis stretches the word מכל far beyond its natural meaning. [96]. *Ps.* xxxvi:7 was ap-plied [97] somewhat obscurely by R. Papa to the maximal duration of the diagnosis of leprosy in humans and in buildings; פשטיה דקרא, as adduced

---

89. *Ibid.* 133a (see Rashi *in loc.*)
90. בשונה לתלמיד שאינו הגון.
91. *Keth.* 111b.
92. חכלילי. is treated as if = Aramaic חיך לי (רבש״ע רמוז לי בעיניך דבסים מחמרא).
93. ʿ*Erub.* 23b on *Ex.* xxvii:18 ורוחב חמשים בחמשים.
94. *Deut.* xiii:7, *Qidd.* 80b.
95. Palestinian Talmud *Pes.* ix, 5, 36d, on *Gen.* vi:19 מכל החי מכל בשר.
96. שיהו שלמין באיבריהן.
97. ʿ*Arakh.* 8b.

by R. Judah and by Rabbah each in his own way, refers the verse (more suitably in the context) to the divine powers of forgiveness. It may be remarked that their respective explanations are coordinated with those of two earlier figures, R. Eleazar and R. Yosē b. Ḥanina, of whom the former was a Tannaite. And finally, we may observe that when R. Isaac sought [98] to discover the biblical principle (the text should probably be corrected to read פשוטיה) by which a man inherits from his deceased wife, he was unable to do so. [99] It is perhaps significant that this follows (though not immediately) on the rejection by R. Yoḥanan of a sophistically inverted argument leading to a perverse conclusion. [100]

According to Bacher [101] it was 'Abbayē (ob. 339) who first distinguished פשט from דרש as separate exegetical approaches; but the substance of 'Abbayē's distinction cannot be established. It is true that in one of the instances labelled as פשט-exegesis discussed above [102] 'Abbayē proferred an explanation which, unlike that of R. Yoḥanan and Ishmael, takes the context into account; but in another [103] he was apparently content to acknowledge as פשט an explanation that merely made explicit the entirely arbitrary application of a verse of *Proverbs*. In his well-known application [104] of *Ps.* lxii:12, [105] מקרא אחד יוצא לכמה טעמים ואין טעם אחד יוצא מכמה מקראות, he does, indeed, allow of a multiplicity of scriptural meanings; but this *dictum* has no bearing on any distinction between פשט and דרש. In the context טעם means an *argument pro* or *con* [in a capital case], and 'Abbayē is concerned to assert that since no biblical text is superfluous, the meanings that may be derived or deduced from two texts can never, for all the multiplicity of each group, overlap. Consequently, an argument advanced coincidentally by separate advocates each basing himself on a different text may be allowed no more force than if it had been put forward by but one of them, inasmuch as the exegesis of one or other of them will necessarily be faulty. There is, how-

98. Palestinian Talmud *Bava B.* viii, 1, 16a.

99. בעי מימר פשוטיה (text פנסטה) ולא אשכח.

100. איתא מן תמן לא אהן גוברא בעי מישמע מילה דאורייא.

101. *Terminologie* (see note 43), ii, p. 112f. L. Dobschütz, *Die einfache Bibelexegese der Tannaiten*, Halle, 1893, p. 11f., regards the term *peshat* as an innovation of the school of Pumpeditha (R. Joseph, ʾAbbayē, and Rava), perhaps introduced there from Palestine by R. Dimi (p. 12, note 4). Cf. end of note 189, *infra*.

102. See note 94.

103. See note 89.

104. *Sanh.* 34a; cf. Bacher, *Terminologie* i, p. 67.

105. אחת דבר אלהים שתים זו שמעתי כי עז לאלהים.

ever, one passage [106] in which 'Abbayē does himself advance two possible interpretations, designated פשט and דרש respectively. The text is an alleged quotation from *Ben Sira* not found in any known recension, [107] and is a maxim advising against the attempt to skin a *gildānā*-fish; since the skin would spoil, the fish should be cooked and eaten unskinned. Defending the suitability of the text for homiletic purposes, 'Abbayē asserts that if it is construed according to the *peshaṭ* (אי מפשטיה) it is paralleled by the deuteronomic prohibition [108] of any wanton destruction of fruit trees during siege-warfare, and if as *derash* (אי מדרשא), it deprecates indulgence in eccentric sexual approach. But the deuteronomic passage strikes an unmistakeable moral tone (כי האדם עץ השדה לבא מפניך במצור). Although this last passage was not quoted by 'Abbayē, who confined himself to the actual words of the prohibition (לא תשחית את עצה) he can scarcely have been unconscious of the moralising note — even though in the *Sifrē* [109] it is not elaborated. If, nevertheless, the content of the prohibition be read on the same level of worldly wisdom as the maxim of pseudo-*Ben Sira*, the parallelism between the two texts to which 'Abbayē will have been pointing will be the occurrence of a word meaning to flay (תינטוש) in *Ben Sira* and one meaning to destroy (תשחית) in *Deuteronomy*. These cannot be said to be near enough in meaning for the *Deuteronomy* passage to throw any light on the other one. If the term פשט signifies exegesis of any type at all, the juxtaposition of not-so-close 'synonyms' can scarcely be reckoned as exegesis; and if, *per contra*, the use of the term פשט indicates a claim that all exegesis is being eschewed and the text left to speak for itself, then to adduce a reference regarding not felling fruit-trees alongside a maxim counselling the avoidance of skinning fish, is effectively to confuse the issue through a stressed juxtaposition of the two verbs. The one common element of the two passages can be reduced to the maxim *'Don't be wasteful with foodstuffs,'* and comparison between them on the basis of this element is not possible unless the deuteronomic *parenesis* is disregarded. Once it is overlooked, the two passages both drop on to the same plane as  the alternative exegesis of *Ben Sira* advanced by 'Abbayē involving sexual practices, and declared by him to be דרש. The net result will be that for 'Abbayē, whereas דרש dispenses with

106. *Sanh.* 100b.

107. לא תינטוש גילדנא מאודניה ולא ליזיל משכיה לחבלא אלא צלי יתיה בנורא ואיכול ביה. תרתין גריצין. See S. Schechter in *J.Q.R.* (old series), 3, 1891, p. 683; M. Segal, *Sefer Ben Sira Ha-Shalem* (Jerusalem, 1953), pp. 38 (§ 50), 40, 66.

108. *Deut.* xx:19.

109. § 203, ed. Finkelstein (1935), p. 239.

with any fortuitous link, פשט requires such link as its starting-point —
here the apparent connection of the fish-name *gildānā* with גלד =
*skin.* [109a]

Yet in 'Abbayē's time there was current the principle, formulated in
Pumpeditha, [110] that a text cannot be distorted from the meaning of its
*'peshaṭ'* (אין מקרא יוצא מידי פשוטו). This formula, which apparently occurs
in the Babylonian Talmud only, seems to have been employed to counter
exorbitant deductions from identity or close analogy of expression (*gezerah shawah*); [111] it constitutes a *via media* between the extravagant
lengths to which verbal analogy might be pressed, and 'Abbayē's principle
(cf. *supra* p. 162) that the richness of scriptural meaning contains no
superfluities, so that convergent results deduced from discrete texts can
only have been arrived at improperly. [112] We find it applied with regard
to two incompatible expressions of opinion on the part of R. 'Aqiba [113]
regarding compensation payable in the case of an unbetrothed virgin
who is seduced. The Biblical texts [114] do not further particularise the
marital state of the victim (אשר לא ארשה), and the Mishnah [115] raises the
question of a victim whose betrothal had been previously terminated.

---

109a. גילדנא is equated with μαινίς, *Sparus Maena* (Jesus bar Bahlul: Payne
Smith, *Thesaurus Syr.*, and I. Löw, *Aram. Fischnamen, Nöldeke Festschrift*, 1906,
i, p. 522 no. 4); A Kohut, however (*Aruch*, ii, p. 293) suggests χελιδών = *flying
fish* or χελιδονίας, a kind of tunny. Dobschütz (see note 101) compares to the
distinction drawn by 'Abbayē that drawn by Rava (*Yeb.* 63b) between the literal
understanding (בגוה) of the word *woman* in *Prov.* xviii:22 and *Eccles.* vii:26 and
its possible allegorical applications (no term, however, being used in connection
with the latter).

110. Bacher, *Terminologie* (see note 43), ii, p. 113. N. Krochmal, *Moreh
Nebochey ha-Zeman,* ed. Zunz-Wolf, Lemberg, 1863, chap. xiv, p. 184.

111. *Yeb.* 11b (*Num.* v:14 and *Deut.* xxiv:4).

112. The three principles may be contrasted schematically thus:
  (i) *Gezerah Shawah.* Text *A* containing *x* points to deduction *Z*, ∴ text
      *B* containing *x* points to Z.
  (ii) *'Abbayē's principle.* מקרא אחד יוצא לכמה טעמים וכו' Text *A* points to
      arguments *XYZ* ∴ *XYZ* cannot properly be indicated by texts *BCD.*
      etc.
  (iii) *The principle* אין מקרא יוצא מידי פשוטו. Deduction by *gezerah shawah*
      from text *A* to *B* is to be applied with circumspection and by no
      means in the teeth of the context of text *B.*

113. *Keth.* 38 a-b.

114. *Ex.* xxii:15, *Deut.* xxii:28. The question is raised as to the admissibility of
a *gezerah shawah* based on the phrase quoted, which occurs in both, as does also
the word *virgin* (בתולה).

115. *Keth.* iii, 3.

R. 'Aqiba asserts that the proceeds of the seducer's fine are due to a victim of this category, and not to her father, [116] construing the above phrase (*who has not been betrothed*) to mean *who has not [at any time] been betrothed* — with the determination of her betrothal her father's rights devolve on herself. However, in a *Baraita* [117] 'Aqiba went on record as holding that in such circumstances a fine is payable, the proceeds being due not to the victim but to her father. 'Aqiba's opinion as represented by the Mishnah is preferred, inasmuch as it does not involve a deduction from analogy that completely distorts the *peshaṭ.* [118] Though stretching the crucial words into the meaning *who has not [at any time] been betrothed,* 'Aqiba nevertheless leaves uncompromised the implied distinction between a victim who is currently betrothed and one who is not — it is this fundamental distinction  that is regarded as the *peshaṭ,* even though the positive case is merely implied in the statement of the negative one. His view in the *Baraita,* by implicitly equating the situation in law of the unbetrothed and the ex-betrothed victim, obscures the distinction between unbetrothed and betrothed which is cardinal to the biblical phrase, and thus invites the criticism that it is a distortion: for the words of the text, according to R. Naḥman b. Isaac, mean *who is not [currently] betrothed,* nothing being asserted with regard to a previously broken engagement. [119] Even though R. Naḥman makes his point by means of a grammatically impossible rearrangement of the verb *betrothed,* this construction of the biblical phrase is palpably more natural than that proposed by 'Aqiba in the Mishnah; and we are left with the conclusion that, at least in this passage, what is meant by the *peshaṭ* is not so much the explicit meaning of the text, as the converse which it naturally implies. Alternatively, the *peshaṭ* which would be compromised by the *gezerah shawah* advanced by R. 'Aqiba in the *Baraita* has nothing whatsoever to do with exegesis and refers to accepted halakhic practice — *viz.* that entitlement to compensation differs according to whether the seduced girl was, or was not, currently betrothed.

For 'Abbayē's contemporary Rava, however, the term *peshaṭ* apparently did mean the natural and explicit meaning of the text, at any rate within the context of this formula. We find him enunciating the principle in

116. The two biblical texts are not quite consistent regarding the rights of the father.

117. *Keth.* 38a.

118. *Ibid.,* fol. b בשלמא ר'ע דמתניתין דלא אתיא ג'ש ומפקא לקרא מפשטיה לגמרי.

119. א"ר נחמן בר יצחק קרי ביה אשר לא ארוסה.

connection with the law of the levirate marriage, [120] in connection with which halakhic practice in a certain particular is in manifest disagreement with the wording of the biblical injunction (*Deut.* xxv:6). The latter plainly declares that the first-born son of a childless widow remarried to her late husband's brother shall 'rise upon the name of his dead brother' (יקום על שם אחיו המת), i.e. be given the name borne by the deceased. It may be granted that the expression is an unusual one for *to be named*; but the context admits of little doubt as to what is intended. The occurrence of a similar phrase in *Gen.* xlviii:6, where inheritance is at issue, has given rise to a *gezerah shawah* which regards the words in the passage relative to the levir as having to do not with nomenclature, but inheritance; and the clause is referred, not to the offspring (although he is explicitly mentioned as the subject of the verb), but to the levir — it is the latter who succeeds to his late brother's property, and not that late brother's posthumously suppositious son, and the obligation to make the child his namesake lapses. Rava asserts that this is a unique case of a *gezerah shawah* being permitted to distort the *peshaṭ* completely. [121] Rava's language is formulated concessively; [122] the exegetical means employed are here tolerated, because (it would seem) the biblical text can thus only be squared with halakhic practice.

But in the next generation the principle was still so far from being generally recognised that it was possible for R. Kahana, though a talmudist of many years' standing, to have remained in ignorance of it. [123] R. Eliezer's contention that weapons may be articles of dress, and consequently legitimate wear for the Sabbath, had been supported by reference to *Ps.* xlv:4, where *sword* apparently stands in apposition to *glory* and *majesty*. To this R. Kahana had objected that *sword* here is figurative for *expertise* in Torah, which should be girded on, i.e. kept ready for instant action by constant study. This exegesis of R. Kahana was countered by Mar b. Rabina through the citation of the principle that a text may not be distorted from its *peshaṭ*. R. Kahana accepts the principle, although declaring that it is new to him, but appears to pass in

---

120. *Yeb.* 24a.

121. אמר רבא אע״ג דבכל התורה אין מקרא יוצא מידי פשוטו הכא אתאי ג״ש אפיקתיה מפשטיה לגמרי.

122. Bacher, *Terminologie* (see note 43), ii, p. 113 asserts that the principle is strongly emphasised (*stark betonte*) by Rava, but this seems to press to undue lengths the force of the formulation that Rava chose to employ.

123. *Sabb.* 63a. See Bacher, *Terminologie*, ii, p. 173, and *Die Aggada der Babylonischen Amoräer*, 1878, p. 145f.

silence over the fact that it would impair his equation of *sword* and *Torah;* what the principle (? or the incident [124]) teaches is that the student should not allow play to his own powers of reasoning until he has assimilated his teacher's conclusions, if necessary taking them temporarily on trust. This would indicate that what is here understood by the *peshaṭ* was not necessarily the natural meaning of the biblical text, but rather the meaning traditionally accepted as authoritative or at any rate familiar, however far from the primary sense of the words it might be. It may be observed that in this last instance of the adducing of the principle אין מקרא וכו׳, no question of any *gezerah shawah* is involved.

Before we make any suggestions as to what may be the cardinal notion inherent in the use of the term *peshaṭ*, it may be helpful to glance briefly at certain other exegetical terms, some of which are possessed of conventional antonyms. It may be that we shall find amongst them some sound appreciation of the distinction between literal or plain, and nonliteral or applied and secondary exegesis; yet we must be constantly on our guard against making any tacit assumption that such distinctions may be read into the term *peshaṭ* as used explicitly or implicitly in contrast to other possible modes of interpretation.

The use of the term כתב, writing, in the phrase דברים ככתבם,[125] as a discouragement of halakhic deviation from an established norm associated with an assumed rigidity of meaning implicit in the scriptural text, appears at first sight to presuppose a conception of the presence of a 'plain' meaning in a text, to the exclusion of all exegesis. [126] Yet where extreme literalism would lead to an halakhic conclusion manifestly perverse, no reluctance is felt in rejecting the כתב, the acceptable exegetical alternative to which is introduced by תלמוד לומר as pointer to another scriptural quotation whose content, if it is to be followed, precludes the pressing of the first one *ad absurdum.* [127] Moreover, in the field of *'aggada* the corresponding expression X *is not written here, but rather*

---

124. במאי קמ״ל דליגמר איניש והדר ליסבר. The formula should refer to a tannaitic *dictum,* and is best referred to the exegetical principle under discussion: but Goldschmidt (unsupported by Rashi) seems to refer it to the *incident,* as would M. Gertner (privately). Were this so, it would desiderate (instead of the explanation advanced) something like 'one lives and learns'.

125. Bacher, *Terminologie* (see note 43), ii. p. 92.

126. E.g. *Pes.* 21b on *Deut.* xiv:21 (R. Judah); *Qidd.* 17b on *Deut.* xv:14 (R. Eliezer).

127. E.g. *Baraita* in *Ber.* 35b, on *Josh.* i:8 לא ימוש ספר התורה הזה מפיך יכול דברים ככתבם ת״ל ואספת דגנך הנהג בהן מנהג דרך ארץ.

Y, [128] is a device for achieving entirely subjective exegetical results through the relentless forcing of linguistic phenomena which, in the context, are incidental to the syntax or accidence. [129] Even though the soil whence alone such interpretation can spring is one of very intimate familiarity with the letter of the text, its results are quite arbitrary; and they cannot properly be classified as literal exegesis. [130]

The terms אם למסורת, אם למקרא, [131] are limited to halakhic contexts, the former maintaining the paramountcy of traditional vocalisation over against whatever degree of equivocation the unvocalised consonantal text may admit. Although אם למסורת is an amoraic coinage, the fact that a group of named Tannaites are recorded to have upheld the alternative principle אם למקרא [132] seems to justify us in assuming that the majority of the remainder subscribed to the other principle. The insistence on אם למקרא would seek to inhibit such halakhic divergence as might claim the support of the consonantal text if the vocalisation is ignored, in order to maintain whatever palpable links might be available between current *halakhah* and the public rendition of the text. Thus we find in a *Baraita* [133] it is applied by R. ʿAqiba in defence of the slightly anomalous infinitive in *Ex.* xxi:8; as against the normal *be-voghᵉdho, be-vighᵉdho* בבגדו must be retained with tradition, although בבגדו is not the same thing as בבגדו (to which ʿAqiba would fain see an allusion), and despite the syntactical impossibility of the latter in the context. If אם למסורת may reasonably be deemed to have been the majority view, it should be borne in mind that wherever the issue of the two rival principles is raised, the possible differences in practice that might follow from אם למקרא carrying

128. ... אין כתיב כאן אלא ...

129. E.g. Pal. Talmud *Ber.* i, 1 2d on *2 Kings* iii:15 (R. Levi) והיה כנגן המנגן כנגן במנגן אכ״כ אלא כנגן המנגן הכינור היה מנגן מאליו.

130. It is worth observing that in the passages in the Babylonian Talmud (*Ḥag.* 14a, *San.* 38b, 67b) where R. ʿAqiba's essays in ʾ*aggada* are ridiculed by the phrase מה לך אצל הגדה כלך וכו׳, the point revolves round a number, the (collective) singularity or plurality of which is, in its context, purely idiomatic (e.g. in the last passage *Ex.* viii:2 ותעל הצפרדע). Both ʿAqiba's own exegesis and that proffered as superior to it take as their starting point the insistence, in the teeth of idiom, on the significance of the occurrence of a singular or a plural. ʿAqiba's exegesis of *Ps.* lxxviii:25 לחם אבירים in a *Baraita* (*Yoma* 75b), though a natural one, is refuted in favour of one that is far more artificial, surprisingly enough by R. Ishmael (אמר להם צאו ואמרו לו לר״ע עקיבא טעית וכו׳).

131. Bacher, *Terminologie* (see note 43), i, p. 119f, ii, p. 115.

132. R. Judah b. Roʿeṣ, *Beth Shammai*, R. Simeon b. Yoḥai, R. ʿAqiba, and R. Judah the Prince. Cf. *San.* 4a/b, *Pes.* 86b on *Ex.* xii:46 (*yēʾākhēl* and not *yōkhal*).

133. *Qidd.* 18a/b דתניא בבגדו כיון שפירש טליתו עליה שוב אינו רשאי למוכרה.

the day are slight ones, with negligible implications of a socially disruptive nature. Once again, the categories 'literal' and 'non-literal' are not pertinent. It may be further remarked that, as the formulation by means of the *lamedh* emphasises, in the case of each of the principles its 'mother' authority (אם) is felt to be external to the medium in which it is expressed; in the case of מקרא the authority is felt to reside in the supposedly constant tradition of practical *halakhah*, including the '*halakhah*' of grammar and phonetics, and in the case of מסורת it attaches to the mystic origin that supposedly guarantees the accuracy of the written text, any degree of equivocation in which is consequently held to be pre-ordained.

If we examine the way in which the term משמעו (*mishma'o*) [134] is used, we seem to find the early Rabbis on the verge of an understanding of what the plain 'letter' of scripture means. Together with *mishma'o* we may take R. Ishmael's well-known exegetical slogan דברה תורה כלשון בני אדם [135] which was intended as a counterpoise, if not indeed as a counterblast, to R. 'Aqiba's stressing of lexical *minutiae* occasioned by the exigencies of syntax. But it should be noted that Ishmael's principle seems always to be advanced apologetically rather than being volunteered, as indeed its very formulation suggests. The same may also be generally true of the term כשמועו. [136] Thus on *Ex.* xvi:23 ולא מצאו מים, the *Mekhilta* [137] records that R. Joshua took it כשמועו: of the interpretations that follow, all except that of R. Eliezer [138] are either allegorical, or press מצאו to arbitrary lengths. But there seems to be no apologetic motivation in its use by R. Levi on *Gen.* vi:13 (חמס); [139] proof-texts are first furnished by him for identifying *violence* with the three cardinal sins of idolatry, inchastity,

---

134. So correctly Bacher, *Terminologie*, ii p. 222; *mashma'*, an *'aphel* participle active according to Bacher (as against Jastrow, who treats it as passive) is used differently (see below).

135. Bacher, *Terminologie* i, p. 98. Cf. also the phrase לשכך (להשמיע) את האוזן מה שהיא יכולה לשמוע as elaborated in the 14th of the 32 Rules of R. Josē (see note 38a), ed. Enelow, p. 25; Bacher, *Terminologie*, i, p. 3.

136. Bacher, *ibid.*, i, 190f., ii, 221f.

137. Ed. Weiss, 53b.

138. כדי ליגען. It may be noted that in the *Mekhilta* of R. Simeon b. Yoḥai, ed. J. N. Epstein – E.Z. Melamed, 1955, p. 102, 1. 21, this is attributed to R. Joshua, the term כשמועו not occurring. R. Eliezer is there credited with כדי לנסותן, i. e. virtually equivalent exegesis.

139. *Gen. R.* § 31,6, ed. Theodor, p. 280. Cf. also § 1,5, Theodor p. 2, on *Ps.* xxxi:19 תאלמנה (R. Huna quoting Bar Kappara). Of possible Aramaic renderings, he says that אשתקקן כשמועו.

and homicide, (*v.l.* כמשמעו) חמס כשמועו following or being identified with
the last of them. But in view of the often subjective interpretations that
are introduced by Aramaic causative form *mashmaʿ*,[140] it seems unwarranted to postulate any firm association between the use of terminology
derived from שמע and a true concept of plain literalism as a proper
branch of exegetical discipline; at the most, we have to do with a semi-
articulate feeling towards one.

With the terms ודאי and ממש[141] we seem to be a stage further in the
same journey. ממש, i.e. what is tactile, sensible, and therefore real, occurs
quite often to distinguish actuality from imaginative interpretation. In
some cases no question of literalism *versus* allegory arises, but simply a
difference of interpretation regarding what is, in both opinions, factual.
Thus R. Judah understands the ערבים by whom Elijah was fed (*1 Kings*
xvii:6) to mean inhabitants of a place correspondingly named, perhaps
El ʿArbaʾin, whereas R. Nehemiah takes it to mean ravens literally
(ממש).[142] There is obviously much scope for divisions of this kind regarding the usage of prepositions, the extended idiomatic application
of which can sometimes be contested, without absurd results, in the
light of the basic meaning. Thus a new-born calf, lamb or kid is to be
left for a week 'beneath'(תחת) its mother (*Lev.* xxii:27); does this mean
'in the company of' (עם), or (by a possible, if indeed forced explanation)
[surviving] 'after' its mother [should she die within the period], or,
quite literally, 'under' [*sc.* its dam's udder] (תחת אמו כמשמעו, ממש)?[143]
Generally, however, both ממש and ודאי distinguish literal exegesis from
applied clearly enough. In the injunction of *Deut.* xx:8 to dismiss from
the army before battle anyone who is 'fearful and faint-hearted,' R. Yosē
sees a reference to the pangs of a guilty conscience;[144] R. ʿAqiba insists

140. Bacher, *Terminologie,* ii, p. 222.

141. Bacher, *Terminologie* i, pp. 113, 148, ii, pp. 60, 105.

142. *Gen. R.* § 33,5, ed. Theodor, p. 309, cf. *Ḥullin* 5a. Similarly regarding
the place-name Succoth in *Ex.* xii:37, *Mekhilta, Boʾ,* ed. Horovitz–Rabin, p. 48,
ed. Weiss. p. 18b: R. Eliezer takes it literally. In the *Mekhilta* of R. Simeon b.
Yoḥai (see, note 138), p. 33, i, 1, the opinions of R. Eliezer and R. ʿAqiba
are transposed.

143. *Mekhilta, Mishpaṭim* on *Ex.* xxii:29, ed. Horovitz–Rabin p. 319, ed. Weiss
p. 103a/b, where see Weiss' note on R. Nathan's discussion (and rejection) of
the possibility of construing the preposition to mean *surviving after.*

144. זה המתירא מן העבירה שבידו. *Tosefta, Soṭah* vii, 22, ed. Zuckermandel p.
309, l. 14.

that cowardice in the face of the enemy is literally intended (הירא ודאי). [145] The 'strange' land (ארץ נכריה) of Moses' sojourning (*Ex.* xviii:3) is taken literally (ודאי) by R. Joshua b. Ḥananiah as *foreign*, whereas R. Eleazar Ha-Modaʻi takes it to mean *idolatrous* (נכריה). [146] The incident of eating in the visual presence of God (*Ex.* xxiv:11) may be understood literally of feasting (אכילה ודאי), with R. Yoḥanan, who was controverting R. Joshua; the latter palliates the anthropomorphism by making it mean that they 'feasted their eyes' on the divine *Shekhinah*. [147] The two women described in the judgement of Solomon (*1 Kings* iii:16) as 'harlots' were, according to Rav, spirits (רוחות), or, as R. Benjamin following R. Judah thought, sisters-in-law with a dispute as to levirate obligations, or, according to Samuel, quite literally harlots (זונות ממש). [148] The well of 'living' water discovered by Isaac's servants (*Gen.* xxvi:19) was identified by R. Nathan on the basis of *Prov.* viii: 35 with the Torah; Rava declared that literal water is meant (מים ממש). [149]

Both ודאי and ממש are quite clearly used to advance controversially motivated exegesis. For example on *Ex.* v:23 [150] הצל לא הצלת R. Ishmael asserts that the infinitive absolute carries its normal (ודאי) reinforcing *nuance — thou hast in no wise delivered.* He will have none of the double time reference, to past and future simultaneously, that R. ʻAqiba attaches to the repeated verbal stem. Although Ishmael's interpretation precedes that of ʻAqiba in the source, in view of their well-known opposing standpoints and the vapidity of Ishmael's comment here if it is isolated from its context, there can be little doubt that it is a rebuttal elicited by ʻAqiba's. There are, however, three passages (all in the Babylonian *Soṭah*) where the alternative views of Rav and Samuel are cited, in all of which the plain interpretation, explicitly labelled ממש, precedes the more *recherché*. It is not essential, it seems to me, to regard the former as apologetic by anticipation; and indeed, if the editor had himself regarded it in such a light, he would presumably have inverted them for the sake of making the rebuttal more marked. In spite of the usual,

145. The parallels in Mishnah, *Soṭah*, viii, 5 and *Sifrē, Deut.* § 197 have *kemishmaʻo*.

146. *Mekhilta, Yithro*, ed. Horovitz–Rabin p. 191, Weiss 65b.

147. שזנו עיניהם מן השכינה. *Lev. R.* § 20, 10.

148. *Midrash Psalms* lxxii, ed. Buber 162b. Variant names are given in the parallels.

149. *Berakh.* 56b. The reading חיים ממש. although maintained in the translations of Goldschmidt, A. Cohen, and the Soncino Talmud, is scarcely possible.

150. Ex. R. § 5, 22.

undifferentiated formulation with this pair of disputants חד אמר...וחד
אמר the literalist may be identified as Rav, inasmuch as in one case [151] he
is explicitly named as such. The passage concerns the urchins who mocked
Elisha, so that he 'saw' them and cursed them (ויראם ויקללם), the issue
being what is meant by 'saw.' Rav, though declaring that he 'simply saw
them' (ראה ממש) in fact does go beyond the letter of the text, for he understands this to mean that Elisha gave them an ominous 'look.' Samuel,
however, with an uninhibited flight of imagination, asserts that he *perceived* that each several child had been conceived on a canonically improper date. [152] Another instance concerns the 'new king' in Egypt, [153] of
whom one disputant, presumably Rav, claims that he was in fact a new
king (חדש ממש) ; according to the other a change of governmental policy
(שנתחדשו גזירותיו) is meant. The third [154] deals with Joseph's chastity, and
the scriptural phrase (*Gen.* xxxix:11) recording that on the crucial occasion during his period with Potiphar Joseph went into the house to 'do
his business' (לעשות מלאכתו). One disputant, again presumably Rav, takes
this at its face value (מלאכתו ממש). According to the other, who follows
R. Yoḥanan, 'business' is a euphemism (לעשות צרכיו) — Joseph was mo-
mentarily mastered by his passions and entered the house with intent to
sin, but recovered himself in time. Rav was himself by no means immune
from mystical speculation regarding the creation story and the *maʿaseh
merkabah*, and in his *ʾaggada* — which is richly preserved — he let his
imagination work fruitfully. [155] But his exegesis is in general character-
ised by straightforwardness; and even though he evinces an occasional
venture into allegory, [156] it may well be that he comes nearer than any
other scholar of the talmudic period to a positive understanding — and
evaluation — of the plain sense of Scripture. Examples to the contrary
taken from his exegesis do not necessarily invalidate this suggestion; it is
unnecessary, and indeed unreasonable to expect that his recorded interpretations should be all of a piece.

The terms אמת and משל are used as antonyms, [157] the essence of משל

---

151. *Soṭah*, 46b, on *2 Kings* ii:24.
152. ראה שכולן נתעברה בהן אמן ביום הכיפורים.
153. *Ex.* i:8, *Soṭah*, 11a.
154. *Soṭah*, 36b.
155. Cf. the instance *supra*, note 148. Bacher, *Die Agada der Babylonischen
Amoräer*, 1878, p. 29f.
156. E.g. *Ḥullin*, 92a on Pharaoh's dream, *Gen.* xl:10 (שריגים).
157. Bacher, *Terminologie* (see note 43), i, p. 122, ii, p. 121. I. Heinemann,
*Altjüdische Allegoristik*, p. 15.

when it is so contrasted being that it is not *factually* true. Thus in an anecdote [158] regarding a presumptuous pupil of R. Eliezer his name and paternity are cited, the reason alleged being in order to prevent the story being regarded as merely poetically, and not historically true. [159] For this reason משל is disallowed in the Pentateuch as a hermeneutic device save in the case of three instances, all of which are halakhic although cited in a context dealing with the rules for aggadic interpretation. [160] In general, the use of משל does not seem to have been frowned upon, unless the injunction not to disparage it [161] is to be deemed to be evidence that it was in fact disparaged; the language is reminiscent of the defence advanced for the rule of *Gezerah Shawah*, [162] which (as the check upon its application suggests) did probably come under criticism because of its exposure to facile abuse. The light that משל can throw on the text is reckoned [163] comparable to the sort of torch — no mere 'penny candle' [164] — that one would be prepared to use in the search for a lost gold piece or a pearl.

As opposed to משל, אמת means *fact*, [164a] and in particular historical fact — patient, indeed, of exegesis and perhaps even demanding it. Thus R. Eleazar, by juxtaposing the words in *Esth.* ix:30 דברי שלום ואמת with *Prov.* xxiii:23 אמת קנה ואל תמכור, could demonstrate the validity of Rav's contention that the book of *Esther* is as fit a subject for exposition as is the very truth of the Pentateuch itself. [165]

The idea that historical truth may be something distinct from historical fact is once fleetingly raised in connection with these two terms, only to be rejected. The passage concerned [166] considers the resurrection of the dead in connection with a *Tana de-vey 'Eliyyahu* which asserts that resurrection, once effected, will be perpetual. [167] But the contrary might, con-

---

158. *'Eruvin*, 63a.

159. שלא תאמר משל היה.

160. No. 26 of the rules in the *Baraita* of R. Eliezer b. Yosē Ha-Gelili, ed. H. G. Enelow, 1933, p. 36.

161. *Cant.* R. § 1,8 on i:1, ed. Wilna 2a, col. b, *infra*, adducing *Prov.* i:1, ורבנן אמרין אל יהי המשל הזה קל בעיניך שע"י המשל הזה אדם יכול לעמוד על דברי תורה.

162. *Kerithoth* 5a לעולם אל תהי גזירה שוה קלה בעיניך וכו'. Cf. *Supra*, note 39, and see Weiss, *Dor Dor we-doreshaw*, i, chap. 18, ed. Wilna, 1911, p. 156.

163. *Cant. R., loc. cit.*

164. פתילה כאיסר.

164a. Cf. Lauterbach (see note 176), p. 331.

165. Pal. Talmud *Meg.* i, 1 80b ז"א שמגילת אסתר ניתנה להידרש .... הרי היא כאמיתה של תורה.

166. *Sanh.* 92a/b.

167. צדיקים שעתיד הקב"ה להחיותן אינן חוזרין לעפרן שנא' וכו'.

ceivably, be deduced (ונילף) from the vision of Ezekiel (chap. xxxvii), it being held that those whom Ezekiel saw resurrected in the valley of dry bones subsequently died again; no, the source must have endorsed the view of R. Nehemiah in a *Baraita* that the vision was quite clearly (באמת) all משל, i.e. not factual. [168] The *Baraita,* which is then cited, asserts that those resurrected in the vision of Ezekiel sang a song (variant versions of which are given) and thereafter died again, and then proceeds to record R. Judah's opinion that the whole thing was *truth in the form of a* משל. [169] To this R. Nehemiah objects that it is a contradiction in terms: [170] if R. Judah's view is to be substantiated, he must put it (or rather quote his source's formulation) in the form '*in* very truth (i.e. quite clearly) it was a משל'. [171] The preposition is held to tbe integral to R. Judah's case. It is not impossible that R. Nehemiah was influenced by the halakhic implications of the formula באמת אמרו as conferring a hall-mark of halakhic authenticity, [172] inasmuch as questions of eligibility for resurrection, upon which R. Nehemiah had some pronounced views, [173] were felt to border upon the realm of *halakhah.* Perhaps his insistence on the wording באמת was intended to assert the unequivocal eligibility of the dry bones of the house of Israel in Ezekiel's vision for the future, general resurrection — irrespective of whether or not he might have to concede R. Judah's view that the whole vision was an allegory, or the view expressed in the *Baraita* that it was indeed factual but that those then resurrected subsequently died again.

It is thus R. Nehemiah, rather than R. Judah, who here represents conventional opinion. That there was no generally accepted understanding of historical truth as something distinct from historical fact, is borne out by a question addressed by the men of Semonias, near Sepphoris, to R.

---

168. ונילף ממתים שהחיה יחזקאל סבר לה כמאן דאמר באמת משל היה. Rashi paraphrases באמת by בברור.

169. אמת משל היה. Goldschmidt renders 'Dies ist eine wirkliche Dichtung gewesen'; the Soncino Talmud, 'It was truth; it was a parable'.

170. א״ל ר׳ נחמיה אם אמת למה משל ואם משל למה אמת אלא באמת משל היה.

171. Goldschmidt renders 'Vielmehr, in Wirklichkeit war es eine Dichtung'; the Soncino Talmud, 'In the truth there was but a parable', adding a note to the effect that the resurrection was both historically factual and foreshadowed the renaissance of the Jewish people. This rendering scarcely does justice to the distinction felt by R. Nehemiah between אמת and באמת, and his rejection of the formulation by means of the former.

172. *B. M.* 60a, א״ר אלעזר עדה אמרה כל באמת אמרו הלכה היא, Pal. Talmud *Sabbath* i, 3, 3b, l. 8 from foot, א״ר לעזר כל מקום ששנינו באמת הלכה למשה מסיני.

173. E.g. Mishnah, *Sanh.* 10, 3.

Levi b. Sisi, which at first stumped him. [174] His questioners, who cited
*Dan.* x:21, *I will shew thee that which is noted in the scripture of
truth,* [175] assumed an incompatibility between אמת, *truth,* and רשום, *noted;*
their assumption derived from the *nuance* of [*allegorically, symbolically*]
*expounded* that had become attached to the term רשום through its connection with the allegorical school of *doreshey reshumoth.* [176] The answer
that he eventually produced went behind this *nuance* to the basic meaning
of *noted,* which R. Levi extended to mean [*provisionally*] *marked down,* as
distinct from *truth,* i.e. a record not subject to cancellation. [177] Alongside
this we may record the scepticism of R. Samuel b. Naḥmani with regard
to the suggestion that the story of Job is a parable (משל), [178] and his endeavours to find proof-texts to the contrary from the book and from the
parable (never explicitly called such in the text) addressed by Nathan
to David (*2 Sam.* xii). These passages show that משל and אמת, insofar as
they are contrasted with one another, lie outside the sphere of practical
exegetics altogether; they concern what may be termed metexegetics. On
the other hand, משל in its own right constitutes a proper hermeneutical
tool — mainly appropriate to '*aggada,* but allowed some scope even in
halakhic matters; an instrument that frankly allows as full a play to the
subjective element as is in fact enjoyed by other principles also, e.g.
אין כתיב כאן אלא..., although these make a show of being allegedly bound
to the 'letter.'

   We may, then, sum up as follows. In the terms other than פשט that we
have been examining, we may observe at the most a semi-articulate feeling towards a distinction between literal and non-literal exegesis, and
this in connection with the terms ממש, ודאי, and (כשמעו) כמשמעו only; the
contrast between משל and אמת lies upon a different plane. Yet even the
terms here mentioned can sometimes be used to draw distinctions of a
lesser categorical order, e.g. as between two possible 'concrete' interpretations; and *kemishma'o* etc. is lexically so closely cognate to terms that
introduce the quite subjective enlargement upon a text, as to render it
a far from unequivocal symbol to denote exegesis that claims to exclude

---

174. Pal. Talmud *Yeb.* xii, 7, 18a.

175. אגיד לך את הרשום בכתב אמת.

176. אם אמת למה רשום ואם רשום למה אמת. See J. Z. Lauterbach's article in the
*Jewish Quarterly Review,* N. S., i, 1910–11, especially p. 302 note.

177. עד שלא נתחתם גזר דין רשום משנתחתם ג״ד אמת. The parallel in *Gen. R.* § 81,
2, ed. Theodor p. 970, reads רשום קודם גזירה אמת משנגזרה גזירה מהו חותמו של הקב״ה אמת.

178. *B. B.* 15a איוב לא היה ולא נברא אלא משל היה (R. Simeon b. Laqish; Cf.
*Gen. R.* § 57, 4, ed. Theodor p. 617).

subjectivity entirely. Whilst it may be with justice asserted that early rabbinic exegesis includes many observations that are sober, pertinent, and
rational, there is not, it seems, sufficient precision in the use of the terms
here examined to indicate that such exegesis was explicitly, or indeed in
general even consciously placed in a category of its own: and the 'straws
in the wind' that we have noticed of a feeling towards such categorisa-
tion are certainly far too insignificant numerically to justify us in superimposing their import upon the use of the term *peshaṭ* up to the end of
the talmudic period, let alone in magnifying that import into such proportions as would make it appear to be the dominant notion present in
the term *peshaṭ* at that period.

In turning, finally, back to the term פשט itself and asking ourselves
what positive notion if any is inherent in its early rabbinic use, we must
avoid the corresponding error of determining for ourselves what it was
that the Rabbis considered the 'plain' meaning of the text and of assuming that they themselves recognised in this the *peshaṭ*. Even so great a
scholar as I. H. Weiss [179] seems to me to fall into this error when controverting the mediaeval *apologia* for early rabbinic exegesis that would
maintain that it was concerned not with the exegesis of the text, but
rather the general tenor of support ('*asmakhta*) that it could give to
familiar ideas and institutions. Weiss insisted, rightly, that what is to be
regarded as plain, straightforward exposition is a question to which different periods, intellectual climates, and even individual temperaments
will give varying answers: so that we should not be justified in disallow-
ing a claim by early rabbinic comment to be prosecuting literal exegesis
merely because it conflicts with our own notions of rationalism. He
further states that the occurrence of such phrases as מכאן אמרו shows that
the deduction was seriously considered to express the true, i.e. the *essential*
meaning of the text; [180] so that *halakhah* and '*aggada* will be the result,
and not the cause, of exegesis believed to be *literal* by the rabbis. Following this up, Rosenblatt [181] points to such cases as *Terumoth* vi, 6 on *Lev.*
xxii:14 [182] as corroboration. As against this it might be urged that in
other cases where two divergent constructions of the same text are cited,
there is sometimes no doubt as to which of the two is, in both modern
and any intelligible ancient sense of the word, the more literal — even if

179. *Dor Dor we-doreshaw,* i, chap. 18, ed. Wilna, 1911, p. 158.
180. ועל כן דבר ברור הוא כי מדרש המקרא היה אצלם פירושו של מקרא וכל דורש חשב
שזה כונת המקרא באמת. The latter phrase corresponds to what Weiss in the wider
context intends by פשוטו של מקרא.
181. *Op. cit.* (see note 39), p. 5.

to follow it might lead to embarrassing or perverse halakhic results, e.g. *Berakhoth* i, 3, on *Deut.* vi:6. The fact that the sources nevertheless not only record both constructions, but often authenticate halakhically the results of the less literal construction, shows that identity of the *essential* meaning (as viewed by the rabbis) with the *literal* meaning has been tacitly and gratuitously assumed by Weiss and Rosenblatt, and this in turn identified by them with the *peshaṭ*. That the identification is not a justifiable one is suggested by the following piece of negative evidence. Although strict conformity with the written prescriptions of the biblical law was an issue as between the Pharisees and the Sadducees, the sources do not retrospectively represent the Pharisees as casting the term *peshaṭ* in the teeth of their excessively literal-minded rivals. [182a] It would seem that it was too closely associated with their own party's exegetical endeavour as well to be patient of pejorative overtones for them. The same holds good of the *doreshey reshumoth*, [183] alternatives to whose allegorical exegesis are sometimes proffered, but never stated to be *peshaṭ*. On one occasion [184] the literal explanation, which precedes, is given in the form *kemishmaʿo*, and when R. Gamaliel, somewhat hesitantly, for once adopted their style of exegesis, [185] he justified himself by saying 'it was nevertheless *plausible*' (*nirʾeh*). Nor do the rabbis ever refer to the *peshaṭ* when reproving each other for perverting or manipulating the text (כתובים, etc.). [185a]

Rosenblatt himself postulates [186] three headings as constituting between them exegesis reckoned in the *Mishnah* as *peshaṭ*, viz. (i) *definitions* introduced by such formulas as כמשמעו, איזהו. (ii) The citation of *conflicting interpretations* of the text, or of single interpretations being

---

182. ממקום שר' אליעזר מיקל משם ר"ע מחמיר שנא' ונתן לכהן את הקדש כל שהוא ראוי. Cf. *B.Q.* iii, 9. להיות קדש דר"א ור"ע"א ונתן לכהן את הקדש קדש שאכל.

182a. Mishnah, *Yadayim,* iv, 6, 7, Tosefta, end.

183. On this school of allegorists see Lauterbach (note 176), especially p. 505, and compare now C. Roth's article *A talmudic reference to the Qumran Sect?* in *Revue de Qumran,* 6, 2, 2, February 1960. Similarly M. Güdemann, *Spirit and Letter in Judaism and Christianity, J.Q.R.* iv, 1892, p. 345 f., regards Mishnah *San.* xi, 1, as elaborated in the Bab. Talmud (99a) relative to the denial of Torah 'from heaven' as being a rejoinder to Paul's assertion (*2 Cor.* iii:6) that *the letter killeth.*

184. On *Rephidim,* Ex. xvii:8, *Mekhilta* of R. Simeon b. Yoḥai, ed. D. Hoffmann p. 82 (not included in the critical text of Epstein–Melamed); cf. *Sanhedrin* 106a.

185. *Sifrē, Numbers* § 8, ed. H. S. Horovitz, p. 14, כמין חומר אבל נראה.

185a. E.g. *Sifrē, Deut.* § 1, end למה אתה מעוית עלינו את הכתובים ed. Finkelstein p. 8.

186. *Op. cit.* (see note 39), p. 5.

implicitly refutations of allegorical constructions. (iii) 'Literal exegesis in a bold sense, including those instances in which the exegesis is only implied in the use made of the [187] verse', by which he means 'exegetical material. . . . in which the Bible is quoted only for the sake of application. . . . i.e. "Schriftanwendung" rather than "Schriftauslegung."' The divisions between these classes are not very precisely drawn; e.g. the distinction between his second, typified by the treatment of *Deut.* vi:6 in *Berakhoth* i, 3 and of *Deut.* xxi:19–20 in *Sanhedrin* viii, 4, and his third, typified by *Jer.* xvii:7 as applied in *Pe'ah* viii, 9, seems quite arbitrary. Exegetically, the two latter cases differ not in kind, but in the degree to which the details are brought into focus and then utilised at will. The real difference between the last example and that in *Sanhedrin, loc. cit.* is not exegetical at all; in *Pe'ah* a piece of more or less general morality is at stake, whereas in *Sanhedrin* the rabbis were confronted with an institution of biblical law, namely the stubborn and rebellious son, the practical implications of which they were determined to stultify. [188] In any case, since the noun *peshaṭ* does not occur in the Mishnah, any detailed assertions as to what may, on tannaitic premises, be regarded as specific to it, are inevitably subjective.

The equation *peshaṭ* = plain and literal exegesis from its earliest occurrences of the word in rabbinic sources has, indeed, generally been assumed by those who have written on the subject hitherto; [189] and in

---

187. *Ibid.*, p. 66, note 57.

188. Cf. *Tosefta, Sanhedrin,* xi 6, Bab. Talmud 71a.

189. Zunz, *Die gottesdienstlichen Vorträge der Juden²*, 1892, p. 62, equates *peshaṭ* with *Erläuterung des Schriftextes nach dem Wortverstande,* being thus more circumspect than many later students. For Geiger it is the *'einfache Sinn des Verses (Das Verhältniss der natürlichen Schriftsinnes zur talmudischen Schriftforschung,* in *Wissenschaftliche Zeitschrift für jüdische Theologie,* v. Leipzig, 1844, p. 74; see also pp. 242f., 248, 254, 257). Geiger did, however, appreciate that the consciousness of a distinction between plain and other exegesis derives not from within, but from external, controversialist factors, references to פשטיה דקרא reflecting a groping towards a conscious distinction. D. Hoffmann apparently dealt with the matter summarily (*einfache Erklärung; Das Buch Leviticus,* Berlin, introduction, p. 3). W. Rosenau, *Jewish Biblical Commentators,* Baltimore, 1906, is similar (p. 18 — the plain interpretation). In his article on *peshaṭ* in the *Jewish Encyclopedia,* ix, p. 652f., J. Z. Lauterbach, though summarising the notion as = simple scriptural exegesis, is careful to point out that 'a distinction between "peshaṭ" as the literal sense of Scripture and "derash" as the interpretation and derivation could not have been made in antiquity for the simple reason that the Tannaim believed . . . . that their "derash" was the actual sense of Scripture, and therefore "peshaṭ"; he did, however, consider that a distinction

some cases apologetic factors have clearly been at work. [190] It is desirable, therefore, to put the matter into its correct perspective. The rabbis were absorbed by the theological dimension of social ethics, their raw material being the Jewish people and its historical experience, and their instrument the Oral and Written Torah — an instrument the revelational character of which placed certain checks on its handling. The categories 'plain' and 'secondary' exegesis of the text are not integral to such a preoccupation; but to assert so much is not to deny that, alongside their principal interest, the rabbis were in a casual way capable of rationalistic analysis of the text and of a profound, almost humanistic insight into the situations that it portrays. In this respect they can stand comparison with most types of person in both ancient and modern times whose minds have not been trained by a system of formal logic or one of the western disciplines closely dependent thereon. Logic controls the thinking of

between *peshaṭ* = simple, literal sense and *derash* = interpretation, was understood by the *'Amora'im*. This is on the lines of L. Dobschütz, *Die einfache Bibelexegese der Tannaim mit besonderer Berücksichtigung ihres Verhältnisses zur einfachen Bibelexegese der Amoraïm*, Halle, 1893.Referring to the view that simple exegesis is a pre-tannaitic phenomenon (Frankel, *Darekhey Ha-Mishnah*, 1859, pp. 3, 6, 17, and also Weiss, *Zur Geschichte der jüdischen Tradition*, 1871, i, p. 69, ii, p. 197), Dobschütz, p. 17, regards the tannaitic period as its *floruit: peshaṭ* was a term introduced at Pumpeditha to describe *'den alten Begriff des einfachen Verständnisses'* (p. 11), possibly by R. Joseph, to distinguish the commonly accepted and simple (*gewöhnlichen, einfachen*) sense from the deeper one henceforth to be styled *derasha* (p. 12), but the concept itself does ascend to the tannaitic period being parallel to *mishmaʿ*, etc. (p. 46). After Rava, and under his influence, Amoraic exegesis becomes dominated by free-ranging *'aggada* (p. 15). S. W. Baron (*A Social and Religious History of the Jews²*, 1952, ii, p. 144) still takes *peshaṭ* in talmudic times as = the plain meaning, but adds in a note (p. 386) 'Of course, the rabbis themselves could not get along without their own system of semi-allegorical interpretation'. The study by G. Aicher, *Das alte Testament in der Mischna*, Freiburg im Breisgau, 1906, was not available to me. M. Gertner (see n. 76a) likewise reaches negative conclusions only.

190. So M. Eisenstadt, *Über Bibelkritik in der Talmudischen Literatur*, Berlin, 1894; the author, whose thesis is that the hints of a plurality of authorship and sources of the biblical books anticipate 19th century bible-criticism, does not mention *peshaṭ* or suggest that the entertaining by some of the early rabbis of markedly critical views is to be equated with it. In this Eisenstadt compares favourably with the latest writer on the subject (I. Frankel, *Peshaṭ in Talmudic and Midrashic Literature*, Toronto, 1956). Frankel takes it for granted that common-sense attitudes as evinced by the rabbis are to be equated with the *peshaṭ*, to the amoraic use of which term he devotes no analysis and but superficial consideration only (p. 72f.) (See the present writer's review in the *Journal of Jewish Studies*, x, 3—4, 1961, p. 188f.).

those who are not logicians to but a partial extent, and some of those who are dominated by an overriding interest (be it material, intellectual, aesthetic or spiritual), may find little place for logic in their own absorbing concern and little occasion to apply it in other spheres. This will not necessarily preclude them from all interest in other matters or from acquiring, through contemporary speech and journalism, some knowledge of other technical vocabularies. In the case of the rabbis, echoes of the technical language of Greek philosophy and even allusions to classical texts can be recognised in their *dicta*, but the familiarity derives not first-hand, from the hellenistic schools, but from the market-place and from the law-courts. [191] If we examine their biblical exegesis, we will sometimes find them evincing not only an intellectual *acumen* but also a poetic insight which, between them, bespeak a commendably common-sense attitude to practical situations, and an enviable understanding of the frailty, the pathos, and the dignity of man. These achievements ought not to be underestimated, and it is true that in the past they have often been ignored or belittled. But they are not the whole picture of rabbinic exegesis, and to make inflated claims for them, and above all to insist that, starting from them as particulars one may infer a general notion of a rabbinic approach which presupposes an articulate distinction between the plain or literal sense of Scripture and other, applied senses, is not merely to misrepresent the rabbis: it is to confuse the issue by raising to a dominating position in exegesis categories which they themselves scarcely bothered to stress at all in their own study of the Bible.

For it seems clear from the foregoing study that notions of 'plain literalism' as a formal branch of rabbinic exegesis ought, up to the end of the period of the Talmuds and the *midrashim*, to be abandoned. As we have seen, [192] gropings in that direction are but sporadic and scarcely ever more than semi-articulate; and what we may style the terminology of refutation, with which an exegete may introduce his own alternative view in controversy with a colleague, for all its inclusion of such apparently or supposedly 'realistic' *clichés* as משמע, ממש, פשט, etc., is in effect patient of much subjective twisting. As regards the meaning of what has by anachronistic confusion been so built up as to become the most spectacular of them, namely פשט, there is no evidence known to me to pre-

---

191. Cf. note 41, and e.g. the occurrence of the Platonic myth of the ἀνδρόγυνος in the Midrash (*Gen. R.* § 8, 1, on *Gen.* i:26 and *Ps.* cxxxix:5, ed. Theodor p. 55). See on the whole subject S. Lieberman, *Greek in Jewish Palestine* (1942) and *Hellenism in Jewish Palestine* (1950).

192. *Supra,* pp. 167 f.

clude our placing it in parallel to the verbal use of the same root. As has been suggested above,[193] the essential element in the use of the verb in connection with exegesis seems to be *authority*, i.e. the *diffusion* of an opinion, by a teacher in a position to express it, amongst a public that is assumed to be receptive towards whatever emanates from him; this being a natural enough semantic development from the primitive meaning of *spread* that attaches to פשט. The noun *peshaṭ* consequently means *authoritative teaching*, but this needs some qualification. As has just been hinted, the corollary of a teacher's power to teach, which may derive from inherent qualifications, or circumstantial sanctions, or from both, is the acknowledgement of that power: indeed, it is upon such acknowledgement that the authority of what he teaches ultimately rests. Within the context of Jewish history, the equipoise which pertains between the spiritual leader or teacher and the community has always been delicately balanced — a good example being the equivocal reception, given to the decree of Rabbenu Gershom establishing monogamy as a rule for Jewish practice, by those Jewish communities that were domiciled amid polygamous environments. What an 'authoritative' teacher has to teach will, it is true, generally secure immediate recognition as being 'authoritative' if it is popularly palateable and palpably in line with tradition; but where innovations are concerned, if they are of a radical character, acknowledgement of the innovator's 'authority' will not usually be forthcoming unless his own transparent sincerity and force of character commands it. The scales are weighed in favour of conservatism.

*Peshaṭ*, therefore, means *authoritative teaching* in two possible senses. Either (as in the case of the verb), teaching propounded by an authoritative teacher, or *teaching recognised by the public as obviously authoritative, since familiar and traditional*. It is noteworthy that where the term occurs, it frequently companies with the citation of tannaitic sources or depends on traditions associated with tannaitic scholars. It is the italicised alternative that is the more important where the noun *peshaṭ* occurs. Granted, the term *peshaṭ* does sometimes proffer a more common-sensical explanation than any alternative with which it may be associated;[194] but instances cited above prove that this is certainly not invariably the case. The notion of *traditional, familiar*, and hence *authoritative* meaning of the text may not, indeed, always be to the fore when the phrase פשטיה דקרא is employed; but I have yet to see its occurrence in a

193. *Supra,* pp. 156, 158 f.
194. E.g. p. 165 and p. 161, note 94.

context which excludes such understanding of it. On the other hand, the conventional assumption that it indicates the *plain meaning* founders upon the submerged rocks of intellectual integrity. Particularly significant as an illustration of this analysis of *peshaṭ* is R. Kahana's case, and the Talmud's rider as to its import, or rather of אין מקרא יוצא מידי פשוטו, [195] *viz.* that the student should assimilate his teacher's meaning before employing his own ratiocinative powers.

The point may be reinforced by consideration of the way in which the *Gemara* [196] glosses the *dictum* of R. Judah b. 'Ill'a'i that to translate a text 'according to its form' (i.e. literally) is to falsify and to add anything thereto is to blaspheme [God's holy Word]. [197] In a *Baraita* regarding the validity of proposals of marriage, R. Judah declares that an assertion of eligibility as a husband on the grounds of the proposer's being a 'Reader of the Bible' (קריינא) is valid provided only that he can translate the text [into the Aramaic vernacular]. The *Gemara*[196] queries this stipulation in the light of R. Judah's expressed views about the ethics of scriptural translation. That the proposer should evince capability of independent translation can never have been his intention; by 'translation' what is meant is 'our own [traditional, authoritative] [198] translation.' It is true that in the case of a 'Reader', who need not necessarily be a scholar, there is no question of his independent translation being deemed to arrogate to itself the character of an authoritative rabbinical *pronunciamento*. But the implied *veto* on a layman's divergence from a traditional, sacrosanct rendering is exactly parallel to R. Kahana's case, and the claim that reason must be firmly relegated to a position where it is subordinate to traditionally authorised teaching [*peshaṭ*]. [198a] It is true that this term and its corresponding verb are used in contexts where halakhic issues are not always immediately apparent. But it is used apologetically, to introduce exegesis that is either in conformity with tradition, or which is subjectively felt by the exegete to carry less dangerous implications for traditional thought patterns or institutions than the alternative which he

195. *Supra*, p. 166 and note 124.

196. *Qidd.* 49a     ר״י אומר [אינה מקודשת לו] עד שיקרא ויתרגם יתרגם מדעתיה והתניא
ר״י אומר המתרגם פסוק כצורתו וכו׳ אלא מאי תרגום תרגום דידן.

197. *Tosefta, Meg.* end (ed. Zuckermandel p. 228f.) המתרגם פסוק כצורתו ה״ז בדאי
והמוסיף ה״ז מגדף.

198. See Rashi *in loc.* relative to the revelational and therefore authoritative character of *Targum ʿOnqelos*. The point holds good even though R. Judah will not have known that particular *Targum*.

198a. See *Supra*, p. 167, n. 124.

rejects. In this half-conscious sensitivity to the possibly disruptive effect of exegetical innovation on the Jewish body politic, it is perhaps legitimate to detect what may be termed halakhic overtones. [199]

If we look for a self-conscious positive concept of plain exegesis up to the end of the talmudic period we shall, I think, look in vain, even though the occurrence of exegetical remarks that qualify for the description 'plain' may be empirically demonstrated. The conventional distinction between *peshaṭ* and *derash* must be jettisoned. The subjective element can never be completely eliminated from the study of a text, as R. Judah b. 'Il'a'i in effect admitted when, speaking in an halakhic context, he defined Torah as מדרש תורה. [200] As has been seen, דרש and פשט can be used indiscriminately as verbs. The real distinction between them as nouns seems to be that *derash* is exegesis naturally, or even experimentally propounded without secondary considerations; if it is popularly received, and transmitted into the body of conventional or 'orthodox' opinion, it crystallises into *peshaṭ*.

But to demolish these two categories as being falsely opposed at once raises the question of what others we can, with propriety, utilise instead. The subjective differences with which we have been dealing in this study cannot be accurately accommodated within the categories קולא and חומרא or *halakhah* and '*aggada*; the former pair is confined to *halakhah* and the boundary between the latter two cannot be precisely drawn. [201] Whatever categories we may propose must be able to embrace both *halakhah* and '*aggada* if they are to be truly applicable.

It seems to me that the true distinction to be drawn is between exegesis that is concerned constantly to enlarge the significance of a given text by relating it to new ideas, conditions, or associations in the mind of the exegete himself, and a concentration on the text that would eschew such accretions. As an example one might point to the two views taken of Joseph and Potiphar's wife. [202] That of (presumably) Rav, which refuses to embellish the story, takes the reference to Joseph's intention to 'do his business' at its face value, whereas the other finds in the words the occasion for heightening the drama of the story of Joseph's temptation and his overcoming it. In this instance the first outlook might be regar-

199. Cf. *supra*, p. 148–149, 157–158.
200. *Qidd.* 49a/b חזקיה אומר המלכות ור' יוחנן אמר תורה מיתיבי איזו היא משנה ר' מאיר אומר הלכות ר' יהודה אומר מדרש מאי תורה מדרש תורה. Rashi may here identify מדרש תורה with the halakhic *midrashim*.
201. Cf. *supra*, p. 150 note 31.
202. Cf. *supra*, p. 172 note 154.

ded as epic, the second tragic. But this distinction is clearly not capable of covering even the whole field of 'aggada, to say nothing of halakhah. In default of a Hebrew terminology, I would tentatively suggest the categories of *static* and *dynamic* exegesis as applicable equally within the spheres of halakhah and 'aggada. It must at once be conceded that such a distinction is not one which the rabbis would themselves have formulated; but it does seem to correspond with the differences of emphasis that we have noticed, and to accommodate them more comfortably than any others so far suggested. The following table arranges some of the more important exegetical terms in their appropriate divisions:

| STATIC | DYNAMIC |
|---|---|
| | מגיד and original sense of הגדה |
| | ללמדך |
| דברים ככתבם | ...אין כתיב כאן אלא... |
| פשט | אל תקרי... אלא |
| אם למקרא | (אם למסורת) |
| דברה תורה כלשון ב״א | גם לרבות אך למיעוט |
| מַשְמָע, כשמועו | לשכך את האוזן מה שהיא יכולה לשמוע |
| ודאי, ממש | משל, רשום |
| | מַשְמָע |

It might have been expected that with the end of the tannaitic period and the main fixation of the halakhah, dynamic exegesis would be allowed to operate in the sphere of 'aggada only; but this is in fact not the case, and the static terminology is in the minority in both halakhah and 'aggada. The fact that exegesis at least theoretically dynamic predominates even in halakhic contexts after the effective freezing of halakhic development, seems to me to reflect the essential vitality of halakhah as a humane discipline — a vitality which conditions might circumscribe, but could not crush. Rather than admit defeat, halakhah chose to hibernate until such time as its exponents might judge that restored conditions of independence again afforded it a climate for advance. Consequently static exegesis remained a minority view, inasmuch as the path to progress, when those concerned should see fit to revert to it, lay with the dynamists. In the aggadic sphere dynamism could, in any case, be allowed free play since no need was felt, up to the end of the amoraic period, to formulate a theology. Essays in the formulation of creeds there were indeed, e.g. אמת ויציב and עלינו לשבח, the wording of the latter at least implying that it was occasioned by apologetic motives. [203] But the challenge to Judaism was proffered, or at any rate understood, in such general terms of opposition to absolute monotheism that close examination of Jewish doctrine as implied in the *'aggada* was not felt to be necessary. It was not until the gaonic period that the formulation of a more sophisticated attitude amongst some of the Arabs towards their own texts and traditions, with the consequential questioning of the exegetical propriety of replacing the plain meaning by an applied one to which primary importance is then assigned, was to stimulate within the Jewish world a more self-conscious attitude towards the exuberant storehouse of the *'aggada*, partly as a result of the challenge that it was meeting from Karaism. But the rabbinic address to this constitutes a chapter of its own.

Raphael Loewe

---

203. I. Elbogen, *Der jüdische Gottesdienst*[2], pp. 80, 143.

# PROLEGOMENON TO THE PESIKTA[1]

By Bernard Mandelbaum

In 1832[1a] Leopold Zunz, in a rare scholarly achievement, demonstrated the existence of a Palestinian Midrash called פסיקתא דרב כהנא. No manuscript or text of the Pesikta[2] was known. On the basis of references and readings in Rabbinic literature, primarily in the Aruch and the Yalkut Shim'oni, Zunz proposed a structure of twenty-nine Piskoth, beginning with the first פסקא דראש השנה, continuing with Piskoth based on Torah or prophetic readings on all the holidays and special Sabbaths throughout the year, and concluding with the פסקא דשוש אשיש, the Sabbath before Rosh Hashanah.

Thirty six years later, in 1868, Solomon Buber published an edition of the Pesikta based on four manuscripts[3] which he gathered. The manuscripts represented a remarkable confirmation of Zunz's basic proposition — the existence of a Pesikta.

---

[1] In the initial stages of this study, I had the distinct opportunity and privilege of having the guidance of Professor Alexander Marx ל״ז. I am deeply beholden to my teachers, Professor Louis Finkelstein and Professor Saul Lieberman who directed me to the study of this Midrash. Their help and encouragement at all times made it possible to bring the study to its present stage of development.

[1a] Zunz' classic work on the Midrash, first published in 1832 is *Gottesdienstliche Vorträge der Juden Historisch Entwickelt*. A second edition was published in 1892 by N. Brüll. In 1946, a Hebrew translation by Chanoch Albeck, הדרשות בישראל והשתלשלותן ההיסטוריה was published in Jerusalem by the מוסד ביאליק. Chapter XI of this work discusses the Pesikta.

[2] Pesikta will be used throughout and refers to what is also known as פסיקתא דרב כהנא, as distinguished from פסיקתא רבתי.

[3] In what follows, there will be a detailed description of each of the manuscripts. However, for the sake of this preliminary discussion it is necessary to note that Buber worked with the following four manuscripts.

Manuscript Safed     (צ)
Manuscript Oxford     (אָ₂)
Manuscript Carmoly     (כ)
Manuscript Parma     (פ)

41

However, despite this confirmation, Buber's work left unresolved many vexing questions about the structure and contents of the Pesikta. The arrangement of Piskoth in Buber's four manuscripts is significantly different from that in Zunz's theory. In three of the four manuscripts are to be found Piskoth which are not included in Zunz's structure. Furthermore, the contents and order of Piskoth in the four manuscripts on which Buber based his work differ from one another, and represent two different families of manuscripts.

Buber's publication, the result of tedious and devoted labor, was an important contribution toward making the Pesikta available as a book. However, the methodology in preparing his edition did not advance the understanding of the character of the Pesikta as a whole, or of the untold number of individual passages which seemed to defy explanation.

To begin with, Buber arbitrarily selected one manuscript א, as his basic text. He made his decision on the basis of the manuscript which happened to reach him first. When an entire Piska was missing he completed it with a Piska from a second manuscript כ.[4] He would frequently insert in the body of the text (i. e. in א, which he used as a base) a variation of the passage as it appears in the other manuscripts or in other sources such as the Yalkut, Babylonian and Palestinian Talmud. He did not always specify in the notes where the changes were made.[5]

---

[4] See פסקא החדש נא: for illustration of unsystematic use of manuscripts. Note קנו points to several lines (taken from ms. א2) that are included in the body of the text. These lines are missing in ms. כ which served Buber as the basic text for this chapter. On the other hand, several equally important lines from ms. א2, which are missing in כ, are quoted in note קנט and not given in the body of the text.

[5] In בחדש השביעי the reading in (א) is as follows: . . . אמר לפני הקב׳ה יכול [באותה שעה נתיירא יעקב], the reading in (כ) is: לעולם אמר ליה אל תחת ישראל . . . אמר לפני הקב׳ה יכול לעולם אמר ליה אל תחת . . . Buber's edition gives the reading as in (כ) without any indication that he was changing (א) which he used as the basic text for the chapter בחדש השביעי. Frequently Buber's edition introduces or concludes a paragraph with a phrase as it appears in a parallel reading in the Yalkut. Buber includes these phrases without indicating in the notes that the manuscript does not have these additions. Many similar illustrations could be given.

Thus a comparison of Buber's basic text, and manuscript צ, which he used, will reveal many minor and several major differences.

After his manuscript was almost completely prepared for publication, Buber learned of the Oxford manuscript א2. In rather irregular and unsystematic fashion, Buber's notes give the variant readings from א2, כ and manuscript Parma פ.

The purpose of these paragraphs is not to minimize the important step forward made by Buber, but rather to underscore the wide gap that exists between what we have and the actual Pesikta.

In 1892, Friedmann (מא״ש — מאיר איש שלום), published a fifth manuscript of the Pesikta in the periodical בית תלמוד, Volume V. In this article, Friedmann also describes, briefly, a second Oxford manuscript of which Buber was unaware. These two manuscripts[6] added important threads of information. However, they still have not been woven with the others into any pattern of a more authentic Pesikta.

Carrying further the studies of Zunz, Buber and Friedmann, it is hoped that these pages will see farther into the structure of the Pesikta. It will serve as a basis for a new edition, with the result that the text, and, therefore, the ideas of this outstanding Midrash will become more available to ever increasing numbers of readers.

## THE MANUSCRIPTS

### 1. *Safed*

Moses Agiman made a copy of a manuscript of the Pesikta which was to be found in Safed; he completed it at מצרים (Cairo) on Tuesday, 19th of Ab 5325 (i. e. 1565 CE). The copyist concludes with the following: חסלת פסקות דרב כהנא שנמצאו בצפת עיר הקודש תוב״ב וכתבתים אני הצעיר משה אגימאן פה מצרים לנבון ונעלה הנדיב ישיע כמה״ר יצחק סרוק נר״י הש״י יזכהו ויזכה להגהות בתורת ה' . . . . ונשלמה העתקתו יום ג' י״ט למנחם (אב) שנת ה'שכ״ה ליצירה.

---

[6] Manuscripts Cassonata ק and א3 in what follows.

In 1703 it came into the possession of R. Shimshon Cohen Modon of Mantua. At a later time it was owned by a physician Samuel Hai די להוולטה (della Volta) who added notes on the margin (example see f. 1a).[7]

Finally the manuscript became the property of Samuel David Luzzatto (רשד"ל) who sent it to Buber for his edition.[8]

The table of Contents of Piskoth is as follows:

1. ויהי ביום כלת משה;   2. פרשת שקלים;   3. זכור;   4. ויהי בשלח;
5. עשר תעשר;   6. בחדש השלישי;   7. דברי ירמיהו;   8. שמעו;   9. איכה
10. נחמו נחמו עמי;   11. ותאמר ציון;   12. עניה סוערה;   13. אנכי
אנכי הוא מנחמכם;   14. רני עקרה;   15. קומי אורי;   16. שוש אשיש בה';
17. ראש השנה;   18. שובה;   19. סליחות;   20. פרשה אחרי מות;
21. ולקחתם ביום הראשון;   22. פרשה אחריתי דסוכות;   23. פרשה
אחרת דרש ר' חיננא;   24. וזאת הברכה;   25. יספת לגוי ה' (מפטיר
שמיני עצרת).

As indicated above, Buber used this manuscript as his basic text. In the new edition this will be referred to as צ, for צפת.

## 2. Oxford Manuscript

It was copied by one Yehozadak B. Elhanan and was finished on Friday, 29 Adar 5051 (1291 CE). The writing reflects a German influence.* It is the oldest of the existing Pesikta manuscripts.

The Table of Contents[9] of Piskoth is as follows.

1. כי תשא;   2. זכור;   3. פרה אדומה;   4. החדש הזה;   5. את קרבני
לחמי;   6. מצות העומר;   7. שור או כשב;   8. ויהי בשלח;   9. בחדש

---

[7] On the 7th of Elul 1830, Samuel copied part of this manuscript for Samuel Reggis. This *one* folio (1a), is Oxford manuscript 2222(2). It corresponds exactly to ויהי בשלח in צ.

[8] This manuscript צ is now the property of the Bibliothèque de l'Alliance in Paris. See M. Schwab in his *Manuscrits Hébreux de La Bibliothèque de l'Alliance Israélite*, p. 25. M. Schwab should correct שאול to שמואל and להזילצה to read די להוולטה.

* I am indebted to Mr. Moses Lutski for his expert judgment of the dating and writing of the various manuscripts.

[9] The pagination of the manuscript in the early pages is incorrect. The actual beginning of the manuscript is on page 4 column 3 as follows: שני

השלישי;  10. דברי ירמיהו;  11. שמעו;  12. איכה;  13. נחמו;
14. ותאמר ציון;  15. ענייה סוערה;  16. אנכי אנכי הוא מנחמכם;
17. רני עקרה;  18. קומי אורי;  19. שוש אשיש;  20. ראש השנה;
21. שובה;  22. סליחות;  23. פרשה אחרי מות;  24. ולקחתם;  25. פרשה
דסוכה;  26. ביום השמיני עצרת.

In what follows this will be referred to as א.[10]

### 3. Carmoly

It[11] was written in the city of Fez. On the margins there are
numerous notes containing omissions, corrections, and comments,
by a later North African hand. A good number of corrections
were introduced into the text proper, erasing the original
readings.

The source of the variants is not indicated, but it seems, from
the certainty of the corrector(s), that they were drawn from
some reliable source, either from a better manuscript of the
Pesikta or from the original sources of the Pesikta (Talmud
Yerushalmi, Midrashim) or from the passages of the Pesikta
found in Yalkut Shim'oni.

The headings of the Pesikta on the top margin are by a later
North African hand.

The first 17 folios are missing. The original foliation begins
with folio י"ח.

Folio I contains an index to the various Piskoth probably by
Carmoly's hand.

---

עשר בקר עגלה על שני הנשיאים. This is a small part of the end of ויהי ביום כלות
משה. It is concluded in the middle of column 4, page 4, and is followed immediately by שקלים. שקלים continues through page 6, column 2 and is then
continued on page 1, through page 3, column 1, (page 2, column 3, and page 3,
column 1, are written in a script that is different from the regular manuscript).
At this point פרשת זכור begins and continues through page 4, column 2, and
then skips to page 6, column 2 for the continuation of זכור.

[10] This Oxford manuscript is to be found in the Bodleian Library (Neubauer
151(1) ).

[11] I am indebted to Dr. Teicher and the University of Cambridge for a
microfilm of the Carmoly manuscript which is in their possession. (Manuscript Add. #1497).

No name of a scribe or date of writing is found in the manuscript. The insertion at the end: לי"י הארץ ומלואה לעמרם השו . . . ע
למתנה (למקנה מס) מיד הסרסור שנת לטו"ב לפ"ק פה פאסיצ'ו is not
by the scribe (המעתיק) as Buber thought, but by a later owner.
The date לטו"ב is probably 5447–1687. The ת as well as the ה
of the thousands is occasionally omitted in dates written in the
Orient or North Africa.

The missing part of the last page might have contained a
colophon with a date, but some owner purposely tore it off to give
the impression that the year לטו"ב is 5047 (1287), as Buber
thought. The line of the tear does not look natural; it does not
form a straight line and the person who tore it off tried not to
touch the inscription with the date.

It is written on paper, (foll. 1–60), with 26 lines to a page,
7 x 5 inches on the script face of the photograph; the writing
reflects a North African Rabbinic hand of the late 15th or early
16th century.

The Table of Contents of this manuscript is as follows:

1. פ' אנכי אנכי; 2. רני עקרה; 3. קומי אורי; 4. שוש אשיש;
5. דרשו; 6. שובה; 7. פרשת החדש; 8. פרשת חנוכה ויהי ביום כלות
משה; 9. פרשת שקלים; 10. פרשת זכור; 11. פרשת פרה; 12. פרשת
כל ר"ח את קרבני לחמי; 13. פרשת ויהי בחצי הלילה; 14. פרשת מצות
העומר; 15. פרשת ויהי בשלח; 16. פרשת בחדש השלישי (למתן תורה);
17. פרשת אחרי מות; 18. פרשת שור או כשב; 19. פרשת עשר תעשר;
20. פרשת ולקחתם (סוכה); 21. פרשת ביום השמיני עצרת (לחג הסוכות);
22. הלכות ניסוך המים (לחג עצרת); 23. פ' וזאת הברכה; 24. פרשת
וה' פקד (לר"ה); 25. פרשת יום ב' ויהי אחרי הדברים האלה (עשרה
נסיונות).

This manuscript will be referred to as (כ) in the sequel.

### 4. Parma**

This manuscript forms part (ff. 184–189) of a volume which
also contains מדרש תנחומא and איכה רבתי.

----

** It is listed in Catalogue De-Rossi N. 261.

The Pesikta is called by the scribe מדרש האפטרות. The spelling אפטרות with an א indicates an Oriental origin so that the scribe's original copy must have had the same title and originated in the East. It is also possible that the entire colophon (fol. 178) from ולדורי דורות to נשלם was copied from the original.

The manuscript contains the Piskoth of 11 Haftaroth, from דברי ירמיה to שובה (ש"ש ש"ק ק"אר ,ע"ונ ,א"רש). The פסקא דרשו is missing.

The entire first column is part of the מדרש תנחומא (by the same hand as the Pesikta) where the scribe states that he wrote it for a certain ר' יצחק. The same person was the owner of the Pesikta manuscript too.

At the end there are a few lines (at the bottom of column 3 of the last volume of the Pesikta) of מדרש איכה רבתי written, however, by a different hand than that of the Pesikta.

The colophon, at the end, reads: נשלם מדרש האפטרות, שבח למוציא אסירים בכושרות, ויצילנו מצוקות וצרות, ויתקדש שמו בתישבחות ושירות, לנצח נצחים ולדורי דורות, אא"ס. ברוך נותן ליעף כח ולאין אונים עצמה ירבה וסימן ב' נ' ד ל' ו'א'ע'י'. Then after some distance another colophon (of clear German origin) is given: חזק ונתחזק, הסופר לא יזק, לא היום ולא לעולם, עד שיעל חמור ושור ושה ואריה בסולם אמן אמן סלה. The first part of the colophon, it seems, was copied from the scribe's original, the second part belongs to the scribe of the present manuscript and is of German origin.

At the bottom of the second column (at the end of the Pesikta) a later owner signed his name: שלי אברהם חיים מלאוידה.

Foll. 184–198, also containing other works, were written on vellum, three columns and 44 lines to each page, 9 ½ x 6 ¾" (of the face of the script on the photograph).* The hand-writing is German (or North Italian) square characters of the 13th or 14th century. Foll. 184ᵛ–189ʳ seem to be of a different hand, though of the same time and place. The headings of the first five Piskoth were left blank and filled in by a later Spanish hand, with the פסקא ותאמר ציון still with no heading.

---

* (Ff. 184ᵛ and 189ʳ appear on the photograph in much smaller script. This was caused by the reducing of the photograph by the photographer: compare the edge of f. 184ʳ with the beginnings of the lines of 185ᵛ).

The Table of Contents is as follows:

1. דברי ירמיהו; 2. שמעו; 3. איכה; 4. נחמו; 5. ותאמר ציון;
6. עניה סוערה לא נוחמה; 7. אנכי; 8. רני עקרה; 9. קומי אורי;
10. שוש אשיש; 11. שובה.

In what follows, this will be referred to as (פ).

## 5. Casanata

This manuscript is the same as that owned by a private party in London and made available to Friedmann by Solomon Schechter for publication in the בית תלמוד. However, the last nine chapters are missing in the Casanata manuscript. The second page is headed by the following: אלה הם רמזי הספר הזה. It includes a table of contents of קל"ח רמזים, beginning with פתיחת הספר רמז א' through the concluding one מדרש פרשת ביום השמיני. All the chapters and רמזים are exactly the same as those described by Friedmann. Many distinct features, such as the punctuation of foreign words,[12] are the same in both manuscripts.

A later hand paginated it in Hebrew numerals and added the דף to each רמז. When this was done, ק, already had the last chapters missing. The foliator drew a line in the table of contents after רמז ק"י and added עד כאן יש בכתב יד הזה.

A cover page of ק has a decorative design and the following inscription above it: פסיקתא מרב כהנא כוס ישועות אשא ובשם השם אקרא ממני יצחק אברהם אבינדור תא . . ., and the following below it: נכתב שנת קמ"ז (1387) לפרט האלף הששי פה נרבונה ע"י אברהם חזק יצ"ו.

Lutzki suggests that this inscription was not written by the original scribe. It was written later than the original text with the possible intention of raising the value of the manuscript by placing it at an earlier date. Inasmuch as the Freedman manuscript has no such cover page, it would seem to be a later addition.

The real name of the scribe was משה as is evident from numerous places in the manuscript where the name משה is decorated on the margin.[13]

---

[12] Example: קהמוקרָטורָין, פרובְטָייא.    [13] See f. 56, 9a, 156, 476.

The script is in rabbinic characters of a Spanish hand with Italian influence of the early 17th century.

The Table of Contents of this manuscript is as follows:

1. הפתיחה;    2. דרשה לפרשת שקלים;    3. דרשה לפרשת זכור;
4. דרשה לפרשת פרה;    5. דרשה לפרשת החדש;    6. מדרש פרשת את
קרבני לחמי;    7. מדרש פרשת ויהי בחצי הלילה;    8. דרשה למצות העומר;
9. מדרש פרשת שור או כשב;    10. מדרש פרשת עשר תעשר;    11. מדרש
פרשת ויהי בשלח;    12. דרשה למתן תורה;    13. פרשתא תנינא;    14. פרשתא
תליתיתא;    15. פרשתא רביעתא;    16. מדרש מזמור הרנינו לאלהים עוזינו;
17. מדרש פרשת בחדש השביעי;    18. מדרש פרשת תקעו שופר בציון;
19. מדרש פרשת וה' פקד את שרה.

This will be referred to as ק[14] in the sequel.

## 6. *Oxford*

As distinct from the Oxford manuscript described above, this will be referred to as אַ[15] in what follows. It is the one described by Friedmann in his article, devoted primarily to ק. All the Piskoth are in an abbreviated form, almost as if they were excerpts from the complete chapters as they appear in the other manuscripts. It was written by Nissim ibn Rosh in Spanish Rabbinic characters and was finished on the 37th of the Omer 5234 (1474). The Table of Contents is as follows:

1. דברי ירמיהו;    2. נחמו נחמו עמי;    3. ותאמר ציון;    4. עניה סוערה;
5. אנכי אנכי;    6. רני עקרה;    7. קומי אורי;    8. שוש אשיש;    9. דרשו;
10. שובה;    11. לר"ה;    12. ויהי אחר הדברים האלה;    13. ליום
הכפורים;    14. ליום ראשון של סוכות ולקחתם;    15. לשמיני עצרת;
16. לשמחת תורה וזאת הברכה;    17. לחנוכה;    18. פרש' שקלים;
19. לפרש' זכור;    20. לפרש' החדש;    21. לפסח (פרשת ויהי בחצ'
הלילה);    22. לעומר;    23. ליום אחרון של פסח;    24. לשבועות;
25. לר"ח את קרבני לחמי;    26. עשר תעשר.

---

[14] A more detailed description of this manuscript is in Gustavo Sacerdote's *Catalogo dei Codici ebraici della Biblioteca Casanatense*, Firenze, 1897, N66. It is listed in Rome as manuscript #3324.

[15] It is listed in Oxford library as Neubauer #152.

## 7. *Unpublished Oxford Manuscript*

In the sequel, this manuscript will be referred to as א‎[16]
Neither Buber nor Friedmann was aware of its existence. It
will serve as the basic text for the new edition. At a later point,
the basic reason for this decision will be discussed.

The Table of Contents is as follows:[17]

1. בחדש השביעי; 2. שובה; 3. סליחות; 4. ביום השמיני עצרת;
5. ויהי ביום כלות; 6. כי תשא; 7. זכור; 8. פרה; 9. החודש;
10. את קרבני לחמי; 11. ויהי בחצי הלילה; 12. העומר; 13. ויהי
בשלח; 14. בחודש השלישי; 15. דברי ירמיהו; 16. שמעו; 17. איכה;
18. נחמו; 19. ותאמר ציון; 20. עניה סוערה; 21. אנכי אנכי;
22. רני עקרה; 23. קומי אורי; 24. שוש אשיש; 25. זאת הברכה;
26. עשר תעשר.

The significance of the order of Piskoth in א, as distinct from
all the others will be discussed later. However, it is interesting
to note the marginal notations of someone who·had it, but also
had in his possession an arrangement of the Piskoth similar to
צ and א₂. For in the margin of ויהי ביום כלות משה (the fifth Piska
in above description of א) there appears the letter "א" in a
script that is different from the manuscript. The following order
of letters continues in the margin. ב — כי תשא, ג — זכור,
ד — פרה, ה — החודש, ו — את קרבני לחמי, ז — ויהי בחצי הלילה,
ח — העומר.

The letter "ט" is missing and so is the Piska of שור או כשב which
is the ninth Piska in manuscripts צ and א₂. העומר — ח is
followed by ויהי בשלח — י. The letter י"א is missing and so is
the פסקא עשר תעשר which is the eleventh Piska in צ and א₂.
י"ב — בחודש השלישי, י"ג — דברי ירמיה, ויהי בשלח is followed by
י"ד — שמעו, ט"ו — איכה, ט"ז — נחמו, י"ז — ותאמר ציון, י"ח — עניה
סוערה, י"ט — אנכי אנכי, כ — רני עקרה, כ"א — קומי אורי, כ"ב — שוש
אשיש. This is followed by זאת הברכה which has the letter

---

[16] It is listed in Oxford Library as Neubauer 2334 (11).

[17] The manuscript begins on column one, folio 70 with an excerpt from
chapter four of מסכת דרך ארץ. Column two begins בשביעי באהר להדש.

ל״ב in the margin. An excerpt from עשר תעשר concludes the manuscript.

The script of א₁ is of rabbinic characters of a Spanish hand of the 16th century.

### Genizah Fragments

ג₁ — In what follows this symbol will refer to a fragment of one leaf of two pages, to be found in the Cambridge University Library.* It contains the end of שמעו and the beginning of איכה. (In Buber's ed. f. 118b, line 2 בתחלה אמר to f. 120 l. 2 ועוד שאל). The leaf is very much damaged, with a loss of text and a number of illegible words. It is written on vellum with a wide reed-pen in square characters by an unprofessional hand of Palestinian, or perhaps Egyptian origin of the 9th or 10th century. Each page has one column of 28 lines.

The vellum on which this text is written is a palimpsest. Originally it had on it a Latin text which was removed by the Hebrew scribe. Traces of the original text are still very distinctly noticeable in some places.

ג₂ — In what follows this symbol will refer to five small fragments (central parts of leaves of ten incomplete pages) to be found in the Cambridge University Library.** They contain parts of Pesikta העומר, כשב, ויהי בשלח, ויהי בחצי הלילה (Ed. Buber, from f. 64b to 79b). The fragments, which are available only in photographs, are very much damaged and stained, so that a number of doubtful words have to be abandoned as illegible. They are written on vellum in square characters by a fine professional hand of oriental, probably Babylonian, origin of the 10th or 11th century. Some words have the old Babylonian superlinear vocalization.

ג₃ — In what follows this symbol will refer to two small fragments to be found in the library of the Jewish Theological Seminary of America.‡ They contain parts of Piska בחודש

---

* Listed as T.S. 12 1a1.
** Listed as T.S. 16, 93.
‡ Listed as Ms. Adler 3665.

השלישי (Buber's ed. f. 101b היה אדם מתאוה — 102b). The text is
well preserved. It is written on yellow oriental paper, in
Rabbinic characters, by an oriental hand of the 13th century.

ג, — In what follows this symbol will refer to four leaves
(some damaged with loss of text) to be found in the library of
the Jewish Theological Seminary of America.‡ This fragment
contains parts of שקלים — זכור. It is written on yellow Or.
paper, each page containing a column of 32 lines. It is written
in oriental square characters of the 12th or 13th century.

ג, — In what follows this symbol will refer to five leaves to be
found in the Oxford Library.*** It contains parts of עשר תעשר
and ולקחתם לכם. It is written on 8 pages of vellum with 18–19
lines to a page. The script is oriental rabbinic characters of the
13th or 14th century.

### Structure of The Pesikta

The Pesikta consists of five basic units of homilies centered
about the following period in the Jewish year:

1. Rosh Hashanah through Yom Kippur
2. Succoth and related holidays
3. Hanukah through Purim
4. Passover through Shavuoth
5. Sabbath after תמוז י"ז — Sabbath
   (before or after[18]) Rosh Hashanah

A consideration of the last group (#5), first, would be in order
because it represents the group by which the Pesikta is best
known. For very often it is referred to as the Midrash of ד"ח
נו"ע אר"ק שד"ש. This mnemonic is made up of the first letters of
the הפטרה readings beginning with דברי ירמיהו through שבת שובה.
Furthermore the name דרב כהנא is perhaps derived from the fact
that the פסקא דברי ירמיהו starts as follows: דברי ירמיהו, ר' אבא
בר כ ה נ א פתח.

‡ Listed as Ms. Adler 3655.
*** Ms. Oxford 2634 (Ms. Heb. C18) ff. 13–16 Genizah.
[18] The reason for this qualification will be explained in what follows.

The various sources[19] which refer to the mnemonic of ד"שח, נו"ע, אר"ק, שד"ש indicate that it is part of a larger work known as Pesikta.

Most, if not all, of the Piskoth in this unit are found in all the manuscripts described above, except ק which only has two versions of שובה. Nevertheless, this unit is not the same in the six manuscripts and the differences between them are of significance. Manuscripts כ and א[20] have the complete unit, along with the rest of the Pesikta. Manuscript פ includes only this unit, with one variation. It is ד"שח נו"ע אר"ק ש"ש; the פסקא דרשו is missing. Although there is a caret sign (∧) in the margin between שוש אשיש and שובה, indicating that something is missing, this may have been the work of a later hand.

Manuscripts א1, צ, א2 (with two missing), and Zunz's construction have this unit in the form of ד"שח נו"ע אר"ק ש, ending with שוש אשיש which is read on the Sabbath before Rosh Hashanah. In this group of manuscripts, שובה is put in the unit of Rosh Hashanah through Yom Kippur (unit #1); they all have the פסקא סליחות instead of דרשו and סליחות is also with שובה as part of the first unit.

The basic question as to the form in which this unit appeared in the Pesikta can be resolved by the following considerations, which weigh heavily in favor of ד"שח נו"ע אר"ק ש as the original unit.

(1) As we shall see later the א1, א2, צ group represents the best manuscripts. Furthermore, Zunz's theory, based on many sources comes to the same conclusion.

(2) ק, which does not have any part of this unit, does have שובה as part of the Rosh Hashanah through Yom Kippur unit.

(3) By putting ד"ש with this unit, the order in the Pesikta overlaps calendar-wise, with Rosh Hashanah coming after שובה, דרשו (as in כ and א).

(4) As collateral support of this contention, it is important

19 תוספות מגילה לא:, סמ"נ עשה י"ט דף ק"נ, ב., ר' אשר למגילה בכוף ארהות חיים דף כ"ז, ס"ד.

20 Several Piskoth are missing, (probably lost), from the first part of the unit.

255

to note that the פיוטי ייני, the poems for the holidays based on Torah and prophetic readings as found in Palestine, refer to תלת דפורענותא (i. e. דש"ח which are read before תשעה באב), and שבעה דנחמתא (i. e. נו"ע אר"ק ש, which are read after תשעה באב through the שבת before ר"ה). פיוטי ייני do not have any reference to ד"ש (which is called תרתי דתיובתא in: תוספות מגילה לא:).

As yet nothing has been found, if anything exists, on readings for ד"ש.

## Rosh Hashanah through Yom Kippur

According to the Mishnah,[21] the Torah reading for Rosh Hashanah is בחדש השביעי and for Yom Kippur is אחרי מות. All the manuscripts and Zunz, except א1 and ק from which they must have been lost, have אחרי מות for Yom Kippur. However, there is a difference in the Piskoth for Rosh Hashanah.

א1, צ and Zunz, in accordance with the Mishnah and in good Palestinian tradition, have בחדש השביעי for Rosh Hashanah as a one day holiday. However, כ and א3, have a non-Palestinian arrangement with two Piskoth for two days of Rosh Hashanah. In כ and א3 the Piskoth for ר"ה are: וה' פקד את שרה, ויהי אחרי, הדברים האלה.

The פסקא דר"ה was lost in the א2, Manuscript ק, which as we shall see later is a composite of many things, has both בחדש השביעי and וה' פקד.

Considering these factors and the earlier discussion of שובה and סליחות, it would seem that the arrangement of this unit in א1, צ, Zunz is the more authentic Palestinian Pesikta. It is further interesting to note this arrangement of a one day reading for Rosh Hashanah in a Palestinian text like the Pesikta throws light on the question raised by רב נסים גאון to רב האי גאון.

In a fragment from a Cambridge manuscript published by Levine in his אוצר הגאונים on ביצה, רב נסים גאון writes to רב האי גאון as follows: ואמר אדוננו כי בני א"י תופסין ר"ה שני ימים ואנו רואים גאון עד עתה אין תופסין אלא יום אחד.

<hr/>

[21] משנה מגילה ג:ה.

It is this passage which the בעל המאור had in mind when he said that there was only one day of Rosh Hashanah in Palestine until very late, that is until after the time of the רי"ף.

### Hanukah through Purim

The unit of Succoth, next in order, will be considered later for reasons which will be clear then. Except for one or two Piskoth which have been lost from א and צ, all the manuscripts and Zunz are in agreement about the following Piskoth which run in order:[22] ויהי ביום כלות משה, כי תשא, זכור, פרה, החודש. In all of them, the reading for שבת ר"ח, את קרבני לחמי follows after החודש.

### Passover through Shavuoth

A consideration of this unit can best begin with Zunz's arrangement. He suggests the following:

בחצי הלילה — first day of Passover

העומר — second day of Passover

בשלח — seventh day of Passover

בחודש השלישי — first day of Shavuoth

עשר תעשר — second day of Shavuoth

Without any references to the manuscripts, there are several difficulties in Zunz's construction. If the Pesikta is Palestinian and the readings[23] reflect the Palestinian tradition, then why is there a Piska assigned to second day Passover and second day Shavuoth? Second day Passover can be explained because it was the day for beginning the עומר count, even if one of the days of חול המועד.[24]

However how does Zunz account for עשר תעשר on the second day of Shavuoth? Furthermore עשר תעשר is also read on the eighth

---

[22] החודש is not in proper order in כ. It is placed before ויהי ביום כלות משה.

[23] See above on Rosh Hashanah.

[24] בבלי מגילה טז. and רש"י there.

day of Passover in the non-Palestinian tradition and why assign
it to one and not the other?

This difficulty is not present in mss., ₁א, כ, ₃א where this unit
appears as follows:

ויהי בחצי הלילה — 1st day Passover

העומר — Beginning of Omer (2nd day)

ויהי בשלח — last day of Passover

בחדש השלישי — Shavuoth

The Ms. צ, with some Piskoth missing has the following:
ויהי בשלח, עשר תעשר, בחדש השלישי. Also Mss. ₂א the order is: שור
או כשב, ויהי בשלח, בחדש השלישי.

In צ and ₂א, the presence of עשר תעשר and שור או כשב respectively
reflect a less authentic Palestinian origin.

Characteristically ק is the composite of both and has the
following:

$$\left.\begin{array}{l}\text{מדרש ויהי בחצי הלילה}\\\text{דרשה למצות העומר}\end{array}\right\}\quad\text{as in}\quad\begin{array}{l}\text{₁א}\\\text{כ}\\\text{₃א}\end{array}$$

מדרש שור או כשב　　　as in　₂א

$$\left.\begin{array}{l}\text{מדרש פרשת עשר תעשר}\\\text{מדרש פרשת ויהי בשלח}\\\text{דרשה למתן תורה}\end{array}\right\}\quad\text{as in}\quad\text{צ}$$

### Succoth and Related Holidays

Beginning with Zunz, we have the same considerations as
above about his arrangement which follows: סוכה (ולקחתם),
שור או כשב, שמיני עצרת, זאת הברכה. Thus he has readings for a
second day of סוכות and for שמחת תורה. Both these days were not
observed in Palestine.

Ms. כ and ₃א, in accordance with the Mishnah[25] have a Piska
only for the first day of סוכות based on ולקחתם לכם. צ and ₂א
have readings for first two days of סוכות as follows:

$$\left.\begin{array}{l}\text{ולקחתם}\\\text{פרשה סוכה}\end{array}\right\}\quad\text{₂א}\qquad\qquad\left.\begin{array}{l}\text{ולקחתם לכם}\\\text{אחריתא דסוכות}\end{array}\right\}\quad\text{צ}$$

[25] מגילה נ:ה.

Unfortunately the Piska for סוכות in ₁א is lost. However ₁א has a פסקה שמיני עצרת and nothing else in this unit.

Ms. כ has

| | |
|---|---|
| ביום שמיני עצרת | אₐ |
| הלכות ניסוך המים (עצרת) | ביום שמיני עצרת |
| זאת הברכה | זאת הברכה |

Also צ has the following יספת לגוי; זאת הברכה. (יספת לגוי is same as שמ' עצ'.) Thus we see that for the first days of סוכות, כ and אₐ reflect a clearer Palestinian source and for שמ' עצ', ₁א alone has this most authentic origin.

In ₂א the Piska for שמ' עצ' was lost and the entire unit is missing in ק.

## SUMMARY AND CONCLUSIONS ABOUT STRUCTURE OF PESIKTA

The following table summarizes the findings described above:

| Unit | דש"ח נו"ע... | ר"ה יו"כ | כוכות | חנוכה – ר"ח | פסח – שבועות |
|---|---|---|---|---|---|
| closer to | ₁א | ₁א | ₁א | — | ₁א |
| early | ₂א | -- | — | — | כ |
| Palestinian | צ | ---- | כ | S | ₃א |
| tradition | --- | צ | ₃א | A | --- |
| | פ | | ק | M | |
| | | | | E | |
| influence of | --- | -- | -- | --- | צ |
| later | | | | | |
| Palestine | כ | כ | צ | — | — |
| or | | | | | |
| diaspora | ₂א | ₃א | ₂א | — | ₂א |

While this has implications for the family relationship of the various manuscripts, that will be considered in another study. It is important to underscore that ₁א is the only manuscript that appears above the line in every instance i. e. indicating its closeness to the original Palestinian source.

Furthermore, ₁א is the only manuscript of the seven which has an order of Piskoth which is almost exactly like that suggested by Zunz. While this is a commentary on Zunz' unusual achievement, there is one difference between Zunz and אۡ which makes a basic difference in the conclusion about the exact contents of the Pesikta.

As noted above, Zunz assigns זאת הברכה תורה שמחת to (i. e. פסקא ח) and עשר תעשר to the second day of שבועות (i. e. פסקא יט). In אۡ עשר תעשר and then זאת הברכה appear at the very end.

It seems correct to assume that the original Pesikta, as reflected in אۡ, with Palestine as its origin did not have עשר תעשר and זאת הברכה which are for days of non-Palestinian holidays. The Pesikta ends with שוש אשיש. However, the scribe found these two, didn't know what to do with them, and tacked them on the end.

In addition to our knowledge from other sources, the manuscripts themselves indicate that there was the practice of taking מדרשים from many sources (ילמדנו, פסיקתא רבתי and perhaps other unknown books) and copying them along with Piskoth to which they were related in content. Thus כ has (לעצרת) הלכות נסוך המים which does not appear in any of the others. In צ we have a פרשה אחרת דרש רבי חנינא. In this same manuscript we have sections quoted from ספר רומי and ספר לומברדיא. In ק, the best example of all, there are chapters from פסיקתא רבתי as well as other sources.

Thus Zunz' construction of the Pesikta, minus one Piska of סוכות,[26] עשר תעשר, and זאת הברכה gives us the picture of the Pesikta as we find it in אۡ — a total of twenty-six Piskoth beginning with בחודש השביעי and continuing through שוש אשיש, the Sabbath before ר"ה.

The uniqueness and greater authenticity of אۡ is also demonstrated by the structure of individual Piskoth, as well as by a comparison of the variant readings of the several manuscripts. All this material, as well as an analysis of the family relationship of the manuscripts will be presented in the introduction to the new edition.

---

[26] It must be kept in mind that אחרי מות for Yom Kippur and ולקחתם לכם for the first day of סוכות are missing from אۡ. This too seems to help explain, אۡ's authenticity. For if anything was lost — and these two were — it would be reasonable to expect that two Piskoth, one following the other would be lost when several pages are misplaced.

# A RABBINIC DEFENSE OF THE ELECTION
# OF ISRAEL

## An Analysis of Sifre Deuteronomy 32:9, Pisqa 312

EUGENE MIHALY

Hebrew Union College - Jewish Institute of Religion, Cincinnati

THE purpose of this study is to demonstrate a variety of methods in the analysis and interpretation of midrashic texts. A close scrutiny of the formal structure of the argument; careful study of the proof-text both in biblical context and as understood in the total rabbinic literature; the ideational and social background of the midrashic lesson, all these are indispensable tools for text study and are too often neglected. Our analysis of the following Sifre passage focuses especially on the rabbinic use of the proof-text and on the form of the syllogism introduced by various technical, exegetic terms.

| *Ed. Horovitz-Finkelstein,* *p. 353* | *Ed. Friedmann (Ish-Shalom),* *p. 134b* |
|---|---|
| (ט) כי חלק ה' עמו, משל למלך שהיה לו שדה ונתנה לעריסים התחילו עריסים גונבים אותה נטלה מהם ונתנה לבניהם התחילו להיות רעים מן הראשונים נטלה מבניהם ונתנה לבני בניהם חזרו להיות רעים יותר מן הראשונים נולד לו בן אמר להם צאו מתוך שלי אי איפשי שתהיו בתוכה תנו לי חלקי שאהיה מכירו כך כשבא אברהם אבינו לעולם יצא ממנו פסולת ישמעאל וכל בני קטורה בא יצחק לעולם יצא ממנו פסולת עשו וכל אלופי אדום חזרו להיות רעים יותר מן הראשונים וכשבא יעקב לא יצאת ממנו פסולת אלא נולדו כל בניו כשרים כענין שנאמר ויעקב איש תם יושב אהלים (בראשית כ"ה) מהיכן המקום מכיר את חלקו מיעקב | (שיב) כי חלק ה' עמו משל למלך שהיה לו שדה ונתנה לאריסים התחילו האריסים נוטלים וגונבים אותה נטלה מהם ונתנה לבניהם התחילו להיות רעים יותר מן הראשונים נולד לו בן אמר להם צאו מתוך שלי אי אפשר שתהיו בתוכה תנו לי חלקי שאהיה מכירו כך כשבא אברהם אבינו לעולם יצא ממנו פסולת ישמעאל ובני קטורה בא יצחק אבינו יצחק לעולם יצא ממנו פסולת עשו אלופי אדום חזרו להיות רעים יותר מן הראשונים כשבא יעקב לא יצא ממנו פסולת אלא נולדו כל בניו כשרים כמותו שנאמר ויעקב איש תם יושב אהלים (בראשית כ"ה) מהיכן המקום מכיר את חלקו מיעקב שנאמר כי יעקב בחר לו יה ישראל [לסגלתו] (תהלים קל"ה) |

103

*Ed. Horowitz-Finkelstein,*
*p. 353—continued*

*Ed. Friedman (Ish-Shalom),*
*p. 134b—continued*

שנאמר כי חלק ה' עמו יעקב חבל נחלתו
ואומר כי יעקב בחר לו יה (תהלים
קל"ה:ד') ועדין הדבר תלי בדלא תלי ואין
אנו יודעים אם הקדוש ברוך הוא בחר
ביעקב אם יעקב בחר בהקדוש ברוך הוא
תלמוד לומר ישראל לסגולתו (שם) ועדין
הדבר תלי בדלא תלי ואין אנו יודעים אם
הקדוש ברוך הוא בחר לו ישראל לסגולתו
ואם ישראל בחרו בהקדוש ברוך הוא
תלמוד לומר וכך בחר בה' אלהיך להיות

ואומר כי חלק ה' עמו יעקב חבל
נחלתו ועדין תלי בדלא תלי אין אנו
יודעים אם המקום בחר לו ישראל
לסגולתו ואם ישראל בחרו להקב"ה
ת"ל [ו]בך בחר ה' אלהיך (דברים ז')
מנין שאף יעקב בחר לו הקב"ה שנאמר
לא כאלה חלק יעקב כי יוצר הכל
הוא וישראל שבט נחלתו ה' צבאות שמו
(ירמיה י'):

לו לעם סגולה (דברים י"ד:ב') ומנין שאף יעקב בחר בו ביה שנאמר לא כאלה
חלק יעקב (ירמיה י':ט"ז)

## I

The verse expounded by the Rabbis in this Sifre passage is Deut.
32:9: "For the portion of the Lord is His people, Jacob the lot of His
inheritance." Note well the context of this verse. Moses, toward
the end of his career, reviews the spiritual odyssey of Israel. He
tells his people that though God chose them, cared for them, led
them, nevertheless "Jeshurun waxed fat and kicked," and "roused
God to jealousy with strange gods..." Therefore, "The Lord saw
and spurned... and He said 'I will hide my face....'" The spirit
of the major portion of Moses' utterance is chastisement, *tokheḥah*,
rejection.[1]

[1] See Sifre Deut. 1 (ed. Finkelstein) p. 1 where the Book of Deuteronomy is
characterized as דברי תוכחות on the basis of Deut. 32:15. It is very helpful, in probing
the meaning of a Midrash, to consider the total context, the "magnetic field," of the
biblical text, especially in the earlier, Tannaitic Midrashim. The Rabbis, it is true,
often disregard context. They derive their lesson not infrequently by treating each
verse and, at times, each phrase or even each word as an isolated entity. This is most
typical of the pleonastic exegesis of the Midrash 'Aggadah. Yet, often, the Rabbis
will cite the first half of a verse when the "proof" is contained in the latter part of
the text or even in the following or preceding verse. On occasion, however, the total
biblical passage is implicit in the subtlety of the exegesis. Our Sifre passage contains
several examples of the significance of context, as will be demonstrated.

A

With the mood of Deuteronomy 32 as background, let us examine the first part of the Sifre comment.[2]

> "For the portion of the Lord is His people..." This is to be compared to a king who had a field and he gave it to tenants. The tenants began stealing it. He (the king) took it from them and gave it to their sons. They turned out to be worse than their predecessors. He took it from their sons and gave it to their grandchildren. They, in turn, were worse than their antecedents. A son was born to him (the king). He said to them (the tenants), 'Go forth from the midst of that which belongs to me. It is not my wish that you be in its midst. Give me my portion that I may make it known as my own.' Thus when Abraham our father came into the world, worthless offsprings issued from him, Ishmael and the sons of Qeṭurah; when Isaac our father came into the world, worthless progeny issued from him, Esau and the princes of Edom. They turned out to be worse than their predecessors. When Jacob arrived, no unworthy offspring issued from him, but all his children were born worthy (kesherim)[3] like himself, as it is stated in Scriptures. "And Jacob was a perfect man (איש תם), dwelling in houses of study (יושב אהלים)." (Gen. 25:27 as translated by the Rabbis.)[4]

---

[2] This passage appears, with minor variants, in Midrash Tannaim, Deut. 32:9, (ed. Hoffmann), p. 190; Yalquṭ Makhiri 135.4 (Buber), p. 254 and Yalquṭ Shim'oni, Jeremiah, Sec. 288. A simplified form of this passage is cited in Sifre Deut., Pisqa 343 (ed. Finkelstein), p. 397, lines 7 ff. Other relevant parallels are Midrash Tannaim, p. 73; Lev. Rabbah 36.5 (ed. Margulies), p. 850, lines 1 ff.; Pesiqta Rabbati 39 (ed. Friedmann), p. 165b; Midrash on Psalms (ed. Buber) 118.20, p. 487.

[3] On the perfection of all of Jacob's children see: Sifre Deut. 31 (ed. Finkelstein), p. 52, lines 5 ff.; Lev. Rabbah 36.5 and parallels cited by Margulies, op. cit., p. 849, note 5. Cf. Gen. Rabbah 99:1, 68:11, Pesiqta Rabbati, loc. cit., Midrash on Psalms, loc. cit., Sifre Deut. 343 reads תמימים instead of כשרים. This reading is more consistent with the proof text איש תם.

[4] The Rabbi characteristically changes the meaning of the biblical verse from "And Jacob was a quiet man, dwelling in tents" (in contrast to Esau, the hunter) by adopting the alternative meaning of תם (perfect, whole, unblemished תמים; the opposite of פסול, בעל־מום) and by understanding אהלים to allude to houses of study, בתי מדרשות. The Rabbis interpret Gen. 25:27 in this sense throughout rabbinic literature, without exception. This verse serves as proof-text for a variety of perfections that the Rabbis attribute to Jacob. He was born circumcised (Avoth d'Rabbi Nathan 2, ed. Schechter, p. 12); he observed the entire Torah (Sifre Deut. 336, p. 386, line 4); he was perfect in good deeds (Tanḥuma, Mishpatim 19); he was upright, innocent of robbery, sin, or any unseemly conduct (Seder Eliahu Rabba [6] 7, ed. Friedmann, p. 32). Similarly יושב אהלים is taken to mean that Jacob studied Torah in the schools of Shem and Ever (Gen. Rabbah 63:9); he studied Torah and was diligent in the performance of commandments (Tanḥuma, Mishpatim 19); he

From what point on does God claim (מכיר, make known) His portion?[5] From Jacob, as it is stated in Scriptures, "For the portion of the Lord is His people, Jacob the lot of His inheritance" (Deut. 32:9). And Scriptures also states, "For the Lord has chosen Jacob for Himself, Israel for His treasure" (Psalms 135:4).[6]

The first part of the Sifre passage, translated above, attempts to determine at which moment in history, at what point in time, God made the choice, "claimed His portion." The Rabbi insists, on the basis of a parable, that Israel became the elect when God chose Jacob. The choice could not have been initiated earlier, with Isaac, because of the unworthiness of Esau and the princes of Edom. Nor could He have chosen Abraham, because of Ishmael and the sons of Qeṭurah. Only Jacob, whose progeny were all worthy, unblemished, could be chosen by God.

The Rabbi clinches his argument, as usual, by citing a biblical proof-text. He understands Deut. 32:9 to say that "God claimed His people as His portion *when* Jacob became the lot of His inheritance." The author of our Sifre passage buttresses his interpretation with a parallel text, a frequent procedure in the literature. He sees an adverbial relationship between the *a* and *b* parts of Ps. 135:4 (a typical exegetic device) and he therefore translates: "When God

---

established houses of study (Pesiqta Rabbati 5, p. 18b); no one studied Torah as diligently as Jacob (Tanḥuma Buber, Wayishlaḥ 9, p. 167). Cf. Tanḥuma, Shemoth #1 and the Targumim to this verse.

Note that we refer to all strata of the literature to form a *gestalt* of rabbinic interpretation of a biblical verse. This should be done with the greatest care. Evidence from the amoraic stratum is certainly not conclusive for the tannaitic period. It is often very helpful, however, to have an integrated view of the total rabbinic tradition and, if properly used, is an indispensable tool for text analysis.

Of relevance to our analysis is the further conclusion drawn from our text that though God chose Jacob, He did not bring him near. "Jacob drew himself near, as Scripture states 'and Jacob was an איש חם, etc.' (Gen. 25:27)." Jacob's study of Torah and his good deeds brought him near to God (Tanḥuma, Ẓaw 8; Tanḥuma Buber, Lev. p. 18; Num. Rabbah 3:2 and Yalquṭ Makhiri, Ps. 65, p. 318).

[5] On the use of מכיר in this sense, see, for example, Sifre Deut. 217, p. 250 and Qiddushin 78b. The term מכיר must be understood in the light of the proof-texts Deut. 32:9 and Ps. 135:4.

[6] Note that I follow the Finkelstein text (along with Midrash Tannaim) in citing the proof-text from Psalms after the verse from Deuteronomy. But I follow the Friedmann version (along with every other available text, except Finkelstein) in not dividing the Psalms text. For the justification of this reading, see below note 7 and note 18.

chose Jacob for Himself, Israel became His treasure." The Psalms text is somewhat more convincing than Deut. 32:9 for it proves conclusively that Israel is God's treasure. The anonymous עמו "His people" of Deuteronomy is definitely identified in Ps. 135:4 as Israel.[7] We shall soon see why the precise identity of "His people" is of crucial significance.

The intent of the passage is thus clear. God chose Israel when He chose Jacob — not earlier. Neither Abraham nor Isaac was free from blemish. They were only tenants. The only one claimed as a son (note well) was Jacob. He earned this choice because he was an איש תם, because he observed the commandments, because all of his progeny were worthy, and because he labored diligently over the Torah, "the law."

Why is the author of our Sifre passage so anxious to prove that the choice was initiated with Jacob?[8] What possible danger did the Rabbi see in the position that God had chosen Abraham? The author

---

[7] This is one of the reasons for our preference of the Finkelstein version where the Psalms verse is cited as the second proof-text. The additional text introduced by ואומר is often cited to forestall an objection based on some weakness in the first proof-text. In the Sifre comment on Deut. 14:2, 96 (p. 158, line 16) immediately after the Deut. verse ובך בחר ה' וגו' the author cites Ps. 135:4. Finkelstein perceptively notes . . . מדברת התורה אחרת כתה או באומה ולא יעקב שבבני להוכחה מתהילים כתוב סביא. This is the function of the Psalms text in our passage. It is, as Finkelstein notes, a later addition in the Sifre to 14:2, but is part of the primary stratum in our passage. Furthermore, since the comment is on Deut. 32:9 we would naturally expect this verse to serve as the primary proof-text. In addition, the pentateuchal text would be cited first and especially so in this instance since the question ending with חלקו (את מכיר המקום מהיכן . . .) is most directly answered by עמו ה' הלק כי.

[8] The superiority of Jacob over Abraham is a recurring theme in midrashic literature. The most elaborate formulation occurs in Lev. Rabbah 36:4: ". . . heaven and earth were created in the merit of Jacob . . . Abraham was delivered from the fiery furnace only because of the merit of Jacob . . . See the parallels cited by Margulies, op. cit., pp. 846 f. Neither Margulies, loc. cit., nor L. Ginzberg in his discussion of this theme (Legends of the Jews, vol. 5, p. 274, note 35) cites any parallels from the tannaitic Midrashim. Ginzberg explains the two conflicting tendencies, i. e., the exaltation of Abraham, on the one hand, and of Jacob, on the other, as follows: "One may safely assert that the older Haggadah (universalistic) favors Abraham. The younger (nationalistic) Jacob." Our Sifre passage and the other tannaitic parallels do not support this distinction. At issue is not a theoretical universalism or nationalism. The rabbinic insistence on the superiority of Jacob is a response to a specific challenge, as will be demonstrated. Note that our concern is only with those passages which affirm the superiority of Jacob over the other patriarchs and not the statements which exalt Jacob by himself. These are of high antiquity and are differently motivated. Cf. Book of Jubilees 19:27 ff. in Charles, Apocrypha, etc., vol. II, p. 42, and Ginzberg, loc. cit.

of our Sifre appears to be arguing on biblical ground against a point
of view, perhaps also based on Scriptures, that the election took
place with Abraham. Somehow, the choice of the first patriarch was
used as an argument to undermine a doctrine close to the Rabbi's
heart. How was this done and who was its author?

The Midrash neither explains the challenge nor does it identify
the adversary. Only the Rabbi's argument is recorded. This silence is
typical of most of the literature. The precise argument of the opponent
and his identity must, in most instances, be inferred from the Rabbi's
reply. (Perhaps this is the reason why many of the significant polemical
passages are overlooked. Our Sifre, as we shall see, is a case in point.)

## B

The fourth chapter of The Epistle of Paul to the Romans is a
typical midrashic commentary on Gen. 15:6, "And he (Abraham) had
faith in the Lord; and He counted it to him for righteousness."
"Now," Paul argues, "if a man does a piece of work, his wages are
not 'counted' as a favor; they are paid as debt. But if without any
work to his credit he simply puts his faith in Him who acquits the
guilty, then his faith is indeed 'counted as righteousness' " (4:4 f.).
Since this righteousness was "reckoned" to Abraham before he was
circumcised, Paul concludes that Abraham "is the father of all
who have faith when uncircumcised, so that righteousness is 'counted'
to them (4:11) . . . For it was not through law that Abraham, or
his posterity, was given the promise . . . but through the righteousness
that comes from faith (v. 13) . . . The promise was made on the ground
of faith, in order that it might be a matter of sheer grace and that
it might be valid for all Abraham's posterity, not only for those
who hold the law but for those also who have the faith of Abraham.
For he is the father of us all, as Scripture says: 'I have appointed
you to be father of many nations' " (4:16 f.).[9]

In the third chapter of Galatians, a similar argument is used to
show that "if you thus belong to Christ, you are the 'issue' of Abraham,
and so heirs by promise" (3:29). Paul builds his case on the same verse
in Gen. (15:6), ". . . 'he put his faith in God . . .' You may take it,
then," Paul reasons, "that it is the men of faith who are Abraham's
sons. And Scripture, foreseeing that God would justify the Gentiles
through faith, declared the Gospel to Abraham beforehand: 'In you

[9] New Testament citations are, with a few minor changes, from *The New English
Bible*, Oxford and Cambridge University Press (1961).

all nations shall find blessing.' Thus it is the men of faith who share the blessing with faithful Abraham. On the other hand, those who rely on obedience to the law are under a curse . . .(3:6 ff.) . . . Christ brought us freedom from the curse of the law by becoming for our sake an accursed thing; . . . And the purpose of it all was that the blessing of Abraham should in Jesus Christ be extended to the Gentiles, so that we might receive the promised spirit through faith" (3:14 f.).[10]

We are not concerned with defining the precise attitude of Paul toward "the law" and toward those who held on to it, a problem raised by the above-cited passages. Nor need we concern ourselves with the reaction toward Paul's doctrine within the Christian group as reflected in the second chapter of the Epistle of James, "Was it not by his action, in offering his son Isaac upon the altar, that our father Abraham was justified? . . . Here was fulfillment of the words of Scripture: 'Abraham put his faith in God, and that faith was counted to him as righteousness'; . . . You see then that a man is justified by deeds and not by faith in itself" (2:21 ff.). Regardless of the interpretation of Paul's attitude toward the legal prescriptions and toward those who lived by the "law," the passages from Galatians and Romans clearly demonstrate that the election of Abraham was used as a pivotal argument for the elect status of the Christians. They were the true heirs of Abraham; the genuine chosen people — a status achieved by faith in Jesus Christ.

But Paul constructs another midrashic argument that is of relevance to our Sifre passage. In the ninth chapter of Romans, Paul reasons: "For not all descendants of Israel are truly Israel, nor, because they are Abraham's offsprings are they all his true children; but, in the words of Scripture, 'through the line of Isaac shall your seed be traced.' That is to say, it is not those born in the course of nature (the children of the flesh) who are children of God; it is the children born through God's promise who are reckoned as Abraham's descendants (9:7 ff.) . . . But that is not all, for Rebekah's children had one and the same father, our ancestor Isaac; and yet in order that God's selective purpose might stand, based not upon man's deeds, but upon the call of God, she was told, even before

---

[10] For a rabbinic comment on this verse (Gen. 15:6), see: Mekhilta deRabbi Yishm'a'el, Beshalaḥ 6, (ed. Horovitz), pp. 114 f. Note especially the comment of R. Neḥemiah (lines 17 f.). The subtlety of the exegesis lies in the rabbinic usage of צדקה which comes to mean more than "righteousness." It indicates an attitude or act performed in addition to the literal requirements of the law, certainly not as a substitute for them — לפנים משורת הדין.

they were born, when they had as yet done nothing, good or ill,
'The elder shall be servant to the younger'..." (9:10 ff.)."

We see here a further development of the argument for the elect
status of the Christians. Not only was Abraham chosen for his faith
and thus became the father of all who seek salvation by faith, but
Isaac and Jacob, as well, were chosen because they were "children
of the promise" not because they were the natural issue of their
fathers, nor because of any meritorious deeds that they performed.
The choice "depends not upon man's will or exertion but upon God's
mercy." Paul is implying that if it were a matter of biologic descent
then Ishmael and Esau would also qualify, perhaps even more so
since they were the elder sons. The fact that the line of descent
is traced through Isaac and Jacob is clear evidence that relationship
of the flesh is not the determining factor in being of the elect.
Furthermore, since Rebekah was told even before Esau and Jacob
were born that "the elder shall serve the younger," the choice of
Jacob could not have been due to any deed or special merit of Jacob.

The various facets of Paul's argument are combined and carried
a step further in the Epistle of Barnabas. In the thirteenth chapter
Barnabas raises the question "whether our people or the former is the
heir, and whether the covenant is intended for us or for them" (13:1).
He bases his answer on the scriptural account of God's response to
Rebekah, "...and the older shall serve the younger." "You should
try to understand," Barnabas explains, "who Isaac is and who Rebekah
and by what means He has pointed out that our people will be greater
than the other" (13:3). An even clearer indication that the Christians
and not the Jews are the true heirs of God's choice, Barnabas continues,
is Jacob's insistence on placing his right hand on the head of Ephraim,
the younger son of Joseph, and blessing him. In reply to Joseph's
protest that Menassah is the elder, Barnabas understands Jacob
to say, "I know, my child — I know; but the older must be subject
to the younger..." (13:5). Barnabas suggests through these two
examples that the preference was given in each case to the younger
to indicate God's choice of the Christians, the younger people. Barnabas

---

" In the light of this passage, a deeper meaning of the rabbinic interpretation of
Gen. 25:23 emerges. First, the Rabbis insist that Esau had a pre-natal tendency
toward idolatry while Jacob was drawn to the synagogue even before birth. Secondly,
the Rabbis interpret ורב יעבד צעיר as a conditional promise: אם זכה יעבד ואם לאו יַעֲבָד
(יַעֲבִיד, יַעֲבֹד). For variants and meaning of this phrase see the discussion in Theodor-
Albeck, Gen. Rabbah, vol. II, p. 686, note 3. See: Gen. Rabbah 63:6-7, 10; 67:7
and often, throughout the literature, cf. the rabbinic interpretation of Gen. 25:27,
note 4, above

concludes his argument with God's charge to Abraham "when he, the only believer, was accounted justified: 'Behold Abraham. I have appointed you the father of the nations which, though not circumcised, believe in God' " (13:7).[12]

The fully developed Christian argument expounded by Barnabas may be summarized as follows: a) Abraham was chosen because of his faith, before he was circumcised, thus becoming the father of all the uncircumcised who have faith. b) The choice of Isaac and Jacob was not due to their natural descent (of the flesh). c) Nor was the election of Isaac and Jacob due to meritorious deeds on their part. Does not Scripture establish the superiority of Jacob over Esau before they are born? d) Isaac and Jacob were chosen as an act of grace on the part of God. So too, the choice of the younger son is symbolic of the election of the Christians; "the elder shall serve the younger."

## C

If we now return to our Sifre passage we will see a point by point refutation of the four-step Christian argument as expounded by Paul and as summarized and supplemented by Barnabas. Consider the parable of the king and its application to the patriarchs. a) Though God (the king) did give his field (elect status) to Abraham, He did so only as an owner gives his property to a tenant, i. e., for a limited period; not as an act of grace but in consideration of an agreed share in the produce. Abraham was chosen conditionally and could only retain his status as long as he fulfilled the conditions. His unworthy children Ishmael and the sons of Qeṭurah, though heir to the tenancy as sons of Abraham, caused the field to be taken from them because of their evil character and to be given to Abraham's younger son Isaac. b) Isaac was chosen also as a tenant, conditionally, as a son of Abraham. He had the merit of being the son of the previous tenant, the friend of the king.[13] Isaac was given preference over his older brother not as a matter of grace, nor because he was the younger, but because Ishmael was unworthy, *pesoleth*. c) Finally the king

---

[12] Note that Barnabas is not translating the verse in Genesis. He constructs a midrashic interpretation of Gen. 17:4 in accordance with Rom. 4:1 f. and Galatians 3:6 ff. Note also that Isaac (on the basis of Barnabas 7:3) symbolizes Jesus. Citations are from the translation of J. A. Kleist, *Ancient Christian Writers*, vol. VI (London, 1957).

[13] On the various kinds of tenancies, including those that were inherited, see: G. Allon, תולדות היהודים בארץ ישראל בתקופת המשנה (Tel Aviv, 1952), pp. 95 f.

had a son of his own, Jacob, and the field was given to him. Jacob was given possession of the field as a son, permanently for himself and his progeny, not as a tenant. God claimed him as a son because he was a perfect man, *ish tam*; he was worthy for he spent his time in houses of study applying himself to the Torah, "the law." He was a *yoshev 'ohalim.*[14] All of Jacob's children were worthy, not only a remnant, or the line of Judah, or Ephraim, but all his issue were unblemished and qualified. d) Jacob was chosen over his elder brother because Esau was unworthy while Jacob had every merit. God preferred Jacob not as an indication of His choosing Christianity, the younger of His sons, but because Esau was unworthy.

Note particularly the difference between the status of Jacob and that of Abraham and Isaac. While the first two patriarchs were but tenants, Jacob claimed "the field" as a son. God's choice of Jacob and his offspring is permanent, irrevocable. This distinction foreshadows the second part of the argument in our Sifre passage, to be analyzed below. Barnabas and Hebrews, before him, draw a similar distinction between Moses who was "faithful as a Servitor" and Jesus, who as "Christ is faithful as a Son."[15] The author of our Sifre appears to be aware of it and subtly responds.[16]

The Rabbi concludes his case by citing the proof-text from Deut.

---

[14] See notes 4 and 11, above.

[15] Barnabas distinguishes between the way Moses received the covenant and the manner in which it was given to the Christians: "Moses received it as a servant but the Lord in person gave it to us .... He appeared in the flesh ... that we may receive the covenant through its destined heir, the Lord Jesus; ... (14:4 ff.)" The same distinction occurs in Hebrews: "Moses, then, was faithful as a servitor (θεράπων) in God's whole household ... (cf. Num. 12:7) but Christ is faithful as a son, set over his household" (Heb. 3:5 f.). Note the similarity between this distinction and the roles the Rabbis ascribe to Abraham and Isaac on the one hand, and to Jacob, on the other. The rabbinic usage of אריס is often very similar to the Greek "therapon." See, for example, Lev. Rabbah 1, where Adam is called the אריס of God referring to his being placed in the Garden of Eden לעבדה ולשמרה.

[16] We do not suggest that the author of our Sifre passage personally confronted the author of the Epistle of Barnabas. Our purpose is to demonstrate that our Sifre passage is a response to a series of Christian arguments current in the second century. By identifying the challenge and giving it precise formulation, many of the subtle nuances in the midrash itself emerge. Justin Martyr, among others, used similar arguments, often more elaborately than Barnabas. However, the argument for the elect status of the Christians as formulated by Barnabas corresponds both in form and content to the response in our Sifre passage, as will be demonstrated. On the existence of compendia of arguments for possible controversies with Jews, see: James Parkes, *The Conflict of the Church and Synagogue*, p. 49 and literature cited in note 6. On Barnabas' use of testimonial literature (*Testimoniallehre*), see H. Windisch, *Der Barnabasbrief*, 1920.

32:9, which he translates, "God claimed His people as His portion when Jacob became the lot of His inheritance." Should anyone claim that "His people" of the Deuteronomy verse refers to the Christians, i. e., that they are the true "seed" of Jacob, the author of our passage cites a second proof-text, Ps. 135:4, where God's treasure is definitely identified as Israel.[17]

Though the discussion in our Sifre passage centers about the point in time when the initial choice took place, this is not the basic issue. Our Rabbi's interest is not a remote, theoretic point nor is it a pedantic, exegetic nicety. At stake is the status of the Jews, and the Christians' right to claim election. The underlying question throughout the discussion is the Jewish claim to be the chosen people. The Christian challenge of this claim, particularly those arguments based on Scriptures, must be refuted. This is the key to our passage in the Sifre.

## II

It would appear that the author of our passage had replied to every point of the Christian challenge as formulated by Barnabas. Our passage, however, continues with a number of additional biblical texts. What other arguments would the Rabbi's adversary muster to evoke a further response, based on another series of proof-texts? The Sifre is somewhat more articulate at this point but the difficult midrashic idiom obscures the Christian counterargument to which the Rabbi is responding.

## A

Immediately following the proof-text from Psalms, the Midrash continues:[18] ועדין הדבר תלי בדלא תלי, ואין אנו יודעים אם הקדוש ברוך הוא בחר לו ישראל לסגולתו ואם ישראל בחרו בהקדוש ברוך הוא. Though the precise

---

[17] The Christians, of course, claimed to be Israel, as well. To Trypho's shocked exclamation, "What, then? Are you Israel?" Justin replies, "Christ is the Israel and the Jacob, even so we, who have been quarried out from the bowels of Christ, are the true Israelitic race..." (Dialogue with Trypho, 123 and 135). The Rabbi was well aware of this claim. However, he proceeds systematically. At this point, he is interested in "proving" only that the choice took place with Jacob, not Abraham, and that the people who inherited the elect status was Israel. He then will consider the identity of the true Israel.

[18] Note that we follow the Friedmann text, as well as every other available version (except Finkelstein), at this point. We cite the full Psalm text, without interruption (see note 6, above) and omit line 11b from ועדין to line 13a ועדין in the Finkelstein text. We read ... ועדין הדבר תלי only once instead of twice. Our interpretation

meaning of ועדין הדבר תלי תלי בדלא תלי which appears but four times in the entire literature, is somewhat obscure, the general sense of the phrase is, "The matter is still in doubt."[19] The continuation of our passage is therefore to be translated:

"But the matter is still in doubt and we do not know whether the Holy One, blessed be He, chose Israel for Himself as His treasure, or whether Israel chose the Holy One, blessed be He."

This is the substance of the new challenge addressed to the Rabbi. He then replies with a proof-text from Deut. 14:2, ". . . and the Lord your God has chosen you to be His own treasure (out of all peoples that are upon the face of the earth)."[20]

---

of the passage follows from either reading; however, the version we adopted appears to be the preferred one. The question . . . ועדין after the first half of Ps. 135:4 is most likely a later gloss by an editor who misinterpreted the passage. The burden of the second proof-text (Ps. 135:4) is to identify עמו as Israel, and this is done only at the end of the verse. Midrash Tannaim 14:2 (p. 73) addresses the question . . . ועדין to the *a* as well as *b* parts of the Psalms text. However, in that case, there is an attempt to identify the first half of Ps. 135:4 with the corresponding *a* part of Deut. 14:2 and the last part of the Psalm text with the *b* part of Deut. 14:2. Therefore the question addressed to both halves of the text is logical. It may well be that some editor was misled into explaining our Sifre passage in like manner. However, the purpose for citing the Psalms text in our Sifre is quite different. In any case, the passage in Midrash Tannaim is a late composite, put together by the author of Midrash Hag-gadol, and is not relevant for our Sifre passage. For a detailed analysis of Midrash Tannaim to Deut. 14:2, see note 26 and Appendix, below.

[19] Sifre Deut. 32:43, 333, p. 383; Sifre Num. 91 (ed. Horovitz), p. 91 (see, how-ever, Ch. Albeck, *Untersuchungen über die halakischen Midraschim*, p. 76. He doubts the authenticity of this formula in Sifre Num.); Mekhilta deRabbi Shime'on b. Yoḥai 12:14 (Epstein-Melamed) p. 16; and, of course, our Sifre passage. It is doubtful whether Sifre Deut. 33:1, 342, p. 393 is to be considered another instance of the same formula. Both the text and the formal structure of the argument would indicate otherwise. The exegetic formulae עדיין הדבר צריך (Sifra, Mezor'a, Pereq II.10 and 'Emor, Pereq XII.8), עדיין אני אומר (Sifre Numbers 116 and 148, ed. Horovitz, pp. 131 and 148, respectively) and (תלוי) עדיין הדבר חלוק (Sifre Zuṭa VII.84, ed. Horovitz, p. 253) introduce arguments that are somewhat different in structure.

David Hoffmann (Mekhilta, etc., p. 14, note 9) translates this phrase עדיין הדבר תלוי במה שאין ראוי; Horovitz (*loc. cit.*) comments הדבר תלוי בדבר . . . שלא נתברר להתלות שאף שם אין הענין מפורש. W. Bacher (*Die Exegetische Terminologie der Jüdischen Traditionsliteratur* (Leipzig, 1899), vol. I, p. 198) explains: "Der Sinn dieser Redens-art (ועדין הדבר תלי בדלא תלי) mit welcher eine Sache als unbestimmt, zweifelhaft bezeichnet wird, ist nicht genau erkennbar." Albeck, *loc. cit.*, follows Horowitz: "Die Sache hängt an etwas, das selbst nicht hängen kann . . . Diese Redewendung dient dazu, um zu erklären, dass ein Bibelvers nicht durch einen anderen, der selbst erklärungsbedürftig ist, näher bestimmt werden kann."

[20] This verse appears twice in Deuteronomy in almost identical form and there is some doubt as to which one is used as the proof-text. The reading ובך corresponds to

Though this translation appears, at first glance, quite reasonable, a closer look reveals a number of logical and textual difficulties. This type of argument appears a number of times in tannaitic literature. In the Sifre to Numbers and Deuteronomy and in the Mekhilta d'Rabbi Shime'on b. Yoḥai, the syllogism is introduced by the aramaized formula עדיין הדבר תלי בדלא תלי. In the Mekhilta d'Rabbi Yishmael, Sifra, Mishnah and Tosefta, an equivalent Hebrew phrase, עדיין הדבר שקול introduces the argument.[21] Regardless of the introductory formula, however, the argument invariably follows a definite form. The structure of the syllogism is as follows:

a) A statement or question.

b) A proof-text. (The proof-text supports the statement or resolves the question.)

c) The formula עדיין הדבר שקול, ועדיין הדבר תלי בדלא תלי) ("The matter is still in doubt.")

d) A definition of the matter still in doubt. (ואין אנו יודעים אם ... ואם ... . This refers without exception to the original statement or question and is based on an ambiguity in the proof-text.)

e) Final proof-text. (This proof definitely decides in favor of the alternative suggested by the original statement.)

Consider two illustrations of this type of argument, one from the Sifre and one from the Mishnah.

1. Sifre Deut. 32:43, Pisqa 343, p. 383.

a) רבי מאיר אומר, כל היושב בארץ ישראל, ארץ ישראל מכפרת. (statement)

b) שנאמר, והעם היושב בה נשוא עון (ישעיה ל"ג:כ"ד)• (Proof text)

c) עדין הדבר תלי בדלא תלי. (Formula)

---

the masoretic version in Deut. 14:2 but the word אלהיך is missing. While Deut. 7:6 does read אלהיך but the verse begins with בך not ובך. Finkelstein cites 14:2 but Friedmann gives the reference as 7:6. Note, however, that LXX, as well as the Targumim and a number of other versions along with the Sifre itself (Sifre Deut. 97, p. 158) read אלהיך in Deut. 14:2. Furthermore, the logic of the argument gives preference to 14:2 as will be demonstrated below. Cf. R. Kittel, *Biblia Hebraica* (Stuttgart, 1952), p. 286.

21 Mekhilta deRabbi Shime'on b. Yoḥai in commenting on Exod. 14:2 uses the phrase תלי בדלא תלי while the Mekhilta deRabbi Yishm'a'el giving the identical comment on the same verse introduces the argument with the formula ועדיין הדבר שקול. Cf. Mekhilta Rabbi Shime'on b. Yoḥai (Epstein-Melamed), p. 16, and Mekhilta deRabbi Yishm'a'el (Horowitz), p. 25. For הדבר שקול see, for example: Mishnah Soṭah 5:5; Sifra (Weiss), p. 14a; Tosefta Menaḥoth 6:19.

d) ‏אין אנו יודעים אם פורקים עוונותיהם עליה ואם נשאים עוונותיהם עליה.‏
(Definition of ‏הדבר‏)[22]

e) ‏כשהוא אומר, .וכפר אדמתו עמו' (דברים ל"ב:מ"ג) הוי פורקים עוונותיהם‏
‏עליה ואין נשאים עוונותהם עליה.‏ (Final proof-text)

2. Mishnah Soṭah 5:5.

a) ‏לא עבד איוב את הקדוש ברוך הוא אלא מאהבה‏ (Statement)

b) ‏שנאמר, .הן יקטלני לו איחל' (איוב י"ג:ט"ו)‏ (Proof-text)[23]

c) ‏ועדין הדבר שקול‏ (Formula)

d) ‏לו אני מצפה או איני מצפה‏(Definition of ‏הדבר‏)[24]

e) ‏ת"ל .עד שאנוע לא אסיר תומתי ממני' (איוב כ"ז:ה'), מלמד שמאהבה עשה‏
(Final proof-text)

At times some of the steps in the argument are not explicitly stated; they are assumed. But whether they are implicit or expressed the formal structure follows a set and universally consistent pattern. Note that "the matter still in doubt" is, without exception, the question dealt with in the first part of the passage. The initial proof-text is not conclusive; both alternatives remain live options (Job could have been motivated by either love or fear; the Land of Israel either atones for the sins of its inhabitants or it may cause them to suffer their sins). The final proof-text decides in favor of the alternative stated in the initial premise (the land of Israel atones; Job served God out of love).

If we now subject our Sifre passage to a similar analysis, the full range of problems becomes apparent.

a) The election of Israel began with God's choosing of Jacob — not Abraham. (Statement)

b) Deut. 32:9 and Ps. 135:4 (Proof-text)

c) ‏ועדין הדבר תלי בדלא תלי‏ (Formula)

d) We do not know whether God chose Israel or Israel chose God. (Definition of ‏הדבר‏)

e) Proof-text from Deut. 14:2; God chose Israel. (Final proof-text)

But at this point our passage continues:

f) How do we know that Jacob also chose God? (Second Alternative)

___

[22] The ambiguity lies in the word ‏נשא‏. Is it a passive participle as the *qere* indicates or is it active ‏נֹשֵׂא‏?

[23] The *kethiv* is ‏לא‏. LXX, Targum, Aquilla, Vulgate, Syriac read ‏לו‏.

[24] Soṭah 31a quotes Isa. 63:9 to show that though ‏לא‏ is written, it means ‏לו‏, which indicates that ‏לא‏ may be either a negative or it may mean ‏לו‏.

g) Scripture states: "Not like these is the portion of Jacob" (Jeremiah 10:16). (Proof for "f")

Now the basic premise, as we have demonstrated is that God's choice began with Jacob, not Abraham. Two texts prove it. We would therefore expect, on formal grounds, a question (step d.) addressed to the original assumption showing that the proof-texts are not conclusive and that either alternative (God chose either Jacob or Abraham) is possible. Instead, we are confronted with a *non sequitur*. The question is on a completely new subject — one not previously mentioned: Did God choose Israel or did Israel choose God.

Furthermore, we have noted that the final proof-text (e) decides in favor of one of the alternatives. But our Rabbi offers a proof-text for both of the possibilities. He proves that God chose Israel (Deut. 14:2) and also that Jacob chose God (Jer. 10:16).

But let us, for the moment, disregard the difficulty posed by the affirmation of both alternatives and let us grant the remote possibility that our passage is, in the formal structure of this type of syllogism, the single exception. We will assume that the texts cited to prove the original contention (Deut. 32:9 and Ps. 135:4) that God chose Jacob, suggested a new difficulty to our author, one not considered heretofore, and he proceeded to explore it. The discussion that follows would, therefore, be independent of the first part of the passage. Well, let us see if the proof-texts suggest the new difficulty.

Deut. 32:9, the point of departure for the Sifre comment, clearly states that "God's portion is His people..." God made the choice. No other meaning is possible. The Rabbis, in fact, continually cite this verse to prove that God chose Israel. A typical comment is: "May the Name of the King of kings, the Holy One, praised be He, be blessed, for He chose Israel from among the seventy nations, as it is stated in Scriptures 'For the portion of the Lord is His people...' "[25] The question whether God chose Israel or whether Israel did the choosing would hardly be suggested by this proof-text.

Consider, however, the second text cited to prove that God chose Jacob and not Abraham, Ps. 135:4. The first part of the verse כי יעקב בחר לו יה is ambiguous. "Jacob" could conceivably be the subject. The verse would then be translated, "For Jacob chose God for himself" and would legitimately raise the question: Who did the choosing? Similarly, the second part of the Psalm text ישראל לסגולתו could, with not unreasonable midrashic license, be rendered: "Israel

[25] Tanḥuma, Noaḥ 3. Cf. Tanḥuma Wayeshev 1, Balaq 12; Num. Rabbah 20:19; Midrash Ps. 2:14, 5:1, 28:1.

(chose God) as its treasure." It is possible, therefore, that the citation of the Psalm text gave rise to the question as to who chose, Israel or God.

When the total midrashic literature is considered, however, even this remote possibility would have to be rejected. Ps. 135:4 is one of the most frequently cited verses in rabbinic literature used to prove that God chose Israel.[26] The Sifre itself in commenting on the verse "... And the Lord, your God has chosen you ..." (Deut. 14:2, Pisqa 97, p. 158), finds no better text to strengthen and make even more explicit God's choice of Israel, than our Psalm text.[27] In order to justify the interpretation that the new question confronting the Rabbi is, "Did God choose or did Israel choose," we would have to assume that this section of our passage deals with a new subject and that it is independent of the first part of the Midrash. We would have to assert, in addition, that contrary to the overwhelming rabbinic tradition, our author finds an ambiguity in the Psalm text (135:4). We would then still be faced with the unique phenomenon that both alternatives are affirmed (God chooses and Israel chooses), in violation of the form of every other similar argument.

Moreover, if the question "who did the choosing" refers to the patriarch Jacob, i. e., that the specific matter discussed in the first part of the passage is not yet decided since the proof-text does not prove conclusively that God chose Jacob, then the answer from Deut.

[26] Gen. Rabbah 76:1; Lev. Rabbah 27:5; Num. Rabbah 3:2, 14:10; Tanḥuma Ẓaw 8, Emor 9; Tanḥuma (Buber) Lev. p. 18 and p. 91; Midrash Ps. 136:1. The use of this verse in Midrash Ps. 119:21 is somewhat ambiguous. The only midrashic passage where this Psalm verse is interpreted to mean either that God chose Jacob or Jacob chose God is Midrash Tannaim 14:2, p. 73. This passage presents a number of textual and structural problems and is, in its present form, a late composite. There is a definite relationship between this comment in Midrash Tannaim and our Sifre passage. The same three texts are used (Deut. 14:2, Ps. 135:4 and Jer. 10:16) and the language is quite similar. However, the author of the Midrash Haggadol (David Hoffmann compiled the Midrash Tannaim by putting together a number of excerpts from the Midrash Haggadol — excerpts which Hoffmann judged to be tannaitic comments on Deuteronomy) used our Sifre passage (Deut. 32:9) as a basis for constructing the commentary to Deut. 14:2. It is a composition by the Yemenite author of the post-Maimonidian period and is irrelevant to the understanding of our Sifre passage. See Appendix below for an analysis of the Midrash Tannaim passage. In any case, the ambiguity of Ps. 135:4 is not the problem in our Sifre, as will be shown. See H. J. Schoeps' analysis of Kurt Emmerich's thesis that God did not elect Israel but Israel chose God as its Volkskönig in *Aus Frühchristlicher Zeit* (Tübingen, 1950), pp. 184 ff.

[27] Though Finkelstein correctly considers the citation of Ps. 135:4 as a later gloss (Sifre Deut. p. 158, note 15), it is nevertheless an indication of the rabbinic use of this text.

14:2 is irrelevant. The context of Deut. 14:2 leaves no possible doubt that the address is to the children of Israel in the desert and not to the patriarch.

Consider further, if it is the Psalm text that casts doubt on who did the choosing, then the Rabbi needs but return to his original proof-text, Deut. 32:9, which conclusively clarifies the issue. He does not do this, however. He goes on to cite a new text, Deut. 14:2. This would indicate that the question facing him cannot be answered by appealing to his original verse. To prove that God did the choosing, no new text is necessary. The problem facing our Rabbi cannot be answered by Deut. 32:9. The question, therefore, must be something other than "who did the choosing."

Every consideration, formal structure, context, logic, demands that we reject the obvious and usually given translation suggested above. Unless, of course, we are ready to state that our passage is a senseless composite or hopelessly corrupt, an alternative to be used only as a last resort. The Sifre text is subtle and is easily misinterpreted. The new question confronting the Rabbi, we would suggest, is not independent of the previous discussion; it is a continuation of it. Nor is the question "still in doubt," whether God chose or Israel chose. The total passage, if properly understood, forms a coherent unit and is a significant response to the Christian challenge concerning the election of Israel. To determine the meaning of the passage, let us again define the challenge, closely examine the Rabbi's answer and then return to the formulation of the question.

## B

After the standard formula תלי בדלא תלי הדבר תלי ועדין and the definition of the matter "still in doubt," the author of our passage responds by citing the verse Deut. 14:2 ". . . and the Lord your God chose you . . ." What may have troubled the Rabbi at this point in his exegesis? He has proved that God chose Jacob and his descendants. What question drives him on to appeal to a new proof-text?

Suppose that some adversary would have challenged the Rabbi as follows: "The biblical record is authoritative for me too. I grant that God chose Jacob and his seed (though I may differ about the role of Abraham). Accordingly Moses offered the covenant to the Jews. But they proved unworthy of the favor, on account of their sins. Did they not turn to idolatry while Moses was yet on the mountain? Moses received the tablets and intended to give them to the people. But the Lord said, 'Arise, get down quickly . . . for your people . . . have made a molten image' (Deut. 9:12). And Moses took the two tablets and cast them out of his hands and broke them before their eyes. The covenant received by Moses was not given to Israel. They rejected it with their idolatry even before it reached them. Therefore God suspended the covenant for the sake of us Christians and revealed it through Jesus, in order that we may be loosed from darkness and, as a holy people, receive the heritage promised to Jacob."[28]

The new challenge would follow logically from the discussion in the first part of our Sifre. God's original choice is not disputed. The Christian also traces his genealogy to the patriarchs who were admittedly chosen by God, though the grounds for the Christian's claim are spiritual. It is, however, Israel's rejection of that choice at Sinai that is now emphasized. Israel rejected its special status at Sinai and, therefore, God withdrew His favor.[29]

The Christian would be led to this argument by the Rabbi's own assumptions. If Jacob was chosen because of his merit and Esau was rejected because of his unworthiness, then the offspring of Jacob too, would retain their elect status only as long as they merited it. The golden calf proved them unworthy. Israel therefore lost its chosenness and it may now be acquired only through faith in Jesus.[30]

Would anyone have raised such a question? The argument summarized above is the substance of the fourteenth chapter of the Epistle of Barnabas. It is the continuation of his argument for the elect status of the Christians and immediately follows Barnabas' discussion of the role of Abraham as "the father of many nations" which we analyzed above (Section I. B.).

But Barnabas carries his argument yet a step farther. If Israel rejected the covenant even before it was given to them, then all

---

[28] Cf. M. Simon, *Verus Israel* (Paris, 1948), p. 180, and H. Lutzmann, *The Beginnings of the Christian Church* (New York, 1937), II.297.

[29] Note in this connection Num. Rabbah 3.2: לא כל הקרוב קרוב ולא כל הרחוק רחוק. יש נבחר ונדחה ונתקרב, יש נבחר ונדחה ולא נתקרב... Cf. Yalqut Makhiri 65:9 and the other parallel passages.

[30] Note that the Rabbi tried to forewarn against this argument by calling Jacob a son (note 14, above). However, this is the very point that is in question and represents the central problem in the Jewish doctrine of election. How is God's irrevocable choice of Israel to be reconciled with His משפט, which implies a reciprocal responsiblity. Much of the rabbinic discussion of this subject stems from the tension implicit in God's choosing Israel in the face of Israel's continous rebellion. If Jacob was chosen because he was an איש תם, because of his merit, then the choice, as the Christian argues, cannot be irrevocable. Cf. note 4, last paragraph, above.

the laws concerning the Sabbath, diet, circumcision — "the law" as the Jews understood and practiced it — are not included in the true covenant. Because of their stubbornness, the Jews could not grasp the purely spiritual meaning of God's commandments. The significance of the biblical laws, Barnabas argues, "are plain to us (Christians) but were obscure to them (the Jews) because they did not understand the meaning of the Lord's voice." Moses did not speak of circumcision of the flesh (9:4). The dietary laws (10:9) and the Sabbath (15:1 ff.) were intended only in a spiritual sense. "They (the Jews) were deluded by an evil angel" (9:5). The judgement that Barnabas "closely approaches Marcion" in his view of the "ceremonies and rites of the Old Testament" is an adequate summary of his position.[31]

A parallel argument against the legal prescriptions was constructed by Justin Martyr. "They (the laws) were enjoined you," Justin tells Trypho in his Dialogue, "on account of your transgressions and the hardness of your hearts (chap. 18)." Adam, Abel, Enoch, Lot, Melchizedek, Justin continues, "though they kept no Sabbaths, were pleasing to God; and after them Abraham with all his descendants until Moses, under whom your nation appeared unrighteous and ungrateful to God, making a calf in the wilderness: wherefore God, accommodating himself to that nation, enjoined them also to offer sacrifices, as if to His name, in order that you might not serve idols ... And you were commanded to abstain from certain kinds of foods ... (chap. 20) ... on account of your unrighteousness and that of your fathers" (chap. 21). The laws given to the Jews, Justin argues, were not a sign of God's favor, but of His rejection; they were promulgated as punishment. The Christians are the true Israel (chaps. 122 and 135).

The question facing the Rabbi of our Sifre, according to our theoretical construction, would be not whether God or Israel did the choosing. The troubling challenge would rather be whether the people of Israel chose God at Sinai (in a specific historic situation) and whether, subsequently, God still chose them. The first part of the discussion proved that God chose Jacob and his descendants. The "matter still in doubt" then, would be the underlying question of

---

[31] A. Lukyn Williams, *Adversus Judaeos* (London, 1935), p. 19. He carefully explains: "Although he is no Marcionite in his doctrine of God, he approaches Marcion in his view of these (ceremonies and rites)." Marcel Simon, *loc. cit.*, explains Moses' shattering of the tablets: "... son geste signifie clairement que la vertu de la Loi réside non pas dans sa lettre, mains dans son esprit." Cf. H. J. Schoeps, *Aus Frühchristlicher Zeit* (Tübingen, 1950), pp. 154 ff., and A. Marmorstein, "Judaism and Christianity, etc." in *Hebrew Union College Annual* (1935), Vol. X, pp. 234 ff. See especially, G. Allon, "הלכה שבאגרת בר־נבא," *Tarbiz* XI (1939), pp. 23–38.

the entire passage, the status of Israel after the golden calf, and its necessary corollary, the status of Israel vis-à-vis the Christians, after Jesus. Neither one of the previous proof-texts, neither Deut. 32:9, nor Ps. 135:4, answers this question.[32] The Rabbi must therefore find a new proof-text.

Consider how naturally such a question would arise in a discussion of Deut. 32, the chapter commented upon by our Sifre. The entire chapter is an elaborate proof-text for the Christian argument and was often used as such.[33] God chose Jacob. He lovingly cared for His people, Jacob's offspring. But they rejected Him and therefore God hid His face (suspended the covenant?). He spurned Israel (?).[34] The Rabbi's proof for the choice of Jacob and his children is of little relevance in the face of this new challenge. The issue is the status of Israel after Sinai, after the golden calf.

Before returning to our Sifre text let us carry our theoretical construction a step farther and consider how the Rabbi would respond to such a challenge. What biblical evidence would he cite to refute the Christian argument? The author of our passage would have to find an unambiguous text which states that God chose Israel, the Israel after Sinai and after the golden calf. The proof-text would be ideal if, in addition, it would speak of the choice through commandments, i. e., that the legal prescriptions given to Israel by Moses after the incident of the golden calf and therefore understood by Israel in a literal sense, were a sign of God's favor. The ideal text would state that the laws were given to Israel because they are a holy people and God's chosen treasure.

Deut. 14:2, the proof-text cited by the Rabbi of our Sifre passage, meets every one of the requirements. It is the perfect text. The fourteenth chapter of Deuteronomy deals primarily with the dietary laws. It begins with the statement: "You are children of the Lord your God: you shall not cut yourselves, nor make any baldness between your eyes for the dead" (14:1). Now follows our text: "For you are a holy

---

[32] Both proof-texts are cited in the first part of our Sifre to show that the choice took place with the patriarch Jacob and his children. They are taken to be historic allusions of the time when God initially elected Israel. The biblical context of both verses supports this interpretation. These texts are therefore inconclusive with reference to the status of Israel after Sinai.

[33] See, for example, Dialogue with Trypho, chapters 20, 119, and 123.

[34] Note the comment of Rabbi Meir on Deut. 32:5 "... שחת לו לא בניו מומם" ... אף על פי שהם מלאים מומים קרויים בנים (Sifre Deut. 308, p. 346). Or a similar exegesis on Deut. 32:19 "וירא ה' וינאץ מכעס בניו ובנותיו", הלא דברים קל וחומר ומה בזמן שמכעיסים קרויים בנים אלו לא היו מכעיסים על אחת כמה וכמה (Sifre Deut. 320, p. 366), cf. Midrash Tannaim 14:1, p. 71.

people unto your God *and the Lord your God has chosen you to be His own treasure . . ."* (14:2). Moses reassures his people toward the end of his career, long after Sinai, that they are the elect. There can be no doubt about the identity of those whom he is addressing. And immediately after Moses tells Israel that they are still God's elect, he continues with a list of the forbidden foods (14:3 f.). This unambiguous statement affirming Israel's status appears between two sets of legal prescriptions. They are to refrain from certain idolatrous mourning customs (14:1) *because* they are a chosen people. Their status as God's treasure is the reason for the laws of diet which immediately follow.[35]

## C

If in the light of our discussion we now examine our Sifre text, a meaning quite different from the one originally proposed and generally assumed will become apparent. Let us recall that the basic problem of our passage is the status of Israel as the chosen people. The first challenge was that the choice took place with Abraham, "the father of many nations," before circumcision. The Rabbi countered this argument by proving that God chose Jacob not Abraham. He cited two texts in support of his position. He thus affirmed the Jewish position that only Israel may rightfully claim to be God's elect. Now follows the formula: "But the matter is still in doubt." And this, in turn, is followed by a definition of the "matter." Now what can the "matter" still in doubt possibly be? It cannot be whether God chose Abraham or Jacob. *That question has been resolved.* Nor is the answer from Deut. 14:2 addressed to this question. The doubt must therefore concern the basic problem of the passage, namely, *whether God chose the Jews or not*. In the light of the challenge by Barnabas, analyzed above, the status of the Jews following the golden calf incident would indeed be open to question. The problem, at this point in the syllogism, would therefore be: Are the Jews after Sinai still the elect or not? The proof-texts cited so far provide no answer. The structure of this type of argument would lead us to expect the formulation: "And we do

---

[35] Note the Sifre comment to 14:2 (Pisqa 97, p. 158). The passage is somewhat obscure. However, both Finkelstein and Friedmann consider it an anti-Christian polemic. The formulation in Mekhilta deRabbi Shime'on b. Yoḥai (Yithro 19:6, ed. Melamed, p. 139) is clearer: הא ,"(דברים י'ד:ב')". "כי עם קדוש אתה לה' אלהיך . . . Finkelstein. כיצד, זו קדושת מצות מצות שכל זמן שהקב"ה מוסיף להם מצה לישראל הוא מוסיף להם קדושה comments (Sifre, *loc. cit.*, note 16): לדעתי שתי הדרשות הן פולמוסיות כנגד הכנסיה הנוצרית. Friedmann (p. 94a, note 5) explains: וכל הענין הוא הקדמה לפ' שלפי מיסדיה היא הסגולה. מאכלות האסורות כנגד תלמידו של רבן גמליאל תלמיד תלמידו של ר' יהושע בן פרחיה.

not know whether God chose Israel or God chose the Christians"; or perhaps: "And we do not know whether God elected Israel or rejected Israel." But our Sifre reads instead, "And we do not know whether God chose Israel or Israel chose God." This is the textual difficulty which has led to the misinterpretation of the entire passage and has obscured the real point of argument.

However, even a cursory familiarity with the rabbinic idiom would immediately rule out the first two suggested formulations. The Rabbis would never overtly express either God's choosing the Christians or His utter rejection of Israel (in the Christian sense) — even as a theoretic possibility. They would suggest such an alternative only with the greatest caution, obliquely or euphemistically. We would suggest that this is the very thing that our Rabbi has done in his definition of "the matter still in doubt."

Let us recall the example of this type of argument cited above (II.A.). The fourth step in the syllogism, the definition of the matter in doubt, is expressed in the form of either/or. Either Job served God out of fear, or he served out of love (Soṭah 5:5); either the land of Israel atones for its inhabitants' sins, or it makes them suffer their sins (Sifre Deut. 343). If one alternative is denied, the other is affirmed and by proving one of the possibilities the other is disproved. They are invariably disjunctive propositions, stating mutually exclusive alternatives. Our case, however, does not follow this form.

The alternatives in our Sifre passage are: a) "God chose Israel," or b) "Israel chose God." Now let us deny a. "God chose Israel," keeping in mind that the reference is to the event at Sinai. By so doing we are also denying b. "Israel chose God," because the only reason for God's not choosing Israel would be Israel's not choosing God. Otherwise, the original choice of Jacob and his descendants would still be in effect. Now if we affirm a. "God chose Israel," we are at the same time affirming b. "Israel chose God." The Rabbi is replying to a challenge which bases itself on the Rabbi's own assumption that the choice is made on the basis of merit, not grace. Therefore, if God chose Israel, they merited the choice, i. e., they chose God.[36]

---

[36] There are numerous passages in rabbinic literature which imply that the choice was conditional. See, for example, the statements of Judah b. 'Illai as opposed to Rabbi Meir (references in note 33, above) and Mekhilta deRabbi Shime'on b. Yoḥai, loc. cit., 19.5, בזמן שאתם בדילים מן העמים אתם לי ואם לאו הרי אתם לנבוכדנצר הרשע וחבריו or the parallel passage in Mekhilta deRabbi Yishm'a'el and Sifre 31:1, p. 331. However, none of these statements implies an ultimate rejection — without hope of reconciliation through obedience to the commandments. Note the introduction of the formula "with an eternal love" (אהבת עולם) rather than "with a great love" (אהבה

Now let us follow the same procedure with b. "Israel chose God." If we affirm it, we also affirm a., and if we deny it, we simultaneously deny a., following the above reasoning.[37] In other words, the stated alternatives in our Sifre passage are not alternatives at all. Both parts of the proposition say exactly the same thing. The true choices are not stated; they are only very subtly implied. Unlike the other examples of this type of syllogism where "the matter in doubt (step d)" is stated in the form of a disjunctive proposition, our Sifre passage states only one of the alternatives (a and b are equivalents). The other alternative, the negative one, is implied by the affirmative form of the stated one. By saying that there is doubt about God's choosing Israel or (the same thing) Israel choosing God, our Rabbi suggests the possibility of God's not choosing and even rejecting Israel. The true alternatives of our passage are therefore to be expressed: "But the matter is still in doubt and we do not know if God chose Israel or (by implication) if He rejected Israel (following Israel's idolatrous behavior)." The final proof-text (Deut. 14:2) then follows and it demonstrates conclusively that Israel remained God's elect

---

רבה) into the daily liturgy by the Rabbis (Berakhoth 11b). Cf. the discussion of H. J. Schoeps referred to in note 26, above.

Note as well the reported prohibition against disputation with the Christians mentioned by Justin (Dialogue, etc. 38, 112) and the Talmud, 'Avodah Zarah 17a, 27b. Yer. 'Avodah Zarah 40d–41a, Yer. Shabbath 14d. This would also explain the subtlety of the polemical rabbinic passages and the reluctance of the Rabbis to name their opponent or express their arguments in any but the most euphemistic language.

[37] If we affirm "Israel chose God" then the original elect state of Jacob's descendants remains in effect and we automatically affirm "God chose Israel," as well. On the other hand, if we deny that "Israel chose God" then Israel no longer merits the choice and we would, therefore, also negate "God chose Israel." However, even if we do not consider the stated alternatives as equivalents, they are obviously not mutually exclusive and, at the very least, would be translated "neither ... nor ..." (and not "either ... or ...") with the possibility of denying both. The concept of Israel as a "God choosing people" with the apologetic background and humanistic context of this concept is largely responsible for the misunderstanding of this passage. It is very well to interpret the doctrine of election as Israel's historic aspiration in line with a contemporary naturalistic, humanistic mood. However, we do violence to the Rabbis if we attempt to impose this concept on a second century text. The thought of "God's choosing" presented no problem to the Jews of the Rabbinic Period. The difficulty for them was how to reconcile the choice with God's justice (*mishpat*) in the face of Israel's sinfulness, with the sad lot of the Jews following the destruction, and with God's universal concern. God, to the Rabbis, acts within a rationally comprehensible ethical framework. Meritorious deeds must, therefore, play a role in God's choosing. The justification of God's choice of Abel, Enoch, Noah, the patriarchs, Moses and Israel is a major preoccupation of the Rabbis in midrashic literature.

and that the legal prescriptions are a concrete expression of God's choice.

The difficulties raised above (II.A.) have now been resolved. The passage is a coherent unit and follows the formal pattern of every syllogism of this type. The question "still in doubt" (step d) is based on the fact that *both* previously cited proof-texts are inconclusive. The final proof-text affirms the original proposition. The argument of our Sifre may now be expressed in the following syllogistic form:

a) The Jews are the chosen people. (The underlying issue in the entire passage.)

b) Proof-texts, Deut. 32:9 and Ps. 135:4. (These proof-texts must be understood in light of the specific challenge to the Jewish doctrine of election which centered on God's choosing Abraham.)

c) But the matter is still in doubt. (Deut. 32:9 and Ps. 135:4 are inconclusive.)

d) We do not know whether God chose Israel or (implied) whether God rejected Israel. (This question must again be understood in terms of the challenge which argues against Israel's chosenness on the basis of the golden calf incident and which questions the validity of the legal prescriptions.)

e) The final proof-text (Deut. 14:2). (This text affirms the original alternative stated in a., God chose Israel.)

### III

#### A

Only one difficulty that we raised above (II.A.) remains unresolved. After citing the final proof text (Deut. 14:2), the author of our passage, contrary to usual form, continues the discussion with another question ומנין שאף יעקב בחר בו ביה and then concludes with a text from Jeremiah (10:16) שנאמר, לא כאלה חלק יעקב. The obvious translation of this final section of our Sifre is: "And from where in the Bible do we know that Jacob also chose God? It is said in Scriptures, 'Not like these is the portion of Jacob, for He is the one who forms all things . . .'" (Jer. 10:16). The last section of our passage would then be interpreted to refer to the alternatives in the preceding discussion. Our Rabbi raised the question "Did God choose or did Israel choose." After proving that God chose (Deut. 14:2), he now proceeds to prove the second alternative, Israel also chose (Jer. 10:16).

We have pointed out (II.A.) the difficulty that this interpretation raises from the point of view of formal structure. The final proof text of this type of argument (step e), invariably affirms one of the alternatives. In no instance are both possibilities proved. How is it then, that our author would prove both alternatives? However, this objection is now mitigated since, as we demonstrated above, every other formulation of the alternatives is a disjunctive proposition where a. and b. are mutually exclusive, therefore only one of the two may be proved. It is logically impossible to prove both. The stated alternatives (not the real ones) in our passage, however, are complementary and our author may logically prove that God chose Israel and then prove also that Israel chose God.

In reality, however, our analysis of the argument up to this point compounds the difficulty. If the two stated alternatives of our passage refer to the covenant at Sinai and are equivalent, as we have demonstrated, why prove the same thought twice? If "God chose Israel" is identical with "Israel chose God" why repeat the demonstration for each one, when by affirming one we automatically affirm the other? The continuation of the discussion would be senseless and confusing.

Consider, as well, some textual irregularities. These are not very serious but they are worthy of note. The alternatives stated by our author are: ישראל בחר בהקדוש or הקדוש ברוך הוא בחר לו ישראל ברוך הוא. He proved that God chose Israel (הקב"ה בחר לו ישראל). Now, if the final argument of our passage is a continuation of the same argument, we would naturally expect the text to read ומנין שאף ישראל בחרו בהקדוש ברוך הוא. Instead, we find ומנין שאף יעקב בחר ביה.[38] Granted that Jacob is used interchangeably with Israel to designate the people of Israel.[39] Nevertheless, since the subject under discussion is Israel, in contrast to the patriarch Jacob referred to in the very first part of our passage, the formulation יעקב בחר ביה (or even Friedmann's reading יעקב בחר בהקב"ה) disturbs and suggests the need for a closer scrutiny of the intent of this question.

---

[38] Note the number of textual variants in this section of the passage as indicated by Finkelstein in his critical apparatus and in the parallel passages (note 2, above). They are indications of the difficulty various editors had with the text and its interpretation. Midrash Tannaim, p. 73, asks the same question in connection with the first half of Ps. 135:4 but refers specifically to the patriarch, ומנין שאבינו יעקב. However, this reading is but further proof of the composite nature of the Midrash Tannaim passage. See Appendix, below.

[39] Jacob, according to the Rabbis, may be designated either as Israel or Jacob unlike Abraham who is not to be called Abram (Berakhoth 13a).

The proof-text from Jeremiah, ... לא כאלה חלק יעקב also leaves one not quite satisfied. Our assumption is that the Rabbi is trying to prove that Israel chose God. Now, we grant that Jeremiah's calling God the חלק יעקב, "the portion of Jacob," is an indication that Jacob chose (or will choose) God, just as the phrase in Deut. 32:9, חלק ה' עמו, is understood to mean "God chose His people." The impression nevertheless persists that a more direct proof-text could have beeen found without leaving the Pentateuch, the source for the other proof-texts.[40] Note also that in the entire midrashic literature we find not one instance of the Jeremiah text being used in this sense.

No one of the foregoing objections is by itself conclusive. When we consider all of them together, however, they are serious enough to justify a search for an interpretation which would yield a smoother reading and would eliminate the above stated difficulties.

We would propose that this final section of our passage is not a continuation of the preceding argument regarding Israel's choosing in the past. That syllogism concluded with Deut. 14:2. It consists of five steps, like every other argument of its kind. The new question and the answer from Jeremiah deal with the third part of the elaborate argument for the election of Christians and against the election of the Jews. We shall again follow the procedure adopted in the previous two sections of our study. After reconstructing the challenge and analyzing the Rabbi's response, the Jeremiah verse, we will then return to the formulation of the question in our Sifre text.

## B

We have analyzed, thus far, two facets of the Christian argument current in the second century. The election of Abraham because of his "faith," before he was circumcised, of Isaac though he was the younger, of Jacob while he was still in his mother's womb, were all indications that God chose the Christians. This was the positive proof for the elect status of those who put their faith in Jesus. The negative aspect of the argument was used to demonstrate that God rejected the Jews, that the Jews were not heir to "the promise." The idolatry of the Jews, Moses' shattering of the tablets proved that the election of the Patriarchs and their descendants did not apply to the Jews after Sinai. These two arguments were effectively refuted by the author of our Sifre passage.

The Christian, however, used one more argument, perhaps the most

---

[40] Ps. 135:4 is only a supporting text. The main proofs are Deut. 32:9 and 14:2.

persuasive to a second century audience. He would reach a climax in his debate by pointing not to an event in the remote past but to the contemporary scene, to the condition of the Jews in his own time. "How do you explain," he would challenge the Rabbi, "the destruction of the temple, the fall of Jerusalem, the miserable lot of your people? Is this not the decisive proof that God has rejected you Jews and has delivered you for destruction at the hand of your enemies? The story of your people is one of continuous rebellion against God. Why, they even made an idol of the temple. Instead of putting their trust in God who made them, they put it in the building, as if it were the house of God. In fact, they almost resembled the heathen in consecrating Him by the temple.... But it has been revealed that the city, the temple and the people of Israel are doomed. Your stiff-necked idolatry has finally resulted in utter rejection. Now there is only one true temple. Not the temple built by hand which was in fact 'a nest of idolatry and a haunt of demons...' but a spiritual temple, in us — that is where God really dwells. Through faith in Jesus and his teachings one is ushered into this imperishable temple."

This is the substance of the sixteenth chapter of the Epistle of Barnabas. Note the sequence of the argument in Barnabas. Chap. 13 — God's choice of the younger sons and His choice of Abraham, "the father of many nations." Chap. 14 — Israel's idolatry at Sinai and their refusal to accept the covenant. Chap. 15 — The purely spiritual meaning of the commandment to rest on the seventh day — and (by implication) of all the other commandments discussed by Barnabas in earlier chapters. Chap. 16 — The destruction of the temple and the fall of Jerusalem, etc.

The Rabbi has successfully countered the arguments in chaps. 13–15. Now how would he answer the final challenge? The Rabbi himself had undoubtedly explained the destruction of Jerusalem and the suffering of Israel as a consequence of the Jews' sinfulness.[41] How could the author of our passage convince his Jewish audience that their degradation is not a sign of God's final rejection? Recall the plight of the Jewish people following the Bar Kokhba rebellion, a not unlikely setting for our Sifre passage. The land lay devastated, the population — decimated, the community — in chaos, the very last hope shattered, seemingly beyond revival.[42] At hand was the

[41] See H. J. Schoeps, "Die Ursachen der Tempelzerstörung," *op. cit.*, pp. 145–53. Note also, G. Allon's analysis of chap. XVI of Barnabas in תולדות היהודים בא"י בתקופת המשנה והתלמוד (Tel Aviv, 1952), pp. 280 ff.

[42] Yer. Peah 7:1 notes: ... לא היו הזיתים מצויין שבא אדריינוס הרשע והחריב את כל הארץ.

Christian group with its ready and plausible explanation and promise of salvation through Jesus. What could the Rabbi reply?

He, no doubt, comforted his fellow Jews by re-emphasizing that God's relationship to Israel was that of a father to his son. A father may punish in anger or even out of love but he never rejects. He may "hide his face" but a reconciliation inevitably follows. The basic relationship remains.[43] Didn't God claim Jacob as His son? Jacob received "the field" not as a "tenant" but as a son, permanently.[44] However, the Rabbi's reassurance will not suffice. His argument is circular; this is the very point that is being challenged; he is begging the question. Is it not the Rabbi's own position that Israel's relationship with God is covenantal and that God's favor must be earned? (Esau and Ishmael were rejected because they were not worthy.) God's attribute of justice demands that sinful rebellion be paid for with banishment and rejection. The Jews had been told again and again that their stubborn sinfulness would be their downfall. The day of final reckoning had come. Israel has fallen never to rise again.

The only effective response would be a clear biblical text which speaks not of an event in the past but one that looks to the future, — a prophecy that sees Israel's degradation as a part of a grand Divine scheme of history which culminates in a final redemption. The Rabbi's scriptural citation would have to give assurance that Israel's option to choose remains open — more so, that Israel shall choose; it is part of the plan, and Israel's ultimate destiny. The ideal proof-text would have to transcend the dismal present and give comfort of a messianic reconciliation. Jer. 10:16 as understood by the Rabbis is such a text. A mere reference to this verse conveyed to a second century audience all that we indicated — and more.

Jeremiah tells Israel in the tenth chapter not to be dismayed by the signs attributed to the idols. They are impotent. Only God is the true God. He created the world by His wisdom and He is responsible for the rain and the wind. Everything functions in accordance with the plan and will of the Creator. This God, the true God, is the portion of Jacob, and Israel is His inheritance. His special relationship to Israel is an integral part of His universal scheme. He is the Lord of Hosts.[45]

But Jeremiah continues in another vein. Immediately following his comforting reassurance, the prophet laments as he sees the temple destroyed ("my tent is spoiled" as the Rabbis would interpret it),

---

[43] See note 36, above.          [44] Note 14 and text, above.
[45] The Rabbis often understand "the Lord of Hosts" to indicate the God of battle, of victory, when His צבאות is triumphant. Exod. Rabbah 3:6 and Tanḥuma, Shemoth 20.

the flocks scattered, "the cities of Judah desolate, a dwelling place of jackals."[46] He pleads (for Israel), that the Lord chastise not by rejection (אל־באפך 10:24), but only to the extent that God's justice (משפט) demands, only to the degree necessary for Israel to merit their choice and destiny. God would pour out his wrath (חמתך, spurn),[47] the prophet prays, on the nations who knew Him not, upon those who have devoured Jacob and have laid waste his habitation. Israel's lot is God. But the people of Israel need *musar* (יסרני ה' אך במשפט...) to cause them to turn from their wayward path. This is the necessary corollary of God's משפט. Regardless of the immediate condition of Israel, God shall be the חלק יעקב just as Israel is the שבט נחלתו.

The Rabbi's invoking the proof-text from Jeremiah recalled to his listeners a total structure of consolation, the prophetic נחמתא.[48] God must chastise Israel so that they will choose and thus help realize God's universal plan. Israel's suffering is proof of their special place in the Divine scheme. (תוכחה and נחמה are the two sides of the same coin within a scheme of משפט.) To reap the benefits of God's having chosen them, they need but choose. The option is live. Israel's degradation is God's מוסר, the father's chastisement of his son so that he will claim his rightful inheritance. Every citation of Jer. 10:16 in midrashic literature indicates that the Rabbis, without a single exception, interpreted this verse as one of messianic consolation.

One of the structural characteristics of the Pesiqta and Tanḥuma homilies (the sermons of Lev. and Deut. Rabbah, the Pesiqtoth, Tanḥuma) is that they conclude with a messianic verse, a biblical text which speaks of the future glory of Israel.[49] These were oft-used verses,

---

[46] Compare the story of the four Tannaim visiting the temple mount. Three of them wept at the sight of jackals but R. Akiba laughed ... Sifre Deut. 43, p. 95 and Makkoth 24b.

[47] Compare the almost identical verse in Ps. 79:6 and the relationship of God to Israel as conceived by the Psalmist.

[48] The rabbinic use of חלק has the overtones of "portion in the world to come," "destiny." Recall the expressions, ... חלק לעוה׳׳ב, יהי חלקי עם, etc. The Midrash often records its message in hints, brief notes — in a form of shorthand. An allusion frequently recalls a complex syndrome of ideas.

[49] Theodor, "Zur Composition der agadischen Homilien," *Monatschrift f. Geschichte und Wissenschaft d. Judenthums* (1879), vol. 28, p. 109: "Endlich schliessen die meisten Piskas mit der Anführung von Bibelversen, die die hoffnungsreiche Zukunft Israels verkünden." M. Margulies, Wayyikra Rabbah, V, p. XII: כאן (בויקרא רבה) כל פרשה מסתיימת בחתימה ברורה, בסיום קצר בדברי ברכה ונחמה, כדרך כל כיוסי דרשות סאו ועד היום... Cf. L. Zunz, *Haderashot Beyisra'el* (tr. Albeck) (Jerusalem, 1954), pp. 79, 85; E. Stein, "Die Homiletische Peroratio im Midrasch," *HUCA*, vols. 8–9, pp. 362 ff.; A. Marmorstein, "The Background of the Haggadah," *HUCA*, vol. VI (1929), pp. 184 ff.

familiar to the audience, which did not require subtle exegesis or
lengthy interpretation. They provided much needed encouragement
and evoked a spirit of hope in the face of an often intolerable present.
Each sermon in the Pesiqta deRav Kahana, a collection of occasional
sermons for the special sabbaths and festivals based on the prescribed
pentateuchal or prophetic lesson, ends with such a verse of consolation.
The homily for the second of the three special sabbaths preceding the
Ninth of Av (תלתא דפורענותא)[50] concludes with our Jeremiah text
לא כאלה חלק יעקב.[51]

An even more explicit messianic interpretation of our Jeremiah
verse is to be found in the Tanḥuma and Lev. Rabbah.[52] In commenting on Isaac's blessing of Jacob (...ויתן לך האלהים, Gen. 27:28), the
Tanḥuma calls attention to the definite article in האלהים and explains
it as follows: "(Isaac said to Jacob), 'God will grant you the blessing
that I invoke upon you when He will perfect His lack (or kingdom,[53]
i. e., when אלהים will be האלהים).' For Jacob is a partner of God in
everything. Rabbi Pinḥas ... said, 'Note what is written in Scriptures, "Not like these is the portion of Jacob for he (Jacob) is the one
who forms all things." (The exegesis is on the word הוא. Rabbi Pinḥas
understands the antecedent of the pronoun הוא to be "Jacob," not "the
Portion of Jacob." Jacob is the creator of everything in the sense that
now it is all up to him).' "[54] The blessing of Isaac will be fulfilled when
Jacob will recognize his duties as God's partner (Jacob is God's inheritance so Jacob must claim God as his), when he will finally choose and
thus perfect God's kingdom and, כביכול, God Himself.

The Jeremiah text is thus a cogent reply to the new Christian
challenge based upon the destruction of the temple and the fallen
state of Israel. The prophetic verse gives clear assurance that Israel's
suffering is divine *musar*, not rejection. Jacob remains God's beloved
son who ultimately shall claim his portion and thus bring God's plan
to fulfillment.

---

[50] See I. Elbogen, *Der jüdische Gottesdienst in seiner geschichtlichen Entwicklung*
(1931), p. 178.

[51] Pesiqta deRav Kahana XIV, p. 119a. The entire passage supports our analysis.
God tells Israel not to hesitate to return to Him because of their fear that their sins
are too grievous. He assures them that He is ready to forgive and forget.

[52] Tanḥuma (Buber) Toledoth 11, p. 132, and Lev. Rabbah 36:4.

[53] Yalquṭ Makhiri 31:23, p. 200, reads כשיטול אלהים מלכותו, instead of כשישלים
אלהים מליותו. See, Tanḥuma, *loc. cit.*, note 72.

[54] Lev. Rabbah, *loc. cit.*, expounds the Jeremiah verse identically, i. e., Jacob
is taken to be the antecedent of הוא.

## C

We may now return to our midrashic text and examine it in the light of our discussion. Deut. 14:2 proved that God chose Israel after their idolatry at Sinai. Israel remained God's son. Now follows a new question, ומנין שאף יעקב בחר ביה. We understand בחר as referring not to a past event. The question is to be translated not, "whence do we know that Jacob chose" — in the past. Were this the intent of the question we should be faced with all the objections raised above (II.A.). The new challenge is rather: "What scriptural proof do we have that Jacob may still choose — that he shall choose? The context of this question is the situation of the Jews in our midrashic author's own time, after Jesus, after the destruction of the temple and probably after the failure of the Bar Kokhba rebellion. The discussion in this last part of our Sifre shifts to the present and future. It responds to a new challenge, as the formal structure of the preceding completed syllogism indicates. The Rabbi replies to the challenge and concludes the discussion with a messianic text, Jer. 10:16, which gives assurance that it is Israel's ultimate destiny to choose God.

This interpretation removes all the difficulties. This final section of our Sifre is not an answer to the stated "second" alternative of the previous discussion, ואם ישראל בחרו בהקב׳ה. It is a new question and therefore may be differently formulated, יעקב בחר ביה.[55] Though the wording of the question is suggested by the Psalm verse cited earlier (135:4) כי יעקב בחר לו יה, it refers neither to the historic Jacob nor to the covenant at Sinai, but to the possibility of Israel's choosing in the present and future. Otherwise the answer (Jer. 10:16) is not in place. The Jeremiah proof-text is convincing only if we interpret the question in a sense that requires a messianic answer.[56]

---

[55] Israel, on the basis of the etymology frequently mentioned by Philo, "the man who saw God" (איש ראה אל), is identified by him with the Logos and is equated in the writings of the Church Fathers with Christ. See, for example, Justin, *Dialogue*, etc., chap. 75: "For, indeed, He was called Israel and Jacob's name was changed to this also." It is likely that in response to this very common equation, the Rabbis preferred the name Jacob as the specific designation for the Jews, especially in discussing their future role. Cf. note 39, above.

[56] Midrash Tannaim 14:2, p. 73 cites the Jeremiah text in response to the question ומנין שאבינו יעקב בחר במקום. The יעקב in Jer. 10:16 is interpreted as the patriarch Jacob (cf. Appendix, below). In our passage, however, the question cannot possibly refer to the patriarch, for that issue was settled in the very first part of the discussion. The Jeremiah proof-text is therefore to be understood in the sense in which it is used in the total literature, namely, as a messianic verse. The question must therefore also refer to the future. Note also that the following Sifre comment on the last part

We are now in a position to reconstruct the full dialogue, both the Christian challenge current in the second century (based on Barnabas' formulation of it) and the Rabbi's response. The Christians argued that they are the true chosen people based on the election of Abraham, of Isaac though he was the younger, of Jacob before he was born. The Rabbi replied in the first part of our Sifre passage that the choice took place not with Abraham but with Jacob because of his meritorious deeds and that he and his progeny were chosen as sons, permanently. The Christian then claimed that God rejected Israel after they turned to an idol at Sinai and that the "law" as practiced by the Jews was not the true covenant. Our author cited Deut. 14:2 which demonstrates that Israel remained the chosen people and that the legal prescriptions were a sign of the choice. The final challenge then centered on the destruction of the temple and the sad lot of the Jewish people. The Rabbi responded with Jer. 10:16 to prove that God is Israel's ultimate destiny; the option is live; the children of Israel need but exercise it, and they will for that is their ultimate role in history.

## D

It is possible to see our Sifre passage as a composite, lacking coherence and unity. The introduction of the Psalm verse as a proof-text may have attracted the entire subsequent discussion. The passage would thus consist of two independent units joined together by a later editor with Ps. 135:4 serving as the connecting link. Such a conclusion, however, is to be adopted, especially without the support of textual variants, only as a last resort. Furthermore, the formal structure of the syllogism would still remain a problem.

There is an obvious hazard in the procedure that we have adopted, as well. The attempt to salvage the unity of a passage at all cost may result in a farfetched pilpulism. The literature abounds in ingenious and imaginative structures built on a textual corruption.

We are persuaded, however, of the soundness of our method and urge its application to other, similar tannaitic passages. The insistence of the author of our Sifre on the choice of Israel having been initiated with Jacob and not Abraham identifies the passage as a polemical one and establishes the ideational context. The three proof-texts, Deut. 32:9, Deut. 14:2 and Jer. 10:16, immediately suggest a direct and cogent response to the prevailing three part argument for the elect

---

of Deut. 32:9 יעקב חבל נחלתו supports our interpretation. It speaks of חבל as גורל and concludes with the assurance that the tie that binds God and Jacob endures.

status of the Christians as expounded in the compendia literature (Testimoniallehre) of the time. The three basic points of our passage, as implied in the three proof-texts, and the three parts of the Christian argument as they appear in Barnabas form a perfect whole. It is like finding the missing half of a dialogue, an exact fit.

Form analysis then leads to the discovery of the precise meaning of the transitional phrases, the Christian argument as restated by the Rabbi. The nature of the subject matter and the character of the literature dictate that the Rabbi's formulation be veiled and euphemistic. The structure of the argument, determined by the introductory technical formula, is an indispensable aid in uncovering the plain meaning.

Our method thus includes the following three steps: a) The discovery of the historic setting and the ideational environment. b) An appreciation of the syndrome of ideas which cluster about a proof-text based on biblical context and on the use of the text in the total rabbinic literature. c) Form analysis of the exegetic syllogism determined by the introductory technical phrase.

# APPENDIX

## Midrash Tannaim to Deut. 14:2 (D. Hoffmann), p. 73

We concluded (II.C. above) that the problem, "And we do not know if God chose Jacob or Jacob chose God," was not prompted by the ambiguity of Ps. 135:4 (i. e., Is God or Jacob the subject of the verse?), but by the fact that neither of the texts (Deut. 32:9 and Ps. 135:4) conclusively proves that God chose Israel after Sinai, after Israel's worship of the golden calf. This interpretation is challenged by a comment of Midrash Tannaim to Deut. 14:2.[57] The question ואין אנו יודעים אם . . . ואם . . . is clearly interpreted in Midrash Tannaim as arising from the syntactical ambiguity of Ps. 135:4. A careful analysis of this passage is therefore necessary to determine whether our interpretation of Sifre Deut. 32:9 can be maintained.

The comment of Midrash Tannaim is as follows:

ד"א בך בחר ה' אלהיך למה נאמר לפי שהוא אומר (תהלים קל"ה:ד') כי יעקב
בחר לו יה ישראל ואין אנו יודעים אם יה בחר ביעקב ואם יעקב בחר ביה ת"ל בך
בחר ה', ומנ' שאבינו יעקב בחר במקום שנ' (ירמיהו י':ט"ז) לא כאלה חלק יעקב:
להיות לו לעם סגלה למה נאמר לפי שהוא אומר (תהלים קל"ה:ד') ישראל לסגולתו
ואין אנו יודעים אם ישראל עושין למקום סגלה ואם המקום עושה להן סגולה לישראל
ת"ל (ישראל לסגולתו) [להיות לו לעם סגלה]

The Midrash Tannaim then continues with a series of other biblical verses (introduced by the familiar formula כיוצא בו אתה אומר) which contain ambiguities similar to Ps. 135:4 and are "clarified" only in the light of other verses (similar to Ps. 135:4 the ambiguity of which is "resolved" by Deut. 14:2).

Now if this passage is from a tannaitic source, it would weaken considerably our analysis of Sifre Deut. 32:9. For here in Midrash Tannaim it is clear that the problem is the ambiguity of Ps. 135:4 — did God choose Jacob or did Jacob choose God; did Israel make God its treasure or did God make Israel His treasure? The series of parallels cited in the continuation of the passage as examples of similar ambiguities in other biblical verses permit no other interpretation. This passage would indicate that the question of who made the initial choice — Israel or God — was, contrary to our contention,[58] a problem suggested by Ps. 135:4. We would therefore have to interpret the similar question in our Sifre passage (Deut. 32:9) in the light of this

[57] Midrash Tannaim zum Deuteronomium, ed. D. Hoffmann (Berlin, 1909), p. 73. Cf. note 26, above.
[58] See Sections II A and notes 18, 26 and 38, above.

rabbinic concern. Though the many problems we raised above (II.A) would still remain, a solution other than the one we suggested would have to be found.

Upon close analysis, however, we find that this passage in Midrash Tannaim is a very late composite, based partially on Sifre Deut. 14:2 and 32:9. These passages were reworked and added to by the author of Midrash Haggadol — the source for Midrash Tannaim — as was his usual practice. The Midrash Tannaim to Deut. 14:2 is therefore of no relevance for the understanding of our Sifre passage. In the process of our analysis we, incidentally, gain additional insight into the manner in which the post-Maimonidean, Yemenite author[59] of Midrash Haggadol treated the classic sources.

David Hoffmann's Midrash Tannaim as well as his edition of the Mekhilta d'Rabbi Shim'on b. Yoḥai are primarily compilations of passages selected from the Midrash Haggadol to Deuteronomy and Exodus, respectively — passages which, according to Hoffmann, were taken from the original Mekhilta d'Rabbi Shim'on b. Yoḥai and from lost Tannaitic Midrashim to Deuteronomy.[60] Hoffmann was aware that the author of Midrash Haggadol made numerous changes in the material which he included in his anthology.[61] The author of Midrash Haggadol, Hoffmann maintains, abbreviated and added; he combined passages from a variety of sources and as a result, it is difficult to determine with any degree of precision the original version of any midrashic passage. "Only the discovery of a manuscript (of the Mekhilta d'Rabbi Shim'on b. Yoḥai)," Hoffmann concludes, "will enable us to make the necessary corrections and to reestablish the original version of the Mekhilta."[62]

The Midrash Haggadol to Deuteronomy, the source for Midrash

---

[59] The authorship of Midrash Haggadol is generally attributed to Dawid b. 'Amram 'Al'adani. Cf. 'Avoth deRabbi Nathan, ed. S. Schechter, Introduction, p. 15, and references given by S. Lieberman in *Midreshei Teiman*, p. 3, note 2, and by M. Kasher, הרמב״ם והמכילתא דרשב״י (New York, 1943), pp. 20 f. Kasher concludes ברור תעלה מכל ספק שר׳ דוד (בן עטרם העדני) חברו.

[60] Israel Lewy, *Ein Wort über die Mechilta des R. Simon* (Breslau, 1889), was the first to note that the Midrash Haggadol quoted extensively from Mekhilta d'Rabbi Shime'on b. Yoḥai.

[61] On the basis of comparison with a few manuscript fragments of Mekhilta d'Rabbi Shime'on b. Yoḥai provided by S. Schechter (cf. Hoffmann's introduction to his Mekhilta, p. ix), and Schechter's introduction to his edition of Midrash Haggadol to Genesis (Cambridge, 1902), p. 13.

[62] Mechilta de-Rabbi Simon b. Jochai, ed. D. Hoffmann, Frankfurt a. Main, 1905. Introduction, p. ix. He felt that only those passages in his Mekhilta were definitely faithful to the original which he could compare with the few manuscripts available to him, or with versions quoted in other secondary sources (Naḥmanides, etc., cf. M. Higger, ספר התנאים בתקופת הגאונים, pp. 32 and 55.)

Tannaim,[63] is based, Hoffmann conjectures, on two ancient midrashim, the Mekhilta to Deuteronomy (now lost) and the Sifre.[64] In his introduction to Midrash Tannaim, Hoffmann again cautions that the author of Midrash Haggadol was particularly attracted to the Mishnah and the Babylonian Talmud. He, therefore, often omitted a passage from the Sifre or Mekhilta and substituted a talmudic or mishnaic comment. He even rejected an ancient midrash, Hoffmann complains, in favor of a halakhah from the Code of Maimonides.[65]

However, due to the efforts of a number of scholars and the discovery of new manuscripts, we have learned considerably more than was known to Hoffmann about the method of the compiler of Midrash Haggadol in his treatment of the sources. The work of S. Horovitz,[66] L. Finkelstein,[67] Ch. Albeck,[68], J. N. Epstein,[69] M. Margulies,[70] E. Z.

---

[63] Hoffmann included in his Midrash Tannaim two Genizah fragments, on Deut. 11:26–12:3; 12:27–13:1 and 13:14–13:19 (Midrash Tannaim, pp. 56–62 and 69–71), published by S. Schechter in *Jewish Quarterly Review*, Vol. XVI, 1904, pp. 446–52 and 695–97. J. N. Epstein republished these two fragments in *Abhandlungen zur Erinnerung an Hirsch Perez Chajes* (Wien, 1933), Hebrew Section, pp. 60 ff. He explains the need to republish these manuscripts as follows: ... אבל הופמן לא ראה את גוף כה"י (שנתפרסמו ראשונה על ידי שכטר) אלא סמך על שכטר שלא דקדק כאן כלל בקריאתו והעתקתו, וביחוד יצא הדף השני משובש טקוטע ומסורס, והופמן שטרח להגיהו ולהשלימו לכתב"יד (ע"פ מה"נ). Note particularly Epstein's analysis of the Midrash Haggadol passage (pp. 73–75) where he shows how the author of Midrash Haggadol combined in the same passage the Mekhilta to Deut., the Sifre, the Mishnah, Babyl. Talmud and the Mishneh Torah of Maimonides. Cf. Epstein, *Prolegomena ad Letteras Tannaiticas* (Tel Aviv, 1957), pp. 631 ff. and his מבוא לנוסח המשנה (Jerusalem, 1948), vol. II, p. 747.

[64] Midrash Tannaim, Introduction, p. vi. Cf. Epstein, *loc. cit.*, and Zunz-Albeck, *Haderashoth Beyisra'el* (Jerusalem, 1954), p. 242, note 49.

[65] *Ibid.* W. Bacher, *Tradition und Tradenten*, pp. 178 ff., lists all the passages in Midrash Haggadol to Deut. introduced by the formula מכאן אמרו (usually followed by a citation from a tannaitic source) taken from the Bab. Talmud and Maimonides' Mishneh Torah.

[66] S. Horovitz, *Beiträge zur Erklärung und Textkritik der Mechilta des R. Simon* (Breslau, 1919). Cf. Horovitz's edition of Sifre to Num., Introduction, p. xix.

[67] L. Finkelstein, "קטע מסכילתא דרשב"י," *Kohut Memorial Volume* (New York, 1935), pp. 102–20. He maintains that "On the basis of these fragments it is clear that one cannot rely on the citations in the Midrash Haggadol from the halakhic portions of the Mekhilta d'Rabbi Shime'on b. Yoḥai. In the haggadic portions, the author of Midrash Haggadol copies the Mekhilta deRabbi Shime'on b. Yoḥai, in most instances, with precision. But in the halakhic portions, he made changes ... (p. 102.)." However, E. Z. Melamed (in his edition of Mekhilta deRabbi Shime'on b. Yoḥai, see below) has shown conclusively that the author of Midrash Haggadol may be relied upon neither in the halakhic nor in the haggadic citations.

[68] Ch. Albeck, *Untersuchungen, etc.*, pp. 151 ff.

[69] See references in note 63, above.

[70] In his excellent editions of Midrash Haggadol to Gen. and Exod.

Melamed[71] and of others,[72] enables us to delineate precisely how the sources were changed by the author of Midrash Haggadol. We thus gain a clearer view, by analogy, of the evolution of our passage in Midrash Tannaim 14:2 (p. 73).

Professor Albeck summarizes the literature as follows: "(The author of Midrash Haggadol) . . . arranges passages taken from a variety of sources one following the other, without distinguishing between them . . . he inserts his own explanation and additions as well as those of the Aruch and Rashi. Similarly, he collected not only from the Talmud and midrashic literature but he took passages from Alfasi, Maimonides and others, clothed them in midrashic garb and introduced them with '*teno Rabbanan*' and similar (typically rabbinic) formulae, so that it is impossible to determine their source. Moreover, he was not exact in quoting the version of the Midrash before him but he changed it as he saw fit so that it is difficult to ascertain on the basis of this anthology what Midrashim he used and what their original version was . . ."[73]

E. Z. Melamed published a new edition of the Mekhilta in 1955. (He completed the work begun by J. N. Epstein.) This edition is based on all the manuscript material available (164 pages out of 224 are from manuscripts). On the basis of this considerably larger body of material, Melamed describes, analyzes and gives examples of the numerous ways in which the author of Midrash Haggadol changed the source material included in his anthology.[74] Some of these methods, noted by Melamed, are of particular relevance to the evaluation of our passage in Midrash Tannaim (Deut. 14:2): a) He summarizes the language of the source — halakhic or haggadic — sometimes compressing a whole page into a few lines. b) He changes the sequence of the passages and the sequence of statements within a passage. c) He changes an unusual or difficult expression into an accustomed or well-known phrase (at times, changing thereby the meaning of the original source). d) When several verses or examples are cited in a source introduced by the phrase כיוצא בו or וכן אתה אומר, the author of Midrash Haggadol separates the various parts and uses them as com-

---

[71] In the introduction to his edition of Mekhilta deRabbi Shime'on b. Yoḥai, pp. 46 ff.

[72] W. Bacher, *Tradition und Tradenten*, pp. 178 ff.; S. Liebermann, *Yemenite Midrashim* (Jerusalem, 1940), pp. 1–7; L. Ginzberg, פירושים וחידושים בירושלמי, vol. III, pp. 240 ff.; M. Kasher, *op. cit.*; and the references in Zunz-Albeck, *op. cit.*, p. 447.

[73] *Ibid.*, pp. 158 f.

[74] Mekhilta deRabbi Shime'on b. Joḥai, J. N. Epstein and E. Z. Melamed (Jerusalem, 1955), Introduction, pp. 47 ff.

ments to different verses. e) He weaves together statements from a variety of sources and combines them into a single passage, at times retaining the language of the original sources and, at times, revising and abbreviating them. f) He inserts into the middle of a passage from the original source statements from the Mishnah, Tosefta, Mekhilta deRabbi Yishm'a'el, Sifre, Gen. Rabbah, Midrash to Psalms, Yelamdenu, Tanḥuma, Pesiqtoth, Babylonian Talmud, etc.[75]

In light of the above analysis, the evolution of our passage in Midrash Tannaim becomes obvious. However, before applying the criteria deduced by Melamed to the Midrash Tannaim passage, we would point to some internal evidence, the formal structure of our passage, which indicates its composite character.

The exegesis of Deut. 14:2 "... the Lord your God chose you ..." begins with the formula למה נאמר. The intent of this question which appears numerous times in tannaitic literature is not to imply that the verse is superfluous but rather that it teaches a special lesson — a lesson necessary because of a possible ambiguity or an erroneous implication in another verse.[76]

---

[75] *Ibid.* Melamed also compared a number of passages of the Sifra quoted in Midrash Haggadol with their version in the extant Sifra. He concludes that all the changes noted in the treatment of the material from Mekhilta deRabbi Shime'on b. Yoḥai occur as well in the passages taken from the Sifra (pp. 56 ff.).

[76] On the formula למה נאמר see: I. H. Weiss, דור דור ודורשיו (Berlin 1924), vol. II, pp. 105 f. (particularly note 1, p. 106); D. Hoffmann, *Zur Einleitung in die hala-chischen Midraschim*, pp. 7 ff.; W. Bacher, *Die exegetische Terminologie etc.*, pp. 6 and 97; H. S. Horovitz, Sifre to Numbers, Introduction, p. xii; Ch. Albeck, *Unter-suchungen über die halachischen Midraschim*, pp. 45 ff. (the most detailed treatment); J. N. Epstein, *Prolegomena, etc.*, p. 568 and his note in *Tarbiz*, vol. VIII (1936-7), p. 380. This exegetic formula is erroneously classified with למה נאמרה פרשה זו (Weiss, Hoffmann, Horovitz) or with א"כ למה נאמר (Bacher) or with מה אני צריך and מה תלמוד לומר (Albeck). An analysis of the form of the syllogisms which each of these phrases introduces indicates that these exegetic terms are not to be identified.

It is of interest, for purposes of stratification, that למה נאמר occurs very often as the introductory formula in expounding a biblical verse in Mekhilta deRabbi Yishm'a'el in the opening Tractate, Pisḥa (pp. 1–71), and from chap. 5 of Tractate Baḥodesh to the end of the Mekhilta (pp. 219 ff.). However, it is not used in Tractates Beshallaḥ, Shirah, Wayass'a and 'Amaleq (pp. 71–218). Similarly, it occurs in the first fifty-three chapters (once in 63) and in chapters 349 to the end of the Sifre to Deut. It does not occur in chaps. 54–348 (cf. Finkelstein's note to chaps. 234, p. 266, line 6 and 235, p. 268, line 5). It is used consistently throughout the Sifre to Num. The phrase is never used in Mekhilta deRabbi Shime'on b. Yoḥai (it occurs a few times in the sections taken from Midrash Haggadol but never in those portions based on manuscripts of the original Mekhilta). Nor does this formula occur in the Sifra. (Albeck is to be corrected in light of the above.)

When a passage is introduced by the question למה נאמר, the exposition usually has the following form:

A. The citation of the verse.

B. The formula — למה נאמר

C. Citation of another biblical verse which is not inclusive enough or from which one may draw a wrong inference which needs to be corrected — usually introduced by לפי שנאמר or its equivalent.

D. The incorrect inference drawn from the second verse (Step C), introduced by אין לי, יכול or similar term.

E. The original verse which clarifies the matter and corrects the possible error, introduced by ת"ל.

Consider a typical example from the Mekhilta deRabbi Yishm'a'el to Exod. 20:7 (ed. Horovitz, p. 227, lines 15 ff.)

A. לא תשא את שם ה' . . . (שמות כ':ז')

B. למה נאמר

C. לפי שהוא אומר לא תשבעו בשמי לשקר (ויקרא י"ט:י"ב)

D. אין לי אלא שלא ישבע מנין שלא יקבל עליו להשבע

E. ת"ל לא תשא את שם ה' אלהיך (שמות כ':ז')

This type of exegetic syllogism occurs close to one hundred and fifty times in the tannaitic midrashim. In all of these instances, without a single exception, the second biblical verse cited (Step C) is from the Pentateuch, i. e., the verse that is being expounded (Step A) is interpreted to forestall a misunderstanding which may arise from another pentateuchal verse (Steps C and D). The confrontation is always between two pentateuchal verses.[77]

---

[77] Whenever the question למה נאמר is asked regarding the verse that is being expounded, the second verse (step C) is from the Pentateuch without exception. We have found one passage in Mekhilta deRabbi Yishm'a'el (Tractate Pisḥa, Bo, XVI, [ed. Horovitz], p. 58, lines 14 and 18), where the second verses (step C) are from Isaiah and Jeremiah and not from the Pentateuch. Note, however, that the verse being expounded in this passage is Exod. 13:2. The question addressed to this verse is למה נאמר and this question is followed by another pentateuchal verse (step C). The Mekhilta then continues with a series of examples from Lev. 6 and Exod. 25, introduced by the formula כיוצא בו אתה אומר. Following the question למה נאמר addressed to these two extraneous verses, the Mekhilta cites verses from the prophets. This latter part of the passage is no longer part of the exegesis of the original verse. Moreover, it is probable that the two cases introduced with כיוצא בו were brought into this Mekhilta passage from another context and belong to a later stratum. At any rate, there is no instance in which the verse in step C is from the Hagiographa. On the phrase כיוצא בו, see M. Friedmann (Ish Shalom) in his edition of the Mekhilta, p. 1, note 5, and Aibeck, *op. cit.*, p. 140, note 2 and p. 142. Friedmann perceptively

In the Midrash Tannaim, however, the second biblical verse (Step C) is, contrary to every other instance, from Psalm (135:4) and not from the Five Books. The passage in Midrash Tannaim follows the form of every other argument of this type but the logic of the exegesis is destroyed by confronting Deut. 14:2 not with another penta-teuchal verse, but with a verse from the Hagiographa. Such pleonastic exegesis, i. e., to explain a pentateuchal verse in the light of an ambigu-ity in a passage from the Kethuvim, never occurs in this type of syllogism in tannaitic literature.

The structure of the argument in Midrash Tannaim appears identical with every other syllogism of this type:

A. בך בחר ה' אלהיך (דברים י"ד:ב')
B. למה נאמר
C. לפי שהוא אומר, כי יעקב בחר לו יה (תהלים קל"ה:ד')
D. ואין אנו יודעים אם יה בחר ביעקב ואם יעקב בחר ביה
E. ת"ל בך בחר ה' (דברים י"ד:ב')

However, a closer analysis reveals that it is a later attempt to imitate the style and the formal structure of the Tannaim. The author gives himself away by overlooking the subtlety of the tannaitic exegesis and citing a verse from Psalms in step C rather than a pentateuchal verse.

Further evidence for the composite nature of the Midrash Tannaim passage may be found by analyzing the continuation of the argument. The question ומנ' שאבינו יעקב בחר במקום is not only atypical but com-pletely illogical within this form of argument.[78] The series of examples introduced by כיוצא בו would, upon close examination of their sources and upon comparison with similar formulation in tannaitic midrashim, also show that they were collected from the Talmud and later midrashim.[79]

In the light of all of the above, both the internal evidence and our knowledge of the manner in which the author of Midrash Haggadol

---

cautions that whenever a series introduced by כיוצא בו occurs, "one must investigate, in each case, whether the source is in this passage or whether it was copied from another source and later attached to this passage."

Of relevance to our analysis of the למה נאמר type syllogism is the talmudic principle דברי תורה מדברי קבלה לא ילפינן (Ḥagigah 10b, Bava Qama 2b, Nedarim 23a).

[78] The syllogism introduced by למה נאמר concludes with the citation of the original verse, the verse being expounded (step E). The fact that the passage in Midrash Tannaim continues with a further question ומנין שאבינו יעקב וגו' and cites yet another text (from Jeremiah) is in itself clear proof of the composite nature of this passage. On the formulation of the question as אבינו יעקב see notes 38 and 56 above.

[79] See the quotation from M. Friedmann in note 77, above.

changed his sources, it is clear that the Midrash Tannaim passage is a product of the Yemenite compiler of Midrash Haggadol. The Sifre to Deut. 14:2 cites Ps. 135:4. This Psalm verse recalled to the compiler of Midrash Haggadol the comment in Sifre Deut. 32:9. In order to weave the two passages together he had to recast the comment to Deut. 14:2 into a למה נאמר type syllogism. He then added a series of examples from the Babylonian Talmud and Midrashim. Beyond doubt, the passage in Midrash Tannaim is of no consequence in understanding Sifre Deut. 32:9.

# HISTORY AND MIDRASH

JACOB NEUSNER

> *"There is no hope in returning to a traditional faith after it has once been abandoned, since the essential condition in the holder of a traditional faith is that he should not know he is a traditionalist..."*
>
> Al Ghazali

## I

Holy Scripture posed to the sages of the Talmudic epoch a more perplexing problem than simply to uncover the plain meaning of the sacred words. Their problem, which still troubles text-centered religions, was how to discover in ancient writings continuing truths and meaning for a very different time. Their answer to this problem was Midrash, the exegesis and exposition of revealed Scripture. In truth, Scriptural interpretation was as old as Scripture, and elements of Midrash are present in the Hebrew Bible itself. The particular achievement of the sages was to explore the implications of Midrash and to exploit its formidable techniques in the

Is the method of Midrash—reading contemporary relevance and ideals into the sacred text—still available to modern man? Or has the establishment of the text's prime factual meaning, by the method of comparative history, made Midrash inadmissible? These questions and their solution form the burden of Mr. Neusner's essay, which was presented, in somewhat different form, as a lecture at the 1957 Week of Work of the National Council on Religion and Higher Education. The author, a senior student at the Rabbinical School of the Jewish Theological Seminary has recently been appointed instructor in the Department of Religion at Columbia University.

cause of a sophisticated and highly contemporary religion.

The rabbis found that they had to expound the religion of a text ascribed to Moses, who had preceded them by more than a millenium, to congregations in the first centuries of the common era. They had to make sense out of the great teachings of the past, and to apply them to the present situation. Far more than this, however, they had come to grips with the *realia* of the Scriptures that conveyed these truths. The sages were concerned not only with the content, but with the very context of revelation. Their inheritance was a record of revelation whose minutest detail demanded assent from the pious man. If these ancient words were to bear truth for all time, they had to make good sense always and everywhere. The rabbis would not, therefore, pass silently over some bothersome detail which did not harmonize with their idea of truth or good manners. They would not deny the Bible's claim to detailed authenticity. "If it is empty—from you," that is, if you find no meaning in a verse, the fault is yours. Scripture could not be reduced to an essence; every word was somehow essential.

Confronted with some Biblical incident which did not accord with proper morals, the rabbis could not dismiss the matter as inconsequential. At the same time, they could not justify an ethical outrage by pointing out the primitive standards of an ancient generation. If like modern critics, they were to explain some improper action as evidence of the antiquity of a given passage, they would thereby have confessed that Scripture bore relevance to the archaeologist or historian of religion, but by no means offered appropriate instruction for a more advanced age. The rabbis would not claim that the more detailed precepts of Scripture were addressed to one particular generation except where the Bible itself makes this clear. They would not admit that its truth was relative, appropriate only to an early and savage time. To them the truth of the Bible was eternal, standing as an imperative to man.

This problem continues to perplex men. The Bible speaks to a primitive and naive universe. Has the passage of time muted its voice? Liberals in days past used to say that the Bible is not a text book for natural science. But liberals did not believe in revelation. Fundamentalists offered ingenious explanations for the real intent of Scripture; for example, the seven days of Creation represent seven aeons of time. But the Bible does not say so. Must a man share the Biblical viewpoint on theology, cosmology, anthropology, in order to hold on to its ultimate consequence of faith in God and in the message of religion? History forced upon the sages a search for harmony between the detailed text and the contemporary view of metaphysics and man. This search was not the consequence of negation but of affirmation. Few men today take the Biblical claim with sufficient earnestness to continue that search.

## II

In the Midrash, the rabbis were not intentionally traditional. They did not wonder how to save a text they might already have come to doubt, nor did they set out in order to sustain Scripture as a possibility for their piety. For the sages, Torah had made manifest the emergent truth that underlies all things. It was the divine design for the universe. To contrive to demonstrate harmony between current truth and Torah would be to reveal the obvious. Revelation was eternal and always in harmony with new visions of the truth. If the rabbis were traditionalists, they never knew it.

The Bible itself made possible Midrashic elucidation. The very first word of God was light. The Talmud says, " 'Is not My word like fire, saith the Lord, and like a hammer which breaks the rock into pieces?' (Jeremiah 23:29). Just as a hammer strikes the anvil and kindles clouds of sparks, so does Scripture yield many meanings, as it is said, 'Once did God speak, but two things have I heard...' (Psalm 62:11)". The rabbis assumed that Torah was the indivisible, exhaustive account of the event of revelation at Sinai. It revealed some truth, and encompassed all truth. Hence it was their task to draw out of the given text the widest possible range of religious insight. They did not need to distinguish between the obvious sense of words and the subtler secondary meanings words might hide. Plain sense (p'shat) is simply what was immediately apparent. Midrash was the level of meaning discovered by search (*d'rash*), by disciplined and careful exegesis. The truth was one, but the rabbis came upon the part uncovered by Midrash with a little more effort. (It is true that the rabbis did distinguish occasionally between a particularly imaginative Midrash of a verse and its plain-sense, but this distinction meant far less to them than it does nowadays.)

A classic exposition of the nature of Midrash is Professor Shalom Spiegel's introduction to *Legends of the Bible* by Louis Ginzberg, in which he writes:

"Just as a pearl results from a stimulus in the shell of a mollusk, so also a legend may arise from an irritant in Scripture. The legend of Cain and Lamech has its foothold in two passages of Scripture. One passage tells of a sign granted by Cain as a warning to all who might threaten his life: anyone that slays Cain shall suffer sevenfold vengeance (Genesis 4:15). The other is the address of Lamech to his wives, reckless with swagger or savagery: I kill a man for just wounding me! (Genesis 4:25).

"This is a brutal and bad boast in a book such as the Bible, but in reality it is less bothersome than the earlier statement in Genesis 4:15 . . . After all, the bluster of a braggart or bully need not be believed literally. . . . Genesis 4:15 cannot be so lightly dismissed . . . The pledge given to Cain presupposes a peculiarly ferocious form of blood-feud: any attack on the bearer of the sign is to be avenged by the slaughter of seven members of the tribe to which the assailant belonged. The archaeologist might conclude . . . that some of the stories in the book of Genesis preserve exceedingly ancient traditions . . . often

antedating by centuries the birth of Biblical religion . . . But in all times men have turned to the Bible not only for antiquarian curiosities, but for spiritual uplift and guidance. To such readers it must be distressing . . . to find the Holy Writ ascribing to the Deity itself the acceptance without protest of an institution of primitive law . . . Many will prefer to believe that this cannot be the meaning of the sacred writings. . . .

"When facts or texts become unacceptable, fiction or legend weaves the garland of nobler fancy. This is how the story of Cain's slaying was born . . .

"The tale runs: Lamech was a burly but blind giant who loved to follow the chase under the guidance of his son, Tubal-Cain. Whenever the horn of a beast came in sight, the boy would tell his father to shoot at it with bow and arrow. One day he saw a horn move between two hills; he turned Lamech's arrow upon it. The aim was good, the quarry dropped to the ground. When they came close to the victim, the lad exclaimed: 'Father, thou hast killed something that resembles a human being in all respects, except it carries a horn on its forehead!' Lamech knew at once what had happened: he had killed his ancestor Cain, who had been marked by God with a horn for his own protection, 'lest anyone who came upon him should kill him' (Genesis 4:15). In bitter remorse Lamech wept: 'I killed a man to my wounding!' (Genesis 4:24).

"... What seemed to be shocking Scripture was made by this legend to yield a moral tale. Genesis 4:24 was turned from a barbarian boast into a cry of contrition: The offensive 'I kill a man for just wounding me' was now read 'I killed a man to my wounding and sorrow.' The Hebrew permits this change by a mere inflection of voice. But above all, the stumbling block in Genesis 4:15 was removed: the assurance of the deity that Cain's vengeance shall be *sevenfold* was made to mean that his punishment will be exacted from him *in the seventh generation.* His sentence was to be carried out by Lamech, the *seventh* in the succession of generations since Adam. The savage reprisal . . . became a deserved but deferred penalty, the merciful Judge, slow to anger, granting the sinner a long reprieve to repent and mend his ways. In brief, two passages of the sacred Writ, disturbing the peace and disquieting the faith of a host of pious readers in every age, were metamorphosed in this legend of Cain and Lamech to yield the edifying lesson: even the arrow of a sightless archer obeys the holy will and word of God. " . . . Any vestige of reprehensible or primitive practices was read away, and Scripture brought to conform to the advanced conscience of a later state in civilization."

A second type of Midrash was inquiry into the legal portions of the Pentateuch to discover laws to apply to a new situation, or to uncover Scriptural basis for an apparent innovation in law. An example of such legal Midrash was the effort to demonstrate the real meaning of 'an eye for an eye.' The sages held that the verse clearly means that one should exact the monetary equivalent of an eye for the loss of an eye, and no more. One proof, among many brought by Talmud, is derived from Numbers 35:31, "Thou shalt not take ransom for the *life* of a murderer . . ." This means, "for the *life* of a murderer thou shalt not take ransom, but thou shalt take

ransom for *limbs.*" Scripture thus means, and has always meant, that a ransom may compensate loss of a major limb.

Midrash represents, therefore, creative philology and creative historiography (in the phrases of Professor Y. Heinemann in *Darchei Ha-Agadah*). As creative philology, the Midrash discovers meaning in apparently meaningless detail. It creates out of the fabric of silence as of speech. Even parts of speech are set out, each by itself, each hiding its special message for some perplexity. As Dr. Max Kadushin demonstrated in *The Rabbinic Mind,* the Midrash uses the elements of language not as fixed, unchanging categories, but as relative, living, tentative nuances of thought. As creative historiography, the Midrash rewrites the past to make manifest the eternal rightness of Scriptural paradigms. What would it be like if all men lived at one moment? This the Midrash sets out to reveal, justifying David by the criteria of Stoic philosophy and even by Roman imperial law, and thundering pious curses at the heads of men behaving fully in accord with the morality of their own age. Midrash thus exchanges the stability of language and the continuity of history for stability of values and the eternity of truth.

In the Bible, the rabbis treasured a many-splendored jewel, now to be admired in one light, now in another. Each word has many modulations of meaning, awaiting the sensitive touch of a troubled soul to unfold a special message for a particular moment in time. Midrash teaches that for all times and to all men, Scriptural values are congruous and consistent. Lamech and a man fifteen centuries later are judged by the same ethics, for Scripture and its people are wholly in harmony with the sophisticated morality of any age. History does not apply to revelation. There are no relative truths. Revelation happened under the aspect of eternity: one God, one Torah, one truth for all men in every age.

## III

Is the technique of Midrashic thought available to bring harmony between the Word and today's world?

It might be argued that Midrash represents speculation in terms of the concrete on the inner nature of reality, a kind of mythopoeic technique. Dr. Henri Frankfort (in *Before Philosophy*) said of myth that its imagery "is nothing less than a carefully chosen cloak for abstract thought. It represents the form in which experience becomes conscious." The Stoic interpreted Homer as allegory, and so made him make sense to their age. If faith speaks out in concrete images, ought Scripture to be understood as the embodiment of cosmic truth in earthly garments? Other men have tried this way before, and come to viable faith. Is this way still open? It is, and it is not.

In a rigorous sense, the techniques of Midrash are unavailable because men have ceased to think only in concrete images. Mythopoeic thought never leaves the concrete, and its concepts exist only in their particular forms. Death does not happen, it is. Yet abstraction is the very soul of the modern intellect. Moreover, men no longer see abstractions in the supple fabric of immediate situations. The rabbis did, using language here in one sense, there in another. The very creative force of Midrash depends on such stubborn particularization. For Mi-

drash, language is finite, its meanings are emergent, but morality is infinite. Long ago, though, men abandoned the relativity of language for the relativity of values.

Not only is the creative philology of Midrash unavailable, but its classic assumptions on history are no longer widely held. Men cannot always come both to perceive the historical setting of Scripture and to assent to its moral rightness. Lamech may teach an ethical truth, but not in the first place. The courts of Israel might always have enforced a merciful form of the *lex talionis,* but Scripture does not say so openly. The Midrash denies relativity between history and morality. Yet if a man today recognizes the primitive in art and literature, he surely cannot refuse to see it in religion and ethics. To the rabbis, creative historiography meant that whatever was discovered in Scripture was the plain-sense from Sinai. They did not mobilize their formidable power of inventiveness and fantasy in order to avoid an apparent heresy. Scripture makes sense, and Midrash merely uncovers it. But if a man today makes the effort to uncover hidden truths and distant meanings, this is the ratification of heresy, for he knows he is trying to restore a tradition and to sustain it.

The idea of history has supplanted the idea of an abiding plain-sense. The historian wonders, what did this text mean to its writer? Midrash asks what meaning is there now, and identifies this meaning with the original intent of the writer. None would claim, though, that his present knowledge of the truth is what the truth has always been. The dilemma of the American Constitution is an obvious consequence of such self-conscious historicism. On the one hand, the unity and continuity of law demand that the twentieth-century judge speak in the name of an eighteenth-century Constitution. On the other hand, the founding fathers could not even remotely have written into their Constitution the subtle intentions discovered by the judges. One result is an ingenious Midrash that creates "The Constitution", a kind of Platonic ideal which is the ultimate referent of Constitutional phenomena. Another is the dogged and progressively less convincing assertion that this was the true intention of the Convention of 1787, or would have been if they were here. A less appropriate case shows what happens when people think that the truth as it is now perceived is what it always was. The article on Beria in the Soviet Encyclopedia was published before his fall. In many columns of text he was extolled as a pillar of Soviet society. After he lost the struggle for succession, he was pilloried as a bestial traitor. The publishers had to supply subscribers with a long insertion to paste over the original article. To Soviet man, this insertion was the new version of the truth as it always was. It was truth discovered, not invented; genuine, not contrived history. For the Western intellect, this is whimsy. What truth there is is finite and provisional. Today, one cannot, therefore, embark on the quest for eternal contemporaneity. A self-conscious man does not see in a given text a truth that was of old, is now, and ever will be, in the sense that a historian understands these words. The truth of old was what the writer meant. The truth now cannot necessarily be what one would have had the writer mean.

The search for an eternal plain-sense for Scripture was the only way to preserve both the historicity and the viability of text-committed faith. That search has found only gall and wormwood for the literalist. Whenever he turns, he meets problems he must somehow explain away. Even if his heart is hard as granite, he must in the end suspect that the phenomena of universe, man, and the day the sun stood still are best explained not by the Bible but by the tentative suggestions of the natural and social sciences.

The recognition of Midrash teaches the distinction between what is history and what is homily. It raises a question to trouble modern exegetes: has Scripture yielded this meaning because this is what it has always meant in its own context? Or has this meaning come in order to make good sense out of a difficult verse?

## IV

While the techniques and assumptions of Midrash are mostly obsolete, the purposes of Midrash are still very relevant. The perception that there is indeed a Midrashic dimension in a text points a way to bring to bear upon present perplexities even the power of a kind of creative philology and imaginative historiography. The Bible has both a plain meaning and an eternal *message* for all men everywhere. These two levels of meaning are not to be confused. The Midrash will teach how to expose the aspect of eternity and to discover the moment of truth.

Its first lesson is to distinguish between history as experienced by believing man and history as observed and elucidated by dispassionate scholarship.

It opens the way to distinguish between the sacred history handed down by creed and faith, and the objective, critical history uncovered by the scholar. (Professor H. Richard Niebuhr makes this distinction in *The Meaning of Revelation*.)

Its second lesson is, in truth, how to endow Scripture with life. This is to be done through homily, anachronism, and especially through the sensitive response of the modern student of religion. When the preacher finds rich and compelling meaning in a verse, this is the living verse. This is Scripture as men may believe in it and live by its message. The faculty of Midrash was not buried with the sages of the Talmud. It is always in the hand of the preacher who comes to create parables and homilies to explain and enhance the text. This secondary level of meaning in Scripture is its sacred history. Plain sense teaches the meaning of the Bible in its time: what the writer wrote and meant. Midrash teaches the meaning for any time: what He-Who-Spoke-and-Created-by-his-Word has to say. The final truth about the Bible surely lies, at the very least, in both places.

Third, Midrash warns scholars not to cross the unmarked frontier between history as it is lived and re-enacted today and history as it is observed. Bible critics have been tempted to impose on it elaborate and ingenious schemes of events; they have reconstructed the history of ancient Israel by blueprints borrowed from alien civilizations; they have thought to find an empty room when they penetrated into the holiest precincts of Jewish faith; they have even ignored the canons of common sense and precise knowledge in their wonderful speculations. Critical history, however, demonstrates what happened, or, most certainly, what could not have happened at a given point in time. Historical material leads to the most delicate of judgments on what actually did happen; even archaeology is mostly useless without corroborating texts. The text itself conveys much more, and yet considerably less, than the facts of what occurred. In the end, however, if the setting of revelation is the concern of normative history, the fact and meaning of revelation are not. Scholars speaking *ex cathedra* need also to keep aware of the idea of Midrash. As men of faith they may very well offer profound insight. As scholars, they ought not to confuse the quality of two very different kinds of truth. The plain sense of an ancient text is not necessarily what makes sense today at all.

Furthermore, scholarship may not offer genuine understanding of a text, at all, at its first level of meaning. Scholars speculate, for example, on what the unknown Prophet of the Exile meant by the story of the suffering servant. Confessional history may indeed impel the Jew to see chapter 53 of Isaiah as the paradigm of Israel's history among the nations. Christians see in the chapter the prefiguration of Christ's life among men. It seems unlikely that scholars will come to determine decisively the original intent of the prophet whose name they do not know. For normative history, it would matter very much if they did. For confessional history, it would simply open the way to new Midrash.

Finally the idea of Midrash teaches the lesson that the Bible, itself, is a kind of Midrash, a confessional history of humanity. It is in the first instance an interpretation of events whose reality is perceived through the veil of time and in the shadowed light of faith. As the Midrash transformed the pragmatic events of Scripture into a paradigm for a later age, so the Bible, and especially the Prophets, transformed the extraordinary history of Israel into a Midrash on life itself.

## V

Men's awareness of history divorces Midrash from plain-sense. The specific techniques of the Midrash are mostly obsolete. Men have lost the capacity to believe that a particular sense of Scripture uncovered today was its eternally present meaning. They do not even expect to find eternal meanings. Even the critical scholarship of one generation has come to seem like Midrash to the next. I think, however, that we might well cling to the faith of the Midrash: the Bible does make some sense to every generation. We look to our ministry to teach that sense. We ought also to explore the resources of our own faith to find it, through mastering the text of the Bible and living with it day by day. Except for the literalist, however, none can look to reconcile his particular Midrash with the plain meaning of Scripture. Although one may recover a harmony between the text and the world,

this is very far away from restoring the detailed historicity of Scripture.

The question arises whether a self-conscious, critical intellect is capable of Biblical faith, and whether such faith will generate genuine piety. The experience of the sages suggests that unencumbered inquiry into the true sense of Scripture will indeed lead to both faith and piety. Self-deception and preconceived commitments cannot. We ought, therefore, never to say, how much better were the old days than these! How much worthier was the age when men believed in mountains that skip like rams and worlds that are made in seven days, when Jews could see the plain meaning of the *Song of Songs* as a poem of love between God and Israel, and Christians, between God and the Church! If this is what the text described and what the tradition of Synagogue and Church expounded, then this was a faithful vision and an honest perception. All that we have, and all we shall ever have, is our own mature vision of the truth. We are left with the poignant teaching of the Talmud: "Rabbi Simon ben Lakish admonished, 'Say not . . . how much better were the old days than these! Say not . . . if only Rabbi Tarfon were alive, then I should go to study Torah with him. In the end, you only have the sages of your own generation'."

# THE DEVELOPMENT OF THE *MERKAVAH* TRADITION

BY

## JACOB NEUSNER

*Brown University,*
*Providence (Rhode Island, U.S.A.)*

It is an axiom among traditional scholars of Talmudic literature that appearance of a saying or story in a late document, such as the Babylonian *gemara* or a medieval collection of midrashim, does not mean the saying or story itself is late. The whole corpus of rabbinic materials, it is alleged, circulated orally before redaction. Hence, what appears in a late document could have been handed on in oral tradition from earliest time, therefore is just as reliable as what is redacted in the earliest compilations. In other words, the theological principle that אין מוקדם ומאוחר בתורה applies as much to the oral as to the written Torah. That axiom cannot be said to run counter to common sense, for the conditions for the transmission of traditional materials are not incongruent to it. If pretty much everything was preserved by memory, then the occurrence in a written document is not consequential in assessing the relative age of materials.

We shall here test that axiom by a comparison of the four versions of the story of Yoḥanan ben Zakkai and the *Merkavah*-sermon of his disciple Eleazar ben ʿArakh. I shall first present a translation of each version, followed by some comments from a historical point of view, and then offer a synoptic study of the several versions [1].

## I

(a) And the story is told that Rabban Yoḥanan ben Zakkai was

---

[1] My *Development of a Legend: Studies on the Traditions Concerning Yoḥanan ben Zakkai* (Leiden 1970) provides similar studies of all materials in which Yoḥanan ben Zakkai appears. In *The Rabbinic Traditions about the Pharisees before 70 A.D.* (Leiden 1971), three volumes: *I. The Masters. II. The Houses. III. Conclusions* I have offered similar studies of all Pharisaic traditions before Yoḥanan's time. My students, Rabbi Moshe Gorelik (Brandeis University), Rabbi Shamai Kanter (Brown University), and Mr. William Scott Green (Brown University) are presently at work on similar studies of Eleazar b. Azaiah, Gamaliel II, and Joshua b. Ḥananiah respectively. My present studies concern Eliezer b. Hyrcanus. We hope eventually to lay the foundations of a critical history of the Yavneh academy and its traditions.

riding on an ass, going out of Jerusalem. R. Eleazar b. 'Arakh his disciple was walking behind him. He [R. Eleazar] said to him [Rabban Yoḥanan], "Rabbi, Teach me a chapter in the Works of the Chariot."

He replied, "Have I not taught you [plural], *And Concerning the Merkavah, not with a single disciple [alone may one study] unless he is a sage and comprehends out of his own knowledge.*"

(b) He said to him, "If not, give me permission that I may speak before you."

(c) R. Eleazar b. 'Arakh was expounding [the Chariot] until fire was licking all around him. When Rabban Yoḥanan ben Zakkai saw that the fire was licking all around him, he descended from the ass and kissed him, saying to him, "Rabbi Eleazar b. 'Arakh, Happy is she who bore you, happy are you, O Abraham our father, that such a one has come forth from your loins."

(d) He [Rabban Yoḥanan] would say, "If all the sages of Israel were in one side of the scale and Rabbi Eleazar ben 'Arakh in the second side, he would outweigh them all."

> (Mekhilta of R. Simeon b. Yoḥai Mishpatim 20:1, ed. EPSTEIN-MELAMED, pp. 158, l. 8-17, and 159, l. 18-21)

*Comment*: Part d is tacked on, having nothing to do with the *Merkavah* story. It stands by itself. I do not know why it should have been important to the Aqibans, responsible for this compilation, to preserve Yoḥanan's praise of Eleazar. Perhaps their *Merkavah*-traditions depended on his, but it is more likely that 'Aqiva's *Merkavah*-traditions come from Joshua. In that case it is all the more puzzling that Eleazar is represented as the chief *Merkavah*-disciple. Furthermore, Eleazar did not come to Yavneh, and probably fell from favor by the time of, if not before, Yoḥanan's death. The *Merkavah*-story therefore was probably given final formulation before that time, for, as we shall see, in other versions, the effort is made to transfer the normative *Merkavah*-tradition to Joshua and others.

I imagine that this account was given final form by the time Eleazar left Yoḥanan's circle and was not altered afterward. That is the only way we can understand the high praise of Eleazar consistently included in the *Merkavah*-materials. But (d) cannot have been added much after formulation of (a) for the same considerations apply without qualification.

It is further to be supposed that the Aqibans preserved the *Merkavah*-story pretty much as they received it, for, as I said, they could not have preferred an account praising Eleazar to one praising Joshua, 'Aqiva's own *Merkavah*-teacher. If these suppositions are sound, then there is evidence that some of the Yoḥaḥnan traditions were given their final and current form not long after the master's death. In this instance it was very likely during his lifetime. Eleazar's disciples in Emmaus would have preserved the story in just this form. ʿAqiva's disciples afterward would have maintained the tradition just as it was taught in Emmaus.

This is the earliest normative version of the *Merkavah* incident. We shall see that details are added in formulations in both Talmuds. Both later versions are clearly Aqiban in origin.

## II

(a) [*One may not teach...about the Chariot to a single individual unless he is a sage and understands of his own knowledge.*] The story is told that R. Eleazar b. ʿArakh was driving the ass behind Rabban Yoḥanan ben Zakkai. He [Eleazar] said to him [Yoḥanan], "Teach me a chapter in the Works of the Chariot."

He [Yoḥanan] replied to him, "Have I not said to you, *One may not teach about the Chariot to a single individual unless he is a sage and understands of his own knowledge.*"

He [Eleazar] said to him, "Give me permission, and I shall lecture before you."

Forthwith Rabban Yoḥanan ben Zakkai descended from the ass and covered himself with his cloak and the two of them sat on a stone under the olive tree and he [Eleazar] lectured before him.

(b) Then he [Yoḥanan] stood up and kissed him on his head and said, "Blessed is the Lord God of Israel who gave a son to Abraham our father who knows how to expound and to understand concerning the glory of our father who is in heaven. Some expound well but do not fulfill well; some fulfill well but do not expound well. But Eleazar ben ʿArakh expounds well and fulfills well.

"Happy are you, O Abraham our father, that Eleazar ben ʿArakh has come forth from your loins, who knows how to expound and to understand concerning the glory of our father in heaven."

(c) R. Yosi b. R. Judah says, "R. Joshua lectured before Rabban Yoḥanan ben Zakkai. R. ʿAqiva lectured before R. Joshua. Ḥananiah b. Ḥakhinai lectured before R. ʿAqiva."

(Tos. Ḥag. 2:1-2, ed. ZUCKERMANDEL, pp. 233-34, ls. 25-7, 1-7)

(d) The story is told that Rabban Yoḥanan ben Zakkai was riding on the ass, and R. Lazar b. ʿArakh was driving the ass from behind... [as above].

R. Lazar b. 'Arakh began to expound the works of the Chariot. Rabban Yoḥanan ben Zakkai descended from the ass, covered himself with his *ṭallit*, and the two of them sat on the stone under the olive and he lectured before him.

He [Yoḥanan] stood up and kissed him on his head and said, "Blessed is the Lord God of Israel who gave a son to Abraham our father who knows how to understand and to expound concerning the glory of his father in heaven. There are some who expound well but do not fulfill well, fulfill well but do not expound well. Eleazar b. 'Arakh expounds well and fulfills well.

"Happy are you, O Abraham our father, that Eleazar b. 'Arakh has come forth from loins, who knows how to understand and to expound in behalf of his father in heaven."

(e) R. Yosi b. Judah says, "R. Joshua lectured before Rabban Yoḥanan ben Zakkai, R. 'Aqiva before R. Joshua, Ḥananiah b. Kinai before R. 'Aqiva."

(Tos. Ḥag. 2:1, ed. S. LIEBER-
MAN, II, pp. 380-81, ls. 1-15)

*Comment*: The differences between Zuckermandel's and Lieberman's texts are not substantial, and at the crucial points there are no variations at all.

First is the circumstance in which Eleazar gives his talk. Second is Yoḥanan's praise of the talk. Third is the saying that it was Joshua b. Ḥananiah, rather than Eleazar, who forms the link in the chain of the *Merkavah*-tradition.

The obvious omission is the record of just what Eleazar had said. This is further excluded in all versions of the *Merkavah*-event. Obviously between (a) and (b) must have been a paragraph containing the content of the *Merkavah*-sermon, and this paragraph has been everywhere suppressed.

Parts (a) and (b) are obviously to be attributed to the Emmaus circle, for reasons stated above.

Part (c) derives from the Joshua-'Aqiva line of Yoḥanan materials. In it, Eleazar is *not* mentioned as having lectured for Yoḥanan. The *Merkavah*-doctrine came to 'Aqiva through Joshua, whose teaching was approved by Yoḥanan himself. None of the other disciples plays a part. Obviously, the Aqibans would have preferred this version. They could (or did) not suppress the Emmaus one, but they were able to correct the "false" impression left by it that the official version of the *Merkavah*-mystery was known in Emmaus only. I suppose, as I said, that once the Emmaus material was given its present form, it was not thereafter altered, for could the Aqibans have suppressed or changed it, they would have done so. They are, to the contrary, *responsible* for its preservation.

Why the Aqibans should have preserved the *Merkavah*-tradition in a form unsatisfactory to themselves I cannot say. The Ishmaeleans said nothing about the event, which is omitted in all their collections. The Abibans regarded mystical experience as important, the Ishmaeleans obviously did not. Yet in handing on the materials, the Aqibans faithfully kept alive the memory of Joshua's rival in *Merkavah*-teaching.

### III

(a) The story is told that Rabban Yoḥanan b. Zakkai was going on the way riding on the ass, and R. Lazar b. 'Arakh was going after him.

He said to him, "Rabbi, Teach me a chapter in the Works of the Chariot."

He [Yoḥanan] said to him, "Have not the sages taught, *And not concerning the Chariot unless he is wise and understands of his own knowledge.*

He said to him, "Rabbi, Give me permission that I may say something before you." He said to him, "Speak."

When R. Lazar b. 'Arakh opened [his exposition of] the Works of Chariot, Rabban Yoḥanan ben Zakkai descended from the ass. He said, "It is not lawful that I should hear the Glory of my Creator and ride on an ass."

They went and sat under the tree and fire descended from heaven and surrounded them. The ministering angels danced before them as members of a wedding rejoice before a bridegroom.

One angel answered from the fire and said, "According to your words, O Eleazar b. 'Arakh, so [indeed] are the Works of the Chariot."

Forthwith all the trees opened their mouths and sang a song, *Then shall all the trees of the forest sing for joy* (Ps. 96, 12).

When R. Lazar b. 'Arakh finished [his exposition] in the Works of the Chariot, Rabban Yoḥanan ben Zakkai stood up and kissed him on his head and said, "Blessed is the Lord, God of Abraham, Isaac, and Jacob, who gave to Abraham our father a son who is a sage and understands [how] to expound the glory of our Father in heaven. Some expound well but do not fulfill well, fulfill well but do not expound well. Eleazar b. 'Arakh expounds well and fulfills well.

"Happy are you, O Abraham our father, that Eleazar ben 'Arakh has come forth from your loins."

(b) When R. Joseph the Priest and R. Simeon b. Natanel heard, they also began [to expound] the Works of the Chariot.

They said it was the first day in the season of Tammuz, and the earth trembled and a rainbow appeared in a cloud, and a *bat qol* came forth and said to them, "Behold the place is vacant for you, and the dining couch [TRYQLYN] is spread out for you. You and your disciples are destined for the third level."

(y. Ḥag. 2:1)

*Comment*: The context is, as to be expected, the Mishnaic teaching, quoted (in italics) in the story itself, that one may not teach the *Merkavah*-mystery to ordinary people, but only to especially well-qualified disciples. The antecedent discussion includes a story told by R. Ḥiyya in the name of R. Judah [the Prince] about a student of R. Judah's who exposited the *Merkavah*-tradition contrary to R. Judah's wishes and was punished with various ailments. "This Torah is like two paths, one of light (fire), and the other of snow (cold). What should one do? Let him walk inbetween them. Then, "The story is told..." Afterward comes the story of Ben Zoma and R. Joshua, concerning the Creation-mystery, then the "four who entered Paradise."

The passage differs from I and II in the inclusion of the *Merkavah*-exposition attributed to two other disciples of Yoḥanan, Joseph the Priest and Simeon b. Natanel (the former appearing in II as Yosi). This is the only instance in which the *Merkavah* mysteries are recited by disciples other than Joshua and Eleazar b. 'Arakh. In I, only Eleazar is mentioned; in II, Joshua is added. As we have observed, the basic account about Eleazar is never suppressed, but is greatly supplemented.

## IV

(a) TNW RBNN: Once R. Yoḥanan b. Zakkai was riding on an ass when going on a journey, and R. Eleazar b. 'Arakh was driving the ass from behind.

[R. Eleazar] said to him, "Master, teach me a chapter of the 'Work of the Chariot'."

He answered: "Have I not taught you thus: *Nor [the work of] the chariot in the presence of one, unless he is a Sage and understands of his own knowledge?*"

[R. Eleazar] then said to him, "Master, permit me to say before thee something which thou hast taught me."

He answered, "Say on!"

Forthwith R. Yoḥanan b. Zakkai dismounted from the ass, and wrapped himself up, and sat upon a stone beneath an olive tree.

Said [R. Eleazar] to him: "Master, wherefore didst thou dismount from the ass?"

He answered, "Is it proper that whilst thou art expounding the Work of the Chariot, and the Divine Presence is with us, and the ministering angels accompany us, I should ride on the ass!"

Forthwith, R. Eleazar b. 'Arakh began his exposition of the Work of the Chariot, and fire came down from heaven and encompassed all the trees in the field; [thereupon] they all began to utter [divine] song. What was the song they uttered?—*Praise the Lord from the earth, ye sea-monsters, and all deeps...fruitful trees and all cedars...* (Ps. 147, 7. 9. 14).

An angel [then] answered from the fire and said, "This is the very Work of the Chariot."

R. Yoḥanan b. Zakkai rose and kissed him on his head and said, "Blessed be the Lord God of Israel, Who hath given a son to Abraham our father, who knoweth to speculate upon, and to investigate, and to expound the 'Work of the Chariot'. There are some who preach well but do not act well, others act well but do not preach well, but thou dost preach well and act well.

"Happy art thou, O Abraham our father, that R. Eleazar b. 'Arakh hath come forth from thy loins."

(b) Now when these things were told R. Joshua, he and R. Yosi the priest were going on a journey.

They said, "Let us also expound the 'Work of the Chariot'."

R. Joshua began an exposition.

Now that day was the summer solstice. The heavens became overcast with clouds and a kind of rainbow appeared in the cloud, and the ministering angels assembled and came to listen like people who assemble and come to watch the entertainments of a bridegroom and bride.

(c) R. Yosi the priest went and related what happened before R. Yoḥanan b. Zakkai, and [the latter] said, "Happy are ye, and happy is she that bore you; happy are my eyes that have seen thus. Moreover, in my dream, I and ye were reclining on Mount Sinai, when a *Bat Qol* was sent to us [saying], 'Ascend hither, ascend hither! [Here are] great banqueting chambers, and fine dining couches prepared for you; you and your disciples and your disciples' disciples are designated for the third class'."

(d) But is this so? For behold it is taught: R. Yosi b. R. Judah said, "There were three discourses: R. Joshua discoursed before R. Yoḥanan b. Zakkai, R. 'Aqiva discoursed before R. Joshua, Ḥanania b. Ḥakinai discoursed before R. 'Aqiva;—whereas R. Eleazar b. 'Arakh he does not count!—One who discoursed [himself], and others discoursed before him, he counts; one who discoursed [himself], but others did not discourse before him, he does not count.

(e) But behold there is Ḥanania b. Ḥakinai before whom others did

not discourse, yet he counts him!—He at least discoursed before one
who discoursed [before others].

> (b. Ḥag. 14b, trans. I. ABRAHAMS,
> pp. 89-90)

> *Comment*: The pericope stands as a comment on the Mishnaic
> teaching cited in its midst. It is related in theme to other materials in
> the same section, mainly discussions of Ezekiel's vision. Immediately
> preceding, however, is a saying about the destruction of Jerusalem, and
> in fact there is no direct connection between the Merkavah-*beraita* and
> the foregoing material. There follows the Tannaitic story (TNW
> RBNN) of the four who entered Paradise. The context therefore is a
> disconnected set of sayings pertinent in some way to mystical visions
> of God. The usual careful, dialectical argument is utterly absent
> (except at the end). It is a collection of *beraitot*, not a *gemara* in the
> usual sense. It could indeed have been put together in pretty much its
> present form in Tannaitic times, and then included by Talmudic
> editors as a complete and final Tannaitic tradition. If so, it was shaped
> in the Aqiban schools, where 'Aqiva's prowess in mystical speculation
> and mystical experience was celebrated.

*The following is a synopsis of the four versions:*

| Mekhilta de R. Simeon | Tos. Ḥag. 2:1-2 | y. Ḥag. 2:1 | b. Ḥag. 14b |
|---|---|---|---|
| And the story is told that Yoḥanan was riding on an ass and going out of Jerusalem | ,, | ,,<br>going on the way riding on an ass | *Teno Rabbanan.*<br>The story is told that Yoḥanan was riding an ass and going on the way, and Eleazar was driving the ass. |
| Eleazar b. 'Arakh his disciple was going behind him | *driving the ass*<br>,, | going<br>,, | ,,<br>,, |
| Eleazar: Teach me a chapter in the Merkhavah | ,, | ,, | ,, |
| Yoḥanan: Have I not *taught* you. Not of the Merkavah...understands of his own knowledge. | *told* | ,, | *taught* |
| If not, give me permission to speak before you. | ,, | ,, | before you *something you taught me.* |
| | Yoḥanan descended from the ass, covered self with cloak; both sat on a stone under an olive tree. | Yoḥanan descended saying, It is not lawful that I should hear the glory of my creator and be riding on an ass. They went and sat under the tree. | Forthwith Yoḥanan descended from the ass, covered himself, and sat on the *stone* under the olive-tree. |

| Mekhilta de R. Simeon | Tos. Ḥag. 2:1-2 | y. Ḥag. 2:1 | b. Ḥag. 14b |
|---|---|---|---|
| | | | He said to him, Rabbi, why why did you descend. He said to him, Is it possible that you should expound the Chariot, and the Shekhinah be with us, and the ministering angel accompany us, and I should ride an ass? |
| Eleazar expounded until flames licked round about. | He lectured before him. | When he opened... Forthwith all trees broke out in song and said Ps. 96. | Eleazar opened on the Chariot and expounded, the fire went down from heaven and encompassed all the trees round about What song did the trees sing? Ps. 145. An angel answered from the fire and said, These, these are the works of the chariot. |
| When Yoḥanan saw the flames, he got off the ass, kissed him, and said, Eleazar, Happy he that bore you. Happy Abraham our father that such has come forth from his loins. | He stood and kissed him and said, Blessed is the Lord God of Israel who gave a son to Abraham our father who knows how to understand and expounds the glory of his father in heaven. Some expound well but do not fulfill well, and vice versa, but Eleazar does both well. Happy are you, Abraham our father that Eleazar b. ʿArakh has come forth from your loins, who knows how to understand and expound the glory of his father in heaven. | When Eleazar finished the Works of the Chariot, Yoḥanan stood and kissed him on his head and said, Blessed is the Lord, God of Abraham. Jacob who gave to Abraham a son wise and knowing how to expound the glory of our father in heaven. Some preach well... Eleazar does both well. Happy are you, Abraham our father, that Eleazar has come forth from your loins. | Yoḥanan stood up and kissed him on his head and said, Blessed is the Lord, God of Israel, who gave son to Abraham our father who knows how to understand and to investigate, and to expound the Chariot. Some preach well etc. Happy are you Abraham our father that Eleazar has come forth from your loins. |
| He would say, If all sages were on one side of the scale and Eleazar on the other, he would outweigh them all. | R. Yosi b. Judah: Joshua lectured before Yoḥanan, Aqiva before Joshua, Hananiah b. Ḥakhinai before Aqiva. | When Joseph the priest and Simeon b. Natanel heard, they too opened a discourse on the Chariot. They said, it was, the first day of summer, | And when these things were told to Joshua, he and Yosi the priest were walking on the way. They said Let us also expound the Chariot. Joshua opened and expounded. That day was the first day of summer, |

| Mekhilta de R. Simeon | Tos. Hag. 2:1-2 | y. Hag. 2:1 | b. Hag. 14b |
|---|---|---|---|
| | | and the earth trembled, and a rainbow appeared and an echo came and said to them, Behold the place is ready for you and your disciples are slated for the third class. | but the heavens clouded over and a kind of a rainbow appeared, and the angels gathered and came to hear like men running to a wedding.<br><br>Yosi and the priest went and told these things to Yohanan, who said, Happy are you, and happy are those who bore you.<br>Happy are my eyes who who have seen such.<br>And also you and I in my dream were reclining on Mount Sinai and an echo came forth to us from heaven, "Come up hither, come up hither. Your disciples are slated for the third class.<br>Is this so? And is it not taught? (TNY'):<br>Joshua lectured, things before Yohanan, 'Aqiva before Joshua, Hanania b. Hakhinai before 'Aqiva.<br>And Eleazar is not mentioned. |

It would be difficult to invent a better example of the development of a tradition from simplicity to complexity, from being relatively unadored to being fully articulated, and from earlier to later versions. In the earliest document the story is the shortest, simplest. The Tosefta represents an obvious expansion. The Palestinian Talmudic account is still further enriched with details and entirely new components. And the Babylonian version, last of all in the age of the document in which it appears, is clearly most fully, carefully worked out.

The Mekhilta's components are:

1. Yohanan riding an ass;
2. Eleazar with him;
3. Teach me—it is illegal;
4. Then let me speak;
5. Eleazar expounded and flames licked round about;

6. Then Yoḥanan blessed him, Your mother and Abraham are
   happy.

The concluding element is, as I said, a separate and unrelated saying.
It plays no integral part whatever in the Merkavah tradition. But it is
therefore all the more important, for presumably this version, in which
no other disciples have any role whatsoever, is how the disciples of
Eleazar would have transmitted the story. In fact, from the viewpoint
of editing, it *is* integral, for after Eleazar's sermon, Yoḥanan's praise
for his exceptional student is in order. Hence the fact that it appears
in no later version should not be regarded as inconsequential. It is
suppressed in favor of other disciples, especially Joshua.

The Tosefta's version is close to the foregoing, but it adds that
Yoḥanan ceremoniously descended from the ass before the lecture
began. Only then did Eleazar say his sermon. The detail about the
flames, on the other hand, is absent. But the blessing is greatly
expanded. The praise now is extended to Eleazar's ability to achieve a
fully realized gnostic experience; he does not merely describe the
*Merkavah*, but presumably is able to go down in it. Then a second, and
separate blessing is copied from Mekhilta, "*Happy are you...*" This
clearly suggests dependence, for the first, invented blessing would
have been sufficient for an independent account. The second blessing
is further augmented: Abraham should be happy because you expound
well and fulfill well. Thus the narrator tied in the duplicated blessing
of the original version. The most important omission is the praise of
Eleazar. In place of it we are told that Joshua did the same before
Yoḥanan, 'Aqiva afterward, and so forth. The later version thus
emphasized that despite the excellence of Eleazar, which no one
denied, the *true* line of transmission extended through Joshua, not
through Eleazar. We may assume the first and simplest version derives
from Eleazar's school, and the second has been altered, then handed on
in Joshua-Aqiva's line.

The Palestinian version begins as do the early ones. But it adds a
careful explanation of *why* Yoḥanan got off the ass. This explanation is
rather fulsome. Only afterward do the master and disciple sit down
—under a tree, the *olive* is lost. Then fire comes down, but this detail,
from the Mekhilta version, is greatly embellished. Angels dance as at
a wedding. They even praise Eleazar's sermon before Yoḥanan has a
chance to say anything. He plays no part in the proliferating details.
Then the trees sing a Psalm. Only after the expanded element has been
completed do we return to Yoḥanan. He now kisses Eleazar and gives

the double-blessing, *Blessed is the Lord . . .* [and] *Happy are you, Abraham*. Then Joseph/Yosi the priest and Simeon are introduced, with further supernatural events accompanying *their* sermon. The echo invites them to the third level of the heaven.

The Babylonian version is augmented in almost every detail. Eleazar is not merely walking, but driving the ass. He wants to teach something *he has already heard*. Not only does Yoḥanan descend, but now Eleazar asks *why* he did so. This is clearly a point at which the Babylonian *beraita* has expanded on a mute detail in the immediately preceding account. Yoḥanan then develops his earlier saying. It is not merely the glory of the creator, but rather both the Shekhinah and the Ministering angels are present. Eleazar speaks, and fire pours from heaven. The trees sing a Psalm, this time Ps. 145. An angel repeats the message of the Palestinian version. The order of the trees' psalm and the angel's message are therefore reversed. Then comes the kiss—now *on his head*—and the blessing is expanded to include *to investigate* after *to understand* and *to expound*. The *Some preach well* formula comes verbatim, then the second blessing. The further report excludes Simeon b. Natanel, who probably left no disciples, certainly no important school, to insure his position in the traditions. Rather Joshua is now the link. The new story depends upon the earlier version. The rainbow is not enough; now the angels come to a wedding, a detail presumably borrowed from the Palestinian dance of the ministering angels. Then Yosi told Yoḥanan, who expressed approval. The heavenly echo of the Palestinian version becomes the whole dream about the circle of Yoḥanan on Mount Sinai, with a direct invitation to heaven, both elements based upon and developments of *Behold the place is ready for you.*

Since the several versions clearly depend on one another, there can be no question as to which comes first, and which later, in time of redaction. Thus, as I said, I can think of no better demonstration that versions of a single event or saying appearing in documents of successive age do proceed from the simpler to the more complex as they pass from an earlier to a later document. Here we may certainly say

יש מוקדם ומאוחר בתורה שבעל פה.

# THE PHILOSOPHY IMPLICIT IN THE MIDRASH

HENRY SLONIMSKY

Hebrew Union College - Jewish Institute of Religion, New York

## I

WHAT Agada or Midrash is the Midrash itself states. In a conspicuous utterance concerning its use and function it characterizes itself as Benedictions and Consolations, ברכות ונחמות. Primarily then, and in its inner core and essence, it is consolation, that is, a feeding of the life-impulse when harassed and threatened by tragic circumstance. Tragic circumstance was the special environment, unexampled suffering the special historic lot, of the Jew. And to guard against despair because of the unremitting enemy from without, and against the temptation to despair because of doubt and weakening faith from within, the Jewish genius prepared for itself, alongside of the code of law which governed its daily living, a great wellspring of assurance and re-assurance, of comfort and ground for faith. That is what the Agada aims to be alongside of the Halakah, the "faith" alongside the "works," which in the Christian world may be contrasted but which here are the twin sources of Jewish being and the twin pillars on which it equally rests.

There are two versions of our initial text and they offer interesting variants which throw light upon each other. In the older version it reads as follows. "In the former days when people had change in their pockets (i. e. when things were leisurely) they liked to listen to some word from Mishnah and Talmud; but now that money is gone, *and especially since we are sick because of the ruling power*, וביותר שאנו חולים מן המלכות, people want to hear something *from the Bible and from Agada*" (Pesikta 101b). The later version, occurring in a later Midrash and possibly after the situation had hardened, has the same text running as follows. "In the past people had some change in their pocket and a man liked to listen to Mishnah and Halakah and Talmud; but now that money is gone, *and especially since we are sick through the oppression*, וביותר שאנו חולים מן השעבוד, nobody wants to hear anything but *words of Benediction and Consolation*" (Cant. R., ed. Wilna, Romm, 15a, Col. 2). The sickness remains the same, through persecution by the מלכות or categorically through *the* oppression, it is in fact

235

perennial; and the healing or therapeutic is in the one case designated as Bible and Agada and in the other as Blessings and Consolations: clearly then the two sets of terms are synonymous.

Consolation however usually carries with it a mere sense of soothing, a mood or tone of feeling without hard body or substance. That is quite definitely not the case here. The consolation and healing offered by Agada to the Jewish people on its hard road is solidly grounded in a powerful pattern of thought and intellect, a worldview and philosophy it might almost be said if these terms were not so academic, in any case a set of themes and imagery and ideas forged in the crucible of a unique and terrible experience and suffused throughout by earnest thinking.

The Midrash is fully aware of the greatness of this its undertaking. It does not play modest. "Dost thou wish to know him who spake and by whose word the world came into being? Study Agada: for through such study thou canst get to understand the Holy One blessed be He and to follow in his ways" (Sifré 85a). These utterances are not peripheral or casual. The first is ascribed to Levi and Yizhak, two central figures in the creation of Agada. And the second so self-conscious statement which we have just quoted stems from the Sifré, one of the oldest and most basic of the Midrashim.

Now the name for the science and study of God and his ways, is Theology, also Philosophy. Is the Midrash then a Theology and Philosophy? We must remember that these terms are Greek in origin and that the categories of thought which they represent are creations of the Greek genius. In a sense these terms are too ponderous and too pedantic. For while there is the most authentic and mature kind of thinking on all the main topics of life present there, on God and man, on time and event, on suffering and the future, it is present in an atmosphere or medium of freedom and unconstraint, not as a set of propositions to be soberly argued in the schools; but rather as themes and images to guide and influence the listener in all the workings of his mind, and still to retain the fluidity of a story, as of the myths to which Plato resorts when his themes outdistance his concepts. In this way speculations which would have been frowned upon or forbidden if set forth as sober creed in Halakic fashion obtain breathing space and an opportunity for emergence; and the audacities without which there is no greatness of thinking achieve room and possibility of expression. It is a subtle device since it succeeds in capturing freedom and substance of thinking without being tied to the numbered paragraphs of a treatise. With this important reservation or qualification one can say that the Midrash is a repository of a

Jewish Theology and of a Jewish Philosophy of History, formidable as these terms may sound, and strange labels as they may be for the living tenderness of Jewish experience.

Always we are to bear in mind that the origin of Jewish speculation is not leisurely intellectual curiosity. There is a difference between Greek and Jew. "All men desire by nature to know," the opening words of Aristotle's Metaphysics, are the words which naturally occur to Aristotle in accounting for the origin of philosophy. Wonder is the emotion, and raising a question is the corresponding intellectual act, whereby philosophy arises, according to the Platonic Socrates (in the Theaetetus 155 d, which Aristotle takes over, Metaph. 982 b). But for Israel it is an acute experience of suffering and of an agonizing perplexity which releases thought. Israel is in the unique position of regarding itself as the chosen people, the beloved of God, and at the same time knowing itself as the most afflicted people: — how resolve that awesome paradox? What thoughts must it frame about God since obviously the received God-idea is rendered untenable? What kind of a God would they in actual fact fashion under the stress? What God, what no-God, what half-God, what man-God, what all-God? How is man to behave? What is the future and is there a future? And what ground is there for faith?

And why the initial affliction? "Sufferance is the badge of all our tribe," *souffrance*, suffering, — the greatest of poets has made his one Jewish character testify. No truer word was spoken, it was spoken with the clairvoyance and penetration of genius. Suffering is involved in the very character of the career on which Israel was launched, is indeed the badge of Israel whenever true to his course. That career is seen to be inevitably tragic. For the core of Jewish belief is that Israel must bear the Torah from God to the world. But the world is unwilling and resists all three, God, Torah, and Israel, and the protagonist who does the actual bearing must also bear the brunt of the suffering. The whole drama is paradigmatic: it is a prelude or prefiguring or archetype of what must take place henceforth everywhere and by all men of good will if a new and higher order is to emerge as reality. The Torah stands for goodness, for the visions and ideals and values, or light of God in which we see light. God, besides being this light and vision which we behold, is also such power, such real actual power in the universe, as is committed and has already been marshalled for the victory of the good; this power is at present still pitifully small, and that fact entails the drama. The power must be increased, the ideal must be translated into the real; and the active agent in this crucial event is man, who is thus destined for tragic heroism by the very nature of his situation. Israel, of course, stands for the ideal Israel, and is paradigmatic of the good and brave man anywhere. That the best man must suffer the most, must assume the burdens and sorrows of the world, constitutes the most awesome phenomenon and paradox of the whole spiritual life. God in the full meaning of the term is seen to stand at the end, not at the beginning. "On that day he shall be one and his name shall be one." *He must be made one*, and man is the agent in whose hands it is left to make or to mar that supreme integration.

To regard God as perfect in power, as he is in vision, at the very beginning, is the most disastrous of superstitions. The "monistic superstition," as William James calls it, has worked havoc, and the most momentous decision which mankind has to make is to re-learn on that score. God and man are a polarity. They are both heroes in the same drama. They need each other, they grow together, but they also suffer together. Hence they need consolation, Benedictions and Consolations. That the Midrash is designed to supply. The Midrash is a vast post-Biblical Bible written on the margin of the Bible to account for the sufferings of God and man in their efforts to reclaim and uplift an unfinished and emerging world. It furnishes the faith which by generating strength helps to create the object of its faith. Its eyes are on the future, on the realized kingdom of God. Hence its proper closing prayer is the Kaddish, which was composed for the schools, not for the Synagogue, and has nothing to do with its later use for the dead. The Kaddish is the briefest formulation of Jewish theology, and it properly terminated every Agadic discourse as the doxology which summed up the very soul of the Agada.

That the Torah will be made real in the end, and that all men will accept it in the end, that there is a far-off goal towards which all history converges, and that time and event are no mere welter or chaos but a meaningful process, and that the protagonist in that progress is a tragic-heroic figure, wounded and smitten but undismayed: that is the theology and the philosophy of history implicit in Midrash and Bible.

Man needs re-assurance on double grounds. He must be saved from despairing that there is meaning in history. He must be saved from despairing over the fact that the good must suffer.

The classic Midrash always concludes with some reminder of the certainty of the Messianic goal, hence very properly the Kaddish is its crown and consummation. The grammar itself is theological. The Ithpaal of the opening words יתגדל ויתקדש connotes gradual process of achievement. "May his great name get to be magnified and sanc-

tified," that is, more and more, in increasing measure. "In the world
which he hath created according to his will," that is, "in a world of
time and effort and growth. Then the climax, "May he establish his
Kingdom," וימליך מלכותיה, corresponding to "Thy Kingdom come"
taken over into the Lord's Prayer in Christianity. And thereupon the
concluding words, unexampled in patience and faith, in heroism and
pathos: "during your life and your days . . . . speedily and at a near
time." For they knew and we know that it is agonizingly remote.
But the course is set and to give up because of delay is despair, and
despair is the cardinal sin in a fighting man's religion, it is the cardinal
sin in Judaism, for it spells the defeat of God. צפית לישועה, did you
continue to hope for salvation, is one of the questions asked of every
Jew at the Judgment Seat, according to one of the great rabbis
(Sabbath 31a).

## II

Before we proceed to the details of our task there must be a dis-
claimer at the threshold, namely, as if Agada excluded or lowered
Halakah. There is a wickedness of human nature which leads man
to think that he cannot praise one thing without denouncing another.
That there can be and indeed on occasion must be, within a given
context of two related but contrasting elements, a cult and cultivation
of both, a mutual supplementation, a perception that they secretly
intercommunicate and feed each other, though on the surface they
may seem to antagonize and negate each other, is the higher and more
adult view, the mark of the genuinely integral and matured mind.
But "all things excellent are as rare as they are difficult" we have
been told by a Jewish thinker; and אלו ואלו דברי אלהים חיים of the
old Rabbis is far more than a homily of easy tolerance, it is a deep
and difficult lesson concerning reality which mankind will have to
teach itself because it is so rare by reason of its excellence.

A wickedness of human nature, we have said, an almost inevitable
temptation to stress one element at the expense of another. We see it
exemplified at every turn in the history of religions and of our religion.
True, in the Bible, i. e. of course in the Old Testament, the ideal of
an equilibrium between Agada and Halakah, as embodying the two
great concerns of the religious mind, is most nearly attained. Taking
Agada as the summary designation for Prophets and Psalms, and
Halakah to stand for the codes, which for all their brevity and bareness
are the backbone of the whole system, we may say that the Halakah
is a product of the Agada: the Agada feeds Halakah in the sense that

the codes are a precipitate and crystallization of Prophets and the Prophetic mind early and late; and that in turn the Prophets rest upon the laws of righteous living for their support, and when these laws have hardened or when they persist in their more primitive phase they tend to be dissolved again into an "Agada" from which they emerge re-fashioned.

But apart from this supreme example of equilibrium in the Hebrew Bible, which however must remain an unstable equilibrium as in any living organism, the rest is a story of a shift from one extreme to another. Jesus and Paul are antinomians. The Protestant Reformation professes itself a revolt of the living faith against the dead works of the Roman Church. With us Hasidism is a similar stress of the soul and spirit, of ecstatic enthusiasm, against the rigidity and dryness of Rabbinic rationalism and routine Mitzwot. And to top them all, Reform Judaism in its first classic phase was a rejection of the whole ritual and pattern of orthodoxy in favor of a few grandiloquent Agadot such as "the fatherhood of God and brotherhood of man."

There is no doubt that codes and patterns tend to harden and to become purely external motions of hands and lips, inspiring recurrent rebellion of the heart and spirit. But there is equally no doubt of the opposite. The most glorious spirit in the world will evaporate into thin air and even into self-righteous gush if not given honesty and reality by a hard discipline of doing and behavior, of observance and performance. This is a basic matter of physiology and psychology. You cannot have a living organism without a skeletal framework, or a building without a scaffolding, and you cannot have a pure life of the spirit without issuance into hands and legs, without articulation and organization of the medium in which it is to work. That medium is the body and time.

In general there is no great feeling without the discipline of high burdens. We can earn our emotions too cheaply. We are never quite willing to pay for them. Hence the danger of all high "Agada," i. e. of music and poetry and prophetic exhortation and ecstasy, which furnish men emotions they have no right to unless they have lived and worked to merit them. Agada is rightly a reward and a זכות for those who have shouldered Halakah.

We must learn to see both sides of both demands, to take the fat with the lean, the danger with the profit. The trouble is that value and danger are distributed unevenly: where the value is apparent the danger is hidden, and conversely where the danger is apparent the value is hidden. In the case of the codes the danger is obvious, namely externalization; but the need and service, though deeper-lying, are utterly indispensable. In the case of the prophecy and poetry the need and service are obvious, for the spirit is goal and essence of the whole set-up; but the danger, though deeper-lying, is deadly. Your organism will die down as your spirit grows less; but your spirit will vanish unless you capture and harness it. You are caught between two necessities equally imperative. It may be a tragedy that pure spirit in man cannot subsist without body; as it certainly is a tragedy when body loses its informing and quickening soul.

Consider, as a classic instance of the intertwining of Halakah and Agada, the rite of circumcision. The supreme Prophet of the Hebrew Bible, Jeremiah, one of the great spiritual seers of all time, demands a circumcision of the heart, i. e. he envisages the replacement and spiritualization of a ritual act which has its beginnings in a dim barbaric past. "Circumcise yourselves to the Lord, and take away the foreskins of your heart, ye men of Judah and inhabitants of Jerusalem" (Jer. 4.4). "Behold, the days come, saith the Lord that I will make a new covenant with the house of Israel and with the house of Judah. . . . I will put my law in their inward parts, and in their heart will I write it" (Jer. 31.31–33). And in Deuteronomy, that great re-statement of the Law under the influence of the Prophets (for the scholars regard it as a product of the Jeremianic School, and it would be a fine example of the purging of Halakah by Agada), the simple injunction "Circumcise therefore the foreskin of your heart" (Deut. 10.16).

All this is superb, but the wisdom of the Jewish genius matches it with grim humor in the daily grace after meals. This prayer enumerates God's various benefactions to Israel, land, redemption from bondage in Egypt, gift of Torah, gift of life and food, and conspicuous in their very midst is the sign and seal of circumcision. "We thank thee O Lord our God because thou didst give as an heritage unto our fathers . . . . as well as for the covenant which thou hast sealed in our flesh. . . ." ועל בריתך שחתמת בבשרנו.

Now which of these two demands shall we go by? Shall it be the circumcision of the heart as the far-off goal of all men and of all aspiration, dropping by the wayside the hard and ineffaceable discipline of the flesh, without which however we collapse and the demand of the heart evaporates? Or shall we retain the discipline of the flesh, knowing full well that the flesh may be weak when the spirit is willing, but also knowing that the flesh is the only vehicle of the spirit if the spirit wishes to abide? Heart is heart, but as the latest and therefore frailest of all human developments it has only the strength of an aspiration; and flesh is only flesh but, if you cut into it, it serves as an everpresent reminder. This is one of many instances in which the Jewish genius shows its poise and power by doing justice to two equally imperative but alternating and jealous claims. The circumcision of the heart is the goal for mankind and for the Jew; and for the Jew the circumcision of the flesh in addition is part of the slow schooling and the inexorable reminder of his special role in the advent of the kingdom of the heart.

The greatest Agadist of our time, Bialik, has written the most powerful defence of Halakah in modern Hebrew letters. He, not only our greatest poet, but also the indefatigable collector and anthologist of the Agada, and its subtle and percipient interpreter, has nevertheless also perceived the danger of the undue emphasis of the merely Agadic, i. e. of the supposedly spiritual, when standing alone and without the counterbalancing action of the Halakic mood and frame of mind, which is of course the willingness to assume disciplines and burdens. And it is because of the special temptation of Agada for the modern Jew, and because of the modern Jew's special unwillingness to accept Halakah, that we indulge here in this divagation in defence of Halakah before we return to an exposition of the values and function of Agada.

Let us see again what is the most telling thing that can be said against the Halakic code and mood. Let us start with the most famous utterances, those of Jesus about the Sabbath being made for man, not man for the Sabbath; about things that come out of the mouth rendering unclean and not the things which enter it; or Paul's summary claim for a man who is truly "in Christ" as having lost the very capacity for sin. It sounds gorgeous, but the problem is by no means solved. The real and serious soul does not need the exemption from the law to gain spirit. Those who are exempted or exempt themselves are not thereby possessors of the spirit. It is precisely those who want to make things easy for themselves who welcome the comforting assurance of exemption. Paul and Jesus say things that sound true, but they only flatter us. They point to the dangers of mere observance without pointing to its indispensable function; and to the value of spirit without pointing to its volatility and its high pretentiousness. When was anyone by believing himself truly "in Christ" freed from the capacity for sin? Was it Paul himself? Is not lapse and relapse the law of our life as it was of Paul's? And was Jesus able to dispense with the Sabbath or with the Law generally? Did he not use the Sabbath for worship and preaching, and by his own express assurance the Law for living? Antinomianism in and by itself is everywhere a self-delusion on the part of those who too easily absolve themselves, those who are impatient with the Nomos but have no Pneuma to match it.

In the case of Reformed Judaism it is wise to remember its origin, the rhythm of its historic course, and its probable future attitude towards the Law. Reformed Judaism is by no means a fixed, static, unchanging religious philosophy. In its beginning (1835–1848) a movement of prophetic fervor, a rebellion against the decrepit and sordid exterior which overlaid the surface of the ancient faith, it was almost perforce a negation of forms and rituals which seemed to have become a dead letter. But negation by itself leads to the emptying of content. It has happened that the extreme of negation was reached when the whole of Judaism was reduced, almost always by laymen who having neither Halakah nor Agada had no right to speak in the name of Judaism, to the single formula of the fatherhood of God and brotherhood of man. That of course is a pompous hollow phrase since it usually does not imply the slightest difference in the mode of life of those who utter it. But the negations of Reform were almost always less extensive and less deep than appeared. Much more of substantive Judaism was retained than was confessed. And while Halakah will never be allowed its old dominion in Reformed Judaism, there can be no doubt that more and more of it will be re-appropriated as time goes on, for there can be no Judaism without Halakah. The only question is, how much.

Moreover the lines of demarcation and mutual exclusion between Agada and Halakah are by no means as real in the history of religions as they seem on the surface. Catholicism is not all "works"; it is full of the richest kind of "faith" from Augustine to Francis of Assisi. Conversely Protestantism is by no means all "faith"; it very soon hardens into an orthodoxy of reform; and there is nothing within Catholicism quite so depressing as the gloomy and morose mood of Calvinistic Halakah. And that in turn was balanced by Pietism and Mysticism. Obviously then something of both Halakah and Agada must enter into every religion, the only problem being how to obtain and maintain the requisite equilibrium.

To return to our own religion, Rabbinic Judaism is by no means all routine Mitzwot: there is the quiet devotion of Kawwana in the most prosaic weekday service, and on Yom Tov and the High Holydays the atmosphere is instinct with it.

Hasidism is so far from being mere spirituality that Shneor Zalman, its finest mind and its theorist, writes a special enriched redaction of the Shulhan Aruch. Then Hasidism itself for all its Hitlahavut or Conflagration settles down to a routine, and the routine alas degenerates often into a magic of intercession.

The problem always is to maintain faith and works both together in their vitality and mutual enrichment, for each is an incomplete half. Works tend to become magic, a mere opus operatum; spirit tends to become hollow grandiloquence, fatuous and complacent. ·Judaism has never failed to insist on the less attractive, the less popular, the prime indispensable of behavior and performance; but it has also the richest kind of enveloping religiosity. *To this latter it has a right* since it has never neglected the former, and we turn therefore with good conscience to a further exposition of Agada.

## III

Hebraism and Hellenism are regarded as the two component factors of our modern Western culture. The formulation was made by Ernest Renan, a thoughtful student of Christian and Jewish origins and of their impact on the modern world, and was rendered current among the English-speaking peoples in a famous essay by Matthew Arnold. It is a grand simplification and still true. The two forces are of course distinctive and different ("doing" and "knowing" says Arnold in his summary way) and for that reason may seek to ally themselves into an integral whole. But there must also be kinship and affinity for alliance; and that general kinship and affinity merges at one particular point into identity. Where the Hellenic genius inclines away from Hellenism and towards Hebraism, in the Platonic Socrates and in the mature Plato, *the primacy of the Good* brings Hellenism into closest proximity with the core and essence of Hebraism. Plato is, in Philo's phrase, a Moses talking Greek.

At the threshold of Midrash Rabbah, which is the most monumental and impressive of all the Midrashim, there stands as prelude and, so to speak, as keynote of all of Midrash, a monolithic Platonic utterance, which bases itself on a similar Platonism in the Bible, namely the passage in praise of the primeval Wisdom in Prov. 8.22–32, and is followed in the Midrash by the Jewish selection among the infinite Platonic essences or forms of the seven which it alone needs and wants. Let us examine the first keynote utterance.

"In the beginning." In explanation of this first verse of the first chapter of Genesis, R. Hoshaya the Elder quotes Prov. 8.30 "Then I was by Him as a nursling, and I was daily all delight." Do not read *Amon* (nursling), read *Uman* (artist or architect). What the Torah or

Wisdom is saying in that verse in Proverbs is this: I was God's architectural tool at creation. In human practice when a mortal king builds a palace he does not build it from his own knowledge but from the knowledge of an architect. And the architect does not build it from his own knowledge but relies on parchments and tablets (blueprints) in order to know how to make the chambers and how to make the doors. *Thus God looked on the Torah as he created the world*, כך היה הקב'ה מביט בתורה ובורא את העולם. And the Torah itself says in confirmation, '*With* the beginning God created,' where "Beginning" can mean nothing but Torah, as is witnessed by the word "Beginning" in Prov. 8.22 'The Lord possessed me (namely the primeval Wisdom or Torah) as the Beginning of his way.' Thus far R. Hoshaya the Elder.

"Beginning" therefore may be a temporal beginning, a beginning in time, but it may also be a logical or intrinsic beginning, a beginning in reality, what we call a principle, just as in Greek ἀρχή may mean a beginning in time, or a first cause and first principle. That principle or timeless beginning is Wisdom or Torah. God created the world in the image and by the instrumentality of that true Beginning which is Wisdom or Torah.

This is not an isolated utterance, it is the common property of the Midrash. Thus the widely known and popular Tanhuma begins on exactly the same note. " 'In the beginning God created.' This is what Scripture has in mind when it says 'The Lord founded the earth with Wisdom' (Prov. 3.19). And as God went on to create his world he took counsel with the Torah בתורה נתייעץ and so created the world." The Targum Yerushalmi translates the opening word בראשית quite simply בחוכמא, as if no further explanation were necessary. The Yalkut on the great text in Gen. 1.26 "And God said, let us make man in our image, after our likeness," has the words "God said to the Torah, let us make man," אמר הקב'ה לתורה נעשה אדם (Yalkut Shimeoni, Article 13, p. 4b, Col. 1, and Pirke Eliezer, Ch. 11, ed. Luria, 27b).

In the Midrash then the Torah, identified with the primeval Wisdom, is the blue-print, the objectified mind of God, but also the instrumental power, i. e. both the plan and the architect, which God employs in the creation of the world and of man.

The idea is already present, if not in such definite terms certainly clearly enough, in the Biblical original to which we have been referring throughout, namely the great poem in Prov. 8.22–32, where Wisdom-Torah, the first of God's works, is present at creation, and not merely delights in the beauty of creation as it proceeds, but is implicitly the means whereby, in contrast to the account in Genesis, creation is not an arbitrary act of divine omnipotence but precisely a cosmos. The exact degree of participation and subordination of Torah-Wisdom in the act of creation, which busies the commentators, need not detain us here, since in any case participation in the act of creation and subordination to God are both true. So likewise, how far the hypostasis of Wisdom-Torah as the mind or intelligent will of God has taken place (here or in the Wisdom of Solomon 9.9 "And with thee is wisdom which knoweth thy works and was present when thou wast making the world") need not concern us; in any case it is sufficiently separate from God to confront God with a degree of independence. Further the Biblical scholars seem on the whole to feel that the poem in praise of Wisdom in Proverbs is indigenous, native to Israel, which would be a welcome confirmation of the view that a certain basic Platonism is one of the original motifs of the human mind whenever it rises to speculation.

But the passage at the beginning of Genesis Rabbah in the name of R. Hoshaya is certainly not independent of Greek influence. Bacher (in the old *JQR* III, 357–360 and in *Agada d. palästin. Amoräer* I, 107, note) has shown the exact parallel to this passage in Philo (De Opificio Mundi, 4), and indicated Origen who lived in Caesarea as the probable source of Hoshaya's knowledge (*ibid.* I, 92). Origen, the Alexandrian Church Father, was precisely the man to be full of Philo, and residing as Bishop in Caesarea, and in constant learned intercourse for his Biblical and exegetical studies with the great Jewish scholars resident in Caesarea, would almost certainly have been in touch with Hoshaya who had his academy in Caesarea.

Philo however is faithfully Platonic. His God proceeds like the Demiurge in the Timaeus (28a). He consults the Torah-Wisdom as pattern like an architect who, in his mind's eye, consults a model, ἀποβλέπων εἰς τὸ παράδειγμα, and then conceives in mind the archetypes or forms of the world before he creates the corresponding empirical things, ἐνενόησε τοὺς τύπους αὐτῆς. And some such conception must have prevailed in the mind of the author of the poem in Prov. 8, since he is concerned with the individual beauties and orders of creation. But Hoshaya is interested in the summary and concentrated meaning of the procedure, which is that the Torah is certainly cause of the world but only its final or purposive cause, its goal and meaning. God created the world for the sake of Torah, i. e. for the sake of goodness, with a view to the realization or domination of Torah or goodness. Similarly in Plato the whole system of "Ideas" culminates in the Idea of the Good, which thus constitutes its ultimate meaning. And shortly after Hoshaya's statement we have a confirmation of this Rabbinic concentration of Plato's thought in the utterance of R. Benaya (which a little later *is put into the mouth of God himself*): "The world and the fullness thereof were created only for the sake of the Torah." העולם ומלואו לא נברא אלא בזכות התורה (Gen. R., ed. Wilna. Romm, 8a and 10a).

Platonism itself is one of the supreme motifs of the history of philosophy, possibly the one single greatest theme in the whole range of philosophical speculation. Its coincidence with the central thought of Judaism is therefore of worldhistoric significance. That all visible things are created and guided by "heavenly" archetypes, according to perfect and deathless patterns ("burning seeds in the hands of God" in Browning's great phrase describing Shelley's Platonism), is only a partial statement of the doctrine, and still does not reach the centre. It is indeed the view of Platonism that the species and genera of the organic world everywhere in their individual exemplars are fashioned in the image of unitary ideal prototypes; and further that planets and stars in their courses and the atoms in their orbits traverse geometrical patterns and obey mathematical laws. But further than that, all mathematical validities, all true relations generally, subsist in a timeless being; *they are*; they constitute the ultimate substance or reality, waiting to be beheld or "discovered" by some chance mind, and waiting for a possible embodiment or translation into empirical reality of at least one portion of their infinite plenitude. But further than that, all moral and aesthetic validities, what we call the moral ideals and the endless shapes and varying types of beauty, "the light of God in which we see light," are a further and even higher region or realm of "Ideas." In his sad, pensive, profound way, Socrates is made to say concerning the ideal commonwealth in the Republic (592 a b), "In heaven perhaps there is laid up a pattern of it, which he who desires may behold and beholding may set his house in order."

The patterns of the true, the beautiful, and the good, the world of values and ideals, if these be considered not as chance thoughts in our heads or soap-bubble aspirations, but the ultimate stuff of reality, of which we get some dim inkling if we have the זכות; infinitely realer than the so-called real things, for sun and stars can burn up, get born and die, but these no fire can burn, no mildew can touch, they are indestructible, they simply are. We call them "the light of God" from which or whom they come as inspiration; but Plato did without a personal God (the later demiurge or creator in the Timaeus is on a totally different and lower plane). His system was indeed Godhead and with a centre, but that centre he designated impersonally as Idea of the Good, the Idea of Ideas. The Idea of the Good as the core of reality occupies the same place within the system of essences and

forms as the sun in our planetary system: as the sun renders things
not merely visible and knowable but is also the source of their growth
and being, so the Idea of the Good is according to Plato the why and
wherefore of all the other ideas, they have their ground in that central
invisible sun (Rep. 509). And it is this central thought which unites
Platonism with Judaism: the Good as the heart and ground of all
being and reality. The Rabbis call it Torah, Plato the Idea of the
Good. R. Hoshaya's opening utterance as the overture to Midrash
marks the august marriage of Hebraism with Hellenism.

A metaphysic whose ultimate principle or final reality is the
Good, a moralistic metaphysic, binds Judaism and Platonism together: that is what constitutes them together the spiritual basis
of our modern world. But in the further development Judaism follows its own nature, its own practical bent. It does not indulge in
the play of ideas. It makes an austere selection. What it takes it
really needs and converts into muscle. Greeks and Germans have
a plethora of ideas, ideas both in the modern depressed and obliterated
sense of thoughts or notions, as in the grand realistic and substantial
sense of Plato, some of them needed and used, but most of them
unused, and cheapening and festering through disuse. In the same
Parasha following Hoshaya's initial declaration there is an enumeration of the seven Ideas which the Rabbis have distinguished
for the high status of primeval forms or essences present before creation. Besides its conspicuous position here, the passage (with some
variations) occurs twice in the Talmud (Pesaḥim 54a; Nedarim 39b),
and many times in Midrashic literature, so it must be regarded as a
known and received doctrine. Our text here in Genesis R. seems to be
the most authentic and serviceable one.

Accordingly we are first told of six Things or Words (a seventh
is later to follow) concerning which it is expressly said that they
preceded the creation of the world. And of these six, two are reserved
for a special first place within the group. These two are Torah and
the Seat of Glory, but concerning both we must make a preliminary
remark at once. The Torah originally, as we saw, stands for the whole
sum of Ideas, for the objectified mind of God so to speak, at least
for the concentration of them all in the purpose of God, in the
"final" cause of creation. Here it seems to be just one of the Ideas
co-ordinated with the others. The Seat of Glory is the veiled designation almost of God himself, certainly of his prime attribute, namely
dynamic power, which as we also saw was at first reserved for Torah,
conceived not merely as plan but also as architect. However, something of the old balance in favor of Torah is presently restored. For

the question is raised as to which of these two firsts has the further priority, and the decision is made in favor of Torah, so that in a sense Torah becomes prior to God himself. After these two absolutely primary Beings, four further forms or essences are enumerated: the Patriarchs, Israel, the Temple, and the Name of the Messiah. These are the constituent categories of history and temporal event, from its beginning in the "founding fathers" of the chosen people to its culmination in the establishment of the Kingdom of God on earth. That Abraham, Isaac, and Jacob are heavenly ideas, above all, that Israel is a timeless and ideal prototype, can mean only the enormous sense of the unique role to be played by this people as the bearer of Torah from God to the world. The Heavenly Temple is of course the ideal prototype of all earthly places of true worship. And the name of the Messiah, in which the virtue and potency of the Messiah is concentrated, assumes the final victorious realization of the Messianic Kingdom.

With pathos and with humor a seventh Idea is singled out for the high status of pre-mundane existence or subsistence, namely Repentance. It is chosen because it is indispensable. Without its beneficent presence and protection men simply could not get on; it is the pathetic reminder of the incessant drama and vicissitude of man's moral life.

The culminating debate as to which of the seven has the real primacy, even after the question seems to have been settled, is the most interesting part of the whole passage. With his tongue in his cheek, one rabbi proves that "the Idea of Israel preceded them all," מחשבתן של ישראל קדמה לכל. Israel takes precedence over Torah itself, as Torah had taken precedence over the Seat of Glory. And therewith the matter is allowed to rest.

What tremendous consciousness of worldhistoric mission animated these men, despite the touch of humor and irony in the expression of the claim: a consciousness supported by the grandeur of tragedy which overshadowed them, but a consciousness which in more relaxed moments they summoned all the resources of great humor to lighten and to render plausible and palatable.


IV

The present section, dealing with suffering and its implications for the varied aspects of Theology and Philosophy, is the most important and most extensive of our entire study. For greater clarity we have articulated it into three parts: 1) a preliminary summary of the

philosophical themes involved; 2) a series of Midrashic texts illustrative of or in some way relevant to these themes; 3) a fuller exposition of the philosophical themes under discussion as well as of related
subjects in philosophy to which they lead.

## I.

"The earth is soaked with the tears of humanity from its crust to
its centre" is the reasoned opinion of Dostoyevsky's profoundest
character in his greatest work (*The Brothers Karamazov*, 256). And
Schelling in his profoundest essay speaks of "the veil of sadness which
is spread over all nature, the deep ineffaceable melancholy of all life"
(*Menschl. Freiheit*, ed. Meiner, 72; ed. Fuhrmans, 64, Eng. tr., 79,
"der Schleier der Schwermut, der über die ganze Natur ausgebreitet
ist, die tiefe unzerstörliche Melancholie alles Lebens.")

It isn't merely the fact of suffering where that is an inevitable
incident in the process of growth, or where it is compensated by fruit
and flower of richer and deeper life. Such things we could understand
and accept. Nor could we object to suffering which comes as inevitable
retribution for foolish and wicked behavior. But where the suffering
is out of all proportion to the spiritual results which ensue; and above
all where the suffering falls to the lot of those who do not deserve
to suffer, first the innocent, and secondly the good and true, that
becomes the most stunning and paralyzing experience of the human
soul, the most awesome paradox of the whole spiritual life.

Transfiguration of suffering therefore looms as the most pressing
task imposed on the thinking mind, and if successful would be the
rescuing of God, the restoring of God to the place he claims in our
reverence.

The Greeks met the problem by inventing the art-form of Tragedy,
the highest of all art-forms as dealing with the deepest of all problems.

The Jews faced it on an even higher plane: in the grand Bible
generation by the invention of the supreme images of the human race,
the Suffering Servant and Job; in the Rabbinic period by the coining
and phrasing of supreme categories in which a sublime solution is
compressed and enshrined, יסורין של אהבה and חביבין יסורין; and finally
in their history, with their own body, with their own living person,
as the most signal and paradigmatic sufferer. They are protagonists
in the most august drama, the making of man. They are the people
whose actual course of life furnishes the material for the apotheosis in
Isa. 53, and the image there conceived is so supreme that it was
borrowed and used to invest the central figure of the Christian religion.

Now what does transfiguration mean? Is it a word or a reality? What does it come to? What do the good achieve in taking over the sins and sorrows of the world, in a word by doing God's work for him?

The assertion of God in a godless world is the supreme act of religion. It is a continuing of the act of creation on the highest plane. It adds slowly to the area and substance of the Kingdom of God and to the stature of God, the translation of God as ideal and vision into the God of empirical embodiment and of power. Man in whom God's creative effort had achieved a provisional pinnacle, so to speak God's own self-consciousness of his aims, becomes from now on God's confronting partner, and the two together a re-enforcing polarity of give and take. They become allies in the most redoubtable of all struggles and for the greatest of all stakes. They are inevitably lovers, and both of them tragic heroes. But in a very real sense the fate of God and of the future rests on the heroism of man, on what he elects to do, for he is the manifesting God and the focus of decision.

The enormously difficult idea of growth, the idea that the reality of a thing can be still in the making and is to be found only in its fullness and completion, only at the end, not at the beginning; the difficult idea of the reality of time in which something genuinely new can come into being, that is, something not explicable merely in terms of what preceded: — these lead to the thought that God cannot possibly be anywhere but at the end, the קץ, the culmination or consummation. And a change in the very character of God must take place. This is due to the re-entrance into himself of the saints and heroes who have lived and died על קדוש השם, so that he becomes more and more like the best whom he has inspired, more and more a lover, from being at first primarily artist and dramatist. Without such an enrichment and deepening in the character of God himself there can be no intelligent religion for future mankind.

And tragedy from being at first a high necessity must in the event continue as mere necessity. It can become a danger, a danger of masochism or sadism, a danger cutting at the roots of life. It must be out-topped by humor, which redresses the balance and renders us sane. And humor leads to the final thought of the charge of Hybris, the charge of delusions of grandeur on the part of man. That thought is the serpent of skepticism sapping the lifeblood of all heroism. The charge of Hybris against man's high endeavor is Satan's most subtle seduction. But man must radically change in order to make himself immune against such seduction. He must stop being conceited in his outward bearing and impotent in his inward substance, as he is at present; he must be overwhelmed by humility in his outward bearing, because inwardly he is filled with a sense of supreme and decisive destiny.

2.

Love stands at the beginning, the lover's love which chooses one amongst many, the beloved's love which returns the love in single-hearted devotion, the love which is proof against the trials and sorrows that love brings in its train because of the hatred aroused in others. The capacity for love is the prime mark of genius, and love is the main means in discovering new areas of truth, in finding new regions of being, which no merely intellectual agency by itself could find. Hence the ecstatic utterance concerning love by the greatest name in all Christian thinking, Augustine: "I loved not yet, yet I loved to love. I sought what I might love, in love with loving. *Nondum amabam et amare amabam, quaerebam quid amarem, amans amare*" (*Confessions*, beginning of Book III). And the Song of Songs has been the classic text of all deeper religiosity from Akiba to Bernard of Clairvaux. "Thou shalt love the Lord thy God," "Thou shalt love thy neighbor," in a word, "Thou shalt love," — although it is known in sober fact that love is an emotion which cannot be commanded.

Our basic text here is accordingly taken from the Song of Songs: "For I am sick with love", כי חולת אהבה אני (2.5): I am love-sick, love has made me sick. Love can be so ecstatic as to invade normal physical health, and this initial paradox that even on the plane of the natural life what should be wholesome and salutary can, when it becomes intense, turn upon itself and threaten the life which it suffuses, this initial conjunction of love with pain, sounds the sombre keynote to all the higher phases of love. For unmistakably on the higher plane of the spiritual life love moves within the shadow of suffering.

The Midrashic exposition of this text unfolds the theme of Jewish history: "All the sicknesses which thou bringest upon me are for the purpose of making me love thee, or in order to make me lovable . . . . all the sicknesses which the nations bring upon me are only because I love thee . . . . . though I am sick thou still lovest me . . . ." (Cant. R., Romm, 15a, col. 2). It is the watchword of Jewish history: they hate me because I love you, and you love me though I am sick and stricken.

Our next text is likewise from the Song of Songs: "Many waters cannot quench love" (8.7). The love which binds together God and his chosen servant by reason of the infinitely precious gift which they together bring to the world, to a world unready and unwilling to accept it; the love which inevitably must subsist between God and his chosen servant in the face of the overshadowing and overwhelming antagonism of this world; the love which ties God and his servant together in closest union and mutual alliance: — that love is an emotion which the world resents and which it tries to dissolve by attempting to separate the two, to turn one against the other. But God's love for Israel is not to be quenched.

"Many waters: these are the nations of the world. Cannot quench love: the love which God bears to Israel, as it says, I have loved you (Mal. 1.2). Or, many waters cannot quench love: these are the idolators, for even if all the idolators were to assemble to quench the love between God and Israel, they would be powerless, as it says, Yet I loved Jacob (Mal. 1.2)." (Cant. R., Romm, 40a; Exod. R., Romm, 79a; Num. R., Romm, 7a).

Thus far the love which God bears towards Israel. But the love which Israel bears God has a far heavier burden to carry, namely disaster, death, martyrdom. How it is to fare under this shadow of death furnishes its most tragic and formidable task of transfiguration and re-interpretation, but they have in Akiba a master of love and martyrdom to speak for them and to set the tone.

Akiba speaks, in a poem in which this master of love and death sums up and transfigures the quintessence of his life. For the nations of the world which appear so eager for God in the poem are a fond anticipation of the poet and in present fact are the Roman executioners flaying him alive; and the God for whom Akiba is so utterly happy to die must surely be a wonderful God if he can so irradiate the martyr's face, though in actual fact that God is still unable to prevent the martyrdoms for his holy name's sake.

Akiba speaks: "I shall tell of the beauties and praises of God before all the nations of the world. For all the nations of the world ask Israel saying, 'What is thy beloved more than another beloved (Cant. 5.9) that you are so ready to die for him and so ready to let yourselves be killed for him? For it is said, "Therefore do the maidens, עלמות, love thee" (Cant. 1.3), meaning they love thee unto death, עד מות; and it is also written, Nay but for thy sake are we killed all the day' " (Ps. 44.23).

At this point in the dialogue the nations turn their gaze in admiration on the tragic heroic lover Israel, and exclaim "You are handsome, you are mighty, come and intermingle with us." But the Israelites say to the nations of the world: "Do you really know him? Let us but tell you some of his praise: My beloved is white and ruddy" (Cant. 5.10). Here the nations express themselves ready to join Israel. But

Israel in the stress and fervor of the emotion and in the language of
true love replies: "My beloved is mine and I am his," דודי לי ואני לו,
"I am my beloved's and my beloved is mine," אני לדודי ודודי לי (Cant.
2.16 and 6.3), i. e. you have no share in him. Any true lovers know
that love is a closed circle, love is lost in its object, lost to all the
world beside. And a mere request on the part of some admiring out-
sider to be allowed to join in, is felt to be, in the face of the red-hot
emotion, unreal and not authentic. Love must first be allowed to take
its own exalted course, and the rest, namely a universal sharing, will
come in due time (Mekilta, ed. Lauterbach, II 26; ed. Friedmann,
37a; ed. Weiss, 44ab).

And now we must put the crucial question. What is it that inspires
this love of Akiba-Israel? What new vision, what higher insight, has
slowly arisen and come to the fore to feed the fire and generate the
power with which to withstand suffering, — to enable man to love
God in a world in which God himself is still lamentably weak, a world
in which God and man both are only like heroes in some tragic drama:
defeated, and victorious only in the spirit?

It is a twofold insight of a new order of being whereby suffering
becomes transmuted and meaningful. In a series of images and parables
the thought is brought home to them in full self-consciousness, to
Akiba, to the rabbis, to Israel, to future men for whom these are the
prefigurations, that, in a growing world like ours, only when the old
self is crushed and broken can a higher self emerge, and only if we
transcend and forget the petty arithmetic of our private life and go
on to include and assume the burdens of others do we rise to a higher
life. This double insight takes the sting out of suffering and completely
inverts its status, raising it from madness to creative heroism.

R. Abba b. Yudan said: "Whatever God has declared unfit in the
case of an animal he has declared desirable in the case of man. In
animals he declared unfit the blind or broken or maimed or having a
wen (Lev. 22.22), but in men he has declared the broken and contrite
heart to be desirable."

R. Alexandri said: "If an ordinary person makes use of broken
vessels it is a disgrace for him, but the vessels used by God are precisely
broken ones, as it is said, 'The Lord is nigh to the broken-hearted'
(Ps. 34.19); 'Who healeth the broken in heart' (Ps. 147.3); 'I dwell
in the high and holy place, with him also that is of a contrite and
humble spirit' (Isa. 57.15); 'The sacrifices of God are a broken spirit,
a broken and a contrite heart O God thou wilt not despise' " (Ps.
51.19). (Pesikta 158b and Lev. R., Romm 11a, col. 2).

R. Alexandri's utterance is so sublime that even slight variants in

the text are to be noted. In Lev. R. the reading is אבל הקב׳ה כלי תשמישו
שבורים, "God's service vessels are broken"; in Pesikta אלא כל שימשיו
כלים שבורים, all of God's servants are broken vessels: the Pesikta
reading seems to be the fuller and the more preferable.

And it may be noted in this connection that the image, the concept,
the phrase "broken-hearted" enters the world-consciousness from these
verses in the Psalms.

We go on. " 'My beloved is unto me as a bag of myrrh' (Cant.
1.13)... Just as myrrh is the most excellent of spices, so Abraham
was the chief of all righteous men. Just as myrrh gives off its perfume
only when brought into the fire, so the worth of Abraham was not
known till he was cast into the fiery furnace".... (Cant. R.,
Romm, 12a, col. 2).

So we read in an English poet writing out of a religious mood:
"Must Thou char the wood ere Thou canst limn with it?" (Francis
Thompson, Hound of Heaven).

And back to our Midrash: "Just as oil is improved only by beating,
so Israel is brought to repentance only by suffering." (Cant. R.,
Romm, 6b col. 1).

When Abraham stayed at home he was like a flask of myrrh with a
tight fitting lid and lying in a corner. Only when opened and scattered
to all the winds can its fragrance be disseminated. Hence לך לך, go
and expend yourself. (Cant. R., Romm, 6b col. 2; Gen. R. 79 a Col. 1).

We now come to the famous group of parables on the text in
Ps. 11.5, "The Lord tries the righteous." The question is, why should
God try the righteous? The righteous do not need to be tried, they
are already "tried and true." It is the wicked who should be tried;
or are the wicked not even good enough to be tried? There is an
inversion here of what one would naturally expect.

"R. Jonathan said: 'A potter does not test defective vessels,
because he cannot give them a single blow without breaking them.
Similarly God does not test the wicked but only the righteous, thus
the Lord trieth the righteous.' R. Jose b. R. Hanina said: 'When a
flax-worker knows that his flax is of good quality, the more he pounds
it the more it improves and the more it glistens; but if it is of inferior
quality he cannot beat it at all without its splitting. Similarly the Lord
does not test the wicked but only the righteous, as it says The Lord
trieth the righteous.' R. Eleazer said: 'When a man possesses two
cows, one strong and the other feeble, upon which does he put the
yoke? Surely upon the strong one. Similarly the Lord tests none but
the righteous; hence The Lord trieth the righteous.' "

And in its purest, almost intolerably poignant form, the exquisite

phrase concerning the lover in the Song of Songs, "He feedeth among the lilies," is transferred from its erotic setting to the awesome tragic plane of the Divine Lover who by preference feeds among the lilies, that is, tries and breaks the tender and noble. . "God's rod comes only ·upon those whose heart is soft like the lily" (Cant. R., Romm, 19a). —
אין שרביטו של הקב"ה ממשמש ובא אלא בבני אדם שלבם רך כשושנים.

These pantragic parables have but one meaning: the good must bear the burden of the bad and the strong that of the weak. The parables occur repeatedly, twice in the Rabbot, twice in the Tanḥuma and once in Midrash Tehillim, so that obviously they were an inalienable possession of the rabbinic mind, part and parcel of the thinking Jewish mind.

The sentiment gradually established itself that it is a mark of the grandeur of man to be asked to bear more than his share of the burden; and by the same token that the supreme degradation of the low and the base is not to be thought worthy of being ennobled through bearing the sins and sorrows of others.

And this theme of vicarious responsibility and vicarious suffering, "in which the heavy and the weary weight of all this unintelligible world is lightened," no matter how honorable for the good and the strong and how derogatory to the drags and the burdens, rises to tragic sublimity in the passages which openly proclaim Israel's atoning martyrdom.

"As the dove stretches out her neck to the slaughter, so do the Israelites, for it is said, 'For thy sake are we killed all day long' (Ps. 44.22). As the dove atones for sins, so the Israelites atone for the nations, for the seventy oxen which they offer on the festival of Tabernacles represent the seventy peoples so that the world may not be left desolate of them; as it says, 'In return for my love they are become my adversaries, but I am all prayer' " (Ps. 119.4). (Cant. R., Romm, 13a and 23a).

A final set of phrases must be considered in which the rabbinic mind enshrined an answer without parable or argument. Such are the great lapidary utterances יסורין של אהבה and חביבין יסורין, "sufferings are a mark of God's love" and "sufferings are precious." They are question-begging, that is, in default of argument they are answers by fiat and decree, they are answers by heroism. The answer to the question why the good must suffer for the inadequacies of the world would be the fact that the world is growing, developing, and therefore inevitably defective, and there must be someone noble enough to assume the burden, as exemplification of a new insight, namely that nobility obligates, noblesse oblige. But the answer to the question as to what kind of a God there is in such a world is a baffling one, since the alternative is that he is unwilling or unable, and neither answer is palatable. Man in his grandeur therefore takes upon himself the odium or onus which would otherwise rest on God and brushes it aside, and the rabbis invent the sublime locution with its flagrant and obvious paradox יסורין של אהבה, sufferings sent by love, chastisements out of love, in which God is allowed to remain the lover, strange though that may sound, and man is willing to take over for him. That had already been the case in the supreme image before their eyes, the Suffering Servant of Isa. 53, the essence of which they sum up in their present phrase. God's love and justice may be veiled and obscured, but man stands forth as all the more heroic. He is willing to take over for God. For what sane mind would not regard as madness the assertion that love can manifest itself by sending sufferings upon the beloved? "And all men kill the thing they love, by all let this be heard" (Wilde, *Ballad of Reading Gaol*) is a saying fit for a crazed pagan penitent, not for the true religious soul. However, because of a crushing dilemma, the rabbis speak of sufferings sent by love, sent by God out of love; they transcend the rational calculus, they save God's face and honor, and they continue the sublime paradox by saying that sufferings are precious. What sane mind would regard sufferings as precious? What sane lover would mark his love by sending sufferings? It is a sublime ecstasy whereby man outdoes God, where man proclaims and postulates God in a world in which God as real power is barely emerging and where God's impotence has to be covered, as Akiba did, the greatest of rabbis and the greatest of Jews, who died with the אחד on his lips in the hope of making the אחד a reality in the world some day, and whose supreme legacy to those who are great among Jews and to all future heroic mankind is the injunction to be עשין מאהבה ושמחין ביסורין, to act out of real love and therefore to rejoice in sufferings.

These are the heights; and the willing acceptance of suffering remains the high-water mark of the religious spirit from Isa. 53 where the image is supremely conceived (and from there borrowed for the central figure of the Christian religion) on to Yehuda Halevi (the deepest Jewish soul of the Middle Ages) who, in words at once the most sober and the most mystical (*Kuzari* I, 115 and IV, 22), asserts that if the Jews were to assume their persecution and sufferings willingly and not merely as a necessary evil, the magic efficacy and sheer suasive power of that truly religious act would overcome nature itself and bring on salvation at once. But, as he recognized himself, it is a sublimity beyond man, it can hardly serve as an everyday pattern of conduct, and a deliberate cult of it would undoubtedly lie in the direction of the morbid. Suffering can be forced on us by fate, and then the best of us may hope to rise by ineluctable grandeur to the willing acceptance of it; but to envisage it as a steady goal is simply inhuman and is out of the question. That way lies masochism.

Hence we shall presently, under the guidance of the Rabbis, have to mark the limits of all suffering: — first, in the simple healthy humorous בשר ודם sense of who wants to suffer? but secondly also as cutting at the roots of life if (as is the danger of the best) it is raised to a tragic-heroic cult.

After that we can undertake as next step the great theme of man and God's mutual need of each other, their mutual implication and mutual cooperation.

However, before developing both of these themes we must bring to our attention God's own special suffering as the Rabbis conceive it: his weeping, his helplessness, his need of comfort. This is indispensable for a weighty reason: because it is the mythological form of expressing the philosophical thought of God's limited power in the world as it stands. In our Halakic creeds we may profess or assert theoretically an omnipotent God (as the great seer of the Exile facing the Zoroastrian dualists whose arguments surely struck home nevertheless insists on a single God though it makes God author of evil as of good, Isa. 45.7); but here in the realm of Agadic freedom we can afford to tell the truth as we feel it with the sharp sting of reality: God is a very finite God in the world of actual things. We can say it if only we say it in the form of images which are not binding as sober formulated creed but which have the supreme value of tacit admission and of irony. Hence the force and justification for the Agadic anthropomorphisms, the human all too human way of speaking the truth as one immediately feels it, and without definitive commitment to the letter.

Now let us look at the weeping God. First a general view: "When God remembers his children who dwell in misery among the nations of the world, he causes two tears to descend to the ocean and the sound is heard from one end of the world to the other" (Berakot 59a).

The weeping stricken God, who says of Israel "I am with him in his distress," עמו אנכי בצרה (Ps. 91.15), can be supremely distressed in his own person. The proems or introductions to Lamentations Rabba contain poems of great pathos and poignancy depicting this bowed and defeated God. It would be the shallowest of rationalisms to dismiss these as anthropomorphic vagaries. Anthropomorphisms are the device of our intelligence to say mythologically what we are afraid or unable to say in bald abstract prose: in the present case, that God and Israel are the emerging higher principle in a world not ready for them, in a world which is still vastly stronger than they. Let us listen to one of the poems.

"In the hour when God determined to destroy the Temple, he said, 'So long as I am in its midst, the nations of the world will not touch it; but I will close my eyes so as not to see it and swear that I will not attach myself to it until the time of the End (the Messianic era) arrives, then the enemy can come and destroy it.' . . . Thereupon the enemy entered the Temple and burnt it. When it was burnt God said, 'Now I have no dwelling place in the land; I will withdraw my Shekinah from it and ascend to my former place.' In that hour God wept, באותה שעה היה הקב"ה בוכה, and said, 'Woe is me, what have I done? I caused my Shekinah to descend for the sake of Israel, and now that they have sinned I have returned to my former place. Heaven forbid that I should become a laughing stock to the nations and a scorn to men,' חס ושלום שהייתי שחוק לגוים ולעג לבריות. Then Metatron came and fell on his face and said, 'Let me weep but Thou must not weep.' Then God said, 'If thou sufferest me not to weep I will go to a place where thou hast no power to enter and I will weep there, as it is said "My soul shall weep in secret places (Jer. 13.17)."' Then God said to the angels of the service, 'Come we will go, you and I, and we will see what the enemy has done to my house.' So God and the angels of the service set forth, Jeremiah leading the way. When God saw the Temple, he said, 'Assuredly this is my house and this is my place of rest into which the enemy has come and worked his will.' In that hour God wept. . . Then God said to Jeremiah, 'Go call Abraham, Isaac and Jacob and Moses from their graves, for they know how to weep' שהם יודעים לבכות. Then they all went weeping from one gate of the Temple to another, as a man whose dead lies before him. And God mourned and said, 'Woe to the King who in his youth succeeded but in his old age failed.'" — אוי לו למלך שבקטנותו הצליח ובזקנותו לא הצליח (Lam. R., Introduction 24, Romm, 6ᵇ col. 2).

The candor here leaves nothing to be desired. God's insistence upon the plain right of the grief-stricken to weep, however unbecoming to the dignity of a God, is especially touching. And as there is no greatness of thinking without audacity, the Rabbis go on to tell the truth about the whole business of comforting. First, it is a very doubtful business at best, of little value and efficacy; and secondly, if anyone can be said to be in need of comfort it is God, not Israel.

There is in the Pesikta de R. Kahana an entire section (ed. Buber, 123b–129a) devoted to homilies for the Sabbath following the Ninth of Ab, the so-called Shabbat Naḥamu, because the Haftarah for the

day is the great text from Isaiah 40, "Comfort ye, comfort ye, my
people." But in the midst of the comforting there is a sudden halt and
a complete about-face in mood, and someone invokes the text from
Job (21.34) "How then comfort ye me in vain? And as for your
answers, there remaineth only faithlessness." The prophets, namely,
at God's request, proceed to Jerusalem to bring the message of comfort,
but as each arrives with his word of consolation, Jerusalem listens
blandly and retorts with another utterance from the same prophet
flatly contradicting the first, whereupon the prophet has to retire
crestfallen. Ten of them by name, from Hosea to Malachi, make their
appearance in order and all receive the same treatment. They then
set forth in company to God, and say to him, "Ribono shel Olam,
Jerusalem refuses to be comforted." He answers, "Let us go together
and bring her comfort" (changing the opening words of Isaiah to read
not *Nahamu nahamu ammi* but *immi*, i. e. with me). And though God,
in addition to himself and the prophets, brings to bear all the powers
and agencies of the world on the same task, namely the upper and
nether regions, the quick and the dead, the life here and the life to
come, there is no indication that comfort is of any avail. On the
contrary, there is so little efficacy in comfort that God himself is
made the object of pity.

Our text proceeds with several parables the purport of which is
unmistakable. When a King's palace is captured by the enemy and
burnt, who is to be commiserated, the palace or the King? Surely
the master of the palace. So with the Temple. God says, "Who is here
in need of comfort? Surely I." Hence the opening words of Isa. 40
should properly read נחמוני נחמוני עמי, "Oh my people, comfort me,
comfort me." And if a King has a vineyard which the enemy captures
and lays waste, who is here in need of comfort? "Surely I," says God,
with the same refrain, "Comfort me, comfort me, my people." And
if a King has a flock of sheep that are attacked and killed by wolves:
again the same refrain, "Comfort me, comfort me, my people" (Pesikta
126b–128b, with supplementary notes).

But comfort either for Israel or for God is of little avail. Tragedy
can be overwhelming. In Pesikta Rabbati (138a–140b), in the passages
corresponding to those cited above from Pesikta Kahana, when the
culmination is reached, Jeremiah and Isaiah are made to vie with
each other, Jeremiah pointing to the agonizing wounds and Isaiah
uttering the words of comfort. But who can fail to feel the greater
force of Jeremiah's outcry, "Let it not come unto you, all ye that
pass by! Behold and see if there be any pain like my pain" (Lam. 1.12).
Tragedy can be so great as to forbid the wish for it to happen at all,

to anyone, not to man, not to God, for it cuts at the roots of life itself.

We had better round out this theme of the opaque limits to all suffering before we pass on to other related themes. And first the pathetic honesty of the Rabbis who cannot bear suffering when it comes as a visitation to their own body, even though they have preached its value to others when they were well themselves. "I want neither the sufferings nor their reward," says Hanina b. Hama to Johanan when the latter visits him in his sickness, although Hanina had urged the same on Johanan when the latter had been sick. No less than three stories with the same pathetic humorous refrain are told on the same page (in Berakot 5b) concerning three of the most distinguished rabbis. "Are the sufferings dear to thee?" asks the visitor who is well (and the sufferings should be dear, according to the theory), but the patient who is sick replies quite brazenly "Neither they nor the reward they bring," although he had been the comforter in a previous instance. לא הן ולא שכרן, or (in the Aramaic version in Cant. R., Romm, 19a) לא אנא בעי להון ולא לאגריהון, had thus become the standing concession to human frailty and human honesty in reply to the high demand of חביבין יסורין.

Transfiguration of suffering indeed, that remains the high task, the supreme achievement, of Judaism, but in the breathing spells there is also the recognition of the intolerable reality. "R. Hiyya b. Abba said: 'If a man were to say to me, "Give your life for the sanctification of God's name," I would give it, but only on the condition that I should be killed at once. But the tortures of the Time of the Persecution I could not endure" and the text proceeds to give in detail the horrors of Roman cruelty under Hadrian (Pesikta 87a and Cant. R., Romm, 16a col. 2). There must be a truce to suffering at the point when it cuts at the roots of life.

And that is expressed in two profound Agadic utterances. The one deals with Job. When God expresses himself as willing to hand Job over to Satan with the bare exception of life, Satan is shocked at the outrage, though it is Satan himself who has tricked God into the offer. "R. Johanan said: 'If it were not expressly written in the Bible, it would be improper to speak of God as behaving like a man whom others can seduce and who can allow himself to be seduced.' .. R. Yizhak said: 'Satan's pain was greater than that of Job, for God's offer resembled that of a master who orders his servant to break the cask but to preserve the wine'" (Baba Bathra 16a). The image of Satan himself secretly sympathizing with Job at the outrageousness of God's methods is one of superb irony. There is such a thing as racking a man up to the breaking point, but it is not for God to do so. Satan himself is better, at least according to R. Yizhak. — אמר ר' יצחק

קשה צערו של שטן יותר משל איוב משל לעבד שאמר לו רבו שבור חבית ושמור את יינה.

The second passage is on the text in Jeremiah (15.17). "I sat not in the assembly of them that make merry nor rejoiced, I sat alone because of thy hand." "I sat alone," says Israel to God, "but there are two kinds of being alone. I am well acquainted with the one and am quite content with it, namely to sit alone in devotion to Thee, to absent myself from felicity a while and for all while, to stay away from their circuses and theatres, to sit alone through all the successive hatreds of the world, alone and not alone, for I had Thee. But when Thou, for whose sake I sat alone, when Thou turnest Thy hand against me, then I am truly alone, alone and desolate" (Pesikta 119b, Lam. R., Proem III Romm 1b, col. 2).

From suffering, which is passive and enforced heroism, we turn to that high active life of which suffering is merely the necessary incidence, we turn to the partnership of God and man in the creation of the new world. This is in truth the peak and the dominating motif of our whole undertaking, for here the mythopoeic power of the Rabbinic mind is most clearly at work.

God and Israel need each other. They are partners in the same enterprise. Therefore he who hates Israel hates God, and if Israel is forced into exile by the powers which for the present overshadow both, God will detach his visible Presence, his Shekinah, from himself and send it into exile with Israel, to return to God only when Israel itself is enabled to return. The love which initially led the two to gravitate towards each other is a primal and opaque urge of the will; but once in operation the love must justify itself in fruits. "God said to Israel, 'You have made me the only object of your love in the world, so I shall make you the only object of my love in the world.' " (Berakot 6a). But Israel must continue to make God the only object of its love. And now read the mythos as to how God closes the circle in return for the love.

The passage is in Sifré on the text from Num. (10.35) "and let them that hate thee flee before thee." The exposition of the Midrash is as follows: "Has God enemies? It means: whoso hates Israel is as one who hates God. . . He who rises against Israel is as one who rises against God. . . . . And he who helps Israel helps God. . . And so each time when Israel is subjected by the empires, the Shekinah as it were is subjected by them. . . . And when it says (2 Sam. 7.23) 'Because of thy people whom thou hast redeemed unto thee from Egypt, a nation and his God,' R. Akiba comments: 'Had we not a direct Scripture it would be impossible to say it, namely this: Israel said to God, "Thou hast redeemed thyself" . . . And thus we find that wherever they went into exile the Shekinah went with them. . . They were exiled into Babylon, the Shekinah went with them . . . to Elam, the Shekinah went with them; to Edom, the Shekinah went with them. . . . And when they return (in the Messianic Age) the Shekinah will return with them. For it says (Deut. 30.3) 'And the Lord thy God will bring back thy captivity.' It does not say והשיב but ושב that is, God himself will return' " (Sifré, ed. Friedmann, 22b; ed. Horovitz, p. 81–3).

The doctrine mentioned last, the mythos of God's going into exile with Israel, or at least God's Indwelling Presence or Shekinah taking exile and captivity upon itself, and waiting for its eventual return or its full restoration to God on the heroic activity of Israel, becomes in later centuries one of the outstanding doctrines in the Kabbala, the great Agada which the Jews developed in the field of the esoteric. We shall have to give it more than passing notice presently.

We come now to the boldest, most forward-reaching thought concerning God in the Midrash, to that conception of God in which the Agada anticipates the most modern speculation concerning the nature of God and his relation to man.

It is this: that God depends on man for his strength and for his failure, for his growth and for his retrogression. In a world in which both are growing or in process, it is man who by his acts increases or decreases the stature of God.

There can be no question of our reading a modern thought into an ancient text: the texts are too unmistakable and unambiguous for that. And on the other hand there can be no asking whether this is the prevailing or predominant view of God in the Midrash. It is not; there is no one prevailing or predominant conception of God. But there can be no question of its presence, of its boldness, and of the full awareness of its boldness on the part of those who utter it. And in general a sense of the interlocking polarity, the mutual implication, of God and man, is one of the ever present features and convictions of the Agadic religious mind.

Let us now look at the texts.

"When the Israelites do God's will, they add to the power of God on high. When the Israelites do not do God's will, they, as it were, weaken the great power of God on high." (Pesikta 166a b and Lam. R., Romm 15a col. 2).

" 'Ye are my witnesses, saith the Lord, and I am God' (Isa. 43.12). That is, when ye are my witnesses I am God, and when ye are not my witnesses I am as it were not God." (Mid. Ps., Buber 255a; Sifré Friedman 144a; Pesikta 102b).

"Unto thee I lift up mine eyes O thou that sittest in the heavens,"

says the Psalmist (Ps. 123.1). To which the Midrash comments: "If
it were not for me i. e. if I did not lift up my eyes, Thou O God wouldst
not be sitting in the heavens." — אלמלא אני לא היית יושב בשמים (Mid.
Ps., Buber 255a; Sifré Friedman 144a, and note; Moore *Judaism*,
III, 181).

One is reminded of modern utterances in the same vein. Thus the
well known lines from the 17th century Baroque mystic Angelus
Silesius:

> Ich weiss, dass ohne mich Gott nicht ein Nu kann leben:
> Werd ich zunicht, er muss von Not den Geist aufgeben.

Or the more modern lines from Rainer Maria Rilke:

> Was wirst du tun, Gott, wenn ich sterbe? . . . .
> Mit mir verlierst du deinen Sinn.

There is no intention of blasphemy here, or of facile Hybris; it is
merely an expression of the thought that God by himself is an abstraction, i. e. an unreality, as of course man by himself is by the same
token abstraction and unreality. The real significance and value of
stressing the correlation, or as we shall say the polarity, between God
and man, is that in our opinion it is the only way, the only directing
guide towards an acceptable, credible and viable theology of the
future. Only if we distinguish God from the rest of the universe (*deus*
from *deitas*) as that part of the universe which not merely has the
insight and will but is also reaching out for the power to implement
its insight and will in order to realize the ideal; and only if we distinguish man from the anthropoid ape which he still largely is, as the
being correlated with God in the high drama of ushering into reality
a new and higher world: only then can the elements of a real authentic
religiosity, worthy of the future and adequate to create a future, have
rocm for deploying their power. Thus prayer as the communication
between two related powers (numerically two, not just autosuggestion
or whistling in the dark) becomes at least possible; thus the relation
between God and man becomes a beneficent circle of give and take,
each growing and profiting by the other; thus God and man can give
each other comfort and forgive each other their mistakes; thus God
and man can insist on an active program and a goal, rather than be
content with a gorgeous and infinite display of imagination and drama.

We turn back to other related texts which may be less challenging
in the wording but which are firmly and solidly founded on the same
high estimate of man's share in shaping the future. There is a text in
Kiddushin 40a, b (and in Tosefta Kiddushin I, 14) which is so expres-

sive of the Jewish ethos as to man's decisiveness with regard to the open and unshaped future of the world, that it was taken over by the Rambam into his Summa of Jewish doctrine and placed in the *Hilkot Teshuva* at the opening of his great code, and though it is a bold and subtle and ever modern thought it has become part of the Jewish religious outlook.

The text reads as follows: "The Rabbis teach: 'Let a man ever regard himself as if he were half guilty and half deserving; then if he fulfils one command, happy is he, for he has inclined the scale towards merit; if he commits one sin, woe to him, for he has inclined the scale to guilt.' . . R. Eleazar b. Simon in the name of R. Meir said: 'The world is judged by the majority and the individual is judged by the majority. If a man fulfils one command, happy is he, for he has caused the scale for himself *and for the whole world* to incline towards the pan of merit; and if he has committed one sin, woe to him, for both himself *and for the whole world* he makes the pan of guilt the heavier.' "

In taking over this old rabbinic doctrine, Maimuni not merely retains this cosmic implication of every man's every act at any time, but focuses attention upon it as constituting the main point of the doctrine. "Every man should look upon himself throughout the year as though his merits and failings were equally balanced, and also to look upon the whole world as though it were half deserving and half guilty. Now if he commit but one sin more, then by this simple sin he causes the scale of guilt to preponderate both with regard to himself *and to the whole world and consequently brings destruction upon it.* On the other hand, if he fulfils but one single commandment more, then by this single good deed he causes the scale of merit to preponderate both with regard to himself *and to the whole world, and consequently brings salvation and deliverance both upon himself and them,* as it is said, The righteous man is the foundation of the world (Prov. 10.25) וצדיק יסוד עולם, meaning that *he who acts righteously causes the merit of the whole world to preponderate and by this means brings about its deliverance.*" — (Hilkot Teshuva, III 4). זה שצדק הכריע את כל העולם לזכות והצילו.

The feeling or conviction, that man has the responsibility and the power to help decide the fate of the world at any moment, could hardly be stated with greater definiteness in a work which is not a formal treatise on metaphysics: a profound notion of the grandeur of man, and of the open future which he is free to make or to mar, of the unfinished creation in which he is a decisive factor, is obviously part of the rabbinic mind and of the Jewish outlook on life, whether they can formulate it in set academic terms and propositions or not.

We read it set forth in modern treatises, say in William James and his school of thought ("that the course of destiny may be altered by individuals, no wise evolutionist ought to doubt," *Will to Believe*, p. 99 and in the essays throughout the volume), but we fail to remember that the world's most memorable and effective thinking has been done informally and by way of intuitive insight and in the form of myth.

And to the myth we turn for a moment. The Kabbala and its later development in Isaac Luria of Safed and its adoption into Hasidism are beyond the scope of the present essay, but it would be a fatal omission while dwelling on this supremely important theme of man's rôle in the cosmos not to allude in passing to the profound and abiding significance of the Kabbalistic mythopoeic thinking on this subject.

Leaving aside the system of Gnostic Metaphysics or Theosophy which explains the relation of God to our present world of darkness and evil, let us lift out and state briefly that part of the doctrine which is relevant to our present purpose. The bold principle of man's responsibility for God's fate in the world, the influence of man through the acts of his life on the destiny of the universe, is felt to be in line with an age-old conception in Judaism, namely that man's heroism adds strength to God. Further, that the Shekinah is in exile and that it is man's function to redeem and restore it to God, now becomes one of the basic themes of Kabbalistic-Lurianic thinking. The process of restitution is called *Tikkun*, and essential parts of that process are allotted to man. The Jew has it in his power, through *Mitzwot* and Prayer, to accelerate or hinder the process. The *Tikkun* restores the unity of God's name. It is the true purpose of the Torah to lead the Shekinah back to her Master, to unite her with him. Prayer is a mystical action with almost magical potency in proportion to its intensity. Everything is in exile. But the Jewish exile, the Galuth of the Jewish people, is a mission to enable them to uplift the fallen sparks of the Godhead from all their various locations. That is why Israel is fated to be enslaved by all the nations of the world, so that Israel may be in a position to uplift those sparks which have fallen among them. The doctrine of *Tikkun* thus raised every Jew to the rank of protagonist in the great process of restitution, namely the extinction of the world's blemish, the restitution of all things in God.

The principle of the cosmic and metacosmic power and responsibility of man was never preached so proudly. Our world is the world of man. Man, in accordance with the original intention of his creation, is to be God's helper. All of freedom has gathered itself into man, he has the full heritage of freedom. All creatures and creation wait for him; God waits for him. All worlds hang on his works, all worlds look and yearn for the teaching and good deeds of man, for that concentration and intensity of acts and prayer whereby alone the Shekinah can be redeemed from its deep humiliation in banishment and united with God.

Man has freedom, he can choose God or reject God, he can lead the world to perdition and to redemption.

The creation of this being Man with such power of freedom means that God has made room for a co-determining power alongside of himself. Man is the cross-road of the world.

To ask whether God cannot redeem the world without man's help, or whether God has need of man for his work, can lead only to quibbling. In history we see that God waits for man. It is clear then that God has willed to use man for the completion of his work of creation and to allow him autonomy in that work.

For further development of these and related ideas the student can consult the great work of Gershom Scholem, *Major Trends in Jewish Mysticism*, and the popular essays on Hasidism by Martin Buber.

We here must pass on from this staggering and immense exaltation of man's function for God and the universe to the more sober and less mystical estimate, none the less high, of Israel's function within history. That more feasible function is to convert mankind to the One God. God is the great patrimony, God the special assignment or "burden" of Israel. Other peoples may have other special and indispensable assignments for the world's economy: the special concern, the special lot and allotment of Israel is God.

"If you do not proclaim my Godhead to the nations I will punish you" — אם לא תגידו אלהותי לאו׳ה הרי אני פורע מכם (Lev. R. Romm 10b col. 1). "God did a kindness to Israel in scattering them among the nations." Pesaḥim 87b. צדקה עשה הקב׳ה בישראל שפזרן לבין האומות.

"Hosea says (2.25): 'And I will sow her unto me in the land.' When a man sows a measure he expects a harvest of many measures. Thus God exiled Israel among the nations only in order to increase the number of proselytes who will join them" — (Pesaḥim 87b). לא הגלה הקב׳ה את ישראל לבין האומות אלא כדי שיתוספו עליהם גרים.

The proselytes are as dear to God as Israel itself. "It is written in Hos. (14.8): 'They shall return, dwelling under his shadow.' 'These,' says R. Abbahu, 'are the proselytes who come and take shelter under the shadow of the Holy One blessed be He... They become the root just like Israel.'.. God said, 'The names of the proselytes are as pleasing to me as the wine of libation which is offered to me on the altar...' " (Lev. R., Romm 2a col. 2 and many other passages in the Midrash).

The ingathering of proselytes in the fullnes of time is the theme of great hymns of the Synagogue, of the second half of the Alenu which concludes every prayer service, and of the magnificent ויאתיו which occupies a place in the Musaf of each of the High Holydays (ed. Birnbaum, pp. 373 and 801).

But that conversion and ingathering of the peoples is of course not the result of intellectual debate and argument, it does not proceed on the plane of peaceful dialogue and persuasion. The suasion is far profounder and bloodier. It is a matter of exemplary life, and its consummation is often a death of martyrdom. It is tragic suasion.

We are not going too far afield in summoning Yehuda Halevi as the witness to the kind and depth of suasion which Israel must practice to bring the world to its side, because he sums up the Jewish experience in this area. In a memorable passage in the Kuzari (IV, 23) he has recourse to one of mankind's supreme images, that of the dying seed. He likens the nations of the world to the soil, and Israel to the seed which is dropped into the soil and trodden underfoot and seems to be completely obliterated and destroyed. But it is only seemingly dead, dead for a greater and more glorious re-birth and life. By the magic alchemy resident within the higher form of the seed it transmutes the lower form of soil and loam into its own higher grade of life, and gradually a tree will grow up in which all will have a part, a single growth in which all will be embodied, due however to the active life-principle within the seed. And in the end those members of the tree which had looked down upon and despised it will acknowledge its supremacy, its inherent transforming power.

This characterizes the Jewish experience at its incandescent white heat, and there is a verse in the Ps. (109.4) which very properly is used as its summing up: "In return for my love they are my adversaries, but I am all prayer." תחת־אהבתי ישטנוני ואני תפלה. — There is definite awareness of what is later known as vicarious atonement, awareness namely of that heart and centre of the religious sentiment whereby we feel that we are all bound together and that the best of us are known by our willingness to bear the burden of the worst.

A formal statement of vicarious atonement occurs in several places in the Midrash, and we have already quoted one such representative statement (Cant. R., Romm 13a col. 1, and 23a col. 1). But there is also a more ominous and profounder touch, namely the intimation of why there should be suffering at all and how much of it must be borne until there can be a turning. Schelling, the last of the world's great theosophists, basing himself on Jacob Boehme and on Gnostic Manichean heresies with a deep sense of the rift at the very heart of things, declared that all evil must be tried out. This is a terrifying prospect for the bravest; and for the easy optimist and progressivist it is so disconcerting as to be unbelievable. But this is the view held in their own way by the Rabbis, and taken over from them by the Kabbala because of its deep sympathy with the tragic dualism informing the heretical Gnostic sects through the ages. It was God's decree that before the Messiah Redeemer can come, Israel must suffer banishment to all and persecution from all the seventy nations of the world. And when the Messiah's coming is prematurely announced they turn in wonderment to the Messiah, and he in the attempt to soften the dread decree re-assures them with the statement that even if only part of Israel had been made to suffer by only part of any one of the seventy Gentile nations (provided all are represented), it will be accounted as full measure both ways (Pesikta 47b, 48a, b and note 98; Cant. R., Romm, 16b, col. 2; Pesikta R. 71b).

There is indeed, both in the liturgy and in the Midrash, a frequent assumption of guilt to account for the suffering; but that is a magnificent and generous gesture of self-castigation which can be and has been misunderstood. The true view is, כי עליך הרגנו כל היום, "For thy sake are we slaughtered day by day." The suffering does indeed purify them from sins, but they are also the lamb כבש or the dove יונה on whom all evil and suffering must be tried out, because of some dread and ominous feature in the scheme of things whereby light can come only after all darkness, and goodness only after all evil, has had its day, and where the elect must bear the burden of the world by taking upon themselves all responsibility and all suffering.

That is the Jewish experience at its incandescent white heat, the truth as it concerns the "remnant" or ideal Israel, into which the great mass are lifted or dragged up in the peak dread moments of history. But the Jewish religion would not be the classic religion that it is, if it did not also have the poise and balance to take a humorous and honest view of the empirical everyday Jew in the broad breathing spaces of life.

Let us take four examples of Agada which give expression to the human, all too human, character of the Jew in four different phases.

The first is one of the most famous of all Agadot. Jacob is asleep out in the open with a stone for a pillow, and he dreams of a ladder propped on to the floor of heaven, with angels ascending and descending. Each angel (the guardian angel of some one people) goes up a certain number of rungs and then descends, but the angel of Edom (i. e. Rome) seems to go up and up without ever turning back. Jacob is afraid that the power of Rome will last forever. "Fear not, Jacob,"

God re-assures him, "even if he rises and sits by my side, from there I will cast him down."

That is the first great half of the story. Small Israel is pitted in a world-historic struggle against all the empires and against mighty Rome, and cannot be defeated in the end.

But the remaining half must also be told. God asks Jacob likewise to ascend. But Jacob is afraid, thinking he too will have to descend like the others. He does not trust God and refuses to try. For that lack of faith he is punished by the miserable oppression of his children throughout their exile, א"ל הקב"ה אלו האמנת ועלית לא היית יורד לעולם. If thou hadst had faith and ascended, there would have been no descent for thee. But now, since thou wast lacking in simple faith in God, thy children will be enslaved by all the four Powers of the world."

Thereupon he is again afraid that the oppression may last forever, and has to be re-assured again with the verse from Jer. (30.10–11): "Fear thou not O Jacob, neither be dismayed O Israel, for lo I will save thee from afar, I am with thee to save thee." (Pesikta 151a; Lev. R., Romm 42a).

The second Agada is even more poignant. The Israelites have just experienced the supreme event of history, the theophany at Sinai. Without further ado they lapse into the idolatry of the golden calf. Moses descends with the Tablets, but as he looks at them he perceives that the Ten Words have disappeared, have gone with the wind, the Tablets are a clean slate. He thereupon shatters them at the foot of the mount and is himself struck dumb and unable to utter a word. At that moment, a decree was issued concerning Israel that they would from now on have to study those Words (i. e. the Torah) in the midst of distress, grief and hunger.

באותה שעה נגזרה גזירה על ישראל שילמד אותן מתוך הצער ומתוך השעבוד מתוך הטילטול ומתוך הטירוף מתוך הדחק מתוך הטירוף מתוך שאין להם מזונות (Seder Eliyahu, ed. Friedmann, p. 117).

There is thirdly the profound legend of Joshua b. Levi's meeting first with Elijah and then with the Messiah himself who is stationed among the sick and the lepers outside the gates of Rome, himself also full of sores and wounds. All the others uncover all their wounds and then bind them all up again, but he uncovers and binds up each one separately, for he thinks "Lest I should be summoned and detained." Joshua b. Levi asks him, "When is the Master coming?" The answer is of the utmost pathos and irony, the single word "Today." Joshua returns to Elijah who congratulates him on the promise to himself and to all Israel. "He lied to me," is the Rabbi's response. "He said he would come today and he has not come." To which Elijah replies with a verse from the Ps. (95.7): "Today, if ye hearken to God's voice." — היום אם בקלו תשמעו. The Messiah could come any day if the Israelites would hearken to God's voice for one single day (Sanhedrin 98a).

The concluding Agada is in a sense the most disconcerting, for it seems to contradict the whole theory of Jewish suffering, namely that Israel suffers vicariously for the rest of the world and thus is the first and major bearer of the brunt of suffering. No less a person than Johanan has the following: "Any affliction in which Israel and the Gentiles are partners (i. e. equally affected) is an affliction, but any affliction of Israel by itself is not an affliction."

כל צרה שישראל ואו״ה שותפין בה צרה, וכל צרה של ישראל עצמן אינה צרה (Deut. R., Romm 103a col. 1).

It is obviously meant as a commonsense salutary correction of any morbid cult of martyrdom. It is not a contradiction of the unique signature of all of Jewish history, but it is a rare and isolated though all the more necessary caution urged by a great Rabbi against overdoing the cult of suffering. For who needs to be told that Israel has had afflictions, untold in number, all by itself, which were the most veritable of all afflictions?

There is one final theme to round out our present series of considerations: the sense of chosenness which the Rabbis have of the Jewish people as the centre of the whole economy of history, and the sardonic humor which the Rabbis have about it, in the attempt to maintain the chosenness as a matter of course and still to be fair with the other nations.

There are two famous passages dealing with this theme, in two of the oldest and most authoritative Midrashim. The one in Mekilta remarks blandly: "The Torah was given in the desert, in no man's land, in all men's land, for all to come and take if they so desired." It would seem that no one but Israel put in an appearance. (Mekilta Lauterbach II, 198; Friedmann 62a).

The passage in Sifré (ed. Friedmann 142b) is much more sardonic: When God decided to reveal the Torah to Israel, it was not to Israel alone that he revealed himself but to all the nations. He first went to the children of Esau and asked them, Will you accept the Torah? They replied, "What is in it?" He answered, Thou shalt not kill. To which they said, "The very essence of our father is killing, as is written 'By thy sword shalt thou live' (Gen. 27.40)." God then went to the children of Ammon and Moab and asked them the same question,

"Will you accept the Torah?" to which they reply with the same
question, "What is in it?" God is wary this time and he quotes a
different commandment, namely, "Thou shalt not commit adultery."
To which they offer the prompt reply: "Adultery is of the very essence
of their being," and they quote in support the story of the compound
adultery and incest of the two daughters of Lot with their father,
ending in the verse 'Thus were both the daughters of Lot with child
by their father' (Gen. 19.36), which children were Moab and Ammon.
God then sought and found the children of Ishmael, and by the same
procedure they hear that the Torah commands, "Thou shalt not
steal," to which they retort: 'That is the very essence of their forbear,
as is written, "And he will be a wild man, his hand will be against
every man and every man's hand against him.' " (Gen. 16.12). There
was not one nation among all the nations, our text continues, whom
God did not visit and knock at their door and speak to, leaving it to
those who were willing to come and receive the Torah. לא היתה אומה
באומות שלא הלך ודבר ודפק על פתחה אם ירצו ויקבלו את התורה.

The spectacle of God peddling the Torah from door to door is
edifying. The Gentiles had their chance. They refused a Torah which
interfered with their favorite pursuits.

But let no one think that the Rabbis indulged in the belief that
the Jews lacked their share of killers, adulterers, and thieves. Such
foolish beliefs are not feasible. And they are bothered to explain the
chosenness of Israel in the face of the common humanity of all men.
The chosenness, the special love God bears for Israel, seems beyond
reason. For are the Jews better than the others? Surely both are
sinners. There is no clear ground for a special predilection. Love must
be an aboriginal arbitrary choice, an opaque attraction.

Thus we read in the Midrash on the text in the Song of Songs
(8.8), "We have a little sister": "In the time to come, all the guardian
angels of the nations of the world will come and accuse Israel before
God, saying, 'Sovereign of the Universe, these worshipped idols and
these worshipped idols, these were whoremongers and these were
whoremongers, these shed blood and these shed blood. Why do these
go down to hell while these do not go down?' God will say to them
' "We have a little sister": just as a child, whatever it does, is not
reproved because it is but a child, so however much Israel may
be defiled by their iniquities throughout the year, the Day of
Atonement comes and atones for them.' " (Cant. R., Romm 40a
col. 2).

We see then, God can find no better reason for indulgent favor
towards Israel than the utterly arbitrary ground that it is an innocent

irresponsible child, for whom in addition the Day of Atonement restores innocence perennially.

Again: "In the time to come the guardian angels of the nations will come to accuse Israel before God and they will say: 'King of the Universe, these worshipped idols and these worshipped idols, these acted lewdly and these acted lewdly, these shed blood and these shed blood. Why then do these go down to Gehinnom while these do not go down?' Then God will answer them saying: 'If that is so, let all the peoples go down with their gods to Gehinnom, and so it is written (Micah 4.5), "For let all the peoples walk each one in the name of its god."' Said R. Reuben: 'Were it not written in the Scripture, it would be impossible to say such a thing, namely "For by fire will God be judged," כי באש ה' נשפט, (Isa. 66.16). It does not say שופט (judges) but נשפט (is judged)'" (Cant. R. 40a and Mid. Ps. Buber 11a and Mid. Ps. to 1:3).

So then all peoples, including Israel, go to hell, each one dragging his own god with him. And there in hell God saves Israel and delivers him; or can it be the other way? The grammar is somewhat tricky here. In any case the Rabbis are under no illusion as to any rational ground they can adduce for God to bear a special love for Israel. There is no reason for love, seems to be their conclusion.

And in truth chosenness is far more than love, it is ineluctable destiny: The individual Jew may drop away, but Israel as a whole is held inexorably fast. Thus Johanan, the prince of the Agada, has the following to say in explanation of God's ontological definition of himself as אהיה אשר אהיה, "I can be whatever I may be to individuals; but as for the mass I rule over them even against their desires and will, even though they break their teeth" (referring to Ezek. 20.33) אהיה לאשר אהיה ביחידים, אבל במרובים על כרחם שלא בטובתם כשהם משוברות שניהם (Exod R., Romm 11b col. 2).

And of course, even though chosen, God so far from playing favorites, imposes special burdens and special responsibilities on Israel. The prophet's stern reminder that special rights bring special duties ("You only have I known of all the families of the earth, therefore I will visit upon you all your iniquities," Amos 3.2) holds with equal force on Israel's later career. The protagonist must bear burdens commensurate with a protagonist's rôle.

### 3

In attempting to state in philosophic terms the main ideas at the core of the Agadot which we have been considering in this long middle section of our essay, certain sobering thoughts as to the value of philosophy must accompany us and must be set forth as premise. And they are, first, that whatever in philosophy is capable of translation or transformation into poetry is alone vital and valuable; and secondly, that whatever has orginally been conceived as myth is alone real and effective, for it is something capable of being believed and therefore loved. With that in mind we can proceed to state, in programmatic fashion, for whatever clarifying and pedagogic value it may possess, the main heads and captions of philosophic thinking present in solution in the Midrash and capable of being abstracted and formulated.

First there is the theory of tragedy implicit in the Rabbinic reflection on Jewish suffering, to be compared and contrasted with other theories of tragedy which have been set forth from academic and from pagan points of view.

Secondly there is the idea of man as the helper of God and co-creator with God, which carries with it implications in two important directions: —

First, metaphysically, to the effect that the future is genuinely open and not pre-determined in advance; that creation is unfinished and continuing; that time is real, against the claims of eternalism that time is an illusion and the perfect present at the start; and that all monism is wrong, meaning that the universe is not a homogeneous single whole and really not a universe, that there is a rift in it, that it is a pluralism or at least a dualism, and its unification in the highest sense has to be achieved, i. e. it is a growing world, a world in process.

The second implication under this important heading lies in the correct apprehension of the mutual relation of God and man: it is a relation of mutual polarity, of give and take or reciprocal enrichment, resulting in the slow change and growth not merely of man but of God, God needing man as much and owing as much to man as the other way about; resulting also in a plausible theory of prayer; and resulting finally in an activistic conception of life, as being more than a dream or a pageant of the imagination, but also more than the emptiness and nothingness which Catholic Christianity and Buddhism conceive it to be at bottom.

The final aspect of Rabbinic thought or reflectiveness and outlook which we single out in our theoretical formulation of its main features we shall call Humor, not of course in the sense of the comic or witty (the small humor), but on the contrary as one of the deepest elements in its attitude towards life (the great humor), something which has gone through tragedy and passed beyond, and is the concluding word in mellowness and perspective and ultimate serenity.

Tragedy arises through our sense of the contrast between what the good man ought to get and what he does get. What he ought to get is happiness; what he does get is pain, disaster and death. Supreme tragedy arises when the best man suffers the worst fate.

Tragedy thus upsets the initial view held as to the relation between virtue and happiness. The initial view is that suffering is a punishment for sin, and that virtue and happiness go together. This is the view, say, of the friends of Job in the face of Job's calamity. And say what we will, it is profoundly rooted; that virtue and happiness imply each other is a basic demand of our conscience. The disturbance which the primitive view suffers is only provisional; it persists after some thought-taking and sober readjustment.

Granted then that the suffering is not a punishment for sin, as must be evident to the thoughtful and honest person, the happiness still demanded to equal or balance the goodness is transferred to another world, it is reserved for a life to come. Thus traditional religion. But thus also philosophy. Kant at the peak of philosophy postulates a God to adjust the balance between our deeds and our rewards, also as assurance of the validity of the moral world-order. And in its last and deepest phase philosophy does not leave the sufferer to himself. The sombre view held by Royce (in whom Hegel culminates) is that the sufferings are taken up into the consciousness of the ultimate world-mind or Absolute, and as details or elements in that grandest setting are seen to be needed for the full experience of God, and are thus explained and justified. The good and the innocent are not allowed to have suffered for nothing. The tragic aspect of the good man's life serves a higher and highest purpose; the tears of the oppressed, דמעת עשוקים, will find their explanation and transfiguration.

But the true theory of tragedy rejects all this. The hero accepts the suffering not for any reward but for growth in greatness. The alleged transfiguration of the hero's suffering within the Absolute is felt to be a cruel farce; because, first, it is not clear how that transfiguration takes place and it looks like verbal juggling or self-delusion, and secondly even if it did take place it does not touch the main point, namely it does not undo the actual suffered anguish. It may be good for the putative Absolute, but not for the sufferer.

The tragic hero accepts whatever suffering that comes to him, as part of his greatness. He acts as the heroic focus of the world. His reward is that he grows in greatness.

With this conception of the grandeur of man which they have in common, the two highest theories of tragedy diverge in a final and supreme respect.

The highest pagan theory of tragedy (as summed up by Nietzsche) would say: the tragic hero ("der tragische Mensch") accepts all the agonies of life because of the wonders of life; if that is the price, he is willing to pay it. But there is no goal or plan and, of course, no God. There is a vast ocean of Becoming, and eternal recurrence, and finally "der tragische Mensch" to face it.

The Jewish theory of tragedy at its highest likewise puts the emphasis on man and man's intrinsic greatness. Man stands on his own and accepts his burden without any view of external reward or relief. Take the great tragic symbolisms and images which Judaism has invented. Thus the Suffering Servant: God is a poor figure in the background, allowing the injustice to be done. Job: God is clearly in the wrong and wins by browbeating. Akiba: God waits for Akiba to assert him, God; otherwise God is muted and impotent.

But the difference of the Jewish from the Pagan view is this: that, in spite of God's inadequacy or absence, the Jewish heroes all proclaim and postulate God, proclaim a belief in God in a godless world, and perhaps in that way help to call him into being and give him strength. That is a capital difference and makes of them the classic of the religious life. They see God through, and so give power to his emerging substance, whereas Prometheus, the greatest creation of Greek tragedy, brushes God aside and is content to be pure humanist and atheist. Man is sufficient unto himself, and the Promethean world-view is a humanism divorced and truncated from the vast background in which it is rooted.

What both views have in common is the refusal to be resigned, a certain activism or dynamism. But if, in the Pagan view, the tragic hero is ready and willing, for the sake of life's grandeur and wonder and beauty, to accept life's horrors and sufferings, even though it will always recur that way without abatement or assuagement, the Jewish view holds that the horrors and sufferings of life are man's task to convert, to make them over and make them other and make them less. God may just be emerging from the vast ocean of Becoming and therefore of little actual power (of great light but of little power); but man emerging with God and through whom God acts, will continue to say "Though God slay me (or suffer me to be slain) yet will I trust in him," (Job 13.15) and eventually there will be no more slaying. Men must be יסורין ביסורין ושמחין מאהבה עושין, they must accept יסורין and call them חביבין, they must save God's face by calling יסורין a mark of God's love, they must insist that there is a God because there can, must and will be one, and by that heroism will help to make God real and extend his kingdom. It will *not* always recur that way as the Pagan maintains; something *is* being achieved as our teachers maintain, namely the *Tikkun* of the world and the *Yiḥud* of God, the rectification of the world and the integration of God, through the labor of the God-inspired and God-bearing man.

There is a stupendous metaphysic of definite type and character implied, a certain kind of world presupposed, in all the various expressions of the Rabbinic mind which we have been passing in review and in Jewish thinking before and after. The Rabbis are of course not aware of any system, for they are not abstract thinkers nor philosophical system-builders; and if we try to lay bare and bring to the surface what is merely implicated and inherent, it may seem like an arbitrary imposition. But we are to remember that the creation is always first, and only after the actual finished achievement can one proceed to unravel the theory or rationale that has been at work in it. So in our present instance of Jewish creative thought we have a bold adventurous imagination making a magnificent anticipation of modern philosophy in its own terms of myth, parable and image; and what needs to be done for a later age to realize what is involved is to translate it into the idiom of abstract terms.

That Jewish thinking is temporalist, not eternalist, is clear to anyone who is at home in it. Eternalism occurs late in isolated cases as a result of mystical and philosophical influence. But, for Jewish thought the victory of God's cause is not a foregone conclusion, hence time as the medium of effort is the most real of things.

That creation is unfinished and that the future remains to be woven, is testified by the one fact of the Messianic ideal. This goal of all time and event has to be achieved and created through the most real and the bloodiest effort. That God has an environment and opposition is indicated by the fact that the unity of God is a postulate and has to be achieved through the whole course of time. "On that day the Lord shall be one and His name shall be one" is the prophetic utterance (Zech. 14.9) which is quite knowingly placed at conspicuous points in our liturgy (in the *Musaf* for Rosh Hashanah at the end of the *Alenu*, of the *Kedushah* and of the triumphant *Kol Ma'aminim* (ed. Birnbaum, pp. 337, 365, 371). On that day God shall be one, that is at the end of time, not before. And the act of making God one, the יחוד השם, is so real and bloody that the locution becomes one of the synonyms for martyrdom.

Of course the formal distinction between God and the rest of the universe (God's "environment"), between הקדוש ברוך הוא and מלך העולם is never made: that would run counter to all psychological need and religious habit. It is implied in fact but never admitted as theory. Only occasionally is there a deliberate identification of the two. Thus,

in the great nature Psalms used for the Friday evening services, the
God of Nature is identified with the God of Justice; the God of the
thunderstorm promises to come to judge the world with righteousness
(Ps. 96.13 and 98.9). And Maimonides identifies his Infinite Unknown
with the God of the Ten Commandments. But the Psalmist is a
gorgeous and sanguine anticipator of the End, and Maimuni does
flagrant and unabashed violence and outrage in forcing Plotinus into
Moses. Actual Jewish religious practice and thought has הקדוש ברוך
הוא fighting a valiant battle against the מלך העולם, mostly with pathetic
results.

The next theme, involving the correlation of God and man in a
polarity of give and take, of mutual influence and reciprocal enrichment, is the crucial chapter in any living and hopeful theology of the
future. If we are to avoid the two great failures and blind alleys of
religion, an utterly transcendent God and a self-sufficient and godless
humanism, we shall have to cultivate and develop the notion of
interaction between the two poles of the emerging higher world. They
must both do something for each other or they don't need each other.
All the various themes of this great area of religion fall into place on
the basis of such a theory.

Thus prayer as the converse between a soul and a great reservoir
of power: two centres dominating an environment and seeking each
other. They must of course find each other and meet; that is their
problem. That they can and do meet is the incontrovertible testimony
of certain souls, whose experience whether subjected to scientific
scrutiny in a book like James's *Varieties of Religious Experience*, or
speaking with unfailing success to all climes and ages and peoples in
so supreme a record as the Book of Psalms, is ample proof. What does
God give? Light and support for faith. What does man give? Faith
and added power.

If they help each other, each must be greater than the other:
that is not a paradox in a genuine polarity. God is greater as source
and giver of light. Man can be greater in what he develops and offers
as return gift to God. Abraham is better than God and tells him what
justice is. The Suffering Servant is more loving, Job more truthful
and courageous, and Akiba more heroic and godlike, than God. They
enrich God with new visions, make him realize his own possibilities
in them. There is nothing absurd in a product being superior to its
own ground or cause: that takes place in every creation. That is what
time and freedom are for. Creation is always inexplicable purely in
terms of what preceded, the effect is always more than the cause.

Only science operates with the initial stupidity that nothing can be gained or lost, that birth and becoming are always merely a reshuffling of given elements. Life is growth and growth is creation and creation is the wonder of something genuinely new.

Now the world gives birth to saints and heroes who are so much grander than anything the world contains that they alone confer upon it meaning and sanctity; and having given birth to them the world allows them to perish.

Here we stand at the crossroads. If we allow God and the world, God and the great creativity of the ocean of Becoming, to telescope together and act as one, we are in a bad way. What could ever change their course? We are where Nietzsche was: the eternal recurrence, an immense pageant of dramatic thrill, terror and beauty, but certainly no hope and no culmination in love and redemption.

But, if we distinguish between the two, we can begin to avoid despair, though the temptation to despair is enormous. Till now there has never been a saint or hero whom God has not allowed to die forsaken. Is the inference that the world gives the lie to the best and highest it produces and is therefore itself a heartless lie? That would indeed be a counsel of despair. Let us take heart and call that inference a *non sequitur*. There is one way out, namely that the creative God can learn through the re-entrance into himself of his highest manifestations, and grow into something as good as his own highest miracles. That would indeed be the most momentous event in all events, the supreme problem for any philosophy and theology to contemplate and the supreme truth to establish. And is it so inconceivable in a world really alive and growing that the great consciousness in which we all participate can receive back into itself and be enriched by its own highest spirits? God from being mere creativity must become light, and from being mere light must become person and from being mere dramatist must become lover.

So then God needs man to redeem and restore the Shekinah, to exemplify God's sublime possibilities, to translate God into the real, and to unify the new God with the old world. And if man needs God to forgive him for failings and shortcomings, God too must be forgiven for whatever share he may have had in the dread fate which is allowed to overtake the Suffering Servant and Job and Jesus and Akiba. It is no idle conceit when the poet addresses that God who is the מֶלֶךְ הָעוֹלָם with the words —

"For all the sin wherewith the face of man
Is blacken'd, man's forgiveness give — and take!"

The sacred heart of man fighting for a God may need forgiveness for its lapses, but must also grant it to a blind, heartless and stupid universe that knows not what it does, whatever Caliban-God or half-blind *élan vital* may be its sovereign.

There are two things further that we must take expressly to heart in this connection. First, that life is more than the mere pageantry which the Shakespearean imagination (a reflex of the divine imagination) would have it, and secondly, more than the emptiness and nothingness which a certain type of religion (Buddhism and Catholic Christianity) would assess it to be. "We are such stuff as dreams are made of and our little life is rounded with a sleep." "Out, out, brief candle, life's but a walking shadow." "All our yesterdays have lighted fools the way to dusty death." These are expressions of an imagination as comprehensive and totalitarian as the world itself, but which, lacking a dominating purpose or bias, ends in resignation and sadness. And when Bossuet speaks of *le vide et le néant au fond*, the nothingness and emptiness of all things at bottom; and when Buddha counsels us to renounce living and desire since desire forsooth ends as ashes in the mouth: they are both of them libellers and calumniators of the glory and wonder and thrill of living. Compare with that the "Go and do," the זיל גמור of the Hebraic hero, whatever language he speaks, Puritan or otherwise, and see which of the two you feel to be the spokesman of the world-spirit.

All these directions in which modern philosophy, in its last great almost contemporary representatives (Scheler, Berdyaev, and above all Whitehead), has been arriving at specific and new revisions of the old concepts of religion and philosophy, show deep kinship and elective affinity with the hidden but active forces of Jewish religious thought.

One last concluding respect we must not leave unmentioned because it is indispensable as rounding out any true and valid world-view, and that is Humor. We mean of course the great humor (as Höffding calls it), the final smile of serenity and understanding, the understanding that is close to forgiveness and acceptance, as experience comes full circle. The Jewish religious experience which has plumbed all tragedy, would end in madness without that final smile and forgiveness of the great humor. Humor sees the element of smallness that hangs on to all greatness, the shadow of pretentiousness it casts, no matter how genuine and authentic that greatness may be; and conversely the element of eternal value present in the most trivial and laughable individual. Humor is a final comprehensive judgment, a thought that comes after the sum has been cast up and the synthesis completed. The Jews regard themselves as the central figure in the whole economy of history, but make fun of it too. God had no special reason for choosing and loving them, but he did. How odd of God!

## V

The proper culmination for a study like the present is the idea of the Messiah. This is a supreme creation of religious genius, for it rests on two new religious insights, on two imperishable thoughts: first, that all men are one, and secondly that they have a future.

But before we go on to this culmination it is worth our while to pass in rapid review certain salient features of Rabbinic thinking in order to complete the picture, — to show its range of interest and to show how wholesome and honest and perennially fresh it is.

And first with regard to that desire or appetite which sets all our activities in motion, and which has such a bad name in almost all religions as the great inciter to temptation. The church name for it is *concupiscentia*, for which I suppose the proper English rendering is "lust"; and what could bring us closer to sin and evil than to follow every object and every direction which we lust after? The Hebrew takes a far more sober and healthy view. The term is *Yezer*. There can be good or bad *Yezer*, but even the bad is good, for *Yezer* means drive, power, indispensable motive force for all action, and with the suppression of Yezer we would have the extinction of life. This is an immense anticipation of modern psychology, an intuition of the very dynamic of life itself.

The opinions and utterances of the Rabbis on this subject of desire and of the field in which it chiefly operates, namely love, constitute one of the most fascinating chapters in the entire range of the Midrash. It is a chapter not indeed extensive or overdone, because the Jews do not make a special cult of love, but it is of vast importance for the understanding of Jewish life and, whenever the Rabbis touch on it and whatever they say, their attitude is always of great depth and interest. The relation of the two sexes in the marriage bond, the importance of children, the intrinsic right of love but also its subservience, the lure of love and its limitations, all the subtle dialectic of love when allowed free course, the temptations which love by its special nature involves for both sexes and the corresponding loyalties and devotion for both sexes, all together constitute a most significant contribution to this great central theme of life and the creation of life. We shall have to content ourselves however with two bare statements. First, the famous utterance "The greater the man the greater his libido" (in Sukkah 52a, as conclusion of a most interesting story). And secondly, the equally famous and bold utterance of R. Samuel b. Naḥman. When the Divine Workman reviewing his six days' labor of creation remarks "And behold it was very good," Samuel b. Naḥman interprets these words of approval as referring to the evil *Yeẓer*. For, he argues, without the evil *Yeẓer* so-called, no man would build a house nor marry a wife nor beget children nor transact business. And he quotes the verse in Eccl. (4.4) concerning "all labor and all excelling in work, that it is a man's rivalry with his neighbors" (Gen. R., Romm, 24b col. 2). Without this rivalry and ambition, without libido and appetite, the business of the world and life itself would come to a standstill.

Education must be the prime concern of any people that wishes to conserve its distinctive character, but quite especially of a people trying to maintain itself without the usual aids of a land and government of its own and trying to conserve a high and unique character under these unusually difficult conditions. Such a people must bend every effort towards shaping and fashioning the soul of its offspring so as to make sure of its future. For education means primarily children and children mean primarily future. And it is this will to the future which marks it off from other peoples, and makes it regard the future as greater than any past no matter how great that past has been. This superlative valuation of a past which must at all costs be conserved, and at the same time the refusal to be overwhelmed by it, the due regard for future creativeness and future responsibility, is likewise a salient feature of Rabbinic thinking. Self-creation at all times, education in this most intense and incisive sense of the will to continued life, is a profound mark of the authentic Jewish character.

Let one Midrash speak for many. "When Israel stood to receive the Torah, the Holy One, blessed be he, said to them: 'I am giving you my Torah, bring me good guarantors that you will guard it.' They said: 'Our fathers are our guarantors.' The Holy One, blessed be he, said to them: 'Your fathers are unacceptable to me... Yet bring me good guarantors and I shall give it to you.'.. They said: 'Master of the Universe, our prophets are our guarantors.' He said to them: 'The prophets are unacceptable to me... Yet bring me good guarantors and I shall give it to you.' They said: 'Behold, our children are our guarantors.' The Holy One, blessed be he, said: 'They are certainly good guarantors. For their sake I give the Torah to you, as is written, "Out of the mouths of babes and sucklings hast Thou founded strength" ' (Ps. 8.3) (Cant. R., Romm, 7a).

Honesty in looking the facts in the face, the refusal to indulge in "soft soap," in lush and saccharine prospects and promises, is another characteristic of the Rabbinic outlook. In the end this stern realism pays off better than the love assurances which the tender-minded so eagerly look for. For these are invariably boomerangs. When today the word is handed out by means of all the instruments of mass communication, during a so-called religious hour, that God is love, what can that mean to the hundreds of millions of the human race for whom the opposite is true? It would be truer to their experience to say that God is wrath or that God is hate. That which should be a sublime goal is changed into a sordid makebelieve, and all honest effort and honest emotion falsified.

We all have to face two ineluctable facts: first, that each one of us is born into a certain status or condition with which we must reckon from the very start: we are born either white or black, bond or free, handsome or ill-favored, gifted or mediocre, and our life is decided for us three-fourths of the way in advance. Secondly, there is no forgiveness for our mistakes: everything is collected, everything paid for, everything recorded, nothing erased, nothing forgiven. Let the Midrash speak its mind on these two themes.

On the text at the beginning of Genesis that "God created the heaven and the earth and the earth was *tohu* and *bohu*," there are two Midrashic parables in which the strange words describing the earth are taken to mean "bewildered and astonished." "R. Abbahu said: 'This may be compared to a king who bought two slaves on the same bill of sale and at the same price. One he ordered to be supported at the public expense, while the other he ordered to toil for his bread. The latter sat bewildered and astonished: 'Both of us were bought at the same price,' exclaimed he, 'yet he is supported from the treasury whilst I have to gain my bread by my toil!' Thus the earth sat bewildered and astonished, saying, 'The celestial beings and the terrestrial ones were created at the same time: yet the celestial beings are fed by the radiance of the Shekinah, whereas the terrestrial beings, if they do not toil do not eat. Strange!'"

R. Yehuda b. R. Simon said: "Compare this to a king who bought two bondmaids, both on the same bill of sale and at the same price. One he commanded not to stir from the palace, while for the other he decreed banishment. The latter sat bewildered and astonished. 'Both of us were bought on the same bill of sale and at the same price,' she exclaimed, 'yet she does not stir from the palace while against me he has decreed banishment. How passing strange!' Thus the earth sat bewildered and astonished, saying, 'The celestial and the terrestrial beings were created at the same time: why do the former live forever whereas the latter have to die?' Hence, 'And the earth was *tohu* and *bohu*,' bewildered and astonished.''

The earth sat bewildered and astonished at the initial inequitableness in the distribution of gifts.

On the text in Joel 2.13 "Turn unto the Lord your God, for he is gracious and compassionate, long-suffering and abundant in mercy and repenteth him of the evil," the Rabbis comment as follows: R. Johanan says, "God is long-suffering before he collects, but once he begins to collect he takes a long time in collecting." מאריך רוחו עד שלא ינבה, בא לנבות מאריך וגובה. R. Hanina says: "He who says that God is lax, his bowels shall be relaxed. He is long-suffering but He exacts his due." א'ר חנינה מ'ד רחמנא ותרן הוא יתוותרון בני מעיו אלא מאריך רוח וגובה דידיה — (Pesikta 161b; Yer. Taanit 65b).

And similarly in the solemn description of the Judgment contained in the famous נתנה תוקף prayer which is the highlight of the *Musaf* for Rosh Hashanah and Yom Kippur, God is described as judge, prosecutor, expert and witness דיין, מוכיח, יודע ועד; and if God is all that in one, it can hardly be called a fair trial, not to say a sympathetic or indulgent hearing. So likewise the Greek proverb concerning anyone who undertakes to appear in a trial before Zeus: Jove's dice are always loaded. Διὸς κύβοι ἀεὶ εὐπίπτουσι. The court is packed, the gods are always right.

With that situation in mind, the old proverb is thrown up to God "not to pull the rope at both ends." R. Levi said: "If it is the world thou seekest, there can be no justice; and if it is justice thou seekest, there can be no world. Why dost thou grasp the rope by both ends, seeking both the world and justice? Let one of them go, for if thou dost not relent a little, the world cannot endure" (Pesikta 125 b. Gen. R. Romm 79b, col. 1).

To which the proper sardonic retort on the part of God would be the variation he gives in the Midrash of the words he utters through Jeremiah. Jeremiah makes Him say "They have forsaken me and have not kept my Torah" (16.11), but in the Midrash God takes the liberty of changing that into the bold invitation, "Would they had forsaken Me, provided they had only kept My Torah." The permission to neglect the religion if they would only practice the morals, is interesting and not so generous as it sounds. For he goes on to add, "The leaven or ferment in the practice of the good would have brought them back to Me" (Pesikta 121a). And that is true. Ethics inevitably leads in the end to religious assumptions: the fate of the good, and of the good man, can never content itself with the defeats this life offers. It demands conservation; it has to have the faith that the best things are also the most eternal. And the dialectic which subsists between the good and the religious is of deep concern to us all and needs to be understood. A man can be said to believe in God only insofar as it is an inference from his behavior, and then his saying so is unimportant. He can say he believes in God and really be an unbeliever and denier by his life. He can in rare cases say he does not believe in God and still have his life belie the denial: there have been great saints who were indifferent to professing God, such were men like Shelley and Eugene Debs and John Stuart Mill and others who were rooted in the divine no matter what they said. The last mentioned is particularly interesting because he is a confirmation of the text in the Midrash. His posthumous "Three Essays on Religion" land in religious belief after a lifetime of agnosticism and freethinking, because his profound interest in the good forced him into religious assumptions, and that is a phenomenon of utmost interest to all students of this question.

We come at long last to the Messiah. This is indeed the zenith or dazzling sun in the whole firmament of Jewish religious thinking. As the prophets had lifted religion from a tribal and particularistic basis to the plane of justice and goodness, and so made it the concern of all men, and indeed thereby discovered the idea of a single man-kind, so the figure and image of the Messiah is the coping stone of that structure. He was indeed originally conceived in national terms as savior and redeemer of the Jewish people, but he presently becomes the savior and redeemer of the world by ushering in a reign of peace and welfare for all men. He heals the wounds of the sorest and most afflicted people, and that is possible only after all other and lesser afflictions have been healed. He is the light of the world, the concrete but symbolic embodiment of the Kingdom of God on earth.

And epoch-making in the maturing of human thought as is the idea of a single mankind, the idea of the future as replacing a golden past is equally decisive in marking the passage of mankind from childhood to manhood, from dreams and nostalgia to hardihood and achievement.

And this is also the line of cleavage between Christianity and Judaism which, starting from a common source, part company on this crucial and fateful question as to whether the Messiah is still to come or has already come. Christianity, by throwing in its lot with the childhood of the race, condemns itself to its immature mythology; and Judaism by severing itself from powerful protection adds woefully to its already tragic lot. The real accentuation of its tragedy stems from a brother's hatred.

What does the Messianic future promise? Everything from the

abolition of war to the abolition of death, i. e. beginning with something so feasible as to be on the agenda of the council of nations today, and ending with something so utterly transcendent as the assault on the citadel of perdition itself.

Naturally the temptation to indulge the fantasy in picturing relief from human miseries is very strong, but it will be found on examination that, in the recital of Messianic measures, the note of sober sense and steady thought prevails even when it seems to hover on the borders and realm of the fantastic.

And first of all the authorized spokesmen for Judaism stress the note of feasibility. Thus Mar Samuel, most sober-minded of Rabbis: "There is no difference between the present world and the days of the Messiah except the oppression by the great kingdoms alone" (Berakot 34b). And Maimonides, who sums up Jewish tradition as no other, adopts and quotes these very words at the end of his code (Hilkot Melakim XII 2). And he says expressly there will be no change in the course of nature, no thaumaturgy, no חדוש במעשה בראשית אלא עולם כמנהגו נוהג (*ibid*. XII 1). The only change will be the absence of hunger, war, envy, and hatred and, in their place, an economy of plenty, so that all will have the leisure to devote themselves to the study of religion. — ובאותו הזמן לא יהיה שם לא רעב ולא מלחמה ולא קנאה ולא תחרות שהטובה תהיה מושפעת הרבה וכל המעדנים מצויין כעפר ולא יהיה עסק כל העולם אלא לדעת את ה' בלבד (*ibid*. XII 4).

These are so to speak Halakic utterances; let us take a glance at the Agada, which allows free scope to imaginative flights. There is an extensive passage in Exodus R., Romm, 29b, describing the ten things which God will "renew" in the Messianic era. The first three are concerned with healing: a greater sun, healing waters, and healing fruits. The fourth deals with the re-building of all waste cities, including Sodom and Gomorrah. The eighth promises no more weeping or wailing, and the tenth likewise, presumably through the abolition of the main causes of wailing and weeping, namely sickness, poverty, hatred and war. So that six of the ten are quite feasible ideals in the program.

The sixth preaches peace in the animal world ("The cow and the bear shall feed together" Isa. 11.7), and the seventh a covenant between Israel and the whole animal world. The fifth is the re-building of Jerusalem, the light of the world, in sapphires. There remains only one more, the ninth, which promises the abolition of death. There are thus only four beyond the realm of the soberly plausible.

As for the sapphired Jerusalem resplendent in light, it is a naive physical rendition of the higher and more difficult thought of "nations shall walk by thy light" (Isa. 60.3).

As for the peace in the animal world it is but an extension, a kind of shadow or reflex, of the peace in the human world. If nature is red in tooth and claw, that holds as much for human nature as for animal nature. The human has been animal so far, and if the human is to get humanized, why not indulge in the further fantasy of the animals getting humanized? If ever poetic license is to be indulged it would be here; it is pathetic and touching to wish the good to invade the animal kingdom itself.

There remains the frank mythology of abolishing death. But even that, with all its proud vaulting surge, or rather because of it, has a deep foundation in sober thought. If the vanishing and perishing of the good is felt to be the heart of evil; if the complete loss of the heroic soul, of the loving soul, of heroism and of love (of "values" as they are heartlessly called in the schools) would be the supreme evil; if the true synonym of evil is death — then death must go. "He hath swallowed up death forever" בלע המות לנצח, (Isa. 25.8) then becomes the proudest, the clearest, the most important demand in religion.

From a far different source and in a different mood, but nevertheless as confirmation, we have the vision of a pagan soul:

"As a god self-slain on his own strange altar
    Death lies dead."

When will the Messiah come? First and foremost when we have made ourselves ready and worthy, and this primarily through conduct and behavior, through changing the past into ripeness for the future. In Hebrew grammar the *vav* conversive changes a past into a future, and the Midrash makes use of this peculiarity of the Hebrew language by making it bear a creative Messianic meaning. The Messianic age will come when a change has been worked on the past, it is something that has to be achieved and earned, and the pivotal words are והיה ביום ההוא, "and it shall come to pass." In Genesis R., Romm, 137a, col. 2, on the words of Jacob (Gen. 28.21), ושבתי בשלום אל בית אבי והיה ה' לי לאלהים, where the two preterite verbs have a future meaning, R. Levi remarks: "God took the manner of speech used by the Patriarchs and made it a key for the redemption of their descendants. Thus God said to Jacob: 'Thou hast said, "Then shall the Lord be (*we-hayah*) my God." By thy life, all the benefits and blessings and consolations which I am to confer upon thy children (in the Messianic age) I will confer with this very expression (*we-hayah*). As it says, "And it shall come to pass (*we-hayah*) in that day that living waters shall go out from Jerusalem (Zech. 14.8)"; "And it shall come to pass (*we-hayah*) in that day that the Lord will set his hand the second time to recover the remnant of his people (Isa. 11.11)"; "And it shall come to pass (we-hayah) in that day that a great horn shall be blown etc. (Isa. 27.13)." ' "

There are of course many other passages making good conduct the specific condition of the coming of the Messiah, in fact the nearness and remoteness of his coming directly dependent on the height and depth of Jewish behavior. But the wait is long and trying, whilst at the same time the eagerness and readiness must never be relaxed. On this theme there is a pathetic and humorous Midrash in Sanhedrin 97b to the following effect: Do not rely on those who compute the exact date of the Messiah's coming, since dates innumerable have been fixed but passed without his coming, so that you may in the end believe he will never come. You must on the contrary trust the Prophet (Habakkuk 2.3) who enjoins us to wait no matter how much he tarries. It cannot be that we expect his coming and he himself does not expect to come. But supposing both Israel and the Messiah desire his coming, what is there to stop it? The answer is, the Attribute of Justice מדת הדין. But if that is the case, why should we keep on waiting? The answer is, לקבל שכר to receive reward: it is good to wait ("they also serve who only stand and wait"), since the prophet tells us "happy are all they that wait for him," (אשרי כל חוכי לו, Isa. 30.18).

The second condition of the Messiah's coming, next to conduct, is the more sombre and ominous one of fulfilling the measure of suffering. Israel must be exiled to all nations and be oppressed by all peoples. We have already heard the Gnostic-Manichean-Jacob Boehme-Schellingian version of the same view: all evil must be tried out in this most tragic-heroic of all worlds before there can be a definite turning. To the eternal glory of Israel be it said that they themselves record and accept this terrifying burden for themselves, professing that a part of the sufferings will serve to purify them of their sins, and the rest are a free gift of atonement to the world by its suffering servant.

The last mark of the Messianic age will be that all men will speak one language. Men spoke a single language at the beginning, namely Hebrew. Then came the confusion at the Tower of Babel, the division of mankind into seventy warring tongues and peoples. The final language spoken will also be one, not one indeed as single linguistic idiom, but one in clarity and sincerity and mutual understanding, namely the שפה ברורה, "the pure language" of the Prophet's promise (Zeph. 3.9) (Tanhuma, Buber I, 28b; ed. Singermann, p. 78). That is the final sign and seal of the unity of human kind.

## CONCLUSION.

The world is young, not old, as the prematurely aged youthful Utopist poet sang because he could not wait. "My Father Time is old and gray with waiting for a better day," says Shelley and dies before his time. The world is young, history has hardly begun, and those who have helped to lay its foundations and have a mind towards the future must bethink themselves how they may perdure through a boundless future in order that they may contribute towards the further building and maturing of historic event. Individuals die, and nations may die but need not die, for nations are not (except by the veriest figure of speech) a concrete physical organism which is perforce doomed to die. On the contrary they may renew their youth perennially, and the ancient Jewish prayer חדש ימינו כקדם, "Renew our days as of yore," is a vivid reflection of this conviction.

However, the art of renewing a nation's days as of yore must be extremely rare and difficult, since it has been so rarely tried with success, and the rhythms and vicissitudes of a nation's life are by no means cumulative and conserving in one progressive direction. Perennial crisis may be said to be the mark of all life, and most peoples have succumbed, and where they have not succumbed they have become stagnant — weary, stale, unprofitable (witness the old China and India).

A tragic destiny has served to keep the Jewish people lean and alert. It has been bad for the nerves but good for the soul. But there are constant imminent dangers; as of today, urbanization, over-sophistication, almost complete absorption into a bourgeoisie, loss of self-respect, loss of belief, and loss of the tragic-heroic sense of destiny. These are dangers which in the case of any other people would be felt as decisive, radical, insuperable. But the Jewish people has always lived in an atmosphere of extremes and not by rules but by exceptions. The incidence of decimation and attrition has been enormous throughout its history; it is the descendant of the minority of minorities; it has always felt its centre of gravity to reside in a "remnant," in an ideal Israel which, like the bird Phoenix, has risen from its own ashes. Heroic measures are needed, but heroic measures will be found by the new great Jewry of this country on which the fate of future Judaism so largely depends.

The heroic measure consists in nothing short of a renewal of life, the rejuvenation of the old life, and we can proceed to specify its elements. First, the warmth of emotion in which alone the religious sentiment can find refuge and love; and religion is one name for that renewal of life. Mythology is another name for it: a high mythology, a high sense of mission, a cult of the Jewish People, like the cult of Jesus in the Christian religion, as incentive to further greatness because of the greatness already given; further, the emotions which feed the sense of calling and distinction, such as tragic protagonism in a heroic drama. Jews need such a climate of the mind to be wooed back to their faith, to feel pride in it and to spearhead it into the future. We need something to believe and love, a great mythos about ourselves, such as we have had since God spoke to Abraham, and such as has continued through Ezekiel's vision of the dry bones' coming to life and Yehuda Halevi's parable of the dying seed transforming the world's soil and mud into a glorious tree: a credible and viable mythos capable of being embraced and loved. I quote in praise of mythos a thinker and poet who has meditated on a similar problem for his own people.

"By myth I do not mean a fiction," says William Butler Yeats, "but one of those statements our nature is compelled to make and employ as a truth though there cannot be sufficient evidence. . . Myth is not a rudimentary form superseded by reflection. Belief is the spring of all action; we *assent* to the conclusions of reflection but *believe* what myth presents; belief is love, and the concrete alone is loved; nor is it true that myth has no purpose but to bring round some discovery of a principle or a fact. The saint may touch through myth the utmost reach of human faculty and pass not to reflection but to unity with the source of his being." (Wheels and Butterflies, N. Y. 1935, pp. 91, 121).

# Hermeneutical Systems of Hillel and the Tannaim: A Fresh Look

## W. SIBLEY TOWNER
### Union Theological Seminary, Richmond, Virginia

Every community which regards as normative certain texts given by the worthies of old must develop a "hermeneutic," a means whereby these fixed standards can be kept in an effective relationship with the ever-changing frontier of day-to-day experience. In the two centuries surounding the turn of the era, six factors impelled Rabbinic Judaism toward the elaboration of a hermeneutic far more self-conscious than anything previously known: the canon of the Scripture was fixed; a body of authoritative Torah not part of that canon had to be kept in fruitful relationship to it; the institutions of *Bet-Kenesset* and *Bet-Midrash* emerged as settings suitable for carrying on the hermeneutical task; sectarian competition increased the urgency for an explicit hermeneutic; Hellenistic culture offered models from its own interpretive tradition; and the normative role of the Temple in religion ceased.

Out of this period emerged a sophisticated system of "hermeneutics," or praxis of interpretation. The essay reviews the traditional lists of seven and thirteen *middot*, together with other methodological devices not part of the lists, and — with the help of illustrations drawn from *Mekilta de R. Ishmael* — offers a logical and literary analysis of each one. A comparison of the results of these analyses with hermeneutical devices found in both Old and New Testaments and in the larger Hellenistic milieu leads to the conclusion that the system of Rabbinic hermeneutics was *sui generis*, and was the indigenous response of the Tannaim and their immediate successors to their own urgently felt need for an effective hermeneutic.

The purpose of this essay is to describe and briefly to interpret the hermeneutical methods employed by the Phariseees and their rabbinic successors in the first two centuries of the common era. However, in order better to appreciate the issues which underlay the rabbinic quest for viable hermeneutical praxis or "hermeneutics," some introductory words must be addressed to the broader question of "hermeneutic."[1] The task of hermeneutic can be expressed very simply: it is to "re-present" the message of the authoritative text in the language and thought-forms of the current

---

(1) Cf. James M. Robinson, *The New Hermeneutic. New Frontiers in Theology*, vol. ii (New York, 1964), pp. x, 1–77, for a discussion of this distinction. A lucid introductory treatment of the issues of rabbinic "hermeneutic" and "hermeneutics" is given by Daniel Patte, *Early Jewish Hermeneutic in Palestine* (Missoula, Mont., 1975), pp. 1–8.

generation.[2] In contrast to exegesis, the task of which is simply to make sense of the text in its own terms and context, the task of hermeneutic is to "prolong in a new discourse the discourse of the text."[3] It is to find "valid contemporary meaning in ancient texts."[4]

A hermeneutical problem exists in any cultural context whenever two factors are present. First, an authoritative text, a written document usually of some antiquity, must hold a place of esteem in the midst of the community. This text, often invested with the sacredness of Scripture, will be the fixed point against which all the moving, changing experience of the community will have to be compared. Second, the community must have a living edge along which events take place which require interpretation in terms of this fixed reference point. Those in society who make it their business to interpret experience from the perspective of the authoritative text may well allege that the "Scripture" provides all the categories and language necessary to cope with experience on the ever-changing frontier of day-to-day. In fact, however, where a living tradition exists, the moving edge will itself be a context in which new norms and new authority are generated. The institutions within the living community in which the process of hermeneutic takes place will be *de facto* loci of new revelation. By virtue of the acceptable "re-presentation" of the authoritative word of Scripture in and by them to new cultural contexts, new light and truth can be expected to break forth.[5]

From the foregoing observations it will be clear that the matter of hermeneutic is far more than a matter of piety (wherein proof-texts are given in support of contemporary acting and speaking). No, in any society which treasures fundamental documents held to have been given by God or by ancient men of great esteem, a viable hermeneutic is essential to contemporary living. Only such a hermeneutic can draw out of the documents the necessary support for commonly held values and a framework for interpreting experience. Since most societies do in fact treasure documents of this sort, the hermeneutical problem is absolutely ubiquitous. It faced the Greek and Alexandrian grammarians in their effort to link the writings of Homer to their own day; it faced the Roman jurists; it faced

---

(2) Cf. M. Noth, "The 'Re-Presentation' of the Old Testament in Proclamation," in C. Westermann, ed., *Essays in Old Testament Hermeneutics* (English trans. edited by James L. Mays, Richmond, 1963), p. 80.

(3) Patte, *op. cit.*, p. 4, citing P. Ricoeur.

(4) Paul J. Achtemeier, *An Introduction to the New Hermeneutic* (Philadelphia, 1969), p. 14.

(5) Similar analyses of the hermeneutical situation of cultures have been made by Page Smith, Jacques Barzun, and others. Cf. Patte, *op. cit.*, p. 8. The applicability of these observations to rabbinic midrash is shown by Geza Vermes in his essay, "Bible and Midrash," in *Post-Biblical Jewish Studies* (Leiden, 1975), p. 88.

Philo, the New Testament writers, the sectaries of Qumran, the rabbis; it faced the scholastics and the Reformers; it faces preachers, literary critics, and constitutional lawyers in our own day.

## THE CONSTITUTIVE FACTORS OF RABBINIC HERMENEUTIC

For the Tannaim and their Pharisaic predecessors the fixed point of reference from which interpretation of experience had ultimately to be derived was, of course, the Bible. The fact that the Bible was itself the product of a long developmental process within which hermeneutical principles were clearly operative was not a matter of significance to them.[6] Of course, the palpable remains of that growth-process posed difficulties for the rabbis just as they have for interpreters ever since. To cope with the lacunae, contradictions, anachronisms, and diverse literary styles of the biblical text, they had to develop text-critical methods and harmonizing devices, some of which must be regarded as hermeneutical methods in their own right. However, except for some lingering questions of canonicity affecting the *ketuvim* (questions which are definitely settled by the Tannaim themselves), the unity and the authority of the Tanakh were recognized by all, and the fixed pole of hermeneutical activity was thus assumed.

The Torah was, of course, regarded as God's own word given to Moses on Sinai. The *nevi'im* and *ketuvim*, too, were words of the Almighty vouchsafed through his chosen spokesmen. It followed, therefore, that no word, no particle, no dot or dash in the sacred text was meaningless or redundant. The divine draftsman wasted nothing, made no mistakes, and intended to communicate some truth even through an apparent pleonasm or a lacuna. Upon these presuppositions would the rabbinic hermeneutic be constructed.

Alongside the Bible, the rabbis were heirs of a large body of extra-biblical but authoritative laws, customs, and precedents which already before the turn of the era could be pointed to as a substantive Oral Torah. Whether or not these materials actually came to Hillel, Shammai, and the

(6) For modern scholars of the Bible it is, of course, a matter of utmost importance, and forms the basis of all the literary-critical theories which have been developed to account for the seams and fissures in the bibilical text. The extent to which rabbinic midrash is in fact an extension of biblical literature itself was explored by I.L. Seeligmann in his noted article, "Voraussetzung der Midraschexegese," *Supplement to Vetus Testamentum*, vol. 1 (Leiden, 1953), pp. 150–181. Even the literary genre of mishnah can be shown to be linearly descended from the juridical processes which gave rise to biblical law, through traces of "rabbinic-type" legal formulations still preserved in the biblical text. Cf. J. Weingreen, "Oral Torah and Written Records," in his *From Bible to Mishna* (Manchester, 1976), pp. 76–99, especially p. 82. An outstanding example of the new work being done in the area of inner-biblical exegesis is Michael Fishbane's book, *Text and Textus* (New York, 1979).

first generation of the Tannaim in oral form is a much debated question which need not detain us here.[7] As far as the matter of rabbinic hermeneutic is concerned, the important fact is that the bifurcation of ancient tradition into two Torahs, Written and Oral, held the potential for a crisis of authority. The Oral Torah was a precious and indispensable legacy of decisions made along the moving edge of Jewish history. It answered questions which the Bible did not, and gave the detail necessary to fill out cryptic biblical law. And yet, the fact remained that the decrees and traditions of the Oral Law were not found in Scripture, and some even seemed to be in open conflict with it.

Of course, not all of the extra-biblical legal traditions which came down to the rabbis from the last centuries B.C.E. carried the same claims of authority. Some of these early "halakhot" were undoubtedly passed on without any attachment to Scripture or named authority, and are still preserved in that form in the Mishnah or midrashim of the Tannaim. Others came down on the authority of the "Men of the Great Assembly," or one of the Zugot. Traditions of this sort are often identified as *gezerot*, "decrees." Other enactments of law from pre-rabbinic times are the *taqqanot*, which differ from the *gezerot* in that they appeal to specific scriptural warrants even when they effectively set aside the prescriptions of Scripture.[8] The assignment of many *taqqanot* to ancient worthies must of course be questioned, and most instances of probably early *taqqanot* come from Tannaitic times. Yet tradition remembers Hillel for his famous *taqqanah* instituting the *prosbul*[9] which effectively set aside the prescription of Deut.

(7) Patte, *op. cit.*, ch. V, "The Use of Scripture in the Schools. Written and Oral Toroth" is a useful discussion of the issue, with bibliography. Weingreen, *op. cit.*, is firm in his conviction that written records of extra-biblical legal discussions were kept and some eventually found their way into the Bible itself. Cf. pp. 83–92.

(8) J. H. Greenstone, "Gezerah," JE, vol. v, pp. 648–649, describes the *gezerah* as a negative ordinance in contrast to the *taqqanah*, a positive ordinance. A. Guttmann, *Rabbinic Judaism in the Making* (Detroit, 1970), p. 257, note 4, distinguishes the two by describing the former as an enactment of a prohibitive nature, and the latter as a supplement to or modification of the biblical law. See his list of the *taqqanot* and *gezerot* of the Men of the Great Assembly, pp. 6–7. Of course, the practice of issuing *gezerot* and *taqqanot* was continued by the rabbis themselves, and in this way the scope of the corpus of authoritative extra-biblical laws was continually enlarged. R. Yohanan b. Zakkai, for example, issued his famous *taqqanah* permitting the blowing of the *shofar* elsewhere than in the Temple (M.R.H. 4:1), thus adjusting cultic practice to conditions as they existed after the Destruction. Cf. JE, vol. xi, pp. 669–76, for a long list of *taqqanot*; also, J. Neusner, "Studies on the Taqqanot of Yavneh," HTR 63 (1970), pp. 183–198; and, more recently, M. Elon, *Hamishpat ha'ivri* (Jerusalem, 1973), chs. xiii–xv, esp. pp. 402–403 on the terminology.

(9) The *prosbul* was a declaration made before the court (i.e., *pros boulē*) by the executor of a loan to the effect that the law of *shemittah*, the cancellation of debts, did not apply to the impending transaction. Hillel's *taqqanah* was designed to protect the makers of loans from losses and to ensure the availability of loan money to borrowers, even at the approach of the seventh year. Cf. J.H. Greenstone, "Prosbul," JE, vol. x, pp. 219–220.

15:1–3 that all loans outstanding between Israelites be forgiven on the sabbatical year.[10] In short, the corpus of extra-biblical but authoritative legal traditions handed down to the Pharisees and the rabbis after them already showed the bi-polar tension between the fixed point of Scripture and the moving point of a living community. Such a situation creates a crisis of authority followed by a demand for a viable hermeneutic; and it was in such a situation that the hermeneutical systems of rabbinic Judaism arose.[11]

During the two centuries of rapid social and religious change which surrounded the turn of the era, all the factors which made imperative the articulation of clear and dependable methods for relating Scripture to the ongoing needs of the living community of the Jews came together. First, as has already been noted, the process of canonization of certain writings as Scripture was completed during this period. Second, a body of rules for community living already existed. That these two Torahs, Written and Oral, already belonged together was a conviction which the rabbis inherited with the two traditions. For them Torah was coextensive with life; therefore, traditional laws and interpretations could be seen as nothing other than projections from that same Torah. As Patte puts it, "There could be no more conflict between the Oral Torah and the Written than between the Pentateuch and the rest of the Bible . . . Scripture had to be interpreted in terms of the Oral Torah. And the discovery of proof texts for the halakhot was nothing but the rediscovery of the interpretations which gave birth to them."[12]

Third, institutional life in Judaism had assumed new forms, two of which were well-suited to be loci of legal and biblical interpretation. The *synagogue*, which after 70 C.E. remained the exclusive liturgical institution among Jews, had long since displaced the Temple as the principal focus of the worship life of the community. In the *Bet-Kenesset* the literary genres of *targum*, *tefillah*, and *derashah* found their home and flourished. Each of these literary activities provided a context in which biblical interpretation

---

(10) M. Shevi'it 10:3–4. Cf. A.Z. Melamed *Mavo' lesifrut hatalmud* (Jerusalem, 1962), p. 7. Patte, *op. cit.*, pp. 102–103; Guttmann, *op. cit.*, pp. 71–74.

(11) A similar crisis confronted Islam as the *sunna*, the body of authoritative legal and ethical traditions representing normative community usage, came into being alongside the written scripture of the Koran. It was the insistence of Shafi'i (ca. 767–820 C.E.), the founder of one of the four orthodox schools of Islamic law, that all authentic *sunna* is really the model behavior of the Prophet which made possible the resolution of this crisis. Of course, various interpretative and hermeneutical devices were necessary to establish the connection between the Prophet, his Companions and Successors on the one hand, and the accepted practices of the *sunna* on the other. Cf. Joseph Schacht, *The Origins of Muhammadan Jurisprudence* (Oxford, 1950), pp. 1–5, 58–61 *passim*.

(12) *Op. cit.*, pp. 97–98.

at a popular level, usually homiletical (haggadic) in character, was carried on. The results, some of which are preserved in the extant Targums, the Amidah and early elements in the liturgical tradition of "normative" Judaism, and in the haggadic midrashim, reveal that informal hermeneutical methods were operative as tradition was generated in the context of synagogue worship.[13] The *Academy* or *Bet-Midrash* came into being after the Destruction of 70 C.E. Prior to the establishment of the *yeshivah* at Yavneh by R. Yoḥanan b. Zakkai, "schools" must have consisted primarily of students gathered around a learned teacher and interpreter of Scripture — much as the twelve disciples gathered around Jesus of Nazareth. As the various small circles of Pharisees coalesced into the larger rabbinical "academies" of the Tannaitic period, their principles of juridical interpretation must have coalesced as well.[14] Halakhah was the subject matter of the discussion, and increasingly articulate hermeneutical methods or *middot* were tools of the learned trade. Thus, the "setting-in-life" of the systematic adjustment of biblical law and ethics to the new conditions of the first and second centuries of our era was the school.

A fourth historical factor which contributed to the emergence of a conscious hermeneutic among the early rabbis was the high degree of sectarianism among the Palestinian Jews of the last century B.C.E. and the first century C.E. Not only were the the well-known parties of Pharisees and Sadducees engaged in controversy over the correct interpretation of Scripture and the status of extra-biblical norms,[15] but conflicting claims about the meaning and proper application of Scripture were undoubtedly heard from other sources: from the Community of Covenanters at Qumran who cherished the special interpretive tradition of their Teacher of Righteousness; from the old priestly groups and Hellenized ruling classes who, at the beginning of our period at least, still sought to accommodate the biblical tradition to the philosophical systems which prevailed in the broader Greco-roman world culture; from Zealots who were prepared to enlist the Bible by means of hermeneutical applications to support their ultra-national cause; and, of course, beginning about 30 C.E.,

(13) The interpretive functions of simultaneous translation (*targum*) and liturgy (*tefillah*) in relation to preaching (*derashah*) are summarized by Patte, *op. cit.*, chapters iii & iv.

(14) A certain degree of tentativeness needs to be maintained in any discussion of the exact institutional form of the Tannaitic "academies," for the sources may project later structures onto the reports of the first and second centuries. David M. Goodblatt argues that, when properly evaluated, the evidence of the Babylonian Talmud will not support the existence of formal "academies" even among the Babylonian Amoraim. Cf. his *Rabbinic Instruction in Sassanian Babylonia* (Leiden, 1975).

(15) Discussion of the hermeneutical issue between these two parties goes at least as far back as Josephus (*Ant.* XIII.x.6; XVIII.i.4).

from followers of Jesus of Nazareth who systematically applied Old Testament tradition by means of informal hermeneutical methods to the new situation created for them by their conviction that the Promised One of Israel had been among them. Such a highly competitive situation demanded that every party give an adequate and convincing account of its way of handling Scripture. Small wonder, then, that the Pharisees and their rabbinic successors devoted serious attention to the problem of hermeneutic right from the beginning. As Vermes puts it, "Halakhic Bible interpretation seems to have accompanied the rise of the religious parties, and in particular of the Pharisaic movement ... Its leaders were ... unable to claim authority by reason of hereditary status or professional training as the older priestly and Levitical scribes had done and wherever their doctrine departed from the accepted norm they were obliged to defend it with argument solidly backed by Scripture. Out of this necessity a technique of exegesis soon arose which conformed to well-defined rules, the *middot*."[16] Their success in identifying their own tradition of hermeneutics with the solution to the problem of hermeneutic which faced all the Jewish sects equally is attested by the fact that only their *middot* are remembered and discussed among us today.[17]

A fifth factor which should be linked to the appearance of an explicit program of hermeneutical methodology among the rabbis is the influence of Hellenism and the intellectual traditions of Greek and Latin letters. Scholars are much divided on the extent of this cross-cultural connection. D. Daube, for example, argues for the essentially Alexandrian and therefore Hellenistic provenance of the seven *middot* of Hillel.[18] After

(16) *Op. cit.*, pp. 80–81.

(17) The contention of this article is, however, that Pharisaic/rabbinical hermeneutical principles were not collected into formal lists until after 70 C.E. (cf. *infra*, p. 18f). By that time the motivation for identifying and systematizing methods of interpretation stemmed no longer from competition between sects but rather from an increasingly sophisticated methodological consciousness and a felt need for clarity in exegetical discussion within rabbinical circles.

It must be acknowledged at this point that differences of opinion regarding proper methods of biblical interpretation arose even among the rabbis themselves. In the exegetical controversies between Bet Hillel and Bet Shammai, not only did the halakhah most frequently go with Bet Hillel, but, in the opinion of later tradition at least, so did the hermeneutical method. (However, Guttmann, *op. cit.*, p. 98 points out that the formal hermeneutical *middot* actually play a very small part in the traditions about Hillel and Shammai. On the one occasion when Hillel was able to introduce three of the formal *middot* into a single discussion, he was rebuffed. Cf. b. Pes. 66a). Out of later interpretive controversies, e.g., between the Schools of Ishmael and Akiba, there arose on both sides hermeneutical methods which came later to be generally accepted.

(18) David Daube, "Rabbinic Methods of Interpretation and Hellenistic Rhetoric," HUCA 22 (1949), pp. 239–264; "Alexandrian Methods of Interpretation and the Rabbis," *Festschrift H. Lewald* (Basel, 1953), pp. 27–44. See the discussion of the latter essay, and partic-

showing the similarity between the formal rabbinic patterns and examples which he draws from Aristotle and Cicero, he asks, "Is the coincidence between Hillel's rhetorical norms and those of the Greeks and Romans accidental or generic?" He answers the question in favor of the latter. "We have before us a science the beginnings of which may be traced back to Plato, Aristotle, and their contemporaries .. Philosophical instruction was very similar in outline, whether given at Rome, Jerusalem, or Alexandria."[19]

S. Lieberman speaks for those who believe that the answer to Daube's question is "accidental" at the most. Although he acknowledges suggestive parallels between the hermeneutical methods of the rabbis and those employed elsewhere in the Hellenistic milieu, he regards the equivalency between two of the thirteen *middot* of R. Ishmael and two of the principles of Hermogenes as a matter of chance. [20] These are natural and primitive logical devices which can be found in use all over the ancient world. Lieberman is willing to concede the possibility that the rhetorical terminology by which the hermeneutical principles were identified among the rabbis might have been borrowed at some relatively late date from the traditions of the Asiatic and Alexandrian rhetors. Such a position would seem to remain open to at least part of the stand taken by Daube, namely, that some impetus toward a conscious effort of "isolation and organization" of rabbinic logical principles came from the Greek side. Yet it would not give credence to any claims of wholesale appropriation of Greek and Roman hermeneutical methodology by the rabbis.

Whether this issue will finally be decided in favor of direct relationship between Athens and Jerusalem on the matter of hermeneutics, or in favor

---

ularly Daube's proposal that the rabbinic device of *seres*, "rearrangement," is borrowed from the Alexandrian interpretive method of *anastrophe*, in W. Sibley Towner, *The Rabbinic "Enumeration of Scriptural Examples"* (Leiden, 1973), pp. 49–50, 103–104. Guttmann makes a sweeping and uncritical application of Daube's proposals when he says, "Hillel was the first Jewish sage officially to introduce a system of hermeneutic rules . . . all of them had been in use among the learned men of the Roman Empire" (*op. cit.*, p. 74).

(19) "Rabbinic Methods," p. 257.

(20) S. Lieberman, *Hellenism in Jewish Palestine*[2] (New York, 1962), pp. 56–68. Lieberman's position generally has been to recognize substantial contact with and knowledge of Greek tradition by the rabbis, but without borrowing of substantive ideological or methodological material. Most borrowing was confined to terms. As to the conventions of rhetoric Lieberman remarks, "The inhabitants of Palestine listened to the speeches of the rhetors, and the art of rhetoric had a practical value" ("How Much Greek in Jewish Palestine?", A. Altmann, ed., *Biblical and Other Studies* [Cambridge, Mass., 1963], p. 134). But again the actual borrowing was, in in his view, confined to terminology.

Louis Jacobs devotes a chapter of his book, *Studies in Talmudic Logic and Methodology* (London, 1961), pp. 3–8, to a refutation of A. Schwartz' contention that the rabbinic argument of *qal vaḥomer* is identical with the Aristotelean syllogism. See *infra*, pp. 25ff.

of chance convergence of like logical formulae performing like functions, it remains self-evident that the rabbinic struggle to link the fixed point of sacred text with the moving point of current experience through the use of dependable hermeneutical methods was a struggle not performed in a vacuum. It was carried on in a world in which others were engaged in the same hermeneutical quest, all within the remarkably international, inter-dependent environment of the Roman Empire. It seems highly probable that the learned rabbinical interpreters of Hebrew Scripture were at least aware that explicit interpretive methods similar to their own were in use among those intellectuals of the Greek-speaking world who studied Homer and the classics in the hope of extrapolating from them lessons for their own time.

The last historical factor which contributed to the appearance of an increasingly articulated hermeneutical method among the Tannaim was the destruction of the Temple in 70 C.E. The destruction of the central authority of the Jews inevitably was both a crisis and an opportunity. The crisis lay in the fact that the Torah, universally regarded among the Jews as co-extensive with life, suddenly was threatened with irrelevancy as the sacrificial cultus and Temple institutions to which Scripture devoted so much attention came to an abrupt end. However, the rabbis who repaired to Yavneh seized the opportunity and gave the future shape of Judaism their own distinctive stamp. They were equal to this task, partly because they had arrived at preliminary agreement about the authority of Scripture and the validity of the methods by which Scripture was to be tied to new practices in their own day. "After the destruction of the Temple and the termination of the authoritative Sanhedrin, exegesis became of paramount importance. . . . The limited power of the Nasi and the *Bet Din Hagadol* was now supplemented by the unlimited realm of exegesis."[21]

Before concluding this discussion of the motivating factors which touch rabbinic hermeneutic in its formative phases, a brief examination of the hermeneutical significance of a pair of rabbinic literary genres is necessary, namely, mishnah and midrash.

Definitions are hardly necessary. The question confronting us here is this: are the hermeneutical functions of mishnah and midrash *au fond* the same, if one's perspective is broad enough? This issue hinges on the degree of consciousness about the hermeneutical dimension that is present in mishnah. The Mishnah proper is a compilation of halakhic decisions organized topically mostly without reference to Scripture. Even traditional commentators have recognized that many of the halakhot of the Mishnah arose independently of Scripture, as decisions made by the rec-

(21) Guttmann, *op. cit.*, p. 75.

ognized authorities were adopted to facilitate the continued adaptation of the community to new conditions. [22] However, the possibility of ultimate rootage in biblical language and thought even of the totally independent halakhot remains. Often this discussion devolves upon the issue of chronological priority. Which came first, the scriptural derivation (midrash) or the legal decision (mishnah)? If one used the prefex "re-" the way S.K. Mirsky does in his remark about "the renewed activity in reattaching halakhot to the written Torah at the time of Hillel . . ."[23] one implies that the relationship of mishnah to Scripture was originally explicit and that that direct relationship is recoverable. If midrash precedes mishnah in this way, then the latter can be described as from the beginning an application of the meaning of Scripture to new human circumstances.[24]

The lack of evidence which faces those who argue the chronological priority of midrash over mishnah has tipped the recent scholarly consensus if not toward the priority of mishnah, at least toward the independent development of midrash and mishnah during the same time period. [25] Even when this view is taken, however, it still seems quite evident that the zeal of generations of rabbis subsequent to those who first issued the halakhot to create viable links with Scripture through the use of hermeneutical methods reveals an ideological commitment at work: mishnah, too, is implicitly an effort to prolong the legal discourse of the Torah within the Palestinian Jewish community of the first two centuries of the common era. Mishnah is not to be seen in conflict with Scripture,

(22) Z.H. Chajes, for example, divided the halakhot into six categories: 1) interpretations traceable to Sinai and supported by biblical texts; 2) halakhot of Sinaitic origin which have no basis in Scripture; 3) rulings which the rabbis inferred through the ordinarily adopted methods of exegesis; 4) halakhot based on ordinary human reasoning; 5) legal rulings derived from post-Mosaic sources; 6) halakhot that bear no relationship to the aforementioned (*gezerot* and *taqqanot*). Cf. the introduction by Jacob Schachter to the second edition of Chajes' *The Student's Guide Through the Talmud*[2] (New York, 1960), p. xxv.

(23) S.K. Mirsky, "Schools of Hillel, R. Ishmael, and R. Akiba in Pentateuchal Interpretation," in H.J. Zimmels, *et al.*, eds., *Essays Presented to Chief Rabbi Israel Brodie* (London, 1967), p. 295.

(24) A classic debate on this subject pitted J.Z. Lauterbach (midrash precedes mishnah — cf. his "Midrash and Mishnah" [1915], reprinted in his *Rabbinic Essays* [Cincinnati, 1951], pp. 163–256) against S. Zeitlin (mishnah precedes or at least develops concurrently with midrash — cf. especially his "The Halaka: Introduction to Tannaitic Jurisprudence," JQR 39 [1948/49], pp. 1–40).

(25) Jacob Neusner speaks more forcefully than most, but clearly represents the position when he writes, "The authorities of Mishnah-Tosefta do not derive their laws from Scriptures. On occasion they do twist Scriptures to make them fit preconceived conclusions. The implicit question of the exegetical compilations on the law is, 'How do we know X from the Torah,' with X the given law or belief, and the problem being to justify it from Scripture, not to find out what Scripture teaches about that subject. If we started with Scripture and asked

but rather as the authentic companion to and fuller statement of Scripture: such is the meaning of Sifra on Lev. 26:46 when it places both written and "oral" Torah on exactly the same basis of authority, as revealed "to Moses from Sinai."

## THE PRAXIS OF HERMENEUTICS AMONG THE TANNAIM

We turn now to an examination of the system of *hermeneutics* which the factors discussed in the previous paragraphs did in fact call forth in rabbinic Judaism.

At least some of the seven hermeneutical principles attributed to Hillel were ancient already by his day. Traditional commentators naturally defend the attribution to Hillel, but even they have a way of recognizing the greater antiquity and ubiquity of the most common of the *middot*. Since they take the position that all of the Oral Torah was revealed to Moses on Sinai, they are obliged to argue that the *middot*, too, were given to Moses, because these rules are mentioned in the midrashic texts which preserve the Oral Torah.[26] The assumption which will be operative here is that the seven *middot* were original neither with Moses nor with Hillel, but evolved through a long process of interpretation of Scripture. Much the same can be assumed about the *middot* attributed to R. Ishmael and R. Akiba. Hillel came to be regarded as the foremost of the early practitioners of the hermeneutics in the development of halakhah; R. Ishmael and R. Akiba came to be regarded as the principal elaborators of the method among the Tannaim. Whether they actually articulated any or all of the *middot* in these lists cannot be known, though the sources suggest that the link between these rabbinical figures and the lists of hermeneutical devices which bear their names was made quite early. Therefore, it remains convenient to treat the *middot* in three blocks, even though it may be possible to show an independent origin and development — in some cases even outside of the literature of the rabbis — for each and every *middah*. The lists can be regarded as traditional collections of existing methods of interpretation, each of which was secondarily attributed as a

---

what it taught, we should never, *never* discover even the simplest datum of rabbinic law. When we start with the answer — the rabbinic law — and ask how Scripture can be made to justify that law, the answers are anything but perspicuous. That the authorities of Mishnah-Tosefta understood these facts full well seems strongly implied by their mythic view of Two Torahs, one written, the other oral." *A History of the Mishnaic Law of Purities*, vol. v (Leiden, 1975), p. 238.

(26) The line of argument is sketched by Chajes, *op. cit.*, pp. 22, 25. It was already advanced by R. Ishmael himself. See also H.L. Strack, *Introduction to the Talmud and Midrash* (New York, 1959), p. 288, note 6.

whole to a prominent interpreter. The usual chronological sequence must in part be a reflection of the relation of the contents of the lists to one another: each of the latter two lists incorporates the previous one and expands upon it.

When listed, as they traditionally are, as seven or thirteen or thirty-two distinct hermeneutical devices, the *middot* appear to be easily distinguishable from one another and very likely individually to give rise to characteristic literary formulations. In actual practice, however, the *middot* often blur into one another. Any kind of "form-criticism" is difficult to employ with them, for each *middah* gives rise to a number of literary forms, subforms, and variations. This blurring of the theoretical distinctions in actual practice may take place in part because the scriptural material being treated is itself of varying formal character and complexity. However, the chief reason seems to be that most of the halakhic *middot* ultimately rest upon the same basis. That basis is *comparability*. Whether comparability is established by terminology, juxtaposition, positioning in a hierarchy of institutions, or simple syntax, the ultimate form and function of the comparison will often appear quite similar to other comparisons elsewhere.

With these caveats in mind, the specific illustration now to be given for each *middah* should be understood neither as exhaustive of all variations of the *middah* in question nor as absolutely distinctive from possible formulations of other *middot*, but simply as a typical example. However, by means of the identification of key terms and formulae which seem to typify each *middah* in operation, together with a brief logical analysis, it is intended that the several components of rabbinic "hermeneutics" will be rendered as distinctly discernible as possible.

## A. The Seven Hermeneutical Rules Attributed to Hillel.

Within the traditional list of *middot* attributed to Hillel,[27] the first two always have priority and appear to be the most ancient and deeply rooted.

(27) The text of the seven *middot* is preserved in Tos. Sanh. 7:11; Sifra, Weiss edition, 3a; Abot d'R. Natan 37 (English translation by Judah Goldin, *The Fathers According to Rabbi Nathan* [New Haven, 1955], p. 154). Brief analyses of the seven *middot* are given by Strack, *op. cit.*, pp. 93–94, with copious references to the secondary literature, pp. 285–287; M. Elon, "Interpretation," in *Encyc. Judaica*, vol. viii (1971), cols. 1422–23. Fuller discussions of each of these rules are given by J.Z. Lauterbach, "Talmud Hermeneutics," *JE*, vol. xii (1906), pp. 32–33; M. Mielziner, *Introduction to the Talmud*[2] (New York, 1903), Part II, "Legal Hermeneutics of the Talmud," pp. 117–187; L. Jacobs, "Hermeneutics," in *Encyc. Judaica*, vol. viii (1971), cols. 366–372; M. Elon, *Hamishpaṭ haʿivri*, vol. ii, pp. 270–302. Cf. also W. Bacher, *Die exegetische Terminologie dur jüdischen Traditionsliteratur*, Part I, "Die Bibelexegetische Terminologie der Tannaiten" (Leipzig, 1899), *ad loc.*, especially מדה, pp. 100–103; S. Zeitlin, "Hillel and the Hermeneutic Rules," *JQR* 54 (1963/64), pp. 161–173.

Hillel himself is reported to have used them in argument with the Bene Bathyra (b. Pes. 66a).

1. *Qal vaḥomer* (קל וחומר). This is the principle of inference *a minori ad maius*, "from the lesser to the greater." It is based on the assumption that a rule which applies to some minor matter will be all the more applicable to a comparable matter of major importance. The converse is also assumed: if a law is applicable to a major case, it will certainly apply to comparable minor instances. When applied to issues of current experience, this rule provided a means of building possible (though not necessary) connections back to the biblical text; however, it could also be used for simple exegetical purposes to relate one biblical text to another.[28]

In the following example, a discussion of the ordinance prohibiting work on the first and last days of the Passover festival (Exod. 12:16) leads to this argument:

(28) M. Elon (*Encyc. Jud.*, vol. viii, cols. 1420–1422; also his *Hamishpaṭ ha'ivri*, vol. ii, pp. 270–302) employs the distinction between "analogical" and "elucidative" modes of interpretation to organize his discussion of the hermeneutical principles of the rabbis. In the former category (*midrash hameḳish*) he includes *qal vaḥomer*, *gezerah shavah*, and *binyan 'av*: these are devices "concerned with the drawing of analogous conclusions from one matter to another with a view to widening the law and solving new problems." The latter category of principles (*midrash hameva'er*), in contrast, is used simply to explain and elucidate scriptural texts. In this category Elon gathers the ten remaining *middot* of R. Ishmael. These two classes of legal reasoning Elon likens, in essential function, at least, respectively to the categories of *interpretatio analogia* and *interpretatio grammatica* of Roman law. Somewhere between "analogical" and "elucidative" reasoning Elon also locates "logical interpretation" (akin to Roman *interpretatio logica*, whereby Scripture can be understood logically and applied to new cases). This *midrash hahiggayon* is not represented among the thirteen hermeneutical principles, but it does give rise, of course, to stereotyped formulations and patterns of discourse. Finally, Elon speaks of "restrictive interpretation," by various means of which the applicability of a law can be narrowed.

Although Elon's typology is useful, it will not be employed here for two reasons: 1) In actual practice, many *middot* have the capacity to function in more than one of the categories which he identifies; 2) the terms "logical" and "analogical" are misleading, at least in the context of the Western philosophical and legal tradition. The rabbinic interpretative devices are not patterns of scientific reasoning by which necessary conclusions are derived from objectively verifiable premises, and in which no presuppositions are involved save the presupposition that arguments structured in the prescribed form will inevitably lead to correct conclusions. On the contrary, rabbinic hermeneutical principles structure arguments which become "logical" only when the unspoken presuppositions of the religious milieu are accepted. These include the *a priori* that Scripture is immutable and utterly authoritative, because it is the very word of God; that that word has direction to give later generations who live along the moving edge of experience even when their experience goes beyond the bounds of any explicit address by Scripture; and that, because the divine draftsman wastes nothing and utters neither error nor redundancy, every feature of the text, every grammatical form, every doublet, every synonym is significant.

As for the term "analogy," we are better served by restricting its use more narrowly than Elon's usage would suggest. An analogy ought to be regarded as something more specialized than simple comparison. Although *heqqesh* ("analogy"; cf. *infra*, pp. 128–30 and a *middah* which must be regarded as one of its sub-types, *davar shehuqqash bishte middot*, etc. ("Something is compared with two things and you attribute to it only the good quality common to

From this I know only with respect to a holiday that you are warned against the work of your fellow-Jew as you are against your own. How about the Sabbath? It can be reasoned by using the method of *Kal vaḥomer*: If on a holiday in regard to which the law is not so rigorous, you are warned against the work of your fellow-Jew as you are against your own work, it is but logical to assume that on the Sabbath in regard to which the law is more rigorous, you surely are warned against the work of your fellow-Jew as you are against your own work.[29]

In this particular example, the line of reasoning intrinsic to the simple *qal vaḥomer* requires four steps. 1) The given (not a hypothetical proposition, but a scriptural institution), introduced by ומה אם, "if" or "if it is the case that," is the biblical regulation governing the first and seventh days of the Passover festival. This regulation prohibits work by anyone in the community of Israel on these days. 2) However (and here the *darshan* introduces a premise, which is, of course, subject to falsification), the laws governing the general category of the יום טוב, "holiday" into which the Passover falls, are הקל, "not so rigorous . . . the less rigorous." 3) If one then considers the Sabbath (on the unexpressed but obvious ground that שבת and יום טוב are both "species" of a broader genus, "sacred days"), . . . ש. דין הוא, "it is but logical to assume that" the scriptural prohibition against the work of a fellow Jew will apply to it as well. Why? 4) Because the laws governing Sabbath obedience are always החומר, "the more rigorous." Therefore, at least whatever is legally true of the "holiday" will be true for the Sabbath.

the two," Rule No. 21 of the 32 *middot* of R. Eliezer; cf. Strack, *op. cit.*, p. 97 and note thereto), are true analogical devices, the other *middot* to which the term has been applied are not — if by "analogy" we mean a subjective, arbitrary, but illuminating impression of the comparability of two events, ideas, expressions,or the like. Athough many of the hermeneutical principles involve comparisons between texts, as their very names indicate, these comparisons are based on formal, verbal congruities between the texts (i.e., on "objective" criteria) and not upon similarity of content (cf. Elon, *Encyc. Jud.*, col. 1421, and S. Lieberman, *op. cit.*, p. 61, whom Elon cites on this point). This even includes *gezerah shavah*, which has been called "Inference by Analogy" (Strack), "Inference from the Analogy of Words" (Elon), and "Analogy of Expressions" (Mielziner). Although interpretation based upon this sort of comparison-drawing, which really involves the fortuitous discovery of identical terms or grammatical features in disparate texts, often appears highly arbitrary to a reader of today, the method makes sense if one accepts the underlying presupposition that the divine draftsman is free to subject the terms of his choice to an infinite number of permutations in a rich array of legal and linguistic contexts.

(29) Mekilta de R. Ishmael, tractate Pisḥa ix:48–52 (edition of J.Z Lauterbach [Philadelphia, 1949], vol. i, pp. 71–72; henceforth *Mek.*). Other notable examples of Tannaitic usage include *Mek.* Neziqin iii:39–50 (vol. iii, pp. 21–22); M. Avot 1:5, Sanh. 6:5, Sot. 6:3, Mak. 3:15. *Qal vaḥomer* is the most frequently used of all the hermeneutical rules. For example,it is used 83 times in Mekilta de R. Shimᶜon b. Yoḥai alone!

Reduced to its most basic form, then, the simple *qal vahomer* runs as follows: if A, the laws governing which are known to be less rigorous, requires Y, it makes sense that B, the laws governing which are known to be more rigorous, will require Y.[30]

Louis Jacobs has shown convincingly why this argument is not a Hebrew version of the Aristotelean syllogism, and why it cannot yield the logically necessary conclusion of the latter.[31] A syllogism is structured as follows: All X is Y. But Z is X; therefore, Z is Y. If the premise of the first clause is correct, namely, that Y is the genus of the species X; and if the assertion of sentence two, which subsumes Z under the species X, is also demonstrably correct, then the conclusion or inference of the last clause is inescapable. Z must be Y.

In the case of the above-cited *qal wa-homer*, however, the conclusion does not follow in the same necessary way because the two institutions being compared are not of the same species (though they can legitimately be compared because they belong to the same genus, "sacred days"). Therefore, the comparison must be made in general terms. If the Sabbath laws are regarded as being *in general* more severe than the laws governing holy days, then, when doubt exists about some point of law regarding Israel's behavior on the Sabbath, *at least* whatever the law requires for a holy day will apply to the Sabbath. This can be affirmed because the laws for holy days are regarded as being *in general* less severe than those applicable to the Sabbath. Such a conclusion, though possible, is not necessary, for logic would permit particular exceptions to general comparisons of this sort. But the rabbis considered the *qal vahomer* convincing, perhaps in part because they were prepared to consider *possible* arguments as sufficient when the results accorded with what was in fact the halakhah; and perhaps in part because they assumed that the institutions which God had ordained were enshrined in biblical law in such a perfect hierarchical fashion that the general relations between them admitted of no exceptions. Within the context of such an ideological outlook, the *qal vahomer*

(30) Louis Jacobs, *Studies in Talmudic Logic and Methodology*, ch. i, "The Aristotelean Syllogism and the *Qal vahomer*," pp. 3–8, identifies a second type of argument *a minori ad maius* which he calls the "complex" form. In it, the severity of the second term of the argument is not self-evident, but must be proved by reference to another factor which operates in its case but not in the case of the first term of the argument. Examples may be found in M.B.Q. 2:5 and Hull. 24a. Jacobs (p. 4) offers the following symbolic analysis of the simple and complex *qal vahomer* arguments (where A is known to be *qal* and B is *homer*):

"Simple: If A has x then B certainly has x.

Complex: If A, which lacks y, has x then B, which has y, certainly has x."

(31) *Ibid.*, arguing against Adolf Schwarz, *Der hermeneutische Syllogismus in der talmudischen Litteratur, Ein Beitrag zur Geschichte der Logik im Morgenlande* (Vienna, 1901), and those who have followed him.

could serve the purpose of reconciling biblical texts with one another and of extrapolating from the fixed point of Scripture to the moving edge of community life quite as definitely as could the logically necessary syllogistic inference.

2. *Gezerah shavah* (גזירה שוה). This principle of "inference by comparison" is based on the assumption that the similarity of expression of two biblical laws implies that they may be interpreted similarly. The rule can be used to solve very basic lexicographical problems by comparing two different instances of rare biblical terms (e.g., Sifra on Lev. 1:15). But, it can also be used much more broadly to solve problems arising from apparent contradictions within Scripture and to expand and apply the law. In fact, the use of this *middah* became so widespread that certain safeguards regarding its use had to be set down.[32]

A good example of the use of *gezerah shavah* comes once again from *Mek*. The context is a discussion of the freeing of Hebrew slaves on the sabbatical year, commanded in the text, "When you buy a Hebrew slave, he shall serve six years, and in the seventh he shall go out free, for nothing" (Exod. 21:2). The plain meaning of the text is asserted to be that "Scripture deals with a slave who is an Israelite." The question arises, however: "Perhaps this law is speaking not of Israelite slaves, but of slaves of Israelites." The question is not one of semantics but of syntax. Is the word "Hebrew" a modifier of the word "slave," as the plain meaning suggests, or are the two in a construct relationship, i.e., "the slave of a Hebrew"? The question is not inappropriately raised. It is, after all, a well-known fact that the law forbids that an Israelite become a slave in the full sense, for it requires the manumission at the sabbatical year of all "brothers" (fellow Israelites) who, because of poverty, have been forced to sell themselves into indentured servitude. (See Deut. 15:12–18; Exod. 21:2–11. In Lev. 25:39–43 the manumission takes place at the "year of the jubilee.")

Even more hangs on the question than this, however. As is noted in the course of the discussion, if the phrase of Exod. 21:2 is read "slaves of Israelites," then one might think that even a gentile slave purchased from a Hebrew (= Israelite) would be subject to manumission after six years. This would not only cause financial hardship to the purchaser of a slave from a fellow Hebrew but would violate the spirit (though not the letter) of Lev. 25:44–46 which allows for the ownership in perpetuity of gentile slaves who have been purchased from gentiles.

A *gezerah shavah* comes to the rescue.

(32) Cf. JE, vol. xii, p. 32; Chajes, *op. cit.*, pp. 9–16. Mielziner, *op. cit.*, pp. 143–149, describes three categories of use of this device: exegetical; constructional (provisions given in one place apply in the other); exorbitant (mostly Amoraic usage, which permits the comparison of two laws even if they have only one word in common).

Scripture says: "If thy brother, a Hebrew man . . . be sold unto thee"
(Deut. 15:12). Now, after having said: "Thy brother," there seems to
be no purpose in saying: "A Hebrew man." Why then does Scripture
say: "A Hebrew man"? Merely to furnish an expression free to be
used in formulating the following *Gezerah shavah*: Here the expression "Hebrew" is used and there the expression "Hebrew" is used.
Just as there when using the expression "Hebrew" Scripture deals
with an Israelite, so also here when using the expression "Hebrew"
(lit., "Hebrew slave") Scripture deals with an Israelite.[33]

When extracted from this particular text, the line of reasoning in the
*gezerah shavah* runs as follows. First, a text other than the *lemma* which
deals with the status of "Hebrew" slaves is called to mind. In that text
(Deut. 15:12), the term "the Hebrew [man]," is set in apposition to "your
brother." The two are thus synonymous and, since "you" and "your
brother" are obviously Israelites, so must "a Hebrew man" be. Now the
*middah* itself enters, establishing a basis of comparability between the two
passages because of the presence in both of them of a common term of
fixed meaning. (A presupposition becomes evident here — if a term, in
this case "Hebrew," can be precisely understood in one context, the precise meaning will be the same in a comparable context. This presupposition can, of course, be challenged.) The argument then proceeds in a basically mechanical way: because the key term "Hebrew" appears in both
passages, the legal conclusion of the one can be extended to the other.
Four steps follow: a) "Here (כאן) the expression 'Hebrew' is used" (i.e., in
Exod. 21:2); b) so also "there" (להלן) it is used (i.e., in Deut. 15:12); c) "Just
as there (מה להלן) when using the expressing 'Hebrew' Scripture deals with
an Israelite"; d) the same intention is present when the term is used "here"
(כאן).

As is evident, the comparative device rides upon a two-fold juxtaposition of "here," כאן , and "there," להלן. The purpose of the comparison is
not to argue about the meaning of the term "Hebrew," but is rather to
clear up any ambiguity about the applicability of the law of Exod. 21:2
which arises because of the double sense of the phrase "Hebrew slave/
slave of a Hebrew." This clarification is achieved by introducing the entire
statement of the law of the Hebrew slave in Deut. 15:12 through the
formal medium of the common term. The conclusions reached are not

---

(33) *Mek.* Neziqin i:35–40 (vol. iii, p. 4). Other clear examples in Tannaitic usage include
*Mek.* Pisha v:93–105 (vol. i, pp. 40–41), xiii: 6–8 (p. 97); M. Beẓah 1:6, Soṭ. 6:3, Naz. 9:5; Tos.
Yom Tov 1:13. A lengthy list of "exegetical" uses of *gezerah shavah* is given by S. Rosenblatt,
*The Interpretation of the Bible in the Mishnah* (Baltimore, 1935), pp. 28–29. A related but more
literally "analogical" device is *heqqesh*, cf. *infra*, pp. 128–30.

necessary at all from a purely logical point of view since the construct of Exod. 21:2 could still be interpreted as "slave of a Hebrew." But the rabbinic interpreter is satisfied that the term in common between the two texts signifies the divine intention that the two be interpreted together. In the process an additional presupposition is supported as well, namely, the conviction that the divine draftsman would not, and, in the case of Deut. 15:12, did not in fact utter a superfluous word. The word "Hebrew" was juxtaposed to "your brother" in that verse for the very purpose to which the halakhah now puts it — to make clear for Exod. 21:2 as well the precise applicability of the law of the Hebrew slave.

This example of a *gezerah shavah* argument demonstrates the exegetical function of the device, for it solves a problem arisng from an apparent inconsistency in Scripture. But it also moves toward the broader hermeneutical task of providing support for the ideology of the coherence of biblical law, and even clarifies the parameters of the applicability of that law to more contemporary social practice. The example given here, of course, represents only one formulation arising from the use of the *middah*. Numerous variations of this same pattern, some amounting to sub-types, can be found.

Moving now into the balance of the list of seven hermeneutical rules attributed to Hillel, we examine those which are not as common nor as closely identified by tradition with Hillel himself.

3. *Binyan ʾav mikatuv ʾehad* (בנין אב מכתוב אחד).
4. *Binyan ʾav mishene ketuvim* (בנין אב משני כתובים).

In the list of *middot* attributed to Hillel, these are treated as two separate principles, but (in this case following the tradition of the 13 *middot*) they will here be treated as one. *Binyan ʾav* is another device for establishing comparability between laws. It is based on the assumption that the presence of a similar obligation in several laws of the Torah must derive from a factor which all share in common, and that cases other than that specified by the text itself may be decided similarly, provided that they share that common factor. By using this *middah*, the rabbis were able to regard as merely illustrative the specific application of a legal principle reported in Scripture. This gave them the freedom widely to apply the principle to the problems of their own age, and thus they "prolonged the discourse" of Scripture.

The following example of a Tannaitic application of *binyan ʾav* is part of a discussion of the text, "Every first-born of man among your sons you shall redeem" (Exod. 13:13). Earlier comments try to prove that a son whose father has not redeemed him should redeem himself. The argument involves comparison of this duty with other duties which have already been mentioned in the larger passage of which this text is a part, namely circumcision (Exod. 12:48) and teaching (13:8, 14–15). The discussion of these three commandments reveals how much they differ in fundamental importance. Compared to the father's duty to teach his son Torah, which is the premier command of the law, and the duty to circumcise, neglect of which is a capital offense, the command to redeem the first-born is of tertiary significance. Yet the three have a basis of comparability which permits the following argument:

> . . . Let me establish a general rule on the basis of what is common to all these three instances: The peculiar aspect of the duty of circumcision is not like the peculiar aspect of the duty of study, and the peculiar aspect of the duty of study is not like the peculiar aspect of the duty of circumcision. Neither have both of them the same peculiar aspect as the duty of redemption, nor has the duty of redemption the peculiar aspect of either. What is common to all three of them is that each is a religious duty affecting the son which should be performed by the father. And if the father does not perform it, the son himself must do it. So also any religious duty affecting the son which should be performed by the father must be performed by the son himself if the father fails to do it.[34]

As employed in this text, the argument of *binyan ʾav* runs as follows. 1) Having examined a series of biblical legal injunctions, the interpreter seeks to deduce a "general rule" (בנין אב) which is "common to all three instances" (מבין שלשתן). 2) After ruling out the "peculiar aspect" of each injunction (and thus showing that no simple analogy between the three commandments exists and that any generalization between the three cannot assume such an analogy), 3) "what is common to all three of them" (הצד השוה שבהן: lit. "the aspect that is comparable among them") is established: "each is a religious duty affecting the son which should be performed by the father." 4) At this point the interpreter makes the hermeneutical move, a move which is neither logically necessary nor convincing unless one accepts the presuppositions that the divine intention revealed in the Torah is one and unvarying; that ancillary considerations which hold true for one commandment therefore hold true for comparable ones; and that the divine draftsman has here located three command-

---

(34) *Mek.* Pisḥa xviii: 104–110 (vol. i, pp. 165–166). Other Tannaitic examples which may be cited include *Mek.* Neziqin ix:43–52 (vol. iii, pp. 72–73), M. Mak. 2:3, Zeb. 9:1. In M.B.Q. 1:1 the device is used to generalize in a similar manner from as many as four separate scriptural provisions.

ments in the same context precisely in order to permit comparison among them and deduction from that comparison. Generalizing from a corollary already affirmed elsewhere in the case of the commandment that the father teach his son Torah, the *darshan* deduces a second "comparable aspect": "And if the father does not perform it, the son himself must do it." 5) This "general rule," which is not an explicit component of the commandment of "redemption" but has now by comparison and deduction been shown to be implicit in it, is finally set forward as a principle of universal application: "*so also any* (אף כל) religious duty affecting the son which should be performed by the father, etc. . . ."

In this example, *binyan 'av* has been pressed into the dual service of clarifying the precise intention of a biblical law (by collocation with two others) while at the same time "prolonging the discourse of Scripture" by articulating a general legal principle based on Scripture but applicable to new situations affecting fathers and sons. As Louis Jacobs points out, the device was in fact often used by the rabbis to provide scriptural support for already accepted halakhah reflecting the practice of later generations.[35]

5. *Kelal uferaṭ uferaṭ ukhelal* (כלל ופרט ופרט וכלל)

Two variations of the same principle are in this case treated as one *middah* in the traditional list attributed to Hillel. The principle here is that "general and particular" stipulations limit one another, as do "particular and general" stipulations. It is based on the premise that if a general statement of law is followed immediately by specifics, further application of the law will be governed by the terms of those specifics. The opposite will also be true. This rule obviously could have special exegetical applications in the elucidation of biblical texts. However, it could in fact be used by expositors to make hermeneutical moves which had significant implications for the practices and laws of their own times, such as limiting the scope of applicability of sweeping biblical legal maxims.

*Mek.* once again provides a good example of this rule in action. The text under consideration, Exod. 12:43, states, "And the Lord said to Moses and Aaron, 'This is the ordinance of the passover: there shall no alien eat thereof.'" The Tannaitic commentator applies the *middah* very directly:

"This is the ordinance of the passover," is a general statement. "There shall no alien eat thereof," is a particular statement. When a

(35) L. Jacobs, *Studies in Talmudic Logic*, p. 13. In his discussion of *binyan 'av* (as in his discussion of *qal vaḥomer* cited earlier, cf. *supra*, pp. 25–7), Jacobs seeks to disprove the contention of Schwarz and others that this *middah* is influenced by Aristotelean logic and is a form of argument by analogy called "Species Induction Reference" or "Genus Induction Reference" (p. 9).

general statement is followed by a particular, it does not include more than is contained in the particular.[36]

As employed in this text, the argument of *kelal uferaṭ* runs as follows. 1) A sentence of Scripture is identified as the "general statement" (כלל). 2) An ensuing clause of scriptural law is then identified as a "particular" (פרט) or qualifier of the general statement. 3) Now the hermeneutical move is made, with the invocation of the principle of the *middah*. To one who asks about the application of biblical Passover legislation, the answer is given: faced with a general statement and a particular statement in that order in Scripture, one must choose the second. There is no question of widening the specific to the entire class indicated by the general; rather, the specific is determinative. "When a general statement is followed by a particular, it does not include more than is contained in the particular" (אין בכלל אלא מה שבפרט).[37]

In the example given here, generated by a series of clauses which are syntactically connected but contain different information, the *middah* does more than simply supply a general statement with exemplars. It serves to create a putatively correct understanding of the proper relationship of a general statement and its exception of specification. The effect is to give specificity to the matter introduced by the *kelal*.

A second example will illustrate the use of the obverse of the rule, namely, *peraṭ ukhelal*. The text under consideration, Exod. 22:9 (v. 10 in English), is one of the regulations of the Book of the Covenant concerning property damages and losses. It says that "if a man delivers to his neighbor an ass or an ox or a sheep or any beast to keep, and it dies or is hurt or is driven away . . .," the neighbor is not liable if he can testify under oath that he did not misappropriate the property. The commentator notes the presence in this text of a list of particulars ("an ass or an ox or a sheep") followed by a general category ("or any beast"). Why is "any beast (or: all beasts)" mentioned when a list of beasts has already been given?

> Because if it had read only: "All beasts," I might have understood that the keeper is liable only if all beasts had been put into his care. Therefore it says: "An ass, or an ox, or a sheep," to declare him liable for each one by itself. And what does Scripture mean to teach by say-

---

(36) *Mek.* Pisḥa xv: 7–8 (vol. i, p. 117). Other clear examples of Tannaitic usage of *kelal uferaṭ* are found in Sifre to Num. 5:15, 6:15, 19:2; Sifra to Lev. 18:6.

(37) The principle of *kelal uferaṭ uferaṭ ukhelal* in the list of seven rules attributed to Hillel undergoes considerable development and expansion into eight distinct *middot* in the list of thirteen principles of R. Ishmael. The particular formulation of the rule given here is that of the fourth rule of R. Ishmael, the first of the eight variations.

ing: "All beasts?" It merely comes to teach you that a general statement which is added to a specific statement includes everything.[38]

The assertion that every "general statement which is added to a specific
statement includes everything" (כל הכלל שהוא מוסיף על הפרט הכל בכלל) clearly
invokes the argument from the particular instance(s) to the general statement. In this case, the biblical phrases at issue do not have the character of
a general statement qualified by exceptions and specifications, but rather
the character of a list followed by its heading. The real purpose of this use
of *peraṭ ukhelal* appears not to be to extend the discourse of Scripture to
new halakhic circumstances, but rather to ward off the false conclusion
that the phrase "all beasts" is redundant. The interpreter undertakes to
show that every component of the list, whether *peraṭ* or *kelal*, has an individual function separable from the components with which it is listed. By
judicious use of the *middah* the perfect consistency of the divine draftsman
can be disclosed to the satisfaction of the rabbinic *darshan*, and the
dependably correct assessment of the function of each component of the
text can be made.[39]

6. *Kayoṣeᵓ bo mimaqom ᵓaḥer* (כיוצא בו ממקום אחר).

This rule might literally be translated "like that which passes with it (in
the same class) in another place" (following Jastrow). It is based on the
very natural and proper assumption that an exegetical problem which
arises with a text may legitimately be clarified by comparison with another
text affected by the same question but which has received adequate exegetical explanation. This *middah* seems to be less fixed in the traditional list
of seven than the others. This is the only one of the *middot* of Hillel which is
not incorporated into the traditional list of 13 rules of R. Ishmael;
furthermore, apart from its mention in the three complete texts of the
seven *middot*, the full title by which it is formally known is rarely if ever
given in the Tannaitic texts. Nevertheless, the principle to which this
*middah* points is commonly employed by the Tannaim for exegetical
purposes, frequently with the variant formula כיוצא בו (בדבר) אתה אומר.[40]

(38) *Mek.* Neziqin xvi: 5–12 (vol. iii, p. 121). The formulation here is that of the fifth rule
of R. Ishmael, which is the second of the eight variations of the principle of *kelal uferaṭ* which
are included in that list.

(39) Deductions can also be made according to the principle of *kelal uferaṭ ukhelal*. In
such cases the particular is held to limit the general statements on either side of it, so that the
law applies only to that which is similar to the *peraṭ*. Such a principle would appear to be
comparable to the Common law *eiusdem generis* rule of statutory interpretation. Cf.
Lauterbach in JE, vol. xii, p. 33.

(40) In its application to an exegetical problem this rule can give rise to an entire list of
analogous instances. For a table of ten types of exegetical lists occurring in Tannaitic
literature, see W. Sibley Towner, *The Rabbinic "Enumeration," op. cit.*, p. 255.

A good example of this principle at work can be seen in *Mek*. The context is a discussion of the commandment of Exod. 13:1–2, "Consecrate to me all the first-born; whatever is the first to open the womb . . . is mine." A question is raised about Deut. 15:19, which in the light of Exod. 13:2 appears to be redundant in commanding, "All the firstling males that are born of your herd and flock you shall consecrate to the Lord your God. . . ." Does this repetition mean that the first-born is not consecrated unless one deliberately consecrates it? If so, how can the Exod. 13:2 phrase, "[it] is mine," be accounted for? The answer: the Deut. statement is given, not because God depends upon your act of consecration to know what is rightfully his, but rather so that you may receive a reward for doing it. The expositor then uses the sixth rule to clear up a number of other apparent inconsistencies and redundancies in Scripture along the same lines of interpretation:

> In like manner you interpret: "And the priest shall kindle wood on it," etc. (Lev. 6:5). Why has this been commanded? Has it not been said: "And Lebanon is not sufficient fuel" (Isa. 40:16)? What then is the purport of the commandment: "And the priest shall kindle wood on it"? Merely to enable you to receive reward for fulfilling it. In like manner you interpret. . . .[41]

The structure of the application of *kayoṣeᵓ bo mimaqom ᵓaḥer* proves in this example to be quite simple. 1) The formula of the *middah* is given at the very outset, serving notice that the ensuing bit of scriptural interpretation is to follow the same pattern as that which has just gone before. 2) The problematical text is then introduced. In Lev. 6:5 the priest is commanded to "kindle wood" on the altar for the burnt offering, and the fire is to be kept burning continually. But why should God require this? Is not his transcendent power so great that, should he really demand his due, "Lebanon would not suffice for fuel, nor are its beasts enough for a burnt offering" (Isa. 40:16)? The suspicion at least of a redundancy, if not an inconsistency, in Scripture is raised. 3) The solution is, however, already at hand having been attained in the comparable case of Deut. 15:19. That solution, that you are to obey the command to maintain a fire on the altar of burnt offering "merely to enable you to receive reward for fulfilling it," is by no means self-evident from the text itself. However, given the presuppositions that Scripture is never redundant, and that every instruction placed in the Torah by the divine draftsman has its independent signifi-

(41) *Mek*. Pisḥa xvi: 38–41 (vol. i, p. 131). The formula כיוצא בו occurs at least 15 times in *Mek*., often in lists which repeat it several times. It is used in both halakhic and haggadic contexts. See also M.R.H. 3:8, Sifre to Num. 6:13.

cance even though other teachings may appear to render the instruction needless, the solution becomes acceptable if not necessary. That solution can be transferred from one textual situation to another by using this *middah*, when the necessary congruency exists.

7.  *Davar halamed meʿinyano* (דבר הלמד מעינינו).[42]

This final rule of Hillel establishes that "a matter [is to be] explained from its context." It is based on the observation that further clarification of the meaning of a word or phrase of Scripture, whether obscure or self-evident, can be discovered through analysis of the modifiers or predicates attached to it, and through attention to the literary structure or larger narrative environment in which it stands. The rule is primarily exegetical in function, although its hermeneutical effect can have ramifications for contemporary legal practice, as is illustrated in the example which follows.

In this example, the very simple observation has been made that the Eighth Commandment, "Thou shalt not steal," has no object. What kind of theft is prohibited here?

> Our Rabbis taught: *Thou shalt not steal* (Exod. 20:13). Scripture refers to the stealing of human beings. You say Scripture refers to the stealing of human beings, but perhaps it is not so, the theft of property [lit., 'money'] being meant? — I will tell you: Go forth and learn from the 13 principles whereby the Torah is interpreted, [one of which is that] a law is interpreted by its general context: of what does the text speak? of [crimes involving] capital punishment; hence this too refers [to a crime involving] capital punishment.[43]

The argument of the *middah* proves to be very simple. 1) The hermeneutical principle is stated at the outset. The question as to the precise meaning of "steal" in Exod. 20:13 can be answered from its context because "a law is interpreted by its general context" (דבר הלמד מעינינו). 2) So, "of what does the larger text speak" (במה הכתוב מדבר)? The prohibitions against killing and adultery which precede the commandment are known from other biblical legislation to carry the penalty of death. Therefore the larger text speaks "of [crimes involving] capital punishment." 3) According-ing to the logic of the seventh *middah*: "hence this too (אף כאן) refers [to a crime involving] capital punishment." Since kidnapping is the only kind

(42) So the text in ARN 37. In the lists of the 13 *middot*, this rule is stated more fully: דבר הלמד מעינינו ודבר הלמד מסופו ("A matter explained from its context and a matter explained from its ending"). The second element provides for the explanation of a biblical passage from further discussion of aspects of its content later in the passage.

(43) b. San. 86a. A truncated version of this same tradition is found in *Mek.* Baḥodesh viii:51–65, (vol. ii, pp. 260–261), where an additional effort is made to show that the apparently redundant "Ye shall not steal" in Lev. 19:11 refers to the theft of money. For other Tannaitic examples see Sifra, Introduction 2b; Sifre to Num. 7:1.

of theft for which the penalty is death (Exod. 21:16), the precise meaning of "Thou shalt not steal" must therefore be "Thou shalt not steal a man."[44] Concern that the result of the argument may in fact be totally contrary to the intention of the original framer of the Decalogue yields to the values of exegetical clarity and the internal consistency with which the divine draftsman has set down the laws of the Torah. The confidence that this consistency is real made possible the formulation of the seventh *middah* to begin with. Now here, in quite a circular but effective way, the application of the *middah* is made in such a way as to allow Scripture to demonstrate its internal consistency!

## B. The Thirteen Hermeneutical Rules Attributed to R. Ishmael.

The traditional list of *middot* attributed to R. Ishmael is expanded over the list attributed to Hillel principally at two points.[45] The fifth rule of Hillel (כלל ופרט ופרט וכלל) is sub-divided into three rules (כלל ופרט. פרט וכלל. כלל ופרט וכלל): five additional modifications of the same principle, general related to particular, are then added.[46] One completely new rule is added as a 13th. With other minor variations accounted for, the two lists compare as follows:

| Hillel | | Ishmael | |
|---|---|---|---|
| 1. קל וחומר | | 1. | Same |
| 2. גזירה שוה | | 2. | Same |
| 3. בנין אב מכתוב אחד } | | 3. | Both are treated as one rule. |
| 4. בנין אב משני כתובים } | | 4-11 | Amplifications and modifi- |
| 5. כלל ופרט ופרט וכלל | | | cations of Hillel No. 5. |
| 6. כיוצא בו ממקום אחר | | — | (Omitted. Function assumed under nos. 2 and 3 above.) |

(44) A critical observer might point out that the "context" at work in this instance has been selectively chosen, and that the commandment which ensues in the Bible itself ("Thou shalt not bear false witness against your neighbor") has not been used to help provide "context." Why not? It might have been chosen as another illustration of a capital crime, if *ᶜed shaqer* is understood as *ᶜedim zomemim* (cf. Deut. 19: 18–19). One can only conclude that the two-word apodictic *form* of the commandments of Exod. 20:13 and 14 contributes to the contextual judgment along with the fact that they are both capital crimes. See the discussion of contemporary use of considerations of *form* to make precise the meaning of the Eighth Commandment in Bernard S. Jackson, *Essays in Jewish and Comparative Legal History* (Leiden, 1975), pp. 207–209, and especially note 21.

(45) The text of the thirteen *middot* is preserved in the so-called "Baraita d'R. Ishmael," printed as the introductory chapter of Sifra. It is also given in summary form in Jewish prayerbooks as part of the preliminaries to the morning service (תפלת שחרית) for Sabbaths and weekdays. For recent discussion in secondary sources, cf. *supra*, note 27.

(46) For a detailed discussion of these rules, see Mielziner, *op. cit.*, pp. 163–173; also *supra*, note 37.

7. ‏דבר הלמד מעינינו‏         12.   Same, with addition of of second
                                   clause: ‏דבר הלמד מסופו‏
——  —  ——                  13.   ‏שני כתובים המכחישים‏
                                   (see below) ‏זה את זה וכו׳‏

As in the case of Hillel's *middot*, it is impossible to assert categorically
that R. Ishmael orginated any of these *middot*, or even assembled the present list. The hermeneutical principle actually most commonly associated
with his name is none of the above, but is instead a broad guideline which
was taken seriously by subsequent generations of interpreters in all
schools: ‏דברה תורה כלשון בני אדם‏ ("The Torah speaks in the [ordinary] language of people").[47] Nevertheless, even early traditions know of a traditional list of thirteen *middot* (e.g., the passage from b. Sanh. 86a cited
above); so we may assume that a list of 13, developed out of an even earlier
list of 7 rules, and generally like the list which we now possess, was known
in Tannaitic times. Certain it is that the "Thirteen Hermeneutical Rules of
R. Ishmael" came in time to be the most authoritative statement of
method for rabbinic interpretation.

Inasmuch as only the last of these rules is completely new, special attention will here be given to it alone.

13.   *Shene ketuvim hamakhhishim zeh ʾet zeh ʿad sheyavoʾ hakatuv hashelishi
wayakhriaʿ benehem* (‏שני כתובים המכחישים זה את זה עד שיבוא הכתוב השלישי ויכריע‏
‏ביניהם‏).

According to this device for reconciling conflicting passages, "two
texts[may] contradict one another until a third text comes and harmo-
nizes them." The logic of the example which follows is largely self-evident,
and hinges on a distinction between ‏צאן‏, "flock" (of sheep), and ‏בקר‏,
"herd" (of cattle).

R. Akiba says: "One scriptural passage says: 'And thou shalt sacrifice
the passover-offering unto the Lord thy God, of the flock and of the
herd' (Deut. 16:2), and another scriptural passage says: 'from the
sheep or from the goats shall yet take it' (Exod. 12:5). How can both
these verses be maintained? You must say: This is a rule about the
interpretation of the Torah: Two passages opposing one another
and conflicting with one another stand as they are, until a third
passage comes and decides between them. Now, the passage: 'Draw
out and take you lambs according to your families, and kill the passover lamb' (Exod. 12:21) decides in this case, declaring that from the
flock only and not from the herd may the passover sacrifice come.[48]

(47) Sifre to Num. 15:31; b. Ber. 31b, Ned. 3a.
(48) *Mek.* Pisḥa iv:42–49 (vol. i, p. 32). Other Tannaitic examples include *Mek.* Pisḥa
viii:34–37 = xvii:50–52 (cf. Men. 66a), Baḥodesh ix: 129–134; Sifre to Num. 7:89; Sifra to

In this example, the application of the principle of "reconciliation between texts" stands forth clearly. 1) Each verse is given at the outset in order to make visible the apparent discrepancy between them. 2) The question to which this *middah* addresses itself is then stated: "How can both these verses be maintained." (כיצד יתקיימו שני כתובים הללו)? 3) Next, the text of the *middah* is given, followed by the introduction of the decisive third text which decides the case. The relevancy of the third text may be apparent on lexical grounds or by virtue of the similarity of its context to the other two passages. It is not really a tie-breaker, for it is thought neither to defeat nor to falsify either of the previous two texts. In fact, in this rather remarkable instance, the *darshan* even recognizes that the texts are using slightly different data and are thus making partially antithetical statements. However, beginning with the presuppositions that Scripture is its own best interpreter, that discrepancies in the text are more apparent than real, and that the divine draftsman will make available elsewhere in the Torah the words and sentences necessary to settle the issue between the texts in question, he proceeds in the confidence that all three texts, properly understood, can be reconciled to one another. In this particular example, the phrase of Deut. 16:2, "and the herd," is simply dropped. The "flock" and not the "herd" is the normative category. Thus is the reconciliation achieved, though with the tacit admission that a phrase of Scripture is not functional. Still, as R. Ishmael taught, "The Torah speaks in the ordinary language of people," and the people, of course, roasted lamb and not veal on Passover. It is better that a word of Scripture should fall into disuse on the evidence of other Scripture than that the discourse of Scripture with later generations should be interrupted.

## C.   The Thirty-Two Hermeneutical Principles of R. Eliezer b. Yose Hagelili.

The list of thirty-two *middot* attributed to this Tanna of the third generation is mentioned neither in the Tannaitic corpus nor in the Talmud itself — though R. Eliezer and his interpretive activity are identified with haggadah (Ḥul. 89a).[49] In fact, this collection of *middot* is itself traditionally identified with haggadah, and some of the more playful rules enumerated in it (e.g., parable, pun, *gematria, notarikon*) are found largely in haggadic contexts. For this reason, further discussion of this list lies outside the scope of this article, although several of the individual

Lev. 16:1; and the two examples given at the conclusion of the "Baraita d'R. Ishmael." Cf. Bacher, *op. cit.*, pp. 86–87.

(49) A text of the 32 rules is now printed in BT after Berakhot, but more fully in H.G. Enelow, ed., *The Mishnah of R. Eliezer* (New York, 1933). For a brief discussion of each rule and older bibliography, see H.L. Strack, *op. cit.*, pp. 95–98.

*middot* are drawn from the lists of seven and thirteen and have already been treated.[50] Let it be said, however, that no hard fast line separates the *hermeneutics* of haggadah from that of halakhah. The majority of the methods are employed in both, and the basic issue of *hermeneutic* confronts the two genres in exactly the same way.

### D.   Other Hermeneutical Methods of the Tannaim.

Although the traditional lists of seven and thirteen hermeneutical principles embody what may be regarded as the "normative" rabbinic hermeneutics, the sources both mention and display a great many other devices both simple and complex, which were employed to "prolong the discourse" of Scripture to later generations. One group of these methods is identified initially with R. Naḥum of Gimzo, but ultimately with his pupil, R. Akiba. The latter is pictured as engaged in methodological controversy with his contemporary of the second generation, R. Ishmael, precisely over the question of the interpretation of Scripture. These methods give substance to the Akiban principle of scriptural interpretation, namely, that the language of Torah differs from human language in that all the apparent redundancies, superfluities, or pleonasms are in reality clues to deeper meaning.[51] Quite naturally, the devices are exegetical, and concentrate on features of grammar and textual structure; however, these too may have great value in making applications of scriptural law to contemporary life. The most noted among them are: (1) *ribbui* (רבוי), "extension" (Eliez. nos. 1, 3), wherein the presence of a certain particle such as כל, אף, את, גם, or a double word, infinitive absolute, or other grammatical feature was held to indicate that a supplementary teaching from tradition should be introduced at that point; (2) *miʿuṭ* (מיעוט), "limitation" (Eliez. nos. 2, 4), wherein the obverse was held to be the case, in the presence of such particles as אך, מן, רק; 3) *semukhim* (סמוכים), "juxtaposition" (an analogical principle related to גזירה שוה), which held that a passage

---

(50) E.g., *qal vaḥomer meforash*, Eliez. no. 5, includes *qal vaḥomer*, Hillel and Ishmael no. 1, and vice versa; *gezerah shavah*, Eliez. no. 7, the second *middah* of Hillel and Ishmael; *binyan ᵓav*, Eliez. no. 8, cf. Hillel nos. 3–4, Ishmael no. 3; *shene ketuvim hamakhḥishim*, cf. Ishmael no. 13. In addition, Eliez. rules 1 and 3 are both forms of *ribbui*, "extension," while nos. 2 and 4 are both forms of *miʿuṭ*, "limitation." These latter rules have considerable play in halakhic texts and are discussed in paragraph D below.

(51) Cf. Lieberman, *Hellenism²*, pp. 95–96. Guttmann, *op. cit.*, pp. 228–229, has some felicitous remarks on the subject of the exegetical method of Akiba: "Most potent and consequential is Akiba's rule that every seemingly 'superfluous' text element of the Torah, such as את... has a specific meaning. ... As a result, Akiba became the foremost champion of *eisegesis*, while other scholars tried to stay (somewhat) closer to the actual meaning of the text, as did R. Yishmael who maintained דברה תורה כלשון בני אדם.... From the scientific point of view Ishmael was right, but Akiba's point of view was more useful and mostly prevailed."

might be explained with reference to neighboring passages (cf. Sifre to Num. 131).

One principle of interpretation employed extensively by both Tannaitic schools is a true analogical device. This rule, which came to be known as *heqqesh* (היקש) "comparison, analogy," is not listed among the seven *middot* of Hillel even though it was reportedly used by him in the abortive debate with the Bene Bathyra (b. Pes. 66a; cf. y. Pes. 33a14). Sometimes called *heqqesh hakatuv*, it starts from an analogy drawn within Scripture itself. It is based upon the basically syntactical premise that to both of the compound subjects of a single legal predicate (or compound objects of the verb or preposition) will be applicable additional halakhic rules known from elsewhere to adhere to just one of the subjects. In other words, the syntactical collocation of terms creates an analogy between them more fundamental than that identified in the immediate context of the legal sentence. This kind of comparison exceeds the general comparability between legal terms established by *gezerah shavah*, with which *heqqesh* is frequently identified.[52]

The very first chapter of *Mek.* provides a good example of an argument based upon the principle of *heqqesh*. The *lemma* is Exod. 12:1, "And the Lord spoke to Moses and Aaron in the land of Egypt. . . ." The interpreter wants to know why both of the ancient leaders are mentioned here. The answer:

> By saying here, "unto Moses and Aaron," Scripture teaches that Aaron was equal to Moses: just as Moses was a judge over Pharaoh [cf. Exod. 7:1], so also was Aaron a judge over Pharaoh: just as Moses would speak his words fearlessly [cf. Exod. 4:11–12], so also would Aaron speak his words fearlessly.[53]

The line of reasoning is very succinct. 1) The combined object of the preposition "unto" in Exod. 12:1 invites the creation of an analogy:

(52) Mielziner, *op. cit.*, pp. 152–155, for example, discusses *heqqesh* in an appendix to his discussion of *gezerah shavah*, though he also acknowledges that it bears some similarity to *semukhim*, "juxtaposition" (p. 177). He contends that the rabbis regarded arguments from *heqqesh* as being usually more conclusive than those from *gezerah shavah*. Bacher, *op. cit.*, p. 45, remarks, "The term היקיש (i.e., the verbal form) may also be used for the comparison of two biblical sentences accomplished on the basis of the deductive rule *gezerah shavah*." As examples he gives the series of analogies offered in *Mek.* Baḥodesh viii: 13–28 between the honoring of father and mother and the honor of God. He concludes that in the School of Ishmael the term להקיש can be used to introduce arguments from *gezerah shavah*.

(53) *Mek.* Pisḥa i: 13–16 (vol. i, p. 2). Among other Tannaitic uses of the device can be mentioned *Mek.* Neziqin viii: 67–72; M. Shev. 1:4, Yev. 3:6, Mak. 1:7, Men. 7:6; b. Ḳidd. 35a, Sanh. 34b, 60b. In b. Zev. 49b the question is debated of whether a law which is derived by *heqqesh* may be used for deriving another law by *heqqesh* — or by *gezerah shavah, qal vaḥomer*, or *binyan ᵓav*!

"Aaron was equal to Moses" (הקיש אהרן למשה — better translated "[The text] compares Aaron to Moses"). 2) The congruence of the two terms of this analogy having been established, the interpreter then applies to Aaron predicates elsewhere assigned to Moses. The underlying presupposition of the consistency of the design of the Torah eliminates, in the mind of the Tannaitic interpreter at least, the possibility that the likening of Moses to Aaron in Exod. 12:1 was given by the Pentateuchal writer for the purpose of that text only. An analogy drawn here by the divine draftsman establishes a relationship of abiding validity available elsewhere for exegetical and hermeneutical purposes.

Other interpretive devices found in Tannaitic halakhic contexts and not already mentioned here include the method of revocalizing a word in order to convey a different meaning (often introduced by the formula אל תקרא, "Do not read. . . .");[54] that principle (later restated as the last two of the 32 *middot*) which allowed interpreters to telescope biblical materials from widely differing time periods into a single discussion, אין מוקדם ומאוחר בתורה ("There is no former or latter in Scripture," i.e., the Torah does not proceed in chronological sequence);[55] and the axiom that אין מקרא יוצא מידי פשוטו ("Scripture does not transcend its plain meaning"), which simply warns that the plain meaning of a text must not be forgotten no matter how ingeniously it may be expounded through the use of various *middot*.[56]

One might go on to list literally hundreds of hermeneutical methods operative in rabbinic texts. When Malbim (R. Meir Loeb ben Yehiel Michael, 1809–1880) did in fact make such a list in his commentary on Sifra, *Ayelet hashaḥar*, he arrived at the figure of 613! Many of these methods can be identified by stereotyped introductory formulae or typical rhetorical patterns such as have been exhibited above. Others would have to be placed in broad functional categories such as "logical interpretation"

(54) The observation of words written defectively and plene (b. Qid. 30a), and the rule of Miqra᾿ vs. Masorah (b. Sanh. 4a) are closely related to this one. Cf. Chajes, *op. cit.*, p. 22. The principle of *seres* or *hefekh* ("interpretation by transposition"), used by the School of R. Ishmael, also involves such manipulation of the biblical text itself. Cf. Daube, *The New Testament and Rabbinic Judaism* (Lieden, 1956), pp. 410–412.

(55) Cf. *Mek.* Shirata vii: 1–16. Patte, *op. cit.*, pp. 67–74 has a useful discussion of this principle under the heading, "The Synthetic View of Scripture and of Sacred History." Also Bacher, *op. cit.*, pp. 167–168; Daube, *New Testament*, etc., pp. 408–410. Lauterbach, JE, vol. xii, pp. 31–32 regards it as R. Ishmael's way of contradicting R. Akiba's principle of "juxtaposition."

(56) b. Shab. 63a. Weingreen remarks that this rule and others like it served "as a healthy deterrent against the over-indulgence in the luxury of Derash interpretation" (*op. cit.*, p. 18). The concept of peshaṭ, usually translated "plain meaning," should be considered a principle of hermeneutics in its own right, though space dose not permit extensive discussion of it here. The term itself may not have been used by the Tannaim (cf. Bacher, *op. cit.*, p. 162,

and "restrictive interpretation," simply on the basis of the tasks which they actually perform in the texts.[57] In fact, new identifications of hermeneutical methods are still being made through analysis of Tannaitic midrashic, targumic, and mishnaic texts. "Allegory," for example, is not formally listed among the ancient *middot* (though the "parable," Eliez. no. 26, is next-of-kin); yet, Vermes can point out allegorical interpretations of texts such as that of Lev. 18:21 reported in M. Meg. 4:9.[58] Jacobs identifies a pattern characterized by the formula אין לדבר סוף ("There is no end to the matter;" cf. M. Pes. 1:2, Yoma 1:1). This he describes as *reductio ad absurdum*, an argument which disproves another by showing that its conclusion is ridiculous.[59]

In short, work remains to be done even yet in discerning the wide variety of devices employed by the Tannaim and their successors to forge the link between normative Scripture and contemporary experience.[60]

## TANNAITIC HERMENEUTICS AND THE BIBLE

The need to "prolong the discourse" of the Scriptures confronted Israel even when the Scriptures were still being written. The traditions of the fathers had to be "re-presented" to the sons and daughters in a way that would claim their loyalty and obedience in the midst of new cultural situations. Evidence of that process of proclamation and expansion of the received tradition is visible in the Pentateuch itself, particularly in the Deuteronomic retelling of the story of Israel's covenant history into the

---

note 3); in fact, if Lauterbach is correct, they may not have had a sharp sense of the distinction of *derash* (interpretation) and *peshat* (literal meaning). (Cf. his article, "*Peshat*," JE, vol. ix, pp. 652–653.) Rosenblatt argues (*op. cit.*, pp. pp. 1–6), however, that the Tannaim were deeply interested in discovering the "simple meaning" of texts, as they understood that "simple meaning." It was precisely the assumption that every Scripture has a basic underlying meaning, and that no "plain meaning" of any Scripture is in fundamental contradiction with any other, that drove Tannaitic interpreters to ingenious methods for reconciling texts.

In recent years, Raphael Loewe has contributed a useful clarification of the discussion of *peshat* ("The 'Plain' Meaning of Scripture in Early Jewish Exegesis," in *Papers of the Institute of Jewish Studies, London*, ed. by J.G. Weiss, vol. i [Jerusalem, 1964], pp. 140–185). The term is best understood as designating a teaching as "authoritative," either because it is propounded by a recognized authority, or because it is "recognized by the public as obviously authoritative, since familiar and traditional" (p. 181). Cf. his catalogue of the recent literature, pp. 178–179, note. 189.

(57) Cf. M. Elon, *Encyc. Jud.*, vol. viii, cols. 1422–1423.

(58) Vermes, *op. cit.*, p. 75.

(59) Louis Jacobs, *op. cit.*, pp. 38–50.

(60) Yet another identifications and discussions of hermeneutical devices operative in Tannaitic texts are given by Mielziner, *op. cit.*, pp. 177–187; Epstein, *op. cit.*, pp. 521–536; Towner, *op. cit.*, pp. 251–254. Rosenblatt, *op. cit.*, gives lists of examples of named and unnamed interpretive devices which are based on lexicographical, grammatical, and critical observations.

ears of a seventh-century B.C.E. Judean community. The Deuteronomistic history is subjected to re-proclamation by the post-exilic Chronicler. There is, in short, a *hermeneutic* at work in the Bible. It is a hermeneutic with which that of the rabbis is in direct continuity.

But there is no defined, explicit *hermeneutics*. The actual methods by which older traditions were taken up and restated are elusive or common-sensical. The authoritative received traditions were not yet treated as canonical texts, fixed and immutable in every semantic detail and to be utilized only through methods which would protect the integrity of the texts themselves. No, older traditions were simply utilized typologically or kerygmatically by later circles for their own purposes; indeed, the teaching of the later circles was sometimes simply substituted for the original. In a broad sense this process of growth can be described as a midrashic one. Glosses and comments which approach the midrashic genre more narrowly construed can also be detected here and there in the text.[61] But no system of hermeneutics at all comparable to that articulated by the Tannaim was operative in the growth of the biblical text.

It is not surprising, therefore, that no biblical precedents exist for any of the formal Tannaitic *middot*, save *qal vahomer*. Although not referred to by that or any name, the argument *a minori ad maius* may be found in the Old Testament as many as 40 times.[62] Its use is purely logical and deductive, however, without exegetical intent.[63] The presence of this type of argument in the Hebrew Scriptures attests not to the beginnings of a system of hermeneutics in pre-rabbinic times, but only to the antiquity and ubiquity of this simple logical device. Neither Hillel nor the Tannaim invented it, though they may have named it;[64] they simply brought it into their collection of interpretive devices. In short, the roots of rabbinic hermeneutics are not to be found in the Hebrew Bible.

Nor does the New Testament shed much light upon the origin and development of the *middot*. It does of course reveal a deep engagement with the problem of *hermeneutic*, and, in its own way, stands very much in a

(61) Cf. Weingreen, *op. cit.*, especially the chapters entitled "Rabbinic-type Glosses in the Old Testament," pp. 32–54, and "Oral Tora and Written Records," pp. 76–99; also his article on "History of Interpretation. A. Within the Old Testament," *Interpreter's Dictionary of the Bible, Supplementary Volume* (Nashville, 1976 — henceforth IDBS), pp. 436–438.

(62) Gen. R. 92:7 gives a traditional list of ten *qal vahomer* arguments in the Old Testament: Gen. 44:8, Exod 6:12, Num. 12:14 (cf. b.B.Q. 25a), Deut. 31:27, Jer. 12:5 (twice), I Sam. 23:3, Prov. 11:31, Esther 9:12, and Ezek. 15:5. For a discussion of this list and as many as 30 other examples discerned in the Bible see H. Hirschensohn, *Berure hamiddot* (Jerusalem, 1939), pp. 39–60; cf. Strack, *op. cit.*, p. 285, note 3.

(63) J.A. Sanders, "Hermeneutics," IDBS, p. 404, points to Ezek. 33:24 as a possible example of a biblical *qal vahomer* argument with exegetical intent.

(64) So S. Zeitlin, "Hillel and the Hermeneutical Rules," *op. cit.*, p. 165.

line of direct continuity with the Old Testament pattern of growth of theological tradition through re-presentation. By reason of this very continuity, the New Testament also shares with the literature of the rabbis a basic principle of hermeneutic, namely, that in the fixed point of Scripture are to be found the truths by which the moving point of the community's experience can be interpreted meaningfully. The Christ-event could be understood by the early Christians only in terms of Old Testament imagery and theology, and their writings everywhere introduce and allude to the authoritative Scripture of the Jews. Like the Pharisees and the earliest of the Tannaim who were their contemporaries, the New Testament writers regarded Scripture as fixed and took its very textual expression to be extremely significant. They were, in other words, dealing with canon. The New Testament writings reflect this conviction in the way they handle the Old Testament — quoting the text with great care, albeit from the Septuagint version, and identifying some exegetical devices as they are used.[65] Indeed, one can speak of the presence in the New Testament of an informal and unsophisticated but nevertheless definable system of hermeneutics.

However, New Testament hermeneutics bears almost no relationship to the sophisticated and precise hermeneutical system of the rabbis represented by the formal lists of *middot* and the scores of other devices. Scholars have struggled to find evidence that the Jews who wrote the New Testament were familiar with the *middot* of Hillel or Ishmael or Akiba.[66]

---

(65) E.g., Gal. 4:24, "This is an allegory," identifies the method being used to apply the stories of Hagar and Sarah to the early Christian theological issue of law versus grace. In Rom. 5:14, Adam is spoken of as "a *type* of the one who was to come." Typology, the simple historical analogy, is probably the single most commonly used hermeneutical method in both the Old and New Testaments. Cf. E. Achtemeier, "Typology," in IDBS, pp. 926–927. The New Testament "prophecy-fulfillment" scheme may also be broadly construed as a hermeneutical method. Cf. David M. Hay, "History of Interpretation. C. NT Interpretation of the OT," IDBS, pp. 443–444.

(66) Many scholars have discerned the presence in both literatures of some of the same informal interpretive moves — typology, allegory, construction of a series of texts around a key word or theme, elucidation of Scripture by various types of analogies to other Scripture. There is no intention here to deny these commonalities of hermeneutical approach to the Old Testament, even though the case could be made that — given the literary devices available to first and second century writers generally, and the commitment to the authority of Scripture in its very textual details held by the New Testament writers and the Pharisees alike — such commonalities were inevitable. Cf. Hay, *op. cit.*, p. 446; Daube, *The New Testament and Rabbinic Judaism* (especially his discussion of Matt. 5:17 ff., in connection with the rule of *kelal uferaṭ*, pp. 63–66); E. Earle Ellis, *Paul's use of the Old Testament* (Edinburgh, 1957) — especially his chapter in "Pauline and Jewish Literary Methods," wherein he states: "Hillel's principles of *a fortiori* and analogy are implicit in many Pauline passages, but here

Among formal arguments, only *qal vaḥomer* can be found, and its presence can be put down to the antiquity and the ubiquity of that simple form of argument.[67] Because of its early date and the familiarity many of its writers probably had with Pharisaic tradition, the New Testament may be regarded as a significant witness to rabbinic tradition in its formative

---

too the rabbinic affinities can be too greatly stressed" [p. 46]. He then proceeds to illustrate only Paul's use of *qal vaḥomer*.

The article by D. Moody Smith, Jr., "The Use of the Old Testament in the New," in J.M. Efird, ed., *The Use of the Old Testament in the New and Other Essays* (Durham, N.C., 1972), pp. 3–66, is a valuable summary of the recent discussion, with references to the works of Tasker, Barrett, Sowers, Doeve, Bonsirven, Davies, Ellis, Lindars, Freed, Stendahl, and others. See also the useful article and bibliography of Merrill P. Miller, "Targum, Midrash and the Use of the Old Testament in the New Testament," *Journal for the Study of Judaism* 2 (1971), pp. 29–82. In all of this discussion, the success at explicating such subjects as the number and order of Old Testament quotations used by New Testament writers, New Testament affinites to *pesher* exegesis and to Philo, and the similarity of New Testament hermeneutical practices to the informal interpretive devices employed in Mishnah and midrash, far outweighs any success at disclosing any New Testament purchase on the formal *hermeneutics* of Tannaitic literature.

One of the most interesting recent attempts to prove that one New Testament writer, Paul, knew and employed at least five of the seven *middot* of Hillel is that of J. Jeremias, "Paulus als Hillelit," in E. Ellis and M. Wilcox, eds., *Neotestamentica et Semitica: Studies in Honor of Matthew Black* (Edinburgh, 1969), pp. 88–94. Aside from *qal vaḥomer*, which Paul does use more frequently than any other New Testament writer, Jeremias' evidence for Pauline use of the five *middot* remains unconvincing. Rom. 4:1–7, which he gives as the lone example of a Pauline *gezerah shavah*, does indeed propose an analogy between Abraham in Gen. 15:6 and the man to whom God reckons righteousness apart from works, whom David blesses in Ps. 32:2. The analogy hinges upon the term *elogisthē*, "reckoned," present in some form in both texts. But does the analogy really perform an exegetical function, clarifying the meaning of the key term in one text by an examination of the other? Or is it simply a line of reasoning seized upon *ad hoc* for the purpose of backing up an argument about Abraham with further support from Scripture? The latter seems more likely to be the case, especially because it is difficult to discern any formal, stereotyped structure in the text similar to that which accompanies the application of a *middah* in rabbinic sources. Similar criticisms of lack of stereotyped form and of clearly comparable function can be made of Jeremias' proposals that Paul uses the argument *kelal uferaṭ* in Rom. 13:9 and Gal. 5:14; *kayoṣe bo mimaqom 'aḥer* in Gal. 3:16; and *davar halamed me'inyano* in Rom. 4:10–11a.

Jeremias' discussion of Pauline hermeneutics has been attacked by Klaus Haacker from another angle in his article, "War Paulus Hillelit?" *Das Institutum Judaicum der Universität Tübingen in den Jahren 1971-1972*, pp. 106–120. Haacker centers his critique upon the unreliability of the attribution of the seven *middot* to Hillel. Why should Paul be linked to Hillel on the basis of his use of certain *middot* when even Hillel "hardy . . . made use of all, or even most, of the rules" (p. 118, note 49, quoting J. Neusner, *The Rabbinic Traditions About the Pharisees Before 70* [Leiden, 1971], vol. i, p. 241). Haacker suggests that contemporary Hellenistic hermeneutical method was the common source for both Paul and the House of Hillel.

(67) Examples include Matt. 6:30 = Lk. 12:28; Matt. 7:11 = Lk. 11:13; Jn. 7:23(?); Rom. 5:15, 17, 11:12; I Cor. 9:9–10(?); II Cor. 3:7–8, 11; Phil. 2:12(?); Heb. 12:9. Cf. H.L. Strack and P. Billerbeck, *Kommentar zum Neuen Testament aus Talmud und Midrasch*, vol. iii (Munich, 1926), pp. 223–226 — a discussion of *qal vaḥomer* in connection with Rom. 5:9f. Examples of *ḥomer vaqal* include Rom. 5:9, 10; 8:32 (?); 11:24; I Cor. 6:2–3.

stages;[68] therefore, the absence in the former of any knowledge of the *middot* of rabbinic hermeneutics suggests that they had not as yet come into being as formally articulated norms.

Because neither the Old Testament nor the New Testament provides significant evidence which might throw light upon the genesis and development of the rabbinic methods of hermeneutics, scholars have turned to the Hellenistic world in search of external parallels. The resulting discussion has already been noted: in brief, it is inconclusive.[69] Some individual *middot* can certainly be compared with methods of juridical interpretation in Roman law, as well as with methods of literary interpretaton among the Alexandrian grammarians. Some terminology may have been borrowed. However, the evidence is much too diffuse to suggest that the Tannaim simply learned their methods of interpretation from the Greek rhetors or grammarians.

There being no other likely external first and second century C.E. sources from which the basic methods of rabbinic hermeneutics might have been drawn, we are left with the inescapable conclusion that the work of formulating their sophisticated system of hermeneutics was done by the rabbis themselves, largely after 70 C.E., in the academies of the Tannaim and their successors.

(68) This proposition is illustrated to good effect by J. Neusner, "'First Cleanse the Inside': the 'Halakhic' Background of a Controversy Saying," *New Testament Studies* 22 (1975–76), pp. 486–495; also found in his *Purities, op. cit.*, vol. iii, pp. 374–381.

(69) Cf. *supra*, pp. 107–109.

# THE DATE OF THE MEKILTA DE-RABBI ISHMAEL

BEN ZION WACHOLDER

Hebrew Union College - Jewish Institute of Religion, Cincinnati

SCHOLARLY papers can derive from any one of a variety of stimuli or a combination of them. The present paper derives from a series of problems which have compelled me to search the material as well as myself. This paper represents a most untraditional approach to a book inordinately precious to me. I found myself resisting the logic of my observations, simply because the conclusion to which I was drawn represents an about-face from my traditional approach to the literature. Nevertheless, the issues are compelling enough to be presented in the arena of notice where my peers can consider my present handling of the array of problems.

The Mekilta de-Rabbi Ishmael contains halakic and aggadic comments on sections of the Book of Exodus. It is the consensus of scholars (to wit, Zunz, Weiss, Friedmann, Hoffmann, Bacher, Lauterbach, Ginzberg, J. N. Epstein, Finkelstein) that the Mekilta of Rabbi Ishmael reflects the second century tannaitic halakah.[1] In his

---

[1] L. Zunz, *Die gottesdienstlichen Vorträge der Juden*[2] (Frankfurt a.M., 1892), pp. 49–53, dates the sources of the halakic midrashim at the latest in the first half of the third century, though he grants that the Mekilta was edited later. I. H. Weiss (ed.), *Mechilta* (Wien, 1865), pp. XVIII f., argues that the anonymous sections of the Mekilta emanated from Ishmael's academy, but that a substantial part was added later, some of it by the amoraim, with Rab (Abba Arikha) as its final editor. M. Friedmann, *Mechilta de-Rabbi Ismael* (Wien, 1870), pp. XVI ff., rejected Weiss' hypothesis that Rab was the Mekilta's editor. Friedmann argues that this book was known to the talmudists as Sifre or Sifra, works which were known as *halakah* and differed in structure from *mishnah*. A. Geiger, *Urschrift*[2] (Frankfurt a.M., 1928), pp. 140 f., regards the Mekilta as a depository of premishnaic halakah. D. Hoffmann, *Zur Einleitung in die halachischen Midraschim* (Berlin, 1886–87), pp. 3 ff., 36 ff., believes that all *baraithot* of the Talmud which present the halakah as it is derived from scriptural verses were originally part of the halakic midrashim, now lost. A substantial part of this tannaitic exegesis, though not preserved in the Talmud, is to be found in works such as the Mekilta. W. Bacher, *Die exegetische Terminologie der Tannaiten* (Leipzig, 1899), tr. into Hebrew (Tel Aviv, 1923), follows Hoffmann's principles. For Lauterbach, see next note. Finkelstein, see note 3. J. N. Epstein (ed. posthumously by E. Z. Melamed), *Introduction to Tannaitic Literature, Mishna, Tosephta, and Halakhic Midrashim* (in Hebrew, Jerusalem, 1957), pp. 501 ff., traces the material of the halakic midrashim, including the Mekilta, to Ezra, LXX, Philo, and to the schools of Akiba and Ishmael, but the anonymous passages of the Mekilta

117

masterly edition of the Mekilta, Lauterbach summed up the prevailing
point of view: "Both in its halakic and haggadic portions the *Mekilta*
shows itself to be one of the older tannaitic works. It contains very old
material and has preserved teachings of the early Tannaim. Its
halakic teachings in many instances reflect the point of view of the
older Halakah, which was different from that of the later or younger
Halakah; hence some of its interpretations of the law are not in agreement with the interpretations accepted in the Talmud."[2] Finkelstein
has raised the question whether the haggadic material was not a later
interpolation, but he endorses the view that the Mekilta indeed
reflects the Ishmaelite school of biblical exegesis which interpreted
Scripture more literally than the rival school of Rabbi Akiba.[3]

In this study the question is raised whether the Mekilta de-Rabbi
Ishmael should be regarded as an authentically tannaitic midrash or
whether this work is instead a posttalmudic compilation or, indeed,
concoction, deliberately using the names of tannaim for authority,
or even inventing names. For the purpose of this paper, it is assumed
that our inherited Mekilta is a unitary work; this assumption will be
defended below. Here it suffices to say that both the halakic and
haggadic sections of the entire Mekilta cite the same names, use a
similar vocabulary, and display the same general characteristics of the
book as a whole.[4] This study discusses only the Mekilta of Rabbi

---

emanate only from the latter (pp. 550–568). E. Z. Melamed, *Halachic Midrashim
of the Tannaim in the Talmud Babli* (in Hebrew, Jerusalem, 1943), follows the path
of his mentor Epstein, but his compilation of the talmudic exegetical comments in
effect has created a new halakic midrash.

[2] J. Z. Laut(erbach), ed., *Mekilta de-Rabbi Ishmael* (New York, 1933), p. XIX
(cf. below, note 28). See also his "Midrash and Mishnah," *JQR*, N. S. 5–6, (1916),
dating the terminology of the halakic midrashim to the pre-Hasmonean period,
subsequent to which the Mishnah form was introduced.

[3] L. Finkelstein, "The Sources of the Tannaitic Midrashim," *JQR*, N. S. 31
(1941), pp. 211–243, reacts to Ch. Albeck's (cited below, note 85) finding that the
halakic midrashim had made use of our talmudic texts. Finkelstein reiterates Hoffmann's thesis (*Zur Einleitung*, pp. 72 ff.), that in addition to Ishmael's Mekilta on
Exodus there existed in the talmudic period an Ishmaelite Mekilta on the remaining
three books of the Torah; the extant Sifre on Numbers belongs also to this school.
The aggadic material of the Mekilta on Exodus, Finkelstein grants, originated from
an independent midrash, subsequently joined with the much older halakic Mekilta.
See also below note 17.

[4] Lauterbach, "The Arrangement and the Division of the Mekilta," *HUCA* I
(1924), p. 434; *Mekilta* I, pp. XVI–XVIII, defends the integrity of the Mekilta.
Epstein, *Introduction to Tannaitic Literature*, pp. 572–588, argues that the nine sections originally were independent treatises, each of which has a different proportion of
Akiba's or Ishmael's school; but he grants that the halakic and haggadic material
within each treatise emanated from the same editor. Cf. the previous note.

Ishmael. Yet much of what is said here of the Mekilta of Ishmael applies also to the Mekilta of Rabbi Simeon ben Yoḥai, possibly an imitation of the former.[5] Respecting the Sifra, Sifré, and Sifré Zutta the question remains open, though obviously the problems confronting the reader of the Mekilta are interwoven with those of the other halakic midrashim.[6]

The nub of the paper involves the question of the date of the author(s) or editor(s) of the Mekilta.

I

The oldest testimony to the existence of a Mekilta comes from the first half of the ninth century. There was written about this time the first extensive rabbinic code, Simeon Kayyara's *Halakhot Gedolot*; it refers to our book as Mekilta on Exodus.[7] Despite this reference,

---

[5] The Mekilta de-Rabbi Simeon ben Yoḥai was first published by Hoffmann (Frankfurt a.M., 1905) from quotations of the Midrash Hagadol on Exodus by the fifteenth-century Saadia ben David al-Adani of Yemen (ed. Margulies, Jerusalem, 1955). This Mekilta was edited on the basis of Mss. by E. Z. Melamed (from J. N. Epstein's notes, Jerusalem, 1955). Cf. now Karl Gottfried Eckart, *Untersuchungen zur Traditionsgeschichte der Mechiltha* (Berlin, 1959), though Eckart used Hoffmann's archaic edition. It is clear that for the most part the Mekilta of Simeon reproduces the one of Ishmael, but sometimes modifies the text to bring the tannaitic midrash into greater conformity with the tannaitic exegesis of the Babylonian Talmud.

[6] Stylistically and structurally all of these halakic midrashim appear to be similar, the differences being mainly in the amount of aggadic material and the names of the authorities listed. But the matter requires detailed analysis to determine whether or not the same author wrote all of these works.

[7] *Halakhot Gedolot* ([ed. Warsaw, 1875], 144a; [Berlin, 1888], pp. 633 f.), lists the number of the biblical books, Mishnah, Tosafot (Tosefta). But both texts, though differing, are corrupt:

| *Warsaw ed.* | *Berlin ed.* |
|---|---|
| ושׁשׁה סדרי תוספות ותשׁעה דבורים תורה | שׁשׁה סדרי תוספות ותשׁעה [דיבורים] שׁל תורת |
| כוהנים וארבעה סדרשׁ סופרים ספרא וספרי | כהנים וארבעה מדרשׁ סופרים חצונות וקטנות אין |
| שׁהם ארבעה ספרי ואלו הן בראשׁית רבה | מספר ספרא וספרי שׁהן ד' ספרי ואילו הן |
| וסכילתא דואלה שׁמות וספר | בראשׁית רבה וסכלתי דאלה שׁמות |
| וידבר ואלה הדברים וכולהו פירושׁם בתורה | וכולהו פירושׁין בתורה כהנים וחיצונות וקטנות |
| כוהנים וחיצונות וקטנות אין מספר .... | לעל .... |

The meaning of this passage (cf. Num. Rabbah XVIII, 21; Tanḥuma, *Koraḥ*, 12) is not clear. Because it is the oldest extant summary of rabbinic literature, a rough paraphrase is offered in English: "And six orders of Tosafot (Tosefta); and nine sections (?) of the Priestly Code (Sifra on Leviticus); and four scriptural midrashim, called Sifre and Sifra, consisting of four books: Genesis Rabbah, Mekilta of Exodus, the Book of Numbers and Deuteronomy. And all of these books are commentaries

the evidence is nevertheless clear that the Mekilta was not used as a source for the *Halakhot Gedolot* (neither in its French nor Spanish version).[8] Saadia Gaon (died in 942) not only refers to the Mekilta on Exodus, but directly cites it, this apparently supplying the first verifiable citation.[9] Samuel Hanagid of Granada (died in 953), in his introduction to the Talmud, appears to be the first who names the book the *Mekilta de-Rabbi Ishmael.*[10] However, Hanagid lists this title among works such as the "Mishnah of Rabbi Eliezer ben Jacob" and the "Alphabet of Rabbi Akiba;" the former is known to us from an obscure talmudic reference to a work lost centuries before Hanagid's time;[11] the latter is a medieval pseudograph parading under Akiba's name.[12] Hence, Hanagid's testimony is necessarily uncertain.

Extensive verifiable references begin to appear in about the year 1000, becoming numerous in the eleventh and twelfth centuries. Hai Gaon (died in 1038) cites the book as the Mekilta of the Land of Israel;[13] the lexicographer Yeḥiel ben Nathan of Rome (died in 1106)[14]

---

(like?) in the Priestly Code (Sifra?); and (in addition to these books there are) numerous apocryphal and minor books...." (The passage goes on to quote B. Sukkah 28a).

Although the meaning is somewhat obscure, it is nevertheless clear that the *Halakhot Gedolot* believed that the Sifra was the oldest of all midrashic works, and that Genesis Rabbah, Mekilta, and Sifre were modeled after it.

[8] Hildesheimer, in the index (p. 136) to his edition of the *Halakot Gedolot,* cites ten references where the Mekilta was presumably used by the geonic author. But an analysis of these passages shows that they were derived from the Babylonian Talmud, not from the Mekilta, though there is no doubt that the *Halakhot Gedolot* did cite the Sifra and Sifre. Thus for example, Hildesheimer cites Pasha, X, p. 34; Laut. I, 77 f., as the source of a passage in *Halakhot Gedolot,* p. 59a (Warsaw ed.); p. 139 (Berlin ed.). But it is likely that the source used here was B. Pesaḥim, 43a, whose wording is closer to that of the *Halakhot Gedolot* than is the text of the Mekilta.

[9] Harkavy in *Hakedem* I (1907), p. 127, citing Mekilta, *Baḥodesh* 10, p. 239; Laut. 2, 276. In citations from the Mekilta, the pagination refers to the editions of Horowitz-Rabin, Berlin, 1930, 2nd ed., Jerusalem, 1960, followed by that of Lauterbach, New York, 1933 (3 volumes).

[10] See Samuel Hanagid, *Introduction to the Talmud,* usually printed at the end of B. Berakhot.

[11] See B. Yevamot 49b; cited also 37a, 60a, etc.: "The Mishnah of R. Eliezer b. Jacob is small but excellent" (משנת ר' אליעזר בן יעקב קב ונקי). This is not to be confused with Mishnat R. Eliezer (or, by its other name, "Midrash Rabbi Eliezer of the Thirty-two Hermeneutic Rules"; also known as Midrash Agur) on Prov. 30, or Pirke de-Rabbi-Eliezer, mentioned below.

[12] See Zunz, *Gott. Vort.,* p. 178 (Hebrew ed., p. 333, n. 67).

[13] A. Harkavy, *Teshuvot Hageonim* (Berlin, 1887), p. 107, Hai Gaon's responsum to Samuel Hanagid.

[14] See A. Kohut's *Index to Arukh Completum* 107b for references to the Mekilta.

and Rashi (died in 1105), refer to the book as Mekilta;[15] and the eleventh-century talmudic scholar of North Africa — Nissim ben Jacob — names it the Mekilta of Rabbi Ishmael.[16]

It remained for Maimonides to give a precise formulation: "The sages of the Mishnah also composed other works which expounded upon the words of the Torah: Rabbi Hosha'ya, the pupil of the saintly Rabbi (Judah Hanasi), wrote a commentary on the Book of Genesis (Rabbah); and *Rabbi Ishmael expounded upon from the beginning of Exodus till the end of the Torah* — and this is called Mekilta. And Rabbi Akiba also was the author of a Mekilta. But other sages authored midrashim as well. All of these works were composed before the Babylonian Talmud."[17] This is not the place to comment upon these enigmatic, and in my judgment, erroneous, words. It would seem, however, that Maimonides already was in possession of the Mekilta de-Rabbi Simeon ben Yoḥai in addition to the Mekilta de-Rabbi Ishmael.[18] Since Maimonides had no inherited tradition by which to explain the authorship of either Genesis Rabbah or of the halakic midrashim, he was the first to infer that the names Rabbi Hosha'ya or Rabbi Ishmael (the first authorities cited in the relevant texts) referred to authorship.[19] He further reasoned that since one Mekilta was authored by Rabbi Ishmael, the other halakic midrash must have been authored by Ishmael's contemporary, Rabbi Akiba. It is evident that the standard assumption of the existence of two tannaitic midrashic works — those by Ishmael and Akiba — rests primarily upon Maimonides.[20]

---

[15] The Mekilta de-Rabbi Ishmael was Rashi's favorite source on the relevant sections of Exod. 12:1 ff.; Rashi did not use the Mekilta of Simeon ben Yoḥai.

[16] See Nissim's commentary on Shabbath 106b printed in the margins of the Wilno editions of the Talmud.

[17] Maimonides, *Yad*, Introduction. Cf. D. Hoffmann, *Midrasch Tannaim zum Deut.* (Berlin, 1909), pp. IV ff. and Finkelstein, above note 3, who uphold Maimonides' statement that the Mekilta of Ishmael extended from Exodus to Deuteronomy.

[18] For the opinion that Maimonides utilized both midrashim (cf. n. 5), see Finkelstein, "Maimonides and the Tannaitic Midrashim," *JQR*, N. S. 25 (1935), pp. 469–517. Kasher, *Mekore Ha-Rambam* (New York, 1943), claims to have traced 100 passages of Maimonides to the Mekilta of Simeon b. Yoḥai.

[19] Cf. Albeck, Introduction to Genesis Rabbah being part of vol. 3 of *Midrash Bereshit Rabba*[2] ... ed. ... by J. Theodor and Ch. Albeck (Hebrew, Jerusalem, 1965), pp. 93 f., who shows that though the early medieval rabbis dubbed our Genesis Rabbah as Midrash of Rabbi Hosha'ya, it does not necessarily follow that they intended to refer to authorship; they merely wished to identify the introductory words.

[20] Maimonides' position is upheld by Finkelstein, *JQR*, N. S. 31 (1941), pp. 211–213. See also Friedmann, *Mechilta*, pp. LXVII ff.

There remains the possibility, however, that the amoraim of the
Babylonian Talmud knew the Mekilta of Rabbi Ishmael but under
different names, such as "The School of Rabbi Ishmael," or Sifra, or
Sifre.[21] In fact, Maimonides, on the basis of a questionable reference
in Berakhot 11b, attributed these latter works to Rab, the founder of
the Academy of Sura in the year 219.[22] I do not know the meaning of
the much-commented-on passage, in Sanhedrin 86a, by Rabbi Yoḥanan
(died 279): "Unless otherwise stated, the Mishnah is by Rabbi Meir;
unless otherwise stated, the Tosefta is by Rabbi Nehemiah; . . . Sifra
is by Rabbi Judah; . . . Sifre is by Rabbi Simeon: all of them follow
(the teachings of) Rabbi Akiba."[23] There seems little likelihood that
these works listed in this passage knew of a midrash emanating from
the School of Rabbi Ishmael.[24] The frequent references in the Babylonian Talmud to a tanna of the school of Ishmael have nothing to do
with either the text or traditions of the Mekilta under consideration.[25]

[21] The "School of Rabbi Ishmael" or "Tanna of the School of Rabbi Ishmael"
(תנא דבי רבי ישמעאל) is frequent in the Babylonian Talmud, but not recorded in the
Palestinian Talmud or other amoraic midrashim. Sifra is mentioned in B. Berakhot
11b where this work (according to the vulgar editions) is identical with Talmud, in
contrast to the halakic midrashim (see Rashi *ad loc.*). But cf. *Dikduke Soferim, ad loc.*;
Friedmann, *Mechilta*, pp. XVI f. See also P. Berakhot, 3c. For other references see
next note.

[22] Berakhot 18b refers to "Tanna Sifra (or Safra) of the School of Rab," commenting on II Sam. 23:20 and Eccles. 9:5. See Maimonides, Introduction to *Yad*;
Aaron ibn Zeraḥ, *Ẓedah Ladderekh*, Introduction (Sabbioneta, 1567), 14b; Weiss,
*Mechilta*, p. XIX. See Friedmann, *Mechilta*, pp. XVI–XXIX, who refutes at length
Weiss' view that Rab authored the halakic midrashim. Friedmann neglects to mention that his own edition of the halakic midrash on Num. and Deut. is named *Sifre
debe Rab* (Vienna, 1864).

[23] None of these books are referred to in the Palestinian Talmud. B. Shabbath
137a, Eruvin 96b, Yoma 41a, Kiddushin 53a, Shav'uot 13a, Bekhorot 61a and
Keritot 22a, mention the Sifra, alluding to Judah ben Illai as its author. Cf. Alexander
Guttmann, "The Problem of the Anonymous Mishna," *HUCA* 16 (1941), 137–155.

[24] So, for example, Weiss, *Mechilta*, pp. XVI ff.; Hoffmann, *Zur Einleitung*,
pp. 15 ff. But it should be remembered that nowhere in the talmudic or midrashic
texts is there a reference to the halakic midrashim as emanating from Ishmael's
school. Because certain parallel passages in the midrashic texts are attributed to
Rabbi Ḥiyya, Malbim proposed that Ḥiyya (a pupil of Judah Hanasi) authored
these works. See next note.

[25] The relevant passages are cited in Friedmann, *Mechilta*, pp. LV–LXVII, of
which only the first two can be discussed here. Commenting on Exod. 12:2, "This
new moon," *Pasḥa* I cites Ishmael to the effect that Moses displayed the new moon
to Israel; Akiba, however, is quoted as saying that the new moon was one of the three
items (the others being leper and lampstand) which Moses had difficulty understanding, so God Himself showed it to him. The Mekilta then quotes: "Some say
that Moses had also difficulty with the manner of ritual slaughtering" (p. 6; Laut. I,
pp. 15 f.). Friedmann cites a number of rabbinic sources which contain parallel passages

II

Scholars have dated the Mekilta on internal evidence. Consistent with the usual dating has been its classification as a tannaitic midrash on the following presuppositions, which I discuss below: a) some of the halakah preserved in the Mekilta antedates the halakah of the Mishnah or the Talmud; b) the arrangement of the halakah according to scriptural verses (Mekilta, Sifra) preceded the topical arrangement of the halakah (Mishnah); c) the authorities quoted in the Mekilta are

---

to Akiba's statement, all of which differ from the Mekilta: Exod. Rabbah (XV, 28) citing an anonymous authority varies the four items, excluding ritual slaughtering, but lists instead the making of the oil for the anointment of the priest; Num. Rabbah (XV, 4) lists three items, also anonymously (also in Tanḥuma, *Shemini* 8 (11); *Baha'alotkha* 3 (4); in the Pesikta de-Rab Kahana (*Haḥodesh*, ed. Mandelbaum I, 104) and Pesikta Rabbati (78a) the three items are attributed to Simeon ben Yoḥai; Sifre Num. 61 follows the Mekilta in referring the text to Akiba; however, Menaḥot 29a attributes the tradition to the tanna of the school of Ishmael. Friedmann, in desperation, resolves the variants thusly: the Pesikta took the passage from the Sifre (if so, why did they vary it from Akiba, as found in the Sifre, to Simeon ben Yoḥai?), but the Babylonian Talmud borrowed the passages from the Mekilta, which the amoraim attributed to Ishmael; hence, Menaḥot 29a refers to the tanna of the school of Ishmael (if so, why did not the Babylonian Talmud cite Akiba as does the Mekilta?), but the late midrashim finding contradictory sources quoted our passage anonymously. An analysis of all the parallels (even those omitted by Friedmann) shows that a direct relationship exists only between the Mekilta and Menaḥot 29a (the other dozen references are too remote to be relevant). The only problem is which of these two is the original text and which the secondary. Only Menaḥot 29a gives a full discussion of the manufacturing of the lampstand of the desert and of Solomon, quoting first Rabbi Yoḥanan that Gabriel the Archangel showed Moses how to make the lampstand and only thereafter mentions Ishmael's school as a source (the passages found in the Mekilta). It follows that the Mekilta borrowed from Menaḥot 29a. The inverse is inconceivable because the Mekilta records a controversy between Ishmael and Akiba; the former claiming that only the new moon was shown to Moses by God, the latter claiming three items. As the Babylonian Talmud attributes the view of the three items to the tanna of the school of Ishmael, the talmudic editor(s) could not have been aware of the Mekilta text; the talmudic editor(s) moreover are not even aware of any controversy in this matter. Thus it would seem that it was the author of the Mekilta who adapted the passage found in Menaḥot 29a into a dispute between Ishmael and Akiba, a dispute not recorded in any other source. Unlike Friedmann, it must be assumed that *Pasḥa* I (p. 7; Laut. pp. 18 f.) was adapted from B. Sanhedrin 42a rather than vice versa. For here again, the quotation seems to be inserted from Sanhedrin 42a where it belongs, into the Mekilta, where it does not. Friedmann (p. LXIII) himself cites a dozen passages from the Babylonian Talmud where the School of Rabbi Ishmael is quoted dealing with comments on the Book of Exodus, but which are *not* in the Mekilta. The conclusion is inescapable that the editors of the Babylonian Talmud did not necessarily know of any book identical or similar to the Mekilta. See note 85.

as a rule tannaim; d) many of the exegetical technical terms of the
Mekilta were already becoming archaic in mishnaic times; and, e) the
Palestinian and Babylonian Talmuds contain direct quotations from
the Mekilta.

Supposition a) was advanced by Geiger and Lauterbach, who
dated much of the Mekilta in the premishnaic period.[26] But the
question immediately arises: where are these premishnaic materials to
be found? One thinks naturally of Jubilees, the Qumran texts, Philo,
Josephus and the Gospels. In none of these is the occasional halakic
overtone or nuance more than something passing and, with the possible exception of the Scroll of Damascus, never is it couched in pure
rabbinic form. It does not seem just to designate this sparse material
as premishnaic or tannaitic. Yet granting that the halakah of the
Mekilta occasionally coincides with such premishnaic or protomishnaic
halakah, the Mekilta follows the text of the Mishnah and Tosefta
precisely as they have come down to us, and thus could hardly be
authentically premishnaic.[27] The passages of the Mekilta cited by

---

[26] See note 2. A. Geiger, *Urschrift²*, p. 141, note, cites the parallel between the
Mekilta (on 23:7; *Kaspa* II, p. 327; Laut. III, pp. 170 f.), that Simeon ben Sheṭaḥ
sentenced to death a false witness, whereupon Judah ben Tabbai accused him of
judicial murder, and the more lengthy description of this incident in the other
talmudic texts (B. Makkot 5b; Tosefta VI, 6, p. 424), which reverse the facts of the
incident. Geiger says that because of its very nature ("wie wir unten ihn kennen
lernen, sowohl als die schmucklose und präcise Erzählung") the Mekilta leaves no
doubt that it alone has preserved the original formulation of the anecdote. However,
an analysis of the relevant texts tends to show that the Mekilta took the anecdote
from the Babylonian Talmud. The Mekilta's version reads הרגנוהו "we have killed
him," when what was meant was מי הרגו לזה או אני או אתה "Who killed this man, I or
you?", as reported in B. Sanhedrin 37b; Mekilta: היודע ובעל מחשבות, "He who knows
and Who is the master of thoughts"; B.T: היודע מחשבות, "He Who knows thoughts."
Hence, the citation of the Mekilta appears to be a tampered version of the story found
in the talmudic texts.

[27] The Mekilta frequently quotes the Mishnah directly, using the phrase מכאן
אמרו. This phrase appears in the first edition of the Mekilta sixty-three times, mostly
citing our Mishnah verbatim or, less often, a Baraitha or Tosefta. Examples: *Pasḥa*
V, p. 16; Laut. I, p. 40, quoting M. Arakhin II, 5; Laut. *ibid.*, p. 17, quoting M.
Berakhot V, 5; Laut. I, p. 42, to M. Pesaḥim V, 5. For a partial list of the Mekilta's
references to the Mishnah, Baraitha, or Tosefta, see W. Bacher, *Tradition und
Tradenten* (Leipzig, 1914), pp. 170 ff.; Epstein, *Mavo lenusaḥ ha-mishnah*, pp. 728 ff.
L. Ginzberg, in a Hebrew article, "On the Relationship between the Mishnah
and the Mekilta," which originally appeared in *Studies in Memory of M. Schorr*
(New York, 1944), and reprinted in *'Al Halakhah Ve-'aggadah* (Tel Aviv, 1960),
pp. 66–103, pp. 284–290, especially pp. 80, 89, 90, 103, argues that the phrase מכאן
אמרו does not necessarily mean that the Mekilta was citing the Mishnah, even
though the wording in the two works is identical. But Ginzberg's reasoning is not

scholars as remnants of the early halakah reveal a subjectivity that precludes the dating of the work as a whole.[28] The occasional apparent difference between the halakah of the Talmud and that of the Mekilta may not be that of priority, but may be due to the latter's misunderstanding of the former, or indeed to our ignorance of both.[29] The basic fact which must weigh in the evaluation of the Mekilta is that its

---

convincing. In the passage cited above (M. Berakhot V, 5), the Mekilta quotes: "From here they say: 'One's agent is like himself'." To which Ginzberg remarks (p. 90) that the Mekilta could not have been quoting the Mishnah because this must have been a common saying. Ginzberg misses the point that the purpose of the Mekilta's citations of the Mishnah was not its novelty but its authoritativeness as a source of Jewish law.

In the reference (cited above) to M. Arakhin II, 5, Ginzberg admits (p. 90) that the verbatim coincidence between the Mekilta and Mishnah should presume interdependence. But he proceeds to argue that since the passage of the cited Mishnah betrays an "old" literary source, it is likely that both the Mishnah and Mekilta were dependent on a premishnaic text. Here again Ginzberg ignores the fact that very frequently "From here they say," in the Mekilta, does coincide with our Mishnah or Tosefta. Only by discrediting the bulk of these citations of the Mishnah in the Mekilta could there be an argument about a certain particular quotation. Ginzberg discusses nine passages of the Mekilta (where the phrase מכאן אמרו does not appear), maintaining that they antedated their mishnaic parallels. When there were variants in the two sources, Ginzberg automatically presumes that the Mishnah altered the text of the pre-Mekilta source. Actually, as in example I (pp. 67–69), the text of M. Kerithot VI, 9 (end) relates but little to the introduction of the Mekilta (see below notes 88–89). It is probable that this final paragraph of the tractate, of aggadic nature and not related to the subject matter of the tractate as a whole, is one of the frequent postmishnaic additions (see end of M. Berakhot, Peah, Mo'ed Katan, Sotah, Eduyot, etc.). Even granting that M. Kerithot VI, 9, is an authentic Mishnah, it is clear that it was not taken from our Mekilta since the instances and the text as a whole do not correspond. Ginzberg's example III (pp. 76–78) merely shows that the text of the Mekilta presupposes the existence of the Palestinian or Babylonian Talmud. For the view that the halakic midrashim used our Mishnah and Tosefta, see Melamed in *Papers: IV World Congress of Jewish Studies* (Jerusalem, 1967) I, pp. 163–166 (Hebrew Section); cf. his *The Relationship between the Halakhic Midrashim and the Mishnah and Tosephta* (Jerusalem, 1967), which I have as yet not seen.

[28] See previous note. Lauterbach, *Hazofeh* IX (1925), pp. 235–241, argues that Mekilta on Exod. 12:46 (*Pasha* XV, pp. 55 f.; Laut. I, p. 124) conformed to the older halakah, which prohibited the breaking of the Paschal lamb's bone whether or not it had meat on it, in contrast to the younger halakah (P. Pesahim VII, 9, p. 35a; B. Pesahim 84b–85a), which presumably prohibited the breaking of the bone only if it contained meat. Actually, the Mekilta's interpretation of 12:46 makes sense only if the existence of the relevant talmudic references are presupposed. As to the different conclusions in the talmudic and Mekilta texts, it seems that the author of the Mekilta follows here Zevahim 97b which in fact prohibits the breaking of a bone under any circumstance.

[29] Cf. I. H. Weiss, *Dor Dor Vedorshav*[2] II (Berlin, 1924), pp. 228 f.

halakah and the Talmud's are virtually identical.[30] It is this overwhelming identity, rather than the variations, which requires explanation for the simple reason that if the Mekilta were very ancient the
variants would be infinitely more striking.

Our ignorance of the methodology of the halakah and its evolution
during the period of the Second Temple prevents the verification of
argument b). But let us accept Lauterbach's thesis that the older,
pre-Maccabean halakah was arranged according to scriptural verses,
and that the topical arrangement began during the Maccabean period.
This thesis does not, however, necessarily support the accompanying
view that the pre-Maccabean formulation of the halakah corresponded
to that of the later halakic midrashim or of the Mekilta. The texts of
Qumran, for example, suggest alternate conceivable methods of presentation.[31] Linguistically and structurally, the formulation of the halakah
in the Scroll of Damascus, though still remote from that of the Mishnah, is more related to it than to the Mekilta. When they cite a biblical
verse, the authors of the Dead Sea scrolls employ formulas such as
אשר אמר "for it is said" or אשר כתוב "for it is written"; in the Mishnah
the formulas are שנאמר and שכתוב, respectively. The hermeneutic
terminology of the halakic sections of the Scroll of Damascus is primitive compared to that of the Mishnah, and is certainly far removed
from the highly developed exegetical idiom of the Mekilta.[32]

Presupposition c), namely, that the texts of the Mekilta (though
not necessarily its final edition) are tannaitic, is based on the names of
the authorities cited in this book. The following is a list of names,
arranged in descending order of frequency, which are mentioned in the
first edition of the Mekilta ten times or more:[33]

---

[30] The scholars who believe that the mishnaic halakah reflects the one promulgated during the Second Temple may argue that the Mekilta preserves traditions of
the pre-70 period. The writer believes that the tannaitic texts reproduce essentially
the halakah as formulated by the rabbis between 80 and 200, frequently differing
from the Pharisaic traditions of the pre-70 oral law. Except in a few instances the
Pharisaic halakah is not known.

[31] The formulation of halakah in the Scroll of Damascus mainly follows a topical
order, using the negated imperative (one shall not). Its relation to the mishnaic texts
has been studied by Ginzberg (*Eine unbekannte jüdische Sekte* I, New York, 1922),
who exaggerated the relationship between the halakah of the scroll and the rabbinic
tradition. Cf. also Rabin, *Zadokite Documents* (Oxford, 1958), index, pp. 87–90.

[32] Cf. p.Hab. III 2, 13, 14; Damascus Scroll IX, 1–XVI, 15; Manual of Discipline
VIII, 14.

[33] For a full list of the authorities cited in the Mekilta, see Weiss (*Mechilta*,
pp. XXIX–XXXV), Hoffmann (*Zur Einleitung*, pp. 83–90), and B. Kosovsky
(*Concordantiae verborum quae in Mechilta d'Rabbi Ismael reperiuntur*, Jerusalem,
1965).

| 83–60 | 54–30 | 29–20 | 18–10 |
|---|---|---|---|
| Ishmael | Nathan | Judah | Eleazar |
| Joshua | Rabbi | Isaac | Simeon |
| Eliezer | Eleazar of Modi'in | Simeon b. Yoḥai | Meir |
| Akiba | Josiah | Jose | Eleazar b. Azariah |
| | Jose of Galilee | | Judah b. Betherah |
| | Jonathan | | Pappias |
| | | | Gamaliel |

If the names listed are treated as identical with those preserved in the Mishnah and the Tosefta (Ishmael ben Elisha, Joshua ben Ḥananya, Eliezer ben Hyrcanus, Akiba ben Joseph, etc.),[34] then the Mekilta would be a significant tannaitic text.

The basic question, however, is not that of the names, but rather, whether the citations in the Mekilta are historical or pseudepigraphic.[35] On the premise that the quotations are genuine, the list of names is puzzling. The scholars who maintain that the Mekilta has preserved segments of the older halakah of the Second Temple ought to explain why (except for one mangled paraphrase of the Babylonian Talmud or Tosefta)[36] the pre-70 *zugot* (pairs) of authorities go unmentioned.[37] Also notable is the role of Rabbi (or Rabban) Yoḥanan ben Zakkai, founder of the academy of Yavneh in the year 70, who is listed in the Mekilta seven times, but only in haggadic texts, some of which are rephrasings from the Babylonian Talmud and postamoraic lore.[38]

[34] The problem whether the author of the Mekilta meant Eleazar to be identical with Eleazar ben Azariah or Eleazar of Modi'in or another person altogether; Jose with Jose ben Ḥalafta or Jose of Galilee; Simeon with Simeon ben Yoḥai, is avoided in this statistical analysis.

[35] The question involves passages which have no talmudic parallels.

[36] See above n. 26.

[37] The *zugot* are listed in M. Ḥagigah II, 2; Avot I, 4–15. Incidentally, Mekilta, *Amalek* III, p. 190; Laut. II, 165 f., alludes to Avot I, 7; or rather to Avot de-Rabbi Nathan IX, p. 42, which the author of the Mekilta regards as identical with the Mishnah. Shema'yah and Avtalyon, though, are cited once in *Beshallaḥ* (p. 99; Laut. I, 220), in an aggadic quotation, where the sequence of authorities is as follows: Rabbi, Eleazar b. Azaryah, Eleazar b. Judah of Bartota (?), Shema'yah, Avtalyon, Simeon of Kitron, a sequence which arouses suspicion as to the authenticity of the traditions. Cf. also the sequence in the Mekilta of Simeon b. Yoḥai (pp. 57–9), note to p. 57, 4.

[38] Mekilta, *Nezikin*, II, p. 253; Laut. III, 16, depends on B. Kiddushin 22b; not on Tosefta Baba Kamma VII, 5, p. 358, where the passage is cited anonymously. Mekilta, *ibid.*, XV, 299; Laut. III, 115, depends on B. Baba Kamma 79b; rather than on Tos. *ibid.*, VII, 2, p. 357; Mekilta *Baḥodesh*, 1, 203 f.; Laut. II, 193 f., seems to follow Avot de-Rabbi Nathan, XVII, p. 33a (a posttalmudic source), rather than B. Ketubot 66b–67a; or Sifre, Deut. 305; or Tos. *ibid.*, V, 10, p. 267; or P. *ibid.*, V, end,

Not one halakah is cited in his name. The oldest material in the tannaitic literature is that respecting the controversies between the
schools of Shammai and Hillel,[39] but the Mekilta knows of only two
disputes, both evidently borrowed from the Babylonian or Palestinian
Talmuds.[40]

Moreover, an analysis of the second and third generations of
tannaim in the list arouses the suspicion that some of the cited authorities are manufactured. Of the second generation, Rabban Gamaliel II
was the most influential figure as the founder of the Hillelite dynasty
of patriarchs during the last decades of the first century. But he is at
the bottom of the list with ten occurrences,[41] all but one in haggadic

---

p. 30c. For only Avot de-Rabbi Nathan, and after it the Mekilta, attributes the story
to Yoḥanan ben Zakkai; the talmudic sources and the Tosefta cite here Simeon ben
Eleazar. Mekilta, *ibid.*, XI, p. 245; Laut. II, 290 is related to Sifra, *Kedoshim* 92d,
rather than to Tos. Baba Kamma VII, 6, p. 358, which reports this passage anonymously. The passage of Mekilta, *Nezikin* XII, p. 292; Laut. III, 99, is related to
Tosefta, *ibid.*, VII, 10, p. 359, but the Mekilta strings together here B. *ibid.*, 67b,
resulting that Yoḥanan ben Zakkai follows Meir and precedes Akiba in a controversy. There is no reason to assume that the author of the Mekilta ever used Yoḥanan
ben Zakkai's name fictitiously, but there is no doubt that his sources were primarily
the Babylonian Talmud or posttalmudic works.

[39] See M. Eduyot I, 1 ff.

[40] P. Eruvin X, 1, p. 26a, records that Rabbi required an annual check of one's
phylacteries, but that Simeon ben Gamaliel did not; the text concludes with a quote
from Hillel the Elder, who, it is said, displayed his maternal grandfather's phylacteries, indicating seemingly that no checkup is required. Apparently, because the
halakah follows Hillel, the author of the Mekilta (*Pasḥa*, 17, p. 69; Laut. I, 157),
"corrected" the Palestinian Talmud, reversing the views of Hillel and Shammai, the
former requiring an annual check, but the latter not; the Mekilta concludes tautologically with Shammai the Elder displaying his grandfather's phylacteries. The
other reference to the two schools is *Nezikin* XV, p. 300; Laut. III, 117, which
abstracts B. Baba Meẓi'a 44a.

[41] Five out of the ten times occurring in an anecdote (adopted from B. Kidd.,
32b; Sifre Deut., 38) about Gamaliel's remarkable hospitality. Like Abraham and
Moses (Exod. 18:12), Gamaliel personally entertained his guests (Amalek III, pp.
195 f.; Laut. II, 177 f.). That Tebi, Gamaliel's slave was permitted to wear phylacteries, the author of the Mekilta (*Pasḥa* XVII, p. 68; Laut. I, 154) found in P.
Eruvin X, 1, p. 26a, as becomes clear from the context. The question of Judah of
Kefar Acco (not recorded elsewhere, but evidently modeled after Simeon b. Judah
of Kefar Akko, B. Sanh. 110b, etc.), addressed to Gamaliel (Amalek IV, p. 196;
Laut. II, 180), why does Scripture say that Moses boasted: "For the people come
*to me* to inquire of God"? (Exod. 18:15) appears to be a manufactured passage.
This inquiry was modeled after the one mentioned in B. Avodah Zarah 54b, which
is found also in the Mekilta (*Baḥodesh* VI, 226; Laut. II, 244–246). In abstracting
the *sugya* of B. Baba Kamma 42b–43a (cf. P. Baba Kamma 4b), the author of the
Mekilta either through carelessness or by design changed the views of the authorities,
inserting the name of Gamaliel, which apparently was not in the sources.

material, though the insignificant Eleazar of Modiʻin, not mentioned in the Mishnah and only rarely alluded to elsewhere, is named in the Mekilta forty-eight times.[42] Gamaliel's rival Eleazar ben ʻAzariah, who became the head of the academy of Yavneh when the former was forced to resign, appears in the Mekilta thirteen times. Joshua, another opponent of Gamaliel, is recorded seventy-two times.[43] It is not only the disproportionate over-representation or under-representation of certain tannaim, but the lack of any discernible pattern respecting the names which raises the great possibility that the names cited in the Mekilta have no historical basis.

This impression that the names cited in the Mekilta are mostly pseudepigraphical is strengthened when one analyzes the third generation of tannaim listed in this book. Ishmael, it is true, heads the list of all the sages mentioned in the Mekilta. But its author appears to be ignorant of the historical Ishmael ben Elishah.[44] In the Mekilta, Ishmael records a tradition in the name of Meir,[45] who lived a generation or two later; he debates with Jonathan or Josiah,[46] who probably lived a century later,[47] and is referred to as a martyr by Akiba.[48]

[42] See above note 34. Eleazar of Modiʻin is mentioned in Avot III, 2, but this tractate names men otherwise not found in, and should not be considered part of, the Mishnah. There is only one halakic reference to him in the talmudic literature (B. Shavuʻot 35b), though the Babylonian Talmud mentions him about a dozen times, occasionally together with Gamaliel. In the other halakic midrashim he is mentioned only twice (Sifre Numb. 137; 157).

[43] See the sources cited in note 33.

[44] In the Mishnah and talmudic texts, Ishmael often debates with Akiba, Tarfon, Jose of Galilee, and less often with Eleazar ben Azariah. Though cited in almost every chapter of the Mekilta, there is no evidence that the author cared who were Ishmael's contemporaries or pupils. See below, p. 130.

[45] Mekilta, *Nezikin* XIV, p. 298, 5; Laut. III, 112, 61, app. crit. This reading of the editio princeps and Ms. Vienna is correct. Influenced by B. Baba Kamma 14a, modern editors, including Horowitz-Rabin and Lauterbach, read Simeon ben Eleazar.

[46] *Pasḥa* III, p. 12; Laut. I, 28 (with Josiah); VI, 22; Laut. 50, (with Jonathan and Isaac); VIII, p. 28; Laut. I, 63 f. (with Jonathan and Jose of Galilee); XI, 37; Laut. I, 84 (with Jonathan and Isaac); *Nezikin* VII, p. 271; Laut. III, 56 (with Josiah and Nathan or, as Lauterbach reads, Jonathan); VIII, p. 275; Laut. III, 64 (with Josiah and Jonathan); IX, p. 278; Laut. III, 70 (*ibid.*).

[47] See below note 65.

[48] Mekilta, *Nezikin* XVIII, p. 313; Laut. III, 141 f., commenting on Exod. 22:22, reports that when Simeon (ben Yoḥai?; Gamaliel?; both lived a generation or two after Ishmael) and Ishmael were to be martyred, the former was wondering what evil deed he had done. To which the latter replied that it must have been because he had let the litigants wait for a judgment while he amused himself. The parallel story is reported in Avot de-Rabbi Nathan XXXVIII, pp. 114 f. and Semaḥot VIII. It is the latter, which also has Akiba's comment and which depicts the ten martyrs, that appears to have been the Mekilta's source. The historicity of

Because neither the Babylonian nor Palestinian amoraic tradition ever refers to Ishmael of the Mekilta, Frankel proposed that the author or editor of the Mekilta was not the famous rival of Akiba, but an obscure amora named occasionally in the Palestinian Talmud as Rabbi Ishmael the father of Judan.[49] Friedmann and Lauterbach are right in rejecting this ingenious identification,[50] but their reasoning that the citations in Ishmael's name record the words of a famous tanna or his school is equally unacceptable. Many of the quotations of Ishmael in the Mekilta are clearly apocryphal.[51]

The same applies to the Mekilta's sixty citations of Akiba. In the Mishnah and the Talmuds, Ishmael and Akiba display differing methods of biblical exegesis. The former adheres more strictly to the plain meaning of Scripture or to formal hermeneutic rules than the latter.[52] But the Akiba of the Mekilta is void of any exegetical personality, except when the Mekilta is clearly dependent upon older mishnaic or talmudic texts.[53] In the latter literature (to cite another

---

Ishmael ben Elishah's martyrdom is, however, defended by some scholars. See the literature cited in G. Alon's *Toledot Hayehudim Bitekufat Hamishnah Vehatalmud*, II (Tel Aviv, 1955), p. 11, n. 85. Although he believed that the Mekilta was tannaitic, Alon rejects the story as a late legend. See also the fictional treatise, the Midrash of the Ten Martyrs.

[49] Z. Frankel, *Einleitung in den Jerusalemischen Talmud²* (Berlin, 1923), 108b–109b, remarks that Rabbi Ishmael of the Palestinian Talmud is usually an amora. P. Pesaḥim II, 4, p. 29b, in the name of this Ishmael, according to Frankel, cites the Mekilta, *Pasḥa* VIII, p. 26; Laut. I, 60; also recorded in B. *ibid.*, 35a, as based on the school of Ishmael. An analysis of the parallel passages makes it clear that the editors of the Babylonian and Palestinian Talmuds had not seen the citation of the Mekilta, but that the latter is based on the Babylonian Talmud. This is necessarily so, as the author of the Mekilta sums up here several sections of the Babylonian Talmud.

[50] Friedmann, *Mechilta*, pp. LXXIV–LXXVII; Lauterbach, *Mekilta* I, p. XXIV, note 19.

[51] Cf. the mystical texts of Hekhalot Rabbati, attributed to Ishmael (A. Jellinek, *Bet ha-midrash* III [Leipzig, 1855'], 83–108.).

[52] See M. Sotah V, 1–2; cf. B. Sanhedrin 51a; M. Kerithot II, 5; Yoma VI, 8; Shevu'ot III, 5. See also Frankel, *Introduction to the Mishnah²* (Warsaw, 1923), pp. 112–130; H. L. Strack, *Introduction to the Talmud and Mishnah* (Philadelphia, 1931), p. 112; Epstein-Melamed, *Introduction to Tannaitic Literature . . .*, pp. 521 ff. (who should be used cautiously).

[53] Mekilta, *Pasḥa* III, p. 11; Laut. I, 26, on Exod. 12:4, *And he and his neighbor shall take.* Ishmael takes the verse that one may bring in new members to partake with him from his paschal lamb; Akiba, that one may offer the sacrifice by himself. There is no apparent difference in the exegesis. In fact, however, the Mekilta seems to have attributed to the latter Jose's view (M. Pesaḥim VIII, 7), in contrast to that of Judah, who sanctions the partaking from the lamb only as part of a group. The author of the Mekilta apparently adopts the gaonic ruling that when Judah and

example), Jose of Galilee emerges as a distinct halakist — he sanctioned the boiling of poultry in milk —[54] whereas in the Mekilta he is named thirteen times with no allusion to his individualism.

In contrast to the Mishnah and other related texts, the most important men of the fourth generation of tannaim — Meir, Judah ben Illai, Jose ben Ḥalafta — play a relatively minor role in the Mekilta.[55] The usual explanation is that these authorities belonged to Akiba's school which rivaled that of the Ishmaelite exegetic tradition. The weakness of this argument is that if Akiba is cited sixty times, why then were his pupils not equally presented? The real problem, however, is not that Meir, Judah, or Jose are not frequently mentioned, but that when they are cited their views and exegesis seem similar to those of the tannaim presumably of the Ishmaelite school.[56] The apocryphal nature of the citations may explain why the author of the Mekilta appears to forget sometimes that Judah with or without his patronymic Illai, Jose and Jose ben Ḥalafta, or Simeon and Simeon ben Yoḥai, are the same person.[57] Some reflections of the *Sitz im Leben*, indeed, the tension behind the exegetic debates frequently so clear in the Mishnah and the Talmud, are absent from the Mekilta.

---

Jose differ, the halakah follows the latter. Incidentally, in B. *ibid.*, 91a, the contrary views are said to be based on the exegesis of Deut. 16:8, indicating that not only did the author of the Mishnah not know of Akiba's position, but that the Talmud did not even know of Akiba's supposed exegesis of Exod. 12:4. *Pasḥa* IV, p. 13; Laut. I, 32 f., cites Akiba as quoting the 13th hermeneutic rule, attributed by the Sifra to Ishmael, but which the Mekilta says Ishmael refuted. On the other hand, the Mekilta (*Nezikin* X, 283; Laut. III, 80) cites a pupil of Ishmael interpreting the particle *et* as an inclusive, supposedly the trademark of Akiba's hermeneutical method (B. Ḥagigah 12a).

[54] See M. Ḥulin VIII, 4; B. *ibid.*, 116a; Shabbath, 130a: cf. *Kaspa* V, p. 336; Laut. III, 190, quoting the Mishnah. One may profit from leavened bread on Passover (Pesaḥim 32b). A second son born from a union of a Jew and a converted Gentile woman is considered legally first-born in regard to inheritance and must be offered to a priest because when she gave birth to their first son, she was not yet converted (M. Bekhorot VIII, 1). Most of the citations of Jose of Galilee in the Mekilta deal with haggadic material in contrast with the talmudic tradition which cites him as a halakist.

[55] Meir is mentioned in the Mishnah 330 times, in the Tosefta 452 times; Judah, in the Mishnah more than 600 times, Jose 330 times.

[56] Sometimes, though, the Mekilta merely reproduces the Mishnah (*Nezikin* X, p. 284; Laut. III, 83, citing M. Baba Kamma II, 4; or *ibid.*, X, p. 284; Laut. III, 84, citing M. *ibid.*, IV, 9).

[57] In the Mishnah, Judah, Jose, and Simeon are never cited by their patronymics. The Mekilta follows this method when citing Simeon in the halakah, but in haggadic passages the patronymic is used. See also in regard to Judah, Mekilta, *Vayyassa* I, pp. 153, 14 f.; Laut. II, 87, 41; on Jose, *Amalek* I, 176; Laut. II, 136, 18, indicating that the Mekilta is dependent on the older texts.

The Mekilta features names such as Nathan, Josiah, Jonathan, Isaac, and Papos (or Pappias), which are never mentioned in the Mishnah,[58] and are comparatively rare elsewhere. In fact, it would appear that Papos is one of the names, listed below, which the author of the Mekilta invented.[59] Nathan is known from the talmudic literature where he is sometimes dubbed the Babylonian.[60] This and the mention of a certain amora from Ḥuẓẓal by the name of Josiah prompted Halevy to propose that Nathan, Josiah, and Jonathan were members of the academy of Ḥuẓẓal, a school which supposedly flourished in Babylonia since the days of Ezekiel, Ezra, and Hillel.[61] Halevy, now followed by Neusner, claims that much of the Mekilta was originated in the Babylonian academy of Ḥuẓẓal.[62] There is no doubt, however, that except for paraphrases from the Babylonian Talmud, the Nathan of the Mekilta is a name of convenience as well as a historical personality. Consider the chronological anomalies: he is said to have debated with Akiba and Ishmael, on the one hand, and with Judah Hanasi, on the other; and he is a pupil of Simeon ben Yoḥai and Jose ben Maḥoz, the latter apparently a fictitious name.[63] Jonathan

---

[58] Excepting Avot, a tractate not properly part of the Mishnah, which mentions Jonathan (Avot IV, 9), and the last Mishnah of Berakhot, which cites Nathan.

[59] Laut. follows most Mss. in reading פפייס (Pappias), but ed. pr. reads פפוס (Papos). In rabbinical literature he is a figure representing heretical views. In B. Sabbath 104b (uncensored texts) Papos ben Judah equals Jesus. In B. Berakhot 61b, he is contrasted with Akiba, both were martyred; the former for rather foolish reasons, the latter for the sanctification of God's name. Gen. Rabbah XXI, 5, p. 200, Akiba challenges Pappias' interpretation of Gen. 2:22, that Adam was created an angel. Mekilta, *Amalek* III, p. 194; Laut. II, 175, citing B. Sanhedrin 94a, quotes Pappias' accusation that it was Jethro (not the Jews) who had first blessed God (alluding to Exod. 18:10).

[60] B. Sabbath 134a. The citations of Nathan in M. Berakhot (end) and Shekalim II, 5, were not in the original text of the Mishnah (see Palestinian Talmud *ad loc.*). He was a younger contemporary of Rabbi. B. Horayot 13b, reports that Nathan and Meir plotted to remove Simeon ben Gamaliel from his office of patriarch, but this is probably not historical. According to B. Baba Meẓi'a 86a, Nathan and Rabbi were the editors of the Mishnah.

[61] I. Halevy, *Dorot Harishonim* (Berlin, 1923) II, pp. 181 ff.

[62] J. Neusner, *A History of the Jews in Babylonia* (Leiden, 1965), I, pp. 179 ff. and *passim*; see my review in *CCAR Journal* XIII, 5 (April, 1966), pp. 74–77.

[63] With Ishmael, Pasḥa XVI, p. 61; Laut. I, 137; *Nezikin* XV, p. 299; Laut. III, 114; with Akiba, *Nezikin* VII, p. 273; Laut. III, 60; as a pupil of Simeon ben Yoḥai, *Beshallaḥ* IV, 101; Laut. I, 225 f.; quoting Abba Jose of Maḥoz, *ibid.*, III, p. 99; Laut. I, 220 f. It should be noted that the Mss. frequently confuse Nathan with Jonathan. It is possible that by Nathan the author of the Mekilta referred to the presumed author of Avot de-Rabbi Nathan, a work frequently quoted. For in *Amalek* IV, p. 200; Laut. II, 186, citing I Chr. 2:55, the Mekilta reports that upon Nathan's death, wisdom disappeared. It is curious that Avot de-Rabbi Nathan

and Josiah were of the generation that bridged the tannaitic and the amoraic periods and may be classified as belonging to either.[64] In the Babylonian Talmud they are occasionally mentioned together, but the author of the Mekilta converted them into leading antagonists:[65] they are said to have debated with Eleazer (80–100), a tanna of the second generation, as well as with Judah Hanasi (circa 200).[66] The well-known debates between Hillel and the sons of Betherah (40–10 B. C. E.?), whether or not the Passover sacrifice may be performed when the fourteenth of Nissan fell on the Sabbath, is rephrased by the author of the Mekilta as a controversy between Josiah and Jonathan.[67]

The name of Rabbi (Judah Hanasi) occasionally appears in the secondary passages of the Mishnah.[68] In the Mekilta, however, Rabbi is one of the most frequently cited names. Sometimes the Mekilta, instead of referring to the Mishnah, refers simply to Rabbi.[69] In some instances where Rabbi is said to have debated with tannaim of different generations, the citations are suspect.[70] Also found in the Mekilta is the epithet Rabbenu Hakadosh, a title of Rabbi of amoraic vintage and in fact recorded elsewhere only in late amoraic or geonic texts.[71]

The following is a partial list of the Mekilta's authorities whose historicity is not attested elsewhere: Abba Ḥanan, Abba Jose of Maḥoz, Jose of Modi'in, Abshalom Hazaken, Issi ben Gurya, Issi ben Shammai, Antoninus, Zerikah, Ḥananya ben Halnisi.[72] It could be argued that

---

XXXV, 53a, also comments in a similar spirit on I Chr. 2:55. The Mekilta seems to say that Nathan's comments on Yabeẓ were applicable to himself.

[64] See Tosafot Yeshanim, to Yoma 57b.

[65] Because of the Mekilta, it is generally assumed that Josiah and Jonathan are tannaim, but it is likely that they were of the first generation of amoraim. Jonathan was a pupil of Ḥiyya (Berakhot 18a).

[66] See *Pasḥa* IV, p. 13; Laut. I, 30 f.; *Beshallaḥ* I, p. 81; Laut. I, 183.

[67] For Hillel's debate with the sons of Betherah, see P. Pesaḥim VI, 1, p. 33a; B., *ibid.*, 66a; Tosefta, *ibid.*, IV, 13, p. 165 (Lieberman). Mekilta, *Pasḥa* V, p. 17; Laut. I, 40 f., attributes the controversy to the interpretation of Exod. 12:6. Cf. Sifre, Num. 65, 142; Sifra (ed. Weiss), p. 103b.

[68] See Frankel, *Introduction to the Mishnah* (Hebrew), pp. 226–228.

[69] Mekilta, *Nezikin* VIII, p. 276; Laut. III, 67, evidently citing B. Sanhedrin 79a; *Shabbatha* II, p. 345; Laut. III, 206.

[70] With Akiba, *Pasḥa* VI, 21; Laut. I, 49.

[71] Mekilta, *Beshallaḥ* II, p. 125; Laut. II, 21; *ibid.*, VI, p. 137; Laut. II, 50. The title Rabbenu Hakadosh was sometimes incorporated from a marginal note. See B. Shabbath 156a; Pesaḥim 37a; P. Megillah III, 2, 74a. Cf. also the medieval treatise, Pirke Rabbenu Hakadosh, ed. Grünhut (Jerusalem, 1898).

[72] The various patronymics of Issi were evidently inspired by B. Pesaḥim 113b; Yoma, 52b: "Joseph of Ḥuẓẓal is identical to Joseph of Babylon, Issi ben Judah, Issi ben Gur Aryeh, Issi ben Gamaliel, Issi ben Mahallel, but what was his real name? Issi ben Akiba." See also Niddah 36b, and Tosafot, *s. v.* "Issi." At least one citation

these and other similar names resulted from scribal corruptions or that the names are historical, but by chance alone are missing from our talmudic records.[73] Yet even the names which are well known in the talmudic literature and which are unquestionably historical appear in questionable contexts in the Mekilta.[74]

The conclusion seems inescapable: the authorities cited in the Mekilta cannot be regarded as historical unless they are confirmed in the more reliable texts of the Mishnah, Palestinian or Babylonian Talmud. Certainly, the names of the tannaim cited in the Mekilta do not necessarily prove the time or place of the work any more than the names Akiba, Eleazer, or Elijah relate to the books known as the Alphabet of Rabbi Akiba, Hekhalot de-Rabbi Ishmael, Pirke de-Rabbi Eliezer, or Seder Eliyyahu. All of these instances only show the existence of pseudepigraphical works during the saboraic and geonic periods. Furthermore, as passages citing authorities are of questionable historicity, so too are those passages which appear anonymously.[75]

With respect to point d), Isaac Hirsch Weiss, in his introduction, described the Mekilta's style as loftier and more pleasing than that of the other talmudic and midrashic texts, and from this he concluded that the Mekilta must be older.[76] Weiss's own taste, however, seemed

---

of Issi found in the Mekilta seems to have originated in geonic times. *Kaspa* II, p. 337; Laut. III, 192, records a curious rationalization of the prohibition of milk and meat, not known in the talmudic literature; the passage in Deut. 12:23 which prohibits blood, it is said, means to include also the eating of milk and meat. Proceeding from B. Niddah 9a, Ẓemaḥ Gaon (*Geonica*, ed. L. Ginzberg [New York, 1909] II, p. 33) explains that milk and blood are of the same substance changing from one to the other, as women do not menstruate during pregnancy. The responsum concludes with proof from Deut. 12:23. Ginzberg (p. 22) missed that this view was abstracted in the Mekilta in the name of Issi. Cf. also *Methivot*, ed. B. Lewin (Jerusalem, 1934), 114, which evidently is older than Zemaḥ's responsum, for it does not have the citation from Deuteronomy.

[73] For attempts to explain the names Issi, see Hoffmann, *Zur Einleitung*, p. 39; Epstein-Melamed, *Introduction*, pp. 571 f.

[74] See above, pp. 129–130.

[75] Frequently, the anonymous suggests the source. See above, note 27 that מכאן אמרו implies as a rule a citation from the Mishnah, occasionally a Baraitha or Tosefta. כיוצא בזה or וכן seems to indicate citations from Gen. Rabba. Cf., for example, Mekilta, introductory section (*Pasḥa* I, pp. 1 f.; Laut. I, 1–3) with Gen. Rabbah (I, 14, pp. 13 f.); Mekilta (*Pasḥa* VII, p. 23 f.; Laut. I, 54; *Beshallaḥ* II, p. 85; Laut. I, 192 f.) with Gen. R. (L, 10, pp. 523 f.); Mekilta (*Shiratha* X, p. 151; Laut. II, 82) with Gen. R. (LXXX, 10, pp. 964 f.) where the former appears to render into Hebrew the Aramaic term דכוותה. Albeck's thesis, Introduction to Genesis Rabbah (cf. n. 19), pp. 58 ff., that the Mekilta and Gen. R. independently used a lost source, is inacceptable because the texts certainly show interdependence, and because it unnecessarily creates a new unknown.

[76] Weiss, *Mechilta* pp. XXI f.

to have improved with the passage of time, for in his masterly history of the rabbinic tradition he completely omits his earlier compliments, and instead refers to the Mekilta's style as childish and therefore concludes that the work was drastically revised by its amoraic editor.[77] Style, however, is too vague and too susceptible of subjectivity to permit the dating of a literary work. The Hebrew of the Rabbis, not a literary tongue, seems to have changed little through the centuries from the completion of the Mishnah to the end of the first millennium.[78] Nevertheless, certain usages of the Mekilta suggest that its author was already far removed from the Hebrew of the tannaim and amoraim. Only a few barbarisms of the Mekilta can be cited here: נדבר (speak), adapted evidently from נדברו, Mal. 3:16; הכתיב (writes), הכתבת (you write); אמרת (you interpret); יוכשר (to be ritually fit).[79] More faulty is the author's rabbinic syntax such as the overuse of pronominal suffixes.[80] Certainly, the Hebrew of the tannaim and amoraim is less stilted than that of the Mekilta.

A reliable method of dating rabbinic works can emerge from the exegetical vocabulary. Judged by this alone, the Mekilta is post-talmudic. The ubiquitous formula used by the tannaim to cite Scripture was שנאמר (for it says).[81] While the Mekilta uses the tannaitic formula, it proliferated into a multiplicity of variants:

| | |
|---|---|
| שכבר נאמר | (it is said once) |
| לכך נאמר | (hence it says) |
| שכך נאמר | (for it says thusly) |
| לכן נאמר | (hence it says) |
| ומה נאמר | (but what does it say) |
| למה נאמר | (why does it say) |
| ועל זה נאמר | (therefore it says) |
| נאמר . . . ונאמר . . . | (it says here . . . but it says there) |
| שנאמר בו | (for concerning it, it says) |
| הוא שנאמר | (this is what it means when it says) |

---

[77] Weiss, *Dor Dor* II, pp. 228–231, esp. p. 228 n. 4.

[78] See E. J. Kutscher, *Studies in Galilean Aramaic* (in Hebrew, Jerusalem, 1952; offprint *Tarbiz*, vols. 21–23); "Leshon Ḥazal" in *Sefer Ḥ. Yalon* (1963), pp. 246–280.

[79] For a full list of citations, see B. Kosovsky, *Otzar Leshon Hatanna'im* (Jerusalem, 1965). For נדבר see Weiss, *Mechilta*, p. XXII. In the Tosefta, this term appears only in Berakhot I, 14 f., p. 5 (Lieberman); cf. Sifra, p. 3d (Weiss).

[80] In general, the Hebrew of the Mekilta is to the Mishnah and Tosefta what Kalir's poetry is to biblical Hebrew, except that much of the Mekilta is made up of quotations from older talmudic texts.

[81] For references, see B. Kosovsky, *ibid*. (n. 79), *a.l.* The English rendition below is only approximate, for the technical meaning of these terms can be understood only in their context.

| | |
|---|---|
| בכלל שנאמר | (to include in what it says) |
| מה שנאמר | (that which it says) |
| כענין שנאמר | (as it says elsewhere) |
| לפי שנאמר | (because it says) |
| מפני שנאמר | (because it says) |
| כל מקום שנאמר | (wherever it says) |
| ממשמע שנאמר | (it implies to say) |

The Mishnah never employs — and other tannaitic texts only rarely — the verb כתב (write) to introduce a Scripture citation. It was standard amoraic to use כתב in its Aramaic form.[82] Not only was כתיב (it is written) or דכתיב (for it is written) borrowed in the Mekilta from amoraic usage,[83] but the term (א)הדה הוא דכתיב (this is what it means when it is written), characteristic of the Palestinian Talmud and early aggadic midrashim,[84] was also taken over by the Mekilta. Aramaic was a living tongue for the tannaim and amoraim, but a foreign language for the author of the Mekilta. Hence, these borrowings must be explained as imitations of amoraic texts.

Moreover the author of the Mekilta shows a genius for borrowing and inventing hermeneutic terms. Here it is only possible to scratch the surface of this problem. But enough has been said to show that the vocabulary incorporates an extension of tannaitic and amoraic technical terms. The fact that the Mekilta attributes the same stereotyped terminology to tannaim of diverse schools or generations shows that the wording is the Mekilta's own rather than that of the authorities to whom it is attributed.

There is no need to deal at length with supposition e), the argument that Mekilta must be regarded as a tannaitic work because it is cited in the Palestinian and Babylonian Talmuds. Chanoch Albeck, in

[82] Proceeding from the assumption that the Mekilta and similar works are tannaitic, W. Bacher (*Exegetische Terminologie*, I, pp. 88 f. II, p. 91) failed to distinguish between basic tannaitic and amoraic terminology. But even he noted the peculiarity that the Aramaic form appears only in some halakic midrashim or so-called amoraic *baraithot*.

[83] כתיב in its many forms appears in the Mekilta more than one hundred times. Because the Mekilta was a rather rarely used text, the contamination from the Babylonian Talmud or midrashim was probably minimal.

[84] See Frankel, *Einl. . . . jer. Talmud*, 9a; 10b; Albeck, Introduction to Gen. Rabbah (n. 19), 26 f. See also Mekilta, *Baḥodesh* IV, 216, 2; Laut. II, 222, 20, for the phrase כמה דאת אמר, a typical formula of Gen. Rabbah (here adopted from Gen. Rabbah XCIX, 1, p. 1272, 2). Note also Albeck, *ibid.*, p. 17, who cites Mekilta, *Amalek*, p. 116; Laut. II, 135, who calls attention to the *petiḥta* in the halakic midrashim. Since the petiḥta is essentially a posttalmudic phenomenon, it attests to the lateness of the Mekilta.

his perceptive study of the halakic midrashim, has shown that the discussions of the amoraim presuppose their ignorance of the Mekilta, but that the author of our Mekilta certainly made extensive use of the amoraic texts of the Palestinian and Babylonian Talmuds.[85] The Mekilta recast amoraic interpretations found in the Babylonian and Palestinian Talmuds into its own style and cites them frequently with tannaitic names.[86] Finkelstein differentiates between the Mekilta's halakic texts, which he regards as tannaitic, and its aggadic material, which he believes to have been inserted. There is no evidence, however, that the Mekilta has been seriously contaminated by extraneous additions.[87] The style of the book is uniform throughout both haggada

---

[85] Ch. Albeck, *Untersuchungen über die halakischen Midraschim* (Berlin, 1927), pp. 91–120. My own studies have independently corroborated Albeck's conclusion. Thus the Mekilta on Exod. 21:33 (*Nezikin* XI, 287 f.; Laut. III, 90–94), dealing with responsibility for damages in case one opens a pit, reproduces amoraic interpretations of B. Baba Kamma 49b ff., sometimes using the term דבר אחר (another interpretation). In fact the Mekilta can be understood (as in fact traditional scholars always have) in light of the Babylonian Talmud. On the other hand, if such presumably tannaitic comments as found in the Mekilta were in existence, the relevant amoraic exertions to explain the halakah do not make sense. See next note.

[86] Cf. for example Mekilta, *Pasha* XV, pp. 56 f.; Laut. I, 127, with B. Yevamot 45b–46a, commenting on Exod. 12:18:

| Mekilta | B. Yevamot |
|---|---|
| רבי נתן אומר<br>שאין תלמוד לומר המול לו אלא להביא את<br>העבד שטבל לפני רבו ויצא לבן חורין מעשה<br>בבלוריא שטבלו מקצת שפחותיה לפניה וסקטן<br>לאחריה ובא מעשה לפני חכמים ואסרו את<br>שטבלו לפניה בנות חורין לאחריה מטועבדות<br>ואף על פי כן שמשוה עד יום מותה. | אמר רב חמא בר נוריא אמר רב הלוקח עבד מן<br>העובד כוכבים וקדם וטבל לשם בן חורין קנה<br>עצמו בן חורין...מתיב רב חסדא מעשה<br>בבלוריא הגיורת שקדמו עבדיה וטבלו לפניה ובא<br>מעשה לפני חכמים ואמרו קנו עצמן בני חורין לפניה<br>אין לאחריה לא. אמר רבא לפניה בין בסתם<br>בין במפורש לאחריה במפורש אין בסתם לא. |

It is obvious that the Mekilta paraphrased the ruling of the sages to conform with Rabba's interpretation of the story. Note also how the Mekilta transformed an amoraic text into a tannaitic one. Cf. also Gerim II, 4.

[87] Contrary to Albeck, *Untersuchungen*, 120: "Ebensowenig wie über die Zeit lässt sich über den Ort der Abfassung unserer hal. Midraschim Bestimmtes behaupten. Einzelne sprachliche Eigentümlichkeiten können in dieser Hinsicht kein Kriterium abgeben, da wir nicht den Urtext, wie er aus der Hand der Redaktoren hervorgegangen ist, besitzen." Weiss, *Dor Dor* II, pp. 228 ff., however, rightly remarks that our text of the Mekilta is substantially the same as it came down from the editor's hand. Certainly the Mekilta is less retouched than, say, the Mishnah, the Babylonian Talmud or Genesis Rabbah. If contamination occurred, it is reflected in the Mekilta de-Rabbi Simeon Ben Yoḥai. The Mekilta of Simeon ben Yoḥai relates to that of Ishmael as Pesikta Rabbati does to Pesikta de-Rab Kahana, Tanḥuma to Tanḥuma Buber, Deut. Rabbah to Deut. Rabbah (ed. Lieberman), or Halakhot Gedolot (ed. Hildesheimer) to standard Halakhot Gedolot. See also note 7.

and halakah. In fact, its legal lore is even more easily traceable to the amoraic halakah than is its legendary or strictly interpretive material. Thus the introductory section of the Mekilta (on Exod. 12:1) attempts to show that though the name of Moses usually precedes in Scripture that of Aaron, the two brothers were in fact of equal status. The text then catalogs other verses where it is claimed that precedence in citation does not necessarily mean precedence in rank. The wording and organization of the passage seems to indicate that the author of the Mekilta copied here the entire section from Genesis Rabbah, which comments on the problem of whether or not Genesis 1:1 implies that the heavens were created before the earth.[88] The text of Genesis Rabbah, however, is in turn traceable in part to the Palestinian Talmud, an expanded form of which is also found in the Tosefta. Because of the multiplicity of possible sources and because the Mekilta's style is distinct from standard rabbinic, the tracing of the source of the passage in the Mekilta to Genesis Rabbah is only probable and not certain. But the next passages of the Mekilta dealing with the calendar are clearly identifiable as adaptations from the Palestinian and Babylonian Talmuds.[89] In general the Mekilta reproduces the halakah of the amoraim, rather than that of the tannaim.

Yet, it should be stressed that the existence of a tannaitic school of biblical exegesis is not questioned in this paper. What is questioned is the claim that the Mekilta of Ishmael and necessarily its variant, that of Simeon ben Yoḥai, are first-hand witnesses of the tannaitic midrash. A compilation of the scattered midrashic passages of the Mishnah could serve as an authentic guide to the tannaitic exegesis of

[88] See above, note 27, for Ginzberg's view that the Mekilta reflects a source older than M. Keritot V, 9. ('Al Halakhah Ve-'aggadah, 67). But it is clear that Gen. Rabbah I, 14, pp. 13 f.; Lev. Rabbah XXXVI, 1, pp. 833–837, Tosefta, Keritot (end), and the Mekilta are interrelated, as Ginzberg says. Hence the relationship of these texts should not be confused with that of M. Keritot (Sifra, beg. *Kedoshim*). See next note.

[89] See previous note. That Gen. Rabbah is here dependent on P. Ḥagigah II, 77c, is clear because the entire chapter I of Gen. Rabbah is built on P. Ḥagigah II (cf. Gen. R. I, 1–14, pp. 2–14, with P. Ḥagigah 77a–c). If so, the concluding section of Gen. Rabbah I, under discussion, must also come from P. Ḥagigah. Hence Lev. Rabbah and the Mekilta must presumably be here dependent on Gen. Rabbah. The latter still retains the wording of the original, which the author of the Mekilta in the manner of the late midrashim simplified by editing out the authorities.

Ginzberg (*ibid.* [n. 27], 76–78), by cutting out key parts of the Mekilta passage, misrepresents the text (p. 7; Laut. I, 17 f.). A great scholar, he felt that he could tell intuitively what was original in a text and what was a later addition. This in turn led him to consider his expurgated text as antecedent to the Mishnah (see above note 27). The reader, however, has no choice but to compare the text of the Mekilta with the Palestinian and Babylonian Talmuds.

the Bible. Of lesser degree of authenticity, but still largely tannaitic, are the thousands of midrashic texts cited in the Palestinian and Babylonian Talmuds, as well as in the Tosefta. An analysis of these exegetical passages suggests that there was no essential difference between the midrash of the tannaim and that of the amoraim; both use the identical methodology and technical vocabulary. The Babylonian Talmud, moreover, with its highly developed methods of citation, uses the identical terms (תנו רבנן, תניא) regardless of whether the reference is to tannaitic midrash or to straightforward halakah. This seems to indicate that the nature of these sources from which the halakic and midrashic passages were drawn was one and the same. Furthermore, of the nearly four hundred tannaitic comments pertaining to the Book of Exodus, compiled from the Babylonian Talmud by E. Z. Melamed, few if any show dependence upon the Mekilta. Even Melamed, who never doubts the tannaitic nature of the Mekilta, grants that there is no reason to believe that the Babylonian Talmud made use of Ishmael's Mekilta.[90] How then is the remarkable kinship between the midrash of the Mekilta and that of the Talmuds to be explained? The conclusion is unescapable that the author of the Mekilta constructed a "tannaitic" midrash from the material he found in the Mishnah, Babylonian and Palestinian Talmuds, and Tosefta.

### III

An analysis of both the halakic and aggadic parts of the Mekilta suggests a fourfold division of its sources: 1) texts such as the Mishnah or Tosefta copied by the author, roughly verbatim; 2) passages taken from the talmudic or midrashic literature, but lightly retouched and put into the mouth of tannaitic authorities; 3) material taken from the last-mentioned sources, but completely recast; and 4) passages

---

[90] See Melamed, *Halachic Midrashim* (n. 1), Introduction, *passim*, esp. p. 36, who notes, however, that there is a linguistic link between the Babylonian Talmud and the Mekilta of Simeon ben Yoḥai. In fact, this is only so because Melamed was then using Hoffmann's edition of this Mekilta, based on the fifteenth century Yemenite Midrash Hagadol, whose author altered the Mekilta's text contaminating it with the wordings of the Babylonian Talmud.

Incidentally, Melamed's *Halachic Midrashim* is a remarkable compilation of the tannaitic midrash, as reported in the Babylonian Talmud. The author's amazing industry, however, was of little avail in describing the nature of this midrash because he proceeded from the premise that the halakic midrashim antedated the Babylonian Talmud. In light of the hypothesis that the midrashic collections based much of their material on the biblical exegesis preserved in the Talmud, Melamed's work assumes added significance.

directly attributable to the author of the Mekilta. It goes without saying that only in regard to 1) and partly 2) may the Mekilta be cited to shed light upon tannaitic and amoraic texts.

There is a basic difference between the composition of the Mekilta and that of the Mishnah, Tosefta, or Palestinian and Babylonian Talmuds. Because of the growth of the latter through accretion, it is not correct to use the terms authors, but only editors. Judah Hanasi retained essentially the form of the Mishnah he had found, using primarily scissors and paste to organize the material. The Tosefta originally consisted of some tannaitic passages omitted from the Mishnah which with the passage of time were labeled *baraithot*. Our inherited Tosefta, however, contains in addition many other tannaitic citations (*baraithot*) taken from the Palestinian and Babylonian Talmuds. The early amoraim (as attested in the Palestinian Talmud) hardly distinguished between a mishnah and a baraitha or, indeed, between tannaitic and amoraic authority. In the later amoraic period, however (as attested in the Babylonian Talmud), a hierarchy was constructed, according to which Judah Hanasi's Mishnah came to be regarded as the most authoritative postpentateuchal text, followed by the less authoritative baraithot, and followed in turn by the amoraic elaborations and comments. In the centuries-long process of making the tannaitic texts intelligible, the amoraim increased the rabbinic literature manifold beyond what it was during the tannaitic period, resulting in the collections known as Palestinian and Babylonian Talmuds. The Mekilta of Ishmael, however, is not a collection of diverse texts, but the work of a real author. And as such it is closer to the eighth century *She'iltot* of Aḥai than to the talmudic texts.[91]

Perhaps an inquiry into the possible date and place of origin of the Mekilta will shed light on why such a pseudograph was concocted. Some clues have already been intimated. The Palestinian Talmud was edited about the year 425; the Genesis Rabbah within a century later.[92] The author of the Mekilta used not only these texts, but also apocryphal tractates such as Gerim (Proselytes),[93] Semaḥot[94] (euphe-

---

[91] Aḥai wrote the *She'iltot* in 747 (*Iggeret Sherira Gaon*, ed. Lewin, 103), sections of which found their way into certain midrashic works (see Tanḥuma, *Bereshit*, 2 — She'ilta I). Though based strictly on the Babylonian Talmud, the *She'iltot* was written in Palestine, where Aḥai migrated. It fuses halakah and aggadah, is arranged according to the pericopes of the Torah, uses an exegetic vocabulary of its own, while mainly reproducing the original passages of the Talmud.

[92] See Albeck, Introduction (n. 19), pp. 93–96.

[93] Cf. Mekilta, *Nezikin* XVIII, pp. 311 f.; Laut. III, 137–141, with Gerim IV, 1–4. For variants in the two texts see commentaries.

[94] Cf. *ibid.*, XVIII, p. 313; Laut. III, 141–143, with Semaḥot VIII.

mistic name for Mournings), and Abot de-Rabbi Nathan, tractates written in the sixth century or later.[95] The Mekilta offers one of the early testimonies to the use of the Babylonian Talmud in the West. Attempts to gather the lore of the academies of Sura and Pumbedita began in the fifth century by Rab Ashi and Rabbina, but the work was abruptly concluded after the Moslem conquest of the Sassanian Empire in 651.[96] Some time must have elapsed before the Babylonian Talmud penetrated into Palestine and North Africa. Since it was utilized by the author of the Mekilta, he could not have lived before the beginning of the eighth century.

Certain passages of the Mekilta give the general impression that we are dealing with a posttalmudic work. The iconoclastic movement which shook the Byzantine empire during the reigns of Leo III (717–741) and Constantine V (741–775) is echoed in a parable of the Mekilta: "A king of flesh and blood who entered a province; the people built icons, formed sculpture, and struck coins for him. After an interval they covered his icons, smashed his sculptures, and defaced his coins."[97] Again, the calendar retrojected to the exodus is that of the posttalmudic period — Nisan has thirty days; Iyyar, twenty-nine — which the Mekilta attributes also to Rabbi Shila, evidently a Palestinian amora.[98]

Commenting on Exod. 20:6, *Baḥodesh*, Chapter Six, alludes to a period of religious persecution. The text extols the righteous men who become martyrs on account of their observance of the commandments, such as circumcision, the recitation of the Torah, the eating of unleavened bread, or the ceremony of lulab. Many, the author suggests, flee the country to save their lives, but God loves the ones who stay in the Holy Land and die sanctifying His name. The persecution alluded to cannot refer to that of Hadrian, which

[95] Substantial sections of the Mekilta have close parallels in Avot de-Rabbi Nathan (e. g., Mekilta, *Beshallaḥ* V, pp. 100 f.; Laut. I, 123 f., with Avot de-R. Nathan XXXIII, 48b–49b. Cf. Zunz-Albeck (n. 12), p. 45; pp. 51 f. Since these tractates drew from the Babylonian and Palestinian Talmuds, they must be later than the sixth century. Even if it be argued that these and similar tractates are younger than the Mekilta, it is clear that the aggada of these treatises is similar to that of the Mekilta. In some instances, it has been shown that our Mekilta is dependent on them (see notes 48, 59, 63, and 100).

[96] Cf. Julius Kaplan, *The Redaction of the Babylonian Talmud* (New York, 1933).

[97] Mekilta, *Baḥodesh* VIII, 233; Laut., II, 262. Cf. P. Shekalim VI, 1, 49d; Cant. Rabbah on 5:14. The latter apparently was the Mekilta's source; the parallels do not have the passage on the icons.

[98] Mekilta, *Beshallaḥ* I, pp. 83 f.; *Vayyassa* I, p. 159; Laut. I, 189; II, 99 f. Cf. B. Shabbath 87b–88a, which evidently forms the basis of this passage, but which is much less definite about the dates of the exodus.

was limited in scope and which was political rather than religious
basically. It follows that the Mekilta refers to the attempts of the
Christian emperors, commencing with Justinian, to uproot the Jewish
religion.

An uncensored text of the Babylonian Talmud relates that before
the people of Israel took upon themselves the yoke of the Decalogue,
God had offered it to the nations of the world, particularly to the
Romans and the Persians (Sassanians).[99] In the Mekilta as well as
in another contemporary book — the Pirke de-Rabbi Eliezer — it is
said that God singled out the sons of Esau (Christians) and the sons
of Ishmael (Moslems). It is clear that the author of this passage lived
when the Arabs ruled the Near East.[100]

Some may argue that all these passages are late interpolations into
an early work or a late re-editing of an old text. But the case for a
posttalmudic dating of the Mekilta does not rest on them alone.
Rather, it is based on an array of considerations: The halakah, the
sources, the names of the authorities, the technical vocabulary, the
tendency towards abstractions, as well as the external evidence, all
point in the same direction — that the Mekilta is a posttalmudic
work. The references to the calendar instituted during the geonic
period or to the Moslem dominance of the Near East must not be
treated as marginal glosses or additions. In fact it is unjust to speak
of a compiler or editor of the Mekilta. This book had a real author,
whose personality is evident in both the formulation of the material
and the architecture of the work. Incidentally, the eighth century was a
particularly productive period of pseudepigraphs among Christians
and Moslems as well. The Mekilta may not be dated much later than
the year 800 because, as noted above, Simeon of Kayyara names the
book in the first half of the ninth century.[101]

The problem of where the author of the Mekilta lived is more
complex, and probably beyond solution. That it was Palestine appears
at first sight to be a good guess. The Palestinian Talmud and midrashim
seem to permeate the Mekilta. Moreover, in geonic texts it is sometimes

---

[99] B. Avodah Zarah 2b. Cf. B. Shabbath 89a–b; Gen. Rabbah XCIX, 1271 f.

[100] See previous note. Mekilta, *Baḥodesh* V, 221; Laut. II, 234 f. Ammon and
Moab are also mentioned to show that all Arab tribes were present at Sinai. In
Pirke de-Rabbi Eliezer XLI, however, only the sons of Esau and Ishmael are cited.
Cf. also Sifre, Deut., 343, which claims that the Torah was given in four languages:
Hebrew, Latin, Arabic and Aramaic. Note the failure to mention Greek, which
would have been inconceivable during the Greek or Roman domination of the Near
East.

[101] See above, note 7.

dubbed as the "Mekilta of the Land of Israel."[102] But other indications suggest that it was published elsewhere. It is difficult to assume that Babylonian influence reached Palestine in the eighth century. Moreover, the Hebrew of the Mekilta appears to be defective when compared with contemporary Palestinian works. Egypt or some other North African location, where both Palestinian and Babylonian roots were planted, appears a more plausible place of the publication of the Mekilta. This might explain the author's selection of the exodus upon which to build his comments. In fact the Mekilta as a whole seems to be dominated by Egypt, perhaps the native country of the author. But I would leave the question open.

The above considerations flow together to suggest that the basic purpose of the Mekilta may well have been to vindicate the rabbinic tradition. Its author invoked the venerable memory of the tannaim, possibly to strengthen the spread of the amoraic halakah of the Babylonian Talmud, a work which was to become the authoritative guide of Jewish law. Possibly, though, the purpose of the Mekilta was to counterpoise the talmudic dialectics, suggesting instead that, with the aid of tannaitic hermeneutic principles, the halakah could be systematically derived directly from the Torah. Another possibility may be that the Mekilta reflects the rabbinic response to the Karaite assaults on talmudic Judaism. About the year 760 Yehudai Gaon of Sura proclaimed the Babylonian Talmud as the only authoritative source of the halakah.[103] Around this time Anan ben David had made an attack upon the entire rabbinic tradition as a distortion and misinterpretation of Scripture. The author of the Mekilta may have responded to the Karaite tendencies he had encountered by showing that the rabbinic traditions arose from a sound and formal exegetical interpretation of the Torah. The earliest attested citation from the Mekilta is used in a polemics against the Karaites.[104] Unfortunately, the knowledge of the tannaitic period and the history of the halakah of the Mekilta's author was rather limited. "Childish blunders" (as put by Weiss) are evident throughout the book. Nevertheless, as an eighth century work it displays a remarkable acquaintance with the

---

[102] See *Responsen der Geonim* (*Teshuvot Hageonim*, ed. Harkavy, Berlin, 1887, p. 107; *Oẓar Hageonim*, ed. Lewin, Baba Kamma, Haifa, 1953, pp. 6–7), a responsum of Hai Gaon. This should dispose of the claim that the Mekilta was written in Babylonia. See above, notes 61–62. Epstein-Melamed, *Introduction* (n. 1), p. 547, n. 20, interprets enigmatically "Mekilta of the Land of Israel," to mean that it was brought from Palestine, not that it was written there.

[103] See *Ginze Schechter*, ed. Ginzberg (New York, 1929) II, pp. 557 ff.

[104] Harkavy, in *Hakedem* I (1907), p. 127, citing Mekilta, *Baḥodesh* X, p. 239; Laut. II, 276.

sources. He constructed a refreshing commentary on parts of the Book of Exodus, fusing it with early medieval haggadah. The author's capacity to build upon the old and invent a new hermeneutic terminology shows some of the similar imaginative genius displayed later by the author of the Zohar.

The traditional halakists (except perhaps Maimonides)[105] rightly paid little serious attention to the Mekilta. In the scale of halakic authority, the Mekilta's position is generally regarded as lower not only than that of the Palestinian Talmud and Tosefta, but also of nonhalakic works such as Midrash Rabbah or Tanḥuma.[106] We can explain this lower position only as their evaluation of the Mekilta as one more apocryphal treatise. Writing in 986, Sherira Gaon (who never names the Mekilta) seems to have alluded to works such as the Mekilta with these words: "When we now find texts of *Baraithot* we do not rely upon them, for they are not studied, because we do not know whether or not they are authentic, except those of Rabbi Hiyya only, which are read by scholars. There are other *Baraithot*, which they call 'minor,' such as Derekh Ereẓ, but they are not to be used as halakic sources."[107]

Sherira Gaon's testimony in regard to the unauthentic *Baraithot* allegedly produced during the geonic period seems to be applicable to the Mekilta as well. Around the year 600 and onward a remarkable revival of the Hebrew literature took place. This becomes evident in the dramatic shift from Greek and Latin to Hebrew in the epigraphical remnants of the period, in the fervent labors of the Masoretes, in the rise of the *piyyut*, and in the adoption of Hebrew (outside of Babylonia) as the language of both the aggadah and halakah. The Mekilta of Ishmael and its variant, the Mekilta of Simeon ben Yoḥai, may be regarded as works which utilize masterfully the hermeneutics of the tannaim and amoraim to summarize the talmudic halakah and aggadah pertaining to the Book of Exodus.*

---

[105] See note 18.

[106] Cf. Responsa of *Tashbaẓ* (Simeon b. Ẓemaḥ Duran) III, No. 52.

[107] *Iggeret Sherira Gaon*, p. 47. See also Hai Gaon's definition of "Mekilta," as a selection of *halakhot* gleaned from the whole Talmud (Ginzberg, *Geonica* II, p. 39). I am indebted to Professor J. Petuchowski for this note.

* My colleagues Lewis Barth, Eugene Mihaly, Jakob Petuchowski, Samuel Sandmel, and David Weisberg have kindly read this essay. I am profoundly grateful for their helpful comments. Naturally, they do not necessarily subscribe to the views, not to speak of the central thesis, expressed in this paper.

# THE LITERARY GENRE MIDRASH

One of the prominent characteristics of biblical studies in this century has been the careful and explicit attention given to the classification of literary genres. Literature has been classified into genres for various purposes at least since Plato, and such classification has become a standard technique for the study of literature in some schools of literary criticism[1] and has found its way into biblical criticism especially through the work of Gunkel and Lagrange.[2] For Catholic exegetes the search for literary forms began in an effort to extricate biblical inerrancy from various difficulties, but the contemporary interest in genres is motivated also by a realization that genre classification is an aid to understanding the individual author in relation both to his social context and to literary techniques which he has used, modified or opposed, and that no work of literature can be understood correctly unless it is put into its proper literary focus in this way. Encouraged by ecclesiastical documents[3] and stimulated by the increasing amount of literature from the ancient Near East available for comparative purposes, this trend in biblical criticism has resulted in many valuable studies of such genres as history, prophecy, apocalyptic, wisdom literature, gospel, etc.

Within the past fifteen years in Christian biblical circles there has been a growing interest in the literary genre midrash in both OT and NT studies and a large number of biblical passages has been assigned to that category. Also the discoveries at Qumrân have raised the question of midrash as a possible designation for the biblical commentaries found there. These recent discussions have by and large attempted in a commendable manner to dispel the lingering ideas of Wellhausen that midrash is a synonym for fable, and to focus attention on some of the primary characteristics of this genre.

[1] For a brief history of genre study see I. Ehrenpreis, *The "Types Approach" to Literature* (New York, 1945) 1-60. Lengthier treatments can be found in the standard histories of literary criticism such as René Wellek's recently completed *History of Modern Criticism* (4 vols.; New Haven, 1955-65).

[2] See for example K. Grobel, "Form Criticism," *IDB*; J. Prado, "La controversia sobre los géneros literarios bíblicos desde fines del siglo pasado hasta nuestros días," *Los géneros literarios de la Sagrada Escritura* (Barcelona, 1957); J. Levie, *The Bible, Word of God in Words of Men,* tr. S. H. Treman (London, 1961), see index "Scripture, literary forms in."

[3] *Divino Afflante Spiritu* (*EB*[2] 558-60), the Letter to Cardinal Suhard (*EB*[2] 577-81), the instruction *On the Historical Truth of the Gospels* (April 21, 1964), and the constitution *De revelatione* of Vatican II (ch. 3).

105

Unfortunately, however, as the situation has developed, it has become more and more evident that there is little agreement among authors on what the genre midrash really is. In the discussions of the Qumrân literature (QL) there has been a tendency among some to use the word in a very limited sense, to use the word only of rabbinic commentaries, and to classify a work as midrash only if it exhibits specific literary structures and/or methods of exegesis of the rabbinic midrashim.[4] In biblical studies on the other hand the term midrash has been used in a very extended sense. Renée Bloch in the article "Midrash" in the *Dictionnaire de la Bible, Supplément,* has defined rabbinic midrash as a homiletic reflection or meditation on the Bible which seeks to reinterpret or actualize a given text of the past for present circumstances.[5] Then in her discussion of the biblical material her definition becomes much broader, and she classifies each of the following as midrash: historical works which gloss Scripture for instruction and edification (the word *midrāš* in Chr);[6] a meditation on history, tending to give to this history a relevance for contemporary preoccupations (Chr);[7] a reuse of traditional sacred texts with a religious reflection on their content and on the past to which they witness, making them relevant for the contemporary situation (Ez 16);[8] anthological style or composition, "which is a reflection or meditation on prior texts that develops, enriches and transposes the earlier message" (Sir, Wis, Prv, 1QH, Lk 1-2, etc.);[9] constant reference to the biblical data, dramatization and reinterpretation of the events and aspirations of the age (Ct);[10] the use of scriptural texts for the purpose of edification in the light of contemporary needs (Sir 44,1-50,24);[11] a work which alludes to earlier history and suppresses, embellishes and rearranges the traditional

[4] E.g., W. H. Brownlee, "Biblical Interpretation among the Sectaries of the Dead Sea Scrolls," *BA* 14 (1951) 76; K. Stendahl, *The School of St. Matthew* (Uppsala, 1954) 184-85, 189-94; K. Elliger, *Studien zum Habakuk-Kommentar vom Toten Meer* (Tübingen, 1953) 163-64; L. H. Silberman, "Unriddling the Riddle," *RevQum* 3 (1961) 323-35.

[5] R. Bloch, "Midrash," *VDBS* 5, 1265-66. Even for rabbinic midrash Bloch gives two definitions, for in discussing the rabbinic use of the word midrash she also states: "le terme midrash désigne une exégèse qui, dépassant le simple sens littéral, essaie de pénétrer dans l'esprit de l'Écriture, de scruter le texte plus profondément et d'en tirer des interprétations qui ne sont pas toujours immédiatement obvies" (cols. 1264-65).

[6] *Ibid.,* 1264.

[7] *Ibid.,* 1271.

[8] *Ibid.,* 1272; cf. also R. Bloch, "Ézéchiel XVI: exemple parfait du procédé midrashique dans la Bible," *Cahiers Sioniens* 9 (1955) 193-223.

[9] Bloch, *VDBS* 5, 1270-71, 1273, 1279.

[10] *Ibid.,* 1273.

[11] *Ibid.,* 1274.

accounts and imposes a new meaning on them (Wis 10-19) ;[12] a work with scriptural reminiscences which proceeds entirely from a meditation on Scripture (Sir 24) ;[13] a development on OT texts (Mt 1-2).[14] Mlle. Bloch also distinguishes between *"midrash* properly speaking" which begins with the Targum of Jerusalem and *"midrashic genre* as such" which is already present in the biblical literature,[15] but the terms are not explained nor is her use of them consistent.[16]

A number of exegetes have taken up one or another of the definitions of Mlle. Bloch and have enlarged upon her brief observations in the *Dictionnaire,* and many other writers have independently proposed examples of OT and NT midrash based on similar, and equally divergent, conceptions (midrash is the glossing of Sacred Scripture, the meditation on previous Scripture in the light of new events, the interpretation of events or themes or persons in the light of previous Scripture, the presentation of data in OT terms, embellished history, didactic fiction).[17] Even the sources underlying the Gospels and the Gospels themselves have been viewed as Christian midrashim (works made up of a series of OT texts each followed by its Christian explication),[18] and the redaction of OT texts has been suggested as the earliest example of midrash.[19] The

[12] *Ibid.*

[13] *Ibid.,* 1273.

[14] *Ibid.,* 1279; although in "Quelques aspects de la figure de Moïse dans la tradition rabbinique," *Cahiers Sioniens* 8 (1954) 283, she prefers to draw no conclusion on the literary form of Mt 1-2.

[15] Renée Bloch, "Note methodologique pour l'étude de la littérature rabbinique," *RSR* 43 (1955) 212.

[16] For example she calls the Canticle "un pur midrash" (*VDBS* 5, 1273), Sir 44,1-50,24 "un midrash aggadique" (*ibid.,* 1274), etc.

[17] Anything like a complete listing would be impossible but typical and influential examples would be R. Laurentin, *Structure et théologie de Luc I-II* (Paris, 1957) 93-119; M. Bourke, "The Literary Genus of Matthew 1-2," *CBQ* 22 (1960) 160-75; P. Ellis, *The Men and the Message of the Old Testament* (Collegeville, 1963) 448-63, 515-29, 533-34; A. Robert et A. Feuillet, *Introduction à la Bible* (2 vols.; Tournai, 1957-59) see index, "midrash"; G. Auzou, *The Formation of the Bible,* tr. J. Thornton (St. Louis, 1963) 200, 207, 237-39, 244; A. Robert and A. Tricot, *Guide to the Bible,* tr. E. Arbez and M. R. P. McGuire, I (2d ed.; Tournai, 1960) 505-509; J. McKenzie, *Dictionary of the Bible* (Milwaukee, 1965) 574-76.

[18] J. W. Doeve, "Le rôle de la tradition orale dans la composition des évangiles synoptiques," *La Formation des évangiles,* eds. J. Cambier et L. Cerfaux (Bruges, 1957) 70-84.

[19] R. H. Pfeiffer, *Introduction to the Old Testament* (2d ed.; London, 1952) 309, 361, 368-73; G. Vermes, *Scripture and Tradition in Judaism* (Leiden, 1961) 127-77; Bloch, *VDBS* 5, 1273, 1275; S. Sandmel, "The Haggada Within Scripture," *JBL* 80 (1961) 105-122.

result is that the word midrash at present is an equivocal term and is being used to describe a mass of disparate material. Indeed, if some of the definitions are correct, large amounts, if not the whole of the Bible, would have to be called midrash. Hence, the word as used currently in biblical studies is approaching the point where it is no longer really meaningful and where some of the material designated as midrash resembles the later rabbinic midrash only in a very superficial way. And surprisingly very few voices have been raised in protest.[20]

The reasons for this confusion seem to be twofold. First, in the studies of rabbinic midrash written before Bloch's article there had been no real attempt carefully to define midrash as a literary form. Studies of the rabbinic midrashim and other rabbinic literature were primarily interested in the content, methods of exegesis and the dating of the rabbinic materials.[21] Definitions of midrash were offered but they were largely nontechnical and failed to sift primary characteristics from secondary features —nor was there an imperative need to, since the studies were concerned not with midrash as a literary genre (i.e., with finding other material similar to the rabbinic and building up a classification), but with analyzing a given body of literature. Secondly, the real contribution of Mlle. Bloch to midrashic studies lay not in her delineation of the classification and definition of the genre but in her effort to point out the history of the genre, i.e., its biblical origins and its development through the biblical and post-biblical literature—something casually mentioned in the earlier

[20] J. Coppens, "L'Évangile lucanien de l'enfance," *ETL* 33 (1957) 733; C. Spicq, "Nouvelles reflexions sur la théologie biblique," *RevScPhTh* 42 (1958) 218, n. 34; E. Galbiati, "Esegesi degli Evangeli festivi. L'Adorazione dei Magi (Matt. 2,1-12)," *BeO* 4 (1962) 26.

[21] E.g., L. Zunz, *Die gottesdienstlichen Vorträge der Juden* (Frankfurt, 1832; 2d ed., 1892); A. Geiger, *Urschrift und Übersetzungen der Bibel in ihrer Abhängigkeit von der innern Entwicklung des Judenthums* (Breslau, 1857); H. L. Strack, *Einleitung in Talmud und Midrasch* (5 editions 1887-1920; an English translation which really is a sixth edition was published in 1931 [Philadelphia: Jewish Publication Society] and reprinted in 1959 [New York: Meridian Books]); W. Bacher, *Die exegetische Terminologie der jüdischen Traditionsliteratur* (2 vols.; Leipzig, 1899-1905); *id., Die Agada der Tannaiten* (2 vols.; Strassburg, 1884-90); *id., Die Agada der babylonischen Amoräer* (Strassburg, 1878); *id., Die Agada der palästinensischen Amoräer* (3 vols.; Strassburg, 1892-99); L. Ginzberg, *Legends of the Jews* (7 vols.; Philadelphia, 1909-38); G. F. Moore, *Judaism in the First Centuries of the Christian Era* (3 vols.; Cambridge, 1927-30); J. Bonsirven, *Le Judaïsme palestinien au temps de Jésus-Christ* (2 vols.; Paris, 1935). Also the pertinent articles in *The Jewish Encyclopedia, Encyclopaedia Judaica,* and the introductions in the various editions of the midrashim.

works but never energetically pursued.[22] The assumption underlying the earlier works had been that the period of great haggadic creativity had been between 100-500 A.D. Between 1930-50 however it had become clear that the Palestinian Targum, including its midrashic elements, was older than the Targum Onkelos and is pre-Christian in date,[23] that a great number of haggadic interpretations figure in works such as the QL, Pseudo-Philo and Josephus and are therefore of pre-tannaitic origin, and it had been suggested by A. Robert that the postexilic biblical phenomenon which he called *style anthologique* was the earliest form of the midrashic genre.[24] In other words, both the nature and the antiquity of haggadic midrash had come to be seen in an entirely different perspective. There was the feeling that the moment was ripe for the elaboration of a new synthesis and Bloch attempted such an undertaking, although her tragic death in 1955 prevented her from doing much more than grapple with the preliminaries.[25] She of course realized that the formulation of this synthesis required a precise definition of midrash and she did isolate admirably some of the primary characteristics of the genre at the beginning of her article in the *Dictionnaire*.[26] But as we have seen, before her study comes to a close her definition becomes very broad indeed, and this undoubtedly out of a laudable desire to show the organic bond between the Bible and the later rabbinic literature.

[22] Save to some extent in the remarkable pioneer works of Geiger and Zunz, *cit. sup.* n. 21.

[23] P. Kahle, *Masoreten des Westens*, vol. 2 (Stuttgart, 1930) 9-13; *id.*, *The Cairo Geniza* (London, 1947) 122-23; 2d ed. (Oxford, 1959) 191-208.—See M. McNamara, "Targumic Studies," *CBQ* 28 (1966) 1-19.

[24] E.g., A. Robert "Les attaches littéraires bibliques de Prov. i-ix," *RB* 43 (1934) 42-68, 172-204, 374-84; 44 (1935), 344-65, 502-25; *id.*, "Le genre littéraire du Cantique des cantiques," *Vivre et Penser*, 3d series (1943-44) 192-213; *id.*, "Littéraires (genres)," *VDBS* 5, 411-17; *id.*, "Les genres littéraires," *Initiation Biblique*, eds. A. Robert et A. Tricot (3d ed. rev.; Paris, 1954) 305-309 (= *Guide to the Bible*, 2d ed., *cit. sup.*).

[25] Cf. "Écriture et tradition dans le judaïsme, aperçus sur l'origine du midrash," *Cahiers Sioniens* 8 (1954) 9-34; "Note méthodologique pour l'étude de la littérature rabbinique," *RSR* 43 (1955) 194-227; "Note sur l'utilisation des fragments de la Geniza du Caire pour l'étude du Targum palestinien," *Revue des Études Juives*, N.S. 14 (1955) 5-35; "Midrash," *VDBS* 5, 1263-1281; "Ézéchiel XVI: exemple parfait du procédé midrashique dans la Bible," *Cahiers Sioniens* 9 (1955) 193-223; "Quelques aspects de la figure de Moïse dans la tradition rabbinique," *Cahiers Sioniens* 8 (1954) 211-85; "Juda engendra Pharès et Zarah de Thamar (Mt 1,3)," *Mélanges bibliques rédigés en l'honneur de André Robert* (Paris, 1956) 381-89.

[26] Cols. 1265-66.

It is not surprising, then, that we find a variety of definitions of midrash in current biblical and intertestamental studies. For the biblical or intertestamental scholar, increasingly desirous of accurately classifying his literature according to literary genres, and alerted to the possibility of midrash in his material by the work of Bloch or by the same new theories and data that occasioned the work of Bloch, is left to draw upon a wide variety of definitions from midrashic studies in which definitions either are not the main point of interest or are not the strongest feature. There is a real need then, for an investigation into midrash as a literary form for the purpose of delineating its primary characteristics, constructing a definition in terms of them, and finding genuine pre-rabbinic examples. It is to this task that we have addressed ourselves in the following pages in the hope that we might offer some contribution to that area of midrashic studies which is of prime importance to the biblical scholar and which has been so long neglected.[26a]

## A Theory of Genre

Scholars are fairly well agreed today that there is no one definition of "literary genre." Any shared characteristics are sufficient basis for putting two or more works together, provided that these works are considered as belonging together only in respect of these characteristics. The classifier must, however, steadfastly keep in mind the basis for his system, or he is likely to confuse more than he clarifies.

Tradition is generally the basis for grouping literary works.[27] As Bruce Vawter remarks in his study of apocalyptic:

However necessary, not to say indispensable, is our determination of literary forms and interpretation according to their canons, we have to recognize that the determination and specification are really ours rather than the ancient writers'. The ancient writer was not precisely conscious of writing in a "literary form," aside, of course, from such obvious genres as prose or poetry, part of the

---

[26a] This article is an outgrowth of the writer's doctoral dissertation, *An Investigation of the Literary Form Haggadic Midrash in the Old Testament and Intertestamental Literature*, presented at The Catholic University of America in 1965. The writer is deeply indebted to Patrick W. Skehan and Roland E. Murphy, O.Carm., for their kind interest and helpful guidance.

[27] On genre theory see Ehrenpreis, *op. cit.* (see n. 1), 1-60; R. Wellek and A. Warren, *Theory of Literature* (3d ed.; New York, 1962) 226-37; L. Alonso-Schökel, "Genera litteraria," *VD* 38 (1960) 3-15; and the bibliography given in each.—Today the novel, the short story, the play, the lyric poem, etc., are called *types*. Early English critics called them *kinds*. In an effort to be precise and to avoid confusion of terms, many scholars have adopted the French term, *genre*, and scholarship in genres is sometimes known as *genology*. The word *form* is also employed, especially in biblical studies because of the influence of the terms *Formgeschichte* and Form Criticism.

mechanics common to all literatures. His lack of conscious advertence makes the literary forms no less definable and applicable, but it should also remind us that his own appreciation of his work ought to be consulted in forming the definition. What the writer was aware of was that he wrote within a particular tradition: it is this that largely decided the literary form to which we have given a name. He was a Deuteronomist, a priestly writer, a follower of the sages, an anthologist of the prophets, or the like.[28]

To the degree, then, that the precise traditions followed by a work can be ascertained, its classification is sure.

Traditions may be characterized by many different elements: plot, subject matter, versification, author's attitude, or any combination of these and other characteristics. Wellek and Warren write:

Genre should be conceived, we think, as a grouping of literary works based, theoretically, upon both outer form (specific meter or structure) and also upon inner form (attitude, tone, purpose—more crudely, subject and audience). The ostensible basis may be one or the other (e.g., "pastoral" and "satire" for the inner form; dipodic verse and Pindaric ode for outer); but the critical problem will then be to find the *other* dimension, to complete the diagram. . . . In general, our conception of genre should lean to the formalistic side, that is, incline to generize Hudibrastic octosyllabics or the sonnet rather than the political novel or the novel about factory workers: we are thinking of "literary" kinds, not the subject-matter classifications as might equally be made for non-fiction.[29]

A single work rarely embodies all the conventions which, through the centuries, have characterized one or another of the many examples of a genre. In fact, the complex of conventions of which a genre consists is not at all stable. From time to time some elements may be changed, dropped, or added as individual writers express themselves within a tradition under the influence of various other traditions. One of the least constant ingredients is the name of the genre, as the terms *elegy* and *movies* suggest. On the one hand a genre may have had as many different names (signifying variously the form, the medium, and the place of performance) as the movies, photoplay, screenplay, cinema, motion picture, or nickelodeon. On the other hand, a single name, the elegy, may have been attached to such different genres as all poems in the elegiac meter, reflective poems in a serious mood regardless of meter, poems on death, or musical compositions of pensive or mournful mood. Irene Behrens has shown that while epic, drama, and lyric may have existed from antiquity, none of them has retained the same name for the same genre.[30] It is also possible for a word

28 B. Vawter, C.M., "Apocalyptic: Its Relation to Prophecy," *CBQ* 22 (1960) 33.
29 Wellek and Warren, *op. cit.*, 231-33.
30 I. Behrens, *Die Lehre von der Einteilung der Dichtkunst* (Halle, 1940) 221 and *passim.*

to have had a non-technical usage before becoming the name of a genre. As Vawter observes in the same article on apocalyptic:

In 1,1 the author of Ap applies the term *apokalypsis* to his work. It is apparent that the term is used by him in no technical way, but not only have we made it the title of his book, we have extended it to a broad body of mainly Jewish literature with which his book shares some striking characteristics. . . .[31]

Genres, then, are literary traditions or institutions within which authors shape their materials, but these traditions, being complex, interwoven and developing, require on our part a precise and scientific description and delineation if our classification of the works in those traditions is to be of intelligible value. And the categories that we form as we look back over the history of a genre from our present vantage point may well be different from those of earlier times.

Do genres remain fixed? Presumably not. With the addition of new works, our categories shift. Study the effect on theory of the novel of *Tristram Shandy* or *Ulysses*. When Milton wrote *Paradise Lost,* he thought of it as one with the *Iliad* as well as the *Aeneid;* we would doubtless sharply distinguish oral epic from literary epic, whether or not we think of the *Iliad* as the former. Milton probably would not have granted that the *Faerie Queene* was an epic, though written in a time when epic and romance were still unseparate and when the allegorical character of epic was held dominant; yet Spenser certainly thought of himself as writing the kind of poem Homer wrote.[32]

The strictness of our classifications will vary with the criteria which the classifier assigns to each genre. The realm of the sonnet, for example, is restricted or expanded as one does or does not require a special relationship between the octave and the sestet, or between the three quatrains and the couplet. Whether the limits of a genre are to be severe or flexible depends on the general reason for using the arrangement. If a biographer is considering the effect of the epic tradition upon Milton, he will probably adopt Milton's own interpretation of that tradition. If a historian of the drama finds that the classical drama of France followed a set of very precise rules, he will modify his own terms in dealing with French plays and not assume Greek or Roman standards. And if an historian of midrash wishes to demonstrate the continuity of rabbinic midrash with the Bible he will perhaps define the genre in terms of the whole tradition back to the first implicit citation of Scripture by a writer, but the literary critic may adopt a more limited definition so as to delineate really similar groups of literature.

Each genre presents its own unique problems of research for the critic due to the way it has developed historically and due to the critical work that has preceded and contributed to the modern concept of the genre. In the

---

[31] *Art. cit.,* 33.
[32] Wellek and Warren, *op. cit.,* 227.

case of midrash it seems best to start with a history of the name of the genre in its technical and non-technical usages.

## I. THE NAME MIDRASH

### A. The Word *Midraš* in the Old Testament

The English word midrash is a transliteration of the Hebrew noun *midrāš* whose first extant occurrences are in 2 Chr where it appears twice as the title of a literary work:[33] "The rest of the acts of Abijah, his ways and his sayings, are written in the Midrash of the prophet Iddo" (2 Chr 13,22) ; "As for his [Joash'] sons, the many oracles against him, and the rebuilding of the Temple, these are written in the Midrash of the Book of the Kings" (2 Chr 24,27). What the Chronicler meant by the term *midrāš* has remained a matter of dispute to this day. From the way the works are cited they evidently contained some historical material, but how it was presented and its relation to the material in Sm-Kgs cannot be ascertained. The books of Chronicles themselves would be our only source of information and it is in no way clear to what extent the Chronicler excerpted from these works or to what extent he may have modified that material. It is certainly gratuitous to say that the Chronicler acquired his method of historiography from the Midrash, as Driver suggests.[34] Furthermore, we cannot even be sure if the Midrash of the Book of the Kings is the only title the book had, or if the Midrash of the Prophet Iddo is a separate work or only a section of the Midrash of the Book of the Kings.[35]

Many have tried to work back to the meaning of *midrāš* through the word itself. Some have assumed that the word in Chr has the later technical, rabbinic acceptation and that it designates an imaginative development of a Scriptural text (Kgs) along didactic, homiletic and edifying lines.[36] This of course is precisely the thing to be proven and is now rendered most unlikely

---

[33] Noth, Galling, Torrey, Pfeiffer and others deny the existence of these works cited by the Chronicler and see them as a parading of authorities, but the majority of commentators accepts them as real works and ones that the Chronicler utilized.

[34] S. R. Driver, *An Introduction to the Literature of the Old Testament* (10th ed.; New York, 1903) 534-35.

[35] Most commentators are of the opinion that "The Midrash of the Book of the Kings" is identical with "The Book of the Kings of Israel" cited in 2 Chr 20,34, "The Acts of the Kings of Israel and Judah" (2 Chr 33,18), "The Book of the Kings of Israel and Judah" (1 Chr 9,1; 2 Chr 27,7; 35,27; 36,8), and "The Book of the Kings of Judah and Israel" (2 Chr 16,11; 25,26; 28,26; 32,32). The Chronicler cites sixteen other works, including "The Midrash of the prophet Iddo," and some would see many of these as sections of "The Book (Midrash of the Book/Acts) of the Kings" (Curtis-Madsen, Rudolph, Goettsberger, Eissfeldt, Bentzen).

[36] Driver, *op. cit.*, 529, and the many who follow him; E. Podechard, "Les références du Chroniqueur," *RB* 12 (1915) 239-41; Zunz, *op. cit.*, 38; R. Bloch, *VDBS* 5, 1264 (the probability).

by the varied and non-technical usage of *midrāš* in the QL (see below). Others, arguing from the meaning of the stem, propose that *midrāš* means "meditation" on Kgs,[37] or "explanation, commentary" on Kgs,[38] but there is no evidence that the stem bears the latter meaning at this time[39] and the relationship to Kgs is certainly not reflected in the other titles the book seems to have.[40] Others, following LXX,[41] suggest that the word means "book, essay, study,"[42] but this fits poorly in 24,27 where "book" is already

[37] A. M. Brunet, "Paralipomènes," *VDBS* 6, 1236-37.

[38] R. North, *Israel's Chronicle* (1st prelim. ed. mimeogr.; St. Mary's, Kansas, 1963) 354-55: a collection of explanations or facts gradually found needful or interesting at the side of the Kgs narrative.

[39] In the OT the verb *dāraš* means basically "to seek" and from this other shades of meaning have developed: "inquire, investigate, beseech, demand, require, avenge, pursue, promote, take care of, search, seek out, examine and study." The verb occurs in the sense of "study" in Ps 111,2; Eccl 1,13, and is applied in this sense to the study of a text in Ezr 7,10 and Sir 32,15 ("study of the Law"). A case could be made for the argument that *dāraš* in Ezr already means "interpret" (as it clearly does at Qumrân) for biblical interpretation was certainly being practiced then. But it seems safer to assign the meaning "study" and to assume that the semantic change in the term's meaning ("study" > "interpret") was the outcome of such practice and not its forerunner.—For a study of the words *dāraš* and *midrāš* see M. Gertner, "Terms of Scriptural Interpretation: A Study in Hebrew Semantics," *Bulletin of the School of Oriental and African Studies, University of London* 25 (1962) 1-27.

[40] See n. 35.

[41] 2 Chr 13,22:

> MT: *kᵉtûbim bᵉmidraš hannābî' 'iddô*
> LXX: *gegrammenoi epi bibliō tou prophētou Adō*
> be²: *gegrammenoi epi bibliou en tē ekzētēsei Addōk tou prophētou*
> Vulg: *scripta sunt diligentissime in libro Addo prophetae*

2 Chr 24,27:

> MT: *kᵉtûbim 'al-midraš sēper hammᵉlākim*
> LXX: *gegrammena epi tēn graphēn tōn basileōn*
> be²: *gegrammena (-oi e²) epi tēn graphēn bibliou tōn basileōn*
> Vulg: *scripta sunt diligentius in libro regum*

Minuscules be² for 2 Chr represent a proto-Lucianic stage of Greek OT revision, probably toward the end of the 1st cent. B.C. (cf. D. Barthélemy, *Les dévanciers d'Aquila* [*VTSuppl* 10; Leiden, 1963] 41-42, 47, 51, 62, 67 for 2 Chr; and the remarks of F. M. Cross, "The History of the Biblical Text in the Light of Discoveries in the Judaean Desert," *HarvTR* 57 [1964] 295). *Ekzētēsei* in be² is used as a mechanical equivalent of *midrāš* and perhaps was an equivalent in common usage (cf. 1 Tm 1,4; Gertner, *art. cit.*, 13). The fact that it is used only in 13,22 in connection with the prophet and not in 24,27 suggests that the revisers may have understood *midrāš* in 13,22 as a book of prophetic responses or biblical interpretations. Jerome apparently understood *midrāš* as a process in both occurrences.

[42] Goettsberger; Galling; Rudolph; Bacher, *Terminologie*, I, 104; O. Eissfeldt, *The Old Testament, An Introduction*, tr. P. Ackroyd (Oxford, 1965) 534.

in the Hebrew text.[43] Zeitlin points out the frequent use of *drš* in the OT in the meaning of "inquire (of a prophet)" and concludes that a *midrāš* was a book in which were recorded the inquiries of the kings and the answers and explanations of the seers and prophets.[44] However, according to 2 Chr "The Midrash of the Prophet Iddo" is made up at least partly of "the rest of the acts of Abijah, and his ways and his sayings" (13,22) and "The Midrash of the Book of the Kings" contains not only the oracles against Joash but also information on his sons and on the rebuilding of the temple (24,27). This does not exclude Zeitlin's concept of the work, but it indicates that the Midrash was not simply a book of questions and answers, nor valued primarily as such. Following Zeitlin's lead, Gertner has proposed that *midrāš* in Chr means "narrative" or "account," concepts for which there were no adequate terms in biblical Hebrew. The noun *mispār* on one occasion means "narrative" (Jgs 7,15) but would not do for the work in Chr which was, according to Gertner, an account of prophecies as well as of historical events, and consequently *midrāš* was used to cover both elements. The root *drš* therefore would already have assumed the connotation of "conveyance" before it came to mean "interpretation," and Gertner points out that this combination of "interpretation" and "narrative" in a single word is paralleled in the corresponding Greek and Latin terms *'ermēneia, exēgēsis, expositio* and *interpretatio*.[45] This would be an attractive theory, if it were not for the fact that it is only later in the rabbinic period that we have evidence for *drš* with any note of conveyance (*drš* meaning "to preach," "to recite a midrash") and that, in view of the basic meaning of the stem ("to seek"), it is hard to imagine *drš* developing that meaning before it meant "interpret." In fine, none of the theories on the meaning of *midrāš* in Chr is without at least apparent difficulties and there is no real basis available yet for deciding between them.

The only other occurrence of *midrāš* in the OT is in the alphabetic canticle which ends the work of Ben Sira:

> Turn to me, you who need instruction
> And lodge in my house of midrash (school).

---

[43] Eissfeldt suggests that *sēper* in 24,27 is a gloss for clarification for it is not represented in LXX. Bacher admits this as a possibility while also suggesting that *midrāš sēper* is a pleonasm (cf. *mᵉgillat sēper*: Jer 36,2; Ez 2,9; Ps 40,8) rendered with one word by LXX and thus the change from *biblion* (13,22) to *graphē* in 24,27. From LXX one might wonder if *midrāš* is not the later gloss except for the fact that *graphē* is never used to render *sēper* in LXX.

[44] S. Zeitlin, "Midrash: A Historical Study," *JQR* NS 44 (1953) 24-25.

[45] Gertner, *art. cit.*, 10-11; also G. Rinaldi, "Alcuni termini ebraici relativi alla letteratura," *Bib* 40 (1959) 277.

> *pᵉnû 'ēlay sᵉkālim*
> *wᵉlinû bᵉbêt midrāši*   (Sir 51,23).

This is the first occurrence of the technical term *bêt-hammidrāš*, common in later Hebrew as a designation of a rabbinical school for the study of the Scriptures, and because of its early appearance here, Israel Lévi suggests that it is a later interpolation and that the original probably read *bêt mûsār*.[46] The mere fact that this would be the earliest occurrence of the expression does not make its appearance here intrinsically impossible, but there is much to be said in favor of Lévi's suggestion on other grounds.[47] However, even if the reading is original, the occurrence is of little importance here since the word *midrāš* is not being used as a literary term,[48] nor does it necessarily indicate that the word at this time connotes the activity of biblical interpretation; the noun could merely mean "study."

## B. The Word *Midraš* in the Qumrân Literature.

The word *midrāš* has occurred five times to date in the published QL and four additional occurrences are reported in unpublished material from Cave 4. The noun means "juridical investigation" (1QS 6,24, and probably in 1QS 8,26), "study" (of the law: 1QS 8,15), and "interpretation" (of the law: CD 20,6, and in two unpublished MSS of CD from Cave 4[49]). It is also used as the title of a *pēšer* on the first lines of Pss 1 and 2 (4QF1 1,14) where it seems to have the generic meaning of "interpretation, exposition."[50] It occurs again as a title in fragments of two MSS of the Manual of Discipline from 4Q which reveal a text differing little from 1QS except for col. 5. In this column the two MSS present a form that is shorter and more primitive than the one we already possessed and they furnish this reading

---

[46] Israel Lévi, *L'Ecclésiastique ou la sagesse de Jésus, fils de Sira*, II (Paris, 1901) 229. Others accept it as original.

[47] First of all the suffix (*midrāši*) is not reflected in the Greek (*en oikō paideias*) or in the Syriac (*bêt yulpānâ'*)—a minor point but one providing a slight cause for doubt. Secondly, the Greek *paideia* is almost a strict equivalent of *mûsār* not only in meaning but also in LXX usage. Moreover, the fact that our Hebrew text of this canticle is a medieval reworking is now clear from 11Q Psª; cf. J. A. Sanders, *The Psalms Scroll of Qumrân Cave 11* (*DJD* 4; Oxford, 1965) 79-85.

[48] The appearance of this canticle in 11Q Psª as a psalm of David seems to indicate that it is a work independent of Sir (cf. Sanders, *op. cit.*, 83). However, it is still possible, as some have suggested, that the phrase *bêt-midrāši* in its context in Sir is intended to refer to Ben Sira's book and not to a school, but the use would be figurative.

[49] J. T. Milik, "Le travail d'édition des manuscrits de Qumrân," *RB* 63 (1956) 61.

[50] "A mi[d]rash of (from?) [m[d]rš m'šry . . .] Happy is the man that walketh not in the counsel of the wicked. The meaning [pšr] of the passa[ge concerns] those who turn aside from etc." For the text and translations see J. M. Allegro, "Fragments of a Qumran Scroll of Eschatological *Midrāšim*," *JBL* 77 (1958) 350-54 and Y. Yadin, "A Midrash on 2 Sam vii and Ps i-ii (4Q Florilegium)," *IEJ* 9 (1959) 95-98.

for the first line of the column: *mdrš lmśkyl 'l 'nšy htwrh hmtndbym*[51] ("A midrash for [of ?][52] the instructor concerning the men of the law who dedicate themselves, etc.") in place of 1QS 5,1: *wzh hsrk l'nšy hyḥd hmtndbym* ("This is the rule for the men of the community who dedicate themselves, etc."). The word *mdrš* appears to mean "an interpretation" (of the Torah) and is used as a title for the section. There is a final occurrence in a MS from 4Q in cryptic script A which preserves on the back of one fragment (probably of the last column of the work) the title in square letters: *mdrš spr mwšh* ("Interpretation/exposition of the book of Moses"). Again we have an example of *mdrš* used as a title, but unfortunately Milik gives no indication of the nature of the work.[53]

By the time of the QL, then, *midrāš* had clearly come to mean "interpretation," as had also the verb *drš*.[54] We may conclude, because of its varied use and the need to express the object *tôrâ* when referring to biblical endeavors, that the stem does not of itself connote *biblical* interpretation. Also, when it is used in that connection the word seems to have a much more comprehensive meaning than *pērûš* and *pēšer*.[55] In the use of *mdrš* as a title nothing indicates that it is employed as a technical term there either. From the

---

[51] Milik, *loc. cit.*

[52] J. Carmignac (*La règle de la guerre* [Paris, 1958] 1) proposes that the *lamed* here is a *lamed auctoris.*

[53] Milik, *loc. cit.* F. M. Cross (*The Ancient Library of Qumran and Modern Biblical Studies* [2d ed.; New York, 1961] 46) remarks that the contents of the cryptic documents belong to well-known categories of literature at Qumrân but does not specify further.

[54] In QL the verb *drš* occurs 41 times, in nine of the OT meanings ("beseech, seek, promote, take care of, seek out, search, examine and study") as well as in the new meaning "interpret" (in the phrase *dwrš htwrh* in CD 6,7; 7,18; 4QF1 1,11; *dwršy [h]ḥlqwt* in 1QH 2,15.32; 4QpNah 1,2.7; 2,2.4; 3,3.6; 4QpIs[c] 10, and *dršw hḥlqwt* in CD 1,18). In all of the occurrences in the meaning "study" and "interpret" (16x) the object has some connection with Scripture (*twrh, mšpt, ḥlqwt*)—40 per cent of the total occurrences of the verb as compared on the one hand with two out of 166 in the OT and on the other hand with the widespread use of *drš* in connection with Scripture in the rabbinic literature.—The Greek verb *zēteō*, by which *dāraš* is so often rendered in LXX, never assumed in pre-NT Greek the meaning of interpretation, nor apparently did the nouns *zētēsis* and *zētēma.* However, in some cases where they occur in the NT the nouns seem to be the equivalent of Hebrew *midrāš* (cf. Acts 18,15; 23,29; 25,19; 26,3; 1 Tm 1,4 [*exzētēsis*]; 6,4; 2 Tm 2,23; Ti 3,9); cf. Gertner, *art. cit.*, 12-14.

[55] *Pērûš* seems to mean "exact interpretation" or a detailed specification of the Torah precepts, and *pēšer* means allegorical historization or actualization of dreams/prophecies (see Gertner, *art. cit.*, 16-18; Silberman, *art. cit.*, 326-35; M. Delcor, "Contribution à l'étude de la législation des sectaires de Damas et de Qumrân," *RB* 62 [1955] 69-72).

limited evidence we have it seems to be simply a common noun. Its occurrence as a title for a *pēšer* happens to be on a complex type *pēšer* which utilizes biblical citations on a secondary level (4QFl),[56] but it is hard to believe that it was limited to this type of *pēšer* alone. Certainly its use was not limited to just the *pᵉšārîm*, for in 4QS *mdrš* is also applied to what apparently is a codified body of inferences from the Scriptures with some possible dependence on explicit biblical citations.[57]

## C. The Word *Midraš* in the Rabbinic Literature

In the later rabbinic literature[58] the noun *midrāš* retained the meaning "study, inquiry," but its main use was in the meaning "Scriptural interpretation." In this sense it designated the procedure, as well as the thing produced: the single interpretative statement (pl. *midrāšôt*). It also designated a collection of such interpretation (pl. *midrāšîm*). Furthermore it was used to designate a branch of Jewish oral tradition. The whole of oral tradition was called Mishnah (in the broad sense) and within Mishnah most rabbis[59] distinguished three objects and activities of study:

a) Midrash—the interpretation of the Bible, especially legislative portions of the Pentateuch.

b) Halakah (or Halakoth or Mishnah [in the restricted sense])—the systematic and topical assembling of halakic (legal) statements ex-

---

[56] Cf. W. R. Lane, "A New Commentary Structure in 4Q Florilegium," *JBL* 78 (1959) 343-46.

[57] Of the three explicit citations of Scripture in 1QS (5,15.17; 8,13-14) two are in col. 5. It will be interesting to see what role if any these played in the earlier version.

[58] Cf. Gertner, *art. cit.*, 4-14; Bacher, *Terminologie*, I, 25-28, 34-36, 42-43, 103-105, 117-21, 201-202; II, 41-43, 53-56, 107, 119-20, 173; *id.*, "The Origin of the Word Haggadah (Agada)," *JQR* 4 (1892) 406-29; *id.*, "Les trois branches de la science de la vieille tradition juive," *Revue des études juives* 38 (1899) 211-19; E. Margulies [Heb. *mrglywt*!], "The Term *drš* in Talmud and Midrash [Heb.]," *Lᵉšônēnû* 20 (1956) 50-61; I. Heinemann, "The Development of the Terms of Biblical Interpretation [Heb.]," *Lᵉšônēnû* 14 (1946) 182-89.

[59] Sometimes in an enumeration of all the parts of the oral tradition the term Haggadah is omitted and the term *midrāš* then designates haggadic interpretation of Scripture as well as halakic. Sometimes, also, *midrāš* was used interchangeably with the term *talmûd*. *Talmûd* (in the period before it became the name of a literary work) had for one of its meanings "the exegetical discussion and proving of halakic statements." In this usage the term *talmûd* was close to the term *midrāš* in the tripartite division above and was sometimes used in place of it. *Talmûd* and *midrāš* were not exactly synonymous, however, and when they were used in opposition to each other a difference in meaning appeared: *talmûd* starts from the halakic statement and seeks to find a biblical foundation or motivation for it, while *midrāš* takes its departure from the biblical text and argues to a halakic statement (Bacher, *Terminologie*, I, 201).

tracted from the Midrash and presented without their biblical proof-texts.

c) Haggadah (or Haggadoth)—non-legal biblical interpretation.

The Midrash, then, was the traditional literature that arranged the rabbinic material in biblical sequence around specific texts. It was that literature which was so structured that it started with a biblical text and then set down in connection with the text edifying thoughts or legislation which the rabbis had drawn out of that text. Midrash in this sense was not so much a technical literary term as a technical theological term based on a literary characteristic, the fact that the works so named were so structured that their discussions took their departure from Scripture and were not structured topically or according to some other plan.

The Babylonian Amoraim apparently were the first to use the Aramaic nouns *peṣat* and *deraš* to designate the plain sense of Scripture and free rabbinic interpretation respectively. From then on, the Hebrew and Aramaic nouns *derāšâ* and *deraš* came to be used more and more frequently to designate this free, homiletic exposition which sought to go more deeply than the plain sense and to draw out the hidden meanings of the Scriptures, and in time even the Hebrew and Aramaic verbs become colored by this usage. In the post-Amoraic period the word *midrāš* also came to designate the *deraš* type of exegesis and was used to set off the earlier homiletic from the later scientific exposition. In this period also, the term haggadah gradually came to include more than non-legal biblical interpretation and designated such things as folklore, sayings of the rabbis, fables, geography, medicine, astronomy, etc.[60] The word haggadah had earlier been used interchangeably with the term midrash (when haggadah had meant only biblical interpretation), and it is apparently for this reason that occasionally, but not frequently, in this later period the same interchange is still made, so that as a result about

---

[60] Gertner, *art. cit.*, 25-27. *Hamburger Realencyclopädie des Judentums* (Neustrelitz, 1896) II, 19.—From this period on Jewish oral tradition could be divided in two ways, one according to *content* and the other according to *form*. According to *content* the oral tradition falls into halakah (legal) and haggadah (nonlegal) material. The halakah is transmitted in two forms: Midrash in which a text of Scripture is interpreted and the law derived from it is given, or Mishna which is a codification of laws presented independently of the scriptural bases. The haggadah is either interpretative (presented as exposition of Scripture—midrash) or free (legends, proverbs, etc., having no connection with the Scriptures and presented independently of Scripture). According to *form*, oral tradition falls into Midrash, Mishna, and free haggadah. The Midrash embraces haggadic and halakic interpretation of the Scriptures. Mishna is the codification of independent halakic statements. Free haggadah is non-interpretative haggadic material.

one to two per cent of the works called midrash have no connection with Scripture but contain merely rabbinic sayings, folk lore, etc.[61]

## D. Modern Usage

The term midrash is used by the Jews in modern Hebrew, and in other languages as a loan word, in the same manner as the word was used in the rabbinic material.

Among biblical scholars today the term midrash has become a technical literary term to designate a literary genre. This is a modern usage of the word and is based on the *rabbinic* term *midrāš*. The word is employed to designate that type of literature called midrash by the rabbis as well as other material judged to manifest the same characteristics. However, as was pointed out in the introduction, there is not much agreement among exegetes on what exactly is called midrash by the rabbis or on the characteristics of midrash; and another reason why this is so is now evident: the Jews themselves have not always been precise in their own use of the term.

## E. Conclusions

At this point the following conclusions may be drawn:

1) The term midrash as used among biblical scholars today is intended as a name for a *literary genre*. The implication in this *literary* usage is that the word is based, not on the rabbinic usage of *midrāš* to designate the *activity* of study or the *activity* of biblical interpretation or a *type of exegesis,* but on that rabbinic usage which designates a specific *corpus of literature* within Jewish oral tradition. This distinction has not always been borne in

[61] For example in A. Jellinek, *Bet ha-Midrasch* (2d ed.; Jerusalem, 1938), one finds the Midrash Maase Tora (II, 92-101) and the Midrash Leolam (III, 109-120) which are really collections of sayings of the rabbis. One also finds various forms of the Alphabet Midrash of Rabbi Akiba (III, 12-49; 50-64, etc.), a discussion of the significance and use of each letter of the alphabet. (It is pointed out in the midrash that these letters are the ones God used to write the Scriptures and perhaps that was the reason the work received the title of midrash. It would not be as far-fetched to the rabbinic mentality as it would be to ours.) There are also assorted versions of the deuterocanonical book of Judith. Some are simply entitled *The Story of Judith* (I, 130-31; II, 12-22) but others are entitled *Midrash for Hanukkah* (I, 132-36). The reason for the title midrash is not clear. Perhaps it is simply an example of midrash being used to designate free haggadah. Perhaps it was felt that the reworking of a revered but non-canonical work of antiquity could be called a midrash as well as the reworking of a biblical text. Perhaps its use as a homily (normally being on the Bible and therefore a midrash) for the feast of Hanukkah was the influencing factor.—For the rarity of midrash as title for non-exegetical works see B. Heller, "Agadische Literatur," *Encyclopaedia Judaica*, I (Berlin, 1928) 979-1036; Strack, *op. cit.* (see n. 21).

mind in recent discussions of the literary form, the word midrash being used within the same discussion to designate biblical study and a type of exegesis as well as a literary classification, as if all were synonymous. And clearly all are not synonymous. There is exegesis of the $d^eraš$ type in the Talmud and yet the Talmud is not called a midrash by the rabbis; and the study of the Bible (midrash) produced all three branches of oral tradition, yet all are not called midrash.

2) In the case of the genre midrash, most of the early works that gave rise to the tradition are not extant, so we are unable to study the genre by way of its historical development. In fact, the bulk of the extant material of the tradition is found in the rabbinic literature of the common era and represents the final stages of the literary tradition. Consequently in building up the modern classification, critics have set up as the exemplar that corpus of literature designated by the rabbis as midrash and then have worked back from there, including in the same category any earlier works that manifest the same characteristics. The method is sound in view of the circumstances, provided that we do not view the rabbinic midrash as a fixed goal toward which the earlier authors had been tending, and see it almost as a Platonic archetype, the pure idea of the genre, of which a writer has a vision, toward which he strives but at which he never wholly arrives.[62] In building up the classification in this manner it will of course be necessary to analyze the rabbinic midrashic literature and to describe its characteristics to provide a basis for grouping other works with it, but we cannot expect all of these characteristics to be found in the earlier works in the tradition. We must distinguish between characteristics constitutive of the form (primary) and the ones that are incidental or acquired in the process of development (secondary). And even in stating the primary characteristics, we must not think that we are thereby describing some sort of heavenly pattern of the genre. Rather we are attempting to provide the basis for recovering the historical development of a tradition of literature in a situation where we must work from the later examples to the earlier. And when we speak of the rabbinic midrash as the exemplar of the genre, we do so only from the point of view of our modern attempts at classification and not from the point of view of the original authors.

3) What is the extent of this corpus of rabbinic literature that is the exemplar and which must be analyzed for its primary characteristics? Is it just the material dealing with the Scriptures, or is it also the folklore, etc., of the later haggadah, since an occasional work of this sort is entitled midrash? Folklore, fables, etc., which have no connection with the Bible or are

---

[62] Neo-classicism is generally blamed for this error. See Ehrenpreis, *op. cit.*, 7-8.

not used in connection with biblical interpretation were regularly called haggadah (modernly: free haggadah in opposition to interpretative haggadah or midrash). Only in a few cases do we find the word midrash applied to such non-exegetical material and it seems legitimate to conclude that this late rabbinic usage is an improper one, occasioned by the gradual broadening of the term haggadah with which midrash had once been interchangeable. Our modern technical term midrash is a term that is intended to be precise and its meaning should therefore be confined to the *proper* meaning of the rabbinic term, and midrash when properly used by the rabbis designated works dealing with Scripture.[63] The exemplar therefore for our modern literary category is that literature which falls under this proper rabbinic meaning.

4)   Some works written prior to the rabbinic material bear the title "midrash" (in Chr and the QL), but one cannot automatically apply to them the modern technical term midrash solely on that account. As best we can tell at the moment from the small number of occurrences extant, the pre-rabbinic word midrash seems to be nothing more than a generic term with a variety of meanings and has not yet taken on the technical meaning found later among the rabbis. If we are to include pre-rabbinic literary pieces under our modern category of midrash, we should do so only on the grounds that they possess the *primary characteristics* of midrash as found in the rabbinic works.

## II. THE CHARACTERISTICS OF RABBINIC MIDRASH

### A. Origin and Content of the Midrashic Literature

A distinctive characteristic of postexilic Judaism was the great importance accorded to the Torah. This was not the introduction of a new element into Israel's faith, but a new emphasis, a greater stress on a feature that had always been of central importance. The exile had naturally resulted in a heightened interest in the Torah. The Torah was the only sacred possession which was left to the Jews in Babylon, nation and cult having vanished. Furthermore, the prophets had explained the calamity of the exile as a penalty for sinning against Yahweh's Law and it is not at all surprising that the Jews felt that the future must be marked by a greater fidelity to the Law's

---

[63] This is clear not only in its use as a title but also in those texts where the word *midrāš* is used by the rabbis with some precision. When the word *midrāš* is deliberately contrasted with another word, it very clearly means that traditional literature whose structure is such that it explicitly or implicitly starts with a text of Scripture and comments on it. *Midrāš* means this when it is used in opposition to *talmûd* (see n. 59) and also when it is set off against the word Halakah (Halakoth), e.g., in the triple division Midrash, Halakoth, Haggadot.

demands. And thus, after the return from the exile and especially from the time of Ezra's reform the Law actually became the organizing principle of the community of the restoration. Moreover, very soon after the return, the living prophetic word had ceased, and thenceforth if anyone was to seek God, inquire of God, determine His will, he must of necessity seek in the Torah. This emphasis on the Torah led to the final redaction of the Pentateuch, and this literary activity created in the succeeding centuries a favorable milieu for the final redaction, composition, and canonization of the remaining books of the OT and for the gradual fixing of the text.

Partly as a result of the exaltation of the Torah and the emergence of a more or less fixed text of the Pentateuch, partly because of the inaccessability of the Temple worship to all, there was gradually introduced into Jewish life the public reading and teaching of the Torah (and later of the Prophets and Writings as well). This new form of public worship existed alongside of the Temple cult and by the Hellenistic era had developed into the synagogue service properly speaking. When the teachers began to read and teach the Torah to the people there was immediately revealed the rift between life as found in the Pentateuch and life as it was lived. Life is always ahead of the written law, there being added in the course of time many different customs, practices, and precepts to meet the needs of a developed and extended society and to specify general laws. And thus there was found the need for interpretation of the legal portions of the Torah to bridge the gap between past and present by justifying existing practices and developing new laws or new interpretations of old laws (halakah). Likewise the nonlegal portions of the Torah and the rest of the Scriptures required interpretation for they had become the primary source of ethical and inspirational teaching; and just as the full meaning and correct application of the legal material of the Torah was searched out, so also the full meaning of the historical records and of the prophecies and the ethical lessons to be derived from the stories of the fathers were drawn out of the Scriptures and applied to the needs of the present (haggadah). And with the destruction of the Temple and the intensifying of persecution an increased demand was made upon the haggadah—namely to supply comfort to the downtrodden and inspire them with hope.

This interpretative activity, first mentioned in connection with Ezra's memorable convocation (Neh 8,7-8) and continued by the teachers of subsequent generations, resulted in an accumulation of a body of traditional legislation as well as explanations and comments on the written Scriptures. Oral at first, this material was later collected and committed to writing. Laws were codified according to subject, generally independently of their Scriptural backing, in collections such as the Mishna of Rabbi Judah; the interpretative material was compiled in other works among which are those collections of the second to the thirteenth century after Christ that are known as the midrashim.[64] By the end of the fifth century (or according to a more recent view, the end of the second century[65]) creative interpretative activity had virtually ceased. Thereafter the tendency was toward elaboration, codification, and compilation until the thirteenth century when, after a gradual process, the midrash was completely superseded by the more modern sciences: history, theology, grammatical exposition, and the counterpart of science, Kabalah.

The primitive *Sitz im Leben* therefore of the halakah was the discussions of the rabbinical schools, and the *Sitz im Leben* of the haggadah (and of the popular halakah) was the preaching which followed the biblical reading in the cultic assemblies on Sabbaths and festivals, and the preaching on important public and private occasions (war, famine, circumcision, weddings, funerals, etc.). The midrashim, which, as we have already said, are compilation works, are therefore collections of material culled directly or indirectly from these sources, and in discussing the general structure of the midrashim we must always remember that we are dealing with artificial structures.

### B. The Literary Structure of the Midrashim

From the point of view of literary structure, the midrashim can be classified under three headings: (1) exegetical midrashim; (2) homiletic midrashim; (3) and narrative midrashim.

1) *Exegetical Midrashim:* When the rabbis undertook to edit, revise, and collect the immense body of exegetical material, one form that suggested itself was to arrange individual interpretations in textual sequence and thus to construct a verse-by-verse exposition of the individual books of the Bible (although in many cases all the verses are not provided with interpretation, especially in the latter chapters of books and in the Psalms). Various long and short explanations of successive passages were strung together and to this running commentary were added at times longer disquisitions and narratives connected in some way with the verse in question or with one of the explanations. Often in these interpretations references are made to other

---

[64] Lists of the extant midrashim with a description of their contents, approximate dates of composition and redactions, printed editions and translations, etc., can be found in Strack, *op. cit.; The Jewish Encyclopedia*, arts. "Midrash Haggadah," "Midrash Halakah," "Midrashim, Smaller"; *Encyclopaedia Judaica*, art. "Agadische Literatur." More recent translations not mentioned there include H. Freedman and M. Simon, eds., *Midrash Rabbah*, 9 vols. (London, Soncino Press, 1951); J. Lauterbach, *Mekilta de-Rabbi Ishmael*, 3 vols. (Philadelphia, 1933-35); W. Braude, *The Midrash on Psalms*, 2 vols. (New Haven, 1959).

[65] Vermes, *op. cit.* (see n. 19), 228-29.

scriptural passages and the text being commented upon is considered in the light of these other citations. There are also references to circumstances and historical events contemporary with the original interpreter—it being characteristic of the midrash to view the personages and conditions of the Bible in the light of contemporary history. We cite a few examples from *Bereshith Rabbah* and *Midrash Tehillim:*[65a]

AND IT CAME TO PASS, AS THEY JOURNEYED FROM THE EAST (*MIKKEDEM*) (Gn 11,2). They travelled from further east to nearer east. R. Leazar b. R. Simeon interpreted: They betook themselves away from the Ancient (*kadmon*) of the world, saying, "We refuse to accept either Him or His Divinity."

THAT THEY FOUND A PLAIN. R. Judah said: All the nations of the world assembled to discover which plain would hold them all, and eventually they found it. R. Nehemiah observed: THEY FOUND: thus it is written, *If it concerneth the scorners, He permits them to scorn* (Jb 3,34).

AND THEY DWELT THERE. R. Isaac said: Wherever you find dwelling mentioned, Satan becomes active. R. Helbo said: Wherever you find contentment, Satan brings accusations. R. Levi said: Wherever you find eating and drinking, the arch-robber [Satan] cuts his capers [is up to mischief].

AND THEY SAID TO ONE ANOTHER (Gn 11,3). Who said to whom? Said R. Berekiah: Miẓraim said to Cush.

COME, LET US MAKE BRICKS, AND BURN THEM (*WE-NISRE-FAH*) THOROUGHLY: This is written *wenissorfah* (and we will be burnt): this people is destined to be burnt out of the world.

AND THEY HAD BRICK FOR STONE, etc. R. Huna said: Their work prospered: a man came to lay one [stone] and he laid two; he came to plaster one [row] and plastered two.

AND THEY SAID: COME, LET US BUILD A CITY, AND A TOWER (Gn 11,4.). R. Judan said: The tower they built, but they did not build the city. An objection is raised: But it is written, *And the Lord came down to see the city and the tower* (*ib.* 5)? Read what follows, he replied: *And they left off to build the city* (*ib.* 8), the tower, however, not being mentioned. R. Ḥiyya b. Abba said: A third of this tower which they built sank [into the earth], a third was burnt, while a third is still standing. And should you think that it [the remaining third] is small—R. Huna said in R. Idi's name: When one ascends to the top, he sees the palm trees below him like grasshoppers. (*Bereshith Rabbah* 34,13).

I WILL MAKE HIM A HELP (*'EZER*) AGAINST HIM (*KE-NEGDO*) (Gn 2,8): if he is fortunate, she is a help; if not she is against him. R. Joshua b. Nehemiah said: If a man is fortunate, she is like the wife of Ḥananiah b. Hakinai; if not, she is like the wife of R. Jose the Galilean. R. Jose the Galilean had a bad wife; she was his sister's daughter, and used to put him to shame. His disciples said to him: "Master, divorce this woman, for she does not act as benefits your honour." "Her dowry is too great for me, and I can-

---

[65a] The translations are from Freedman and Simon, *op. cit.*, and Braude, *op. cit.* (see n. 64).

not afford to divorce her," was his reply. Now it happened once that he and R. Eleazar b. 'Azariah were sitting and studying, and when they finished, the latter asked him, "Sir, will you kindly permit that we go to your home together?" "Yes," replied he. As they entered, she cast down her gaze [in anger] and was making her way out, when he looked at a pot standing on the pot-range and asked her, "Is there anything in the pot?" "There's a hash in it," she answered. He went and uncovered it, and found in it some chickens. Now R. Eleazar b. 'Azariah knew what he had heard, and as they sat together and were eating he observed, "Sir, did she not say it was hash, yet we have found chickens?" "A miracle has happened," replied he. When they finished he said to him: "Master, abandon this woman, for she does not treat you with proper respect." "Sir," he replied, "her dowry is too great for me and I cannot divorce her." "We [your pupils]," said the other, "will apportion her dowry among ourselves, so you can divorce her." And they did so, etc. etc. (*Bereshith Rabbah* 17,3)

[A PSALM] OF DAVID. UNTO THEE, O LORD, DO I LIFT UP MY SOUL (Ps 25,1). These words are to be considered in the light of the verse *In the same day thou shalt give him his hire, neither shall the sun go down upon it; for he is poor, and he lifteth his soul unto him* (Dt 24,15). The Holy One, blessed be He, asked David: "David, why dost thou lift up thy soul unto Me?" David replied: Because upon Thine earth I am a hireling before Thee: *A servant that eagerly longeth for the shadow, and . . . a hireling that looketh for the reward of his work* (Jb 7,2). And it is written of a hireling in the Law of Moses *In the same day thou shalt give him his hire.* And so *Unto Thee, O Lord, do I lift up my soul.* For in the world's use the hireling who completes his work for a householder asks the householder for the wage of his work, and the householder gives it to him. And shall it not be so with the Holy One, blessed be He? Shall not the words *neither shall the sun go down upon* [*a man's hire*] apply also to the Holy One, blessed be He? Now if it is said of a hireling who asks the wage which the householder owes him, *He lifteth his soul unto him,* how much more ought this be said of us whose lives depend on Thee! (*Midrash Tehillim* 25,1)

The Tannaitic midrashim (generally classified as halakic but containing haggadic material as well: *Mekilta, Sifre, Sifra,* etc.) follow this exegetical form throughout. However, many of the later haggadic midrashim differ in this that the several "parashiyyot" (sections, chapters) are introduced by proems such as characterize the beginnings of homilies. Thus they are a combination of running commentary and homily. There are also minor haggadic works that use the exegetical format but treat of selected passages of Scripture rather than of entire books of the Bible. There are even some midrashic works that are completely folklore, tales of the rabbis, etc., but they take their departure from a single biblical text and thus present the material in such a way that it is in the service of the Bible; e.g., the Midrash *'Elle Ezkerah* which describes the execution of ten noted Tannaim but in connection with Ps 42,5.

In none of these exegetical compilations was an attempt made to reproduce in full the contents of the original sermons. The midrashim merely record in an abbreviated form the central ideas from which flowed the whole process of thought of the preachers and around which they wove their homilies. This accounts for the style of these collections being laconic, pithy, and terse at times to the point of obscurity, so that the reader feels that he is faced with a kind of super-shorthand. As William Braude has remarked, "the world of Midrash may thus be described as a garden of dried flowers. And at times only a combination of love, reverence, and learning can breathe life into leaves and blossoms which to a hasty and unsympathetic eye appear to be dead."[66]

2) *Homiletic Midrashim:* Not all of the midrashic works arrange the haggadic material in textual sequence. Some of the compilations—the homiletic midrashim—present the traditional interpretative material in the form of homilies. The homiletic midrashim therefore contain more extended discussions of texts than the exegetical midrashim, but on the other hand present exegetical material only for selected verses of the Bible, usually the verses that form the beginning of the Scripture readings in the synagogues.[67]

Bacher defended the position that the homiletic midrashim contain hardly any authentic homilies but are rather a collection of proems to homilies.[68] Others like Philipp Bloch think that actual homilies are preserved in these midrashim.[69] Recent study seems to indicate that both of these viewpoints are inadequate, that real sermons are not preserved in these midrashim, but that the structures or patterns used in the real homilies have been employed in a rather mechanical way to collect the units of traditional material within them and form artificial homilies.[70] Many of these homiletic patterns have been described,[71] but a discussion of these would take us beyond the scope

[66] Braude, *op. cit.,* I, xx.

[67] The Scripture readings are either Pentateuchal pericopes according to the triennial Palestinian cycle which divides the Pentateuch into 154-175 Sedarim, or Pentateuchal and prophetic pericopes according to the Pesikta cycle for festivals and special Sabbaths. Both "Sedarim and Pesikta homilies" are found in the extant midrashim.

[68] W. Bacher, *Die Proömien der alten jüdischen Homilie* (Leipzig, 1913) 1-4.

[69] Ph. Bloch, "Studien zur Aggadah," *MGWJ* 34 (1885) 174-84, 210-24, 257-64.

[70] P. Borgen, *Bread From Heaven* (Leiden, 1965) 56-57. Cf. the similar viewpoint of Zunz, *op. cit.* (see n. 21) 359-60.

[71] J. Theodor, "Zur Composition der agadischen Homilien," *MGWJ* 28 (1879) 97-113, 164-75, 271-78, 337-50, 408-18, 455-62; 29 (1880) 19-23; Ph. Bloch, "Studien zur Aggadah," *MGWJ* 34 (1885) 166-84, 210-24, 257-69, 385-404; 35 (1886) 165-87, 389-405; S. Maybaum, *Die ältesten Phasen in der Entwicklung der jüdischen Predigt* (Berlin, 1901); W. Bacher, *Die Proömien . . .* ; A. Marmorstein, "The Background of the Haggadah," *HUCA* 6 (1929) 141-204; E. Stein, "Die homiletische Peroratio im Midrasch," *HUCA* 8-9 (1931-32) 353-71; J. Mann, *The Bible as Read and Preached*

of this article where we are concerned simply with the genre's primary characteristics or gross qualifications. However, attention to these sub-traditions within the genre would be necessary if one is to classify a given work with precision and certainty; and studies of this nature such as those of Silberman[72] and Borgen[73] show that this literary labor can be exegetically rewarding as well.

3) *Narrative Midrashim:* These works exemplify what Geza Vermes has called the "rewritten Bible" type of midrash: a completely rewritten biblical narrative embellished with legends and non-biblical traditions (e.g., *Sefer ha-Yashar, Pirke de-Eleazar, Midrash Wayyissaʿu, Dibre ha-yamim shel Mosheh, Midrash Wayyosha', Midrash Petirath 'Aharon, Midrash Petirath Moshe,* etc.).

In this type the interpretative material is not given at the side of the Scripture text, as it were, but is worked right into the biblical text to form a continuous narrative.[73a]

## C. The Purpose and Techniques of the Literature

The purpose of the midrashic literature was to make the Bible relevant and meaningful, to interpret it and to draw out from it all of the lessons contained therein. The exegesis that we find in the midrashim is of a twofold character. There is first of all a considerable amount of literal exegesis (exposition of the *p<sup>e</sup>shaṭ* or plain meaning) which shows evidence of fine linguistic sense, good judgment, and acute insight into the biblical text.[74] But side by side with this there is an even larger mass of expositions far removed from the actual meaning of the text (*d<sup>e</sup>raš* interpretations): biblical accounts are embellished with fanciful details; many things are drawn out of the Bible which the original authors clearly never intended; the biblical text is even altered in many daring ways and apparently without hesitation.

The methods used for the exposition of the *p<sup>e</sup>shaṭ* we need not dwell upon here. They are in many ways the same as the techniques of our own day (based on grammar, lexicography, critical analysis of the text) and while they are not identical with modern techniques they can be understood on the

*in the Old Synagogue,* I (Cincinnati, 1940); M. Smith, *Tannaitic Parallels to the Gospels* (*JBL Monograph Series VI;* Philadelphia, 1951) 101-109; H. Thyen, *Der Stil der jüdisch-hellenistischen Homilie* (Göttingen, 1955).

72 Silberman, *art. cit.* (see n. 4) on the Qumran *pēšer.*

73 Borgen, *op. cit.* (see n. 70) on Jn 6.

73a See, for example, Vermes' discussion of *Sefer ha-Yashar* in *Scripture and Tradition in Judaism,* 67-95.

74 Cf. I. Frankel, *P<sup>e</sup>shaṭ in Talmudic and Midrashic Literature* (Toronto, 1956); Braude, *op. cit.* (see n. 64), I, xvi-xvii.

basis of our own biblical research. Requiring some comment are the methods employed for the $d^e ra\check{s}$ exegesis. Isaac Heinemann in his study of the methods of the haggadah[75] divides the $d^e ra\check{s}$ methods into two general categories: creative historiography and creative philology;[76] and this provides a convenient schema for our treatment here.

*Creative historiography* is the complementing and amplification of the available facts in an imaginative manner. The method is found in all three forms of rabbinic midrash—the only difference being that in the narrative midrashim the amplifications are worked in with the original data to form a new running account, while in the exegetical and homiletic midrashim the embellishing of history remains external to the original text and is done in the form of outside "data" brought to the text for exegetical purposes. Creative historiography is, of course, not peculiar to midrash. It is found in free haggadah (Jewish folk literature) and in popular history, as well as in the folk literature and popular history of other nations where its use has a variety of motives underlying it.[77] In midrash its use is an exegetical and homiletic one primarily, its purpose being to clarify the Scriptures and make the biblical text relevant in one way or another for the writer's audience. Thus, embellishments are used to clarify stories and to answer questions raised by lacunae in the text, to aid in the understanding of the text, to eliminate historical and doctrinal problems raised by the Bible itself, and to satisfy curiosity. As a homiletic technique amplifications on the text serve to illustrate abstract truths which one wishes to join to the text or which are suggested by the text. They are means of imparting instruction and inspiration. They make the biblical narrative more attractive, more contemporary, more edifying, more intelligible, and, by filling out many of the briefly mentioned and shadowy figures of the Bible, they make the narrative much more real.[78] This is not to say, however, that exegetical and homiletic motives were the only ones operative. Some of the embellishments in the midrashim were also prompted by the motivation behind any folk literature —the desire to tell a good story—for, undoubtedly, in the course of exegeting and moralizing, the midrashist warmed to his task and elaborated to some degree merely for the sake of elaboration and out of a delight for imag-

---

[75] I. Heinemann, *Darkê ha-Aggadah* (2d ed.; Jerusalem, 1954). For a summary and review of the book see *Jewish Social Studies* 13 (1951) 181-84, and J. Bonsirven, "Interpretatio Aggadica," *VD* 30 (1952) 349-52.

[76] In his choice of terms Heinemann is influenced by subjective idealism (cf. *op. cit.*, 4-11). We retain the terms here without subscribing to the philosophical presuppositions.

[77] Heinemann, *op. cit.*, 1, 24, 27-28, 35, 39, 44-46.

[78] *Ibid.*, 21-25, 27-29, 34-37, 56-57, 60, etc.

inative details.[79] But this was not the primary purpose. It might be helpful here to cite Marc Connelly's *Green Pastures*[80] as a non-rabbinic parallel to illustrate, *servatis servandis,* something of the process and mentality involved and to provide a basis for sympathetic understanding of the rabbinic counterparts.

The term *creative philology* would cover all of those techniques of the rabbis whereby they made deductions from the Scriptures and drew out hidden meanings. In the case of creative historiography it is almost impossible to give methodological formulae from the rabbis themselves. The permission to *develop and expand* the biblical material seems to have been self-evident. The situation appears to be somewhat different concerning *deduction* from the biblical text, for here the rabbis actually formed certain exegetical rules by which the Torah was to be interpreted.[81] However, these rules are primarily concerned with halakah and were looked upon as merely a helpful guide for the haggadist, and so are not an exhaustive list of the rabbinic techniques. Two general principles, however, governed the rabbis' approach to the text of Scripture.[82] (1) *One must interpret all the minute details in Scripture.* This principle was based to some extent on the conviction that the Torah is a divine book and that it does not speak in human language. Unlike the language of men, God's word has many meanings for he can say many things at once. Hence in this divine language everything is significant and is there to impart knowledge: e.g., anything superfluous in the text, any omissions, the order in which things are referred to, any deviations from common language and spelling, etc. (2) *All parts of the Bible* (the letters, the words, the verses, and the sections) *may be explained not only as a continuity in relation to the context* (as with human documents), *but also as autonomous units,* for the parts retain an independent significance as well as unlimited possibilities of combination with each other. Thus we find the letters of words being scrutinized for meaning through their numeri-

---

[79] *Ibid.,* 23, 49, etc.

[80] New York, 1929.

[81] Cf. Strack, *op. cit.* (see n. 21), 93-98. On this aspect of rabbinic interpretation, in addition to the work of Heinemann cited, see also I. Heinemann, *Altjüdische Allegoristik* (Breslau, 1936); J. Bonsirven, *Exégèse rabbinique et exégèse paulinienne* (Paris, 1938) 1-259; D. Daube, "Rabbinic Methods of Interpretation and Hellenistic Rhetoric," *HUCA* 22 (1949) 239-64; *id.,* "Alexandrian Methods of Interpretation and the Rabbis," *Fest. Hans Lewald* (Basel, 1953) 27-44; A. Kaminka, "Bibel VII, Bibelexegese," *Encyclopaedia Judaica,* IV (Berlin, 1929) 619-28; S. Lieberman, *Hellenism in Jewish Palestine* (New York, 1950) 47-82; J. Weingreen, "The Rabbinic Approach to the Study of the Old Testament," *BJRylL* 34 (1951-52) 166-90; M. Kadushin, *The Rabbinic Mind* (New York, 1952) 1-142.

[82] Heinemann, *Aggadah,* 96-107.

cal values, being made into acrostics, being rearranged to form other words, etc. We find the words of sentences being rearranged, revocalized, assigned alternate meanings; and we find sections being interpreted allegorically, being connected with unrelated sections in other parts of the Bible, etc.

The existence of large quantities of *d⁴raš* exegesis in the midrashim poses the question of how the rabbis could have departed so drastically from the obvious meaning of the text. The question is an old one—discussed even by Maimonides.[83] Modern writers in discussing the problem have rightly called attention to the rabbinic conviction mentioned above that God's word can and does express at once many different things and thus every word and every verse has "49 (or 70) aspects" (*Bemidbar Rabbah* 2,3; 13,15-16) or hidden meanings and the exegete can draw out all these meanings over and above the plain sense if only he knows how to do it. It is like striking sparks out of a rock (*Sanhedrin* 34a-b). However, some of these recent writers have seized upon this belief and have made it more or less the basis of their explanations of the biblical interpretation of Rabbinic Judaism.[84] The belief in hidden meanings is indeed a part of the explanation of the *d⁴raš* exegesis, and an important part, but not a premise upon which one can construct a whole theory of interpretation, for it tends to put the hidden meanings on a par with the plain sense and this is something that the rabbis did not do.[85]

It would seem that the true explanation of this dual phenomenon of *p⁴shaṭ* and *d⁴raš* exegesis in the midrashim is to be sought primarily in the homiletic and religious preoccupations of the interpreters.[86] The purpose of the midrash was the instruction and edification of the masses, and consequently the midrashist by reason of this religious rather than purely scholarly aim endeavored not so much to seek the original meaning of the text as to find religious edification, moral instruction, and sustenance for the thoughts and feelings of his audience. The text of Scripture was the point of departure,

---

[83] *Moreh Nebukim* 3,43.

[84] E.g., S. Horovitz, "Midrash," *The Jewish Encyclopedia* 8 (New York, 1904) 548; Lauterbach, *op. cit.* (see n. 64) I, xv.

[85] Witness the sober tone of the exegesis in the Mishnah (see S. Rosenblatt, *The Interpretation of the Bible in the Mishnah* [Baltimore, 1935]). Furthermore, the rabbis taught that "a biblical verse never loses its literal meaning" regardless of how the verse may be employed in rabbinic interpretation. This principle affirms that the literal meaning is stable and primary, that rabbinic interpretations are added matters and secondary, and that each interpreter should bear in mind the literal meaning of the verse regardless of what his predecessors have done with it.—On this whole question see Heinemann, *Aggadah* 129-30, 136, 153-56; and especially Kadushin, *op. cit.*, 131-42.

[86] See Weingreen, *art. cit.* (see n. 81) 173-74, 190; Kadushin, *op. cit.* (see n. 81) 98-121; Heinemann, *Aggadah, passim;* Zunz, *op. cit.* (see n. 21) 337-38; *et al.*

for it was God's word, valid for all time. The interpreter would begin with
the plain sense. If it was useful religiously, it would be thus expounded. But
if in the course of his reflection the biblical text suggested some idea other
than that immediately apparent, then this idea would be set forth in connection with the text. If the plain sense contained a difficulty and thus an ob-
stacle between the text and the audience, the difficulty would be solved and,
if possible, some religious value also derived. If the plain sense was obvious
or if it was not useful religiously, then a hidden meaning would be sought.
Throughout the whole process the belief in hidden meanings was not the
primary motivating principle, however. It seems to have been a secondary
consideration that helped the process along and served to justify the whole
activity. The primary aim was to make the Bible relevant, to make the
Bible come alive and serve as a source of spiritual nourishment, refresh-
ment and stimulation.

It is sometimes said that the interpretations in the midrashim are in reality
attempts by the rabbis to justify or confirm their concepts, ideas, and teachings and to find for them a biblical foundation. Occasionally this is the situation, but it is not the general rule by any means, and to make it such would
be to do the rabbis a grave injustice. Actually the biblical texts played a
rôle in the development of rabbinic ideas and were not employed simply as
pegs for ideas that had already been thought out—and midrashic statements
were precisely what they claimed to be: interpretations of the biblical text.
We can best describe this interplay between Bible and midrash as one in
which the Bible acts as a stimulus for homiletic material, and in this connection there is a certain kinship between midrash and poetry.[87] Both the poem
and the midrash are touched off by a stimulus. In poetry it is an object perceived; in midrash it is usually the plain sense of the biblical text. In both
cases the stimulus is non-determining: it can produce a multiplicity of effects, for, once the stimulus functions, the poet and the midrashist develop
the ensuing thoughts in their own personal and individual ways. Thus it is
possible to have many poems on the same object and many interpretations
on the same verse. And neither a poem nor a midrash is an integral part of
a system of thought, an idea logically inferred from other ideas. On the
contrary, both are discrete and individual entities.

Just as with the poem, so also with the midrash, the stimulus may play a
more extensive role in the development of the thought than that of a mere
initial impetus. The resulting ideas may be more or less cast in the terms
of the stimulus and thus the ideas are concretized and their development in
some way controlled. Sometimes, however, the ensuing ideas may be quite

[87] See especially Kadushin, op. cit., 113-21, 132ff.

different from the stimulus. In any case both the poet and the midrashist are obliged to give the "sequence of thought" to show the connection between the stimulus and its effect. Often in the case of midrash the connection with the original text consists of hardly more than a play on words but this verbal connection would be quite sufficient.

Here, of course, the analogy between midrash and poetry ceases. It is the nature of poetry to communicate aesthetic experience, while the midrash is concerned with religious and ethical values, and the thought touched off by the biblical verse is not intended to be judged by standards of style, beauty, and form. But the analogy does help us to see the midrashic comments in their proper relation to the biblical texts and also to account for the multiple and contradictory interpretations often given to a single text.

### D. Conclusions: The Primary Characteristics of Rabbinic Midrash

From this brief description of the literary structure, content, methods and aims of the rabbinic midrash, we are now in a position to attempt a statement of the primary characteristics of the literature.

1) *Literary structure:* From the point of view of structure there are several rather diverse forms of literature that are designated as midrash. There are the exegetical, homiletic and narrative midrashim. Presumably the original synagogue homilies which gave rise to so much of this material were looked upon as a form of midrash too. Moreover, as was pointed out above, every midrashic statement is a logically independent unit that is complete in itself—even to the extent that contradictory interpretations can be placed side by side in the midrashim. The various collection forms (the exegetical and homiletic midrashim as well as the homilies themselves) are merely attempts to unify otherwise independent units so as to make for sustained interest on the part of the audience. Hence an individual midrashic statement can be and was called a midrash also.

A primary characteristic of a genre should be able to be verified in all the manifestations of that genre, and characteristics that are found only in one or another type should be classified as secondary characteristics. We would conclude, therefore, that the basic midrashic structure, common to all forms that can be labeled midrash down to the smallest independent unit, is merely that one begins with a text of Scripture and proceeds to comment on it in some way. The midrashic unit must be so structured that the material contained therein is placed in the context of a Scripture text, and is presented for the sake of the biblical text. Midrash, then, is a literature about a literature.

2) *Aim:* The aim of midrash is to comment on the Scriptures, to make

them religiously relevant to the contemporaries of the interpreter, to make yesterday's text (which is the word of God for all time) meaningful and nourishing for today. Midrash has primarily, therefore, a religious and edifying aim and not a speculative one.

3) *Content:* Content is the basis for the distinction between halakic and haggadic midrash (legal *vs* nonlegal discussion of a text), and therefore content enters into a definition of these two species of midrash. However, content does not appear to be a factor in the definition of the genre midrash, for there seem to be no topics or themes that are peculiar to midrash or that flow from the very nature of the literature. We can find in the midrashim discussions of everything from cabbages to kings—literally—and it is very risky to say that a particular theme or topic is not represented in the literature.[88] And for the same reason no aspects of content other than "legal and nonlegal" should enter into the definition of the species halakic and haggadic.

4) *Type of Exegesis:* Is *dᵉraš* or creative exegesis among the primary characteristics of the literary form midrash?[89] The question is not easy to answer. On the one hand it would seem that *dᵉraš* exegesis is not among the primary characteristics. It is true that the rabbinic midrashim contain a vast amount of non-literal exegesis and that as time went on more and more of it was employed in them, but there is also a substantial amount of literal exegesis. It is also true that to a certain extent *dᵉraš* exegesis flows from the nature of midrash (in so far as midrash is a popular and devotional type literature and therefore prone to this type of exegesis). But to some extent the *dᵉraš* exegesis is due to the concept of Scriptural inspiration in antiquity, i.e., that when God speaks in human language He says hundreds of things at once and thus there are many hidden meanings to be uncovered, and for this reason the *dᵉraš* type of exegesis is seemingly an accidental characteristic due to time of composition and other circumstances.

On the other hand there is one fact that suggests that "creative exegesis" is one of the primary characteristics. The production of midrashic literature is commonly thought of as ceasing around the 13th century after Christ with the last of the great compilations, and the word midrash is not used today to describe any modern homiletic exposition of Scripture. Hence the word mid-

---

[88] E.g., Lane's claim ("A New Commentary Structure in 4Q Florilegium," *JBL* 78 [1959] 346) that messianic and eschatological orientations are lacking in rabbinic midrash cannot be supported (cf. the conclusions of the homilies). Nor can Silberman's statement (*art. cit.*, p. 329) that contemporizing is lacking in rabbinic midrash be supported. For example, the identifications of Edom with Rome, so frequent in the midrashim (and cited by Silberman—p. 331), were contemporizing comments at the time the particular interpretations were composed.

[89] *Dᵉraš* exegesis is of course essential to midrash when the word midrash designates a *type of exegesis.* Here we speak of midrash in the sense of a literary genre.

rash is by convention reserved for the earlier predominantly creative exegetical literature, and it seems legitimate to conclude that creative exegesis is so
frequent and prevalent in the genre that it has become a constitutive element.

For our study the point has little practical importance since the authors
of the pre-rabbinic literature in which we shall seek examples of midrash
shared the creative exegetical mentality with the later rabbis. The point is
of practical importance only if one is seeking to incorporate post-13th century works in the classification, in which case, because of conventional usage,
the note of "predominantly creative exegesis" must be expressly stated as a
primary characteristic. We should note, however, that in the case of both
pre-rabbinic and post-13th century midrash it is a matter of *predominantly*
creative exegesis; any single midrashic statement could be of the literal or
*peshaṭ* type.

5) *Exegetical Methods:* The techniques of exegesis found in rabbinic
midrash are not among the primary characteristics of the literary form, and
one is not justified in demanding that a literary work must employ one or
another of these techniques before it can be called a midrash. To fasten attention on the individual devices (e.g., gematria, notrikon, etc.) and to set
them up as criteria of midrash is to become fascinated with a multiplicity of
techniques and to miss the basic operation underlying all of them. The exegetical methods were employed by the rabbis in order to show the sequence
between the Scripture text and the midrashic thought, and it is this indication of sequence which is the only primary characteristic of midrash in the
area of method. How it is accomplished is secondary and contingent upon
the background and talents of the interpreter and upon the particular period
in the history of the development of midrash that the work comes from.[90]

---

[90] That the specific rabbinic methods are secondary characteristics is borne out by
the fact that in haggadic interpretation the rabbis were not bound to specific rules.
Rules of interpretation were given (which were apparently no more than statements
of accepted practices of previous rabbis) but they were used only as helpful guides,
and the haggadist was free to use whatever means suggested themselves in order to
establish sequence. In other words the important thing was the indication of sequence;
the method was secondary and up to the individual to find a cogent way to do it.
Moreover, many of the rabbinic rules of exegesis were derived from pagan sources.
As Saul Lieberman has demonstrated (*op. cit.* [see n. 81] 68-82) a number of the
rabbinic rules for biblical interpretation were current in the literary world at that
time and even relate back to hoary antiquity, for they were used by both Jews and
non-Jews in the interpretation of dreams and by non-Jews in the interpretation of
oracles as well. Hence many of the rules (and thus to a certain extent the whole
method in which Scripture was approached) were not developed within the framework
of midrash with an organic relationship to that literary form. Rather they were well-
established devices that were resorted to by the rabbis in order to satisfy one of the
demands of midrash, the indication of sequence between the text and the midrashic

It should be further noted here that the indication of sequence between text and midrashic statement is really less a requirement of midrash than it is a demand of the human mind. In other words for the comment on the text to be meaningful to the audience it must appear to be related to the text in some way. Often in the midrashim the indication of sequence is not always explicit. The connection between comment and text is sometimes left unstated and the audience is expected to see the connection. And sometimes, as for example in the case of the frequent identification of Edom with Rome where the value assigned appears to be quite arbitrary, the interpretation is in fact based on a conventional value assigned to a term in the text. Consequently the explicit indication of sequence will not always appear in an interpretation and we must not make the indication of sequence a necessary element of the visible structure. The indication of sequence is necessary only logically and it may be accomplished implicitly.

We might also note that just because one finds rabbinic exegetical methods being employed in a given work, one is not necessarily in the presence of a midrash. For example, the methods of creative historiography can be and were used in the service of free haggadah, and some of the methods of creative philology were used for the interpretation of dreams (see n. 90).

With regard to exegetical method, some have proposed that *careful analysis* of the text is a primary characteristic of midrash.[91] In the rabbinic midrash this certainly is a prominent feature. However, every midrashic statement is not based on *careful* analysis, and it is conceivable that pre-rabbinic material might be found which does comment on a text but without attentive analysis of the words, etc. It would seem that such material should not thereby be excluded from the category midrash. As with the note "creative," perhaps the best way to express the matter is that midrash *frequently* is characterized by a careful analysis of the biblical text, but any single midrashic statement may be an exception to the general rule.

6) Is *the note "Jewish"* a primary characteristic of midrash? It would seem that Christian discussions of the OT in the NT and later Christian homiletic discussions of the Bible which manifest the other primary characteristics of midrash could legitimately be called midrash also. Such literary works stand in the same tradition as the Jewish material as an offshoot of the parent stem, and the mere fact that the word midrash is Hebrew and that we have set up as the exemplar of our modern literary category the

idea. And these particular methods were chosen simply because the argumentation produced by them would be familiar, understandable, and forceful to the interpreter's contemporaries.

[91] Bloch, *VDBS* 5, 1265-66; J. A. Fitzmyer, " 'Now This Melchizedek . . .' (Heb 7,1)," *CBQ* 25 (1963) 305.

Jewish midrashim, should not deter us from seeing the two groups of literature as being two species of the same literary genre. Samaritan works of the
same type could also be called midrash.[92]

In her article in the *Dictionnaire de la Bible, Supplément,* Mlle. Bloch
states that the fact that midrash takes its departure from Scripture excludes
all possibility of finding parallels to this literary genre outside of Israel.
Faith in a revelation which is consigned to sacred books is an essential pre-
requisite for writers of this literary form.[93] Recently, however, François
Daumas has called attention to several previously published Egyptian works
which seem to bear witness to the existence of a prophetic literature and the
exegesis thereof in ancient Egypt.[94] One demotic papyrus dating perhaps
from the beginning of the Ptolemaic period is a section-by-section commentary on an apparently prophetic document of the same period and bears
strong resemblance to the Qumrân *pešārîm* in form and aim. Other material
from Egypt bears witness to the explanatory glossing of prophetic texts as
far back as the Middle Kingdom and the glossing of other material even
earlier. The dependence of later Jewish midrash on such Egyptian material
has yet to be established, but, if such a dependence does become clear, we
can see no reason for refusing to classify the Egyptian material as midrash.
Like the Christian material, the Egyptian would stand in the same tradition.
If, however, the Egyptian material stands in a tradition independent of
Jewish midrash, then the term midrash should be avoided—or if it is used,
it should be seen as an improper and analogous use in lieu of a better title.

We may summarize the discussion to this point by saying that rabbinic
midrash is a literature concerned with the Bible; it is a literature about a
literature. A midrash is a work that attempts to make a text of Scripture
understandable, useful, and relevant for a later generation. It is the text of
Scripture which is the point of departure, and it is for the sake of the text
that the midrash exists. The treatment of any given text may be creative or
non-creative, but the literature as a whole is predominantly creative in its
handling of the biblical material. The interpretation is accomplished sometimes by rewriting the biblical material, sometimes by commenting upon it.
In either case the midrash may go as far afield as it wishes provided that
at some stage at least there is to be found some connection, implicit or explicit, between the biblical text and the new midrashic composition. At times
this connection with the text may be convincing, at times it may be desper-

---

[92] E.g., the Midrash of Marqah; cf. M. Heidenheim, *Der Commentar Marqah's des
Samaritaners* (Weimar, 1896).

[93] Bloch, *VDBS* 5, 1265.

[94] F. Daumas, "Littérature prophétique et exégétique égyptienne et commentaires
esséniens," *A la rencontre de Dieu: Mémorial Albert Gelin* (Le Puy, 1961) 203-21.

ate; it is sufficient merely that a connection be there. Frequently the midrashic literature is characterized by a careful analysis of and attention to the biblical text.

Thus far we have been led by our investigation to concur with the statement of Renée Bloch that rabbinic midrash is homiletic reflection on the Bible which seeks to apply a given text of the past to present circumstances.[95] We would prefer to say "work" or "composition" or "literature" rather than "reflection" to make clear that we are speaking of the literary genre midrash and not of the exegetical method midrash or of the activity of biblical interpretation in general (an ambiguity frequent in Bloch's work); but aside from that we would agree with this one definition of Mlle. Bloch and with her statement that two primary characteristics of rabbinic midrash are "le rattachement et la référence constante à l'Écriture" and "l'adaptation au présent."[96] The task which remains is to go back into the pre-rabbinic literature and find truly similar works in the same tradition with the same basic characteristics. In this way we will build up our literary classification, and at the same time, by accepting or rejecting works for it, come to an even clearer notion of the genre.

*(to be continued)*

ADDISON G. WRIGHT, S.S.
*St. Mary's Seminary*
*Roland Park*
*Baltimore, Maryland*

[95] Bloch, *VDBS* 5, 1265-66.
[96] *Ibid.*, 1266.

# THE LITERARY GENRE MIDRASH

## (Part Two)*

### III. Examples of Pre-Rabbinic Midrash

In this final section we will indicate what in our judgment are true examples of the literary genre midrash prior to the rabbinic collections. The discussion here is in no way intended to be a complete inventory of all the examples in the literature of that period. Rather, we will point out significant examples of a variety of types of midrash to serve as a guide for future work and as an occasion for enunciating various principles and elements implicit in our conclusions above. At the same time and for the same purposes we will also discuss some works and passages which in our judgment are not midrashic but which have been classified as midrash in recent criticism. The procedure will be that of analysis and comparison, the twofold method of genre study—analysis of the intentions of the author as manifested in the structure, content and tone of the literary piece under consideration, and comparison with other works to situate the piece in its proper tradition.

### The Midrash of the Passover Haggadah

The most natural piece to single out first is the midrash on Dt 26,5-8 in the Passover Haggadah, the liturgy for Passover eve. Louis Finkelstein argues that the work dates from the last half of the third century B.C. or the first half of the second and inclines toward the former date.[97] Daube[98] and Seeligmann[99] opt for the latter. We give here the beginning of the midrash in Finkelstein's translation:[100]

Go forth and learn. What did Laban the Aramaean intend to do to our father, Jacob? For Pharaoh decreed the destruction only of the males, while Laban sought to destroy the whole family. Thus it is written, *The Aramaean sought to destroy my father and he (my father) went down into Egypt and sojourned*

---

* For Part One, see *CBQ* 28 (1966) 105-38.

[97] L. Finkelstein, "The Oldest Midrash: Pre-Rabbinic Ideals and Teachings in the Passover Haggadah," *HarvTR* 31 (1938) 291-317.

[98] D. Daube, "The Earliest Structure of the Gospels," *NTS* 5 (1959) 176, 179, n. 4.

[99] I. L. Seeligmann, *The Septuagint Version of Isaiah* (Leiden, 1948) 85-86.—S. Stein, "The Influence of Symposia Literature on the Literary Form of the Pesaḥ Haggadah," *JJS* 8 (1957) 13-44, dates it in the second or third Christian century, but his argument is from silence and is extremely weak.

[100] Finkelstein, *art. cit.*, 295-98.

*there, few in number, and he became there a nation, great, mighty, and populous.
And he went down into Egypt;* compelled thereto by the word of God.

*And sojourned there.* This teaches us that he did not go down into Egypt to
settle there, but only to sojourn, as it is said, "And they said unto Pharaoh: To
sojourn in the land are we come; for there is no pasture for thy servants' flocks;
for the famine is sore in the land of Canaan. Now therefore let thy servants
dwell in the land of Goshen" (Gn 47,4).

*Few in number,* as it is said, "Thy fathers went down into Egypt with threescore
and ten persons; and now the Lord thy God hath made thee as the stars of
heaven for multitude" (Dt 10,22).

*And he became there a nation.* This teaches us that the Israelites were distinguished there.

*Great and mighty,* as it is said, "And the children of Israel were fruitful and
multiplied, and waxed exceedingly mighty, and the land was filled with them"
(Ex 1,7).

*And populous,* as it is said, "I caused thee to increase, even as the growth of the
field; and thou didst increase and grow up, and thou camest to excellent beauty"
(Ez 16,7).

*And the Egyptians dealt ill with us,* as it is said, "Come let us deal wisely with
them lest they multiply, and it come to pass that, when there befalleth us any
war, they also join themselves unto our enemies, and fight against us, and get
them up out of the land" (Ex 1,10).

*And afflicted us,* as it is said, "Therefore they did set over them taskmasters to
afflict them with their burdens. And they built for Pharaoh store-cities, Pithom
and Raamses" (*ibid.* 1,11). . . .

The work comments on each detail of the text, enriching it and applying it
to the contemporary situation,[101] often with the help of other Scripture
passages. It is similar in form to the later exegetical midrashim, although
much simpler in that multiple citations from the Scriptures and assembling
of interpretations of the rabbis are lacking.

## The Pᵉšārîm

Soon after the discovery and publication of the biblical commentaries
from Qumrân the question arose as to whether or not these commentaries
(or *pᵉšārîm* as they have come to be called) should or could be called
midrash. Three positions have been taken over the years: that they are not
midrash, that they are midrash, and that they are midrash pesher (in contradistinction to midrash haggadah and midrash halakah). The discussion is
still joined from time to time, authors siding with one or other of these
positions.

Those who deny the propriety of the use of the term midrash in connection with the *pᵉšārîm* have done so for various reasons. Millar Burrows

---

[101] See Finkelstein, *art. cit.,* where he discusses at length the historical background
of the midrash and the possible significance of the interpretative remarks.

states that "midrash is a homiletic expansion of a biblical book or part of a book for the purpose of edification" and that its method of exposition is either like a popular expository lecture in which the opinions of various authors are cited and problems of exegesis discussed or like the telling of a Bible story. The Habakkuk *pēšer* does not have this structure and form and therefore is better labeled a commentary.[102] J. L. Teicher refused to call the Habakkuk *pēšer* a midrash because its aim is different from that of the midrashim in that the purpose of the *pēšer* is to show how certain significant events represent the unravelling of the mysteries of the prophetic utterances. Thus the *pēšer* should be called an apocalyptic commentary.[103] Geza Vermes writing in 1951 agreed with Teicher because he felt that midrash is an exegetical research either to establish law from the Bible (halakah) or to discover in the Bible moral or religious teachings (haggadah).[104] In 1954, Vermes again held that the *pēšer* is not a midrash, but this time because the *pēšer* differs in structure from the midrashim in that the *pēšer* is a paraphrase of a biblical text and not a "more or less independent development as is often the case in *midraš*." Moreover, the *pēšer* does not cite other biblical books or the opinions of teachers.[105] Karl Elliger in his work on the Habakkuk *pēšer* insisted that the *pēšer* differs from midrash in that the interpretations of the *pēšer* are not derived essentially from the text but merely stand "neben dem Text." Moreover, the structure of the *pēšer* is less detailed and developed than that of the midrash.[106] Cecil Roth felt that the attempt to characterize the *pēšer* literature as midrash leaves out of account the principal characteristic of the *pēšer:* that it does not elucidate the biblical text as does midrash but determines the application of certain biblical prophecies to current and even contemporary events.[107] Dupont-Sommer defines midrash as "stories depending on 'haggadic' tradition" and "purely imaginary developments" on Scripture and sees this as differing radically from the genre of the *pešārîm*. The *pešārîm*

[102] M. Burrows, *The Dead Sea Scrolls* (New York, 1955) 211. Cf. also Burrows' further remarks in W. H. Brownlee, "Biblical Interpretation Among the Sectaries of the Dead Sea Scrolls," *BA* 14 (1951) 76.

[103] J. L. Teicher, "The Dead Sea Scrolls—Documents of the Jewish-Christian Sect of Ebionites," *JJS* 2 (1951) 76.

[104] G. Vermes, "Le 'Commentaire d'Habacuc' et le Nouveau Testament," *Cahiers Sioniens* 5 (1951) 344-45.

[105] *Id.,* "A propos des Commentaires bibliques découverts à Qumrân," *La Bible et l'Orient: Travaux du premier congrès d'archéologie et d'orientalisme bibliques (Saint-Cloud 23-25 avril 1954)* (Paris, 1955) 96-97.

[106] K. Elliger, *Studien zum Habakuk-Kommentar vom Toten Meer* (Tübingen, 1953) 163-64.

[107] C. Roth, "The Subject Matter of Qumran Exegesis," *VT* 10 (1960) 51-52.

"aim at discovering predictions in the biblical text relating to the end of the world, whereas the *midrashim* endeavor to make the story of the past more vivid and full."[108] Carmignac refuses them the name midrash (which he defines as edifying glosses to make the word of God relevant) because the *pešārim* seek to reveal the hidden meaning of prophetic texts to which are attributed symbolic values.[109]

Another group of authors has insisted that the *pešārim* are very definitely midrash, and again for a variety of reasons: Brownlee because the exegesis of the *pešārim* is midrashic;[110] Seeligmann[111] and Delcor[112] because the *pēšer* actualizes Sacred Scripture; Bloch because it actualizes Scripture and uses midrashic techniques;[113] Silberman because the aim of the *pēšer* and its method and structure can be found in the midrashim;[114] Michel because it is history written in the light of earlier history as found and interpreted in a book of the Bible.[115] Milik,[116] Allegro,[117] and van der Ploeg[118] call the *pešārim* midrash but in Qumrân's generic sense of the term ("exegesis, interpretation") and not in the rabbinic or modern technical sense. Daumas follows van der Ploeg but also sees in the *pešārim* a genuine midrashic search for hidden meanings in the Scriptures.[119] Lane reserves the term midrash for the complex type *pēšer* only (4QFl), since Qumrân used it and since this is a convenient way to distinguish this type of *pēšer* from the simple ones—but midrash "in the Qumran rather than the rabbinic sense of the term, i.e., with the same messianic, eschatological orientation as much of the rest of their literature."[120]

[108] A. Dupont-Sommer, *The Essene Writings from Qumran*, trans. by G. Vermes (Cleveland, 1962) 280-81, 310.

[109] J. Carmignac, É. Cothenet et H. Lignée, *Les textes de Qumran*, II (Paris, 1963) 46.

[110] Brownlee, *art. cit.*, 76.

[111] I. L. Seeligmann, "Voraussetzungen der Midraschexegese," *SupplVT* I (Leiden, 1953) 171, n. 1.

[112] M. Delcor, *Essai sur le midrash d'Habacuc* (Paris, 1951) 77.

[113] R. Bloch, "Midrash," *VDBS* 5, 1277.

[114] L. H. Silberman, "Unriddling the Riddle," *RevQum* (1961) 323-64.

[115] A. Michel, *Le Maître de Justice* (Avignon, 1954) 26-28.

[116] J. T. Milik, "Fragments d'un midrash de Michée dans les manuscrits de Qumràn," *RB* 59 (1952) 413, n. 4.

[117] J. M. Allegro, "Fragments of a Qumran Scroll of Eschatological *Midrāšim*," *JBL* 78 (1958) 350.

[118] J. van der Ploeg, "Le rouleau d'Habacuc de la grotte de 'Ain Fešha," *BO* 8 (1951) 2; *id.*, "Les manuscrits de Désert de Juda. Livres récents," *BO* 16 (1959) 163.

[119] F. Daumas, "Littérature prophétique et exégétique égyptienne et commentaires esséniens," *A la rencontre de Dieu: Mémorial Albert Gelin* (Le Puy, 1961) 204-5.

[120] W. R. Lane, "A New Commentary Structure in 4Q Florilegium," *JBL* 78 (1959), 346.

In 1953, Brownlee suggested a new classification, midrash pesher, by which the *pešārîm* might be both related to (on the basis of type of exegesis) and distinguished from (on the basis of style and content) the previously known rabbinic midrashim of the classes midrash halakah and midrash haggadah.[121] This classification has been adopted by Krister Stendahl who uses it apparently to relate the *pešārîm* to rabbinic midrash on the basis of the "realistic nature" of *pēšer* interpretation and to distinguish them from rabbinic midrash because of their sectarian character.[122] The same classification is used by Grelot who sees the midrash pesher as differing from haggadah and halakah in that it actualizes prophetic Scriptures (and eventually other types) in showing their accomplishment in the events of the near past and present in order to infer what will happen in the future.[123]

From all of these discussions it becomes clear that the problem lies in two areas: the definition of midrash and the mode of expressing the very real differences between *pēšer* and midrash. An assortment of definitions of midrash has been brought to the discussion, and sometimes the definitions of midrash have been rather limited and restricted; one wonders if it is not sometimes a case in which authors, seeing the real difference between the *pēšer* and the midrash and trying to express this difference, consciously or unconsciously construct definitions of midrash which result in the exclusion of the *pēšer* from the genre midrash.

We would unhesitatingly classify the *pešārîm* as belonging to the literary genre midrash—simply because the *pešārîm* actualize biblical texts, make them meaningful for the sect, and show where the secrets of the sect are to be found in the Scriptures. The biblical text is the point of departure throughout the material and that for the sake of which the *pēšer* exists, and that is sufficient to make it midrash. Moreover, the striking similarity in structure, method and aim between the *pēšer* and the *petirah* found in the later midrashim[124] confirms the judgment that the *pēšer* stands in the midrashic tradition.

How should the secondary differences between the *pēšer* and rabbinic midrash be expressed? Certainly the threefold division: midrash haggadah, midrash halakah and midrash pesher is not satisfactory and should be

---

[121] W. H. Brownlee, *The Dead Sea Habakkuk Midrash and the Targum of Jonathan* (mimeographed; Duke University, Feb. 2, 1953). Cf. also the same article, somewhat revised: "The Habakkuk Midrash and the Targum of Jonathan," *JJS* 7 (1956) 179, n. 38.

[122] K. Stendahl, *The School of St. Matthew* (Uppsala, 1954) 184.

[123] P. Grelot, "L'interprétation catholique des livres saints," *Introduction à la Bible,* ed. A. Robert et A.Feuillet, I (Tournai, 1957) 175.

[124] Silberman, *art. cit.*

abandoned.[125] The classifications halakah and haggadah are based upon content (legal v. non-legal discussion of a text) and are mutually exclusive terms as set up by the rabbis. There is not room for another classification according to content—least of all for one that signifies messianic, eschatological content, for that sort of thing can be found in the rabbinic midrashim as has been pointed out above.[126] The *pĕšārîm* then are haggadic midrash. Perhaps the terms "Qumrân" or "Essene" midrash could express the secondary differences. Or since the term *pēšer* (which is our modern designation and not Qumrân's) will probably continue to be used to designate the Qumrân commentaries, perhaps it can serve as a convenient designation for the secondary characteristics peculiar to these works (whether these be in the area of method, or the sectarian aspect, or even content provided that in the latter case the term *pēšer* is not seen as opposed to haggadah and halakah). Even the term midrash pesher would not be unacceptable if it is freed from the tripartite content division it has been associated with and used in some other connection.

## The Palestinian Targums

Unlike the Targum Onkelos and the Targum on Job from Qumrân, the Pentateuchal targums from Palestine in so far as we can recover them (and to some extent the Targum Jonathan on the prophets) contain, in addition to the Aramaic rendering of the biblical text, narrative and other expansions on the text, probably reflecting the synagogal homilies which followed the reading of the Bible. Renée Bloch has suggested that the Palestinian targums on the Pentateuch especially are for this reason much closer to a midrash than to a version,[127] and that they are in fact the point of departure of midrash properly speaking since they contain, in a less developed stage, its structure and its essential themes.[128] Certainly the sections of expansions in these targums are midrash, but that the whole targum should be called a midrash is open to question. It is true that the material brought to the text comes from the same synagogal tradition as does much of the material in the later midrashic collections and that the targums as a whole actualize Scripture, but to call these targums midrash and thus distinguish them from the more literal ones is to use as a criterion of genre solely the

---

125 Thus similarly Silberman, *art. cit.*, 328, n. 10.
126 In Part One p. 134 and n. 88.
127 R. Bloch, *VDBS* 5, 1278-79.
128 R. Bloch, "Note sur l'utilisation des fragments de la Geniza du Caire pour l'étude du Targum Palestinien," *Revue des études juives*, Nouvelle Série 14 [114] (1955) 6-7. For a more detailed description of the characteristics of these targums see R. Le Déaut, *La nuit pascale* (Rome, 1963) 58-62.

ratio between text and expansion. The distinction between targum and midrash, however, is much more basic. The purpose of the targum is to give translation plus incidental material; the purpose of the midrash is to give homiletic material with incidental connection to the text. And this purpose is often reflected in the outward form: a targum sets out to give the full biblical text whereas a midrash frequently does not. There is good reason then to retain the traditional title targum for the more fulsome ones and to speak of them as targums with midrashic sections.

### *The* Biblical Antiquities *of Pseudo-Philo*

Pseudo-Philo's *Liber Antiquitatum Biblicarum* (LAB), which is at least as old as the first Christian century,[129] is a retelling of biblical history from Adam to the death of Saul. The narrative follows closely that of the OT but passes rapidly over many incidents and omits many sections, while on the other hand it elaborates certain portions (especially the period of the Judges) and furnishes many novel additions to the narrative of the Bible including genealogies, lengthy speeches and songs. Because in all the MSS the work ends rather abruptly with (in the midst of?) the speech of the dying Saul, it has been suggested that Pseudo-Philo's story originally went beyond Saul and that the ending has been lost.[130] On the other hand, Riessler and Spiro insist that the work as we have it is integral and, because LAB ends where the narrative of Chr begins, they suggest that it was intended as a supplement to Chr for the earlier history and that it is of the same historical genre.[131] Spiro speculates that it was intended as a popular work for circles which were not familiar with Jos-Sm but only with the highlights of the Pentateuch and with Chr. The material in Gn-Sm told of many strange things in the days of old (the escapades of various

---

[129] The work is known to us only in a Latin translation based upon a lost Greek translation made at the end of the first Christian century from a likewise lost Hebrew original which was perhaps older. The *editio princeps* is that of J. Sichardus (Bâle, 1527). The work has been translated into English by M. R. James (*The Biblical Antiquities of Philo* [London, 1917]) and into German by P. Riessler (*Altjüdisches Schrifttum ausserhalb der Bibel* [Augsburg, 1928] 735-861). The Latin text has been republished by G. Kisch (*Pseudo-Philo's Liber Antiquitatum Biblicarum* [Notre Dame, 1949]). Useful studies of the work are L. Cohn, "An Apocryphal Work Ascribed to Philo of Alexandria," *JQR* 10 (1898/99) 277-332; A. Spiro, "Samaritans, Tobiads, and Judahites in Pseudo-Philo," *Proceedings of the American Academy for Jewish Research* 20 (1951) 279-355; O. Eissfeldt, "Zur Kompositionstechnik des Pseudo-Philonischen Liber Antiquitatum Biblicarum," *Interpretationes ad vetus testamentum pertinentes Sigmundo Mowinckel septuagenario missae* (Oslo, 1955) 52-71.

[130] Sixtus Senensis, *Bibliotheca Sancta* (Cologne, 1576) 314. James (*op. cit.,* 19-20, 61-65, 185, 187) and Kisch (*op. cit.,* 29) accept this as a fact.

[131] Spiro, *art. cit.;* similarly Riessler, *op. cit.,* 1315.

figures, opposition to the monarchy, lack of Mosaic institutions, etc.) and there was a need for someone to handle this history in the same selective way that the Chronicler had handled the later period. LAB was the result. Spiro also suggests that LAB is a polemical work against Samaritans and Tobiads.

The polemical dimension of LAB seems quite secondary. However, there is no doubt that Pseudo-Philo is concerned about many of the strange things in early Israel and that he is using the same techniques as the Chronicler (selection of narratives, insertion of extra-biblical material) and like the Chronicler he is using history as a basis for exhortation. But the more basic questions are: did Pseudo-Philo see himself as writing a book like Chr or did he see himself as a midrashist gathering material of interest on the margin of the biblical text? These are extremely difficult questions to answer. Our task would be made somewhat easier if we were sure of the condition of the ending of LAB. But even if LAB as we now have it is intact and even if Chr suggested the terminus of the work, this need not indicate that LAB is of the same genre, for Pseudo-Philo could have conceived of it as a supplement to Chr but a supplement by way of a midrashic collection. And this in fact seems to be the case. If Pseudo-Philo was trying to do for Gn-Sm what Chr did for the later material, he has done a very skimpy job in many areas, and all the omissions of material from the biblical story are not accounted for on polemical grounds as Spiro attempts to do. Moreover, a large amount of the content consists of amplifications on the biblical narrative. On this account LAB seems to be some distance from the type of work Chr is (regardless of how Chr affected LAB in extent or method), and with the work as we have it as our only clue it seems better to see it primarily as a summary retelling of the biblical account for the purpose of inserting where desirable extra-biblical material for edification and for expansion's sake. With regard to extent of coverage there is a certain similarity between LAB and the much later *Sefer ha-Yashar* which runs from Adam to the Judges. On the basis of the present evidence then we would call LAB a narrative midrash.

### The Genesis Apocryphon

The *Genesis Apocryphon* (GA) has been classified by some as a targum because it presents a rendering of the Hebrew text of Gn into Aramaic.[132] Because of its expansions on the biblical text[133] the work has been called by

---

132 M. Black, "The Recovery of the Language of Jesus," *NTS* 3 (1956-57) 310-13; M. R. Lehmann, "1Q Genesis Apocryphon in the Light of the Targumim and Midrashim," *RevQum* 1 (1958) 251 (a midrashic targum).

133 The nature of the text and its relation to Gn can be seen clearly in G. Vermes'

others a midrash, a primitive and simple forerunner of the later more elaborate rabbinic narrative midrashim.[134] Milik refuses to classify it as either targum or midrash and sees it as a compilation of traditional lore on the patriarchs. preserving the popular literary form of the pseudepigraph (the patriarchs themselves being the narrators).[135] The editors of the preliminary edition have termed it an apocryphon since it is a sort of apocryphal version of stories from Gn.[136]

For a discussion of literary genre we are at a distinct disadvantage in not possessing the beginning and end of GA. From what we do know of the work it very much resembles a targum in that it sets out to give the full

*Scripture and Tradition in Judaism* (Leiden, 1961) 97-110 where he arranges GA, cols. 19-22, and Gn in parallel columns.

In some cases the embellishments on Gn serve to make the biblical account more real and vivid. Thus, in 19,11-13 geographical data are given to fill in the biblical lacuna; in 20,2-8 the summary statement of Gn (12,15) is expanded to explain how the Egyptian princes praised Sarah's beauty, as well as to give the number of princes and the name of one of them. Other embellishments serve to make the account more edifying, such as the addition in 20,12-16 on Abraham's confidence in God and in 22,25 on the benevolence of Abraham. Other expansions seek to harmonize the Gn account with other biblical texts: hence the mention of Hagar in GA 20,32 (to harmonize with the note in Gn 16,1 that she was an Egyptian maid); hence, also, the addition in GA 21,15f. (to make Abraham take the journey that he was just commanded to take and which the Bible seems to imply that he didn't), and the addition of the escape of the King of Sodom in 21,32 (to explain his reappearance in Gn 14,17). In some cases geographical locations are identified (GA 21,23-25.29). Some additions provide reasons for actions. Thus, in 19,10 it is explained why Abraham went to Egypt and not elsewhere: he had heard there was corn in Egypt; in 19,14-17 the dream of Abraham is supplied to explain what prompted Abraham to fear for his life and thus conceal Sarah's identity; and in 20,22-23 it is explained how Pharaoh discovered Sarah's identity: Lot told him. Finally, the author of GA is at pains to allay any doubts that the biblical text might raise (e.g., in GA 20,17 it is emphasized that Sarah was protected) and also he seeks to remove anything unfitting in the text (e.g., in GA 20,10 Abraham owes his life to Sarah but not his wealth as Gn states; in GA the gifts come to Abraham in return for his curing the Pharaoh [20,31-33]).

For a discussion of these and other features of the text see N. Avigad and Y. Yadin, *A Genesis Apocryphon. A Scroll from the Wilderness of Judaea* (Jerusalem, 1956) 23-37; Vermes, *op. cit.*, 110-121; Lehmann, *art. cit.*; G. Sarfatti, "Notes on the Genesis Apocryphon," *Tarbiz* 28 (1959) 254-59; Carmignac, *et al.*, *op. cit.*, II, 221-40.

[134] P. Kahle, *The Cairo Geniza* (Oxford, [2]1959) 198, having previously termed it a targum; Vermes, *op. cit.*; H. Lignée in Carmignac, *et al.*, *op. cit.*, II, 215; Dupont-Sommer, *op. cit.*, 280; G. Lambert, "Une 'Genèse Apocryphe' trouvée à Qumrân," *La secte de Qumrân et les origines du christianisme* (*Recherches Bibliques* IV; Bruges, 1959) 105.

[135] J. T. Milik, *Ten Years of Discovery in the Wilderness of Judaea* (Studies in Biblical Theology 26; London, 1959) 31.

[136] Avigad and Yadin, *op. cit.*, 8, 38.

biblical text,[137] rather literally for Gn 14, and elsewhere in much the same free and paraphrastic way that characterizes many sections of the Pentateuchal Palestinian targums. But the autobiographical form found in some sections of GA is not a normal targumic feature, and this may be an indication that the nature of the work is other than targumic. The autobiographical feature is one held in common with testaments and other literature[138] and may indicate that GA is a collection (the autobiographical feature is not constant) of assorted material to elucidate the biblical text and expand on it in the spirit of LAB, for certainly a large number of alterations and additions to the biblical text are for exegetical purposes. GA seems to stand somewhere between a targum and LAB and its resemblance to a targum may be due to its primitive and simple form. Perhaps the nature of the work will become clearer when the complete MS is published as well as other similar texts from Qumrân. At present, it can be said that the expansions on Gn in GA are certainly midrash and that there is some degree of probability to the view that the whole work is.

## Some Non-midrashic Narratives

Other writers also retold the biblical accounts by excerpting from the Scriptures and enlarging upon the biblical data, but the literary form of many of these works is not midrash.

A.   A clear example is Josephus' *Jewish Antiquities* (JA), especially in the part of JA that deals with the period from creation to the exile (Bks. 1-10), where Josephus uses as his source the biblical books as well as a considerable amount of traditional lore on Jewish history. JA is not a midrash on the historical books of the OT; it does not stand in relation to the biblical books utilized as for example GA does to Gn. Rather, Josephus has written a history of the Jewish people and this is evident from two features of the work. First of all, JA is clearly modeled after the *Roman Antiquities* of Dionysius of Halicarnassus (as to title, number of books, and in some cases style[139]), and the author evidently sees himself as writing in that tradition. Secondly, in the preface the author does not indicate any intention of interpreting the Jewish Scriptures but states explicitly that he is writing a history (JA I,1) and that the primary motive for writing the work was to inform the pagan world of the history of the Jews (I,3-4), a secondary motive being to show that God blesses those who keep His law (I,14). In order to accomplish these aims he will set forth the details as found in the Scripture record (I,17). Hence, the biblical material utilized

[137] Save for Gn 13,6.8-10.13.
[138] See Ligne, *op. cit.*, 212-15.
[139] H. St. J. Thackeray, *Josephus*, IV (London, 1930), ix-x.

by Josephus is not looked upon as an object to be clarified, interpreted and made relevant; it is rather a source from which to draw material. Josephus does not intend his work to contribute anything by way of understanding to the biblical account; it is the biblical account which contributes to the work of Josephus. Therefore, JA as a whole is not a midrash, nor are those sections which contain fictional embellishments taken from targums and similar works. This legendary material was very likely used to interpret the biblical narrative in Josephus' sources in the manner of GA and is very useful for tracing the history of midrashic traditions, but Josephus has taken it over and used it as data for his history; hence, the material, now no longer in the service of the biblical text, ceases to be midrashic.

JA exemplifies very clearly the role that context plays in some literary genres—to the extent that in some cases the genre of a composition, or of an element of it if it is a composite work, is determined entirely by its context.[140] For example, the little story that Nathan tells David in 2 Sm 12,1-4 about the poor man and his ewe lamb is in itself true enough to life to be a narration of fact and indeed is so understood by David at first ("The man who has done this deserves to die"). In the context of ordinary factual speech, then, it would be a factual narrative. When it is put in the context of "You are the man," the same composition becomes an allegory. The same story could be put in another context and could conceivably become a parable with a moral lesson for anyone. The story would be textually the same in each case; only the context would change and with it the literary form. In 2 Sm 14 the literary form of the plea of the woman of Tekoa is "drama" and this because the context so determines it (vv. 2-3 for the reader; vv. 13ff. for the king). In another context the same words could be a narration of fact. Context, then, plays a role in the determining of the literary form of a composition, and this is especially true of midrash. Conceivably, both of the above compositions could be prefixed by some appropriate biblical text and, thus put into the context of a commentary on Scripture, would become a midrash. And conversely the embellishments in Josephus which were once probably in the context of the interpretation of Scripture now are in the context of a history and cease to be midrashic.

B. Another example of the non-midrashic rewriting of the biblical text are the Books of Chronicles—*pace* Robert, Bloch and others.[141] The usual

140 Cf. L. Alonso-Schökel, "Genera litteraria," *VD* 38 (1960) 1-15.

141 A. Robert, "The Literary Genres," *Guide to the Bible*, vol. 1 (Paris, ²1960) 508; R. Bloch, *VDBS* 5, 1271; P. Ellis, *The Men and the Message of the Old Testament* (Collegeville, 1963) 260; H. Lusseau, "Les livres des Chroniques," *Introduction à la Bible*, I (Tournai, 1957) 722-23; L. Hartman, *Encyclopedic Dictionary of the Bible* (New York, 1963) 365; J. Myers, *I Chronicles* (New York, 1965) xviii; etc.

reason for classifying Chr as a midrash is that Chr is an elaboration on and a free handling of ancient texts and traditions in order to edify, teach, and explain. It is pointed out that the Chronicler is an historian and the work is to some degree a history; but it is also pointed out that the Chronicler "selects, emphasizes, and imaginatively embroiders the facts at his disposal and to this degree he is a midrashic author."[142]

It is true that about half of Chr is dependent upon prior Scripture[143] and that the Chronicler has reworked and added to that Scripture and with a certain freedom in some areas—although not in the wholesale fictional manner that some like Pfeiffer would suggest,[144] for today we realize that some of the Chronicler's additions contain reliable historical material. But was the purpose of the Chronicler to fill out the data of Sm-Kgs as GA did for Gn? Is he truly a midrashic author?

The question of the primary objective of the Chronicler is not an easy one to answer. Freedman has analyzed the structure and themes of Chr and concludes that the principal objective of the Chronicler was to write a history of the dynasty of David, especially its accomplishments in the religious and specifically the cultic areas, and to establish legitimate patterns of institutions and their personnel for the people of God. It is around these fundamental points that the Chronicler constructs his history and theology.[145] Freedman's conclusions are rather convincingly argued. But even if one does not agree with him in every detail, it seems hard to construe the Chronicler's work as anything other than a history and a theology of history quite independent of the Deuteronomic history. In borrowing material from Sm-Kgs and combining it with material from elsewhere, the Chronicler has not sought to make a fuller, clearer, more interesting, trouble-free version of Sm-Kgs and, thus, to write something for those books similar to GA. He has written a new work, a history of the Davidic dynasty, which has

---

[142] Ellis, op. cit., p. 260; the same ideas are expressed by the others.

[143] A list of the passages the Chronicler selected from Sm-Kgs is given in Myers, op. cit., xlix-lxiii; id., II Chronicles (New York, 1965) xxiv-xxxii; E. L. Curtis and A. A. Madsen, The Books of Chronicles (ICC; New York, 1910) 17-19. The method of the Chronicler and his use of his sources can be studied most easily in P. Vannutelli, Libri Synoptici Veteris Testamenti (Romae, 1931), and a useful guide for the study is A. Brunet, "Le Chroniste et ses sources," RB 60 (1953) 481-508; 61 (1954) 349-86. The Chronicler has of course used the Old Palestinian text of the Deuteronomic history current in Jerusalem in his day, and it is by no means identical with the received text; see F. M. Cross, "The History of the Biblical Text in the Light of Discoveries in the Judaean Desert," HarvTR 57 (1964) 292-97.

[144] R. H. Pfeiffer, Introduction to the Old Testament (London, 1952) 806; id., IDB 1, 578-80.

[145] D. N. Freedman, "The Chronicler's Purpose," CBQ 23 (1961) 436-42.

preoccupations which are not those of Sm-Kgs as well as new doctrinal themes which he is attempting to illustrate. The work is structured not on Sm-Kgs but according to the themes of the Chronicler. And all indications point to the fact that in taking material from Sm-Kgs the Chronicler is using those books as sources and not as an object of interpretation. He takes selected passages in accord with his interests, sometimes rearranges their order, abbreviates them, supplements them from extra-biblical sources or his own imagination, and practically all of his additions to the biblical text are for the purpose of throwing into relief one theme or another that is dear to the Chronicler.

It is true that some of the methods used by the Chronicler are the same as those to be used later by the author of GA and the rabbis in their narrative midrashim. But this is not a reason to call Chr midrash, for these methods are used by the authors of many literary forms. Selection of material and emphasis of details are methods employed by all historians, ancient and modern; and fiction in its various uses is a device that is common to several genres (e.g., popular pre-history, popular history, parable, apocalyptic, folklore, didactic fiction, and midrash if the fiction is at the service of a biblical text). As Seeligmann has pointed out, many of the techniques used in rabbinic midrash (alteration of traditions, play on words, adaptation of biblical texts) are found in use in the OT.[146] But they are all techniques and can be used for many purposes, and the literary form midrash does not have a monopoly on them. Technique and method, therefore, are not to be confused with literary form.

Nor should we classify Chr as a midrash because the Chronicler used the Midrash of the Book of the Kings and the Midrash of the Prophet Iddo as sources for his extra-biblical material. As was already stated, we have no idea of the nature of these two midrashim mentioned in Chr, but even if they were something like GA and were to be classified under the modern literary category, midrash, this would still not mean that Chr is midrash any more than JA is a midrash because Josephus borrowed material from midrashic works. The material borrowed would have been at the service of the Bible in the original midrash, but in Chr it is used as data to fill out a new work of history. The context of the material is now entirely different.

It must be admitted that midrash and history are not always easy to distinguish. History is concerned with the interpretation of events; midrash is concerned with the interpretation of texts. Whenever the object of discussion is clearly one or the other, there is, of course, no difficulty in ascertaining the genre of a work. Frequently, however, the texts which are the

---

[146] I. L. Seeligmann, art. cit. (see n. 111) 150-81.

subject of a midrash are narratives dealing with events and, thus, there is an interest in the events related (GA, and Wis 11-19 discussed below). Likewise, the events which are the subject of a history are not infrequently known to the historian from earlier texts and are recounted by reproducing these earlier sources in part or in whole (Chr and JA). In borderline areas such as these it is sometimes very difficult in practice to classify a work according to genre. In theory, at least, the general rule can be given that a midrash will be distinguishable by its interest not in events *simpliciter* but in events as related in a specific way in a given text, and that a character-istic feature of a midrash will be either its skimpy presentation of the text to provide a framework within which to introduce ample embellishments at various points (LAB) or its attention to details of a narrative (GA) as opposed to a recasting and restructuring of older material in one way or another (JA, Chr) as is characteristic of a history.

C.  It has been suggested that the historical psalms (Pss 78; 106; etc.) should be classified as midrash,[147] but these are actually recitals of salvation history. In Ps 78,5-7 the psalmist states the *lex narrationis:* "He set it up as a decree in Jacob and established it as a law in Israel that what he com-manded our fathers they should make known to their sons . . . that they might not forget the deeds of God but keep his commands" (cf. Ex 13,8; Dt 4,9; 6,20ff.; Jgs 6,13); and it is in this light that the historical psalms and other similar short narrations of biblical history such as Sirach's Praise of the Fathers,[148] Wis 10, CD 2,14-3,19, Acts 7 and Heb 11 should be read. These works are much closer in genre to the credos of Dt 6,21-23; 26,5-9 and to the historical prologue of a covenant renewal (Jos 24) or of a prayer

---

[147] Bloch, *VDBS* 5, 1275.

[148] Siebeneck (*CBQ* 21 [1959] 416), following Bloch (*VDBS* 5, 1274), calls Sirach's Praise of the Fathers (44,1-50,24) an historical psalm but says it should also be called haggadic midrash because Sirach uses Scripture, exploits and reorganizes it to make it an instrument of edification in the light of contemporary needs. It is also pointed out that "midrash is what Sirach himself calls his teaching in 51,23." It would be more accurate to say that, if the text as we have it is original, Sirach calls his book or his teaching a *bêt hammidrāš* or school, and, of course, this is irrelevant to a discussion of the literary genre of any part of Sir, even prescinding from the fact that Sirach's use of the word *midrāš* is quite different from our modern technical literary term. In fact, the Praise of the Fathers is a recital of events similar to the historical psalms. Sirach begins his praise of Israel's ancestors with a statement of purpose (44,1-15) in conformity with the literary procedure of his time. He intends to "praise those godly men, our ancestors" (v. 1) in the same way others had done: "at gather-ings their wisdom is retold and the assembly sings their praises" (v. 15). This is the tradition in which he is writing. The poem addresses Solomon (47,14ff.) and Elijah (48,4ff.) in the second person and for this reason some have chosen to speak of the Praise of the Fathers as a eulogy.

(Neh 9,6-31) than they are to GA and LAB, for it seems clear that it is the events and personages themselves and not some specific biblical narration of them which are the object of interest. The works are not a literature about a literature.

D.  Besides those works which retell the biblical narrative there is another group of literature which is frequently termed midrash, namely, works of didactic fiction such as Est, Tb and Jon.[149] Apparently the sole reason for classifying these writings in this manner is that these works freely elaborate for didactic purposes an historical nucleus of one sort or another or are simply fiction. It is hard to see how this type of writing can be called midrash. Est, for example, stands in relation to no biblical text as, say, GA does to Gn, yet this is the essential note of midrash. If we are to be precise in our classification of literary works, we must avoid using midrash as a euphemism for biblical fiction and we should borrow from the rabbis the term (free) haggadah as well as the term midrash and use the term haggadah to describe works such as Est.

We would suggest the same classification of haggadah for Tb, even though there is some relation with Gn since some details in Tb have been borrowed from the stories of the patriarchs. But it is a standard technique of fiction to borrow details from other stories; here it is done to create the atmosphere of patriarchal times and there is no suggestion in the story that Tb is intended to be a rewritten patriarchal story brought up to date. It is a matter of simple borrowing of details and no different from the other borrowings in Tb—of phraseology from elsewhere in the OT and of details from folklore.[150]

The situation in the case of the book of Jonah is not so clear-cut because there are potentially significant relations with two texts: the mention of the prophet Jonah in 2 Kgs 14,25 and the text of Jer 18,8 alluded to in Jon 3,10. But what sort of relation is it? Did the author of Jon merely borrow the name of Jonah from Kgs, as he did details from the stories of Elijah and Elisha and other material from Jer and from folklore,[151] to compose a bit of free haggadah with a didactic purpose, or did the author wish to embellish on 2 Kgs 14,25 in the manner of GA and write a midrash? Or, is Jon a sermon in story form based on Jer 18,8 ("If that nation concerning

[149] Thus Robert, *Guide to the Bible*, 508; Lusseau, "Les autres hagiographes," *Introduction à la Bible*, I, 692; Ellis, *op. cit.*, 454-61; and others.

[150] See D. C. Simpson, "The Book of Tobit," *The Apocrypha and Pseudepigrapha of the Old Testament in English*, ed. R. H. Charles (reprinted ed.; Oxford, 1963) I, 187-94.

[151] A. Feuillet, "Les sources du livre de Jonas," *RB* 54 (1947) 161-86.

which I have spoken turns from evil, I will repent of the evil that I thought to do it") since the Jer text is clearly alluded to in Jon 3,10 ?[152]

Surely if Jon were found in a rabbinic midrash after the text of 2 Kgs or Jer there would be no question that it would be a haggadic work applied to Scripture in order to indicate interpretation or to provide illustration or expansion and would truly be a midrash. But since it is not placed in such a context in the Bible, we must decide if the mere use of the prophet's name or the Jer citation is enough to create that context. The writer would consider the allusions to 2 Kgs and Jer far too weak to give the impression that Jon is a midrash on either of them. One would expect a few more allusions to a particular text if the book were intended to be a midrash on that text; also the borrowings from elsewhere in Kgs and from folklore would suggest that the name Jonah and the Jer text are simply borrowings in the same spirit. In any event, the point we wish to make here is that it is on these grounds that one should determine whether Jon is a midrash or not—and not on the grounds of the fictional or didactic elements, or because Jon "prolongs the doctrine of Jeremiah" as Bloch would have it.[153]

### Some Homilies

Peder Borgen has isolated in the works of Philo a number of homilies (*De Mutatione nominum* 253-263; *Legum allegoriae* III, 65-75a; 162-168; 169-

---

[152] Thus L. H. Brockington, "Jonah," *Peake's Commentary on the Bible,* eds. M. Black and H. H. Rowley (London, 1962) 627.

[153] Bloch, *VDBS* 5, 1275. If the prolonging of a theme constitutes midrash, then most of the Bible is a midrash for one reason or another, since much of it prolongs the themes of the Pentateuch and it is not uncommon for later biblical writers to take up themes of earlier writers and restate or develop those ideas. This prolonging of a theme is frequently done in such a way that it focuses the reader's attention on no particular text of the past and therefore there is no justification to classify such literature as midrash. The prolonging of a theme is something that is found in every genre and is a characteristic that is quite secondary, if indeed it is correct to speak of it as a genre characteristic at all.

K. Budde ("Vermutungen zum 'Midrasch des Buches der Könige,'" *ZAW* 12 [1892] 37-38) has suggested that Jon was originally part of the Midrash of the Book of the Kings mentioned in 2 Chr 24,27 and that Jon originally stood in relation to 2 Kgs 14,25 in that work but has since been excerpted and stands alone. The suggestion has found few adherents, for there is no evidence to support the assertion, nor even to support Budde's presuppositions on the nature of the Midrash of the Book of the Kings. In the same vein, H. Winckler (*Altorientalische Forschungen,* 2d series 2 [1899] 260f.) proposes that Jon is a fragment of a midrash on all the prophets, the one called the Chronicles of the Seers in 2 Chr 33,19; but again the assertion is pure speculation. However, granting for the sake of discussion that Jon once was a midrash because of the context given it, it is not a midrash now because it is no longer in its original context (unless of course one feels that the original context is still preserved by the strength of the allusions to 2 Kgs or Jer).

173; *De sacrificiis Abelis et Caini* 76-87; *De somniis* II, 17-30) which are similar in structure to the homily in Jn 6,31-58, and he has demonstrated that they are all constructed on a homiletic pattern found in the later Palestinian midrash.[154] The pattern is to begin with a citation of Scripture usually from the Pentateuch (in the homily of Jn 6 it is in v. 31: "he gave them bread from heaven to eat"). This is followed by an exegetical paraphrase of each part of the text in a successive sequence (e.g., first the theme of "he gave them bread from heaven" in Jn 6,32-48, then the theme "to eat" in Jn 6,49-58). The closing statements refer back to the main statement at the beginning and at the same time sum up points from the homily as a whole. Commonly within the homily there is a subordinate citation (e.g., Jn 6,45) to which a few lines of commentary are devoted.[155] These pieces discussed by Borgen are fine examples of midrash in homily form, compositions which take a text and apply it or adapt it to contemporary needs. The same homiletic pattern is also observable in Gal 3,6-29 (on Gn 15,6) and Rom 4,1-25 (likewise on Gn 15,6) and these Pauline passages are examples of midrash too, regardless of whether they are homilies that have been incorporated into the text as Borgen suggests.

Those homilies of the Fathers which set out to comment on biblical texts and which have been influenced directly or through the NT by their Jewish counterparts can also be classified as midrash, and this tradition should be seen as an offshoot of the parent Jewish tradition.[154]

However, there are some sermons in the pre-rabbinic literature which are not midrashic. An example would be 4 Mc. The work is a discourse on the supremacy of religious reason over the passions and is a splendid piece of Hellenistic oratory. It has on the one hand been assessed as a synagogue sermon because its reference (1,10) to the feast being celebrated (Hanukkah?) and its religious tone including the use of doxologies (1,12; 18,24) argue strongly for its deliverance in a context of worship. On the other hand it has been classified as a lecture because it has as its point of departure a philosophico-religious thesis and

---

155 In Jn 6 the pattern is complete in 6,31-50 and perhaps this was the original discourse, 51-58 being a later addition. For this and a slightly different treatment of the whole discourse see R. Brown, *The Gospel According to John, I-XII* (New York, 1966) 277-78, 293-94.

156 Cf. Bo Reicke, "A Synopsis of Early Christian Preaching," *The Root of the Vine: Essays in Biblical Theology,* ed. A. Fridrichsen (Westminster, 1953) 128-60; W. B. Sedgwick, "The Origins of the Sermon," *HibbJ* 45 (1946-47) 158-64; art. "Predigt" in *RGG*³ (5,516-19) and *LTK*² (8,705-13). Also many of the reworkings and embellishments on the NT Scriptures in the apocryphal material were the Christian midrashic counterpart to Jewish material on the OT. For a discussion of the evidence for the existence of ancient Jewish-Christian exegetical midrashim see J. Daniélou, *The Theology of Jewish Christianity* (Chicago, 1964) 97-107.

not a biblical text—a departure from the seemingly regular synagogue practice of beginning with a scripture text. It is true that for the non-biblical point of departure we have no parallel to 4 Mc (save in a sense Heb 11 and Wis 10) but it is doubtful if we know enough about Judeo-Hellenistic practice to judge the question of the synagogal origins of 4 Mc on that basis. It is even possible, as Thyen suggests,[157] that the Scripture text was not part of the homily but was simply the synagogue reading (from 2 Mc ?) that preceded. However, regardless of its original *Sitz im Leben*, as 4 Mc stands now (i.e., without that Scripture reading) it is not a midrash because it is not a discourse on a text but on a religious thesis. And the same should be said for the embellishments on 2 Mc contained in the discourse: these could be embellishments in the spirit of GA and LAB but it is not clear from the work that the discourse is to be taken in the context of 2 Mc and it seems better to view the embellishments as existing for oratorical effect to heighten the thesis being discussed.

## The Homily of Wis 11-19

The structure of this work we have discussed elsewhere.[158] The composition begins with a brief narrative summing up the desert journey (Wis 11,2-4) and then, apropos of the incident of the water from the rock, a theme is enunciated: "For by the things through which their foes were punished they in their need were benefited" (11,5). This theme is then illustrated with five antithetical diptychs (11,6-19,22) which are punctuated with digressions of various lengths:

Introductory narrative (11,2-4)
Theme (11,5)
Illustration of the theme in five diptychs
   1. Water from the rock instead of the plague of the Nile (11,6-14)
   2. Quail instead of the plague of little animals (11,15-16,15; with three digressions: 11,17-12,22; 13,1-15,17; 16,5-15)
   3. A rain of manna instead of the plague of storms (16,16-22; with a digression: 16,23-29)

[157] H. Thyen, *Der Stil der jüdisch-hellenistischen Homilie* (Göttingen, 1955) 13-14.
[158] "The Structure of Wisdom 11-19," *CBQ* 27 (1965) 28-34. There we showed that the beginning of the composition is 11,2 and not 10,1, that the theme of the whole composition is 11,5, and that this theme is illustrated not by seven antithetical diptychs, as is frequently stated, but by five. Since then, James M. Reese has pointed out that many of the sections of Wis have been marked off by the author with inclusions ("Plan and Structure in the Book of Wisdom," *CBQ* 27 [1965] 391-99). In a forthcoming article in *Biblica* we will review the structure of the whole book and show that the limits of all the sections as well as of the paragraphs within the sections are marked with inclusions. With regard to the major divisions of the homily of 11-19 we would here reaffirm for the reasons already stated (*art. cit.*, 32, n. 11) that 16,5-15 and 18,20-25 (which have been set off with inclusions by the author) are digressions and not diptychs, but it is now clear that the fifth diptych extends from 18,5 to 19,22 (inclusions: *laou sou/laon sou* [18,7 and 19,22] and *edoxasas* [18,8 and 19,22]) and that 19,6-21 is a digression within it (inclusion: *genei/genos* 19,6 and 21).

4. The pillar of fire instead of the plague of darkness (17,1-18,4)
5. The tenth plague and the exodus by which God punished the Egyptians and glorified Israel (18,5-19,22; with two digressions: 18,20-25 and 19,6-21)

The work, then, is structured on the narrative and theme of 11,2-5 and resembles very much a homily[159] (regardless of whether or not it was ever delivered as such). It recalls for the encouragement of afflicted Jews in Alexandria that once before Israel had suffered in Egypt and the Lord had come to their rescue. It spells out in great detail the marvelous fidelity and providential workings of the Lord and in this way attempts to stir up hope for another similar intervention on behalf of the just—perhaps an eschatological intervention.[160]

The homily is an excellent example of a midrash. It is true that it is not structured on an explicit citation of a specific text, but this is much too rigid a criterion. The narrative of 11,2-4 is a digest of Ex 12,37-17,7 (somewhat influenced in its formulation by Ps 107,4-6 which apparently was understood as referring to the exodus) and the author is really calling to mind these chapters of Ex as his point of departure. (The same sort of digest is used as the point of departure for the midrash in Heb 7 [cf. 7,1-3] and in 1 Cor 10 [cf. 10,1-5] mentioned below.) After the narrative the author then states the pattern he has detected in comparing those events with the plagues on Egypt in Ex 7-12 and proceeds to help his audience to the same insight. Throughout the discussion there is on the one hand careful attention to the details of the biblical texts and a desire to explain the reasons for happenings (e.g., 11,7.8-9.15-16; 16,3-4.6.11; 18,5) and to draw out applications for the present (e.g., 16,23-29; 19,22), and on the other hand a creative handling of the biblical material: details are altered to fit the purposes of the author, events are idealized and embellished upon with legendary and imaginative material to make them more ample, vivid and edifying (e.g., 11,4; 16,2-3.18.20; 17,1-21; 18,12.17-19; 19,7).[161] Because

---

[159] The frequent direct address to God whose salvific actions are being recalled finds a homiletic parallel in 4 Mc where Eleazar and the Mother, whose actions are there being recalled, are addressed by the speaker (4 Mc 7,6-15; 15,16-20.29-32; 16,14ff., etc.).

[160] Because of the present juxtaposition of 11-19 to the eschatological chs. 1-6 the intervention of God at the exodus is perhaps being used as an image of His eschatological intervention. The idea is explicit in 17,21. See G. Kuhn, "Beiträge zur Erklärung des Buches der Weisheit," *ZNW* 28 (1929) 334-41; J. Fichtner, "Die Stellung der Sapientia Salomonis in der Literatur- und Geistesgeschichte ihrer Zeit," *ZNW* 36 (1937) 113-132.

[161] This aspect is well described by R. Siebeneck, "The Midrash of Wisdom 10-19," *CBQ* 22 (1960) 176-82. For contacts between Wis 11-19 and Jewish midrashic traditions see E. Stein, "Ein jüdisch-hellenistischer Midrasch über den Auszug aus

the whole work is structured on 11,2-4 the whole work is a midrash and not just the embellishments and interpretative remarks. It has been suggested that these chapters at one time constituted a Passover Haggadah recited in Egypt,[162] but perhaps there is more precision in this judgment than one is entitled to by the evidence.

The homily is not developed on any Jewish homiletic pattern but in a *synkrisis* (or comparison), and some speak of *synkrisis* as the genre of Wis 11-19.[163] Even if *synkrisis* is a genre (it would seem to be simply a technique) and the work is of a composite genre (synkristic midrash), the more basic genre is midrash, for even on the level of external form it is more basic that the diptychs are structured on 11,2-4 than that the diptychs are antithetical.

Wis 11-19 is a very useful biblical illustration of what a midrash is. The fact that it is classified as a midrash first and foremost because it is structured on the biblical paraphrase of 11,2-4 and is throughout a discussion of the Ex texts sets in relief the note of "literature about a literature" as a primary characteristic of the genre. The fact that it is a homily helps to focus attention on "homiletic actualization of Scripture" as another basic characteristic. In addition Wis 11-19 (which as a whole is an example of one form of midrash, the homily) contains a fine example of another type of midrash, rewritten Bible or narrative midrash, in 17,1-21 where it can be pointed out with clarity that fiction which is midrashic is fiction at the service of the biblical text; and since this feature is not constant in the work but is quite secondary and can therefore in no way be mistaken as the basic reason for classification, one can easily convey the idea from it that fiction is but one of many techniques used by the genre and is by no means synonymous with the word midrash.

### Smaller Midrashic Units

The literary genre midrash is not made up exclusively of works of considerable size and of homogeneous content. Just as in the rabbinic usage of the term midrash a single interpretative statement was called a midrash,

Ägypten," *MGWJ* 78 (1934) 558-75, and G. Camps, "Midraš sobre la història de les plagues," *Miscellanea biblica B. Ubach* (Montserrat, 1953) 97-113.

[162] K. Kohler, "Wisdom of Solomon, Book of the," *The Jewish Encyclopedia* 12 (New York, 1907) 539.

[163] Cf. F. Focke, *Die Entstehung der Weisheit Salomos* (Göttingen, 1913) 12 and the many who follow him. For the classical use of this figure see F. Focke, "Synkrisis," *Hermes* 58 (1923) 327-68, and for its use in Jewish literature see Stein, *art. cit.*, and I. Heinemann, "Synkrisis oder äussere Analogie in der 'Weisheit Salomos,'" *TZ* 4 (1948) 241-52.

so it is legitimate to use the modern literary term in the same way and classify in the genre interpretative units found within works of other genres. For example in CD 4,12-19 we find the following passage:

And in all those years (13) Belial shall be unleashed against Israel;
as God said by the hand of the prophet Isaiah son of (14) Amoz, *Terror and pit and snare are upon thee, O inhabitant of the land.*
The explanation of this [*pišrô*] (is that) (15) these are Belial's three nets, of which Levi son of Jacob spoke,
(16) by which he (Belial) ensnared Israel,
(17) and which he set [be]fore them as three sorts of righteousness:
the first is lust,
the second is riches,
(and) the third (18) is defilement of the Sanctuary.
Whoever escapes this is caught by that,
and whoever escapes that one is caught (19) by this.[164]

Here in a description of the years before the consummation of the end-time we have a citation from Is 24,17, and following it an interpretation of the text. The author introduces his interpretation with the word *pišrô*, so that as a result the section looks like an excerpt from a *pešer* in form as well as in method and content. Ll. 14b-19 then constitute a midrash within a work of another genre. Similar midrashic units constructed on explicit citations can be found in CD 4,2-4; 6,4-11; 7,12-8,2; 8,10-12; 19,9-14.22-24; 1QS 8,15-16; Heb 3,7-4,11 (the midrash on Ps 95); Heb 7,10-28 (on Ps 110,4); 1 Cor 1,18-2,14 (on Is 33,10.18; Ps 33,10); 1 Cor 9,8-12 (on Dt 25,4); Eph 4,8-14 (on Ps 68,18).

Midrashic units built on implicit citations are found in Heb 7,1-10 (on Gn 14,18-20);[165] Gal 4,21-31 (on Gn 21,2-13); 1 Cor 10,1-13 (on the exodus traditions); 2 Cor 3,7-18 (on Ex 34,29-35). In 2 Esd 7,132-40 the biblical text (Ex 34,6) is cited word by word and explained:

(132) I answered and said, "I know, O Lord, that the Most High is now called *merciful,* because he has mercy on those who have not yet come into the world; (133) and *gracious,* because he is gracious to those who turn in repentance to his law; (134) and *patient,* because he shows patience toward those who have sinned, since they are his own works; (135) and *bountiful,* because he would rather give than take away; (136) and *abundant in compassion,* because he makes his compassions abound more and more to those now living and to those who are gone and to those yet to come, (137) for if he did not make them abound, the world with those who inhabit it would not have life, etc.[166]

---

[164] The translations of the QL are taken from Dupont-Sommer, *op. cit.* (see n. 108).

[165] Cf. J. Fitzmyer, "'Now This Melchizedek . . .' (Heb 7,1)," *CBQ* 24 (1963) 305-21.

[166] Cf. D. Simonsen, "Ein Midrasch im IV. Buch Esra," *Festschrift I. Lewy* (Breslau, 1911) 270ff.

Even the brief lines in Sir 7,27-28 could be considered a midrash on Ex 20,12, providing motives for the observance of the commandment:

> With your whole heart *honor your father;*
> *your mother's* birthpangs forget not.
> Remember, of these parents you were born;
> what can you give them for all they gave you?

### Non-midrashic Passages

Mlle. Bloch speaks of meditation and reflection on Scripture, the reworking and citing of texts and especially anthological style as midrash,[167] and the implication seems to be that almost every citation of Scripture, especially if it is multiple, indicates the presence of the literary form midrash, and indeed the citations themselves seem to be viewed as midrash.

There is, of course, a certain element of truth in the idea and this makes it plausible on first sight. Every citation of Scripture contains an implicit exegesis since the citation expresses the author's understanding of the text and sometimes even his exegetical methods. Furthermore, all uses of Sacred Scripture can be seen as a result of meditation and reflection on prior texts. An author's ability to cite presupposes some acquaintance with the material and one can presume that a certain amount of thoughtful consideration has been given to the text prior to its use. Moreover, every citation from the Bible is made because the text is seen as relevant to the topic being discussed; otherwise the citations would be meaningless. Thus, behind every use of Scripture there lies interpretation, reflection, and the perception of relevancy.

However, there are several important distinctions to be made:

1) A text of Scripture may be cited by an author to contribute something to a new composition (as in Chr), or it may be cited so that a new composition may contribute something by way of understanding to the Scripture text (GA, the *pešārîm*). The first type of citation may occur in any literary form (even in midrash, e.g., the secondary citations in the *pešārîm*) but it does not make a composition midrash. The work containing the second type of citation is midrash because of the nature of the composition.

2) Meditation on Scripture can be a *pre-literary process* which underlies the use of citations in a given work and makes it possible for the Scripture citations to be used to full advantage in the new composition; or the *new work itself* can be a meditation on a biblical text and be written to lead the reader to insights into that text. Only the latter is midrash, because only in that case are we concerned with a composition and, therefore, with a literary form.

---

[167] See above in Part One, pp. 106-7.

3) An author can cite or paraphrase a text and, while the text is understood in a certain sense (material exegesis), no emphasis is put on the interpretation and it is assumed that the reader will concur in the interpretation; or an author can cite a text in a certain sense and intend by the way he uses or paraphrases the citation to contribute to an understanding of that text (formal exegesis). Only the latter is midrash since only there does the new composition add to the understanding of the text.

Thus, we see that in biblical citations two directions of movement are possible: either a biblical text contributes to the new composition and is for the sake of the new composition or the new composition contributes to an understanding of the text cited and is for the sake of the biblical citation. Only the latter is midrash since only there does the composition actualize Scripture. In the former case (which is mere literary dependence) the author may have put attention on a text and made it relevant in his own mind but he does not write a midrash. He merely uses the results of a previous midrash (written or mental) as he proceeds to write a composition of another genre.[168]

The following are examples of non-midrashic passages containing Scripture citations. In Sir 48,9-11 the author cites Mal 3,23-24 as part of the narrative:

You [Elias] were taken aloft in a whirlwind,
in a chariot with fiery horses.
You are destined, it is written, in time to come

[168] M. Gertner ("Midrashim in the New Testament," *JSemS* 7 [1962] 267-92) distinguishes only between overt and covert (or invisible) midrash. In the former the text is quoted and the interpretation is given separately and explicitly. The latter is presented either in the form of a concise paraphrase of the text or of an expanded paraphrastic composition. The midrashic nature of the latter is not therefore easily recognized and to establish such a piece of writing as a midrash, Gertner states, one must find the scriptural text involved, the particular notion and meaning of the text contained and established by that interpretation, and the specific hermeneutical technique by which the interpretation has been achieved. To set up these as criteria is to make a midrash out of every paraphrase of a biblical text that can be related to some hermeneutical principle. There is a confusion here between midrash as method and midrash as genre (which Gertner himself senses when he speaks of the covert midrash as being "demidrashized" in its form); three of his four examples of covert midrash (Mk 4,1-22; Lk 1,76-79; Jas) are not literary pieces that can be classified as midrash at all, for in their present form Mk 4 and Jas are not in the context of a biblical text and the Lucan selection is better taken as an OT text contributing to a new composition (see below, n. 171). We do not restrict the literary genre midrash to overt midrashim alone and we quite readily admit the covert as a midrashic form (e.g., Sir 7,27-28 above and CD 20,17-20; Bar 2,20-25, etc., below), but we would require that in a paraphrase the allusions to the text be strong enough to set the whole thing in the context of that text for the reader and we would insist on the distinctions in our text above as the more basic criteria for establishing a piece of writing as midrash.

to put an end to wrath *before the day of the Lord,*
*To turn back the hearts of fathers toward their sons*
and to re-establish the tribes of Jacob.
Blessed are those who saw you, etc.

and in Tb 8,5-7 a citation from Gn (2,18) is incorporated:
And Tobias began to pray,
Blessed art thou, O God of our fathers,
and blessed be thy holy and glorious name for ever.
Let the heavens and all of thy creatures bless thee.
Thou madest Adam and gavest him Eve his wife
as a helper and support.
From them the race of mankind has sprung.
Thou didst say, *"It is not good that the man should be alone;*
*let us make a helper for him like himself"*
And now, O Lord, I am not taking this sister of mine, etc.

In both of these cases the text is of course cited in a specific sense and thus materially exegeted, but there is no question of the new composition formally exegeting the texts and being written for that purpose. The text is simply contributing something to the new work. (Cf. also the citations in the antitheses of the Sermon on the Mount, Mt 5,21ff.) And the same is true of many implicit citations;[169] they simply contribute ideas, terminology, authority, etc., to a new literary production:

CD 5,15-18
    (15) For formerly &lt;also&gt; God visited (16) their works,
    and His anger was kindled against their forfeits.
    *For this is a people without understanding*        (Is 27,11)
    (17) *they are a nation void of counsel*
    for *there is no understanding among them.*        (Dt 32,38)
    For formerly (18) Moses and Aaron arose
    by the hand of the prince of lights, etc.

1QS 10,16-17
    (16) I will confess Him because He is marvelous
    and will meditate on His might;
    and I will lean on His favors every day.
    I know that *in His hand* is judgment (17) *of all the living*    (Jb 12,10)
    and that all His works are truth, etc.

Jb 7,17-18
    What is man, that you make much of him
      or pay him any heed?
    You observe him with each new day
      and try him at every moment.

---

[169] I.e., those without introductory formulae, whether they be virtual citations (exact reproductions of biblical texts with the intent to cite but without the introductory formulae) or allusions. The practice of indicating OT quotations with formal introductions became common only in the latter part of the first century B.C. Hence most of the citations of the OT in the OT are implicit.

How long will it be before you look away from me,
    and let me alone long enough to swallow my spittle?
Here a hymnic motif from Ps 8,4 is changed into a rebellious statement; the
same psalm text apparently also inspired 2 Esd 8,34-35 where it becomes a call
upon God's mercy:

> But what is man, that thou art angry with him; or what is a corruptible race,
> that thou art so bitter against it? For in truth there is no one among those who
> have been born who has not acted wickedly, and among those who have existed
> there is no one who has not transgressed.

None of these passages is a midrash.

Likewise a proof or fulfillment text is not a midrash. It is necessary to
distinguish between *mere* application of a text to a new situation and exposition of a text to show *how* it applies to a new situation. Only the latter is a
composition and deserving of the name of a literary genre. Hence the proof/
fulfillment texts in 1 Mc 7,16-17; 1QM 11,11-12; CD 1,13-14; 6,11-14;
Mt 3,3; 4,14-16 and the many others like them in the QL and the NT are
not a midrash in themselves nor do they make the passage midrashic. Occasionally, however, there is added to a proof/fulfillment text an explanation, and such a brief explanation is a midrash (e.g., 1 Cor 15,56).[170]

Sometimes of course it is difficult to tell in which direction the movement
is between text and citation. An example would be CD 8,14-18:

(14) But that which Moses said,
*Not because of thy righteousness or the uprightness of thy heart*
*art thou going in to inherit* (15) *those nations,*                      (Dt 9,5a)
*but because He loved thy Fathers*
*and because he kept the oath,*                                           (Dt 7,8a)
(16) so is it with the converts of Israel
(who) have departed from the way of the people;
because of God's love for (17) the first
who <testified> in His favour
He loves those who have followed after,
for theirs is the (18) Covenant of the Fathers.
But because of His hatred for the builders of the wall
His Anger is kindled.

In this passage the author cites the texts and then goes on to say that an

---

[170] On the midrashic nature of this text see M. Gertner, *art. cit.*, 282-83.
It is, of course, possible to conceive of the gospels being, in whole or in part, a series
of testimonia interspersed with narrative to show fulfillment or Christian interpretation
of OT texts, and thus to call a gospel or a part of it a midrash (e.g., J. W. Doeve, "Le
rôle de la tradition orale dans la composition des évangiles synoptiques," *La formation
des évangiles*, eds., J. Cambier et L. Cerfaux [Bruges, 1957] 70-84; F. F. Bruce, "The
Book of Zechariah and the Passion Narrative," *BJRylL* 43 [1960-61] 336-53). But this
raises the very real question if testimonia plus narrative and Christian interpretation is
an adequate description of the gospel material.

analogous situation obtains in his own day. On the one hand, the texts cited may have been merely recalled so that a conclusion might be drawn from them and, thus, are merely contributing data for the new composition. On the other hand, the piece could be understood as an application of the ancient text to a new situation followed by a midrashic attempt (ll. 16-18) to bring out the message that the text should have for the sect.

In 1QS 2,2-4 it is again difficult to decide in which direction the movement lies between citation and composition.

And the priests shall bless all (2) the men of the lot of God who walk perfectly in all His ways, and shall say:

> May He bless thee *with all* (3) *goodness,*
>    and keep thee *from all evil*
> May He enlighten *thy heart with understanding of life,*
>    and favor thee *with everlasting knowledge.*
> (4) May He lift His *gracious* face towards thee
>    to grant thee *eternal* bliss.

Here, in a description of the ceremony of entry into the community, we find an embellishment (given above in italics) on the Aaronic blessing of Nm 6,24-26. In a sense the additions are interpretative[171] and the new composition could be seen as a midrash to expand the old text and bring out its implications. It is, however, possible (and much more plausible to the present writer) that the new composition does not exist for the sake of the text but for the sake of a liturgy, and that both Nm 6 and the author (and Ps 121) have contributed something to the formula.[172] This is clearly the case in 1QS 2,8-9 where the same Aaronic blessing is turned into a curse against the men of the lot of Belial:

> May God not favor thee when thou callest upon Him
>    and may He be without forgiveness to expiate thy sins.
> May He lift His angry face to revenge Himself upon thee,
>    and may there be for thee no (word) of peace
>    on the lips of all who cling (to the Covenant) of the Fathers.

---

[171] Thus Brownlee, *art. cit.* (see n. 102), 60, and Gertner, *art. cit.* (see n. 168) 277. —Gertner points out that the seven concepts of the Aaronic blessing are contained in the *Benedictus* (blessing [v. 68]; keeping [save and deliver in vv. 71 and 74]; face [vv. 75.76]; *ḥnn* [give v. 77; mercy v. 78]; lifting [= forgive v. 77]; shining [v. 79]; peace [v. 79]). He suggests that the first part (vv. 68-75) is a psalmistic poem based on the blessing and the last part (vv. 76-79) is a covert midrash on the blessing in the form of a paraphrase shaped as a liturgical piece. Since the seven concepts are distributed through both parts, it is hard to see why both parts are not simply a poem based on the blessing. Gertner himself says that the only clue to the midrashic nature of 76-79 is its differing in style and structure from the poem. This simply means it is an addition, not a midrash.

[172] In the same way Nm 6 has contributed to Ps 67 and 121.

and in 1QS 2,12-18 where Dt 29,18-20 provides the wording.

Again, Sirach takes Prv 11,4a

Wealth (*hôn*) is useless on the day of wrath

and expands it to

Do not rely on deceitful wealth (*nksy šqr*)
for it will be useless on the day of wrath.                    (Sir 5,10)

Perhaps it is an attempt to elucidate the proverb and to bring out the full meaning of "wealth" in Prv as Ben Sira understood it, or perhaps Ben Sira merely took the proverb and used it for his own purposes without intending to focus attention on the original text. Only the former would be midrash.

Sirach also takes Prv 12,9

Better a lowly man who has a servant (*w'bd lw*)
than the boaster who is without bread

and restates it thus

Better the worker who has plenty of everything
than the boaster who is without sustenance.                    (Sir 10,26)

Here there is the added difficulty of an ambiguous consonantal text in Prv. The phrase *w'bd lw* can be translated "who has a servant" (thus MT) or as "and works for himself" (thus 1 MS, LXX and Syr). Ben Sira can be merely borrowing from the proverb or he could be explicitly interpreting in a midrash either of the above readings—and perhaps precisely in order to eliminate the ambiguity.

### Anthological Style

Anthological style, in the words of André Robert, "consiste à réemployer, littéralement ou équivalemment, les mots ou formules des Écritures antérieures."[173] It is of course well known that this process was frequently used in the postexilic period in the canonical and non-canonical literature. The postexilic period brought new problems and needs, and the responses to these needs were sought in the Scriptures. This seeking in and meditating on the Bible often resulted in new works which would take up expressions and ideas of predecessors, develop, enrich and transpose the earlier message and thus pass to a new stage of thought while still speaking in the language of the ancients.

Bloch and Robert and subsequently others have equated anthological style with midrash.[174] They see in it the two basic characteristics of the

---

[173] A. Robert, "Littéraires (genres)," *VDBS* 5, 411.
[174] See nn. 9 and 24.

midrashic genre: meditation on Scripture and actualization of Scripture for contemporary needs. From our remarks above it should be clear that such an automatic equation of anthological style with the literary form midrash is not valid. As with single citations, so also with multiple ones there are two possible directions of movement between a citation and the new work in which it is found. Only if the audience's attention is focused on the prior text and if the new composition exists for the sake of the old text can the work be called a midrash. The borrowing, adaptation and transformation of older material in such a way that the older material merely contributes to the new work as a source is not midrashic. Moreover, anthological style can be a process resorted to merely out of a desire to speak in the language of the Bible for one reason or another, and this can hardly be conceived of as an attempt to make earlier Scripture relevant for a later age. Thus, in discussing the possibility of midrash in a given passage, one has not exhausted the question when one establishes the anthological character of the passage, but one must then carry the investigation further to see whether the anthology is a sign of mere literary dependence or an indication that texts are being cited in order to contribute some understanding to them.

The *Benedictus*,[175] the *Magnificat*[176] and 1QM 12[177] are good examples of non-midrashic anthology. All three are a veritable mosaic of biblical citations and by no stretch of the imagination could they be conceived of as in any way being written for the benefit of the original texts or even of some of the texts. Not only the number of texts cited but also, and especially, the way they are cited clearly indicates that it is a case of prior texts serving as a source and providing terminology and atmosphere for a new work.

Examples of midrashic anthological style are difficult to find but perhaps CD 20,17-20 could be so classified:

(17) ... But *those who are converted from the sin of J[a]c[ob]*,    (Is 59,20)
who have kept the Covenant of God,
*they will then speak one* (18) *with another*    (Mal 3,16)
to justify each man his brother
by supporting their steps in the way of God.
*And God will heed* (19) their words *and will hear,*
*and a reminder will be written [before Him] of them that fear God*
*and of them that revere* (20) *His name,*    (Mal 3,16)
*until salvation and justice are revealed* to them that fear [God].    (Is 56,1)

[175] See A. Plummer, *A Critical and Exegetical Commentary on the Gospel According to S. Luke* (*ICC*; Edinburgh, ⁵1922) 39.

[176] *Ibid.*, 30-31, and R. Laurentin, *Structure et théologie de Luc I-II* (Paris, 1957) 82-85.

[177] For the textual analysis see J. Carmignac, "Les Citations de l'ancien testament dans 'La Guerre des fils de lumière contre les fils de ténèbres,'" *RB* 63 (1956) 254-60; id., *La Règle de la guerre* (Paris, 1958) 171-87.

> [*And*] *you will distinguish anew between the just* (21) *and the wicked*
> *between him that has served God and him that has served Him not.* (Mal. 3,18)
> *And He will be merciful to* [*thousands*]     (Ex 20,6)
> *to them that love Him* (22) *and to them that heed Him.*
> *for a thousand generations.*     (Dt 7,9)

The passage first of all identifies the *šby pš‘* of Is 59,20 with those "who have
kept the Covenant of God" (the sect). It then goes on to identify the sect with
the "they," "them that fear God," and the "you" in Mal 3,16.18 (which is apparently seen as a prophetic text). If the allusion to Is 56,1 is intended, then the
text also states that the sect will be the recipient of the promises of Is 56,1. The
repetition of the phrase "them that fear God" in line 20 supports this interpretation of the use of the Isaian quotation. The subsequent citations from Ex and Dt
merely contribute to the new composition. They may have been understood as
referring to the sect but CD does not point up that aspect. It merely cites them
in a certain sense and uses them for what they can contribute to the work.

Perhaps another example of the midrashic use of anthological style is found
in Bar 2,20-25:

> For thou hast sent thy *anger* and *thy wrath* upon us, as     (Jer 36,7)
> thou didst declare by thy servants the prophets, saying:
> "Thus says the Lord: *Bend your shoulders and serve the*
> *king of Babylon, and you will remain in the land* which     (Jer 27,11.12)
> I gave to your fathers. But if you will not obey the voice
> of the Lord and will not serve the king of Babylon, *I will*     (Jer 7,34; 16,9;
> *make to cease from the cities of Judah and from the region*     33,11)
> *about Jerusalem the voice of mirth and the voice of glad-*
> *ness, the voice of the bridegroom and the voice of the*
> *bride, and the* whole *land will be a desolation without*
> *inhabitants.*" But we did not obey thy voice, to serve the     (Jer 33,10)
> king of Babylon; and thou hast confirmed thy words,
> which thou didst speak by thy servants the prophets, that
> *the bones* of our *kings* and the bones of our fathers *would*     (Jer 8,1)
> *be brought out of their graves;* and behold they have been
> cast out *to the heat of day and the frost of night.* They     (Jer 36,30)
> perished in great misery *by famine and sword and pesti-*
> lence.     (Jer 14,12; 38,2)

In this passage if our analysis is correct, it is not a question of texts simply being
applied to a new situation as in the case of a proof/fulfillment text, nor is it a
question of texts supplying vocabulary and ideas. Rather, there is here an arrangement of textual elements from a single chosen biblical author to apply them
to a new (or fulfillment) situation, and the arrangement then provides us with
a composition which explains how the biblical texts apply to the new situation,
thus accomplishing implicitly what, for example, the midrash in 1 Cor 15,56 does
for its text explicitly. Similar midrashic passages can be found in Bar 2,27-35
and Dn 9,1-19; also Is 60-62 can be seen as a reinterpretation of the oracles of
Deutero-Isaiah.[178]

---

[178] For a compendium of the prophetic material which Trito-Isaiah took over and
actualized and a discussion of the alterations which he made see W. Zimmerli, "Zur
Sprache Tritojesajas," *Schweizerische Theologische Umschau* 20 (1950) 110-22.

It could perhaps be argued that Wis 3-4 should be classified as a midrash because of its anthological style. The first five chapters of the book are structured as follows:[179]

a. Exhortation to justice (1,1-15)
b. The wicked invite death (speech of the wicked and author's comment) (1,16-2,24)
c. The hidden counsels of God (3,1-4,20)
　　1. On suffering (3,1-12)
　　2. On childlessness (3,13-4,6)
　　3. On early death (4,7-20)
b.* The final judgment (speech of the wicked and author's comment) (5,1-23)
a.* Exhortation to seek wisdom (6,1-21)

In the central section the author gives the "hidden counsels of God" (2,22) on the three topics central to the Jewish thought on retribution. His teaching is the fruit of meditation on these chapters in their LXX form and he sets forth that teaching in a series of characters or types taken from Is, presented in their Isaian sequence and embellished with additional details from elsewhere.[180] In 3,2ff. the author is drawing on Is 53,4-11 on the subject of suffering. In 3,13ff. he has moved on to Is 54,1ff. and 56,2-5 and the subject of childlessness, and in 4,7ff. he has moved on to Is 57,1-2 and the subject of early death. The Isaian texts, originally referring to Jerusalem, are thus by implicit citation recalled and are reinterpreted and transferred to the individual order with the help of other implicit citations from Is and elsewhere. The significant thing here is that in the midst of the anthology there are principal texts cited in their Isaian order, so that as a result the central section could be viewed as a midrash on these texts accomplished by an anthological presentation. However, the sequential dependency on Is really begins in 2,13 (with Is 52,13) and ends in 5,22 (with Is 55,19) and therefore cuts across the structure which the author has given his material. This would seem to indicate that the author is not concerned with interpreting specific texts in the central section, but that in chs. 1-6 he is presenting a doctrine and citing the Isaian material as a source of images for that presentation and by way of appeal to the authority of that earlier book, as, for example, he does again with Is, Dt, Hos, Jer and Pss in chs. 13-15 on idolatry. This would not be midrash.

---

[179] See n. 158.
[180] Cf. P. W. Skehan, "Isaias and the Teaching of the Book of Wisdom," *CBQ* 2 (1940) 389-99; M. J. Suggs, "Wisdom of Solomon $2_{10}$ — 5: A Homily Based on the Fourth Servant Song," *JBL* 76 (1957) 26-33.

Another use of anthological style is found in Prv 1-9. As Robert has pointed out[181] the author of Prv 1-9 has reused words and phrases of earlier biblical books (Dt, Jer, and Deutero-Isaiah especially) in order to present wisdom in the garb of a prophet, in order to identify wisdom in some way with God, and also, although not in the explicit manner of Ben Sira and Baruch, to identify wisdom with the Torah, and to make the *ḥăkāmîm* heirs of the prophets. By such a presentation the author of Prv 1-9 apparently wished to further incorporate into Judaism a wisdom tradition which was of foreign and secular origins, and to present wisdom as a legitimate vehicle for describing the good life under the Law. The method which the author of Prv 1-9 used to accomplish this was the method of allusions. He does not cite earlier texts properly speaking or juxtapose texts, but he employs images and phrases associated with the Torah and the prophets and uses them in connection with wisdom to show that the wisdom tradition is the modern counterpart of ancient realities.

Allusive theology of this sort is not midrashic as Bloch has suggested.[182] Specific texts of earlier Scripture are not cited as a point of departure for a discussion that attempts to make these texts relevant for a new generation. Rather, images and vocabulary strongly associated with the Law and the prophets are now associated with wisdom, and the implication is thus made that there is a continuity between them, and that wisdom is the successor of the prophet and the equivalent of the Law. There is no attempt to make earlier texts refer to wisdom. Rather, the earlier texts bestow the Deuteronomic and prophetic mantle upon wisdom personified. And this is not midrash.[183]

Another variety of this allusive use of anthological style is found in 1QS 8,4-10. Unlike Prv 1-9 where it is a question merely of the employment of vocabulary that is associated with institutions of the past, here specific texts are alluded to:

---

[181] See n. 24.

[182] *VDBS* 5, 1273.

[183] G. W. Buchanan's attempt to describe Prv 2,20-7,3 as a midrash on Dt 11,18-22 ("Midrashim pré-tannaïtes. A propos de Prov., i-ix," *RB* 72 [1965] 227-39) is not convincing. In addition to the allusions to Dt in Prv 2-7 one must take into account the allusions in these chapters to Jer and Deutero-Isaiah in order to evaluate properly the use of the Deuteronomic vocabulary. Moreover, the author of Prv 2-7 has not structured his material according to the themes in the Dt text as Buchanan supposes but almost certainly on quite another plan (cf. P. W. Skehan, "The Seven Columns of Wisdom's House in Proverbs 1-9," *CBQ* 9 [1947] 190-98). Nor are any of the units within Prv 2-7 a midrash. The one text for which a case could seemingly be made and which Buchanan emphasizes is 6,21-22, and apparently 6,22 is out of place and should follow 5,19 (cf. Skehan, "Proverbs 5:15-19 and 6:20-24," *CBQ* 8 [1946] 290-97; CCD; and R. B. Y. Scott, *Proverbs, Ecclesiastes* [New York, 1965] 55, 58).

(4) ... When these things come to pass in Israel,
(5) the Council of the Community shall be established
in truth as an everlasting *planting*.                    (Is 60,21)
It is the House of holiness for Israel
and the Company of infinite (6) holiness for Aaron;
they are the witnesses of truth unto judgment
and the *chosen of loving-kindness*                       (Is 42,1 perhaps)
appointed to offer expiation for the earth
and to *bring down* (7) *punishment* upon the wicked.      (Ps 94,2 perhaps)
It is the *tried* wall, the *precious cornerstone;*
(8) its *foundations* shall not tremble
nor *flee* from their place.                              (Is 28,16)
It is the Dwelling of infinite holiness (9) for Aaron
in <eternal> knowledge unto the Covenant of justice. ...

In lines 7 and 8 there is clearly an allusion to Is 28,16: the community is the cornerstone of which Isaiah spoke. In line 5 we have an allusion to the "planting" of Is 60,21. Of itself the occurrence of *mt't* here does not necessarily suggest the Isaian passage, but the term is used elsewhere to designate the sect (1QS 11,8; CD 1,7) and, thus, was apparently a popular term, and in 1QH 6,15 and 1QH 8 the connection is clearly made with Is 60,21. In line 6 the *bhyry rṣwn* may have been inspired by Is 42,1: *bhyry rṣth npšy.* If so, it too would be an allusion by which the community is identified with the Servant of Yahweh who is "appointed to offer expiation for the earth." This passage could be considered a midrash (a pointing out of the fulfillment of the respective prophecies) but the anthological technique does seem to be of the sort found in Prv 1-9, and perhaps the passage is better conceived of not as a literature about a literature (midrash) but as literature about the sect in which Scripture is used in an allusive manner to interpret the significance of the community.

It is perhaps in this connection that the genre of Jdt should be discussed. As Patrick Skehan has pointed out, the Book of Judith is based in an extraordinary way on Ex, perhaps on Ex 14,31 if one were to single out a particular verse.[184] The Canticle of Judith echoes the Canticle of Miriam and the narrative portion of Jdt reflects primarily the exodus events, so that both in the prose and the poetry what is done by Judith's hand is set forth as a revival of what was done by the hand of God and the hand of Moses at the exodus.

These findings raise anew the question of the literary form of Jdt. Is the book a midrash on Ex 14,31 (the hand of God in Ex is ever active)? Or is it an example of allegorical haggadah, a meditation on God's providence and another example of the allusive category of anthological style (the ideal event described in Jdt being equated or likened to the exodus event)? It is very difficult to decide. If Jdt were found in a Jewish midrashic work after Ex 14,31, it would clearly be a midrash and a very beautiful one. But

---

[184] "The Hand of Judith," *CBQ* 25 (1963) 94-110.

are the allusions to Ex strong enough to create that context on their own? The allusions when perceived are striking, but they are not immediately recognizable nor are they the only allusions to Israel's history, and the repeated idea that as long as Israel does not sin against God it will prosper (4,12-21; 8,18-20; 11,10; 16,15) suggests that perhaps this was the point of the work in the mind of the author; in this case he did not write a midrash.

One final passage should be mentioned, not so much for its own sake but because it has been so emphasized by Bloch[185]—the allegory of Ez 16. She points out the many similarities of thought between Ez 16 and Hos (2; 8,1-9,10), Jer (3; 12,7-17) and Dt (4,1-31; 8,11-20; 32), and concludes that these earlier texts were reused anthologically, and in this manner were completed and clarified one by the other and transposed to highlight certain points in the sources for the needs of a later generation. Thus the passage, according to Bloch, would be similar to the midrashic examples of anthological style pointed out above. But the fact of the matter is that the passage is not an example of anthological style (i.e., the use, literally or equivalently, of words or formulae of earlier Scripture). It is really an anthology of ideas and images culled from some[186] of the texts mentioned, plus a good deal of originality. No text is cited; in many cases it is not clear exactly which earlier text has provided the image, and a large number of the details of all of the previous texts involved are in no way taken up. Without entering into a detailed discussion of these points here,[187] let us simply remark that once Hosea and Jeremiah uttered their oracles on Israel the faithless wife, anyone who later simply takes up that image to exploit it literarily is not thereby exegeting and actualizing Hos and Jer. Now, if Ezekiel were to exploit the ideas of Hos and Jer in this way, it is hard to see how such an effort would differ from what we have in Ez 16; and before affirming that Ezekiel was commenting on or updating Hos and Jer, one would like to see a good deal more concern for the details of the earlier texts

---

185 R. Bloch, "Ézéchiel XVI: exemple parfait du procédé midrashique dans la Bible," *Cahiers Sioniens* 9 (1955) 193-223. Within the article (p. 216) she speaks of Ez 16 belonging to the midrashic genre, a term that she evidently equates with midrash (see above n. 16).

186 That Dt 4 and 8 provided the background could probably be denied.

187 To say nothing of the probability that Ez 16,16-21.26-34.44-63 are later additions to the allegory to update its application (see the commentaries of Eichrodt, Fohrer and Zimmerli *ad loc.*), something that Bloch does not take into consideration in her discussion of the chapter. W. A. Irwin (*The Problem of Ezekiel* [Chicago, 1943]) and E. Vogt ("Textumdeutungen im Buch Ezechiel," *Sacra Pagina* [Paris, 1959] I, 475-78) speak of such additions in Ez as midrashic, but this is not a correct evaluation (see below on redaction and glosses).

(in whatever form Ezekiel knew them). Ez 16 is not a midrash, but it does provide the opportunity to enunciate the principle that the reworking of ideas found in earlier literature does not necessarily produce a midrash.[188]

### Redaction and Glosses

Geza Vermes writes:

The final redaction of the Pentateuch, performed in the spirit of the most recent revision, affected, therefore, the significance of the older material, and established the meaning of the compilation as a whole according to the then contemporary understanding of biblical history. This implicit harmonization and interweaving of scriptural tradition may be termed biblical midrash or haggadah.[189]

And Vermes illustrates these remarks with a discussion of the story of Balaam and shows how P's supplement to the Balaam story puts a pejorative interpretation on the story and makes Balaam a villain. Pfeiffer calls later explanatory and interpretative additions to Jos and Sm midrash,[190] and Camps suggests that similar additions in Jgs and Kgs are midrash.[191] In the same vein Bloch proposes that glosses are midrash.[192]

[188] The same sort of non-midrashic reworking of ideas is operative in the anthological style of Mi 4-5. Cf. B. Renaud, *Structure et attaches littéraires de Michée IV-V* (Paris, 1964), who, however, classifies the chapters as midrash.—The Canticle of Canticles has been termed a midrash because of the allegorical character it supposedly possesses from the alleged anthological process used in its composition (Bloch, *VDBS* 5, 1273, based on the works of Robert and Feuillet on Ct). The arguments for the existence of *style anthologique* in Ct are extremely tenuous (cf. R. E. Murphy, "Recent Literature on the Canticle of Canticles," *CBQ* 16 [1954] 5-8).

[189] Vermes, *op. cit.* (see n. 133), 176.

[190] Pfeiffer, *Introduction* . . . , 309, 361, 368-73.

[191] Camps, *art. cit.* (see n. 161), 98 n.—Samuel Sandmel ("The Haggadah Within Scripture," *JBL* 80 [1961] 105-22) sees the doublets in Gn, Ex, Jgs, and Sm, not as variant traditions, but as examples of midrash: one story is the primitive version, the other a midrashic retelling of it in the manner of GA. Thus, Gn 20 is a midrash on Gn 12,9ff.; Gn 15 expands Gn 12,1; Gn 21,8-21 is a retelling of Gn 16; 1 Sm 24 is a midrash on 1 Sm 26, etc. As Sandmel remarks: "Were we to find this story [Gn 20] in Genesis Rabbah instead of Gn 20, we would promptly recognize it as a haggadah based on Gn 12,9ff." (p. 111). According to Sandmel we are not dealing with sources blended but with successive haggadic recastings of a single source. Bit by bit over the years embellishments have been added on to the primitive narrative, neutralizing, correcting and interpreting what was already present. Thus, the Abraham of Gn 20 determines and clarifies the character of the Abraham of Gn 12, etc. It may be that some of the doublets were *used* in this manner by the various redactors, but as a systematic solution to the problem of the *origin* of the Pentateuchal material it is an impossible one. Cf. ideas similar to Sandmel's in J. Weingreen, "Exposition in the Old Testament and in Rabbinical Literature," *Promise and Fulfilment*, ed. F. F. Bruce (Edinburgh, 1963) 187-201.

[192] *VDBS* 5, 1276.

The equation of redaction with midrash is nothing else than the logical result of the confusion of method with literary form, and it clearly demonstrates the error of such a confusion. There is a vast difference between the stages in the composition of a book and a commentary upon that book, between the adapting and interpreting of material and a composition that adapts and interprets another composition. The first is a method that can be used in many literary operations (to assemble oral material into various literary forms, to put out new editions of such a book, or to write a new work commenting on a former one). The second is a literary work with a specific literary form, and the fact that it uses a certain method does not necessarily allow one to classify under that literary genre other works that utilize the same method.

As Mlle. Bloch rightly notes, the gradual fixing of the sacred text in the postexilic period was of the greatest importance for the birth of the midrashic genre.[193] Prior to this period of fixation Israel felt free to re-edit her sacred traditions and to add to them and in this way make them relevant to the needs of the community at that time and to bring the traditions into accord with developed religious practices. Once, however, the sacred text was looked upon as unalterable, successive editions were no longer possible, and, yet, the need to bridge the gap between the sacred literature of the past and the needs of the present still remained. Thus it was that a separate literature grew up—the midrashic literature—which accomplished by means of works distinct from the Scriptures being commented upon what redaction had accomplished during the state of textual fluidity. There is an organic bond between the redaction of the OT and the early midrash (and this, of course, is what Bloch, Vermes, *et al.*, are at pains to point out), but we should not attempt to express this organic relation by means of literary genres, grouping under one genre both those works which are the result of several editions and the later interpretative works, solely because both the editing and the later works were interpretative. The interpretative works belong to the literary genre midrash; the final redaction of the Pentateuch (to take an example) still belongs to the same genres (sacred history and pre-history, Torah, etc.) as did the earlier redactions.

For this reason glosses strictly speaking should not be classed as midrash. They are really successive additions (albeit often interpretative and at times even characteristic of certain types of rabbinic midrashic exposition[194]) to a book which intentionally or accidentally have become part of

---

[193] *Ibid.*, 1268.
[194] Cf. J. Weingreen, "Rabbinic-Type Glosses in the Old Testament," *JSemS* 2 (1957) 149-62, who, however, does not call them midrash.

that book and are absorbed by the literary form of that book. They do not constitute a literary work separate from the text commented upon.

### Apocalyptic and Midrash

Renée Bloch has stated that there is a very close relationship between apocalyptic and midrash. She first of all points out the similarities between the two: both literary forms instruct and edify; they hark back to Scripture or oral traditions to reinterpret the past for the sake of the present and the future; both manifest a deep sense of the supernatural and are characterized by hyperbolic style. The difference between the two is that midrash is a work of reflection on traditions and therefore is oriented toward the past, whereas apocalyptic is concerned with revelations and is oriented toward the eschatolcgical future. This difference, though, is only apparent because in reality midrash is concerned with the past for the sake of present and future needs, and apocalyptic, in order to justify its eschatological predictions, scrutinizes the history of the past or recounts some alleged prophecy of the past. Bloch then concludes that apocalyptic is really only a variety of midrash.[195] Needless to say this discussion of the two literary forms is not a very satisfying one to the writer.

It is apparently more difficult to isolate the primary characteristics of apocalyptic than of midrash,[196] but for our purposes a general descriptive definition of apocalyptic should suffice. Apocalyptic is prophecy about the imminent eschatological future. In its pure form (i.e., without true prophetic vision behind it) it presents itself in the guise of revelations which were allegedly given to some personality of the past and which have been hidden for a long time and are now published. It is frequently characterized by lush imagery (because it is dealing with the distant future) and mysterious symbols (because it was often "resistance literature" and it had of necessity to be cryptic). It is a literature whose purpose is to stir up hope during days of crisis by demonstrating that things will get better soon (and hence there is a fondness for the calculation of times, etc.). To establish confidence in this demonstration, something of the past is set forth and interpreted in order to give credence to what is said about the future. It is at this point that we come to the area where apocalyptic and midrash may be combined in a given work. If the apocalyptic work scrutinizes past history for a key to the future, it is simple apocalyptic. But if the apocalyptic work

---

[195] *VDBS* 5, 1276-78. Similarly Robert who, however, states that the two forms are distinct but that sometimes the distinction is difficult to make in practice (*Guide to the Bible*, I, 509).

[196] Cf. B. Vawter, "Apocalyptic: Its Relation to Prophecy," *CBQ* 22 (1960) 33-46 and the bibliography there.

scrutinizes biblical texts from the past for the answers to the future and reinterprets these texts in the manner proper to apocalyptic, then the work is of a composite genre; it is both apocalyptic and midrash. As always, the factor that determines if midrash is present or not is whether or not the discussion is for the sake of some biblical text; and the deficiencies of the discussion of Bloch on apocalyptic and midrash are that she has introduced into the discussion other characteristics which are not constitutive of midrash and which, as a matter of fact, are secondary characteristics of many literary forms. In conclusion, then, apocalyptic and midrash are distinct literary forms, but sometimes they exist together as a compound literary form when apocalyptic is scrutinizing a text of the past (or conversely, when midrash is interpreting a text in an apocalyptic manner).

To illustrate the above remarks from Dn: Dn 1-6 contains stories about Daniel, a hero of the past. The stories are recounted to attribute the subsequent visions of the book to Daniel and thus give them some authority. The stories also of themselves set forth Daniel as a model of perseverance in adversity and thus encourage the reader in time of persecution. There is nothing midrashic here—although sometimes these stories are called the midrashic section of the book (along with chs. 13-14) because they are didactic fiction;[197] but the remarks made above in the case of Est and Tb are valid here also: the genre is not midrash but haggadah, at the service of apocalyptic. Dn 7-8 are visions allegedly received by Daniel. These chapters are simple apocalyptic, scrutinizing the history of the past and imposing a pattern upon it which indicates that deliverance is at hand. Dn 9, however, is apocalyptic and midrash. Daniel seeks an understanding of the 70 years in the prophecy of Jer (25,11; 29,10), and the interpretation of Jer is presented in an apocalyptic manner—an alleged vision and revelation (Dn 9,20-27). This is the midrashic section in Dn, and not cc. 1-6; 13-14.

Another example of midrashic apocalyptic is 4 Esd 12,10ff. where the vision and its interpretation in Dn 7 is reinterpreted apocalyptically with alleged revelation. Possibly Ez 38-39 is a midrashic apocalypse, if it is an attempt to reinterpret eschatologically the "foe from the north" in Jl 2,20; Jer 1,14; 4,6; 6,1. In the NT, the anthological style of Ap, however, is of the non-midrashic variety.[198]

---

197 E.g., J. McKenzie, *Dictionary of the Bible* (Milwaukee, 1965) 575; Ellis, *op. cit.* (see n. 141), 451, 517-23; etc.

198 A work which offers difficulties in the discussion of both apocalyptic and midrash is the Book of Jubilees. The question of the literary form of Jub is a complex one, for it is a book of composite genre: history (in the ancient sense), apocalyptic (it makes Moses the recipient of disclosures on the pattern of history), testament (the several spiritual testaments of the patriarchs) and perhaps midrash (the large amount of

*Are the Infancy Narratives Midrash?*

The infancy narrative of Lk has been classified as midrash because of its anthological style,[199] and the narrative of Mt as midrash for various reasons: because it is a development on OT texts,[200] because it is a commentary on OT texts,[201] because of Mt's dependence on midrashic traditions, the presence of elements apparently legendary and the construction of five

embellishments which may be for the sake of the biblical text). One need only look at the various titles the book has been given to see the difficulty involved in ascertaining the literary form: Jubilees, The Little Genesis, Apocalypse of Moses, Testament of Moses, etc. To the present writer apocalyptic seems to be a primary dimension of the work. Jub purports to be a revelation given to Moses and handed down secretly about the fixed pattern of history and its periods. The first period is set forth with a fixed numerical pattern. The second period, in which the author lived, is not recounted or provided with a numerical pattern, but it is described in a summary manner, and it is hinted, undoubtedly to offer encouragement and hope, that the present sufferings are to be interpreted as the tribulations that mark the end of the second period and usher in the third. The primary purpose of retelling the biblical story up to the exodus seems not to have been that of GA, namely, to give a vivid and trouble-free version of Gn, but rather to impose the schematized chronology on Gn, to indicate that the author possessed a knowledge of the rhythm and order of past history, and thereby to reinforce the apocalyptic section (23,9-32) and inspire confidence in its suggestions that it was the Messianic woes which had arrived.

So much for the apocalyptic nature. Is the work also midrashic since in the course of retelling the biblical narrative much legendary material has been incorporated? On the one hand the work is presented as material given to Moses in addition to what is contained in the Bible; it is presented as a separate and independent work containing the secret pattern of history and could thus be understood as an interpretation of history. On the other hand the work is obviously based on the biblical text and in the re-telling, difficulties in the biblical narrative are solved, gaps supplied, offensive elements removed and the spirit of later Judaism infused into the primitive history. This would suggest that the author had a midrashic aim as well as an apocalyptic one. There is no compelling reason that would prevent us from looking upon the embellishments as midrashic and we would be inclined to see Jub as another example of an apocalyptic-midrashic work.

[199] Bloch, *VDBS* 5, 1279; *id.*, "Écriture et tradition dans le Judaïsme," *Cahiers Sioniens* 8 (1954) 31; Laurentin, *op. cit.* (see n. 176) 95, 116-19; R. Dillon, "St. Luke's Infancy Account," *The Dunwoodie Review* 1 (1961) 5-37; McKenzie, *op. cit.* (see n. 197) 575.

[200] Bloch, *VDBS* 5, 1279; *id.*, "Écriture . . . ," 31; Laurentin, *op. cit.*, 100-1. What they mean by "development" is not clear: perhaps a semi-fictional piece taking its inspiration from details in the OT text, perhaps a construction of episodes upon texts with no implication as to history or fiction.

[201] A. H. McNeile, *The Gospel According to St. Matthew* (London, 1915) 23; G. H. Box, "The Gospel Narratives of the Nativity and the Alleged Influence of Heathen Ideas," *ZNW* 6 (1905) 80-101; F. C. Grant, *Ancient Judaism and the New Testament* (Edinburgh, 1960) 110, 112; McKenzie, *op. cit.*, 575.

episodes on five texts with the referring of OT Scripture to Jesus in whom they are fulfilled.[202]

Of course, neither the fiction nor the anthological style of itself makes these narratives midrash, nor does the fact that allusions are made to midrashic material. The fundamental question is: do the narratives under discussion actualize biblical texts? It is hard to see how the infancy narrative of Lk does. It does not exist for the sake of the many biblical texts alluded to; rather it is concerned with interpreting the Christ-event by means of OT analogies (the same sort of thing that is done by the heavy overlay of OT allusions in the Baptism, Temptation and Transfiguration narratives), and the anthological style is of the non-midrashic variety that we have seen, for example, in 1QS 8,4-10.

Mt's narrative could be called a midrash if one sees the five texts in the five episodes as the primary point of interest in the narrative. Viewed in this way each episode would be a commentary worked up primarily to show the fulfillment of the text contained within it. But in fact are the OT citations the primary point of interest? They are no different from other fulfillment texts in Mt and the rest of the NT—texts which are simply applied to a new situation. Moreover, these five texts are not the only citations in the narrative. There are some implicit citations from the LXX of Ex (Mt 2,20 from Ex 4,19 and perhaps Mt 2,13f. from Ex 2,15), as well as allusions to the Moses birth story as found in biblical and extra-biblical accounts. These other biblical and non-biblical texts also shaped the narrative as well as the five explicit citations, and all (explicit citations, implicit citations and allusions) seem to be used not to direct attention to OT material so that it might be explained but to explain the person of Jesus. Hence, in fact, Mt's narrative does not seem to be midrash.

In what literary genre are our narratives written? Because of the comparisons being made between old and new and the fact that the true significance of the new is an enigma to be discovered by meditation, Laurentin speaks of the Lucan narrative as a *mashal*[203] and the same category could be suggested for Mt 1-2 on the same grounds. The suggestion is no more satisfactory than the classification midrash. *Mashal* has its own range of meanings within biblical literature, none of which is this new and modern denotation. Whatever else may be said of OT *mashal,* it is certain that when it does represent a parable/allegory/extended comparison, it is regularly the anterior, lesser, prototypical term of the comparison which is described in a

---

202 S. Muñoz Iglesias, "El Género literario del Evangelio de la Infancia en San Mateo," *EstBib* 17 (1958) 243-73; M. Bourke, "The Literary Genus of Matthew 1-2," *CBQ* 22 (1960) 160-75.

203 Laurentin, *op. cit.,* 117-18.

self-consistent manner and in detail, and it is the subsequent, primary, typified term which is left for the reader/hearer to fill out from those data. Our material does the exact opposite. Perhaps the best classification of our material is simply *infancy narrative,* for these chapters seem to have been written in the tradition of infancy stories, biblical and extra-biblical, sharing with them many of their motifs.[204] The Jewish stories of biblical figures were of a composite genre, midrashic infancy stories, because they were at the same time embellishments on the biblical text. The NT stories are not midrashic.

## Summary

The word midrash in biblical studies today has come to possess two connotations: it is used on the one hand to designate a method of exegesis (a creative and actualizing handling of the biblical text) and on the other as the name of a literary genre. Both usages are legitimate borrowings from the rabbinic vocabulary, but they must be kept distinct, else in classifying literary works into genres we will not delineate really similar groups of literature, for distinction in genre is something more basic than the methods employed within it, and the creative and actualizing handling of biblical material can produce works of various genres.

As the name of a literary genre, the word midrash designates a composition which seeks to make a text of Scripture from the past understandable, useful and relevant for the religious needs of a later generation. It is, thus, a literature about a literature. Midrashim exist in three forms, exegetical, homiletic and narrative, and they are accomplished in two ways: explicitly (the biblical text is presented and additional homiletic material and comments are assembled at the side of the biblical text) and implicitly (the interpretative material is worked into the text by means of a paraphrase).

Examples of midrash in the pre-rabbinic literature include the Midrash of the Passover Haggadah, the Qumrân *pešārîm,* the Biblical Antiquities of Pseudo-Philo, the homilies in Wis 11-19 and Jn 6, and probably the Genesis Apocryphon.

In addition, isolated midrashic sections occur in the Palestinian targums and in works of other genres in connection with explicit and implicit biblical citations. However, an implicit or explicit citation from Scripture does not of itself indicate that the surrounding passage is midrashic, for the text may be merely contributing to the new composition. Only if the new com-

---

[204] S. Muñoz Iglesias, "Los Evangelios de la Infancia y las infancias de los héroes," *EstBib* 16 (1957) 5-36; M. S. Enslin, "The Christian Stories of the Nativity," *JBL* 59 (1940) 317-38; Vermes, *op. cit.* (see n. 133) 90-95; etc.—L. Cerfaux and J. Cambier (*VDBS* 5, 590-91) suggest that the literary genre of the infancy narratives of Mt and Lk is "l'histoire populaire."

position contributes something by way of understanding to the text cited is the composition midrash. In the same connection, the mere citation of a text of Scripture in a specific sense is not a midrash. An interpretation of the original text has taken place in the mind of the author, but the composition that he writes does not interpret it and therefore the composition is not midrashic.

Just as context is a determining factor of literary form in the case of parable and allegory, so also with midrash. A midrash is always explicitly or implicitly placed in the context of the biblical text(s) upon which it comments. Works like Chr and JA which rework biblical material in what appears to be the same manner as GA are not midrash because these works are not to be read in the context of previous biblical texts. They are not a literature about a literature; they are works of history which exist for their own sake. Likewise, works of didactic fiction which are not placed by the author in the context of a biblical text are not midrash. If we are to be precise in our classification of literary genres, we should borrow from the rabbis the term haggadah as well as the term midrash and use the term haggadah to describe works of didactic fiction.

Anthological style does not necessarily make a composition midrash. It can be employed to create a composition that focuses attention on earlier texts and elucidates them (midrash); it can also be used in a non-midrashic manner to contribute vocabulary images and the biblical atmosphere to a new work of any genre.

Redaction is not to be confused with midrash. Redaction is a process or a stage in the production of a work of any genre; midrash is a composition with specific characteristics. Frequently, redaction and the writing of a midrash are undertaken for identical motives but the work resulting from redaction is not thereby a midrash. Glosses should not be classified as midrash, for they are really successive additions which intentionally or accidentally have become part of the sacred text and are absorbed by the literary form of that text.

Apocalyptic and midrash are distinct literary forms, but an apocalyptic work or a section of it can at the same time be a midrash if it manifests the primary characteristic of that genre by interpreting a sacred text of the past and showing its relevance for a later situation and a later age.

ADDISON G. WRIGHT, S.S.
*St. Mary's Seminary*
*Roland Park*
*Baltimore, Maryland*

# Volume Index

William Chomsky, "What Was the Jewish Vernacular During the Second Commonwealth?"

Louis Finkelstein, "The Transmission of the Early Rabbinic Tradition."

Nahum N. Glatzer, "Hillel the Elder in the Light of the Dead Sea Scrolls."

Judah Goldin, "Hillel the Elder."

Judah Goldin, "The Three Pillars of Simeon the Righteous."

David Halivni, "On the Supposed Anti-Asceticism or Anti- Nazritism of Simon the Just."

Armand Kaminka, "Hillel's Life and Work."

Baruch Kanael, "Notes on Jewish Art in the Period of the Second Temple."

Aryeh Kasher, "The Historical Background of *Megillath Antiochus*."

Jacob Z. Lauterbach, "Misunderstood Chronological Statements in the Talmudic Literature."

Hugo Mantel, (Haim Dov), "The Dichotomy of Judaism During the Second Temple."

Hugo Mantel, "Ordination and Appointment in the Period of the Temple."

Jacob Neusner, "In Quest of the Historical Rabban Yohanan ben Zakkai."

### 5:2. History of the Jews in the Second and First Centuries B. C.

George Foot Moore, "Simeon the Righteous."

Ellis Rivkin, "Beth Din, Boulé, Sanhedrin: A Tragedy of Errors."

Ellis Rivkin, "The Utilization of Non-Jewish Sources for the Reconstruction of Jewish History."

Cecil Roth, "Historical Implications of the Ethics of the Fathers."

Daniel Sperber, "Palestinian Currency Systems During the Second Commonwealth."

Eugene Taeubler, "Jerusalem 201 to 199 B.C. on the History of a Messianic Movement."

Ben Zion Wacholder, "Pseudo-Eupolemus' Two Greek Fragments on the Life of Abraham."

Ben Zion Wacholder, "The Calendar of Sabbath Years During the Second Temple Era: A Response."

Ben Zion Wacholder, "The Calendar of Sabbatical Cycles During the Second Temple and the Early Rabbinic Period."

Ben Zion Wacholder, "The Letter from Judah Maccabee to Aristobulus: Is 2 Maccabees 1:10b–2:18 Authentic?"

Luitpold Wallach, "Alexander the Great and the Indian Gymnosophists in Hebrew Tradition."

Solomon Zeitlin, "Prosbol, A Study in Tannaitic Jurisprudence."

Solomon Zeitlin, "Slavery During the Second Commonwealth and the Tannaitic Period."

Solomon Zeitlin, "Synedrion in the Judeo-Hellenistic Literature and Sanhedrin in the Tannaitic Literature."

Solomon Zeitlin, "The Book of Jubilees, Its Character and Its Significance."

Solomon Zeitlin, "The Origin of the Synagogue."

### 6. History of the Jews in the First Century of the Common Era

S. J. Bastomsky, "The Emperor Nero in Talmudic Legend."

Baruch M. Bokser, "Rabbinic Responses to Catastrophe: From Continuity to Discontinuity."

W. M. Christie, "The Jamnia Period in Jewish History."

Louis H. Feldman, "Josephus' Portrait of Saul."

Louis H. Feldman, "The Identity of Pollio, the Pharisee, in Josephus"

Judah Goldin, "A Philosophical Session in a Tannaite Academy."

Erwin R. Goodenough, "Early Christian and Jewish Art."

Jehoshua M. Grintz, "Hebrew as the Spoken and Written Language in the Last Days of the Second Temple."

Alexander Guttmann, "Hillelites and Shammaites—a Clarification."

Alexander Guttmann, "Akiba, 'Rescuer of the Torah'."

Alexander Guttmann, "The End of the 'Houses'."

Alexander Guttmann, "The End of the Jewish Sacrificial Cult."

David Halivni (Weiss), "The Location of the Bet Din in the Early Tannaitic Period."

Sidney B. Hoenig, "Historic Masada and the Halakhah."

Sidney, B. Hoenig, "Synedrion in the Attic Orators, The Ptolemaic Papyri and Its Adoption by Josephus, The Gospels and The Tannaim."

R. A. Horsley, "Josephus and the Bandits."

Samuel. Krauss, "The Great Synod."

Hugo Mantel, "The Removals of the Sanhedrin from Yabneh to Usha."

S. K. Mirsky, "The Schools of Hillel, R. Ishmael and R. Akiba in Pentateuchal Interpretation."

Jacob Neusner, "From Enemy to Sibling: Rome and Israel in the First Century of Western Civilization."

Jacob Neusner, "Judaism in a Time of Crisis: Four Responses to the Destruction of the Second Temple."

Jacob Neusner, "Max Weber Revisited: Religion and Society in Ancient Judaism."

Jacob Neusner, "The Conversion of Adiabene to Judaism: A New Perspective."

Pinchas Hacohen Peli, "The Havurot That Were in Jerusalem"

George Alexander Kohut, "Abraham's Lesson in Tolerance."

Jacob Neusner, "A Zoroastrian Critique of Judaism: (Skand Gumanik Vicar, Chapters Thirteen and Fourteen: A New Translation and Exposition)."

Jacob Neusner, "Jews and Judaism Under Iranian Rule: Bibliographical Reflections."

Jacob Neusner, "The Jews in Pagan Armenia."

Jacob Neusner, "New Perspectives on Babylonian Jewry in the Tannaitic Age."

Jacob Neusner, "Politics and Theology in Talmudic Babylonia."

Jacob Neusner, "The Phenomenon of the Rabbi in Late Antiquity."

**8:2. History of the Jews in the Second through**
  **Seventh Centuries of the Common Era**

Saul Lieberman, "The Martyrs of Caesarea."

Saul Lieberman, "Palestine in the Third and Fourth Centuries."

Saul Lieberman, "Roman Legal Institutions in Early Rabbinics and in the Acta Martyrum."

Saul Lieberman, "The Martyrs of Caesarea."

Jacob Mann, "Changes in the Divine Service of the Synagogue Due to Religious Persecutions."

A. Marmorstein, "Judaism and Christianity in the Middle of the Third Century."

Jacob Neusner, and Jonathan Z. Smith, "Archaeology and Babylonian Jewry."

Jacob Neusner, "Babylonian Jewry and Shapur II's Persecution of Christianity from 339 to 379 A.D."

Jacob Neusner, "Rabbis and Community in Third-Century Babylonia."

John T. Pawlikowski, "Roman Imperial Legislation on the Jews: 313–438 C.E."

J. B. Segal, "Jews of North Mesopotamia Before the Rise of Islam."

Ben Zion Wacholder, "Chronomessianism: The Timing of Messianic Movements and the Calendar of Sabbatical Cycles."

Luitpold Wallach, "Church and State in the Later Roman Empire."

Abraham Weiss, "The Third-Century Seat of Calendar Regulation."

Solomon Zeitlin, "Encyclopaedia Judaica: The Status of Jewish Scholarship."

Solomon Zeitlin, "Judaism and Professors of Religion."

Solomon Zeitlin, "Spurious Interpretations of Rabbinic Sources in the Studies of the Pharisees and Pharisaism."

Solomon Zeitlin, "The Encyclopaedia Judaica: A Specimen of Modern Jewish Scholarship."

Solomon Zeitlin, "The Plague of Pseudo-Rabbinic Scholarship."

**9. The Literature of Formative Judaism:**
  **The Mishnah and the Tosefta**

Shaye J. D. Cohen, "Jacob Neusner, Mishnah, and Counter-Rabbinics: A Review Essay."

Shamma Friedman, "Two Early 'Unknown' Editions of the Mishna."

Louis Ginzberg, "Tamid: The Oldest Treatise of the Mishnah."

Judah Goldin, "The First Chapter of Abot de Rabbi Nathan."

Mayer I. Gruber, "The Mishnah as Oral Torah: A Reconsideration."

Alexander Guttmann, "Tractate Abot—Its Place in Rabbinic Literature."

Alexander Guttmann, "The Problem of the Anonymous Mishna: A Study in the History of the Halakah."

R. Travers Herford, "Pirke Aboth: Its Purpose and Significance."

Hyam Maccoby, "Jacob Neusner's Mishnah.".

Henry Malter, "A Talmudic Problem and Proposed Solutions."

Samuel K. Mirsky, "The Mishnah as Viewed by the Amoraim."

Jacob Neusner, "The Mishnah and the Smudgepots."

Jacob Neusner, "Transcendence and Worship Through Learning: The Religious World-View of Mishnah."

Joshua Starr, "A Fragment of a Greek Mishnaic Glossary."

P. R. Weis, "The Controversies of Rab and Samuel and the Tosefta."

Ernest Wiesenberg, "Elements of a Lunar Theory in the Mishnah, Rosh Hashanah 2:6, and the Talmudic Complements Thereto."

Meir Ydit, "A Case Study in Mishnaic Theodicy."

**10. The Literature of Formative Judaism:**
  **The Talmuds**

Moshe Aberbach, "Educational Institutions and Problems During the Talmudic Age."

Ludwig Blau, "Methods of Teaching the Talmud in the Past and in the Present."

Gerson D. Cohen, "The Talmudic Age."

Nina Davis, "The Ideal Minister of the Talmud."

Lewis N. Dembitz, "Babylon in Jewish Law."

Ian Gamse, "The Talmud of Babylonia, XXIII: a Review."

Judith Hauptman, "An Alternative Solution to the Redundancy Associated with the Phrase Tanya Nami Hakhi."

Louis Jacobs, "Are There Fictitious Baraitot in the Babylonian Talmud?"

Hyman Klein, "Gemara and Sebara."

Hyman Klein, "Gemara Quotations in Sebara."

H. Klein, "Some General Results of the Separation of Gemara from Sebara in the Babylonian Talmud."

Saul Lieberman, "A Tragedy or a Comedy."

# Author Index